AFRICA AT THE CROSSROADS

AFRICA AT THE CROSSROADS

Between Regionalism and Globalization

Edited by John Mukum Mbaku
and Suresh Chandra Saxena

Westport, Connecticut
London

Library of Congress Cataloging-in-Publication Data

Africa at the crossroads : between regionalism and globalization / edited by John Mukum
Mbaku and Suresh Chandra Saxena.
    p.   cm.
    Includes bibliographical references and index.
    ISBN 0–275–98020–0 (alk. paper)
    1. Africa—Economic policy. 2. Regionalism—Africa. 3. Globalization—Economic
aspects—Africa. 4. Africa—Economic integration. 5. Africa—Economic conditions—1960–
6. Africa—Politics and Government—1960– I. Mbaku, John Mukum, 1950– II. Saxena,
Suresh Chandra, 1933–
HC800.A55332   2004
337.6—dc21   2003057997

British Library Cataloguing in Publication Data is available.

Library of Congress Catalog Card Number: 2003057997
ISBN: 0–275–98020–0

First published in 2004

Praeger Publishers, 88 Post Road West, Westport, CT 06881
An imprint of Greenwood Publishing Group, Inc.
www.praeger.com

Printed in the United States of America

The paper used in this book complies with the
Permanent Paper Standard issued by the National
Information Standards Organization (Z39.48–1984).

10 9 8 7 6 5 4 3 2 1

This book is dedicated to our colleagues in Africa who continue to work under very difficult political and economic conditions, and to friends of Africa in India, Sri Lanka, and other parts of the Asia-Pacific Region.

Contents

Tables   ix

Acknowledgments   xi

Acronyms   xiii

1   Africa at the Crossroads   1
    John Mukum Mbaku and Suresh Chandra Saxena

2   Africa at the Crossroads of Globalization   21
    Emmanuel Nnadozie

3   Globalization and Popular Disenchantment in Africa   49
    Francis B. Nyamnjoh

4   A Tale of Three Images: Globalization, Marginalization,
    and the Sovereignty of the African Nation-State   93
    Paul L. Ehioze Idahosa

5   Regionalism and Regional Cooperation in Africa:
    New Century Challenges and Prospects   121
    Paul-Henri Bischoff

6   The New East African Community: A Defense and
    Security Organ as the Missing Link   147
    P. Godfrey Okoth

7   The African Union: Africa's Giant Step toward
    Continental Unity   163
    Suresh Chandra Saxena

8   Fighting Poverty and Deprivation in Africa: The Continuing
    Struggle   191
    John Mukum Mbaku

9   Internet Connectivity and Development in Africa:
    Look before You "Leapfrog"   211
    Lyombe S. Eko

10 Decentralization and Privatization of Infrastructure   233
    Mwangi S. Kimenyi and Wilson S. K. Wasike

11 Beyond Rhetoric: Peacekeeping in Africa in the
    New Millennium   267
    Korwa G. Adar

12 Cultural Diversity, Societal Conflict, and Sustainable
    Peace in Africa: Consociational Democracy Revisited   287
    Ufo Okeke Uzodike

13 State Repair and Democratic Development in Africa   315
    'Kunle Amuwo

14 Ethnicity, Agonism of Difference, and National
    Imagining in Postcolonial Africa   337
    Nantang Jua

15 The Struggle for Stability in Nigeria's Contemporary
    Politics (1990–1999) and the Lessons for the Fourth
    Republic   371
    E. Ike Udogu

16 Imperialism and Militarism in Africa: The Political
    Economy of French Arms Sales and Military
    Interventions, 1960–1980   387
    Immanuel Tatah Mentan

Selected Bibliography   429

Index   443

About the Editors and Contributors   461

Tables

2.1	The Benefits and Costs of Globalization	34
2.2	Africa's Problems Compared with the Rest of the World	39
8.1	The Thirty Least-Developed Countries in the World	197
8.2	Regional Comparisons in Human Development	198
10.1	Selected Private Participation in Infrastructure in Africa	238
10.2	Investment Risk in Africa	240
11.1	African Peacekeeping Training Capacity: African–U.N. Initiatives, 1997–1998	275
16.1	French Arms Deliveries, 1972–1977	409

Acknowledgments

This book grew out of a suggestion by coeditor Suresh Chandra Saxena, retired professor of African Studies, University of Delhi, who at the time was assistant editor of the highly regarded *Africa Quarterly*, published by the Indian Council for Cultural Relations, New Delhi. He had just completed work on a special issue of the journal (Volume 40, no. 3, 2000) on Africa's preparedness for life in the new century, and believed that an expanded examination of the choices faced by Africa as it enters the new millennium was warranted. He then contacted John Mukum Mbaku, a contributor to the special issue of *Africa Quarterly*, to help bring together a group of African scholars to examine from different perspectives the choices that Africans and Africa face as they enter this important period in their development. In bringing together scholars to tackle the different issues faced by the continent at this point in its evolution, the editors had one overriding goal: to produce policy relevant analyses that would provide policy makers in the continent with the tools to make those choices that will enhance peaceful coexistence in particular and the quality of life for Africans in general in the new century and beyond. We hope that we have succeeded in meeting this important goal.

The present project could not have been completed successfully without the enormous assistance provided by the institutions that employ the contributors. We send words of thanks and gratitude to Truman State University (Nnadozie); University of Botswana and CODESRIA (Nyamnjoh); York University, Canada (Idahosa); Rhodes University, South Africa (Bischoff); Africa Institute of South Africa (Adar); Moi University and Maseno University (Okoth); Delhi University and Jawaharlal Nehru University (Saxena); Weber State University (Mbaku); University of Iowa (Eko); The Kenya Institute for Public Policy Research and Analysis (Wasike); The Kenya Institute for Public Policy Research and Analysis and The University of Connecticut (Kimenyi); University of Natal (Uzodike); University of the North, South Africa (Amuwo); University of Buea, Cameroon (Jua); and University of Yaoundé, Cameroon (Mentan). We hope that these institutions will continue their generous support of the important work that these scholars are doing.

Suresh Chandra Saxena acknowledges and extends words of gratitude to the Departments of African Studies at both Delhi University and Jawaharlal Nehru University, which for many years have provided him with the opportunity to explore his interests in African studies. He also wishes to acknowledge the inspiration that has been provided to him by the India Africa Society (IAS), for which he served as founding secretary for many years. The IAS has done significant work in improving the study of Africa in India and in developing friendly relations between India and many African countries. In addition to providing a forum for open, frank, and rigorous examination of African problems, the IAS has provided support for Africa-friendly policies in India and the subcontinent and significantly improved the teaching of Africa at Indian institutions of higher learning. The Society continues to generate interest in Africa among Indians and other citizens of the sub-continent.

John Mukum Mbaku acknowledges the financial support of the Willard L. Eccles (Charitable) Foundation of Utah, which has supported his work financially for several years. In addition, he thanks the Department of Economics at Weber State University (Dr. Cliff Nowell, chair) and the John B. Goddard School of Business and Economics at Weber State University (Dr. Michael Vaughan, dean) for invaluable research support.

The views expressed in the chapters that follow are those of the authors and should not be ascribed to any of the universities and institutions mentioned here or to their trustees, officers, or other staff.

Acronyms

AATUF	All-African Trade Union Federation
ACP	African, Caribbean, and Pacific (countries)
ACRF	African Crisis Response Force
ACRI	African Crisis Response Initiative
ADB	African Development Bank
AEC	African Economic Commission
AF-RTDC	African Telecommunications Development Conference
AGOA	Africa Growth and Opportunities Act (of the U.S. Congress)
AIDS	Acquired Immondeficiency Syndrome (disorder of the immune system)
AISI	African Information Society Initiative
AMBs	Agricultural marketing boards
AMU	Arad Maghreb Union
ANAD	*Accord de non-aggression et d'assistance en matière de défense*
ANC	African National Congress (South African political party)
API	African Peace Initiative (U.K.)
APSC	African Political Security Council
ARPANET	Advanced Research and Projects Network
ASEAN	Association of Southeast Asian States
ASTD	African Symposium on Telematics for Development
ATI	*Agence Tunisienne d'Internet* (Tunisian Internet Agency)
ATNV	*Association Tchadienne pour la non-violence* (a Chadian human rights organization)
ATPSG	African Telecommunications Policy Study Group
AU	African Union
CCC	Committee of Concerned Citizens
CD	Campaign for Democracy (Nigerian political organization of the post–Cold War era)
CDHR	Committee for the Defense of Human Rights
CEAO	*Communauté économique de l'Afrique de l'ouest*
CEEAC	*Communauté économique des états de l'Afrique centrale*
CERN	*Centre européen de recherche nucléaire* (Geneva)

CFA	*Coopération financière en Afrique centrale* and *Communauté financière Africaine* (as in CFA franc, common currency for the Franc Zone in Africa; the former is used in central Africa and the latter in West Africa)
CLO	Civil Liberties Organization (Nigerian human rights organization)
CLOs	Civil liberties organizations
CNC	Committee for National Consensus (Nigeria)
COMESA	Common Market for Eastern and Southern Africa
COSATU	Congress of South African Trade Unions
CPDM	Cameroon People's Democratic Movement (Cameroon political party)
CRG	Control Risk Group
CRP	Constitutional Rights Project
DA	Democratic Alternative (Nigerian political organization of the post–Cold War era)
DARPA	Defense Advanced Research Projects Agency (an agency of the U.S. Department of Defense)
DBSA	Development Bank of South Africa
DFI	Direct foreign investment (also FDI, foreign direct investment)
DFID	Department for International Development
DNS	Domain Name Server
DPN	Democratic Party of Nigeria
DRC	Democratic Republic of Congo (formerly Zaire)
EAC	East African Community
EAHC	East African High Commission
ECA	(U.N.) Economic Commission for Africa
EC-ACP	European Community–African, Caribbean, and Pacific (countries)
ECCAS	Economic Community of Central African States
EC-DC	Electronic Commerce for Developing Countries
ECISAS	Executive Committee for Information and Strategy Analysis Secretariat
ECOMOG	Economic Community of West African States Monitoring Group
ECOWAS	Economic Community of West African States
ECPS	Executive Committee on Peace and Security
ECSC	European Coals and Steel Community
EEC	European Economic Community
EMIROAF	Ethnic Minority Rights Organization of Africa
EU	European Union
EWS	Early warning system
FDI	Foreign direct investment

FIS	*Front islamique du salut* (Islamic Salvation Front [Algerian political party])
FPI	*Front populaire ivorien* (political organization in Côte d'Ivoire)
GATT	General Agreement on Tariffs and Trade
GDM	Grassroots Democratic Movement
GDP	Gross domestic product
GNP	Gross national product
GOMU	*Groupe d'observations militaires neutres*
GWPA	Gabonese Written Press Association
HDI	Human development index
HIPC	Highly indebted poor country
HIV	Human immunodeficiency virus
HRFOB	Human Rights Field Operations in Burundi
HRFOR	Human Rights Field Operations in Rwanda
IBT	Increasing block tariff
ICFTU	International Confederation of Free Trade Unions
ICJ	International Court of Justice
ICT	Information and communications technology
IDPs	Internally displaced persons (also industrialization decentralization points)
IFC	International Financial Corporation
IFI	International Financial Institutions
IGAD	Intergovernmental Authority on Development
IGADD	Intergovernmental Authority on Drought and Desertification and Development
IMF	International Monetary Fund
ING	Interim National Government (Ernest Shonekan's interim government in Nigeria during the Babangida era)
ISDSC	Inter-State Defense and Security Council (SADC)
ISI	Import substitution industrialization
ISPs	Internet service providers
IT	Information technology
ITU	International Telecommunications Union
JACOM	Joint Action Committee (Nigerian political organization of the post–Cold War era)
KANU	Kenya African National Union
LDC/LDCs	Least developed country/least developed countries
LGA	Liptako–Gourma Integrated Development Authority
LRA	Lord's Resistance Army
MCPMRS	Mechanism for Conflict Prevention, Management, Resolution and Security
MDC	Movement for Democratic Change (Zimbabwe political party)
MDM	Mass Democratic Movement

MINURCA	U.N. Mission in Central African Republic (French acronym)
MIOBU	Military Observer Mission in Burundi
MNCs	Multinational companies or multinational corporations
MOBU	*Mission d'observation au Burundi*
MONUA	U.N. Observer Mission in Angola
MONUC	U.N. Mission in the Democratic Republic of Congo (French acronym)
MOSOP	Movement for the Survival of the Ogoni People (of Nigeria)
NAACP	National Association for the Advancement of Colored People (U.S. civil rights organization)
NADECO	National Democratic Coalition (Nigerian political organization)
NAFTA	North American Free Trade Area
NAI	New African Initiative
NAM	Non-aligned Movement
NATO	North Atlantic Treaty Organization
NBA	Niger Basin Authority
NCCC	National Constitutional Conference Commission (of Nigeria)
NCPN	National Center Party of Nigeria
NGOs	Nongovernmental organizations
NLC	Nigerian Labor Congress
NMOG	Neutral Military Observer Group
NOW	New World Order
NRA	National Resistance Army (of Uganda)
NRC	National Republican Convention (Nigerian political party of the Babangida era)
OAS	Organization of American States
OAU	Organization of African Unity
ODA	Official development aid (assistance)
OECD	Organization for Economic Cooperation and Development
OLF	Oromo Liberation Front
O&M	Operation and maintenance
OMIC	Observer Military in Comoros
OPDS	Organ for Defense and Politics (SADC)
PANA	Pan-African News Agency
PPI	Private-sector participation in infrastructure
PSOs	Peace support operations
PSP	Private-sector participation
PTA	Preferential Trade Area for Eastern and Southern Africa
PTC	Permanent Tripartite Commission
RE	Rural electrification (program)
Recamp	*Renforcement des capacités Africaines de maitien de la paix*
RECs	Regional Economic Communities
REU	Rural Electrification Unit

RMA	Rand Monetary Arrangement
RPF	Rwandan Patriotic Front
RPTC	Regional Peacekeeping Training Center
SACP	South African Communist Party
SACU	South African Customs Union
SADC	Southern African Development Community
SADCC	Southern African Development Coordination Conference (now defunct and replaced by SADC)
SADR	Sahawari Arab Democratic Republic
SAPs	Structural adjustment programs
SDF	Social Democratic Front (Cameroon political party)
SDNP	Sustainable Development Network Program
SDP	Social Democratic Party (Nigerian political party of the Babangida era)
SNC	Sovereign National Conference
SNGs	Subnational Governments
SPLA	Sudan Peoples Liberation Front
SSA	Sub-Saharan Africa
SWAPO	South West Africa People's Organization
TNCs	Transnational corporations
TRC	Truth and Reconciliation Commission
TRIMS	Trade-related investment measures
TRIPS	Trade-related intellectual properties
UAD	United Action for Democracy (Nigerian political party)
UAM	Union of Arab Maghreb
UDEAC	*Union douanière et économique de l'Afrique centrale*
UDFN	United Democratic Front of Nigeria
UEMOA	*Union économique et monetaire ouest Africaine*
ULGS	Unified Local Government Service
UNAMIR	U.N. Mission in Rwanda
UNAMSIL	U.N. Mission in Sierra Leone
UNAVEM	U.N. Angola Verification Mission
UNCHS	U.N. Center for Human Settlements
UNCIVPOL	U.N. Civilian Police
UNCP	United Nigeria Congress Party
UNCTAD	U.N. Conference on Trade and Development
UNDP	U.N. Development Program
UNDPKO	U.N. Department of Peace Keeping Operations
UNDRO	U.N. Disaster Relief Office
UN-ECOSOC	U.N. Economic and Social Council
UNEP	U.N. Environment Program
UNESCO	U.N. Educational, Scientific, and Cultural Organization
UNFPA	U.N. Population Fund
UNHCR	U.N. High Commissioner for Refugees

UNICEF	U.N. Children's Fund
UNITA	National Union for the Total Independence of Angola (Portuguese acronym)
UNITAF	U.N. Task Force
UNOSOM	U.N. Operations in Somalia
UNTAT	U.N. Training Assistance Team
UNTSI	U.N. Training School in Ireland
USAID	U.S. Agency for International Development
VCRs	Video cassette recorders
VSWP	Voice of Somali Women for Peace, Reconciliation and Political Rights
WARDA	West African Rice Development Association
WSCs	Water and Sanitation Committees
WTO	World Trade Organization
WUAs	Water Users' Associations
WWW	World Wide Web
ZANU-PF	Zimbabwe African National Union-Patriotic Front

1

Africa at the Crossroads

JOHN MUKUM MBAKU AND SURESH CHANDRA SAXENA

Decolonization and independence represented an important crossroads for Africans: It was an opportunity for them to choose the "right" path, one that could enhance governance and the creation of the wealth that the people needed to deal effectively with mass poverty and deprivation. In fact, during the struggle for independence it was generally believed that the latter would allow Africans to rid themselves of Europeans and their oppressive, exploitative, and repressive laws and institutions. In their place, the African people, with the help of their new leaders, would develop and adopt, through a democratic process, institutional arrangements based on their own values and designed to maximize their own interests (see, e.g., Mbaku 1997). The hope was that the state inherited or captured from the colonialists would be dismantled and reconstituted through democratic constitution-making processes to provide the people with transparent, participatory, and accountable governance and economic structures. Both the economic and political systems anticipated for the postindependence society were to be such that would enhance popular participation, encourage indigenous entrepreneurship and maximize wealth creation, and generally allow for a more socially equitable allocation of resources. A critical and very important function of the new postindependence state would be to design and implement policies to improve the welfare of the African people. In other words, the welfare of the indigenous people, which had been neglected during the colonial period, would be made an important part of public policy.

What path, then, did the Africans choose at independence? In economic growth and development, most African countries chose statism, a development model that emphasized government ownership of productive resources and significant levels of intervention in private exchange. Eventually, the state came to dominate most economic activities in these countries. What were the reasons advanced to support the abandonment of the market system, which had been inherited from colonialism, in favor of statism? First, at independence many Africans considered the state as the most capable entity to deal effectively with massive poverty and deprivation. Thus, many citizens were willing to grant the government significant power to intervene in economic activities so that it could more effectively deal with poverty. Second, a significant number of the new independence leaders (e.g., Ahmadou Ahidjo of Cameroon, Julius Nyerere of Tanzania, Kwame Nkrumah of Ghana) argued then that the state was the only organization that had the wherewithal to rebuild societies that had been torn apart by decades of colonial exploitation. Third, a state now controlled by indigenous elites was considered the only entity powerful enough to hold together competing (and often feuding) ethnic groups, provide the appropriate environment for national integration and nation building, enhance the effective management of ethnic conflict, and ensure sustainable development. Fourth, many development economists of the time argued that the state was the only organization capable of undertaking the large, complex, and relatively expensive development projects that were required to provide jobs for the people, create enough wealth to confront poverty, and help the new economies become globally competitive. Finally, many of Africa's new leaders had been educated in Europe, where social engineering had become quite pervasive. As a consequence, many of these leaders favored development models that emphasized state intervention in private exchange while minimizing the functions of the market.

What exactly was statism supposed to do? Among the important goals that statism was supposed to meet were the following: (1) significantly improve the ability of the state to secure the resources it needed to eradicate poverty and improve the living conditions of the indigenous people, especially historically deprived groups and communities such as women, children, and rural inhabitants; (2) empower the state to promote rapid economic growth and development; (3) enhance the state's ability to meet certain societal goals, including the equitable distribution of resources, alleviation of poverty, sustainability in the management of the environment, and the protection of the rights of individuals and their property; (4) enhance the government's ability to reduce and eventually eliminate the country's dependence on primary commodities and the economies of the industrial countries; (5) improve trade and other forms of exchange with other African countries; (6) protect local industries from foreign competition, allowing them to mature and become globally competitive; and (7) provide the government with the wherewithal to deal with a legacy of discrimination and marginalization inherited from the colonial state (Ihonvbere 1996; Mbaku 1997).

How has statism performed? As the evidence from the last forty years shows, it has failed to meet these goals. Instead, it has enhanced the ability of Africa's postindependence ruling elites to engage in opportunistic behaviors—that is, plunder their economies for their own benefit. Historically marginalized groups (e.g., women, children, and rural inhabitants), who had expected the government to rescue them and provide them with the facilities to use their resources and talents productively to improve their living conditions, soon found themselves being subjected to similar types and levels of exploitation as they had suffered under colonial rule. In fact, the new governments developed and implemented perverse economic policies, which while generating significant benefits for those who controlled and monopolized national political spaces, actually impoverished the people and subjected them to relatively high levels of material deprivation. In most African countries the new development model enhanced the ability of urban dwellers to exploit the rural farming areas, further making development in these already impoverished areas virtually impossible (see, e.g., Bates 1981, 1987). Thus, today, as Africans stand at another crossroads, the choice of a resource allocation system, one that can significantly enhance indigenous entrepreneurship and promote the creation of the wealth that the people need to meet their needs, is as critical now as it was in the 1960s.

In the area of politics and government, many of the African countries chose the one-party political system. The argument advanced at the time to support this choice was that the only viable way to bring together feuding ethnic groups to provide the appropriate institutional environment for peaceful coexistence and sustainable development was through the imposition on each country of a unitary political system with a strong central government. Many of the early leaders (e.g., Modibo Keita, Sékou Touré, Ahmadou Ahidjo, Kwame Nkrumah, and Julius Nyerere) considered the one-party political system the only system of governance capable of ensuring the proper and effective management of ethnic diversity and allowing for the kind of rapid economic growth that was needed to generate enough resources for each country's poverty-alleviation efforts. Competitive politics as promoted by the Western countries and undertaken through a multiparty system, many of these leaders argued, would become a vehicle for the politicization of ethnic, religious, and other social cleavages. A multiparty system was believed to exacerbate ethnic conflicts, increase levels of political instability, and, hence, contribute to poor economic performance. As argued by Siaka Stevens, late president of Sierra Leone, multiparty competition is "a system of . . . institutionalized tribal and ethnic quinquennial warfare euphemistically known as elections [which] contributes an open invitation to anarchy and disunity" (Quoted in Decalo 1992, 10). As Julius Nyerere of Tanzania argued then, "where there is one party, and that party is identified with the nation as a whole, the foundations of democracy are firmer than they can ever be where you have two or more parties, each representing only a section of the community" (Decalo 1992, 10; also see Nyerere, 1966). Thus, shortly after gaining independence, many of the new African countries chose the single-party political system, with such a party expected, as forcefully promoted by Nyerere, to represent "all streams of opinions and societal groups" (Decalo 1992, 10).

How well did the one-party political party function? Instead of enhancing the ability of the government to deal effectively with pressing societal issues (e.g., alleviation of poverty, more effective management of ethnic diversity in order to enhance peaceful coexistence, national integration, rapid economic growth, etc.), the one-party system, along with statism, provided those who had captured the governmental structures at independence the wherewithal to (1) monopolize political power, rule by decree, and effectively deprive the people of the opportunity to develop a democratic culture; (2) exploit vulnerable groups (e.g., women, children, minority ethnic groups, and inhabitants of the economically peripheral areas), and marginalize and further impoverish them; (3) intimidate, suffocate, and destroy civil society, which could have served as a check on the exercise of government agency; (4) plunder, steal, illegally appropriate, and confiscate national resources for their own use; (5) stunt, through the promotion of perverse economic policies, the development of a viable indigenous entrepreneurial class; (6) retard and in many cases prevent the creation of the wealth that these countries needed to eradicate poverty; (7) significantly increase corruption and public malfeasance, as well as rent seeking and other forms of opportunism; (8) enhance the ability of foreign actors (e.g., transnational companies) to over-exploit the country's natural resources and severely damage the agroecological system; and (9) generally increase national levels of poverty and push these countries to the periphery of the global system. In fact, as indicated by recent data from the United Nations Development Program (UNDP 2000), Africa remains the poorest region in the world, with most Africans poorer now than they were in the 1960s. By the mid-1980s, most countries in sub-Saharan Africa were no longer able to meet their rising public obligations and were forced to seek external assistance, especially from the Bretton Woods institutions and the developed-market economies. Unfortunately, most of the aid and loans provided by these external organizations were not used to improve domestic wealth-creating structures. The resources were "allocated" through highly corrupt state systems and spent mostly on politically motivated projects—primarily to subsidize highly inefficient and poorly managed state-owned enterprises and to provide benefits for a bloated, parasitic and mostly unproductive civil service (see, e.g., World Bank 1996; Ihonvbere 1994; van de Walle 1994).

Today, Africa stands at another crossroads, and like the 1960s, it must decide which political path to take. Whatever choice it makes, it must be one that provides a dispensation that will (1) enhance the peaceful coexistence of population groups and improve popular participation in governance; (2) bring government closer to the people and make it more relevant to their daily lives; (3) improve the allocation of resources; (4) encourage the development and sustaining of indigenous entrepreneurship; (5) promote wealth creation; (6) significantly reduce inequities in the distribution of resources; (7) guarantee the rights of all citizens; (8) provide more effective ways to manage the environment; and (9) generally enhance each country's ability to participate in and benefit from the new global economy.

In this book the contributors examine, from different perspectives, the choices faced by the continent as it stands at this important crossroads and contemplates what to do, which development path to take, and which governance system to adopt in order to achieve the many goals that Africans have made for themselves in the new millennium. Some of these goals include, but are not limited to, (1) transition to democratic governance systems; (2) greater respect for human rights; (3) sustainable management of the ecosystem; (4) eradication of poverty; (5) greater and more enhanced participation by Africa in both the global economy and global affairs; (6) minimizing the negative effects of the new globalization on the continent ("new globalization" as used here refers to post–Cold War efforts to make "capitalism" a universal resource allocation system, and democracy as practiced in the West, the universal governance system); (7) finding more effective and efficient ways to deal with the HIV/AIDS pandemic; (8) significantly improving the participation of women and other historically deprived groups in both political and economic activities; (9) finding sustainable solutions to destructive ethnic conflict and finally achieving peaceful coexistence of each country's population groups; and (10) making the continent's governors more accountable to the governed. These are only a few of the problems that confront Africa today, and can only be dealt with effectively if the right choices are made. Thus, whether Africa moves on from the present crossroads into a "state of the world" characterized by more democratic and participatory dispensations, as well as economic systems that guarantee economic freedoms and, hence, maximize wealth creation, or refuses to learn from its past mistakes and continues with authoritarianism and resource allocation systems that discourage entrepreneurship will have a significant impact on the quality of life in the continent for most of the new century. In the rest of this chapter we bring into focus the several contributions in this book and how they have attempted to examine the road traveled by Africa during the last fifty years and how choices made now can affect the continent in the years to come.

Since the end of the Cold War and the cessation of superpower rivalry, trade has emerged as the most important determinant of East–West relations. The phenomenal increase in international flows of goods and services, capital, people, and information, now generally referred to as globalization, has come to dominate relations between nations and regions. Unfortunately, due to many constraints, both internal and external, Africa has been unable to participate gainfully in this phenomenal expansion in global economic activities. In Chapter 2 Emmanuel Nnadozie presents a study of Africa at the crossroads of this new globalization or, as some analysts call it, the triumph of global capitalism. He argues that in order to enhance the ability of the continent to participate in the new global economy, many of its traditional benefactors (e.g., the IMF, the World Bank, and the industrial market economies, especially of the EU) have imposed neoliberal therapies on the African countries. The hope is that such therapies would improve domestic economic conditions in the African countries and enhance their ability to participate more effectively in the new globalization. Unfortunately, Nnadozie argues, these therapies, some of them quite harsh, have failed to achieve the desired results. Instead, they have created many problems for the continent and its inhabitants, including increased poverty and deprivation.

The response of many African countries to the new globalization, Nnadozie continues, has been to adopt policies that emphasize self-reliance. Hence, there has been an increased interest in the continent in regional economic integration, a process many Africans believe would create larger markets and allow domestic industries to more effectively exploit technological economies of scale. In addition, regional integration is expected to improve the ability of African countries to participate in the global economy (e.g., through an enhanced negotiating position at such international forums as the World Trade Organization). Nnadozie argues, however, that so far regional integration does not seem to be helping Africans improve their domestic economic conditions as well as their participation levels in the global economy. He then poses a series of questions regarding what Africa should do at this crossroads of globalization. What, for example, should African policy makers do now, given the fact that despite the efforts of the last decade, the continent remains on the periphery of the global economy? If they do nothing, they risk being left permanently on the periphery of the new globalization. However, should they embrace neoliberalism, they risk further economic deterioration and subsequently, social, and political instability. He then argues that the choice for the continent is not between complete openness and autarky. He concludes with the following policy suggestions: (1) Africans should continue and intensify their regional cooperation efforts in order to develop and sustain a solid foundation for eventual integration into the global system. (2) Africans should carefully control their entry into the global economy, making certain that such participation is designed to maximize their values. (3) Africans should make sure that they adopt an approach to globalization that allows them to maximize the benefits while at the same time minimizing the costs. Thus, it might be more appropriate for policy makers in the continent to think not of integration into the global system, but of some form of cooperation that allows the African people to limit their participation only to welfare-enhancing global activities or projects.

In Chapter 3, Francis B. Nyamnjoh continues with the discussion of globalization and its impact on Africa begun in Chapter 2 by Emmanuel Nnadozie. However, in Nyamnjoh's disquisition much more than the economic dimensions of globalization are examined. He also looks at what he calls the "standard-bearers of globalization," the information and culture industries. The traditional literature on globalization does pay a lot of attention to its economic dimensions—how the "internationalization and integration of economic activities" impacts the authority and sovereignty of nation-states, especially when one considers the level of global power now enjoyed by transnational companies. The latter are, of course, the agents of this new global capitalism. In many developing countries, especially those in Africa, these nonstate actors have become very strong challengers to the authority of the state, especially in the development and implementation of public policy. In Chapter 3, Nyamnjoh takes a critical look at globalization "from the standpoint of the African experience of the West." He discusses "modernization," "development," and "globalization" and argues that these are different labels for the same basic concept: that of dispossessing the African of "his natural and cultural Africanness, and inviting him or her to partake of the 'standardized, routinized, streamlined and global' consumer culture, of which McDonalds, Coca-Cola, CNN and satellite entertainment television are harbingers." Due to high levels of poverty and deprivation in African countries, only a small number of people, mostly corrupt civil servants and politicians, are able to afford the goods and services brought by this new globalization. Most Africans, however, must make do with what trickles down from relatives and patrons at the center of political and economic power. Given such fantastic inequities in the distribution of resources, Nyamnjoh argues, it is difficult to see how popular forces in the continent can relate to the new globalism in any other way than the frustration, disillusionment, and disenchantment that it brings to them. Today, throughout most African countries, the poor and deprived masses have come to equate globalization with corrupt and bloated bureaucracies that are unwilling to perform even the most basic of services; broken-down and nonfunctioning public services (e.g., telephones that do not work, collapsed bridges, roads in total disrepair, etc.); schools with no textbooks or teachers; and hospitals with no medicines, just to name a few. Nyamnjoh's discussion, however, is not focused on cultural resistance but on "the processes and effects of co-optation or assimilation of the elite few by consumer capitalism, and how these elite few, in turn, use their consumption of things foreign as an identity, and as a source of prestige, status, and power." Thus, the main focus of the chapter is on how the new globalization has captured the continent's ruling classes and turned them into instruments of torture and marginalization of the continent's masses, turning the latter into a powerless, disillusioned, and frustrated group. He concludes by suggesting ways in which the plundered African heritage can be reconstructed and the people provided with participatory, accountable, and transparent forms of governance.

In Chapter 4, Paul L. Ehioze Idahosa continues the discussion on globalization and thoroughly examines how it relates to Africa in general and to African marginalization in particular. He outlines the major features of globalization, sets out globalization's design with respect to Africa, and identifies the many ways in which some Africanist commentators on Africa often "buttress the practice of accepting limiting the sovereignty" of many of the continent's nation-states. He concludes by identifying what he believes to be a very special kind of "globalization" that he believes can minimize African marginalization while at the same time enhance the continent's ability to participate in and benefit from the international system.

Some scholars and international organizations, as well as policy makers in Africa, have argued that if Africa does not join the new global movement it would suffer further marginalization. Idahosa argues that if we subscribe to this thinking then we must see globalization not just as an economic project, but as one with political as well as ideological dimensions. Such a multifaceted project, he argues, is constantly being reenforced through many mediums, including the press, its principal source of representation, and academics (i.e., Africanists), its primary source of legitimacy. The choice for Africa, Idahosa argues, should not necessarily be between marginalization and globalization; rather, it should be about alternative conceptions of each. For one thing, he argues, there was a time in Africa when globalization was not about marginalization but about opportunities for Africans to enhance national development through access to larger foreign markets. Over twenty years ago, Idahosa argues, *The Lagos Plan of Action* was developed by the Organization of African Unity (OAU) with the aim of fully integrating Africa into the world economy. Such integration, however, was only expected to be undertaken after African states had significantly improved their national capacities and regional integration had been fully exploited. He goes on to argue that the plan was abandoned because of the lack of political will and also because "at the center of its identity lay choices that put people, not markets first." This approach to development, one that placed the African people (not markets or capitalism) at the center of all public policies, of course, was not acceptable to external actors, who by the mid-1980s, had brought structural adjustment programs to the continent and destroyed any chances for a bottom-up, home-grown, people-driven charter for development in the continent. The abandonment of *The Lagos Plan of Action* was a road not taken and, it may be necessary to remind Africans, especially given the marginalization suffered by the people at the hands of the IMF and World Bank imposed structural adjustment programs and other externally imposed programs of economic "salvation," of the consequences of dependence. The efforts by the Bretton Woods institutions at globalizing Africa have not only failed but have imposed significant hardship on the people. In fact, as Idahosa argues, the SAPs created new dependencies that actually proscribed the underlying principles that would have formed the foundation for an African model for sustainable economic growth and development. Today, many scholars are beginning to re-air *The Lagos Plan of Action* as an alternative to the failed Western-led effort to force the continent into the new global system.

Africa is at a crossroads and has the opportunity to look back at what has not worked, and as a result, where not to tread. Most Africans know now that they do not want to go back to (1) military dictatorship, (2) one-party political systems, (3) governance structures characterized by the absence of the rule of law, and (4) rule-making processes not governed by democratic constitutionalism. At this crossroads, then, Africans must choose the path that maximizes their values and enhances development in the continent, as well as their ability to participate in and benefit from the new globalization.

Regional economic integration is seen by many, including both the OAU and the U.N. Economic Commission for Africa (ECA) as a way to improve economic conditions in Africa and enhance the ability of the continent to participate more effectively in the new global economy. In Chapter 5, Paul-Henri Bischoff takes a look at the challenges posed by as well as the prospects for regionalism in Africa. First, he examines the concept of regional integration as it applies to Africa. Second, he presents what he believes are the major challenges to regionalism and regional cooperation in the continent. Third, he analyzes several of the continent's major efforts at integration, including the Union of Arab Maghreb

(UAM), the *Union économique et monetaire ouest Africaine* (UEMOA), the *Communauté économique des états de l'Afrique centrale* (CEEAC), the Economic Community of West African States (ECOWAS), the Southern African Development Community (SADC), the Common Market for Eastern and Southern Africa (COMESA), the East African Community (EAC), and the Intergovernmental Authority on Development (IGAD), assesses the level of success of these integration schemes, and advances reasons to explain why most of them have failed to meet their goals. Finally, he analyzes the challenges that Africa faces as it struggles to implement more effective integration schemes, which are expected to enhance its ability to develop and become a more active member of the global community.

Since the end of the Cold War and the cessation of the bipolar superpower rivalry that dominated global affairs from 1945 to 1991, there have emerged many regionally based political and economic arrangements designed to ensure the peaceful coexistence of groups and nationalities and enhance development. These new organizations, as argued by P. Godfrey Okoth in Chapter 6, lack a worldview and do not have the appropriate structures for them to cooperate for the mutual benefit of their constituents. As a result, Okoth continues, unhealthy competition has arisen among these regional groupings, resulting in relatively high levels of insecurity among nations and regions of the world.

In order for these regional organizations to produce benefits for their members and enhance the move toward a sustainable global system, there must be peace in each subregion. Hence, security (military, economic, societal, environmental, and political) is a very important and critical concern of regional integration schemes. In this chapter, Okoth analyzes the East African Community and how it can serve as a framework for the improvement of economic conditions in the subregion and prepare the latter to more effectively participate in the new globalization. It is now generally accepted that regional economic integration is very important for African countries, given the fact that most of these countries have relatively small and often nonviable economies. Integration schemes such as the EAC can significantly improve the ability of member states to participate more effectively in the new global economy (e.g., through an enhanced negotiating presence at such international forums as the WTO).

In order for regional integration schemes to benefit Africa, however, there must be peace in the region. This, as argued by Okoth, calls for the establishment within each regional organization of a security organ, one that can effectively resolve conflict and minimize political violence within the community, defend member states against external aggressors, and provide foreign investors with the assurance that they will be able to operate in an environment characterized by law and order. Okoth warns, however, that one must understand that threats to security do not only come from military incursions; they can also come from poverty, inequality, and inequity in the allocation of resources, environmental destruction, and other social and economic phenomena (e.g., HIV/AIDS). Hence, it is important that each regional organization consult the relevant stakeholder groups so that regional policies reflect the needs, desires, and concerns of the latter (i.e., the people). It is only through a *participatory process* that an integration scheme such as the EAC can be able to fulfill its mission of improving the welfare of the citizens of the member states and enhancing their ability to benefit from the new globalization.

During the colonial period, Africans believed that unity and cooperation among the indigenous people would be the only way they could free themselves from European exploitation and domination. As a consequence, many of the post–War War II freedom fighters (e.g., Kwame Nkrumah of Ghana, Nnamdi Azikiwe of Nigeria, Ruben Um Nyobé of Cameroon, and Sékou Touré of Guinea) saw continental unity as an important way to fight colonialism and further oppression by Europeans. From their perspective, then, part of the struggle for real independence involved efforts to unite Africans and design and adopt political and economic arrangements that transcended the boundaries established by European colonialism, ethnicity, and language, as well as religious and cultural preferences. The main goal was to provide Africans in the postindependence society with structures at the continental level that could help them negotiate more effectively at the global level and enhance their ability to participate in the international economy.

However, as argued by Suresh Chandra Saxena in Chapter 7, the idea of African unity was part of the worldwide movement to unite all peoples of African ancestry and improve their ability to fight against European oppression (specifically in the African colonies) and continued discrimination against black people in the United States. The movement for African unity, Saxena argues, spearheaded by such intellectuals as Dr. Kwame Nkrumah, benefited significantly from such freedom fighters of African ancestry as Dr. W.E.B. DuBois, Marcus Garvey, and Sylvester Williams, as well as from several European- and American-based organizations, such as the National Association for the Advancement of Colored People (NAACP), founded in New York in 1909, and the Pan-African Federation, founded in Manchester in 1944. Although the aim of the NAACP was to fight discrimination and racism in America, that of the Manchester group was to improve living conditions for Africans and peoples of African ancestry throughout the world.

In Chapter 7 Saxena first examines the historical context of African unity and the latter's origins to the early days of the growth of the movement generally referred to as "Pan-Africanism." Second, he takes a look at the different approaches to African unity. Third, he discusses the many setbacks to the goal of African unity. Fourth, he examines the Organization of African Unity (OAU), its formation in 1963 in Addis Ababa, Ethiopia, and its inability to deal effectively not only with African unity but also with the multifarious development and political problems that plagued the continent in the postindependence period. Since the OAU was not granted the power by its founders to take punitive actions against recalcitrant members, many of the member states took positions on several issues that were in violation of the decisions and policies of the organization. For example, in the 1970s and 1980s many African countries acted contrary to the position of the OAU on the question of apartheid and sanctions against the pariah South African regime. Malawi, under H. K. Banda, established diplomatic relations with apartheid South Africa and engaged in both trade and other types of exchanges with the oppressive and exploitative regime in Pretoria. In addition, Banda's government opposed the armed rebellion, led by the African National Congress (ANC), against the apartheid government. Thus, for many years Banda and his government openly ignored pleas from the OAU for African countries to boycott the racist regime in Pretoria. As another example of the inability of the OAU to effectively unify the continent, many Francophone countries openly ignored pleas from the OAU to condemn France for its nuclear weapons tests in the Sahara. These former French colonies considered their economic and political cooperation with France more important than their solidarity with their fellow Africans. Saxena then examines some of the reasons why the OAU was not successful in uniting Africa. Finally, he advances the need for a new organization and follows that discussion by taking a look at the African Union (AU), which was formed in the summer of 2001 and is expected to replace the OAU.

In recent years an important challenge for countries in Africa has been the emergence of powerful economic blocs such as the European Union (EU) and the North American Free Trade Area (NAFTA). Should these trading blocs become protectionist, this could spell disaster for Africa, since most of the countries in the continent presently carry out most of their trade with the countries of these two economic and political arrangements. Another issue of concern to Africa is globalization and the emergence of a new post–Cold War global economy. However, given the relative economic strengths of NAFTA and the EU these two trading schemes are most likely to dominate global economic and political affairs in the years to come. How well the African countries are able to participate in and gain from the global economy will be determined by their ability to form a strong and viable continental economic and political organization, one that can negotiate effectively with NAFTA, the EU, and other such economic unions for the benefits of global trade. Since the late 1980s Africans have come to realize that the OAU, in its present structure, cannot meet the challenges posed by globalization and emerging regional economic integration schemes such as the NAFTA and the EU. Hence, the desire to form a new organization.

It is hoped that the new organization, the AU, will provide a more enabling environment for increased unity and cooperation in the continent. To enhance the AU's ability to perform the many tasks assigned to it, it is being armed with many structures that were lacking in the OAU. However, as Saxena argues in his conclusion, if the AU is to succeed in its mission, member states must pay their dues regularly and must comply with the policies and decisions of the AU government. Of course, the AU must function democratically, providing all relevant stakeholder groups with the facilities to participate fully and effectively in policy design and implementation, so that policies adopted fully reflect the interests and concerns of member states. Such an approach to AU policy will encourage compliance and minimize the chance that member states will adopt positions contrary to those taken by the AU.

Today, Africa is considered one of the poorest regions of the world (see, e.g., UNDP 2000, 2002). Many researchers have attempted to determine why most postindependence efforts to deal with poverty and deprivation in Africa have failed. Among the reasons advanced to explain continued policy failure in Africa (and hence, increasing levels of poverty, especially among women, rural inhabitants, and other vulnerable groups) is incompetence and ineptitude on the part of civil servants and the politicians whose job it is to design and implement policies to deal with underdevelopment. In Chapter 8, John Mukum Mbaku revisits the debate on poverty eradication in Africa and argues that it is the absence of an enabling institutional environment that is primarily responsible for policy failure and the inability of African policy makers to deal effectively with poverty in the postindependence period.

According to Mbaku, in order for poverty eradication programs to work effectively and meet their goals they must be undertaken within an institutional environment that (1) properly constrains civil servants and politicians and minimizes their ability to engage in opportunistic behaviors (e.g., rent seeking and corruption); (2) enhances indigenous entrepreneurship and, hence, wealth creation; and (3) promotes peaceful coexistence of population groups. To enhance the ability of African countries to deal with poverty in the new millennium, Mbaku concludes, each country must engage in state reconstruction through democratic (i.e., people-driven, participatory, inclusive, and bottom-up) constitution-making to arm itself with a new dispensation characterized by transparent, accountable, and participatory governance structures and an economic system that guarantees economic freedoms.

One of the most important challenges to development in Africa today, as examined by many contributors to this volume, is the new globalization, a phenomenon that began to receive serious attention in the continent shortly after the end of the Cold War and the cessation of superpower rivalry in the late 1980s and early 1990s. In Chapter 9, Lyombe S. Eko examines how Africans have reacted to one of the most important aspects of the new globalization: rapid and phenomenal changes in mass communication and telecommunications technologies. Specifically, he discusses the emergence of the Internet and Africa's reaction to it. Eko argues that the importance of the Internet as an instrument of development was impressed upon African policy makers by the international community. In the beginning, African governments were not very enthusiastic about the Internet because they believed they could not control its content due to its extremely decentralized nature.

Under pressure from the international community, Eko continues, sub-Saharan African countries adopted the Internet and, using legislation, facilitated its diffusion into their specific territories. The North African countries opted for an adoption program that allowed the government to have significant control over content by making certain that a government agency served as the gate-keeper.

The Internet is arguably one of the most important inventions of the twenti-eth century and promises to be a powerful development tool. While agreeing that the Internet has the potential to revolutionize communications in Africa, significantly improve the continent's ability to interact with the rest of the world, and provide enormous opportunities for trade and development, Eko ar-gues that African policy makers should not allow the IMF, the World Bank, and other international actors "to shove them willy-nilly into the vortex of an ever-accelerating technological whirlwind." Africans need to determine for them-selves how to best benefit from this new technology. Determining how to best utilize this new communication and development tool called the Internet, how-ever, should be part of the larger effort to improve the continent's participation in the new globalization. The overall goal should be to maximize benefits flow-ing to the continent from the new globalization, which include the Internet and other emerging technologies. Eko reminds us that throughout history the devel-opment of communication technology has been "incremental and systematic." He believes that technological "leapfrogging" without first providing society with the enabling political, economic, social, and cultural environment will pro-duce few or no benefits for the societies involved. For example, African socie-ties that really want to benefit from the Internet and other emerging communi-cation technologies (e.g., cell phones), first need to provide electricity and the needed telecommunications infrastructure, as well as an institutional environ-ment that enhances the efficient functioning of such technologies and improves their ability to function as instruments of development. Such an environment should allow Africans to adapt the imported technologies to local needs and prevent them from becoming agents of cultural annihilation. Eko makes a very important point about the adoption of the Internet and other technologies in Af-rica, a point that also applies to Africa's entry into the global marketplace. First, Africans should adequately prepare themselves (e.g., through the provision of needed infrastructure, institutions, etc.) to adequately benefit from the Internet in particular and the new global economy in general. Second, Africans should take a long-term view of technology and globalization and design entry (into the global economy) and adoption (of new technologies) strategies that provide them with net benefits. It is only through such an approach that Africans can make sure that their net benefits from participation in the global economy are maximized.

One of the most important constraints on economic growth and develop-ment in Africa during the last fifty years has been the absence of viable eco-nomic infrastructures. Many African countries are landlocked and find it very difficult to export their products. Throughout the continent, vast distances and low population density make government provision of infrastructure very diffi-cult. In several countries, state capacity has been overstretched or even undermined so much that provision of services is no longer capable of meeting demand. In fact, throughout the continent, rural inhabitants are almost cut off from the urban centers because of the absence of functioning roads, telephones, and other communications infrastructures. In the urban areas, many people lack access to clean water, the streets are overcrowded, sewage disposal systems are inadequate, endangering sanitation, provision of electricity is sporadic at best, and the phone system rarely works. Throughout most of Africa, few countries have been able to provide their citizens with viable and sustainable infrastructures that can enhance economic growth and development.

What have been the reasons for the inability of the African countries to provide their citizens with the appropriate infrastructure for development? Several reasons have been advanced to explain this failure of the postindependence government to provide important social overhead capital. Some of them include vast distances and low population density, making provision very difficult; division of the continent into many states, most of which are landlocked, making it very difficult for public provision to benefit from economies of scale since many of these countries are quite small and have nonviable economies; poor and to a certain extent perverse economic policies and the absence of institutions that enhance entrepreneurship; and weak states, many of which have actually become constraints to service provision. As part of the transition to democratic governance that began in the continent in the late 1980s and early 1990s, it has been suggested that adopting a decentralized form of provision, as well as privatization, would significantly improve infrastructure provision in Africa. In Chapter 10, Mwangi S. Kimenyi and Wilson S. K. Wasike examine decentralization and privatization of infrastructure in Africa. First, they review the problems associated with Africa's highly centralized service provision structure. Second, they tackle the issues that make decentralization and privatization of infrastructure provision in Africa imperative. Third, they assess private-sector participation in infrastructure provision in the continent, how this can be undertaken, and why it is necessary. As part of this assessment, they also look at the emerging field of information technology and how Africans can enhance their ability to benefit from it. Fourth, they examine the problems and challenges that lie ahead. Some of these include political constraints, bureaucratic roadblocks, institutional weaknesses, and the risks associated with fiscal decentralization and the financing of huge construction projects. Finally, they provide practical recommendations for countries interested in decentralizing and privatizing their infrastructure provision.

Since the 1960s, Africa has been unable to deal effectively with poverty. As a consequence, it remains the most underdeveloped region of the world today. Against this background of very high levels of poverty and deprivation, as Korwa G. Adar argues in Chapter 11, lie significant levels of violence (the outcome of ethnic and ethnoregional conflicts, as well as inter- and intrastate conflicts). Adar argues that these conflicts serve as significant constraints to economic growth and the alleviation of poverty in the continent. Specifically, conflicts endanger the peace, significantly raise the cost of investment, and, hence, drive away both domestic and foreign investors. In addition, they create a refugee problem that has contributed to the misallocation of human resources, forced countries such as Kenya and Tanzania to absorb a lot of refugees, placing an extra burden on already very fragile economies.

In some countries, sectarian conflict has forced the disintegration of the state (e.g., Sierra Leone, Democratic Republic of Congo, Liberia, Rwanda, and Somalia). An economy ravaged by violent conflict is hardly a place conducive to investment and the productive use of resources. Thus, as argued by Adar, resolving these conflicts peacefully and bringing about peace in the continent is a sine qua non for economic growth and development.

In Chapter 11, then, Adar examines peacekeeping and peacemaking in Africa. First, he examines peacekeeping in the continent during the Cold War and shows how the Cold War protagonists (the West, led by the United States and the East, headed by the USSR) constrained the ability of Africans to maintain a peaceful environment for the allocation of their resources. Second, he examines peacekeeping in the continent in the post–Cold War era, a period characterized by increased economic interaction between countries and regions of the world. However, Adar cautions that despite increased global economic interaction, the Western countries are no longer willing (as they did during the Cold War) to commit their national resources to global peacekeeping efforts. Instead, they are now more likely to contribute to a U.N. effort, allowing the multilateral organization to serve as the mechanism for global security and peacekeeping.

While Africans, Adar continues, are now more involved in peacekeeping efforts in their own continent, they still lack a continental peacekeeping institutional framework. As this book goes to press, African leaders have launched a continental organization called the African Union, which has replaced the Organization of African Unity. The AU, unlike the OAU, is expected to be provided with the appropriate framework for peacekeeping in the continent. Adar's discussion, however, is limited to the OAU. He carefully analyzes the OAU's Mechanism for Conflict Prevention, Management and Resolution (MCPMR), adopted in Cairo in 1993. What is important about the MCPMR is the fact that for the first time since the OAU was founded in 1963, African leaders are now willing to consider the possibility of intervention in the internal affairs of member states as a way to secure the peace.

Adar also looks at how external actors (e.g., the United Nations and industrialized countries) can help Africans develop and sustain effective structures for peacekeeping in the continent. He takes a look at African peacekeeping capacity-building initiatives, with special emphasis on regional efforts (e.g., ECOMOG and its work in Liberia and Sierra Leone). Finally, he provides practical policy recommendations.

During most of the postindependence period, Africa's rich cultural diversity has served primarily as a major constraint to peace and as a result has contributed to underdevelopment in the continent. How to manage diversity and provide each country with an environment within which citizens can use their resources, including their talents, productively has been one of the most important areas of investigation by scholars of African political economy during the last fifty years years.

In Chapter 12, Ufo Okeke Uzodike revisits the concept of consociational democracy and proposes it as an institutional structure capable of enhancing the peaceful coexistence of the continent's population groups. In other words, argues Uzodike, consociational democracy can be used to significantly improve governance in Africa's segmented societies, cushion cultural cleavages, and effectively provide an enabling environment within which sustainable economic growth and development can take place.

Postindependence African politics has been preoccupied primarily with the struggle for resources, a process that can be linked to "one-man" rule, overcentralization of governance structures, venality and malfeasance in public office, and the monopolization of political power by ethnoregional coalitions. Political control has come to be synonymous with access to economic resources. Thus, those ethnic groups that control political institutions and governance structures enjoy a comparative advantage in the competition for wealth and income. During most of the last fifty years in Africa, then, Uzodike argues, political participation has been characterized by violent struggles among societal groups to capture political power and use it to plunder the economy for their own benefit. In such an environment, disadvantaged groups have tended to rally around their shared lines of affinity and demand redress from the state or violently attempt to capture the state. Many of these historically marginalized groups often come to see that their security and their very survival can only be guaranteed through a capture of the state. Uzodike argues that in order to maintain peace in these countries, cultural diversity must be managed effectively. He then suggests that consociational democracy can provide the appropriate tools to manage diversity properly, minimize destructive conflict, and enhance the productive use of resources.

At independence, Africans inherited from the colonial powers a state that was constructed for the sole purpose of exploiting Africans and their resources for the benefit of the metropolitan economies. Such a state was supposed to be dismantled, and then reconstructed and reconstituted, once it was in the hands of indigenous elites and its structures made more relevant to the needs of the African people. Unfortunately, few countries in the continent undertook such a reconstruction process. Where such a process was undertaken, it was reluctant and opportunistic and designed primarily to produce governance structures that enhanced the ability of the new custodians of the state to (1) monopolize political power and (2) plunder the economy for their own benefit. Thus, during most of the postindependence period political economy in the majority of African countries has been characterized by suffocation of civil society, high rates of corruption and public malfeasance, political violence, marginalization of certain sectors of society (especially women, children, rural inhabitants, and many minority ethnic groups), and poor economic policies.

In Chapter 13, 'Kunle Amuwo tackles the critical issue of "state repair" and how government can be made transparent, accountable, participatory, and more relevant to the lives of the citizens. The point of departure for Amuwo's analysis is that the African state, at the dawn of the twenty-first century, is basically a public institution whose structures have been effectively privatized and are being used by state custodians (i.e., the ruling elites) for private capital-accumulation purposes. As Africans struggle to bring about structural changes that can improve popular participation and make government more relevant to the lives of the people, entrenched groups, all of which are beneficiaries of the status quo, have been bitterly opposed to such reforms. To counter the efforts of grassroots organizations to make government more democratic, entrenched groups and their foreign benefactors, Amuwo argues, have developed and are implementing so-called transformation projects, which only serve to enhance their ability to monopolize political power and the allocation of resources. Hence, many of the so-called liberalization projects that several African countries are currently involved in will not significantly improve governance or resource allocation in the continent. They, however, will reinforce the hegemonic positions of entrenched groups and further push to the political and economic periphery historically marginalized and deprived groups and communities.

Amuwo indicates that the present state in Africa is torn between two contradictory pressures: one from citizens, especially the poor, to deal effectively with worsening living conditions, and the other from the international community (as represented by the IMF and the World Bank) to make capitalism the new "deity" in Africa. What is the way out? Amuwo's answer is the introduction of a people-driven democracy, a dispensation that would bring government closer to the people and make it more relevant to their lives. Such a popular substantive democracy would, in Amuwo's opinion, produce a state that is responsive, responsible, and accountable to the people.

In the immediate postindependence period the new African leaders embarked on a process of nation-building. In doing so, however, most of them rejected ethnicity as an organizing concept. In fact, leaders such as Julius Nyerere of Tanzania rejected ethnicity as the foundation for nation-building and argued that ethnic groups were moral enemies of the new state. Others, like Samora Machel, argued that in order for the state to survive, the tribe must be killed. There were, however, dissenting voices, as evidenced in Nnamdi Azikiwe's (first president of the Federal Republic of Nigeria) argument that it takes tribes to make a nation. Azikiwe's argument, supported by several others of his day, was to use the tribe as the "matrix for a politics of national imagining." In Chapter 14, Nantang Jua examines ethnicity and its role in national imagining in the postcolonial period in Africa. After presenting an historical review of the reasons given in favor of exorcising ethnicity from the process of state construction in Africa, he goes on to argue that ethnicity should be allowed to form an important building bloc of the postcolonial state.

In Chapter 15, E. Ike Udogu examines the struggle for stability in Nigerian politics, with specific emphasis on the period from 1990 to 1999. As is familiar to most students of Nigerian political economy, the country, which gained independence from Great Britain in 1960, has been ruled by military regimes during most of its existence as a sovereignty. During this time, military coups d'état came to be the most dominant method for regime change. Udogu's work reveals the extremely difficult and torturous road that Nigeria has traveled during the last forty years in its quest for political stability and economic growth. During this period, Udogu argues, the country has made a lot of mistakes and, he hopes, has learned from them. Given its status as the most populous country in Africa and one that has the potential (through its enormous endowments of human and natural resources) to lead the continent in the new century, Udogu argues, Nigeria must work diligently toward establishing stability and a democratic governance system that can be emulated by others in the continent. He then suggests some things that Nigerians and their leaders can do to move the country forward and ensure peace and sustainable development. He concludes that in the final analysis only those proposals that provide for maximum participation by the country's relevant stakeholder groups are likely to gain the legitimacy required for them to bring about the expected outcomes. In other words, unless Nigerians are enfranchised and provided the facilities to participate fully and effectively in state reconstruction, the outcome is not likely to be viable laws and institutions and the country will fail to achieve the peace and stability that it seeks.

Through so-called cooperation agreements signed between France and its former colonies prior to independence, France has managed to maintain a dominant position in the economies of most of the Francophone African countries. In addition, French influence in postcolonial Africa has also extended to the former Belgian colonies, especially Zaire (now called Democratic Republic of Congo). In recent years, France has courted many Anglophone African countries, and during the Cold War it conducted significant levels of trade (especially in military equipment and technology) with apartheid South Africa.

The French presence in post–Cold War Africa has been maintained through (1) trade; (2) investments (both portfolio and direct foreign investment, including the presence, in some Francophone countries, of large numbers of French entrepreneurs); (3) cultural and educational exchanges; (4) development aid (including food aid); (5) military aid (including arms transfers, provision of military experts to train African militaries, and the granting of "scholarships" for African military elites to engage in further study at French military academies); (6) direct military intervention to prevent the collapse of regimes friendly to France and its strategic interests in the region, as well as to help such regimes crush domestic insurrections; and (7) technical assistance (in the form of expatriate staff) to help train senior-level civil servants in administrative procedures, accounting, and other aspects of "governance."

In Chapter 16, Immanuel Tatah Mentan tackles an important aspect of French presence in Africa: its arms sales and military intervention in the continent, with specific emphasis on the period from 1960 to 1980. The exhaustive study determines that (1) French leaders of all political persuasions are united on the policy of arms production and export as a critical part of the country's economic growth strategy; (2) French military sales to Africa continue to represent a major portion of the country's merchandise exports to the continent; (3) training of African militaries by French experts keeps the armed forces of these countries connected to France and the latter's strategic interests in the region; (4) by using so-called development aid to train the police and paramilitary forces of the African countries, the French are assured of continued loyalty by the African ruling elites who must depend on these "security" forces to maintain law and order and retain their political positions; (5) French military bases in Africa and the cooperation agreements signed with African countries guarantee French businesses access to critical raw materials; (6) payment for imports of military equipment from France drains the meager foreign exchange reserves of poor African countries, forcing them to deepen their dependence on France; and (7) the proliferation of arms industries in France creates jobs for citizens, improves economic performance, enhances the development of technology, and generally improves the welfare of French citizens.

French economic and military activities in Africa during most of the postindependence period, as Mentan's analysis indicates, have generated enormous benefits for France and its citizens, and to a lesser extent, African ruling elites. The African people have been severely impoverished by most of these economic transactions, many of them have been killed by the soldiers trained by the French and with French guns, and the agroecological systems of many rural regions of the continent have been destroyed by the exploitation of raw materials for export to France.

What should Africans do to bring to a halt such destructive French interference in the African economies? First, as Mentan argues, African ruling classes need to rid themselves of the "enemy-thy-neighbor" mentality, which partly accounts for the obsession with military expansion in many countries throughout the continent. In fact, in most African countries today the armed forces, which consume a significant portion of the public budget, serve virtually no productive role. They do not contribute positively to the maintenance of peace. Most of them are actually used by the ruling classes to suffocate civil society, disenfranchise popular forces, and abuse human rights, all in an effort to help the incumbent ruling coalition maintain a monopoly on power. Unfortunately, the enormous amounts of resources devoted to military spending could actually be used to increase spending on welfare-enhancing areas such as health, nutrition, education, transportation, water, and HIV/AIDS education. Second, the adoption by Africans of a self-reliant approach to development should significantly reduce their dependence on France and other external actors. Finally, African countries should increase trade and other exchanges with each other. Such increases in regional economic cooperation should significantly reduce intercountry conflict and minimize the need for arms imports.

In line with the title of this book, contributors have attempted to deal with some of the problems that Africa faces at this point in its existence. While Africa as a continent has a lot of problems, the most important, as illustrated by the discussions in this book, is how to arm each country with accountable, transparent, and participatory governance structures and an economic system that encourages and enhances indigenous entrepreneurship and maximizes wealth creation. Africa is at a critical crossroads and the decisions made by its policy makers today can move the continent toward peace and sustainable development or toward increased poverty and further marginalization in global affairs. Whether the continent ends up at the periphery or the core of global affairs during the new century will be determined by the road chosen today. Of course, unless the people (i.e., the relevant stakeholder groups) are fully and effectively consulted and provided facilities to participate, meaning that choices are made through a democratic process, the continent is unlikely to move in the right direction. It is hoped that the contributors to this book have provided the African people in general and the continent's policy makers in particular with tools to make the right choice, one that will enhance the ability of the continent to finally achieve peace and sustainable development.

REFERENCES

Bates, R. H. 1981. *Markets and states in Tropical Africa*. Berkeley and Los Angeles: University of California Press.

Bates, R. H. 1987. *Essays on the political economy of rural Africa*. Cambridge: Cambridge University Press.

Decalo, S. 1992.. The process, prospects and constraints of democratization in Africa. *African Affairs* 9 (362): 7–35.

Ihonvbere, J. O. 1994. Nigeria: *The politics of adjustment & democracy*. New Brunswick, NJ: Transaction.

Ihonvbere, J. O. 1996. Where is the third wave? A critique of Africa's non-transition to democracy. *Africa Today* 43 (4): 343–368.

Mbaku, J. M. 1997. *Institutions and reform in Africa: The public choice perspective*. Westport, CT: Praeger.

Nyerere, J. 1966. *Freedom and unity*. Dar-es-Salaam: Oxford University Press.

UNDP. 2000. *Human development report, 2000*. New York: Oxford University Press.

UNDP. 2002. *Human development report, 2002*. New York: Oxford University Press.

Van de Walle, N. 1994. The politics of public enterprise reform in Cameroon. In *State-owned enterprises in Africa*, edited by B. Grosh and R. S. Mukandala. Boulder, CO: Lynne Rienner.

World Bank. 1996. *African development report, 1996*. Washington, DC: World Bank.

2

Africa at the Crossroads of Globalization

EMMANUEL NNADOZIE

Today, perhaps no issue elicits as much passion as globalization. Globalization is not just the most significant "socioeconomic phenomenon" in the late 1990s and early 2000; it is expected to be the most serious challenge for the world economy in the years ahead.[1] Trade, capital, and information flows have increased dramatically. For instance, global merchandise exports have increased from $3.2 trillion to $5.2 trillion (World Bank 2000, 313–315). There has been an increased integration of the world financial markets and dramatic expansion in financial flows. Today, American Express, Visa, and MasterCard provide worldwide credit card services. Direct foreign investment (DFI) has more than tripled in just eight years! From $193 billion in 1990, DFI rose to $619 billion in 1998. With recent advances in information technology, this trend is likely to intensify.

Yet globalization means different things to different people. To the antiglobalization interests—which massively manifested their strong opposition to globalization in Seattle, Washington, DC, Prague, and Davos[2]—it means job loss, sweat shops, child labor, limited national sovereignty, environmental destruction, economic exploitation, increased poverty, cultural domination, and more. These antiglobalization forces are not alone; many analysts of globalization also now believe that the developing countries will actually be worse off within a highly competitive global economy (Castells and Henderson 1978). There are fears that globalization may result in the disruption of the social fabric and further marginalization of whole regions (Swamy 1994).

To the proglobalizationists, otherwise known as the One Worlders, globalization means unlimited economic opportunities, economic growth, higher incomes, and improvement in labor and environmental standards. Along these lines, many information technology analysts believe "that the current trends are beneficial to the developing world, offering opportunities for economic growth to all countries" (Avgerou 1996, 148). Whose view is correct when it comes to the effects of globalization on Africa? What are the benefits and costs of globalization? Will globalization as it is presently conceived and proposed be beneficial to African countries, and why? What are the implications and lessons of the current globalization craze for African countries and what conclusions can we draw from these implications?

In this chapter we are mostly interested in Africa's neoliberal immersion into the global economy because of its germaneness as one of the most significant phenomena of contemporary discourse and its potentially serious consequences for Africa's development imperatives. The chapter focuses on the impact of economic globalization on the development prospects of African countries. Specifically, we examine the African experience with globalization and attempt to provide a balanced picture of globalization's pros and cons and its potential impact on economic development in the continent. The chapter is divided into five sections. Following this introduction, section two presents the conceptual and theoretical foundations for globalization in Africa to show the inapplicability of neoliberal theory in Africa's globalization reality. Section three deals with globalism and Africa's encounter with globalization. This section provides a brief historical overview of Africa's encounter with, and quest for, globalization, noting that the continent's experience with globalization dates back to the time of the African empires. This historical review is critical because it places Africa's globalization experience in the proper perspective.

The question of the costs and benefits of globalization is the object of section four. Evident from section four, and as much of the recent literature concludes, is Africa's overwhelming net losses from globalization. Section five presents the key policy implications and lessons learned and provides some recommendations that policy makers can implement to enhance the ability of their countries to participate in and benefit from the new globalization. This section also deals with the real dilemma surrounding globalization, which is not whether Africa should embrace globalization, but rather what type of globalization and under what terms. The critical recommendation is that African countries embrace globalization but only after taking into consideration (1) their individual specificities and (2) their historical experience with it. In any case, each country should engage in globalization on its own terms and in a way that maximizes net benefits from the process.

THE CONCEPT AND THEORY OF GLOBALIZATION

Although much has been written about globalization, until recently the focus has mainly been on the relationship between international capitalism and the nation-state through a political economy approach. The literature that looks at the economic angle focuses mostly on trade and economic integration. But what really is globalization? Is it a new phenomenon? Is it an all-encompassing buzzword and a new fad "that has political, economic, social, and institutional dimensions" (Edoho 1997, 3)? How has it unfolded and what has been its economic impact?

The Concept of Globalization

From a political viewpoint, globalization is seen as "the multiplicity of linkages and interconnections between the states and societies which make up the modern world system" (McGrew and Lewis 1995, 23). Globalization, in the political sense, is also a "process by which events, decisions, and activities in one part of the world can come to have significant consequences for individuals and communities in quite distant parts of the globe" (McGrew and Lewis 1995, 23) such that actions or incidents in the Middle East create political and economic ripples in Europe and the U.S. Hence, it is difficult to consider globalization from a purely economic perspective without considering global politics. In fact, multinational corporations (MNCs)—the major engines of globalization—have, in Sklar's (1999) view, become political and economic institutions such that one cannot separate their political and economic roles. He argues that in the postimperialist world MNCs have emerged to become "engaged in the exercise of power as well as in the creation and distribution of wealth" (Sklar 1999, 2).

According to Baker, Epstein, and Pollin (1998, 2) globalization is nothing but *globalized capitalism*, which has led to three things: (1) increase in international economic interactions, (2) qualitative changes in the way nation-states operate within any country's economy, and (3) a decrease in the power of nation-states and an increase in the power of private business and market forces. The extent of these changes is disputable because "globalization does not mean that the world is becoming more politically united, economically interdependent or culturally homogenous" (McGrew 1995, 23). In fact, "the international economy" is today "characterized by a fractured globalization" in that, contrary to the dictates of pure and full globalization, trade is conducted mostly within trading blocs, and global prices and rates in the financial and commodity markets are not harmonized and do not maintain parity (Harris and Michie 1998, 416). Hence, the current stage of global integration "is that of interdependent hyper-cycles of contemporary societies of developed, underdeveloped, and emerging economies" that are in a transition period characterized by "interdependency, some degree of chaos, and randomness" (Abedian and Biggs 1998, 7).

Since the main focus in this chapter is economic globalization, we can therefore define globalization as increasing economic interdependence among the countries of the world in which global politics plays a key role. This multiplicity of linkages, interconnections, interdependence, and dependence has been facilitated by improvements in transportation and communications and the removal of trade barriers. Contemporarily, global economic powers interested in extending their spheres of influence and control use globalist organizations and multilateral agencies and multinationals to internationalize capitalism. This is done through such programs as the shift to free-market economic reform, trade liberalization, and structural adjustment, the so-called neoliberal reforms imposed and managed by the multilateral agencies, including the International Monetary Fund (IMF), the World Bank, General Agreement on Tariffs and Trade (GATT), and the World Trade Organization (WTO).

The IMF uses conditionality to advance stabilization and adjustment loans, the Bank introduces policy-based loans, while the WTO practically removes any preferential trade regimes that African and other developing countries enjoy. All these coincide with the interest of the rich nations. With the support of their governments, the transnational corporations (TNCs), located mostly in rich industrial countries, contributed to globalization through mergers and acquisitions, thereby controlling most of the trade in the developing world. Hence, globalization is a term couched in neoliberalism, which denotes international capitalism or economic liberalization. More specifically, globalization involves the flow of capital, technology, people, ideas, and information, which means the increasing role of multinationals and increasing partnership among companies around the world. It can equally involve trends in mass media and institutional patterns of behavior, which lead to the spread of mass culture.

The pervasiveness of the current globalization trend is no accident. Perhaps Dunkley (2000) best captures the main tenets of globalization effort: a powerful push for global integration and global free trade that he refers to as "free trade adventure." This, according to him, is supposed to be accomplished through regionalism and multilateralism, two agendas mostly founded on the GATT and the WTO. The expected outcomes "range from a glorious new dawn of globalism and a massive stimulus for the world economy, to an economic, social and environmental disaster or the creation of a world-dominating bureaucracy which will enable giant TNCs to make the world their oyster" Dunkley (2000, 3). Through the IMF and the World Bank, he argues, neoliberal policies will be implemented in countries in the form of structural adjustment programs, which usually involve heavy economic and social costs.

However, the critical juncture in the emergence of globalization is the Uruguay Round of GATT, which according to Dunkley (2000) resulted in the emergence of a new world trading order and the extension of the concept of free trade. In Dunkley's view, the success of the Uruguay Round was due to the influence of very powerful corporate vested interests that had become quite interested in globalization. This raises questions about the influence and "coercive" power of the corporate groups that have so far backed neoliberal international economic policy and the motivations behind their strong lobby.

Yet the neoliberal proponents are not monolithic; if anything, their positions come in different forms and many of them have modified their positions following the Asian miracle (MacEwan 1999). Following the Asian financial crisis, divisions have appeared among their ranks. But the clear failures of neoliberalism, MacEwan concludes, have given rise to revisionism in the Bank and the

IMF—the strong bastions of globalization—even though revisionism, qualifications, and caveats have not, in his opinion, affected core Bank and IMF policies.

The Theory of Globalization

We need to understand globalization's theoretical underpinnings and relevance. From an economic standpoint, what could be considered a theory of globalization is the extension of the classical trade theory, the sum total of which is that international trade and integration into the global economy contribute to economic growth, improved allocation of resources, and improved overall welfare. The theory upon which the neoliberal vision of globalization rests states that free movement of goods (free trade), services, and capital, unimpeded by government regulations, will lead to rapid economic growth. According to neoclassicism, this will increase global output and international efficiency because the gains from comparative advantage-based division of labor and specialization will improve overall welfare. In its dynamic form, neoclassicists argue that trade raises domestic levels of income, which, in turn, raise the level of saving. Since investment depends on saving and leads to growth, trade will, therefore, lead to growth. Likewise, international mobility of financial capital will ensure that foreign capital will augment domestic saving and investment and lead to national economic growth.

The neoliberal position is not new, because the role that trade and international cooperation play in fostering economic growth has been identified throughout the history of economic thought. The Mercantilists believed in gold, encouraged exports, and discouraged imports. Following mercantilism, the classical economists undertook a comparative-advantage-based analysis (mainly by Adam Smith, David Ricardo, and J. S. Mill) to show the importance of international trade to economic growth.

Adam Smith observed in 1776 that specialization and trade increase the productivity of a nation's resources. His observation was related to the principle of absolute advantage, whereby a country should buy goods from other countries that can supply them cheaper. Following Adam Smith, the basic principle of comparative advantage was first observed and explained in the early 1800s by David Ricardo. According to this principle, it pays for a person or a country to specialize and exchange, even if that person or nation is more productive than potential trading partners in all economic activities. Specialization, Ricardo argued, should take place if there are relative cost differences in production of different items.

Modern trade models (such as the Heckscher–Ohlin Theory), which are based on the neoclassical trade theory, assume perfect competition and argue that trade enhances welfare by improving the allocation of productive resources across economic sectors (Nnadozie 1997, 158–160). Trade also improves productivity since "returns to entrepreneurial effort increase with exposure to foreign competition" (Tybout 1992, 190). Likewise, economic integration and cooperation are considered necessary for small fragmented economies to lower per unit production costs and to increase economic viability. Thus, integration of industrial production must accompany integration of markets.

Neoclassical trade theories and integration theories are of little relevance to Africa, because the fundamental neoclassical assumptions of full employment and perfect competition are absent in Africa, which is instead characterized by market segmentation and information asymmetries. The problem, as the case of Africa illustrates, is that although trade may increase total global output, equitable distribution of the gains from trade is far from guaranteed. This is because trade policy always has interpersonal, intersectoral, and intergroup redistributive consequences. Likewise, the returns-to-scale argument can move in both directions. Krugman (1985) and Rodrik (1998) have shown this with regard to pre-existing imperfect competition, in which case a domestic firm already enjoying market power faced with foreign competition may expand or exit. Furthermore, MacEwan (1999) argues that the Ricardian foundation of the neoliberalist theory is ideologically based. The claim that the neoclassical theory is validated by the history of economic development of Western Europe, the United States, and the newly industrialized countries is only mythical in MacEwan's view. "An examination of these experiences," he states, "quickly demonstrates that the neoliberal claims are but myths, having only a vague connection to reality" (MacEwan 1999, 35).

To support this pointed argument, MacEwan (1999) refers to the exclusion of labor in the neoliberal advocacy for unfettered and unregulated international flow of resources as a major flaw in the neoliberal theory and asks why there is not a comparable advocacy for the movement of labor across nations as there is for capital. MacEwan feels that the neglect of the social and political dimensions of globalization is a serious oversight because of their importance in the context of developing countries. In other words, there is an unequivocal support for the movement of goods and services and physical resources but not of people, because it is politically less palatable. Another criticism of neoclassical-based trade theory is that it could be interpreted to mean that Africa and other developing countries "should under welfare maximization and free trade continue to be producers of primary commodities, exchanging them for imports of manufactures" (Krueger 1984, 521). Hence, one cannot but conclude that the neoliberal foundations of globalization are inadequate in the African context and will lead to undesirable consequences. It seems, therefore, that therein lies the fundamental problem.

But where does Africa stand in this new conception of globalization? In the neoliberal globalization arrangements, "TNCs determine which countries participate in the new global re-division of labor" (Edoho 1997, 4). Since Africa is perceived as lacking attractive investment opportunities and due to the continent's lack of strategic interest to rich nations, Africa's role in global affairs remains marginal. Indeed, in all measurable respects Africa is the marginalized continent of the global economic system. Subjected to the dictates and whims of the global economy, Africa neither fully participates in the global environment nor benefits from its economic advantages. In short, as we shall see in the next sections, in the new globalization order, like the old one, Africa shares and disproportionately bears the costs but not the benefits of globalization.

GLOBALISM AND AFRICA'S ENCOUNTER WITH GLOBALIZATION

Looking at globalization in the African context, it is important to clarify the different modes of globalization that form the historical continuum under which the term has evolved. There is, first, Africa's preindependence insertion into the global marketplace. Then, there is Africa's globalism, its intentional geopolitical attempt at operating on the world stage. More recently, there is the neoliberalist (forced) immersion (albeit an incomplete one) of Africa into the global economy. Hence, globalization, in general and as far as Africa is concerned, is a multifaceted process. There is imposed or forced globalization as opposed to intentional globalization (or the taking by national elites of a globalist policy stance). There is also beneficial as opposed to nonbeneficial globalization, and Western conception or interpretation as opposed to African conception or interpretation of globalization.

We also note that Africa's globalization has been both externally and internally driven. In externally driven globalization, an African country has no control over its insertion into the global economic system and therefore can neither dictate nor control the terms of globalization. In contrast, internally driven globalization resulting from a deliberate decision by a country to adopt globalism or to become globalist permits the country to control the terms of its globalization. African countries have always sought to globalize and regionalize. Hence, the internally driven African model of globalization is old, dating back to the period of the great African empires as shown in the next section. This reality should not be ignored in formulating globalist policies.

The externally driven model is largely the consequence of precolonial, colonial, and postcolonial relationship with imperialist powers that African countries experienced with the rest of the world, Western Europe and the U.S. in particular. In this model, during the precolonial period, African producers of primary products, especially small agricultural households, were thrust into the global economy in which they were ill-equipped to compete. Also, colonial and imperialist powers established the rules of the game and controlled product prices. There is equally a new model of the externally driven globalization, which Chaliand (1999, 4) identifies as the "postimperialist" era characterized by "a class-based rather than a state- or system-centered" situation. The postimperialist globalization era also involves a move from "the domination of one people, nation, or country by another" to the domination of one people, nation, or country by international organizations, which "gradually supersede [national] economic, political, and social organizations" and in this situation, the transnational companies rule supreme, accompanied by "transformational class formation

based on the coalescence of dominant class elements across national boundaries" (Sklar 1999, 11). McGrew (1995, 23) distilled from the literature four
"fundamental processes of globalization" in the post–World War II period:
great-power competition, technological innovation and its diffusion, the internationalization of production and exchange, and modernization, or what Giddens
(1990, 6) calls "dynamism of modernity" (cited in McGrew 1995, 24).

ORIGIN AND FOUNDATIONS OF GLOBALISM AND GLOBALIZATION IN AFRICA

The term "globalization" in its literal sense is not a new phenomenon for
Africa and the rest of the world. What is new to Africa is the neoliberalist conception of globalization. In fact, "far from being a completely novel or primarily
twentieth-century phenomenon, a globalizing imperative has been evident in
many previous periods of history, and is, perhaps, most powerfully visible in
nineteenth century imperialism" (McGrew and Lewis, 1995, p. 23).

African history is replete with expansionism and integration through in-
tracontinental colonization and annexations that reached a crescendo in ancient
Egypt. Thus, contrary to Smith's (1995) argument that globalization began with
the strengthening of the global reach of Western Europe from the seventeenth to
the nineteenth centuries, Africa's experience with globalization predates this
period. Long before the rise of the European empires, African Sudanese empires
were expansionist states that cooperated with or integrated neighboring economies and the rest of the world. For instance, long before the eighth century the
Ghana Empire expanded to integrate much of Western Sudan. About 300 B.C.,
as the Ghana Empire flourished during its Iron Age, there was an influx of trad-
ers from the North and from the Nile region, thus marking the exposure of the
Ghana Empire to global forces through trade. By exporting gold, salt, and other
products, Ghana flourished through this newly found globalism.

All the Western Saharan empires were expansionist in nature and hence
globalist. As in the case of Ghana, Mali, and Songhay, Africa's encounter with
globalization was achieved through international trade, territorial expansion,
international relations, Islamic expansion and pilgrimages, foreign invasion, the
slave trade, and European colonization. It was also achieved through Africa's
encounter with capitalism, communism, and European/Christian expansionism.

However, since the formation of the European Coal and Steel Community
(ECSC) and the European Economic Community (EEC) in the 1950s, the propensity for regionalism and global integration has dramatically increased, especially in postcolonial Africa. Indeed, the Treaty of Rome (Article 131) explicitly
specifies the dynamics of the relations between African countries and the EEC.[3]
The Treaty of Rome provided for the association with the EEC of the colonies of
Belgium, France, Italy, and the Netherlands, the majority of which were in Africa (Okigbo 1967). The TNCs and the multinational companies (MNCs) have
also played significant roles in the integration of African countries into the

global economy. Other nongovernmental and international organizations and the former colonial governments have also contributed to Africa's global integration. At present, African countries are members of many regional, subregional, and international organizations.[4] Such multilateral organizations as the World Bank, the United Nations Development Program (UNDP), and the African Development Bank (ADB) have all contributed to Africa's insertion into the global economy.[5] The UNDP and the U.N. Economic Commission for Africa (ECA) have played major roles in enhancing African regional cooperation, thanks to their nature and constitution, which allows them to make resources available for intercountry activities. UNDP assistance is mainly in the areas of institution building, training, and provision of resources for start-up projects, as well as technical know-how.

The recognition and acceptance of the need for regional cooperation and a globalized worldview led to the creation of the African, Caribbean, and the Pacific (ACP) countries, based on the declaration of the Georgetown Agreement (1975) and the Suva Declaration (1977). Since these declarations there have been three Lomé Conventions (named after the capital city of Togo, where the European Community first met with ACP countries) to reinforce the objectives of the EC–ACP relationship. One of the aims of Lomé and of the ACP countries is to improve regional cooperation and gradually create larger integrated economies. Assistance by the EC for cooperation among ACP countries comes in the form of financing of regional multicountry projects in these developing countries. It is expected that regional cooperation funds will act as incentive for cooperation between ACP states, which will help in their eventual integration into the global economy. The EC support for regional cooperation began with Lomé I and continued to Lomé III.

The latest globalization instrument is the Africa Growth and Opportunities Act (AGOA), which spells out U.S. policy toward Africa. The AGOA authorizes the U.S. government to pursue a foreign policy that seeks to promote stable and sustainable economic growth and development in Africa through trade, investment, debt reduction, technical assistance, and infrastructure development. Although not purely a trade bill, the AGOA greatly emphasizes trade in a way that portrays the policy as being fundamentally and uniquely trade-oriented and designed to promote a trade-led African development policy.

Even though the AGOA is likely to boost exports for the "winners" in Africa, eligibility for participation in the program depends on the fulfillment by the African country of certain conditionalities, including the restructuring of the domestic economy to make it more market-driven, with special emphasis on the way capitalism is practiced in the United States. This presupposition presents several problems. First, it assumes that the American economic system is the best for everyone. Second, it assumes that the market-based economy as it is practiced in the United States, will succeed in Africa if African countries were willing to adopt it. Third, it neglects the length of time—hundreds of years—it took the U.S. market system to evolve into its present form of efficiency. The

AGOA focuses too much on opening African markets to U.S. exports. In this regard, one wonders if there is really any significant shift in U.S. policy toward Africa. Suppose that as a result of this bill Africans open their markets to U.S. exports and that the United States subsequently reduces or eliminates tariffs on goods originating in the African countries for sale in U.S. markets. What will be the most likely results? In the African markets, American goods will out-compete those produced in Africa in both price and quality, and in the U.S. market the same is true. The results are that U.S. producers will become dominant in African markets, forcing most African producers into bankruptcy and at the same time maintaining their economic positions in the U.S. economy. It is obvi-ous that the only beneficiaries from this state of affairs would be U.S. transna-tional companies, most of whom would use the new trade openings in Africa as a source for cheap raw materials and Africa's markets as dumping grounds for excess output from their U.S. factories, as well as their technologically obsolete products. In the process, Africa's opportunity for diversification of industrial base, industrialization, attracting foreign investment, and generally strengthen-ing the private sector would be squandered. In fact, a close look at the so-called trade act shows that it is most likely to sabotage Africa's efforts to create for itself a viable industrial base.

THE PROHIBITIVE COSTS OF GLOBALIZATION IN AFRICA

Since trade is the centerpiece of globalization, it is appropriate to pose the following question: How has Africa, which has 10 percent of the world's popu-lation and only 2.5 percent of the world's GNP, fared in global trade? Africa remains an insignificant player in global trade. For example, despite more than fifty years of independence, in 1998, the region called sub-Saharan Africa (SSA) accounted for less than 1.35 percent of world exports of $5.2 trillion and 1.5 percent of global imports of $5.3 trillion. In fact, the absolute increase in SSA exports between 1990 and 1998 was a mere $3.9 million dollars, whereas global exports increased by $1.9 trillion during the same period (World Bank 2000). In addition, Africa's international trade has a history of high volatility, especially from 1972 to 1982. There is lack of commodity diversification (primary prod-ucts are by far the dominant export commodity—oil, agricultural goods, timber, minerals); and most African countries remain almost totally dependent on the West European countries and the U.S. for the sale of most of their exports. It is interesting to note that most African countries do not trade with each other, pre-ferring instead to carry out most of their export and import trade with their for-mer colonizers (see, e.g., Mbaku 1997, 33–60).

How do trends in global trade affect the fifty three African countries, espe-cially since they are party to several important international trade agreements, such as the Uruguay Round of GATT, the agreement on textiles and clothing, the agreement on trade-related investment measures, and trade-related aspects of intellectual property? Very few African countries have benefited from these agreements. Except for Mauritius, Swaziland, Botswana, and Zimbabwe, few other countries have been able to reap any benefits from these "cooperation" agreements. Mauritius, Kenya, and Lesotho may increase textile exports under the agreement on textiles and clothing (USAID 1999a). In terms of the WTO, since most African countries are ill-equipped to participate in the WTO's areas of interest, "there is a real danger that some African countries will end up worse off than before" (USAID 1999b, 1). Based on the foregoing discussion, it is difficult to believe that the current global arrangements are of any significant benefit to African countries. Although it is true that globalization is not the root cause of many of Africa's economic and social troubles, it is not difficult to see that neoliberal globalization has not helped Africa and its citizens.

In adopting neoliberal economic reforms, one of the expectations of African countries is increased and, indeed, unfettered capital flows from the rich countries in the form of direct investment, which they perceive to be extremely beneficial to national development.[6] The reality, following over a decade of economic reform, is utterly disappointing. Dunning (2000, 20–21) confirms that developments in the global economy have deeply affected the pattern of foreign investment, leading to a "new geography of foreign direct investment" to the detriment of African countries. He speaks of "a spectacular increase in investment to Asia and to Central and Eastern Europe, modest increases to Japan and the EU, and relatively smaller gains" to the rest of the world.

Although during the post–Cold War era investment from the industrialized West into the developing countries has been increasing, Africa as a region has failed to benefit from such increased flows. For example, in 1997 sub-Saharan Africa received only 1.3 percent of the world's $394 billion in total direct foreign investments, a drop from 1.5 percent in 1996. In 1997, low- and middle-income countries received a total of $160,579 million, while SSA received only $5,222 million or 3.3 percent of the total (World Bank 1999).

A closer look at foreign investment in Africa reveals that most of it is concentrated in the extractive industries, primarily in petroleum and petroleum-related activities. It is only in South Africa that the majority of American investments exhibit some level of diversification (Williams 2000). In this one country, U.S. investment can be found in extractive as well as manufacturing concerns. In the International Financial Corporation's (IFC) ranking of developing country recipients of FDI for the period from 1970 to 1979, three African countries—Nigeria (3rd), South Africa (7th), and Algeria (12th)—appeared in the top twelve. For the period from 1980 to 1989, only Egypt (5th) and Nigeria (10th) appeared in the top twelve. For the period from 1990 to 1996, no African country appeared in the top twelve developing country recipients of FDI. Similarly, no African country ranked among the top twelve recipients in 1996 (IFC 1997, 17).

Many factors contribute to Africa's marginalization in a globalized world. Even though there are many internal constraints (including bad economic policies, corruption, financial mismanagement, political instability, including destructive ethnic conflict; see, e.g., Mbaku 2000) to the flow of investment into the continent, external factors have also contributed to Africa's present inability to attract foreign flows. For instance, in justifying his policy of engagement in China, President Clinton argued that a policy of "strategic partnership"—which has so far ignored the constraints posed by the Chinese economic sys-tem—would benefit both China and the United States. The U.S. administration's China policy was to use its economic and political relationships with the com-munist country to bring about fundamental changes in the latter. The American business community has responded accordingly, pouring some $167 billion dollars into China between 1990 and 1996 (IFC 1997, 17). Hence, in the case of China, U.S. investment is expected to bring about change, not follow it. How-ever, when it comes to Africa, the story is different. African countries are ex-pected to change before they can benefit from massive U.S. investment. It is often said that U.S. investment is low in Africa because of Africa's low absorp-tive capacity, inadequate economic structures, political instability, inadequate policies, and unfavorable business environment. Why is U.S. policy on foreign investment different when it comes to Africa? Why is it that when it comes to Africa, there is a tendency to assert that the business environment is not condu-cive enough for U.S. investment, while a similar environment in China is not a problem?

These painful facts notwithstanding, the neoliberal argument is that eco-nomic expansion and universalism of market capitalism and neoliberal democ-ratic norms will result in political and economic benefits for the world. Is this really the case for Africa? Many recent publications provide damning evidence of the gross failures of neoliberalism. Among these are Korten (1995), Rodrick (1997), MacEwan (1999), Dunkley (2000), and Ugarteche (2000). Essentially, these authors have argued that neoliberal policies have been detrimental to eco-nomic development in developing countries. Because of the human, environ-mental, social, and political costs, other analysts reject neoliberalism simply on ethical and moral grounds. However, not all researchers agree with criticisms of globalization.[7] For instance, Gilpin (2001, 367) believes that "many of the problems alleged to be the result of economic globalization are really the conse-quences of unfortunate national policies and government decisions." Many of these contributors argue against the existence of a third way, believing that such problems as the East Asian financial crisis were caused by wrong regulatory intervention, not by global forces.

Notwithstanding the polemics, history is essential to understanding the im-pact of globalization in Africa. This is because when the artificially created countries of Africa, exploited by slavery and colonialism (together with the gravely undermining political, social, and economic legacies of these two phe-nomena) are forced through neoliberal globalization imperatives to confront global market forces, they are bound to experience disastrous consequences, as Africa's current marginalization shows. Four historical facts are at play here. First, the human catastrophe and economic and social disaster created by the slave trade depleted Africa's human resources. Second, the unparalleled colonial physical and human resource exploitation, which included massacres, forced labor, and taxation, left Africa in a state of political and humanitarian disaster before independence. Third, the remote economic control and manipulation of the independent African states "locked into the extraction or production and export of raw materials," squarely placed the continent at the whim of unstable commodity markets and the policies of various development institutions (Thomas and Wilkins 1999, 10). Fourth, the more recent crushing debt burden and debt service exacerbated the continent's development problems and intensified the massive resource transfers from the continent to the creditor nations, making Africa a net capital exporter. Ugarteche (2000) shows evidence of what he calls systematic crisis and worsening of the LDC debt burden by IMF loans. In 2000, over half of the countries in Africa were no longer able to service their debts, let alone reduce them.

African dependency derives, therefore, from its historical experience with globalization through the slave trade, colonialism, and imperialism—the foundations of dependency. In modern times, the international debt crises and the IMF's SAPs have not only created new dimensions of dependency, but have also intensified traditional dependency. Because African countries and other LDCs owe Western institutions a lot of money, they were constrained in their efforts to restructure their economies, improve macroeconomic performance, and enhance development. Institutional reforms imposed by the IMF and World Bank have produced only disaster for the African economies: currency devaluation led to inflation, wage freezes intensified poverty, and cuts in government spending caused untold hardships, reduced the physical quality of life, and caused massive unemployment. In addition, trade liberalization worsened the terms of trade for the countries involved in structural adjustment. This continued dependence created the yearning for self-reliance by African countries as a strategy in the global economy. Notwithstanding the efforts made so far, the power of inherited dependency has made it very difficult for these countries to attain self-reliance, even though most of them are now politically independent. But what is the verdict on the neoliberal globalization order? Table 2.1 summarizes the major arguments on both sides of the debate.

One important argument being put forth is that neoliberalism has grossly overstated the economic benefits of globalization and understated its costs, especially where noneconomic costs are concerned (see Table 2.1). Hence, Dunkley (2000) states that if we consider noneconomic costs the virtues or so-called benefits of globalization may become degraded; hence the rise in international opposition and resistance to free trade and globalization. To this end, Rodrick (1997, 85) sees globalization and its consequential interlinking of national economies as part of a broader trend of "marketization" whose domestic counterparts are "receding government, deregulation, and the shrinking of social obligations."

Table 2.1
The Benefits and Costs of Globalization

Benefits According to the Proponents of Globalization	*Costs According to the Critics of Globalization*
Increase in the respect for human rights and political liberties	Control of the rules of engagement with national governments by multinational companies that force the latter to compete with each other for investment
Decrease in inequalities within and between states	Lessening of regulation, wage deterioration, and environmental degradation fueled by competition for foreign investment
Increase in cooperation through economic interdependence and an interlinked global civil society	Reduction in public spending by African governments in an attempt to create an inflation-free favorable business climate
Strengthening of international institutions as states perceive that their interests are met better through cooperation than competition	Erosion of state autonomy
Individualism that engenders self-interest and helps to unleash the human creative and productive potential	Increased state complicity with international capital. The coercion of the state to work for the interest of capital instead of the interest of the people, which leads to decrease in democratic accountability and in the supply of public goods
Universalism	Increase in poverty
The defense of property rights	Serious environmental damage
Limitation of state intervention	Increase in ethnic conflict
Economic regulation through market forces	Declining sense of community
Emphasis on efficiency and competitiveness that drives the penchant for divestment and cost-based decentralization of production	Unusually negative impact on women

Source: Synthesized from Tickner, J. A. 1999. Feminist perspectives on security in a global economy. In *Globalization, human security, and the African experience*, edited by Caroline Thomas and Peter Wilkins. Boulder, CO: Lynne Rienner. Also see World Bank. 1999. *World development indicators, 1999.* Washington, DC: World Bank.

Contrary to the argument that neoliberal policies are inevitable, economists (e.g., MacEwan 1999) use historical evidence to show that there is an alternative to neoliberalism and SAPs. Free trade, he argues, cannot be defended as an optimal policy on purely economic grounds because the choice is not necessarily between openness and autarky. Besides, globalization "is exposing a deep fault line between groups who have the skills and mobility to flourish in global markets and those who either don't have these advantages or perceive the expansion of unregulated markets as inimical to social stability and deeply held norms" (Rodrick 1997, 2). The result is different types of tensions and "seemingly insoluble societal conflicts that cut across national boundaries" (Rugumamu 1999, 4, citing Amin 1992, 1999). This is exemplified by severe tension between the market and such social groups as workers and pensioners (Rodrick 1997), as well as conflict with respect to religion, cultural autonomy, the environment, security, and individual and collective rights (Rugumamu 1999).

It is also important to note that the force of unfettered flow of capital, while good, could lead to such problems as intensification of inequality and division and "global openness undermines the already precarious position of subaltern groups and intensifies domestic inequalities" (Adams, Gupta, and Mengisteab 1999, 2, 6).

Globalization can equally lead to significant deindustrialization through import liberalization, as exemplified by the following: "A process of deindustrialization has taken place in many countries such as Zambia. Our once-flourishing textile industry has been wiped out by imports from Asia; several small industries such as tire manufacturers and medical supply companies have folded in the face of competition from large South African firms" (Henriot 2000, 3). Hence, the reemergence of globalization-led multinationalism has undoubtedly had severe negative impacts on Africa's small-scale entrepreneurs, the working poor, and agricultural small holders, the "passive subjects of globalization" in the words of Amin (1999, 19). Rugumamu (1999, 90) adds that "understandably, the significance and impact of globalization differs from one individual to another, from one group to the other, from one class to another, and from country to country." Nevertheless, "there is a growing awareness of the tensions between global economic forces and those who seek to maintain a civil society and human society; between global corporations and national democracy; and between efficiency and social contract" (Ash 1999, 90).

Hence, the costs of Africa's encounter with globalization are real and significant and should not be underestimated. There are social, economic, and environmental costs, but there are also potential benefits, although so far these have clearly bypassed the African continent. Given the immense price that Africans have paid for globalization, should African countries embrace it? The answer is a qualified yes. Africa must embrace globalization provided the benefits outweigh the costs and that Africans define the basis and conditions of participation in the global economy.

POLICY IMPLICATIONS AND LESSONS

To Globalize or Not to Globalize

To globalize or not to globalize, this is the question; or is it? The discussion about Africa's encounter with neoliberal globalization tends to center on whether or not the continent should globalize or embrace globalization. In reality, this question is inherently flawed. It is utterly fallacious to present Africa's globalization debate in terms of whether or not African countries should embrace globalization when they are already deeply entrenched in global economic arrangements, either by choice or by circumstance. Rather, a more appropriate question should be, Do African countries have a choice to globalize or not? To what extent should they continue to embrace neoliberal globalization under the current terms and conditions? Should African countries devise their own approach to globalization based on their own realities? Hence, the debate should be framed in terms of degree and type of globalization and on what terms and conditions.

As we saw in the preceding section, globalization is not new to Africa as African countries are already members of several global organizations (e.g., the U.N. and the WTO), albeit often in a nominal manner.[8] They contribute to and participate in the programs of several (global) multilateral organizations, including the World Bank and the IMF. African countries are heavily influenced by global phenomena, over much of which they have little control. Also, the globalization adventure has been extremely costly to Africa, even though there are potential benefits, as Table 2.1 shows. Hence, instead of focusing on the false debate of whether or not to embrace globalization, African countries must try to weigh the costs and benefits in order to effectively manage the reality of the globalization in which they find themselves. They must redefine globalization from their own point of view, and, according to their self-interest, dictate the terms of global relations and cooperation and maximize the benefits related to globalization while at the same time minimizing the costs.

The debate on globalism and Africa should center mainly on the structure of the relationship African countries should adopt with the rest of the world. On the one hand, the main question is whether African countries should aspire for integration or coordination within the African continent or a subregion. On the other hand, the question is whether African countries should strive for more global integration or cooperation.[9] Regardless of whether it is integration or cooperation, the critical issue is whether to adopt an isolationist posture and risk marginalization or embrace neoliberalist globalization and subject domestic economies to the vagaries and exploitative tendencies of the global markeplace. If an African country opts for a globalist approach to development, should it strive for total integration into the global economy or should it adopt a more cooperative (or coordinated) globalist posture? "Cooperation" and "coordination" are now preferred to the more rigid and probably less realizable "integration," which requires more drastic changes and shifts in the loci of political and economic control, with a new center exercising control over preexisting state authority. In contrast, global cooperation involves opening up to trade and technology through trade liberalization, building institutions for technological development, and fostering appropriate technology transfer. Cooperation can occur in the cultural, political, diplomatic, and economic spheres. It seems, therefore, more realistic for African countries to strive for cooperation rather than integration into the global economy.

Advocacy for globalization is mostly based on the benefits of free trade, which is believed to maximize internal and global welfare under a laissez-faire regime. For Africa, the need for global cooperation is economic (i.e., the need to engender national, continental, and regional economic growth) and political, in order to foster and preserve independence and democracy. The main argument in favor of global cooperation is that trade has played an important role in the economic growth of many nations. To grow rapidly, therefore, African countries must take trade seriously. Another argument in favor of global cooperation is that the absence of such cooperation causes a loss of markets, technology transfer, and capital, as well as the global interrelationships necessary to foster economic development. It appears that African countries must work harder to increase the flow of capital and technology into their countries.

Furthermore, global cooperation fosters political stability through induced democratic reforms and mutual political reinforcement by regional and global political organizations. Efficiency gains result from the use of scarce resources and improved quality of goods and services, improved resource allocation, and increased competition and product specialization. Although losses may result mainly from comparative and absolute advantages that will accompany a more globalist posture, openness, if properly engaged, will ensure net gains to participants in the form of cheaper imports, more effective utilization of technological economies of scale, and increased competition.

Africa inevitably needs some form of global collaboration, cooperation, or coordination. This is because such active involvement in the global economy improves information, labor, and capital flows for increased investment and encourages technology transfer. Moreover, Africa's inability to generate enough resources domestically to meet its investment needs implies that it has to seek assistance in the global economy so that it can secure the resources needed to augment domestic capital-formation efforts. Foreign investment can also be useful in improving management, productivity, total output, and economic growth. A good example is the case of Costa Rica, whose original exports were traditionally coffee and bananas. Through its assembly plant, Intel has generated a veritable economic transformation in Costa Rica. Costa Rica's "GDP surged by 8.4 percent, with output from the Intel plant making up half of that growth and 37 percent of the country's exports" (*Newsweek*, August 28, 2000, 42).

To What Extent Should Africa Embrace Globalization?

In determining to what extent to embrace globalization and the best approach to use, African leaders must examine the impact that globalization has already had in the continent. To do this, they must pose some key questions. How does increased globalization affect the growth and structure of African economies? For instance, how much power do African countries have to determine the terms and conditions of increased globalization? How will mining, agriculture, and manufacturing be affected? What impact will globalization have on income distribution? What effect will globalization have on national policy in the African countries? What will be the reaction of international markets to domestic policy measures? What are the likely development issues for African countries, and will globalization enhance, impede, or be neutral to these issues?

Providing appropriate answers to these questions should assist African countries in determining whether or not the pursuit of globalization is a desirable goal. For sure, the effects of globalization should be viewed in terms of the impact of capitalism and unfettered global capital on Africa's political, sociocultural, economic, and environmental conditions. Hence, while remembering their experience with globalization, African countries must ask themselves to what extent global capitalism addresses/alleviates or exacerbates the continent's critical long- and short-term concerns. This question is important because the main concerns that African countries have today are the HIV/AIDS epidemic, poverty, corruption, political instability and ethnic conflict, low growth, and a relatively heavy debt burden. As Table 2.2 shows, in all these categories Africa is either disproportionately negatively affected or has performed worse than the rest of the world. Sub-Saharan Africa's debt burden in 1998, measured by external debt/GNP ratio, was 67.9 percent, compared to 41.3 percent for all developing countries and 43.6 percent for the world (UNDP 2000). To determine the efficacy of globalization, therefore, one must examine to what extent these problems have been mitigated or exacerbated by globalization or to what extent globalization has created more problems. This is because globalization will mean nothing to Africans if it cannot contribute to the alleviation of the continent's perennial malaise.

In the 1960s a good number of African countries, such as Nigeria, experimented with inward-oriented development strategies involving import substitution as opposed to outward-oriented (export promotion/globalist) strategies adopted by some other LDCs. Those countries that opted for export-led growth experienced relatively high growth rates. Growth rates showed a remarkable temporal jump once export promotion measures were adopted, and noticeable dynamic effects were created in their economies due to improved resource allocation (Bhagwati 1978; Balassa 1982; Krueger 1990; McCarville and Nnadozie 1995). Another issue is the overwhelming evidence in favor of openness rather than protectionism. Countries grow more and faster when they are open than when they are closed. This does not mean that the practice of protectionism may not be beneficial in some instances, as Krugman (1985) shows. This is because protectionism could create a permanent shift in comparative advantage in the home relative to foreign country in terms of productivity growth.

This is especially true of labor-abundant economies, of which African countries are the majority. However, a combination of evidence from research and the net benefits of the outward-oriented approach make the latter better than import substitution industrialization. African countries must learn the implicit and explicit lessons of their encounter with globalization, make the necessary adjustments, and become more engaged in the global economy. They should participate in the global arena, especially to the extent that global cooperation helps fulfill strategically defined short- and long-term interests. To deal with the seemingly insurmountable obstacles shown in Table 2.2, Africa needs the support of the rest of the world. African leaders need to heed Asante's (1986, 11) advice: "Economic integration in the case of developing countries should be treated as an approach to economic development rather than a tariff issue." Of course, it is important that African countries prepare themselves well for any type of engagement in the global economy so that cooperation with international actors brings the continent net benefits.

Table 2.2
Africa's Problems Compared with the Rest of the World

	Sub-Saharan Africa	*Other Developing Countries*	*World*
AIDS[1]	7.8%	1.18%	0.99%
Human Welfare[2]	0.464	0.642	0.712
Poverty[3]	46.3%	—	24.0%[4]
Corruption[5]	4.97	6.03	—
Conflict	1.27	0.72	—
Annual Growth of GNP, 1990–1998	-0.4%	3.3%	1.0%

Notes: [1]People living with AIDS, measured as a percentage of people aged 15 to 49 years in 1997.
[2]Measured by the UNDP's human development index, which ranges from 0 to 1. The higher the index, the greater the level of human development. Data are for 1998.
[3]Proportion of the population living on less than U.S. $1.00 per day. Data are for 1998.
[4]Excludes China and North America.
[5]The lower the score, the higher the level of corruption within the country.
Sources: UNDP. 2000. *Human development report, 2000.* New York: Oxford University Press; World Bank. 2001. *World development report, 2001.* New York: Oxford University Press; Collier, P., and J. W. Gunning. 1999. Explaining African economic performance. *Journal of Economic Literature* 37 (March): 67.

LESSONS AND RECOMMENDATIONS

From this chapter we can learn two important things: (1) There are no absolute solutions and (2) instead of a heavy ideological or political focus, each African country must adopt a pragmatic choice of policies based on its historical, social, political, economic, and environmental realities. Policies could carefully mix interventionist and laissez-faire strategies. Collier and Gunning (1999, 64) identify five factors responsible for Africa's poor growth performance: lack of social capital, lack of openness to trade, deficient public service, geography and risk, lack of financial depth, and high aid dependence. In particular, they conclude, "[n]either households nor firms have as yet sufficiently created the social institutions that promote growth." Likewise, the World Bank (2000) asks if Africa can claim the twenty-first century, and recommends, among other things, diversifying exports, reorienting trade policy, pursuing regional integration, and reducing aid dependence and debt. Very strikingly, these two important contributions to the literature ignore the external dimensions of Africa's poor economic performance. They ignore the colonial legacy and the impact of global economic policy on Africa's lackluster growth performance. They do not address the role, responsibilities, and implications for non-African development stakeholders and partners, especially with regard to the policies of multilateral organizations, increased access to rich countries' markets, and overall international support for African development initiatives.

Other analysts recognize the external dimension of Africa's problems and give a variety of recommendations. Some suggest radical liberalism concerned with justice and development from below. Mengisteab (1996) calls for autocentricity and an autocentric development approach that ends fragmentation and duality. MacEwan (1999, 147–148) recommends a "democratic economic development strategy," which entails increased taxes and government spending, expansion of social programs, targeted investment incentives, recognition of the value of local production, and land reform.

The UNDP calls for globalization with a human face, arguing that globalization represents a tremendous opportunity to deal with global challenges and problems. But the UNDP recognizes that globalization has potential negative economic, social, environmental, and political consequences.[10] Clearly, the UNDP would not have advocated for globalization with a human face were globalization not perceptibly bereft of consideration of the human element. All said and done, even the World Bank now recognizes that globalization can exacerbate poverty by causing shocks and disruptions to domestic economies and recommends the following methods for addressing this externally induced poverty (World Bank 2000, 37):

- expanding market access in rich countries for developing countries' goods and services;
- reducing the risk of economic crises;

- encouraging the production of international public goods that benefit the poor; and
- ensuring a voice for poor countries and poor people in global forums.

But how specifically can African countries increase their clout and make their voices heard? For a start, they must aggressively seek to have an African country become a permanent member of the U.N. Security Council. To attract and retain foreign capital, African countries must establish the appropriate or enabling environment for such investment to be profitable and contribute to national development. At the same time that governments are working hard to reduce political risk and strive for political stability and investment protection, they must aggressively recruit investors and court DFI.

One area in which many African governments have failed is in mobilizing and tapping the expertise and resources of African émigrés, especially those living in the West. These highly skilled and knowledgeable individuals can help Africa in many ways. However, for them to do so they must be made welcome in the African countries, especially considering the fact that many of them were forced, by either a high level of political violence or perverse economic policies, to flee abroad. For example, Americans of African origin (those born in the United States, as well recent immigrants from the continent now residing in the United States) can play a major role in the crusade to significantly increase American investment in Africa. These private citizens can act as individuals, as groups, or as professionals if African governments are willing to tap into this resource. The advantage is that this will help in reversing the brain drain that has plagued the continent. With some encouragement, these overseas Africans can specifically make significant contributions in the following ways:

- Choosing investment portfolios with a strong consideration for Africa-friendly firms and purchasing African stocks, African-focused stocks, or Africa-friendly stocks.
- Investing in African capital markets.
- Using one's expertise and knowledge of the American business environment and financial markets to promote American investment in Africa.
- Identifying African businessmen and businesswomen with whom one can develop a partnership or who can become suppliers and clients or with whom one can do business.
- Organizing professionally to undertake direct volunteer action to expand and strengthen the private sector of African countries and to promote U.S. investment and economic development in Africa.

Regardless of which strategy they wish to adopt or what they choose to do, African countries must handle globalization very carefully and see it as a means, not as an end. In fact, they need to rethink their growth strategies given the current increasingly globalized environment (Wallace 1999). They must learn from the East Asian experience of adeptly managing globalization. Amin (1999, 23) argues that "East Asian countries have been successful precisely to the extent that they have subjected their external relationships to the requirements of their internal development and have refused, at least until recently to 'adjust' to dominant tendencies at the world level." This is precisely what Africa needs to do.

Because the impact of globalization varies among individuals, countries, and regions, the approach used to embrace globalization must also differ. Therefore, there is a need and basis for adopting a multidimensional, internally driven, Africa-oriented approach to globalization. Regional cooperation must be strengthened in addition to public- and private-sector cooperation and partnership. In addition, Africa must make its voice heard in the international arena, be it through the U.N. or the WTO.

Hence, African countries must strategically position themselves to take advantage of the opportunities presented by the global markets in which they have found themselves. They must negotiate from a position of strength to eliminate some of the bottlenecks and conditionalities encountered in their attempt to access global markets and resources. They must identify their areas of comparative advantage and establish appropriate strategies for developing the relevant sectors of their economies associated with these areas.

African countries must have reasonable exchange rate policies and focus on export promotion and production of manufactures for export rather than on import substitution. They must maintain a country-specific approach in the operational aspects of programs and avoid accepting any one-size-fits-all proposals that come from the multilateral agencies. Finally, they must maintain a degree of consistency, especially in policy matters, and seriously boost regional cooperation and intra-Africa trade. Because of the smallness of the private sector in most African countries, public–private partnerships will be needed in most cases.

CONCLUSION

This chapter examined the phenomenal expansion in global interrelationships, the concept and theory of globalization, and Africa's experience with neoliberal globalization. The chapter asks a series of questions: Does the neoliberal theory of globalization apply to Africa? What is globalization's record in African history? What is the impact of neoliberalism? What policy implications do these issues have for Africa and should Africa embrace neoliberal globalization or not? Based upon available evidence, the chapter concludes that although globalization is one of the most important phenomena of the 1990s and 2000s, it is still a difficult concept to define because it means different things to different people. Nations perceive globalization from their strategic interest. For the high-income countries, it is a means of fostering economic expansion and enhancing national security. To Africans, it is a means of addressing basic human and development needs. Notwithstanding its tendency to stir significant polarization and controversy, the so-called globalization is not really globalization because it tends to ignore the continent of Africa. Its impact varies around the globe. For one thing, it is creating interconnections and economic and political linkages. It creates unequal gains and pains, and in the case of Africa, the pains outweigh the gains. Africa's response to globalization has been mostly to pursue regionalism. African countries must adopt a globalist approach, not be driven by, or become victims of, increased globalization over which they have no control. In harnessing the benefits of globalization, they must view globalization in terms of global cooperation rather than global integration. In other words, maximize the benefits of globalization while at the same time minimizing its costs.

ACKNOWLEDGMENTS

The author is indebted to Professors John Quinn, Seymour Patterson, and John Ishiyama for their invaluable insights and comments on earlier drafts of this chapter. I also thank Teresa York, Summer Battles, Martha Miricho, Annette Hoskins, and Lisa Miller for their important contributions at various stages of the development of this chapter.

NOTES

1. According to the views of Christian Avgerou (1996, 147). Rodrick (1997, 2), states, "The most serious challenge for the world economy in the years ahead lies in making globalization compatible with domestic social and political stability or to put it even more directly, in ensuring that international economic integration does not contribute to domestic social disintegration."

2. In Seattle during the World Trade Organization ministerial meetings in December 1999, in Prague during the annual meeting of the World Bank and the IMF, and in Davos, Switzerland during the World Economic Forum.

3. The Treaty of Rome was signed in 1957, establishing the foundation for the formation of the EEC. The African territories referred to, according to Okigbo (1967, 26), were French West Africa (Senegal, the Sudan, Guinea, Ivory Coast, Dahomey, Mauritania, Niger, Upper Volta), French Equatorial Africa (Middle Congo, later known as Congo Brazzaville, Ubangi-Shari, Tchad, Cameroon), and dependencies, Togo, Belgian Congo, Rwanda-Urundi, and Somaliland under Italian Trusteeship.

4. Examples of regional organizations are the African Economic Community and the Organization of African Unity; subregional organizations include Economic Community of West African States and the Southern African Development Community.

5. Of notable contribution are the following U.N. agencies that are active in Africa: United Nations Disaster Relief Office, United Nations Center for Human Settlements, United Nations Children's Fund, United Nations Conference on Trade and Development, United Nations Environment Program, United Nations Population Fund, United Nations Development Program, and the Economic Commission for Africa.

6. Such benefits include increased economic growth and a positive spillover from transferring technology to domestic firms (Caves 1982; Helleiner 1989; Haddad and Harrison 1993). Furthermore, foreign presence accelerates productivity growth (Aitken and Harrison 1999) and transnational corporations had direct and indirect positive employment effect in manufacturing and service (Haddad and Harrison 1993; Lal 1995; Chitraker and Weiss 1995). Direct foreign investment is also more stable and "less vola-

tile (as measured by the coefficient of variation) than commercial bank loans and foreign portfolio flows" (World Bank 1999, 37).

7. See, for instance, Gilpin (2001, 367). See also Sahn, Dorosh, and Younger (1997). For the proponents of globalization, see also Vasquez (2000).

8. As of November 2000, 41 of the 140 members of the WTO were African countries, with the majority of them joining the organization right at inception on 1 January 1995.

9. The literature on the theory of integration posits two schools of thought: federalism, based on political determinism, and functionalism (orthodoxy) as proposed mainly by Viner (1953), based on economic determinism. The two schools of thought differ essentially on the basis of whether political integration should precede economic integration or vice versa. The ultimate goal of the traditional integration theory—increases in global welfare—may not be the primary concern of African countries. African countries' dynamic goals are to improve trade within their region and to change the structure of their trade and their economies for long-run gains, not necessarily to increase aggregate welfare in the short-run. Hence, cooperation between African countries and the rest of the world will, in part, be to create the preconditions of integration suggested by the orthodox model.

10. The *Human Development Report, 1999* of the UNDP (1999) provides a very compelling and detailed analysis of the impact of globalization, as well as a comprehensive discussion on the solution to these problems.

REFERENCES

Aitken, B. J., and A. E. Harrison. 1999. Do domestic firms benefit from direct foreign investment? Evidence from Venezuela. *American Economic Review* 89 (3); 605–618.

Abedian, I., and M. Biggs. 1998. *Economic globalization and fiscal policy*. New York: Oxford University Press.

Adams, F., S. D. Gupta, and K. Mengisteab. 1999. Globalization and the developing world: An introduction. In *Globalization and the dilemmas of the state in the south*, edited by F. Adams, S. D. Gupta, and Mengisteab. New York: St. Martin's Press.

Amin, S. 1992. *The empire of chaos*. New Monthly Review Press.

Amin, S. 1999. For a progressive and democratic New World Order. In *Globalization and the dilemmas of the state in the south*, edited by F. Adams, S. D. Gupta, and Mengisteab. New York: St. Martin's Press.

Asante, S.K.B. 1986. *The political economy of regionalism in Africa: A decade of the Economic Community of West African States (ECOWAS)*. New York: Praeger.

Ash, R. 1999. *The Third World in the age of globalization: Requiem or new agenda*. Delhi, India: Madhyam Books.

Avgerou, C. 1996. How can information technology enable developing countries to integrate into the global economy? In *Global information technology and systems management: Key issues and trends*, edited by P. C. Palvia, S. C. Palvia, and M. E. Roche. Nashua, NH: Ivy League.

Baker, D., G. Epstein, and R. Polin. 1998. *Globalization and progressive economic policy*. New York: Cambridge University Press.

Balassa, B. 1982. *Development strategies in semi-industrial economies*. Baltimore: Johns Hopkins University Press.

Bhagwati, J. N. 1978. *Foreign trade regimes and economic development: Anatomy and consequences of exchange control regimes.* Cambridge, MA: Ballinger Press.

Caves, R. W. 1982. *Multinational enterprise and economic analysis.* Cambridge: Cambridge University Press.

Castells, M., and J. Henderson. 1978. Techno-economic restructuring, socio-political process and spatial transformation: A global perspective. In *Global restructuring and territorial development*, edited by J. Henderson and M. Castells. London: Sage.

Chaliand, G. 1999. Foreword. In *Post-imperialism and world politics*, edited by D. G. Becker, and R. L. Sklar. Westport, CT: Praeger.

Chitrakar, R., and J. Weiss. 1995. Foreign investment in Nepal in the 1980s: A cost benefit evaluation. *Journal of Development Studies* 31: 451–466.

Collier, P., and J. W. Gunning. 1999. Explaining African economic performance. *Journal of Economic Literature* 37: 64–111.

Dunkley, G. 2000. *The free trade adventure: The WTO, the Uruguay Round and globalism—A critique.* London: Zed Books.

Dunning, J. W. 2000. Globalization and the new geography of foreign direct investment. In *The political economy of globalization*, edited by N. Woods. New York: St. Martin's Press.

Edoho, F. M. 1997. Globalization and the New World Order. In *Globalization and the New World Order: Promises, problems and prospects for Africa in the twenty-first century*, edited by F. M. Edoho. Westport, CT: Praeger.

Giddens, A. 1990. *The consequences of modernity.* Cambridge: Polity Press.

Gilpin, R. 2001. *Global political economy: Understanding the International Economic Order.* Princeton: Princeton University Press.

Haddad, M., and A. Harrison. 1993. Are there positive spillovers from direct foreign investment? Evidence from panel data for Morocco. *Journal of Development Economics* 42 (1): 51–75.

Harris, L., and J. Michie. 1998. The effects of globalization on policy formulation in South Africa. In *The effects of globalization on policy formulation in South Africa*, edited by D. Baker, G. Epstein, and R. Polin. Cambridge: Cambridge University Press.

Helleiner, G. K. 1989. Transnational corporations and direct foreign investment. In *Handbook of development economies*, edited by H. Chenery, and T. N. Srinivasan. Amsterdam: North-Holland.

Henriot, P. 2000. Globalization: Implications for Africa. Lusaka, Zambia: Jesuit Center for Theological Reflection. http://www.sedos.org/english/global.html.

IFC. 1997. *Foreign direct investment: Lessons of experience.* Washington, DC: IFC.

Korten, D. C. 1995. *When corporations rule the world.* West Hartford, CT: Kumarian Press.

Krueger, A. O. 1984. Trade policies in developing countries. In *Handbook of international economics*, edited by R. W. Jones and P. B. Kenen. New York: Elsevier Science.

Krueger, A. O. 1990. Import substitution versus export promotion. In *International economics and international economic policy: A reader*, edited by P. King. New York: MacGraw-Hill.

Krugman, P. 1985. The narrow moving road, the Dutch disease and the competitive consequences of Mrs. Thatcher: Notes on trade in the presence of dynamic scale economies. *Journal of Development Economics* 27: 41–45.

Lal, S. 1995. Employment and foreign investment: Policy options for developing countries. *International Labor Review* 134 (4–5): 521–541.

MacEwan, A. 1999. *Neoliberalism or democracy? Economic strategy, markets, and alternatives for the 21st century.* London: Zed Books.

Mbaku, J. M. 1997. *Institutions and reform in Africa: The public choice perspective.* Westport, CT: Praeger.

Mbaku, J. M. 2000. *Bureaucratic and political corruption in Africa: The public choice perspective.* Malabar, FL: Krieger.

McCarville, M., and E. Nnadozie. 1995. Causality tests for export-led growth: The case of Mexico. *Atlantic Economic Journal* 23 (2): 140–145.

McGrew, A. G. 1995. Conceptualizing global politics. In *Global politics: Globalizataion and the nation-state*, edited by A. G. McGrew and P. G. Lewis. Cambridge, MA: Blackwell.

McGrew, A. G., and P. G. Lewis, eds. 1995. *Global politics: Globalization and the nationa-state.* Cambridge, MA: Blackwell.

Mengisteab, K. 1996. *Globalization and autocentricity in Africa's development in the 21st century.* Trenton, NJ: Africa World Press.

Nnadozie, E. 1997. Trade and regional cooperation strategy for African economic development in the twenty-first century. In *Globalization and the New World Order: Promises, problems and prospects for Africa in the twenty-first century*, edited by F. M. Edoho. Westport, CT: Praeger.

Okigbo, P.N.C. 1967. *Africa and the Common Market.* Evanston, IL: Northwestern University Press.

Palvia, P. C., S. C. Palvia, and M. E. Roche, eds. 1996. *Global information technology and systems management: Key issues and trends.* Nashua, NH: Ivy League.

Rodrick, D. 1997. *Has globalization gone too far?* Washington, DC: Institute for International Economics.

Rodrik, D. 1998. Globalization, social conflict and economic growth. *World Economy* 2 (2): 143–158.

Rugumamu, S. M. 1999. *Globalization, liberalization and Africa's marginalization.* Occasional Papers. Harare, Zimbabwe: African Association of Political Science.

Sahn, D. E., P. A. Dorosh, and S. D. Younger. 1997. *Structural adjustment reconsidered: Economic policy and poverty in Africa.* Cambridge: Cambridge University Press.

Sklar, R. L. 1999. Post-imperialism: Concepts and implications. In *Post-imperialism and world politics*, edited by D. G. Becker and R. L. Sklar. Westport, CT: Praeger.

Smith, M. 1995. Modernization, globalization and the nation-state. In *Global politics: Globalization and the nation-state*, edited by A. G. McGrewand and P. G. Lewis. Cambridge, MA: Blackwell.

Swamy, D. P. 1994. *The political economy of industrialization: From self-reliance to globalization.* New Delhi: Sage.

Thomas, C., and P. Wilkins, eds. 1999. *Globalization, human security, and the African experience.* Boulder, CO: Lynne Rienner.

Tickner, J. A. 1999. Feminist perspectives on security in a global economy. In *Globalization, human security, and the African experience*, edited by C. Thomas and P. Wilkins. Boulder, CO: Lynne Rienner.

Tybout, J. R. 1992. Lining trade and productivity: New research directions. *World Bank Economic Review* 6 (2): 189–211.

Ugarteche, O. 2000. *The false dilemma: globalization: Opportunity or threat?* (Translated by Mark Fried). London: Zed Books.

UNDP. 1999. *Human development report, 1999.* New York: Oxford University Press.

UNDP. 2000. *Human development report, 2000.* New York: Oxford University Press.

USAID. 1999a. *Africa's opportunities in the new global trading scheme.* EAGER Policy Brief 38 (January). Washington, DC: USAID.

USAID. 1999b. *Implications for Africa of Initiatives by the WTO,* European Union, and U.S. EAGER Policy Brief 39. Washington, DC: USAID.

Vasquez, I., ed. 2000. *Global fortune: The stumble and rise of world capitalism.* Washington, DC: Cato Institute.

Viner, J. 1953. *The customs union issues.* New York: Carnegie Mellon Endowment for Peace.

Wallace, L. 1999. *Adjusting to the challenges of globalization.* Washington, DC: International Monetary Fund.

Williams, S. 2000. Globalization and the new South Africa. *African Business* 252: 32–34.

World Bank. 1999. *World development report, 1999/2000.* London: Oxford University Press.

World Bank. 2000. *World development report: Attacking poverty.* New York: Oxford University Press.

World Bank. 2001. *World development report, 2001.* New York: Oxford University Press.

3

Globalization and Popular Disenchantment in Africa

FRANCIS B. NYAMNJOH

Defined as the compression of time and space or "the intensification of world-wide social relations which link distant localities in such a way that local happenings are shaped by events occurring many miles away and vice versa" (Giddens 1990, 63–78), globalization is seen as a process of accelerated flows of capital, consumer goods, people, and products of culture and knowledge (especially in the form of electronic audiovisual images) (cf. O'Brien 1993; Appadurai 1996; Thompson 1999; Geschiere and Meyer 1998; Meyer and Geschiere 1998; Gray 1998). While international flows could be traced back to when humankind first attempted the domestication of time and space, it is generally agreed that the rapid advances in communication and information technologies of the last twenty years have had the greatest impact on the process.

It has been argued that due to the emergence of the information superhighway, the way wealth is created has been changed remarkably (Jussawalla 1988). There has been a shift from real cash to electronic "cash" and electronic payment systems, which has radically transformed the way banking and commerce are conducted (Moore 1997/1998, 277–278; Lynch 1997/1998, 295–296). In almost all information societies, the information sector, whose function is "to satisfy the general demand for information facilities and services . . . is growing much faster than the overall economy" (Moore 1997/1998, 272). Experts believe that "the long-term success of many commercial organizations will be determined by their capacity to use and manage information to reduce costs, to extend their range of services, to reduce risk and to become more sensitive to customer demands" (Moore 1997/1998, 278).

However, others have pointed out that the rush to create new information and communication technologies is, to a large extent, driven by the irresistible drive to accumulate and to maintain economic, political, and cultural privileges and advantage (cf. Schiller 1983). In what concerns the Internet, for example, some maintain that if the business world is promoting it, "their motive is to create a sense of need" for their products, and "once this perceived need is cultivated, some organizations then require a membership or annual subscription fee for the information or service that you initially accessed without cost" (*Awake*, July 22, 1997, 8), a tendency which has led others to wonder if the information superhighway can ever truly become as available and affordable as is fashionable to claim, given the fact that information, as commodity and power, is often to be paid for and to be controlled (Lee 1995, 2; P. Hamelink 1995, 16). If it were, indeed, to become available and affordable, "the question of the quality of the information" on the Internet would still be raised, for an easily accessible and relatively cost-effective Internet could boast of little more than "information rubbish" or "scrap opinion" (Becker 1996, 11). Even now already, "there is . . . an awful lot of junk, trash, and trivia" on the Internet (C. J. Hamelink 1996, 19). The debate is, however, open. But Africa is yet to really experience such technology, the attractions of which are increasingly highlighted by local communication and development scholars (cf. Masmoudi 1995; Nkwi 1995; Uche 1997; Mukasa 1998; Ouma-Odera 1998; Berger 1998; Braman 1998; Ras-Work 1998; Nyamnjoh 1999a). Could the relative lack of this technology explain, in part, the continent's current record of accounting for less than 5 percent of the volume of international trade? To Moore (1997/1998, 273) and others, there is no doubt, for "technological change is a major contributor to this process of economic development."

The growth of the information superhighway has revitalized debate on international flows of news, information, and cultural products. While some view it as rapidly forwarding the globalization process, others sympathetic to the predicament of those financially and psychologically incapable of achieving these sophisticated technologies see their development as fostering media and cultural imperialism (cf. Van Audenhove 1998; Golding and Harris 1997), although it is worth noting that "[g]lobalization does not necessarily or even frequently imply homogenization or Americanization," as different societies tend to be quite creative in their appropriation or consumption of the materials of modernity (Appadurai 1996, 17; Warnier 1999; Gray 1998). That notwithstanding, it is apparent that Third World countries stand to "bear the brunt of the risk and instability associated with the exploitation of information industry technologies and markets" (Melody 1987, 26). Thus goes the argument that the new telecommunication technologies have made dependency in and stereotypical news coverage of Africa a fait accompli (Uche 1988, 1997; Okigbo 1995, 1997; Paterson 1998). Nevertheless, many argue that these revolutionary media technologies are rapidly shrinking the world into Marshall McLuhan's prophesied "global village." Jussawalla (1988) observes that "the proliferation of global information systems and the rapid transmission of data flows across national boundaries" have rendered the nation-state meaningless and raised the prospects of the eventual creation of a global "republic of technology" (Jussawalla 1988, 11–12), a view and optimism shared by America and other leading industrialized countries—the G7.[1] The German government, for example, in its position paper on the "global information society," argues that advances in information and communication technologies have made knowledge mobile worldwide, geographic location and time restrictions to lose their meaning, and the world to grow closer together (*Nord-Sud Aktuell*, Vol. 10, 4 (1996), 835). Wriston (1994, 20) argues that with the advent of an information superhighway, human rights or democratic freedoms will not be denied people of remote places, for "a global village will have global customs" (Wriston 1994, 20). This will be made possible by the "McDonaldization" of societies the world over through emphasis on efficiency, calculability, predictability, and control (Ritzer 1996).[2] The "information society" (cf. Moore 1997/1998) is synonymous with George Ritzer's "McDonaldized" society.

The tendency is to claim that these interactive technologies offer more control over the media by consumers, and to present media audiences as having a greater opportunity to choose and consume what they want when they want. These assumptions are clearly euphoric and much of the optimism quite unfounded. There is need for careful ethnographic research on how different cultures in different regions of the world actually experience and relate to these new technologies and their ramifications; hence my call for mitigated euphoria (cf. Nyamnjoh 1999a).

Although its standard-bearers have been the information and culture industries, discussions on and about globalization have tended to be dominated by its economic dimensions. Much emphasis is placed on the internationalization and integration of economic activities and its implications for the authority and sovereignty of nation-states, especially as global capitalism means global power for multinational corporations and calls for a new way of public governance. While some see in globalization a requiem for the nation-state, others believe that the state would continue to be relevant but must work in conjunction with nonstate actors to facilitate trade and investment. Such private and international agencies include multinational corporations, NGOs, and international intergovernmental institutions such as the United Nations, World Bank, IMF, WTO, and other international standard-setting bodies that are often unofficial, informal, and not clearly recognized as such. This challenges the idea of the self-regulating free market economy, for, as Thompson (1999) argues, big business needs public support and regulation as "an insurance against the full vicissitudes of a turbulent and potentially self-destructive system" as global capitalism, especially as big "business does not want to go about its activity totally unprotected." In other words, the "free flow" of capital needs an ordered global environment to function properly and in a sustainable manner. It needs "public governance of the world trading and investment system," for "a pure free market economy is so fragile, volatile and vulnerable that the implications of its operation on a truly global scale could be disastrous" (Thompson 1999, 142). Thus, Thompson sees "a modified minimal multilateralism based upon the strengthening trilateral relationship between North America, the European Union and Japan" as repre-

senting "the most likely prospect (but not the only one) for the effective governance of the world economic system" (Thompson 1999, 144–150).

These concerns imply that globalization is not all about "unregulated flows"
or the disappearance of political and social boundaries, as enthusiasts of the
global village or the global republic of technology seem to imply (cf. Appadurai
1996; Geschiere and Meyer 1998; Gray 1998; Nyamnjoh 1999a). It is a "deeply
and starkly inegalitarian" process (Golding and Harris 1997, 7) that still favors a
privileged minority as it compounds the impoverishment of the majority through
closures and containment.[3] Increasingly, "we are witnessing a convergence of
economic thinking and policy as well as technologies," with the growing power
of multinational corporations and "their abilities to dictate the terms of competition" through hostile take-overs, megamergers, or "by forcing weaker players
out of the game" (Murdock 1994, 4–6; McChesney 1998; Gray 1998). Their
objective is to control not only global markets, but also global consciousness, by
encouraging "the emergence of a small number of monopoly concerns which
command a disproportionate share" of the global market (cf. Thomas and Lee
1994; Murdock 1982, 1994; McChesney 1998; Gray 1998). As Murdock (1994)
argues in connection with the media and information market, "the new media
mogul empires" are "empires of image and of the imagination" in that "[t]hey
mobilize a proliferating array of communications technologies to deliver a plurality of cultural products across a widening range of geographical territories
and social spaces, and are directed from the center by proprietors who rule their
domains with shifting mixtures of autocracy, paternalism and charisma" (Murdock 1994, 3). The tendency is to mistake plurality for diversity, oblivious of the
possibility that an appearance of plenty could well conceal a poverty of perspectives.

While capital is enabled to "seek competitive advantage and the most secure
and largest returns by roaming the globe for cheap but efficient production locations" (Thompson, 1999, p. 40), labor is denied the same privilege.[4] If capital
can search the globe for competitive advantage, why cannot labor? In their editorial to a special issue of *Media Development*, "Migrants, Refugees and the
Right to Communicate," Pradip Thomas and Philip Lee (1998) highlight the
predicament of migrants and refugees in a world where globalization seems to
generate an obsession with boundaries and belonging. In EU countries where
"the dominant accent and concern is the protection from rather than the protection of refugees and asylum seekers" (Thomas and Lee 1998, 2), no amount of
integration appears enough to qualify immigrants for citizenship or to limit the
powers of individual states as critical players in this area (cf. Bhabha 1998). In
the words of an immigrant in Germany, "It doesn't matter if you've read
Goethe, wear lederhosen and do a Bavarian dance, they'll still treat you as an
immigrant" (cited in Thomas and Lee 1998, 2).

In general, migrants and refugees who for one reason or another attempt to
flee from various insecurities—economic downturns, impoverishment, growing
gaps between the rich and the poor, conflicts over national and personal identi-

ties, civil strife—are among the primary victims of globalization. Enforced migrations often affect people who are vulnerable in the first place. The danger of "once a refugee, always a refugee" becoming a reality is borne out by the increasingly large numbers of people who live all their lives in refugee camps without any hope of permanent settlement.

Where does one flee to in a world that is closing its borders to refugees and asylum seekers? Equally important, what does a person flee to? From a situation characterized by total negation to one where there is the possibility of freedom? More likely from relative insecurity, to relative security although in the present context of xenophobic nationalism in Europe and elsewhere, even minimum rights are by no means guaranteed (Thomas and Lee 1998, 2).

The tightening of immigration conditions in the West and other vibrant centers of accumulation, is clear evidence that labor is not given the same opportunity to globalize as is capital. It must be added that not all labor gets confined in the same way. For example, "the overwhelming black poor" are the most discriminated against by Western politicians keen on ensuring that the advantages gained by their peoples are maintained (Seabrook 2000, 22). Thus, while even mediocre labor from the North usually finds its way to the South at Western salary rates, labor from the South is both devalued and confined by stiff immigration policies in the North. This and other factors discussed in this chapter make globalization only marginally beneficial to the South, if at all. Far from breaking down boundaries and structures of inequality, as widely claimed, globalization is yet to prove that it is not simply a new way of perpetuating the same age-old divisions that have polarized societies and the world for centuries. "It looks as if, in a world characterized by flows, a great deal of energy is devoted to controlling and freezing them: grasping the flux often actually entails a politics of 'fixing'—a politics which is, above all, operative in struggles about the construction of identities" (Geschiere and Meyer 1998, 605).

This chapter takes a critical look at globalization from the standpoint of the African experience of the West. It discusses "modernization," "development," and "globalization" as different labels for the same basic process or mission: that of freeing the African of his or her natural and cultural Africanness, and inviting him or her to partake of the "standardized, routinized, streamlined and global" consumer culture, of which McDonalds, Coca-Cola, CNN, and satellite entertainment television are harbingers (Golding 1994, 7). However, granted the level of poverty in Africa, only an elite few do qualify (largely through corruption, embezzlement, and abuse of state power and office) to consume first- or second-hand, for global availability is not synonymous with global affordability. The majority of people have to content themselves with what trickles down (in hand-me-down or worn versions) to them in the ghettos and villages (if at all), from relatives and patrons at the center of power and resources. In the face of such inequities, it is difficult to envisage how ordinary Africans can relate to the global consumer culture in any other terms but the frustration and disenchantment it brings them.[5] Their experience of globalization is the "misery and incoherence of life in the suburbs" and villages; "the collapse of public transport, state-run educational and public health services; the breakdown of electricity and sewage systems; the serious degradation of . . . infrastructure and the sheer abuse of power by self-serving functionaries" (Devisch 1999a, 5). This notwithstanding, this chapter focuses not on cultural resistance, *bricolage* (patchwork), or *métissage* (hibridity) (cf. Appadurai 1996; Geschiere and Meyer 1998; Warnier 1999; Nyamnjoh 1999b), but on the processes and effects of cooptation or assimilation of the elite few by consumer capitalism, and how these elite few, in turn, use their consumption of things foreign as an identity and as a source of prestige, status and power.

In Africa, modernity or development, since contact with Europe, has traditionally been conceived, presented, and pursued as something induced from without, a process that favors imitation over originality. Such a concept of modernity to Africans has entailed self-denial, self-abandonment, or self-humiliation, and the adoration of most things Western—packaged and presented as the norm in a variety of ways, both crude and subtle. Salvation, comfort, or self-betterment has been seen as something possible only with Westernization, as African civilizations or cultures are perceived as a hindrance to progress to be crusaded against at every level by every means.

Such devaluation of Africans, their institutions, and their cultures has meant the institutionalization of consumerism and the enshrinement of dependency by a Westernized elite who have seen in consuming Western a source of power and identity. The result has been disillusionment at the grass roots, especially among the rural populations, who have been forced to mark time with so-called African traditions for the gratification of the powerful. Such a situation explains the current stalling democratic transition and diminishes hope that the process could crystallize in a veritable culture of participatory democracy.

In this chapter my focus is on modernity, leadership, marginalization, and disillusionment in Africa as they relate to the phenomenon of globalization. The chapter examines the pretensions, phoneyness, humbug, and sores that underlie the veneer of African modernity, particularly among the elites and their sad counterparts, the underclasses (both rural and urban). At the end of the chapter one may well ask whether or not there is hope for the future. What ways forward do we have to the reconstruction of the plundered African heritage? What hope for participatory democracy, social justice, and the empowerment of the powerless? The vision is indeed sombre, the sense of despondency profound, whatever the imagined future for Africa, I hope this chapter provides some insight, provocative or not, into the downtrodden and forgotten bulk of the darkened continent—their complex web of despair, frustration, paradox, and hope. The chapter calls on all who have Africa's interests at heart to listen to the heartfelt cry of "The Disillusioned African" (Nyamnjoh 1995) as an incentive to set about the task of "redeeming the time" and of building a better future for a continent sidestepped by globalization.

These themes are articulated in six parts: (1) modernity as cultural superiority, (2) modernity as consumerism and dependency, (3) the modern leadership, (4) the predicament of the rural and urban poor, (5) social classes, and (6) by way of conclusion, the future of democracy in an Africa trapped by the globalization of poverty.

MODERNITY AS CULTURAL SUPERIORITY

Western cultures have been forced onto the peoples of Africa as "the culmination of all human progress" (Ajayi 1966, 606), a model to be followed without equivocation or reservation. Supposedly universalistic and achievement oriented, Western cultures are expected to penetrate the backward-looking cultures with their values through a unilinear process of intercultural communication (Himmelstrand, Kinyanjui, and Mburugu 1994, 3). In other words, there is no question why the rules of existence, elaborated in the West, could not be applied in exactly the same way in other parts of the world with different backgrounds and experiences. By presenting science as a predicament-free exercise, proponents of modernity have been able to argue in favor of unilinearity. They advocate social change in non-Western societies, and consider as progress everything new—from blue jeans and chewing gum to commodified sex and swear words diffused by Hollywood or Western tourism in search of "the three s's: sun, sea and sex" (cf. Sreberny-Mohammadi 1997, 63–64)—as long as the new is the uncritical reproduction of the "McDonaldized" and "Cocacolized" versions of society perfected in the West and spearheaded by America (cf. Ritzer 1996; Roach 1996; Warnier 1999).

Thus, as a paradigm, such a perspective presents development as something exogenously induced (Golding 1974), a process that requires the sacrifice of creativity and originality. Development to the Africans thus entails self-denial, self-evacuation, or self-devaluation and the glorification of everything Western. Salvation, comfort, or self-betterment is seen as something possible only with Westernization, as every other civilization or culture is perceived as constrictive and conservative—a crushing opponent of progress (Lerner 1964, 54–55) that must be countered with the assistance of the media and culture industries as "magic multipliers" of knowledge, information and propaganda (Schramm 1964, 246–247). Africans have thus been invited to devalue themselves, their institutions and their cultures by cultivating an uncritical empathy for Western economic, cultural, and political values that are glorified beyond impeachment. They are presented as having little chance of progress as Africans or blacks, and invited to intensify their assumed craving to become like the whites in Europe and North America. The entire paradigm is impatient with alternative systems of thought and practice, and seeks monoculturalism by imposing the Western consumer outlook and approach as the one best way of achieving betterment or higher level of welfare (cf. Laburthe-Tolra and Warnier 1993, 15–52; Warnier 1999). Modernity, as hegemonic "modes of social life and organization" of

European origin (cf. Giddens 1990), thus, poses as a giant compressor determined to crush every other civilization in order to reduce them to the model of
the industrialized West. As Seabrook (2000, 22) puts it:

Europe has contributed spectacularly to the global disturbance of regions and peoples,
has, since colonial times, been an agent of vast uprootings, has exported its own migratory spirit, has sought to snuff out all alternative ways of answering need, has filled the
world with economic migrants, many of them from within its own borders. . . . The
economies of almost every country in the world have been influenced by Western international financial organizations, by transnational companies, by the diktats of the International Monetary Fund and the World Bank, by "democratic institutions," in which
those whose lives are wrecked by them have no say.

This is a model that mistakes the globalization of capitalism for development by ignoring the growing polarization and marginalization of peoples and
societies that result from the process (Amin 1997b, 38–40). The model is quite
oblivious of the fact that increasing coexistence and seeming competition at airports and city centers between Western consumer goods and tourist art from the
remotest corners of Africa (cf. Davis 1999) are hardly enough to credit global
capitalism with harmonizing "seemingly disparate and incompatible zones of
accumulation and production" (Surin 1995, 1191–1196). Much remains to be
done, even in the domain of African art (despite its impressive export record), to
promote the type of meaningful and mutually rewarding encounters between
African artisans and their Western customers that Elizabeth Davis (1999) discusses in her paper, "Metamorphosis in the Culture Market of Niger."
    Modernity as cultural superiority has often implied, on the part of its theo-
rists, paying a deaf ear to empirical evidence and confusing ideal types with
reality, a tendency just as true of its latest label, globalization, as Thompson
(1999, 140) points out in his introductory essay to a UNESCO collection on the
topic. Thus, some Westerners, even scholars, have often given the impression
that what they want of Africa and Africans are stereotypes, not meaningful
knowledge. When one reads some of the Western literature on slavery and colonialism in Africa, the question usually arises if there was not a sort of conspiracy
between ideology and science to justify Western penetration, devaluation, and
devastation of Africa, the Africans (cf. Chinweizu 1987), and their once en-
slaved kin in the Diaspora (cf. Hare 1991; Woodson 1990; Wilson 1993;
Maduno 1994). Belief in one's superiority or the inferiority of others is seldom
informed by science; yet even though such beliefs are often repugnant to reason
and common sense, in the twenty-first century a good number of Westerners
continue to think of Africa in tantalizingly "tarzanic" and essentialist terms.
Similarly, a good number of books on Africa today published by Western scholars would seldom pass the scrutiny of rigorous science (cf. Bryceson 1999;
Young 1999).

Instead of recognizing the fact that "people are fiercely proud of their heritage, language, customs, religion and traditional ways of life" (Halloran 1993, 4), some Europeans set about suppressing African pride, creativity, and self-esteem through physical conquest, coercion, and persuasion, as Vernon February's (1981) brilliant study of the "colored" stereotype in apartheid literature in South Africa demonstrates. There was, even by social scientists, "the unconditional condemnation of African culture[s]" and "the unconditional affirmation of the colonizers' worldview" (Nnoli 1980, 2). The African, as "a primitive savage," was judged fit to be studied not under sociology, but under ethnology and anthropology as the science of "other" [meaning lesser] societies (cf. Mafeje 1998). That ethnological studies of Africa were Eurocentric can be seen in the fact that when Western scholars referred to the societies they studied as "non-literate," "non-state," "simple," "traditional" or "primitive," this was done in contrast to, or in comparison with, the Western societies, which they saw as "literate," "centralized," "complex," "modern" or "civilized." It was more scholarship by analogy than seeking to understand African societies in historical perspective (cf. Mamdani 1996, 12–13). Rejecting, a priori, African experiences, cultures, social values, and political organization offered scholars of modernity the opportunity to analyze African efforts at development from the insensitive position of a supposedly value-free social science informed by Western experiences exclusively.

Thus, even though "multi-ethnicity is a quality of all societies," the Western bias of the anthropologists led to the imposition of a false dichotomy between the "tribal" societies of Africa and their "ethnic" or "national" opposites of the developed world (Cohen 1978, 399). Some scholars have argued that contemporary notions of "tribe" and "tribalism," like many customs and traditions in Africa today, were an invention of colonialism (cf. Ranger 1983; Vail 1989), an "illusion" (Southall 1997), a "false consciousness" (cf. Hadjor 1987, 60–65) with little or no indigenous roots, fostered in order to divide and rule, both in the colony and postcolony. Those, like anthropologists, who had adopted "tribal" perspectives were deluded and thus became, consciously or unconsciously, the agents of oppression or cultural devaluation of Africa (cf. Mafeje 1998). Although scholarship has since evolved on the issue of ethnicity and tribalism in Africa (cf. Vail 1989; Berman 1998), there remains a noted reluctance in certain circles to graduate from a perception of African ethnicity as an atavasm, or from the view that Africans, unlike Europeans, are essentially tribalistic, doctrines of ethnic and racial cleansing generated in Yugoslavia and by the far right in France, Germany, Belgium, England, Austria, and the rest of Europe notwithstanding (cf. Geschiere and Nyamnjoh 2000; Seabrook 2000).

The perpetuation of Western cultures as the standard of measure not only dispossessed Africans of their own cultures, it infanticided and disempowered them by forcing them to learn afresh, under the guidance of condescending and overbearing Western overlords, new ways of seeing, doing, and being. Undermining, marginalizing, and distorting African cultures were intended to minimize the empowerment that Africans and their communities could draw from these cultures to fight domination (Ngubane 1996, 4–7; Biko 1996). This, as Franz Fanon (1976b, 169) has argued, created the myth of the inferior native and a justification for colonialism. The Westerners, by alienating the Africans from their traditions through "cultural estrangement," reinforced in the Africans' self-hatred and a profound sense of inferiority that compelled them "to lighten their darkness" for white gratification. Skin lightening creams and culture-bleaching products were made available to blacks as if to suggest that "black cannot be the ideal of beauty" (C. J. Hamelink 1983, 2), or that black cultural achievements could not be pace-setters. Today skin-lightening products manufactured mainly in Britain and the United States continue to be "smuggled into Africa in a multi-billion Rand underground industry" (Busisiwe Mosieman 1999, 16). The production and proliferation of such bleaching products is a pointer to how whiteness remains internalized as an ideal that blacks must aspire to willy-nilly. By painting white as the ultimate judgment of all aesthetics, good and beauty, the black man and woman are made to understand that they are far from being equal to their white counterparts, and that they can be salvaged only through a pursuit of the liberating cultures of the West. As Fonlon (1967, 20) has argued, from the first day of contact,

[t]he white man strove, might and main, to despoil the black on his own continent, strove to keep him down lest he should rise and become a rival. And to make this new implacable thraldom more complete, they decided to enslave his soul, to inculcate into his mind, through raillery and contempt the idea that he was inherently despicable and inferior and that all excellence, all nobility, all that is beautiful and sublime was white. And thus they were able to make him detest himself and the works of his hands.

The consequence is that today, in every country south of the Sahara, thousands of black men and women strive to develop a lighter complexion with assorted skin-poisoning, cancer-causing, mercury- and hydroquinone-ridden toners and soaps, and have devised hairstyles (including the wearing of imported natural and artificial white-like hair) that bring them nearer to whiteness, the ideal. Thanks also to cultural bleaching facilitated by the modern culture industries and mass media of the West (e.g., films, recorded music, videocassettes, specialized magazines, children's comics and electronic games, radio, TV, the press, and books), blacks have been made to understand that with white skin and Western cultures go all sorts of advantages. Whiteness has come to symbolize power, authority, status, and, above all, the good life, even for the most fragile or the most mediocre of whites.

Dervla Murphy (1989, 56), in her book, *Cameroon with Egbert*, gives us an idea, through the person of a Cameroonian, George Charles Akuro, of how the feeling of inferiority, self-hatred, and yearning for most things Western in order to be seen and rewarded as a progressive are articulated at an individual level:

"Cameroon is very bad," insisted George. "All these bush people, they don't know how to live—they are backward stupid people! In Hamburg I have everything—big home, big car, deep freeze, fridge, cine-camera, television, stereo-system, swimming-pool for my kids. See! I show you!" . . . He drew a thick wallet of photographs from his briefcase and the children crowded eagerly around to marvel yet again at his achievements. There was George, leaning nonchalantly on the roof of a Mercedes by the open driving door—and George removing a silver-foil-wrapped dish from a face-level microwave oven—and George posing by an open refrigerator taller than himself and packed with colorful goodies—and so on. There were dozens of photographs, all of a professionally high standard and looking remarkably like advertisements for the objects illustrated. . . . Watching the children staring with awed incomprehension at these emanations from another world, I remembered those who are working hard and patiently, without publicity or luxury funding, to introduce "appropriate technologies" to rural Africa. Ease of communication, when it means bright pictures of the enviable unattainable circulating in Cameroonian villages, is not necessarily beneficial.

The persistent craving to be Western or to go West in Africa today attests to such exogenously induced self-hatred and inferiority. Perhaps what Ali Mazrui (1996, 134) has referred to as "Africa's culture of tolerance" or its "short memory of hate," can be explained by this Western devaluation of the African cultural identities that has made of the Africans "people more sinned against than sinning," and people keener to forgive and forget than to exact restitution and rehabilitation. Not even apartheid and its monstrous indignities would push Africans to go beyond "truth and reconciliation" with those who for decades debased and violated their humanity with little compunction. As president of South Africa's post-apartheid Truth and Reconciliation Commission, Archbishop Desmond Tutu (1996, v) acknowledged this when he wrote: "We have been humbled and deeply touched by the nobility and generosity of spirit of those who, despite so much pain and anguish, have amazed the world by their willingness to forgive the perpetrators of all these dastardly deeds of darkness" sponsored by apartheid.

Justifications for such sins against Africa were usually in the form of assumptions to the effect that African cultures and traditions are incompatible with development (cf. Kabou 1991). Yet more and more we are overwhelmed with indications from Asian experiences (e.g., Japan, South Korea, and China) that the so-called traditional cultures need not necessarily be "modernized," for there to be economic development (cf. Gray 1998, 55–60). There is "evidence that a modern economic system is also reconcilable with other than European–North American values and social structures" (Kunczik 1993, 47–48), and that the fruit of scientific discovery need not be confused with its domestication in the culture of its first consumers. Unlike Asia (the Orient), which the West, upon initial contact, credited with some degree of civilization and therefore opted for cultural interpenetration, Africa (the Dark Continent) was considered virgin ground in matters cultural, with little to boast but savagery and babyishness. Thus, instead of cultural interpenetration, the West went for wholesale cultural conversion (cf. Bryceson 1999), and if it has succeeded more with the modern elite, this by no means implies that only they were targeted.

MODERNITY AS CONSUMERISM AND DEPENDENCY

By defining development in terms of an excruciating craving for Western institutions, cultures and products, Western advocates have lured and/or coerced the Africans, their cultures, and creativity to become consumed by the giant compressors of the West. The ultimate effect being, as Wole Soyinka (1994a, 209) has so aptly observed, that Africans are encouraged "to develop an incurable dependency syndrome and consume themselves to death," for the consumerist culture propagated in the name of development can only guarantee productivity at home in the West by vigorously exporting itself to Africa and the rest of the Third World. Thus, capitalism as a way of life cannot leave the Africans free to perform their work at home, nor their duty in the world (Fanon 1967b, 78; Amin 1997a, 40–41). The outcome, Soyinka (1994a) argues, is that peoples of different cultures, often of poorer societies, "are inducted into this unequal exchange," and "feeding the foreign consumerist machine becomes a way of life for countries whose consumer habits hitherto trailed an umbilical cord from their productive technologies, however, rudimentary, and were, indeed, rooted in the totality of the nation's culture." Youths, mothers, values, and tastes are all victims, ravaged by the elite few of the consumer club:

the self-respecting youth dare not be seen without a Walkman. The hybrid shuts out the world and enters another world, so wrapped up in that world that he sometimes steps into the gutter or fails to hear the warning sounds of a speeding vehicle and crosses the road at a fatal instant. Mothers are encouraged to get their children hooked on powdered milk, mashed food substitutes, the so-called baby nutrients. Toiletries and other forms of body enhancement are now legitimized only by their appearance in air-conditioned supermarkets; the traditional unguents are deemed uncivilized; the marketplaces where they normally preside are uncultured (Soyinka 1994a, 209–210).

Colonialism succeeded in creating the myth of the Westerner as "superman" or omniscient by whom the desperate African was to be teleguided in every sphere of life, even to the point of aiding and abetting the very deconstruction of his own humanity, with the negative consequence being the creation of "a pathological case of xenophilia" by bringing Africans to value things Western "not for their efficacy but simply because of their foreignness" (Nyang 1994, 434), and to measure development "more by the capacity to consume imported Western goods than by the capacity to produce local equivalents" (Rowlands 1995, 119).[6] Being human would be measured also by how much of a patchwork of whiteness one had succeeded to render oneself, through consumption of second-hand white hair, skin-bleaching creams, white dress codes, white food and eating habits, and, ultimately, the white body.

This consumerism and the power it brings to its disciples at the periphery in relation to their fellow countrymen and women, it must be echoed, are limited to a minority. While global capitalism caters for the needs of investors, advertisers, and the affluent consumers of the world as a whole, this tends to be a substantial portion of the population in the developed West but only a distinct minority in the underdeveloped South (McChesney 1998, 6). Hence, Amin's (1980, 31–32) argument that, unlike in the industrialized West where there is a good chance that modernization, development, or globalization could accelerate homogenization of some kind, in underdeveloped and heavily plundered Africa it is only by marginalizing the masses that the power elite are able to afford the "growing income" that encourages it to adopt Western models of consumption, the extension of which "guarantees the profitability of the luxury production sector and strengthens the social, cultural, ideological, and political integration of the privileged classes" (Amin 1980, 138). This is an argument echoed by Sharp (1998) and Comaroff and Comaroff (1999) in relation to post-apartheid South Africa, where structural inequalities are yet to be resolved in a way that benefits more than just a black elite by a state that has opted to play according to the diktats of global capitalism. As Comaroff and Comaroff (1999, 19) put it,

There is widespread evidence of an uneasy fusion of enfranchisement and exclusion, hope and hopelessness; of a radically widening chasm between rich and poor; of the effort to realize modern utopias by decidedly post-modern means. Gone is any official-speak of an egalitarian socialist future, of work-for-all, of the welfare state envisioned in the Freedom Charter that, famously, mandated the struggle against the ancient regime. Gone, too, are the critiques of the free market and of bourgeois ideology once voiced by the anti-apartheid movements, their idealism re-framed by the perceived reality of global economic forces.

Thus, while a small but bustling black elite can today wallow in the conspicuous consumption of prized commodities such as houses, cars, TVs, cellphones, and Jacuzzis, most ordinary South Africans, who are still trapped in shacks, shantytowns, joblessness, poverty, and uncertainty, can only marvel at the "indecent speed and . . . little visible exertion" with which the black elite have come by their riches and prosperity. These inequities have given rise to the belief "that it is only by magical means, by consuming others, that people may enrich themselves in these perplexing time," and consequently, to a resurgence in accusations of witchcraft and zombification and to the scapegoating of immigrants—*makwerekwere*—whose readiness, like homozombies, to provide devalued labor is seen as compounding the disenchantment of the autochthonous populations in the face of rapidly diminishing prosperity in South Africa (Comaroff and Comaroff 1999, 22–26).[7]

In Zaire (current Democratic Republic of Congo), getting involved in the dollarized diamond economy as an alternative to collapsed state structures seems to create more problems than it solves among villagers who have come to believe that "to be considered in Zaire, you got to have money!" with some going even further to assert that "you need money to be considered in the eyes of God, for God only recognizes the rich" (De Boeck 1998, 793). Thus, driven by desperation to capture and tame the wild, unpredictable, and ambivalent diamonds and dollars, the young males of *bana Lunda* (an ethnic group), who are at the heart of this economy, are ready to sacrifice (by means of sorcery and otherwise) their work power and productivity, their youth, strength, and beauty, their fertility and sexual prowess, and their friends or family members. Diamonds and dollars "totally isolate one and invert the normal ties of solidarity and reciprocity into the destructive internal mechanisms of redistribution by sorcery. The longing or hunger for dollars and diamonds is . . . like an incurable festering sore which re-opens every time one runs out of money," which happens pretty often, since diamond dollars tend to "evaporate," to be wasted away on beer, cigarettes and women ("economy of ejaculation"). This is an "uncontrolled and wild flow of money and commodities . . . that does not correspond to accepted patterns of self-realization" (De Boeck 1998, 789–799).

For being a very restricted club, global capitalism is attracting its fair share of opportunists and gatecrashers from among the side-stepped, not least in Africa. Today, "the Nigerian-based letter scam" and the Cameroonian "feymenia" are wreaking havoc all over the business world (from the United States, through Europe, to Southeast Asia), making as many victims as there are men and women hungry enough for "a quick buck" to be able to risk a little fortune. Known locally as "4–1–9," the Nigerian letter scam operates from Lagos and other centers of accumulation in Africa (e.g., Johannesburg) and the world.[8] Their strategy, similar to that of the Cameroonian "feymen" and Liberian fraudsters, consists in luring unsuspecting businessmen (both local and foreign) with fake deals, and then robbing them.[9] Elliott Sylvester (1999, 23) explains,

The scam is dangerous but ingeniously simple, as Van der Westhuizen [police Superintendent of the commercial crime branch in Johannesburg] explained. . . . A company or individual receives a letter by mail, usually from a fictitious Johannesburg [or any other] security company. "In the letter, the sender claims to be in possession of large sums of money from a foreign government which overspent on its arms budget. They then ask the victim to come to the country and help move the money to a safe account. But first it has to be cleaned." It is during the "cleaning" process that the victims are fleeced. . . . The fraudsters set up dummy companies and show the businessmen the money, usually sprinkled with a white powder, claiming it is marked and requires a special cleaning fluid. "They show the victim how to clean the money with a fluid but then tell him they have run out of it and will cost about $100,000 to buy more," Van der Westhuizen said. . . . The "special fluid" is often just colored water or, in some cases, a weak cool drink mixture but, faced with a 30% commission for helping the fraudsters, victims hand over the money in the belief they will make even more. Once money changes hands, the fraudsters disappear. . . . The financial crimes division of the U.S. Treasury Department has established a special "Operation 4–1–9" unit to deal with the problem. Its investigators have found that hundreds of millions of dollars are being lost each year.

It is naïve to imagine that any amount of policing could eliminate these alternative ploys of seeking to make it, within a global capitalist structure obsessed with closures and inequalities. While such scams eventually become a way of life, a business of some sort, one must not lose sight of the fact that the assimilation and exclusion logic of global capitalism is largely to blame for them in the first place.

The majority of Africans, on the other hand, are not as smart as the Nigerian "4-1-9" or the Cameroonian "feymen," so they seldom come close to escaping the misery imposed on them. Thus, only the blanketing misery of the masses blunts Africa's craving to consume Western things, for many are those who simply cannot afford what it takes to excel in consumerism, pervasive mass-mediated images of desire notwithstanding. Even then, misery can only stop most from consuming the best and first-hand, but not from second-rate consumption (in the form of second-hand cars, second-hand clothes, second-hand underpants, second-hand hair, second-hand shoes and socks, second-hand refrigerators, second-hand television sets and VCRs, second-hand computers, second-hand technology of all types, second-hand drugs, second-hand beef, second-hand knowledge, etc.). Because of misery, Africa has become the dumping ground for obsolete Western technologies and consumer products. Brussels and Utretch, for example, are Europe's leading centers for exporting used cars, or what I prefer to call "reconditioned comfort," to Africa. Africans, unconsciously, have become a solution to many an environmental problem in the West by dying to consume what Westerners are dying to dump. Western waste unfit for Western consumption finds ready markets in desperate Africa, from cigarettes, through a host of outdated consumer items, to toxic chemicals and infected beef. What globalization is doing is to intensify the divisions between consumer "citizens" and consumer "subjects," first between the North and the South and then within different countries of the North and the South. The overall effect is that nothing is too old or too worthless to be consumed, and everyone is deluded into thinking that they do not need to enter the consumer market at the same level to qualify as "bona fide" consumers. Global capitalism creates markets and opportunities for rejects even among the dead and the forgotten, who normally should be fighting it. Slum dwellers may not afford first- or second-rate consumption, but they can scavenge the rubbish heaps of rich residential areas for leftovers and for disposable tins, plastic containers, dumped household effects, and other rejected consumer items that they recycle to keep hope alive. Similarly, villagers wait for urban-based relatives to hand down to them what they have got tired of consuming in the cities, battered or intact. Nothing is too old or too used to be used. Globalization thus provides for the endless recycling of consumer products, and, consequently, of the poverty, misery, and voicelessness of the majorities of the world, North and South.

The local bourgeoisie or power elite have, therefore, capitalized upon such a sterile craving to consume foreign culture, using it as an identity for themselves and a source of power and status (Rowlands 1995; Warnier 1993, 163–196), and by so doing they foster, sometimes unwittingly, the Machiavellian designs of the giant compressors of global capitalism. Consumerism was so much at the fore that at independence what mattered most to the modern elite was political power, not economic power. The economic power was largely retained by the Europeans and expatriates (mainly from Lebanon and India), a situation that remains true also of post-apartheid South Africa where the economy, despite the integration of a handful of black elites, is still largely under white control (cf. Sharp 1998; Comaroff and Comaroff 1999). It is little wonder, therefore, that in most of Africa today the elite exploit and manipulate the rural and urban poor in order to sustain their consumer appetites. Had the African leadership been sensible enough to think seriously of economic power as well, African countries today would certainly not be this dependent upon the unmechanized efforts of the rural poor, and they would also be in a position to carry out their own development efforts without necessarily posing as beggars of the world. One can imagine Karl Marx writing, "beggars of the world unite," had he been African! The African leadership remain indifferent to the fact that no country can borrow its way to prosperity under the current international financial system, which is simply not integrated enough to guarantee that (Thompson 1999, 148). If this is true of countries in general, it is even truer of African countries, where endemic corruption has become a national culture (Hope and Chikulo 2000; Reno 1995; Mbaku 1998, 2000), where kleptocracy has been enshrined by the "big men" of power, and where loans are seldom put to effective use (cf. Russell 1999, 6–126).

The identity and power conferred by consuming foreign things explains why, despite much rhetoric about cultural renaissance in many an African country (e.g., *authenticité* of Mobutu [Zaire], *négritude* of Senghor [Senegal], *African communalism* of Nkrumah [Ghana], *Ujammaa and African Socialism* of Nyerere [Tanzania], *Harambee* of Kenyetta [Kenya], *African Renaissance and Ubuntu* of Mbeki [South Africa]), the ruling elites continue to acculturate themselves and to "progressively take on the look of strangers in their own country due to their daily lifestyle, modeled on that of *homo consumens universalis* (the global consumer subject) (Amin 1980, 175). With a ruling elite whose weakness and marginality vis-à-vis global capitalism and its institutions of legitimization have been certified, consuming foreign things becomes a major way of staking claim to power locally and of further mystifying the disaffected populations with whom they have lost credibility.

THE MODERN LEADERSHIP: FRIEND OR FOE OF AFRICA?

By leadership here I refer to African pacesetters and wielders of power in various domains of life, from politics to academics through economics and culture.

Inasmuch as we recognize colonialism as a cause of Africa's present impasse, it would be wrong to sound as if colonialism is all that there is to it. This type of myopia is too dangerous to harbor, because it fails to give sufficient account of the postcolonial malaise brought about by "*les drames internes*" (internal conflicts and tensions). With a little bit of thought one immediately sees that, just as historical events always have their remote causes as well as the immediate antecedents, we must think of Africa's present dilemmas as the outcome of a historical process, not the result of a single point in time. In this way we would avoid the mistakes of the modernization theorists, yet complete the thinking process of the dependentists. The causes of Africa's problems are neither simply external nor exclusively internal, but a combination of both. Africans have been, and still are, both dependent and autonomous agents in relation to the historical forces that have impinged and are impinging upon them and their continent. While it would be too simplistic to see Africans entirely as zombies totally overwhelmed by external forces, one must also be careful not to credit them with utopic agency, which is certainly not feasible within the current global structures and relations of unequal exchange championed by the giant compressors of the West.

If you can picture a cow down in a valley being milked by a herdsman under instructions from a distant patron, then Africa is best seen as milked by external forces with the active collaboration of internal counterparts conditioned to act like zombies. Just like in traditional accounts of sorcery, where one cannot become a victim unless one is offered by one's very own relative to be "eaten," so too Africans cannot be exploited by so-called multinationals and Western states if they are not, in the first place, sacrificed as victims by their very own "brothers and sisters" in power. If external forces were entirely to blame, as some would want us to believe, where do we classify the leadership (in the broadest sense of the word), who not only prefer to embezzle and bank abroad in Europe, but who sometimes are mad enough to show off "their" riches by helping to construct free hostels for European school children, as did Banda of Malawi, while the children in their own miserable and highly plundered countries are languishing in the ignorance and poverty of the overburdened villages and the ghettos? Or those who shower money on French politicians seeking (re)-election (as do Francophone presidents), while civil servants are starved of pay and the poor left to die without medication? Or those who reproduce basilicas in their native Yamoussoukro or sponsor the construction of Rosicrusian lodges in France with so-called personal fortunes, while their toiling peasants and slum-dwellers hunger and thirst to death in darkness and the illusion of prayer?

The power elite in Africa have been contaminated by the haunting rapacity of high office and/or prominence (cf. Russell 1999). Almost everywhere on the continent people seek power in order to empty public coffers into private pockets. They take refuge under the public-interest banner to pursue personal goals with capitalist impunity. Thus, it is not unusual to find African leaders doing abroad what they consider not feasible in "our young fragile nations." Public ownership and control is good in Africa because of limited resources, but some African leaders can afford money not only to buy personal shares and stocks in foreign companies, but sometimes to own or take over these companies.[10] In this way, Africa is presented as a dense swampy forest with incredible riches, but where the hostile jungle and its primitive aborigines would allow nothing good to be undertaken, and so all avenues must be sought to siphon the riches to the West, where conditions are deemed forever favorable. They give life and meaning to such sayings as Aristotle's *Semper aliquid novi ex Africa* [There is always something new coming from Africa] (cf. Barrett 1968, xix).

This gives one reason to think that at the level of the continent, the people's greatest enemy is their leadership, with barely a few exceptions, regardless of what domain we scrutinize. In the political domain, most of this leadership would virtually give up their ambitions for power and prominence if there was nothing for them to embezzle once unfairly elected or catapulted into supremacy by dubious coups d'état. They are driven into excesses of greed by the false idea of their own importance or adequacy, a delusion of superiority, and a bizarre nose for red herrings as strategy for mass repression. How elated some are to have villas and mansions in Europe or North America, where they can afford to live better than the middle-class whites who stubbornly claim to be superior to them![11] How can the average middle-class housewife in the West claim superiority when every bank holiday she jostles in the giant supermarkets with the wives and girlfriends of African presidents and ministers who have flown over specially to shop at Harrods and to have their grafted hair and wigs retouched at the Ritz? Some twenty years or so ago, it was not uncommon to sight limousines with Kinshasa number plates on the streets of Brussels, specially flown over by the super rich of the Zairean bourgeoisie on holidays in Europe. How many so-called superior whites are in the financial position to buy off designers' rights for particular dresses, the way some African leaders have done, in order to stop other women dressing like their wives? How many of their wives or mistresses can boast of a thousand pairs of shoes and more, or rings of ruby, diamond, and sapphire? Just how many of them can earn enough money to take a holiday abroad, let alone dart from country to country, sampling toiletries and designer wear, and fishing for where prices are highest so that the value of what one buys may be read from the price one pays? Just how thrilled some African leaders and their mistresses are with self-delusion to the effect that without them Swiss banks would be out of business! Some prominent African leaders are known to be so madly in love with Europe that they would fly there to lunch, to wine and dine in luxury hotels, or to dry clean their suits and buy special cigars and vintage wines, then fly back to continue with the arduous but prestigious task of purging the masses of "ignorance" and making them contribute in the chase after "civilization" through "nation-building" and "sustainable development" with the determined assistance of structural adjustment programs (SAPs) pre-packaged by "our" friends in the West.

Does this not reveal that no matter what they might say to the contrary, the modern African elite still acknowledge their internalized or induced inferiority to whites? Otherwise, why would someone with any self-esteem underrate and denigrate what is theirs in matters cultural? What superiority to or equality with someone is there if you constantly denounce your own values and ways of thinking, doing, and being? Would someone, no matter how well-meaning and modest, not ask themselves, without arrogance perhaps, but with legitimacy, whether you would be so keen on them, their ways and values, if there was anything worth preserving in yours? And would you blame them and their folks for believing in the inherent superiority of their culture and values, when you yourself have exhibited such damaging impatience with what, to them, could well have been a valid alternative to the shortcomings of their own social organization and outlook? How can you turn around and speak meaningfully against the one-way flow of cultural products that globalization has exacerbated? And would you be surprised if the side-stepped and dispossessed of your marginal republics found little to believe in your rhetoric about the need for cultural renaissance, rehabilitation, diversity, and/or pluralism?

All this is indicative of the superficial understanding the African leadership has of its mission, of Africa, and of the world. Most are callous to their subjects' (I hesitate to say "citizens," since some have never been made to feel they were anything but subjects) and their countries' problems because they know next to nothing about the latter. Of the intellectuals amongst them, imagine individuals who received Western education when they were kids of their country, and later they assumed leadership of their country. What they know best is American history, English history, French history, or European history in Africa—Western history, in short. They excel in the classics, Greek philosophy, and Elizabethan literature, uphold Victorian values, and remember with nostalgia and native emotion the good old days when they could recite all volumes by Shakespeare, chuckle at Chaucer's tongue-in-cheek humor, praise the psychology and genius of Dickens's plume, criticize Racine's sentimentalism, and agree with Corneille's heartlessness or fanatical commitment to "La Patrie." They are generally proud to have spent their childhood years learning to dissolve their Africanness, and to fill themselves up afresh, with Europeanness. They only think of their grandparents while acknowledging the foresightedness of the latter to have sent them to the colonial school years ago to be purged of primitive savagery. Apart from that passing reference, which often takes the form of a footnote, they know little else about their people or "tribes," and don't really care to, except, of course, when it comes to manipulating these for political ends. As most of them love to say, people must be forward-looking; Africans must part with the past and pair with the present. "We must beat Westerners at their own game!" That is how diasporic scholars are known to justify their flight abroad at the slightest inconvenience, or their slavish mastery of Western intellectual traditions.

How can a leadership fail to cherish a deeper knowledge of its people, yet hope to succeed? Ask some African leaders to name the ethnic groups that constitute their constituency and country, and they wouldn't be exact on anything. Force them to give a press conference, and they could not tell you where for sure the country is said to be afflicted by drought, famine, floods, or quakes. When there is a natural disaster, that is when they send word around for information to be made available about the populations affected, they ask to know the location of the village or "tribe" concerned, the number of "elites" from the area, and whether or not the afflicted are party affiliates, peace loving and respectful of their sacralized leadership. But ask the very same leaders the same questions about France, Britain, or Belgium, and they would bombard your ears with detailed facts, even when taken unawares, thanks largely to a lifelong history of cultural alienation thanks to the ubiquity of Western educational institutions and epistemological traditions, and thanks to the aggressive exportation of Western cultural products through the mass media (cf. Gareau 1987; McChesney 1998). Ask them to name the major traditional kings (whom they derogate and undermine) in their countries and they would betray an ignorance unpardonable even in foreigners. But ask them to name English, French, Belgian or American kings, queens, or presidents from inception and they could easily score 100 percent with nostalgia. One must admit that in these matters they baffle even the Americans, the French, and the English. The misfortune is that the average American, Belgian, French, or English person is made to believe that their national cultures and values must be universal, since even savages from as remote a continent as tarzanic Africa appear to share them. Little wonder that they cannot always understand what fuss academics and activists of peripheral countries tend to make about globalization as a process of one-way flows that must be resisted. Just how can the average Westerner understand arguments to the effect that the global culture some presume to observe today is nothing but "the transnationalization of a very national voice, the universal triumph of a supremely local and parochial set of images and values" (Golding and Harris 1997, 9), when it is possible to find your McDonalds, Coca-Cola, Fish & Chips, Mars Bar, English or Continental breakfast and five-course meal, John Lennon, Elvis Presley, Spice Girls or Madonna tune, Barbie, Batman, or Mickey Mouse even in the remotest corners of the Dark Continent? It is largely thanks to facilitation by the African leadership (again in the broadest sense of the word), that such unmitigated one-way flows are perpetuated, and everyone becomes trapped by the Western consumer culture in one way or another, at one level or the other.

The paradox with the African leadership or "elite" is that they know what they do not need and need what they do not know. This is as true of the politician as it is of the academic. It is a similar situation to that in economics, where the leadership encourages the production of what they do not consume and consume what they do not produce. Just how they can succeed seems impossible to predict. Hence, this popular joke about an African president who went to God and asked in prayer, "When shall my country be developed?" to whom God replied, "Not in my lifetime."

Concerning foreign aid, the mismanagement of which has been criticized so much in the West (cf. Hancock 1989), and with good reason, given the overwhelming evidence of corruption in Africa (cf. Hope and Chikulo 2000; Mbaku 1998, 2000; Reno 1995; Russell 1999), is it not a shame that concerned outsiders have often shown much more commitment to the plight of our forsaken masses than have our own leadership? How do they feel when tons and tons of wheat, maize, milk, and rice marked: "USA Aid to Famine-stricken Victims"; "*Aide Française aux victimes des catastrophes naturelles*" (French aid to victims of natural catastrophies) or "British Aid to Disaster Victims" are found in local shops and supermarkets, when those for whom these foodstuffs were intended have died unattended?

It is not a coincidence that this leadership begs and banks only in American dollars, English pounds, German deutsch marks, or French francs. Aid, which never leaves the donor countries, finds its way into one private account or another in Zurich, California, or elsewhere in the West. It is as if whenever an African president visits the West it is to perform the two B's: beg and bank. This is a theme in popular literature and *radio trottoir* (pavement radio or rumor), well loved by the cynical masses of most towns and cities in Africa, who relish every opportunity to laugh at or ridicule those who have enshrined corruption and crime at their expense (cf. Sekoni 1997; Mbembe 1997a; Nyamnjoh 1999d; Toulabor 1981; Diamani 1995). Such literature and informal broadcasts illustrate the fact that ordinary folks "can see beyond the mask or veil of deception worn by people in power" (Sekoni, 1997, p. 143). As Sekoni (1997, 143) puts it in his discussion of politics and urban folklore in Nigeria, such popular accounts are a bitter indictment of leaders who repose little trust in the stability of the local economy that they have been elected (or elected themselves) to protect, but who do not hesitate to rush "the products of their primitive accumulation to other countries, thus giving the impression that the economy of their country is to be plundered rather than promoted."

There is reason to feel worried that outsiders have appeared to be more committed to the cause of Africans than have their leadership. What philanthropic organizations have brought in through the front door has often gone out through the back door in the form of checks addressed to foreign banks. From Côte d'Ivoire to Kenya, through Nigeria and Cameroon, the media are full of stories on embezzlement and corruption in Africa, not all of which are exaggerations. Added evidence is provided by Transparency International's yearly reports on corruption, and also by scholarship (cf. Hope and Chikulo 2000; Mbaku 1998, 2000; Reno 1995; Ellis 1996; Good 1994; Bayart, Ellis, and Hibou 1999). Such sickening disregard for their people makes it difficult either to contest the conclusion that in Africa "the only thing which grows is MISERY," or to blame those who now argue against the whole idea of aid. How convincingly can we seriously dismiss books on kleptocracy, corruption, patronage, and the criminalization of the state in Africa, unsubstantiated in their allegations though some may be (cf. Bryceson 1999; Young 1999), when our leadership makes no secret of the vices that have championed their sterile love of power, prestige, and hollow pretence (cf. Mbembe 1992; Russell 1999)?

You perhaps have asked yourselves why it so happens that almost every African leader that falls out of political fortune ends up in the West or elsewhere abroad? Is it because, having facilitated the zombification of their own people by the West, they cannot see themselves staying to face the wrath of those whose patience they have stretched to the elastic limit? Does it mean that the only way they believe they can contribute to nation building is as politicians? It sounds as though once they realize they cannot contain the mess they occasioned, they flee the country for a peaceful life abroad. What about those who cannot afford a journey even to the local city, but whose hard work helps sustain the powerful? What are these forsaken peasants to do, they who cannot afford the luxury and freedom of being political refugees in countries of their choice?

THE PREDICAMENT OF THE RURAL AND URBAN POOR

If modernity in Africa has enriched the white man and the local bourgeoisie, it has frustrated the black masses. As Basil Mathews (1924) remarked many years ago in his book *The clash of color: A study in the problem of race*, the white man owes the soil of Africa and the laboring hands of the black "an inexhaustible catalogue of necessities," ranging from the cup of coffee or cocoa, the box of chocolates and the bunch of bananas on the dinner table, to the timber for office furnishings, the ivory on knife handles and billiard balls, the rubber on balls and tires, the leather for shoes, bags, and jackets, and much of the gold used as currency. But because the white man has both the yam and the knife, as the reputed Nigerian novelist Chinua Achebe (1959) would put it, he refuses calls for indexation and thereby reifies unequal exchange. And so the poor and their progeny toil till death, so that the white man must never know discomfort.

No one would deny that the way to independence in Africa was and has remained rough, even where decolonization was chiefly a smooth transition of power to an indigenous political elite carefully chosen by the retiring colonialists. Where the struggle for independence was violent, tiring, and demanding, people were mobilized right from the grass roots to support nationalism with all their might. Peasants and urbanites were called upon to sacrifice body and soul and win for themselves a place in the future years of democratic and material abundance. At last, their struggles were said to have born fruit when "flag independence" was granted. The whites, who had been ready to consider independence only for those willing to sacrifice that very independence, withdrew to the background and were replaced by their shadows, the black skins with white masks (cf. Fanon, 1967a). The dance of the puppets was on, as simulation took center stage.

It soon became apparent that the independence that mattered was economic and not political. Faced with the exacting world capitalist system, the ruling elite of Africa, reluctantly or not, opted to sacrifice their democratic ideals and the welfare of their citizens and subjects, instead of revolting against the international system. The implications of limited independence for the continent were economic dependence and marginality in global capitalism, neocolonialism, and dominance for Western epistemes and *manières de faire* (way of doing). Weakened by their status as dependent capitalists, the ruling elite in Africa have had to resort to ethnicity and obsession with belonging; corruption, patronage, and kleptocracy; sacralization and personalization of power; and bureaucratic authoritarianism in order to service what has become a sterile craving for power.

Amin (1997b, 22) captures this well when he argues that the polarization of power and wealth produced by global capitalism makes democratic rule at peripheries like Africa virtually impossible, as global capitalism needs autocratic powers to be able to penetrate the peripheries with its inequalities. This renders economic life in Africa "little more than an appendage to the exercise of state functions, which directly and visibly occupies the front of the state." It also explains why "civil society is feeble or even non-existent." However, the power of the state in Africa is only illusory, because the "true strong state" is "the state of the developed center," as economic activities in the continent seem perpetually in "a process of adjustment to the demands of accumulation at the center." To Amin (1987, 1–13), the reluctance of African states to yield to private enterprise is proof of their "real weakness." In other words, the African state "must be strong enough in relation to its internal forces to assure the constant outflow of economic surplus from across its boundaries" to the West, but in relation to which "it must be weak enough to be incapable of blocking such flows" (Tussie 1983, 4). This perspective explains both economic underdevelopment and stalling democracy essentially in terms of the assimilation and exclusion logic of global capitalism, according to which only the handful of power and economic elite in Africa stand to benefit from its internalization and reproduction.

Thus, although popular movements played a key role in the struggle for independence in many a country, the ruling elite have since then seldom allowed these movements to germinate as counterforces with the mission of curbing repressive tendencies and/or articulating issues outside of their suffocating grip. The strategy has been for them "to reorganize the structure of domination while at the same time deflating the movement against [them]" through delegitimization of all struggles autonomous of the state, cooptation, and the imposition of state-centered initiatives and solutions (Mamdani 1990, 47–55). In this way the international legitimacy of the state has often counted more than its internal legitimization.

It is evident that things have worsened, instead of getting better, for the rural and urban poor. Instead of democratic abundance and populous grandeur, the masses have barely been able to eke out a living under scorching dictatorships for most of the time. The elite have created and sustained political institutions not so much to mobilize and conscientize the masses for collective interests, but to curb mass involvement, to control and to strengthen their own omnipotence in national life (cf. Bayart 1993; Geschiere 1995, 125–163; 1997, 97–131; Mamdani 1990; Beckman 1992), with the result being widespread passivity and cynicism in the masses in general, in particular the villagers who were led to believe that "politics is the business of the big people [*l'affaire des grands*]" of the cities (Geschiere 1995, 126; 1997, 70). The worsening state of things has reached a stage when ordinary people asking for nothing more than their daily bread increasingly find themselves threatened or eliminated by famine. And it has become common for people to complain in the following way captured by René Devisch (1995, 608) among Kwaangolese slum dwellers in Kinshasa: "In the days of the Belgian, we could eat three times a day. During the First Republic [1960–1965] one ate but two meals. With the Second we can afford only one. Where will progress end?" Throughout the continent, people have continued to wonder what happened to all the promises made at independence. Today, South Africans have become the latest to join the ranks of those who are wondering about why their leaders have completely forgotten about the welfare of the masses (cf. Sharp, 1998; Comaroff and Comaroff 1999). More and more, the peasants and slum dwellers have asked one another: "When will this *'ndependa* end?" and have wondered whether it had been a wise idea to chase away the white man after all. It is less painful to die by the hands of a stranger, than to be killed by someone whom you've always believed a soul brother. Remember Caesar's "Et tu Brute?" (Even you Brutus?). The heartfelt cries and calls for help by the disillusioned African masses go unheeded because the elite leadership that they seek to chase away mediates their relations with global capital.

That is the position of the African poor today, a most pathetic position indeed. They toil or hunger "under the sun, moon and stars," like Jimmy Cliff's slave ancestors did in the Americas, in order to sustain their exploiters and urban-based bunches of consumerist (un)civil servants and professional idlers. In most countries it is still thanks mainly to the food and cash crops of the rural poor that bureaucrats and the ruling elite are able to excel in barren consumerism. They have simply failed to see the need to produce before they spend. Where they are less successful in making the villagers dance to their tunes, or where the latter have simply said enough is enough, that it is better to die than to toil in vain, widespread famine and malnutrition are the inevitable consequence. Yet even then the peasants are doomed, for foreign aid intended to relieve everyone is misappropriated by their urban-centered exploiters.

The only other sector that could claim to produce and, therefore, to be taxpayers is the business sector. But unfortunately the state and its bureaucrats have swallowed the country's businesses almost everywhere. Little business is in private hands, and the few private operators choose to bank abroad for safety's sake, to avoid the caprices of the unstable political arena wherein they operate, granted that even local embezzlers are untrusting enough to bank abroad. The state-owned businesses are everything short of profit-making enterprises; they are in fact run as "public–private" businesses for the benefit of patrons and clients in power, and more often than not, instead of making money for the state, the state is forced to borrow to keep them going, for what matters at the end of the day is patronage, not prosperity. The state is keener on patronage as a check against popular modes of politics than on the pursuit of economic policies committed to the eradication of misery (cf. Bayart 1993; Mbembe 1992; Berman 1998; Olukoshi 1998b).

Thus, in real economic terms the heavy and, in most cases, the only tax-payer is the highly marginalized, overexploited rural poor. The civil servants, instead of creating wealth in a similar manner, are like the inflated queen of the termites, comfortably seated in her fattening chamber, waiting to be fed by her toiling and selfless soldiers. It is thanks to the peasant's food and cash crops that these uncivil servants excel in consumerism. Most African countries owe a large part of their foreign exchange to the sole effort of the peasant community.

The tragedy of the African poor today is that, unlike in the past, they are exploited by two forces. If the metaphor is allowed, their blood is sucked by two parasites: the one swimming inside the blood and the other attached like a tick to their bodies. In the case of the rural poor, the problem is that they produce cotton, groundnuts, cocoa, coffee, and tea, the prices of which are not determined by them, but by some remote reality called "international market forces." Handicapped by their supposed ignorance and the inability of their own leadership, they have struggled in vain to book an audience with this all-important "superman" of a tick.

ON SOCIAL CLASSES IN AFRICA

Given the largely underdeveloped nature of most African economies, which has retarded the crystallization of class differentiation and afforded the state a pervasive and repressive presence, it is hard to talk of social classes in terms Marx envisaged for capitalist societies. By the sheer fact of its monopolization or control of avenues of accumulation and social reproduction, the state succeeds in stifling civil society with strategic offers of power, privilege, and wealth to critical members of interest groups, and by encouraging the elite into thinking that they stand more to gain by investing in ethnoregionalism or the politics of belonging/primary patriotism (cf. Geschiere and Gugler 1998; Nyamnjoh 1999b).

With perhaps the exception of South Africa, it is incorrect to attribute to African societies the classic notion of two classes in constant opposition to one another, given the fact that most of Africa has failed to develop "a trans-ethnic public arena grounded in universalistic norms and the essential relations of social trust in the disinterested competence and probity of millions of unknown and unseen others" (Berman 1998, 339), and given the influence of "the evil triumvirate of patronage, corruption and tribalism . . . in African societies" (Berman 1998, 306). However, if we absolutely must speak of classes, I suggest we see Africa as a pyramid of three fluid classes (given widespread networks of patronage and clientelism), where the class at the base is the most exploited. We can identify, first, those without the opportunity to steal either from others or from the state: This class is made up of the toiling peasants who live in the rural areas despite themselves, and who are closely attached to their ancestral prescriptions of the good, normal, and upright life; again, despite themselves. They are largely confined and contained as rural subjects. When one is in a position of weakness, most of what one does is despite oneself.

This is the case, though African elites would like to idealize and romanticize the "traditional African" in order to perpetuate their suppression of this unfortunate class of the sidestepped. For the simple truth, believe it or not, is that most of those vociferous about preserving African cultures and values, whether on the continent or in the Diaspora, are the least endowed with these, and who at best visit their villages once a year, either to consult the diviner on their prospects for job promotion, to campaign for the reelection of "sons and daughters of the soil" in high office, or to bury one of their urban dead. My contention is that the "traditional Africa," allegedly epitomized by the rural poor, is a symbol of tradition despite itself; African peasants have been forced to pose as custodians of a tradition of which few, least of all the leading elite, are proud. The villagers are not interested in preserving tradition any more than their urban counterparts are; they are also preoccupied with enhancing the chances of attaining their objective interests even as foragers and scavengers for crumbs underneath the dining tables and refuse mountains of peripheral consumer capitalism.

Tell me how many times the young men and women of the rural areas have been coerced to remain in their villages under the pretext that the cities are centers of vice, crime, and bad habits. Why should some people be allowed to live in the cities at all, if cities are as bad as constantly painted to the rural poor? The truth is, for their power to have any meaning, the urban-based elites or leadership must make the peasants their scapegoats. They give the impression that the peasants have something they ought to be proud of, but their daily activities and behavior are such that they undermine the very doctrine of the importance of upholding African traditions, cultures, and values. At best, these elites want only what they term "traditional dances" or "*les danses folkloriques*," which they can use for their personal amusement or to entertain their foreign friends and counterparts. Thus, one of the rare times one actually hears of "our cultural heritage" is when Rousseau's "noble savage" is pulled out of the "happiness" and "naturalness" of his village (like the bullfighters of ancient Rome) to entertain his urban lords and masters, either during the national day celebrations, revolution anniversaries, or at the occasion of the visit of a foreign head of state or director of the World Bank or the International Monetary Fund (IMF). Performances, which were reserved for solemn occasions in the past, have today been trivialized and in certain cases commodified for touristic consumption (cf. Sreberny-Mohammadi 1997, 64–65; Geschiere and Meyer 1998, 607; Davis 1999), partly because the new breed of leaders know next to nothing about the societies they so claim to represent, but also because of the desperate quest by sidestepped rural communities to survive through feeding Western tourism.

Second, we can distinguish those who have the opportunity to steal from others, but who find it difficult to steal directly from the state because they are constantly under surveillance by their bosses and their prior claims. It takes a thief to catch a thief! This class consists of the low-ranking civil servants and literate or semiliterate urban dwellers. They are midway between the abject poverty and hardship of the village and the filthy riches and sumptuous plenty of the self-elected few who form the higher rungs of the urban community. Because of the uncertainty in their stealing opportunities, they are forced to have one foot in the city and the other in the village. Some of them live buried in the deplorable squalor of menstruating ghettos in divided cities, or in what some men and women of modern learning have termed "urban villages" (see René Devisch's (1995, 1996, 1998, 1999a, 1999b) detailed studies of "villagization" among slum dwellers trapped by "misery and hardship" in the "tragic spaces" of Kinshasa, and how they seek to contain their disillusionment with consumer capitalism, aggressive inflation, and crumbling state structures. Because their financial prospects are often unpredictable—even when they are involved with an apparently lucrative dollarized economy like the diamond diggers/dealers among the bana Lunda of the Zairean–Angolan border (cf. De Boeck 1998), their links with the villages are still strong, and they are forced from time to time to rush home to half-forgotten peasant relatives for food, protective charms, and other types of favors. But on the whole they are better off, because they live where they choose to live; unlike the villagers, they have not been forbidden the benefits of modernity, no matter how tiny or how devalued their share of these.

Our third and final class is the petty bourgeoisie, a class which includes the group of Africans who rule without legitimacy. It comprises those who have the near exclusive opportunity to steal from or "to criminalize" the state (cf. Bayart, Ellis, and Hibou 1999), and who believe that what matters is the fact that one is rich, not how one gets rich (cf. Reno 1995). They make no secret of their motto: Get rich or perish. These are the self-elected watchdogs of the national cake. They are constantly mediating between themselves and the outside world, and never stop preaching to the peasants how dangerous rural exodus is and how sacred life in the village has always been. This group comprises national political figures along with their provincial and regional representatives, top civil servants (easily identifiable in their thick woolen suits and well-polished Italian shoes, or in their gorgeous gowns, elaborately designed and imported from the Middle East), and pseudointellectuals who forge poems, compose songs, and kill the aggressive instinct in their pen or provide dictators with the "conceptual noises they need" (cf. Soyinka 1994b) to justify their excesses, with the hope of being appointed director of this or that public institution (which perhaps explains why African governments have the chronic tendency to nationalize, turning everything into a patrimony of some sort, in order better to satisfy the obliging and the yesful). This, in fact, is the class entrusted with the Herculean task of developing Africa, a class wherein the greater one's influence, the greater one's chances of stealing from the state and of making empty promises to one's people and the outside world. The current continentwide endorsement of World Bank policies and IMF-driven structural adjustment programs (cf. Ellis 1994, 120–121; Mkandawire 1996; Mkandawire and Olukoshi 1995) and their poor implementation shows to what extent this class has been successful with the task of (under)developing Africa.

THE FUTURE OF DEMOCRACY IN AFRICA

If one were to endorse Samir Amin's argument, that there is little prospect for democracy in dependent and peripheral states within the current international capitalist system, then there would not be much to hope for in this regard until the present structures of inequality are redressed. But then, ending the debate at that level would amount to a summary and uncritical dismissal of certain internal factors that have tended to worsen the predicament of ordinary Africans already disfavored by the logic of global capitalism; hence, my decision to examine how African states have fared even as boxers with their hands tied behind their backs. What prospects are there in Africa, even for "liberal democracy" in the twenty-first century?

Prior to 1990, most Africans lived under political systems where the genuine and popular was circumvented. Democracy remained confined to a few ambiguous statements in constitutions that were fashioned, often capriciously, by civilian dictators or military regimes. This was a cynical world of tyranny, a shadowy world of fear and insecurity designed by those in power for whom power was all that mattered. During this period the state's contradictions and pathologies, epitomized by the head of state, placed the whole of society under siege. Executive freedom, secure and at peace with a *folie de grandeur* (megalomania) required that the rest of society had to be shackled and deprived in the absolute. The peculiar consequence of African dictatorships was society's forfeiture of the freedom to resist through intricate networks of patronage connecting the small and poor to the big men at the center of power and wealth (Bayart 1993; Mbembe 1992; Berman 1998). This "competitive alienation" of the masses by tyrants all over the continent was achieved by "conceptual noises" furnished by pseudointellectual apologists (Soyinka 1994b, 7–9), the impoverishment and disillusionment of the masses by structural adjustment (cf. Olukoshi 1998b), the sacralisation of power (cf. Bediako 1995; De Boeck 1996; Blake 1997, 255–257), and the neutralization of shared pain and misery (Nyamnjoh 1999b).

The Eastern European revolution in 1989 and the euphoria of the South African struggle for liberation encouraged the African masses to believe that the time had come to be liberated from dictatorial complacencies, endemic corruption, and suffocating mediocrity. They were no longer willing to tolerate autocrats who, while promoting obscure notions of national development and stability, deterred all forms of opposition. Most had come to know that such stability was fraudulent and development elusive. They wanted democracy—multiparty democracy, some argued—with the hope that this would bring about pluralism and popular democratic participation in practice. Clearly, military regimes and the single-party state had failed to deliver. If thirty years of sacrificed freedoms was not time enough to attain national integration, welfare, and human dignity, then monopartyism and militarism were problems, not solutions.

By the 1990s the feeling grew, even among pessimistic scholars (see the overview of literature on democratization in Africa by Buijtenhuijs and Rijnierse 1993, and of the democracy debate in Africa by Olukoshi 1998a), that however entrenched, repression in Africa was something that popular disillusionment, international pressure, and the growing recognition by the masses of the importance of organized resistance would overcome. Such optimism notwithstanding, it rapidly became obvious that the African people would still have to anticipate the reality of participatory democracy. The present state of current democratization efforts in Africa (cf. Buijtenhuijs and Rijnierse 1993; Buijtenhuijs and Thiriot 1995; Mbaku 1999; Olukoshi 1998a, 1998c) strongly suggests that there is goodwill and genuine commitment to collective betterment neither with those in power nor with those seeking to replace them. "Faced with many grievances and demands from poor social groups, the supply of ideas from political leaders has remained limited" (Monga 1995, 365–366). The general concern of the opposition parties is to replace the gluttons at the table rather than redistribute the "national cake" (cf. Berman 1998; Nyamnjoh 1999c). It is like the war of the gourmands, where the opposition is more concerned with "the bellies" at the dining table than the fact of gluttony, as those of them who have managed to assume power have taken on the same predatory contradictions. "Often resorting to arm-twisting and increasingly authoritarian ways in order to push their views through, many of these governments have not shown themselves to be different from the discredited politicians whom they replaced" (Olukoshi 1998b, 27). Decriers of malfeasance in high office within the opposition employ mere political gimmickry, as even the most radical of them have seldom gone beyond what Monga (1995, 371) has termed "slogans in line with populist illusions." The consequences of these developments have been a profound disillusionment and "a growing problem of popular de-participation in the political process of most African countries" (Olukoshi 1998b, 28).

In light of this, one may ask what prospects there are for an active civil society and real participatory democracy in Africa. It is true that political liberalization is well under way in a number of countries, and that, in the course of this "second liberation" struggle for the continent, some achievements have been made (cf. Ellis 1994), but there is no certainty over its future direction or the impact it may have on the underlying political structure. There is doubt about the true extent and likely beneficiaries of political reform, because in the absence of a democratic culture, multiparty democracy is likely to remain confined to competition among political elites to the exclusion of the disaffected masses (Nyong'o 1988; Buijtenhuijs and Rijnierse 1993; Good 1999). Currently there is widespread popular disillusionment with politics, since multipartyism seems to differ little from monopartyism and military regimes as a vehicle for establishing a truly democratic culture in Africa. In the face of repeated frustrations at elections, opposition parties have either become dupes of the ruling party "to lure them with the carrot of state patronage," or have "simply splintered into factions and/or faded into irrelevance" (Olukoshi 1998b, 31–34). Similarly, undemocratic NGOs have profited by the tendency among Western donor agencies and governments to "assume that NGOs are by definition democratic simply on account of the fact that they are non-governmental" (Olukoshi 1998a, 38–39).

Observers of African affairs have borne witness that enfranchisement does not necessarily lead to empowerment and universal suffrage does not guarantee access to political decision making. As a Cameroonian political satirist, Tchop Tchop (1997), points out in a sketch, "Elections are like a football match where one must prepare one's players physically and psychologically. One can consult the Pygmy witchdoctor, corrupt the referee, or motivate [bribe] one's opponents. . . . You organize your elections knowing full well that you are going to win them."

Political equality has been confined to the right to vote, as autocrats have chosen to ignore the right of most to be elected or to enjoy civil liberties. Although statements have been made to the contrary, ordinary people and alternative social and political organizations continue to face, in practice, enormous difficulties exercising their rights: "to hold and express opinions contrary to those of the state, or regimes and leaders; to assemble freely and organize within the framework of the law: to publish contrary opinions about public affairs, to suggest alternative political strategies, and to expect the protection of the state itself from arbitrary arrest and abuse of power" (Goulbourne 1987, 46). The state remains "an interfering irritant, a source of corruptly obtained advantage or a massive irrelevance for many people" (Barnett 1997, 45), floating with impunity above civil society like a balloon in mid-air (Hyden 1983, 19). Thus, as Olukoshi (1998b, 33) asserts, multipartyism does not seem to have led to good governance even in countries like Zambia, where the opposition came to power on the ticket of popular expectations, as such new governments have tended to conduct themselves like the erstwhile single ruling parties which they replaced. In Burkina Faso, an "upbeat official rhetoric" on political democratization that has earned praise from Western governments "masks a more complex—and sobering—reality" of corruption and patronage; in this instance, "the most outspoken critics continue to face threats, harassment and occasional detention," and "the police have been known to torture and kill suspects," while "the authorities have pushed through legislation to restrict the right to demonstrate" (Harsch 1998, 626). In South Africa, democracy is seriously threatened by "misguided loyalties and a culture of silence," not least among academics: "White academics do not speak out on issues of national concern any more because they are afraid that they will be labeled racist. Black academics do not criticize the government because of misplaced loyalty born out of a comradeship with its roots in the struggle against apartheid—they cannot be seen to be criticizing their own. These misguided loyalties and a culture of silence is putting South Africa's democracy at risk" (Ramphele 1999, 31). It remains to be seen to what extent a post-apartheid state, amenable to the exclusion and assimilation logic of global capital, will succeed in redressing structural inequalities in ways that are beneficial to more than just a black elite (Sharp 1998).

In the absence of a vigorous civil society and creative initiatives, African political leaders continue to perceive the state as the sole source of personal enrichment and reward. They are apt to use political power for private ends, guided by a sort of "mercenary ethos" (Eyoh 1995) or kleptocratic instincts (Bayart, Ellis, and Hibou 1999). As such, they are reluctant to commit themselves to popular democracy and, hence, with few exceptions, they are least likely to adopt genuine democratic instruments or concede power even when defeated at the polls. Only eight heads of state—Kérékou and Soglo of Benin, Kaunda of Zambia, Sassou-Nguesso of Congo, Ratsiraka of Madagascar, Pereira of Cape Verde, Da Costa of São Tomé, and De Klerk of South Africa—"have conceded power more or less gracefully as a result of defeat in democratic elections" (Ellis 1994, 119). Democratic participation in the continent has yet to mean respect for the ballot or a meaningful extension of the franchise "into areas where ordinary people do not normally participate" (Hamelink 1995, 19). For, while passive participation might guarantee privileges for individuals and groups, only "the active inclusion in public politics of those who have in the past lost out, and whose presence continues to be ignored in corrupt and crumbling states" (Von Lieres 1999, 143) would render the notion of democracy meaningful and popular with the masses. Hence Olukoshi's (1998a, 38) contention that "the most crucial factor for the sustenance of democratic reform and governance in Africa" would have to consist of "the enthronement of a popular sovereignty that touches the daily lives of the populace, gives life and meaning to the notion of citizenship, and goes beyond the constitutionally defined form of rule." For democracy can only survive in the continent if and when it becomes "a lived experience that is worth defending." In other words, "there must be a culture of robust open and public debate, tolerance of different viewpoints and people with the courage of their convictions to express their views, even if these might not be popular" (Ramphele 1999, 31).

Until then, contemporary manifestations of political liberalization are, in the perception of most ordinary Africans, little more than cosmetic reforms designed by reluctant autocrats to retain legitimacy in the eyes of Western supporters and lending agencies, and to ensure their continued dominance in the face of popular disaffection (cf. Ellis 1994, 119–121). As Peter Wanyande (1996, 5–7) aptly observes, even the emerging civil society is being infiltrated by organizations "that are undemocratic in orientation," some of which may have been created by ruling parties, cliques, juntas, or oligarchies "to protect the state against its adversaries" by countering the activities of other associations fighting for undiluted democracy. Thus, at the dawn of the twenty-first century we cannot resist revisiting Ayi Kwei Armah's (1969, 79) question of thirty years ago; namely, "How long will Africa be cursed with its leaders?"

It is indeed discouraging to note that ten years into the democratic transition most of Africa's political environment is still characterized by the one-party logic, for which government, the opposition, interest groups and sometimes even the public are culpable. All parties employ a logic that has prevented multi-partyism from addressing the issue of how best to bring about genuine political equality that P. Hamelink (1995, 19) argues is only possible with "the broadest possible participation of all people in processes of public decision-making."

From all that has been said, it should be evident that there is an urgent need to empower the masses, especially as—lip service to democracy notwithstanding—Africans are still subjected to the sort of post-totalitarian control that Václav Havel (1986, 44–45) described regarding Czechoslovakia prior to the 1989 East European revolution, and that is still true of many African countries today. Borrowing from Havel, therefore, we could consider the one-party logic of the power elite in Africa as a system that "serves people only to the extent necessary to ensure that people will serve it," with those failing to play their predetermined roles risking indictment as enemies of the system. Because its diversionary markers touch people at every level of society, the system has succeeded in tainting civil society with hypocrisy and lies.

A need exists, therefore, to provide for public control of power in Africa through public competition for power. Political affairs and social life should be organized and conducted in such a way that allows for effective access to decision making for all and sundry, and for an equitable distribution of the fruits of progress among the various social groups (cf. Mbembe 1997b, 1999). P. Hamelink (1995, 19) argues that there is nothing wrong with the delegation of powers to politicians, experts, or market forces as such. What is important, however, is to provide for "rules, procedures and institutional mechanisms to secure public accountability," as well as "the possibility of remedial action by those whose rights to participation and equality are violated." For "there can be no rights without the option of redress in case of their violations," and the option must be both accessible and affordable (P. Hamelink 1995. 24). As Amin (1997a, 43) puts it, for any meaningful revolution (whether agrarian or technological) to take place in Africa there must be a new type of power in which the masses are no longer passive spectators in decision making, but organized social forces with a contribution to make. Only by returning power to the people in this way could Africans hope to stop "living within a lie" and start "living within the truth" (Havel 1986, 36–122).

According to Ellis (1994, 120–121), "The fact that African politicians are unable to articulate any original or critical view on economic policy," given how committed to World Bank policies they virtually all are, means that "there is little to choose in ideological terms between rival parties." This not only implies that political parties tend "to compete for the same social constituencies as their rivals," but also that they "find it hard to identify and represent any social or economic interest group which has been previously under-represented, unless, of course, such a group is ethnically defined." This would explain "the tendency for rival parties to recruit ethnic constituencies, just as the barons of the old ruling parties tended to do." It also raises the question of the relevance of the party as a mode of political organization in Africa.

If political parties in Africa tend to appeal to ethnic loyalties rather than seek to establish a shared ideological consensus, and if their partisans have consistently tended to vote along regional and ethnic lines, it is perhaps time we look beyond political parties as the way of organizing politics and government in Africa. The recognition that there is nothing inherently authoritarian about monopartyism and nothing inherently democratic about multipartyism (Neocosmos 1998; Wiredu 1997), coupled with the fact that most of Africa has failed to develop a culture of commonwealth and public interest that transcends ethnicity and is "grounded in universalistic norms and the essential relations of social trust in the disinterested competence and probity of millions of unknown and unseen others" (Berman 1998, 339), ought to push African social scientists to explore other models of political organization informed by African cultural, political, and historical experiences, on the one hand, and the reality of its economic dependence and lightweightness, on the other. For this quest to be creative and fruitful, African intellectuals and political classes must desist from a view of "African ethnicity as an atavism" (cf. Eyoh 1995, 50; Berman 1998, 306) and envision a democracy that guarantees not only individual rights and freedoms, but also the interests of communal and cultural solidarities (Eyoh 1995, 50). They must provide for a creative "mix between the individual legacy of liberalism and collectivist legacy of ethnicity" (Von Lievres 1999, 143), as well as for the containing reality of Africa being at the fringes of global capitalism (cf. Amin 1987, 1997a, 1997b). Wiredu's (1997, 308–311) suggestion that Africans revisit the idea of "consensual democracy" as a possible solution to stalling "majoritarian democracy" deserves to be taken seriously. Referring to consensual democracy in the traditional Ashanti system, Wiredu argues that this was "a democracy because government was by the consent, and subject to the control, of the people as expressed through their representatives." Thus, while majoritarian democracy might be based on consent without consensus, the Ashanti system ensured that "consent was negotiated on the principle of consensus." Guided in part by this idea of consensual democracy, it is time to investigate possible alternatives, such as a confederation of regional or ethnic associations (elite or otherwise) staking claim to national resources without dissemblance or equivocation for the benefit of their regions or ethnic groups (cf. Nyamnjoh and Rowlands 1998). This is more likely to yield positive results than the current practice, whereby politicians and intellectuals "take comfort in ancestral traditions at the same time that they stubbornly refuse to concede to the formal representation of the interests of cultural solidarities" (Eyoh 1995, 50).

Social scientists must seek a better understanding of, and inspiration from, popular responses to state delinquency and the elitism of consumer capitalism. The growing number of studies and critical scholarship on Pentecostalism (Meyer 1995, 1998a, 1998b; Van Dijk 1992, 1993, 1997; Van Dijk and Pels 1996), healing charismatic churches (Devisch 1995, 1996, 1998, 1999a, 1999b), witchcraft and zombification (cf. Geschiere 1997; Eyoh 1998; De Boeck 1998; Comaroff and Comaroff 1999; Ciekawy and Geschiere 1998) are signposts in the direction where contemporary African studies ought to go toward understanding the creative agency of ordinary Africans in the face of repeated contradictions and frustrations with global capitalism and its seesaw of flows and closures, assimilation and exclusion, seduction and rejection (cf Appadurai 1996; Geschiere and Meyer 1998). More of such studies are likely to inform the collective imagination on how to seek redemption from victimization.

Yet only a certain quality of leadership and citizenry can return power to the people in this way. Quality leadership is scarce in Africa, where, as Akin Mabogunje (1991) of Ogun State University (Nigeria) remarks, there has been a most striking paucity of attention devoted to the socialization of leadership. But as he warns, "Africa cannot afford to continue with ill-prepared and unassisted leaders . . . if they are to meet the challenges that will face them." African societies must, he argues, like their Western counterparts, invest tremendous resources in "inculcating, nurturing and promoting the right leadership qualities" among their members, so that the continent's future leaders comprehend fully their responsibilities, duties, and obligations. They cannot afford to be "lackadaisical and indifferent to the type of qualities evinced by those who seek to lead" them if they are to avoid "the agonies of purposelessness, deprivation and insecurity." Africans, he maintains, need leaders who are "knowledgeable, dedicated to some ideals, visionary, selfless in commitment to the aspirations of the populace, astute, and critical of cant, rigorously honest and tolerant of alternative opinions." They need leaders armed with moral, spiritual, intellectual, and physical integrity, for "popular democracy requires responsible leaders and enlightened followers" (Ndulo 1996, 12). Responsible leadership entails recognizing the correlation between democratic practices and socioeconomic development, rather than the widespread tendency of wrongly asserting, as do many leaders on the continent, that political stability—not democratic governance (including respect for the rule of law)—are the preconditions for economic growth and development (Nyong'o 1987). Only such leadership can guarantee a new social contract for individual African countries, one that focuses on the social welfare of the people, reinforces political and cultural pluralism, emphasizes democratic accountability, guarantees the protection of human and peoples' rights, and ensures representation for competing interests in the political process (cf. Olukoshi 1998b, 34–35).

Academics—both on the continent and elsewhere, black and white—with Africa's future at heart, must help destroy once and for all the myth of "noble savage" and earn respect for the peasants and slum dwellers (the urban villagers), not as custodians of "traditional dances" and "recreational savagery," but as the genuine pillars of the African economy, without whom the ruling minority would starve to death. We must help the peasants and urban villagers make political and economic capital out of their sweat, toil, and patience, and out of the ignorance and lazy habits of their privileged overlords. Only by joining forces with sympathizers the world over, and through the "social shaping" and appropriation of new communication and information technologies (cf. Lyon 1986), can Africans fight off the globalization of poverty by making a strong case for the effective globalization of opportunities and the riches of their universe. Such unity and creative domestication of new technologies hold the key to the end for globalization as a process where "many are called but few are chosen."

NOTES

1. President Clinton, in his last State of the Union address, devoted a lot of time to globalization as an information technology–driven process that would mark the twenty-first century and revolutionize human societies.

2. For a critical look at the impact of globalization on Africa and its culture, see Eko (2001).

3. According to *The Financial Times* (cited in Seabrook 2000, 22), "At the start of the 19th century the ratio of real incomes per head between the world's richest and poorest countries was three to one. By 1900, it was 10 to one. By 2000, it had risen to 60 to one."

4. Although some have argued that multinational corporations in the South pay better wages than does the state or local businesses (cf. *The Economist*, January 29–February 4, 2000), the tendency remains to take advantage of cheap labor, to the point that these days it is possible to buy a "pair of Reeboks, the left shoe of which was made in the Philippines and the right in South Korea" (cf. O'Brien 1993, 67), probably to prevent local workers stealing from the stock to supplement low wages.

5. Globalization might imply that "the noses of the poor are always pressed against the television screens of the rich," but it does not diminish the fact that "at the touch of a button they can be made to disappear," unless, of course, they actually start knocking at the doors of one's borders (cf. Seabrook 2000, 22).

6. This is so prevalent that a patient in Cameroon once asked her doctor to be administered "an imported anesthesia" in place of the "local anesthesia" that the doctor suggested (Warnier 1993, 164).

7. Zombification means "rendering a mindless and passive subject" and Makwerekwere is a Tswana term for those who cannot speak the local language properly, now used derogatorily in South Africa and Botswana, especially to refer to immigrants from fellow African countries. See *Mail & Guardian* (November 26–December 2, 1999, 11) and *Saturday Star* (October 23, 1999, 2), for reports on the "Nigerian 4-1-9"; see *Libération* (November 1998, 14–15, 18), for a report on the leading "Cameroonian feyman," Donatien Koagne.

8. This refers to an article in the Nigerian constitution against fraud and corruption, but popular usage has corrupted it to refer to anyone involved in corrupt deals and fraud.

9. In Cameroon it refers to tricksters and fraudsters who pose as businessmen in order to defraud others with fake deals. Like the 4-1-9, they are involved in all sorts of business ventures, from letter scams to money doubling, and so on.

10. Interviewed once on TV in the West about Zaire's foreign debt, late President Mobutu, one of the world's richest men at the time, is noted to have replied that the problem was not whether or not he could lend his country money, but rather what guarantees there were that Zaire would repay the loan.

11. See De Boeck (1998) for more on such ostentatious spending and its impact among young Zaireans involved with the dollarized diamond economy.

REFERENCES

Achebe, C. 1959. *Things fall apart.* New York: Anchor Books.

Ajayi, J.F.A. 1966. The place of African history and culture in the process of nation-building in Africa South of the Sahara. In *Social change: The colonial situation,* edited by I. Wallerstein. New York: John Wiley and Sons.

Amin, S. 1980. *Class and nation: Historically and in the current crisis.* London: Heinemann.

Amin, S. 1987. Preface: The state and the question of "development." In *Popular struggles for democracy in Africa,* edited by P. A. Nyong'o. London: Zed Books.

Amin, S. 1997a. L'Afrique et le développement. *Jeune Afrique Economie* 234 (February 3): 36–43.

Amin, S. 1997b. Reflections on the international system. In *Beyond cultural imperialism: Globalization, communication & the New International Order,* edited by P. Golding and P. Harris. London: Sage.

Armah, A. K. 1969. *The beautiful ones are not yet born.* New York: Collier.

Appadurai, A. 1996. *Modernity at large: Cultural dimensions of globalization.* Minneapolis: University of Minnesota Press.

Barnett, T. 1997. States of the state and Third Worlds. In *Beyond cultural imperialism: Globalization, communication & the New International Order,* edited by P. Golding and P. Harris. London: Sage.

Barrett, B. D. 1968. *Schism and renewal in Africa: An analysis of six thousand contemporary religious movements.* London: Oxford University Press.

Bayart, J.-F. 1993. *The state in Africa: The politics of the belly.* London: Longman.

Bayart, J.-F., S. Ellis, and B. Hibou. 1999. *The criminalization of the state in Africa.* Oxford: James Currey.

Becker, J. 1996. The Internet, structural violence and non-communication. *Media Development* 43 (4): 10–12.

Beckman, B. 1992. The liberation of civil society: Neoliberal ideology and political theory in an African context. Paper presented at the workshop on "Social Movements, State and Democracy," New Delhi, October 5–8.

Bediako, K. 1995. De-sacralization and democratization: Some theological reflections on the role of Christianity in nation-building in modern Africa. *Transformation: An International Evangelical Dialogue on Mission and Ethics* 12 (1): 5–11.

Berger, G. 1998. Media and democracy in southern Africa. *Review of African Political Economy* 78: 599–610.

Berman, F. B. 1998. Ethnicity, patronage and the African state: The politics of uncivil nationalism. *African Affairs* 97 (388): 305–341.

Bhabha, J. 1998. Enforcing the human rights of citizens and non-citizens in the era of Maastricht: Some reflections on the importance of states. *Development and Change* 29 (4): 697–724.

Biko, S. 1996. *I write what I like.* Randburg, South Africa: Ravan Press.

Blake, C. 1997. Democratization: The dominant imperative for national communication policies in Africa in the 21st century. *Gazette* 59 (45): 253–269.

Braman, S. 1998. The information society, the information economy, and South Africa. *Communication* 24 (1): 67–75.

Bryceson, D. F. 1999. Review article: Of criminals and clients: African culture and Afro-pessimism in a globalized world. Leiden, Netherlands: Center for African Studies Discussion Paper.

Buijtenhuijs, R., and E. Rijnierse. 1993. *Democratization in sub-Saharan Africa (1989–1992): An overview of the literature.* Leiden: African Studies Center.

Buijtenhuijs, R., and C. Thiriot. 1995. *Democratization in sub-Saharan Africa (1992–1995): An overview of the literature.* Leiden: African Studies Center.

Busisiwe Mosieman. 1999. Skin-lightening creams resurface. *Mmegi/The Reporter*, December 17–23, 16.

Chinweizu. 1987. *The West and the rest of us: White predators, black slavers and the African elite.* Lagos: Pero Press.

Ciekawy, D., and P. Geschiere, eds. 1998. Containing witchcraft: Conflicting scenarios in postcolonial Africa. *African Studies Review* (Special Issue) 41 (3): 1–14.

Cohen, R. 1978. Ethnicity: Problem and focus in anthropology. *Annual Review of Anthropology* 7: 379–403.

Comaroff, J., and J. Comaroff. 1999. Alien-nation: Zombies, immigrants, and millennial capitalism. *CODESRIA Bulletin* 3–4: 17–28.

Davis, E. A. 1999. Metamorphosis in the culture market of Niger. *American Anthropologist* 101 (3): 485–501.

De Boeck, F. 1996. Postcolonialism, power and identity: Local and global perspectives from Zaire. In *Postcolonial identities in Africa*, edited by R. Werbner and T. Ranger. London: Zed Books.

De Boeck, F. 1998. Domesticating diamonds and dollars: Identity, expenditure and sharing in southwestern Zaire (1984–1997). In *Globalization and identity: Dialectics of flows and closures*, edited by B. Meyer and P. Geschiere, *Development and Change* (Special Issue) 29 (4): 751–776.

Devisch, R. 1995. Frenzy, violence, and ethical renewal in Kinshasa. *Public Culture* 7 (3): 593–629.

Devisch, R. 1996. "Pillaging Jesus": Healing churches and the villagization of Kinshasa. *Africa* 66 (4): 555–585.

Devisch, R. 1998. La violence à Kinshasa ou l'institution en négatif. *Cahiers d'Études Africaines* 150–152: 441–469.

Devisch, R. 1999a. Mimicry, parody, and the "cannibalization" of the French master language in the prophetic healing churches of Kinshasa. Paper presented at the Department of Anthropology, University of Cape Town, April 30.

Devisch, R. 1999b. Therapy choice, utilization, and satisfaction by low-budget health-seekers in suburban and rural Bantu Africa. Keynote paper presented at the Pan African Association of Anthropologists (PAAA) Conference, Yaoundé, Cameroon, September 2–8.

Diamani, J. P. 1995. L'humour politique au phare du Zaire. *Politique Africaine* 58 (June): 151–157.

Eko, L. 2001. Jerry Springer and the Marlboro Man in Africa: Globalization and cultural eclecticism. *Ecquid Novi* 22 (1): 25–40.

Ellis, S. 1994. Democracy and human rights in Africa. In *Poverty and development: historical dimension of development, change and conflict in the south*, edited by R. Van den Berg and U. Bosma. The Hague: Ministry of Foreign Affairs.

Ellis, S. 1996. Africa and international corruption: The strange case of South Africa and Seychelles. *African Affairs* 95: 165–196.

Eyoh, D. 1995. From the belly to the ballot: Ethnicity and politics in Africa. *Queen's Quarterly* 102 (1): 39–51.

Eyoh, D. 1998. Through the prism of a local tragedy: Political liberalization, regionalism and elite struggles for power in Cameroon. *Africa* 68 (3): 338–359.

Fanon, F. 1967a. *Black skin, white masks*. New York: Grove Press.

Fanon, F. 1967b. *The wretched of the earth*. Harmondsworth: Penguin Books.

February, V. A. 1981. *Mind your color: The "colored" stereotype in South African literature*. London: Kegan Paul.

Fonlon, B. 1967. Idea of culture (II). *ABBIA: Cameroon Cultural Review* 16 (March): 5–24.

Gareau, F. H. 1987. Expansion and increasing diversification of the universe of social science. *International Social Science Journal* 114: 595–606.

Geschiere, P. 1995. *Sorcellerie et politique en Afrique*. Paris: Karthala.

Geschiere, P. 1997. *The modernity of witchcraft: Politics and the occult in postcolonial Africa*. Charlottesville: University of Virginia Press.

Geschiere, P., and J. Gugler. 1998. Introduction: New ways of belonging. *Africa* 68 (3): 309–319.

Geschiere, P., and B. Meyer. 1998. Globalization and identity: Dialectics of flows and closures: Introduction. *Development and Change* 29 (4): 601–615.

Geschiere, P., and F. B. Nyamnjoh. 2000. Capitalism and autochthony: The seesaw of mobility and belonging. *Public Culture* 12 (2): 423–452.

Giddens, A. 1990. *The consequences of modernity*. Cambridge: Polity Press.

Golding, P. 1974. Media role in national development: Critique of a theoretical orthodoxy. *Journal of Communication* 24 (3): 39–53.

Golding, P. 1994. The communications paradox: Inequality at the national and international levels. *Media Development* 41 (4): 7–9.

Golding, P., and P. Harris, eds. 1997. *Beyond cultural imperialism: Globalization, communication & the New International Order*. London: Sage.

Good, K. 1994. Corruption and mismanagement in Botswana: A best-case example? *Journal of Modern African Studies* 32 (3): 499–521.

Good, K. 1999. Enduring elite democracy in Botswana. *Democratization* 6 (1): 50–66.

Gouldbourne, H. 1987. The state, development and the need for participatory democracy in Africa. In *Popular struggles for democracy in Africa*, edited by P. A. Nyong'o. London: Zed Books.

Gray, J. 1998. *False dawn: The delusions of global capitalism*. London: Granta Books.

Hadjor, K. B. 1987. *On transforming Africa: Discourse with Africa's leaders*. Trenton, NJ: Africa World Press and Third World Communications.

Halloran, J. D. 1993. The European image: Unity in diversity—Myth or reality. A presentation at the IAMCR Conference, Dublin, June.

Hamelink, C. J. 1983. *Cultural autonomy in global communications: Planning national information policy*. London: Longman.

Hamelink, C. J. 1996. Globalization and human dignity: The case of the information superhighway. *Media Development* 43 (1): 18–21.

Hamelink, P. 1995. The democratic ideal and its enemies. In *The democratization of communication*, edited by P. Lee. Cardiff: University of Wales Press.

Hancock, G. 1989. *Lords of poverty*. London: Macmillan.

Hare, N. 1991. *The black Anglo-Saxons.* Chicago: Third World Press.

Harsch, E. 1989. Burkina Faso in the winds of liberalization. *Review of African Political Economy* 25 (78): 625–641.

Havel, V. 1986. *Living in truth: Twenty-two essays published on the occasion of the award of the Erasmus Prize to Václav Havel* (edited by Jan Vladislav). London: Faber and Faber.

Himmelstrand, U., K. Kinyanjui, and E. Mburugu. 1994. Introduction: In search of new paradigms. In *African perspectives on development: Controversies, dilemmas & openings,* edited by U. Himmelstrand, K. Kinyanjui, and E. Mburugu. London: James Currey.

Hope, K. R., and B. C. Chikulo, eds. *Corruption and development in Africa: Lessons from country case-studies.* London: Macmillan.

Hyden, G. 1983. *No shortcuts to progress.* London: Heinemann.

Jussawalla, M. 1988. The information revolution and its impact on the world economy. In *Information economy and development,* edited by D. I. Riddle. Bonn: Friedrich-Ebert-Stiftung.

Kabou, A. 1991. *Et si l'Afrique refusait le développement?* Paris: L'Harmattan.

Kunczik, M. 1993. *Communication and social change.* Bonn: Friedrich-Ebert-Stiftung.

Laburthe-Tolra, P., and J. P. Warnier. 1993. *Ethnologie, anthropologie.* Paris: Presse Universitaires de France.

Lee, P. 1995. Introduction: The illusion of democracy. In *The democratization of communication,* edited by P. Lee. Cardiff: University Press of Wales.

Lerner, D. 1964. *The passing of traditional society: Modernizing the Middle East.* New York: Free Press.

Lynch, M. D. 1997/1998. Information highways. In *World Information Report,* Paris: UNESCO Publishing.

Lyon, D. 1986. From "post-industrialism" to "information society": A new social transformation. *Sociology* 20 (4): 577–588.

Mabogunje, A. 1991. The African leadership forum. *The Guardian* (Nigerian), July 29: 33.

Maduno, C. O. 1994. *White magic: The origins and ideals of black mental and cultural colonialism.* Hampton, VA: UB and U.S. Communication Systems.

Mafeje, A. 1998. Anthropology and independent Africans: Suicide or end of an era. *African Sociological Review* 2 (1): 1–43.

Mamdani, M. 1990. State and civil society in contemporary Africa: Reconceptualizing the birth of state nationalism and the defeat of popular movements. *Africa Development* 15 (3/4): 47–70.

Mamdani, M. 1996. *Citizen and subject: Contemporary Africa and the legacy of late colonialism.* Cape Town: David Philip.

Masmoudi, M. 1995. Africa facing the information highway. Paper presented at the ACCE Conference on Traditional Communication in Africa, Nairobi, November 28–December 1.

Mathews, B. J. 1924. *The clash of color: A study in the problem of race.* New York: Missionary Education Movement of the United States and Canada.

Mazrui, A. 1994. Development in a multicultural context: Trends and tensions. In *Culture and development in Africa,* edited by I. Serageldin and J. Taboroff. Washington, DC: World Bank.

Mbaku, J. M., ed. 1998. *Corruption and the crisis of institutional reforms in Africa.* Lewiston, NY: Edwin Mellen Press.

Mbaku, J. M., ed. 1999. *Preparing Africa for the twenty-first century: Strategies for peaceful coexistence and sustainable development.* Aldershot, UK: Ashgate.

Mbaku, J. M. 2000. *Bureaucratic and political corruption in Africa: The public choice perspective.* Malabar, FL: Krieger.

Mbembe, A. 1992. Provisional notes on the postcolony. *Africa* 62 (1): 3–37.

Mbembe, A. 1997a. The "thing" & its double in Cameroonian cartoons. In *Readings in African popular culture*, edited by K. Barber. Oxford: International African Institute and James Currey.

Mbembe, A. 1997b. The value of life and the price of death: Persons and things in African contemporary debates on rights. Keynote address delivered at the Conference on Cultural Transformations in Africa: Legal, Religious and Human Rights Issues, Center for African Studies, University of Cape Town, South Africa, March 11–13.

Mbembe, A. 1999. *Du gouvernement privé indirect.* Dakar: CODESRIA.

McChesney, R. W. 1998. The political economy of global media. *Media Development* 45 (4): 3–8.

Melody, W. H. 1987. The information society: Implications for economic institutions and market theory. In *Transborder data flow and development*, edited by J. Becker. Bonn: Friedrich-Ebert-Stiftung.

Meyer, B. 1995. Translating the devil: An African appropriation of Pietist Protestantism: The case of the Peki Ewe in southeastern Ghana, 1847–1992. Ph.D. dissertation, Amsterdam: University of Amsterdam.

Meyer, B. 1998a. Commodities and the power of prayer: Pentecostalist attitudes towards consumption in contemporary Ghana. *Development and Change* 29 (4): 751–776.

Meyer, B. 1998b. "Make a complete break with the past": Memory and postcolonial modernity in Ghanaian Pentecostalist discourse. *Journal of Religion in Africa* 28 (3): 316–349.

Meyer, B., and P. Geschiere, eds. 1998. Special Issue on "Globalization and identity: Dialectics of flows and closures." *Development and Change* 29 (4).

Mkandawire, T. 1996. Economic policymaking and the consolidation of democratic institutions in Africa. In *Domination or dialogue: Experiences and prospects for African development cooperation*, edited by K. Havnevik and B. van Arkadie. Uppsala: Nordiska Afrikainstitutet.

Mkandawire, T., and A. Olukoshi, eds. 1995. *Between Liberalization and repression: The politics of structural adjustment in Africa.* Dakar: CODESRIA Books.

Monga, C. 1995. Civil society and democratization in Francophone Africa. *Journal of Modern African Studies* 33 (3): 359–379.

Moore, N. 1997/1998. The information society. In *World Information Report.* Paris: UNESCO.

Mukasa, S. G. 1998. Towards a global knowledge for environmentally sustainable development agenda in 21st century southern Africa. *Communicatio* 17 (1): 1–27.

Murdock, G. 1982. Large corporations and the control of the communications industries. In *Culture, society and the media*, edited by Michael Gurevitch, Tony Bennett, James Curran, and Janet Woolacott. London: Methuen.

Murdock, G. 1994. The new Mogul Empires: Media concentration and control in the age of divergence. *Media Development* 41 (4): 3–6.

Murphy, D. 1989. *Cameroon with Egbert.* London: Arrow Books.

Ndulo, M. 1996. Constitution making in Africa: Postindependence arrangements. In *Africa Notes*, Ithaca, NY: Institute for African Development, Cornell University.

Neocosmos, M. 1998. From people's politics to state politics: Aspects of national liberation in South Africa. In *The politics of opposition in contemporary Africa*, edited by A. Olukoshi. Uppsala: Nordiska Afrikaninstitutet.

Ngubane, B. S. 1996. Dr. B. S. Ngubane: Minister of Arts, Science and Technology: Symposium: Culture, Communication, Development. Pretoria, South Africa, August: HSRC.

Nkwi, P. N. 1995. Electronic mail: The experience of the Network of African Medical Anthropology (NAMA). *African Anthropology* 2 (1): 154–161.

Nnoli, O. 1980. *Ethnic politics in Nigeria*. Enugu: Fourth Dimension.

Nyamnjoh, F. B. 1995. *The disillusioned African*. Limbe, Cameroon: Nooremac.

Nyamnjoh, F. B. 1999a. African the information superhighway: The need for mitigated euphoria. *Ecquid Novi* 20 (1): 31–49.

Nyamnjoh, F. B. 1999b. African cultural studies, cultural studies in Africa: How to make a useful difference. *Critical Arts* 13 (1): 15–39.

Nyamnjoh, F. B. 1999c. Cameroon: A country united by ethnic ambition and difference. *African Affairs* 98 (390): 101–118.

Nyamnjoh, F. B. 1999d. Press cartoons and politics in Cameroon. *International Journal of Comic Art* 1 (2): 171–190.

Nyamnjoh, F. B., and M. Rowlands. 1998. Elite associations and the politics of belonging in Cameroon. *Africa* 68 (3): 320–337.

Nyang, S. S. 1994. The cultural consequences of development in Africa. In *Culture and development in Africa*, edited by I. Serageldin and J. Taboroff. Washington, DC: World Bank.

Nyong'o, P. A., ed. 1987. *Popular struggles for democracy in Africa*. London: Zed Books.

Nyong'o, P. A. 1988. Political instability and prospects for democracy in Africa. *Africa Development* 13 (1): 71–87.

O'Brien, J. 1993. Ethnicity, national identity and social conflict. *Nordic Journal of African Studies* 2 (2): 60–82.

Okigbo, C. 1995. National images in the age of the information superhighway: African perspectives. *Africa Media Review* 9 (2): 105–121.

Okigbo, C. 1997. Media ownership and control: The challenges of communication in Africa. Paper presented at the Regional Workshop on Media Ownership and Control in West and Central Africa, Yaoundé, Cameroon, September 8–10.

Olukoshi, A. O. 1998a. The democracy debate in Africa: An outline. In *Towards a new partnership with Africa: Challenges and opportunities*, edited by S. Kayizzi-Mungerwa, A. O. Olukoshi, and L. Wohlgemuth. Uppsala: Nordiska Afrikaninstitutet.

Olukoshi, A. O. 1998b. Economic crisis, multipartyism, and opposition politics in contemporary Africa. In *The politics of opposition in contemporary Africa*, edited by A. O. Olukoshi. Uppsala: Nordiska Afrikaninstitutet.

Olukoshi, A. O., ed. 1998c. *The politics of opposition in contemporary Africa*. Uppsala: Nordiska Afrikaninstitutet.

Ouma-Odera, D. 1998. Superhighways to governance in the Third Millennium: Selected global perspectives. Paper presented at the Eleventh Biennal Conference of the ACCE, Nairobi, October 9–15.

Paterson, C. A. 1998. Reform or recolonization: The overhaul of African television. *Review of African Political Economy* 25 (78): 571–583.

Ramphele, M. 1999. When good people are silent. Vice chancellor's address at the graduating ceremony at the Faculty of Humanities, University of Cape Town, South Africa, *Mail & Guardian*, December 10–16, 13.

Ranger, T. 1983. The invention of tradition in colonial Africa. In *The invention of tradition*, edited by E. Hobsbawm and T. Ranger. Cambridge: Cambridge University Press.

Ras-Work, T., ed. 1998. *Tam Tam to Internet*. Johannesburg: Mafube.

Reno, W. 1995. *Corruption and state politics in Sierra Leone*. Cambridge: Cambridge University Press.

Ritzer, G. 1996. *The McDonaldization of society*. London: Pine Forge Press.

Roach, C. 1996. New perspectives in global communications. In *North–South information culture: Trends in global communications and research paradigms*, edited by L. U. Uche. Lagos: Longman Nigeria.

Rowlands, M. 1995. The material culture of success: Ideals and life cycles in Cameroon. In *Consumption and identity*, edited by J. Friedman. London: Harwood Press.

Russell, A. 1999. *Big men, little people: Encounters in Africa*. Basingstoke: Macmillan.

Schiller, H. I. 1983. The communication revolution: Who benefits? *Media Development* 30: 18–20.

Schramm, W. 1964. *Mass media and national development: The role of information in the developing countries*. Stanford, CA: Stanford University Press.

Seabrook, J. 2000. Racists and hypocrites. *Mail & Guardian*, February 18–24, 22.

Sekoni, P. 1997. Politics & urban folklore in Nigeria. In *Readings in African popular culture*, edited by K. Barber. Oxford: International African Institute and James Currey.

Sharp, J. 1998. "Non-racialism and its discontents: A post-apartheid paradox. *International Social Science Journal* 156: 243–252.

Southall, A. W. 1997. The illusion of tribe. In *Perspectives on Africa: A reader in culture, history, & representation*, edited by R. R. Grinker and C. B. Steiner. Oxford: Blackwell.

Soyinka, W. 1994a. Culture, memory and development. In *Culture and development in Africa*, edited by I. Serageldin and J. Taboroff. Washington, DC: World Bank.

Soyinka, W. 1994b. Democracy and the cultural apologia. *Afrika Spectrum* 29 (1): 5–13.

Sreberny-Mohammadi, A. 1997. The many cultural faces of imperialism. In *Beyond cultural imperialism: Globalization, communication & the New International Order*. London: Sage.

Surin, K. 1995. On producing the concept of a global culture. *South Atlantic Quarterly* 94 (4): 1179–1199.

Sylvester, E. 1999. Nigerian letter scam envelops SA. *Saturday Star*, October 23, 2.

Tchop Tchop 1997. *Candidat unique de l'opposition* 1 (audio sketch). Douala, Cameroon.

Thomas, P., and P. Lee. 1994. Editorial: Public communication—Superhighway or one-way street. *Media Development* 41 (3): 2.

Thomas, P., and P. Lee. 1998. Editorial on migrants, refugees and the right to communicate. *Media Development* 45 (3): 2.

Thompson, G. 1999. Introduction: Situating globalization. *International Social Science Journal* 51 (160): 139–152.

Toulabor, C.-M. 1981. Jeu de mots, jeu de villains. *Politique Africaine* 1 (3): 55–71.

Tussie, D. 1983. Introduction. In *Latin America in the world economy: New perspectives*, edited by D. Tussie. Aldershot, UK: Gower.

Tutu, D. 1996. Preface. In *I write what I like*, by S. Biko. Randburg, South Africa: Ravan Press.

Uche, U. L. 1988. Mass communication and cultural identity: The unresolved issues of national sovereignty and cultural autonomy in the wake of the new communication technologies. Paper presented at the IAMCR Conference, Barcelona, July 24–29.

Uche, U. L. 1997. The economic and emancipative potentials of the information super-highway regime for Africa South of the Sahara. Paper presented at the Regional Workshop on Media Ownership and Control in West and Central Africa, Yaoundé, Cameroon, September 8–10.

Vail, R., ed. 1989. *The creation of tribalism in southern Africa*. Berkeley and Los Angeles: University of California Press.

Van Audenhove, L. 1998. The African information society: Rhetoric and practice. *Communicatio* 24 (1): 76–84.

Van Dijk, R. 1992. Young puritan preachers in postindependence Malawi. *Africa* 62 (2): 159–181.

Van Dijk, R. 1993. Young born-again preachers in Malawi: The significance of an extraneous identity. In *New dimensions in African Christianity*, edited by P. Gifford. Ibadan: Sefer Books.

Van Dijk, R. 1997. The Pentecostal gift: Ghanaian charismatic churches and the moral innocence of the global economy. Paper presented at the Colloquim on African Religion and Ritual, Manchester, April 19–22.

Van Dijk, R., and P. Pels. 1996. Contested authorities and the politics of perception: Deconstructing the study of religion in Africa. In *Postcolonial identities in Africa*, edited by R. Werbner and T. Ranger. London: Zed Books.

Von Lievres, A. 1999. Review article: New perspectives on citizenship in Africa. *Journal of Southern African Studies* 25 (1): 139–148.

Wanyande, P. 1996. The media as civil society and its role in democratic transition in Kenya. *Africa Media Review* 10 (3): 1–20.

Warnier, J.-P. 1993. *L'esprit d'enterprise au Cameroun*. Paris: Karthala.

Warnier, J.-P. 1999. *La mondialisation de la culture*. Paris: Editions la Découverte.

Wilson, A. N. 1993. *The falsification of African consciousness: Eurocentric history, psychiatry and the politics of white supremacy*. New York: Afrikan World InfoSystems.

Wiredu, K. 1997. Democracy and consensus in African traditional politics: A plea for a nonparty polity. In *Postcolonial African philosophy: A critical reader*, edited by E. C. Eze. Oxford: Blackwell.

Woodson, C. G. 1990. *The mis-education of the Negro*. Trenton, NJ: Africa World Press.

Wrinston, W. B. 1994. The inevitable global conversation. *Media Studies Journal* 8 (1): 17–25.

Young, T. 1999. Review article: the state and politics in Africa. *Journal of Southern African Studies* 25 (1): 149–154.

4

A Tale of Three Images: Globalization, Marginalization, and the Sovereignty of the African Nation-State

PAUL L. EHIOZE IDAHOSA

"Globalization" is a concept which performs very important and powerful political functions—above all legitimating the international pressures for states in the South to accept the hegemony of international capital within their borders—but which stands on shaky empirical ground as a descriptor of an economic process (its capacity to attract research funding notwithstanding) (Bush and Szeftel 1998, 176).

The past twenty years have demonstrated that in the short run, nothing is politically more dangerous for the state than the pretension of being able to control the future. The desire to make the future, to plan it, influenced the legitimacy not only of the leaders but also of the whole political system. In citizens' eyes, the state did not escape from being responsible for the present while becoming also accountable for the future. In both black Africa and Central Europe, state legitimacy collapsed around 1989 over the issue of the future (Jewsiewicki and Mudimbe 1995, 205).

Crossroads are places where we make choices about where we want to go. We have a limited number of options facing us and can go in different directions, some of which we may or may not know about, others that we might select because of previous knowledge, or because of the map and the promise of something better that others who have gone before us have given us. Upon reaching the possible forks in the road we may decide to turn back, either out of fear for the known challenges we face or because the roads ahead are just too difficult. We may very well not return to where we came from because we know what a bloodied, oppressive, and impoverished road we left behind. There may be resources, people, and practices worth picking up from the past that, however useful, are simply unacceptable to those whom we meet and who are willing to assist us on the road ahead.

The metaphor of being at the crossroads can be broadened and its applications made almost limitless. However, like many metaphorical dilemmas, it is locked into a rationality of prisoner-like, either-or choices, such that one is forced to take the choices available. There is a kind of moral spatial-fatalism of the metaphor. Even though there are four options, they are mutually exclusive and are assumed to be choices effected by a sense that the selection we are asked to take might be a misstep with serious consequences for one's future well-being. If there is a weary resignation about speculative theoretical choices, one can imagine how it must be even more so in practice, as messy and empirical that it is. However, when it comes to the choice between globalization and marginalization, then it would appear that Africa's choices are easy. How could one possibly choose the latter, with its insinuation, fuelled by millennial fear, of being left out and being left behind at the advent of the new epoch?

The globalization-marginalization dichotomy is all part of a new resignation. One finds it in many of the circles of international political economy, international relations, other social sciences, and even in studies of technology and culture. It also exists especially in the most present and powerful, if simplifying, of discourses, popular culture, the pervasiveness of which so many of our constructed images and understanding of others are both derived and filtered through. While proponents of economic globalization offer hope of salvation and freedom, the language of globalization, like the language of the market, is decidedly deterministic and political.

At its worst, and most especially for Africa, the language of globalization is defeatist and disabling, as it recommends restricted volition; it appears to contract authority and disregards the autonomy of those who suggest alternatives or who will not submit to it. Both its language and its practice feed into and off the circumstance of much of the continent's economic and political predicament. There is an obvious correspondence between this language of globalization and the popular images of Africa in the media. In part this agreement lies in the popular and distorting image of marginalization, of selective images and information received and the narrowed and limited choices available, of unsustainability faced by those nation-states that are identified as not following one or more of the norms of globalization. This agreement also draws upon the real substance behind the image of incapacity and incompetence, which further nourishes, while feeding off of, a language of questionable, even failed sovereignty that some Africanists, de facto or by default, equally and explicitly assert. In some instances these are more academic versions of how Africa's position plays out in the popular and mass media, and both views confirm an Afro-pessimistic image still commonplace in many Africanist circles. It is what I call global knowing as "homogenous" thinking, which does not recognize its subjects, or facets of them, and presents them as other than they might see themselves. At the crossroads, Africa needs to reflect on these images that act as a medium through which the sources of the understanding of globalization and marginalization take shape. There is a need to think about not just the "fact" of globalization and the conditions of marginalization, but also the language of this dichotomy itself and the implications for the choices that Africa faces.

In what follows I will attempt to elicit these associations, first by summarily outlining the apparent features of globalization; second, by setting out its design with respect to Africa, and through pointing to the program of legitimating-delegitimating that it fosters and is nourished by—that of crisis, especially with respect to the role of nation-states; and finally I will identify some ways in which some Africanist commentators on Africa often buttress the practice of limiting the sovereignty of many nation-states. In conclusion, I will also try to identify a case for a very specific kind of "globalization." If we can make sense of globalization and ask whether or not it should be embraced lest Africa be marginalized, we need to see globalization not just as an economic project, but as a political and ideological project that gets reenforced through many mediums, not least of which is the media, its principal source of representation, and by some Africanists, its primary source of legitimacy.

THE HORIZON FOR LIMITED SOVEREIGNTY: GLOBALIZATION AS MARGINALIZATION

Globalization, which is often characterized as any number of interdependent economic, political, military, technological, and cultural processes on a world scale, is not an uncontested notion. For many, however, it appears to have significantly reduced the ability of states to have dominion over wide areas of decision making within their nation-space. David Held (1995, 20) describes globalization as

dense networks of regional and global economic relations which stretch beyond the scope of any single state (even of dominant states); extensive webs of transnational relations and instantaneous electronic communications over which particular states have limited influence; a vast array of international regimes and organizations which can limit the scope for action of the most powerful states; and the development of a global military order, and the build-up of the means of "total" warfare as an enduring feature of the contemporary world, which can reduce the range of policies available to governments and their citizens.

These networks and their institutional embodiments have resulted in the weakening of the prevailing expression of territorial sovereignty, and they have become subversive of the economic, political, cultural, and social meaning of the nation-state. We are presumed to be presently undergoing a more intensive interconnectedness among different people than before. In addition to the fact that the world economy has grown rapidly, world trade has expanded enormously and financial systems are now highly integrated. In a world where transactions in the foreign exchange market run into the trillions of dollars, and in a world where multinational companies appear to dominate national and international economic transactions, the diminution of sovereignty appears a given, and to some, even necessary. By some reckoning it appears that the unprecedented growth in intensity and expanse of the various facets of globalization—economic, political, and cultural—has made somewhat clearer the choice between global, national, and local methods of governance, citizenship, and identity.[1] Some, like, David Rothkopf (1997, 46–47), unapologetically celebrate the official view of globalization and its supposed positive effects on culture. Those who try to resist globalization are like King Canute. Providing no evidence, he asserts,

Business leaders in Buenos Aires, Frankfurt, Hong Kong, Johannesburg, Istanbul, Los Angeles, Mexico City, Moscow, New Delhi, New York, Paris, Rome, Santiago, Seoul, Singapore, Tel Aviv, and Tokyo all read the same newspapers, wear the same suits, drive the same cars, eat the same food, fly the same airlines, stay in the same hotels, and listen to the same music. While the people of their countries remain divided by culture, they have realized that to compete in the global marketplace they must conform to the culture of that marketplace.

Sovereignty is also diminished because of the decline in the recognition of what most states, and the elites within them, can or should unilaterally do in their interest, and because of the decline in the recognition of the capacity of states to decide events within and without borders in their own interests. These diminished capacities are especially, but not only, so with regard to economic policy. Indeed, what one might call the strong version of globalization is essentially an argument about economic integration.

At least since the early 1970s, transformations in communications and electronic technology and the change to neoliberal political economy have achieved what many on the left and many economic nationalists have argued capital has always wanted to do: to greatly extend its propensity to create one "free market" and have an unregulated world of finance, production, wage labor, and investment. As of the early 1990s, ideologically emboldened by the collapse of communism, multinational capital in particular has used its power in unprecedented ways. First, in the area of investment, employment, pricing, and industrial location, to shrewdly introduce new technologies to stay ahead of the ability of some states and social movements to regroup and defend their interests against the encroachment of multinational capital. Second, multinational capital increased its influence over states, which have been in search of foreign investment to enhance their ability to participate in the new global economy. The net effect appears to have been, along with state retrenchment, the diminishing of the ability of national states and local actors to intervene in economic and political decision making in an effort to circumscribe the power of capital.[2] Central to all these processes has been multinational corporations, global managers of supra-state finance and development (e.g., the World Bank and the International Monetary Fund—IMF), as well as the General Agreement on Tariffs and Trade (GATT) and the World Trade Organization (WTO), which have attempted to multilaterally (some might even say unilaterally) regulate trade processes and internal investment decisions. Economic governance has moved from the nation-state to homeless corporations and global institutions, which, from the vantage point of national economic space, have "disembodied economic relationships" (Thompson 1999, 140).

However, a lot of questions remain as to the extent to which today's world is actually globalized. Some commentators question the extent of a global order and the allegation that we live in a fully integrated world where the world economy and all nation-states, their cultures, and societies are inextricably linked. To be sure, there is indeed an acute disparity of power and resources between these states and societies in a hierarchical global order, and there are transnational mediums and patterns of economic and cultural consumption. However, those who question globalization's pervasiveness are apt to see (at least in the industrialized world) the nation-state form as healthy and connected to its nation-space as it ever was; they are likely to question both the methods by which analysts arrive at their conceptions and measurements of globalization, to query whether globalization is a new phenomenon at all, and to ask about the sources of knowledge where these conceptions of globalization come from.[3] Some even refer to "inter-nationalization," rather than globalization, claiming that by some measures there is a lack of integration in the world economy, at least at the level of trade and direct foreign investment (DFI), two of the principal measures of strong globalization (Thompson 1999). In fact, a number of commentators point to the world economy currently being configured through major trading blocks, and not only through supranational institutions. Indeed, globalization presents a contradiction of sorts, inasmuch as there is a propensity toward regionalization in trade and investment through the growth and expansion of the economic superblocs, or the "triads"—Japan and the Asian-Pacific Rim countries, the European Economic Community, and North America—that has in effect stalled the full integration of the world economy, between which there has always been the specter of possible trade barriers and into (and behind) which many developing countries have tried to insert themselves (Thompson 1999).

Clearly, one can debate the status of globalization's existence. However, as all of the demonstrations from Seattle on have confirmed, for many activists and commentators alike, what is all too apparent and needs to be resisted on a world scale are the increasingly asymmetrical interconnectedness and diminished authority of most states, especially their limited capacity to redistribute income and wealth downward, and the inability to control the movements of capital, the increasing inequality between people, and the acute disparities in wealth between the economic North and South. Such disparities in the distribution of wealth and income are even more of a problem in Africa. For others, it is not so much the need to resist globalization as some form of an extension of a more fully extended international commerce and trade, which few doubt can be avoided but which can even increase the well-being of people and states. Nor is the issue that Africa ought not to participate; the issue has always been about a particular globalization in its neoliberal form. As Arthur MacEwan (1999) has put it, the point is less "*whether* we take part in world commerce, but rather *how* we take part.[4]

It is often asserted that African countries "are by and large bystanders in the globalization process," which to some is also inclusive of the formation of the super-trading blocks, and from which most African countries have been and continue to be "excluded," especially in the burgeoning manufacturing and value-added new informational technology sectors (Edoho 1997b, 5; Ekanem 1997). More radical African and critical perspectives on globalization, such as that of Bernard Founou-Tchuigoua (1996), claim that Africa has been histori-cally marginalized because of its model of development—the unsuccessful modernization of the economy and society in countries with weak states. The latter, he claims, resulted from a deliberate effort to marginalize Africa and to confine it to the role of a cheap commodity and labor reserve through partial industrialization. He also views African states as economically nonviable, and that given the fragmented, small, and frail economies of Africa, regional inte-gration and regional trading unions have a lot to offer in the form of substates that can provide the foundation for wider economic integration and advantage on the continent.[5]

Whether it is this model of trade and development or any other that has pro-duced Africa's current predicament, and whether alternative models of regional development are feasible in the world political economy, to many Africa must appear to be the best place to observe the incapacity of the nation-state to sustain its principal role, until recently, as the site of the construction of economic space, identities, and cultures. African states are also therefore in many ways the best candidates to be identified as having all of the symptoms and consequences of marginalization. Putting it differently, African countries would therefore benefit from being integrated into global economic processes, the absence of which would make—and, as some claim, has made—them exemplars of mar-ginalization. There are, however, problems with this formulation, not least of which is the fact that it is not clear whether marginalization is the cause or con-sequence of adopting a feature of internationalization or neoliberal adjustment policies.

If so much of the continent has increasingly fallen prey to the numerous and intensifying economic and cultural dependencies, it has done so through the governance of multilateral agencies and multinational banks. The ability of multilateral agencies such as the International Monetary Fund and the World Bank to set policy priorities and prescribe economic goals for the African coun-tries is derived from the weakness of African economies and these agencies' control of access to international sources of finance (including development aid) for the African countries. The representing complicity here, whether academic or popular, lies in an Afro-pessimism of a homogenized Africa in deep crisis. The collusion also lies in what Africa must be constrained to do for itself, by itself, or with the assistance of others to ameliorate these conditions in a world where it is assumed determinations, like the market, are essentially made, and where, too, states constantly need the practical and conceptual assistance of others to make it right. The fundamental premise is that the failure of Africa to integrate into and keep up with adjustments in the global economy is a crucial factor in explaining Africa's continued fragile economic performance, "and that unless steps are taken to remove the external and internal barriers to integration, Africa faces the prospect of being further marginalized as the inexorable pace of globalizations continues or even accelerates" (O'Brien, 2000, 1).[6] However, it is equally evident that for many the pitfalls of incorporation into globalism appear no clearer—and, to many, with often catastrophic consequences—than in the rapid trade liberalization in most Third World countries, and Africa in particular.

For example, agricultural price liberalization, a key part of so many adjustment programs in Africa and a foundation of expected export-led growth and Africa's reintegration into world markets, has not always increased incomes of producers.[7] According to a recent U.N. report written by the United Nations Conference on Trade and Development (UNCTAD) secretary-general, Rubens Ricupero (1997), in many countries that have implemented reforms the expected improvements in the domestic terms of trade for agriculture have not been realized. Producer prices for export crops have remained well below initial calculations, and middlemen rather than producers appear to have been the primary beneficiaries of liberalization. Indeed, in most African countries structural adjustment programs (SAPs) have not increased production or investment or improved balance of payments (see Ricupero 1997; Gibbon 1996).

African economic marginalization does not seem to appear to be in dispute. What is in dispute is its significance and what caused it. I should add the obvious caveat here; namely, that I'm not in any way trying to suggest that many African leaders and the management of states are without culpability in contributing to the continent's economic and political deterioration. On the contrary, they obviously played a central part in Africa's poor economic performance. One cannot blame dictatorial rule, greed, and corruption on global economic downturns alone. What is not in dispute either is that so many African politicians have concentrated political power in the center, adopted and sustained authoritarian, one-party, military, personal systems of governance, as well as encouraged corrupt, highly centralized and inefficient forms of economic decision making that have had a destructive impact on economic well-being. However, among the many issues that do not appear to have been seriously worked out, beyond the typical blaming the victim, is the contribution of world recession and Cold War alignments and realignments.

With regard to world recession, among the many attempts that go beyond the somewhat self-serving analyses undertaken by the IMF in its *Finance and Development* (see e.g., Greene 1989; Ouattara 1999; Calamitsis 1999; Hernandez-Cata 1999; Harris 1999; Sharer 1999) and, more popularly, the London-based *Economist* (see e.g., issues for May 13, 2000; February 24, 2001) are the works of Sayre Schatz (1994), and, more recently, Mkandawire and Soludo (1999). What is so useful about the analyses undertaken by Schatz and Mkandawire and Soludo are the exemplary demonstrations of how to navigate between the oft-repeated extremes that depict Africa as the hapless victim of colonialism and imperialism or one of the pathologies of chop and quench patrimonialism. By carefully charting the origins of much of the contemporary crises in an earlier form of integration and internationalization (i.e., the oil price hike and shock of the mid-1970s), they show that the subsequent recession that it augured in acted as a catalyst for the abandonment of rural development. Moreover, they also cogently illustrate how many African states were convinced by the global counselors of development assistance, the many development consultants and/or many economists, to engage in both borrowing and later economic reform precisely at times when world economic recessions were taking place (see Schatz 1994, 1996; Mkandawire and Saludo 1999; cf. Green 1998). Adjustment policies followed on from bad advice and recession, and at a time that African states were being counseled to amend their macroeconomic policies to take advantage of increased liberalization of trade and thereby become the beneficiaries of globalization.

Despite some recent small gains, production has decreased over the decade and a half since most SAPs were introduced in Africa. Budget deficits have grown and a larger ratio of export earnings now goes to debt servicing. By the year 2015, by some estimates, the debt to export ratio of the poorest nations of the world, most of which are in Africa, will be three times more than in 1994.[8] In addition, there is the increasing diminution of aid, and financial commitments (especially official development assistance) to Africa seem to have declined. At the same time, there has been an increase in the privatization or subcontracting of aid through nongovernmental organizations (NGOs).[9] Yet while receiving $14 billion in foreign aid in 1997, Africa paid out $12 billion in interest on its foreign debt alone, a figure that represents about 25 percent of the continent's annual export earnings since the mid-1980s. This enormous amount of money was sent to the international financial institutions and, ultimately, to the wealthy class in rich creditor countries. Because of missed payments, accumulated debt arrears alone in the last nine years has amounted to $56 billion (UNECA 1998).[10]

The financial figures are fatiguing enough; to many, what is even more dismaying is their impact on Africa's poorest. While there are often denials about the role of adjustment in bringing about poverty (Sahn 1996; cf. Sahn, Dorosh, and Younger 1997), no one denies that poverty continues within a context of adjustment. At present, with twenty-nine out of the fifty-three African countries classified as severely indebted and another thirteen as moderately indebted, it is not surprising that spending on the social sectors has fallen significantly.[11] In 1992 the United Nations Children's Fund's (UNICEF) World Summit on Children estimated that it would take $9 billion to decrease the incidence of infant mortality in Africa by a third, lower mortality rates by half, and supply universal primary education in Africa by the year 2000. Zambia, a liberalizing and privatizing star in Africa, has in three years (1990–1993) spent thirty-five times as much on debt repayment as it has on primary education. Over the next four years, Tanzania, one of the world's poorest nations, has to pay some $1.24 billion in order to service its debt. Yet according to recent data from UNICEF (1999) and the World Bank (1999a), the infant mortality rate in Tanzania is 105 per 1,000, while 27 percent of its children under five are malnourished and half the population has no access to clean water. A recent briefing by Oxfam (2000) points out,

Some countries—including Senegal, Tanzania and Zambia—will emerge from the HIPC debt relief process in the perverse position of paying more on debt servicing. Debt repayments will continue to absorb a disproportionately large share of government revenue, amounting to more than 15 percent in six countries, and to over 40 percent in Zambia, Cameroon and Malawi. All but three of the twelve countries reviewed in the Oxfam research will continue to spend far more on debt servicing than on health and primary education after they have received debt relief.

Yet as Muchie (2000, 12) has recently pointed out,

Diverse debt forgiveness agreements have brought no tangible and real relief. The rate of development of the debt is faster than that of major economic variables. Such levels of debt and debt servicing ratio reckoned as total debt service as percent of exports of goods and services are known to impact adversely on imports, and funds for new investment for industry. They are not only unsustainable but also they have created their own peculiar political economy contributing to the weakening of the African state to manage and lead industrialization. Debt service payments have imposed a political economy of dereliction and despair complicating the region's development future.[12]

Creditors expect countries like Tanzania to continue to liberalize, retrench, and repay their debt at the current rate, even when the outcome appears to be more poverty, even though there has been a decline in the availability of "soft" loans to poorer countries, like Tanzania, and even though they have demonstrated all of the prerequisites of a "firm commitment to improved economic management" (Bush and Szeftel 1998, 175).[13]

These demands appear as consequences of the relentless neoliberal determination to make every factor that moves on or sits in the ground "competitive," efficient, and flexible, especially given the emphasis on export-oriented growth in the international marketplace. What the radical Canadian economist Michel Chossudvosky (1997) has called the "globalization of poverty" is taken to be one side of the complexly integrated character of global market liberalization, which magnifies the increasingly acute asymmetries in power and importance between Africa and the rest of the world, and which is also reflected in Africa's limited and diminishing and apparently insignificant role in world trade and investment, two major measures of economic integration or marginalization.

Africa's importance to global trade has declined over the last forty years. In 1955, on the eve of independence for many colonies in the continent, Africa accounted for 3.1 percent of world exports; that declined to 1.2 percent by 1990, which, at current prices implies trade losses of about $65 billion.[14] Africa, most especially sub-Saharan Africa, has understandably now become the center of attention in aid programs. For some African economies, aid and migrants' remittances now make up their principal form of involvement in the world economy. Sub-Saharan Africa, in particular, receives about five times the amount of net official transfers per capita as does South Asia, accounting for 9.3 percent of African GNP in contrast to 2.1 percent of South Asia's. From the early 1970s to the early 1990s, net transfers approximately doubled as a proportion of GNP. By 1991, sub-Saharan Africa was receiving about a third of global net aid transfers. Yet as we have noted, Africa's share of world exports has fallen steadily, and by comparison with South Asia, in the decade from 1970 to 1980 the growth in the quantity of Africa's exports was 2.8 percent per annum against 3.6 percent for South Asia, and between 1980 and 1992 African export growth declined to 2.4 percent against South Asia's increase to 6.8 percent. While in many developing countries exports have grown faster than national output, this has not occurred in Africa. Direct private investment into developing countries increased significantly over the past decade (to around $200 billion per annum). However, regardless of recent events in East and Southeast Asia, the share of foreign private investment going to Africa has shrunk to apparently insignificant proportions. By some estimates, less than 5 percent of this investment is going to sub-Saharan Africa, half of which goes to Nigeria and Angola, primarily to exploit oil and natural gas. Even the rate of investment is declining; it is less in real terms than it was in 1985, the depths of economic crisis for most of the continent.[15]

Whether seen in the official version—and these are more or less official figures—or used as a critique of current economic orthodoxy, these figures become one part of Afro-pessimism and the other side of the marginalization thesis: Africa's meaning to the world economy is peripheral, even and indeed especially where the human dimension to this suffering calls for intervention. If there is no consensus over solutions, the official view, nevertheless, continues to suggest targeted assistance, contingent upon liberalization, in order to reintegrate Africa into international markets.[16] That is, it takes this aspect of what some understand as globalization to mean as given. Globalization, as integration, is the reverse of marginalization.

This was precisely the message, expressed in the media, that U.S. President Bill Clinton's trip to Africa signified, and which is also the gist of the now defunct Africa Growth and Opportunity Act, which emphasized a "radical shift . . . from sustainable development strategies to a private sector and market incentives approach to stimulating economic growth and reducing poverty in those countries in sub-Saharan Africa who are committed to economic reform." These countries should have "established or be making continual progress towards establishing a market-based economy," which should then make them "eligible for participation in the new U.S.-Africa economic institutions and agreements."[17]

Africa goes global, even if the relationship here is bilateral, once again through the mantra of liberalizing market reforms. It is here where the world of policy, representation, and the production of knowledge begin to coincide.[18] In the so-called global village, or at least in the town square where most of the decisions are made by the self-governing modern burghers of economic finance, Africa is consigned to being like the village idiot, the last to become conscious of itself and often represented by an image primarily of someone else's making.

THE CONFORMITY OF MEDIA CONSENSUS AND POLICY

If there is controversy among academic commentators over the meaning and significance of market-induced or market-imposed reforms in Africa, there is little controversy in saying that contemporary images of Africa thrown up by media have deep historical traces (Fair 1993).[19] More recently, these images have been attached to and reinforced by the seemingly intractable political, social, and economic problems that postcolonial African states have faced. Among those who have presented distorted images of Africa is Robert Kaplan (1996), whose work has not really been concerned with Africa's suffering and increased marginalization in global affairs. Instead, his interest has been in the impact that such distorted images of Africa has on his Western audiences.

What exactly is the impact that these global images actually have on Africa? I suspect that few of us can answer this question in some specifically measurable social science way, except to assert that these "global" images are having some impact on Africa in policy terms, and indeed they must in some indirect way. They can certainly be used as images of racist reinforcement, of the disastrous, inept, incompetent, "childlike" Africa, waiting to be rescued by the West; and perhaps, too, they fortify the decision by the industrial countries (e.g., the U.S.) to consider Africa as marginal and insignificant to their national security interests and hence not worthy of consideration in international policy.[20] I think that the task is not only to counter these stereotypical images, but to build a much more positive image for the continent and its people.[21] When we can and do make sense of these media distortions we must understand that most of them are about the weakness that comes from limited sovereignty; about the loss of the ability of Africans to intervene in affairs that they have little control over, or at least some say in. The global media, like the discourse of strong globalization, is about the lack of choice. In this there is at least symmetry, and in this sense the numerous recent media studies and commentaries addressing the distorted projection of Africa's image in the Western, and most especially the U.S. media, seem to me to miss the point.[22]

We live in the globalizing world, a world of structured asymmetries of meaning and the consumption of meaning, of unequal locations in an international division of labor, whether as producers or consumers, of disproportionate capacities in economic decision making. Africanists, however unintentionally or otherwise, contribute to this intensification of the widespread popular belief that somehow Africans are both irresponsible and incapable of managing their own affairs and therefore in constant need of outside intervention and assistance. We have already seen how this works implicitly and explicitly in the discussion about economic options, of what I referred to as global knowing as homogenous thinking; that is, seeing what we want others to see, which is what we want for ourselves. In doing so, are we not, especially in developing a theory directed toward practical or policy ends, also part of a normative thinking that views interlocking global processes or procedures as being either good or inevitable? In so doing, are we fortifying the view of African incompetence and illegitimacy?

If we move from media to global conceptions in other, more academic spheres, again with respect to the production of knowledge (Hountonji 1995), rather than just images and information, we have part of the answer about how the sovereignty of Africa is not only being restricted, but in fact should be. To take three examples of what is symptomatic of both the underscoring of popular perception and the academic shift in the conception of the legitimacy of African states as nation-states are the debates a few years ago in *International Security* initiated by Jeffrey Herbst's (1996–1997) proposal to dissolve African states unable to manage their political and socioeconomic affairs effectively (Joseph 1997; Herbst 1997); the new wave of post–Cold War international relations perspectives on Africa (see, for example, Harbeson and Rothchild 1999; Deng, Kimaro, Lyons, Rothchild, and Zartman 1996; Keller and Rothchild 1996), which identify the failure of many states to perform the litmus test of responsible (i.e., sovereign) government; and even and especially Wole Soyinka's (1996a) passionate depiction of the miserable "crisis of our-nation being," wherein rapacious dictators use the "nation space" as "a gambling space for opportunism, adventurism and power."[23]

FROM GLOBAL IMAGE TO MARGINALIZED REALITY?

If the nation-state has been the principal cultural-political and economic form within which to situate the modern conception of sovereignty, then this sovereignty is hardly any longer unquestionable. Soyinka's (1996a) resplendently intense literary depiction particularly captures well the underlying moral, legal, and political science reasons why, among other things, African states cannot be considered "organic" sovereign entities like those of most of Europe and elsewhere in the world, and why, too, one should withdraw legitimacy from states, as under Abacha's Nigeria, that should forfeit their sovereign status. Why so? Because of the absence of democracy, respect for human rights, and good governance; that is, because of these states' incapacity to guarantee basic human rights through (1) liberal democratic rule, (2) the rule of law, (3) the recognition of all ethnic identities, and (4) economic justice, they have forfeited their right of sovereign status.[24] African states, in short, lack legitimacy because of their inability to manage their own affairs.

Like so much else today, the language of democracy, human rights, good governance, and the status of legitimate government appears to have been globalized. It has become so, it must be added, in part because of neoliberalism, which under certain conditions disseminates the need for freedoms and the rule of law; but it has equally come from below, through demands from and within local and international civil society. Both the international and locally coordinated or spontaneous transformations have shifted and reshaped our conceptions of the appropriate, if contestable, form of the democratic political community. In these changes it is no longer possible to view sovereignty as a static notion reducible to the part where it is located, but rather one that is constantly renewed; that the process of globalization, as a form of synchronized international integration, has intensified and demanded Africa partake in and be accountable to. In its most ideological moments, "prodemocracy" and "reform" are invoked to validate someone, some groups, or some state commonly engaged in market reforms, while the converse results in the demonization of those who are not.[25] This is a piece of the configuration of world politics that is currently being sought and assigned based upon one that mirrors Western conceived vistas; it is a view that is commonly appealed to and accepted, and with which few, including myself, would disagree: where all citizens are guaranteed human rights, and where minimum requirements of responsibility that states exercise must exist for them to deserve to be legitimately sovereign. Only by effectively discharging its responsibilities for good governance can a state now be said to legitimately claim sanction for its national sovereignty. If a state transgresses these norms, it has infringed on its own right of sovereignty, and it is now the responsibility of the international community to intervene in the interests of the threatened or suffering community as a whole. In short, sovereignty is now conditional and contingent; it can now only mean what one text (Deng, Kimaro, Lyons, Rotchild, and Zartman 1996) calls "responsible sovereignty."

This version of sovereignty is very different from the "Westphalian" model, which most African countries at independence assumed they had adopted. The Westphalian model was one that assumed a given state's externally recognized right to exert definitive authority over its affairs, and that the state acted as the guarantor of both the security and welfare of its people.[26] Thus, the historical salience of the nation-state, and its subsequent nationalist and postcolonial identification of being home to the promise of equal citizenship regardless of ethnic belonging, class, or religious disposition, is one that, as we have said, appears to have lost much of its value, most especially for many of those in Africa who appear not to have the capacity to ensure what citizens want.

The inclusively optimistic view of nationalism and the nation-space sovereignty can be seen, somewhat implicitly, in Soyinka's (1996a) discussion, though barely in some and sometimes not at all in the other discussions mentioned. He does not overromanticize the past, earlier postcolonial condition of African nation-states, especially Nigeria's, though some might disagree with his depiction of nationalist intention. He does, however, evoke a more tolerant past, of, for instance, religious "cohabitation, that was not riven by present uncertainties"; and a period during which there was at least the expectation of the benefits of minimal and redistributive welfare that, for most of the principals involved, informed the varied forms of nationalist movements and their understanding of nationalist citizenship in the 1950s and 1960s and especially, I would add, the Lusophone (Guinea-Bissau and Cape Verde, Angola and Mozambique) and Southern African liberation (Zimbabwe, Namibia, and South Africa) movements of the 1970s, 1980s, and 1990s, whatever the revisionism about them now.

This essentially social democratic nationalist citizenship for the most part was broadly articulated through a view of the people's right to equal self-development and a tolerance of others. To be sure, in many instances the languages of citizenship were elite and class bound, although just as often they were not. Today there are more nuances around gender and more subnational and local identities, as there has been everywhere. More women and representatives of local or regional identities have inserted their voices into the configuration of citizenship, a development that was noticeably absent at independence, and now citizenship, in theory, is more sensitive to the needs of those not identified in the sometimes more relatively abstract citizenship of nationalism. Nevertheless, however important such amendments are, the core assumptions of nationalist citizenship that Soyinka (1996a) envisaged, and which today remain a wistful desideratum in his writings, were part of a presumed social exercise.

This exercise assumed choices; these were choices of planning and redistribution that were not exclusively market driven, which, however fanciful they may seem now, would also be one of the foundations for social values that directed citizens to identify with the state, and which remain at the center of the more devolved reconceptions of citizenship and sovereignty reemerging today, while others, such as the redistributive, have apparently been purged.[27]

Why so purged? The answer should be obvious, even if it is contestable.[28] The nature of the role of the state has changed from what Steven Gill (1995, 81) has called the mercantilist and developmentalist states, which marked the regulatory, planning, Keynesian postwar and early postcolonial decades of nationalism, toward the rise of the neoliberal state structures, so consonant with adjustment programs and coincident with Africa's perilous economic condition. Globalization, as it is currently applied to Africa, implies liberalization by compulsion and where all other views have become marginal. If the continent's political status and conditions are certainly not multiple epiphenomenona of this shift, they are certainly causally linked, and are a piece of what Christopher Clapham (1996, 196–195) has called the "externalization of political accountability." This phenomenon is one part of a set of conditionalities that comes from one facet of globalization and is also bound up with it: the shift not only in our practice, but also in our conception of external sovereignty and the practice of the traditional welfare and developmentalist states (such as they were) to the would-be liberal state. For example, we might after all agree on limitations on sovereignty, and even enact the limitations to do it, but we might not believe in what we are doing as a principle, simply because that sovereignty has been reduced. The new wave of leaders in Africa, so triumphed, until very recently, by liberal pundits a few years ago as part of the so-called African Renaissance for their flexible, pragmatic (i.e., their "nonideological"), noninterventionist view of economic policy, allow for an abridgment on sovereignty, which is acceptable to those doing investment and supplying aid.[29] Do these African leaders, however, actually believe in it beyond a kind of defensive Westernism; that is, the adoption of certain Western values in order to maintain themselves as recipients of aid?[30] The attempt to find various approximations to Westernism as a vindication of sovereignty can even be a way of asserting one's independence, and one can sometimes even keep various degrees of one's authoritarianism in place as long as there are some core cognates of reform, lest one becomes marginalized and excluded from whatever benefits Western reforms supposedly bring.[31] In other words, despite the talk about globalization in the current regulatory discourse about the new sovereignty, few are willing to talk about, let alone seriously theorize, the interconnectedness between globalization and diminished sovereignty in areas other than the obvious with respect to nation-space decision making. That is, there is always talk about the fact that marginalization can force African countries to the periphery of the global economy, a process that would negatively affect their ability to attract badly needed foreign investment. If that happens, economic growth in the continent could suffer significantly. Few, however, talk about the relationship between abridged sovereignty and economic marginalization in the global economy or identify the relationship between this marginalization and the marginalization of the state.

Thandika Mkandawire (1998, 27; 1999, 119–136), Director of the U.N. Research Institute for Social Development, speaks of the minimalist, almost choiceless African state. This is where newly elected "democratic" governments and the diminished development states that they inherited have little right, let alone much capacity, to determine their own budgets and policy priorities through the state. Given the conditionalities imposed by external financing agreements, the nature of shrunken resources they have to work with, but also their own proclivity towards an antistate ideology, they too become beholden to the consequences of adjustment that lie in accepting practices because there appears to be not much else at hand.[32]

CONCLUSION

Even if they can be deemed analytically distinct, one cannot separate globalization and marginalization when they are rooted in the language of Afro-pessimism and derive from a practice of neoliberalism. Often they all share in common the taking for granted of the marginalization and disablement of Africa, as they do with Africa's inability to deal with the so-called challenges that globalization generates. It is this conceptual slippage that makes a choice between globalization and marginalization appear required, as if the two were separate paths and choices. Liberalization, after all, is the reverse side of the language of failed sovereignty, and therefore, paradoxically and paternalistically, the need for others to act on your behalf. The wish to see Africa removed from its current state, for it not to be "marginalized," is contingent upon Africa accepting both practices and norms that, notwithstanding the new language of "ownership" and stakeholding of the recent rethinking on adjustment, will undermine a capacity to make decisions on its own behalf up until outside intervention and assistance acknowledge the achievement of those conditions. Until such a point, Africa's sovereignty is abridged, as much of it is born of the compulsion to make Africa sovereign in our eyes, all of which combine and underscore the limited range of representations with the narrow range of options open to Africa through the restricted range of mediums available.

In constantly emphasizing the need for taking on the challenges of globalization, what is emphasized is how unprepared and marginalized Africa is. Such a view ends up implicitly and repeatedly endorsing the Afro-pessimising of dependent Africans. Such images effectively further demit the impression of Africa to what Africa cannot and should not do and what it should do. The state cannot redistribute; it must open markets; it must reenter the world of global trade; it must depend on the Western industrial countries, thereby reinforcing Africa's status as incapable of having a conception, let alone a practice, of citizenship and development that is its own. These images, including the usual ones of war, chaos, starvation, the "except Africa syndrome" and so on contribute to the refusal by the international community to accept the African nation-state as an effective arena for public policy.[33]

For Africa, globalization as freer trade, as more open markets, as general trade liberalization, need not necessarily be subversive of the meaning of sovereignty to the extent that it does not rule out choices that are compatible with the regulation of that commerce and trade and to the degree that it implies and operationalizes "generalized reciprocity."[34] If it does not allow this, then globalization is inimical to it to the extent that it exposes Africa, once again, to the demands that others place upon it, but also the lack of accountability to no one other than those who set it.

That there is, of course, cause for pessimism and that Africanists will and should question the sovereignty of states that cannot and will not provide for their people is only part of the issue. What is at issue, rather, is the forms that the doubt takes, the uses to which they are put, and who uses them. Globalization is, like crisis scenarios—or as Emory Roe (1995) has called them, crisis narratives—a means by which development experts, and the institutions for which they work, claim custodianship over the land and the resources that are not their own, and it is a medium through which unaccountable global governance is partly legitimated

Besides, globalization can also suggest possibilities as much as perils and opportunities for collaboration that come from interconnectedness, and the chance for an engagement across the parochialism of localisms and constrictive states.[35] This can be especially so for the ordinary peoples of Africa, most especially workers and the rural poor, who so often are spoken for but increasingly not spoken about in discussions of globalization except as consequences and objects, rather than as agents and subjects of real participatory practices of political and economic democracy (Founou-Tchuigoua, 1996, 158–161). One rarely, for example, hears about workers, their needs, and *their* connectedness, or their possibility, in discussions about the necessity for or adaptation to globalization. There is rarely talk of the need to insert the demands of global labor under an international global regime, which generally seeks to diminish the power of labor and its cost as a way of making them more competitive and therefore "global." To talk of labor, of course, is to talk of redistribution and injustice locally and globally; to talk of the rural poor is not only to talk of ameliorating poverty through market reforms—that is, the problem lies elsewhere in distorted markets—but in the fundamental distributive arrangements in society. Thus, for those who oppose globalization as a panacea for the marginalization of Africa, globalization can also be about integration and connectedness rather than a synonym for increasing inequality.

Until recently, however, the prevailing image was one of Africa not having any choice, which was an ascription of the absence of sovereignty, and in fact the denial of African global citizenship. This is a discourse within which there has been an uncritical celebration of globalization, and where one constantly countenances the enduring impression of Africa's choices appearing irrelevant, or relevant only to the extent that they are ones that conform to a particular arrangement of globalization.[36] This is a globalization where unaccountable global institutions make choices that have dire consequences over people who have little or no say. This, as Richard Falk (1999) has put it, a "negative globalism."[37] We are now at a juncture where this negative globalism is being questioned, and where new vistas are being formed; the issue is whether those within the citadels of negative globalism will allow them to be executed.

If Africa is at a crossroads, it is one where she is looking back on what has not worked and where not to go again. We know for certain that the military dictatorship, one partyism, and overcentralization of economies are bad things; that the absence of the rule of law and of meaningful constitutionalism have all played a role in undermining political stability and economic well-being, and are therefore roads that we do not wish to revisit. To reiterate, the problem is that what we want and what is available is not independent of what others on the road allow us to act on and what they know is available as a choice. The choice is not so much between globalization and marginalization, as between alternative conceptions of each and where the former does not necessarily entail the latter; indeed, as we have repeatedly suggested, globalization as it is usually constructed in Africa has been about marginalization. There was a time when it was not always viewed so.

To date, nearly twenty years after its publication and nearly twenty years after the first adjustment programs were introduced into Africa, *The Lagos Plan of Action for the Economic Development of Africa 1980–2000* (OAU 1981) still gathers dust, a footnote to failed intellectual history and a poignant reminder of the paths not taken. Twenty years ago was as much a crossroads as being at the advent of the new millennium or just the other side of it. This plan was cancelled, despite it being approved by the OAU, and despite the fact that it was in favor of Africa being more fully integrated into the world economy, but only after national capacities and regional integration were established. It was shelved precisely because of the weakness of the volition of African governments, but also because at the center of its identity lay choices that put people, not markets first.[38] What adjustment subsequently brought were not just loans, but also ideas that precluded Africans and their intellectual production from formulating and executing their own charter to the future. This was a road not taken, and perhaps one that people need to be reminded of after twenty years of a marginalization that Africa might have had a chance of avoiding. The new dependencies that adjustment had created proscribed the five underlying principles that would have formed the foundation for an African model of economic growth, but which today are beginning to be aired again in light of twenty years of what many consider to be failed, marginalizing attempt at globalizing Africa.[39]

NOTES

1. The recent literature on globalization, its meaning, its significance, and its future, most especially for national states, is now voluminous and is growing exponentially. I cite here only a few of the texts that I have found useful. For a useful introduction, see Scholte (1997); Crane (1997); Appandurai (1996); Sassen (1996); Falk (1999). For an African perspective, see Edoho (1997a); Ekanem (1997); Amin (1998).

2. For a debate, see Tabb (1997); Du Boff and Herman (1997). For a summary of the contestation, see MacEwan (1999), especially Ch. 1 and pp. 26–30.

3. For a critical view of the ahistoricity of the discussion about capital flows and the powerless developed, industrialized welfare states, see Weiss (1997); Rieger and Leibfried (1998). For an African perspective, see Edoho (1997a). With regards to the production of knowledge about Afro-pessimism and the circumstances that lead to specific policy choices and a perception of marginalization, see Mkandawire and Soludo (1999); Ochwada (1996). Also see the discussion between Kassimir (1997) and Davis (1997). Of interest should be the collection by Martin and West (1999).

4. See, for example, the comment by one critic of the tendency of the market to globalize: "Supra-national institutions have to be strengthened so that they can curb the excesses of markets, and deal with social exclusion, impoverishment and environmental degradation. Supra-national institutions must be made accessible and democratic, to re-

flect the needs and aspirations of the world's people. In the long run, a world society needs a global polity." The issue is not globalization or certain aspects of it, but rather one economic version of it. See Castles (1998).

5. Cf. Amin (1998, 103–107). See also Nnadozie (1997). This is a very complicated and difficult issue that I cannot explore fully here. At least nominally, Africa has a number of regional trading blocks, and intuitively, by standard economic measures, they appear to make a great deal of sense. However, their failure has much to do with the concern of primarily poor countries that what little capital and industry they have might move to their comparatively more prosperous neighbors. See Foroutan (1993). However, as a claim or a strategy, and however difficult, there is every reason to believe that this is one way for Africa to confront some forms of globalization.

6. Notice the deterministic language again, with the emphasis that unless, then watch out. If Africa is at the crossroads, there isn't much room, deliberation or alternative.

7. Most of the figures here are taken from various issues of "official" publications, including those of the World Bank (1997, 1998, 1999a, 1999b, 2000); U.N. Economic Commission for Africa (1998, 2000); and O'Brien (2000).

8. "The external debt of African countries rose from $340 billion in 1996 to $349 billion in 1997, an increase of nearly 3 percent. The debt service amounted to $33 billion, up from $31 billion in 1996, absorbing 21.3 percent of earnings from the export of goods and services" (see UNECA [1998], I.A.5, Section 39 [no pagination]). Note, however, that it has since declined slightly (1998 figures) to $325 billion at the end of 1998.

9. Recent pledges for new loans by the "Bank to sub-Saharan Africa 1996–97 fell by 36 percent to $1.73 billion—the lowest figure for the 1980s (the average annual figure 1987–91 was $3.2 billion). Actual disbursements for 1996–97 were 17 percent down to $2.47b." See Bush and Szeftel (1998, 176).

10. The ratio of total external debt to GNP is approximately 75 percent for sub-Saharan Africa and somewhat lower (ranging from 45 percent to 68 percent) for North African countries. Still, there are nineteen African countries with debt/GNP ratios of greater than 100 percent and seven with ratios in excess of 200 percent, capped by the Democratic Republic of Congo at 720 percent. The unsustainable debt problem for more than half of Africa's countries persists despite almost twenty years of debt relief efforts from the Paris and London Clubs, from bilateral aid donors, and, more recently, from the Bretton Woods institutions. See O'Brien (2000, 7).

11. Severely indebted countries are identified as countries with debt-to-GNP and debt-to-export ratios larger than 80 percent and 220 percent, respectively, and GNP per capita less than $675. See Muchie (2000, 12, fn. 8).

12. The same point was made by Ernest Aryeetey, Julius Court, Machiko Nissanke, and Beatrice Wedern (1998) in *Strengthening Africa's Participation in the Global Economy: Report from Expert Consultative Meetings*, organized by the United Nations University and the African Economic Research Consortium, Tokyo and Nairobi, respectively. Interestingly, at the conclusion of this report, which lists the usual afflictions of many of Africa's economies—corruption, inefficiency, why it continues to be indebted, fails to attract investment, and expand trade—the authors ask what the developed world can do to facilitate the integration of Africa into the global economy. They identify transforming the nature of aid, reducing the debt burden, and guaranteeing open markets for African goods, as among the principal extraneous impediments to growth, but also globalization. In other words, constraints on integration are external as well as internal.

13. Between 1996 and 1997 the World Bank's "soft" loans, usually bestowed to poorer countries, declined by over one-third, from $2.74 billion to $1.68 billion (Oxfam 2000; Bush and Szftel 1998).

14. It is unlikely that the increased oil prices for African oil-producing states have offset this ratio, as they would be compensated by higher prices.

15. These figures come variously from Collier (1995); Bhattacharya, Montiel, and Sharma (1997); Yeats, Amjadi, Reincke, Ng (1996); Ng and Yeats (1997). Typically, the evidence supplied by these global articles "suggest[s] that anti-competitive domestic policies rather than trade barriers played a key role in this decline." Yates, Amjadi, Reincke, and Ng, F. (1996). Also see African Development Bank's (ADB) *African Development Report, 1997*. What these data also represent are the huge disparities within Africa, something that I cannot explore in detail here.

16. Indigenous African alternatives, such as they are, are likely to get short shrift by the World Bank and IMF. See Green (1998). Also, the academic critiques are unlikely to be acknowledged, or more often dismissed as "much posturing but little serious analysis." See Paul Collier's (favorable) review of Sahn (1996). Again, they might be deemed "unconvincing," or based on "unrealistic assumptions." See Van de Walle (1994).

17. Cited in a draft of *The African Growth and Opportunity Act* of the U.S. Congress (http://www.agoa_legislation.html). The paternalistic zero-sum and no-choice tone of the proposal was sufficiently annoying to former President Mandela to incur his outrage. He was also brave enough, and had the moral force, to say that it was unacceptable to Africans. Other African leaders may have thought so, but few would likely say as much publicly. Compare his remarks with those of Thabo Mbeki and the other African leaders in *Africa Recovery* (1998). Similar consensus, although the tone was somewhat milder, emphasizing more the vapid language of partnerships in its Washington form, come out of the Denver G7 *Summit Communiqué* (cited in *Africa Recovery*, Vol. 11, No. 1, 1997), where it was asserted that "increased prosperity ultimately depends upon creating an environment for domestic capital formation, *private sector-led* growth and *successful integration into global markets*" (emphasis added).

18. The remarks by Kenneth P. Jameson (1998) are worth citing in full:

Discourse on development has narrowed perceptibly in the past 15 years. Macroeconomic concerns have dominated the development problem in Latin America and Africa. . . . The technical values of efficiency and market driven allocation have controlled research and writing on everything from privatization of industry to population growth and land reform. An important contributor to this narrowing has been the dominant role of the World Bank and the International Monetary Fund (IMF) in *allocating capital for development efforts and in funding and publishing research on development.* I calculated the adjusted article pages in the five main development journals between 1984 and 1986. World Bank authors were the most published, accounting for 1.6 times the pages of authors affiliated with the Institute of Development Studies at Sussex. Adding in IMF authors raised the multiple to 2.25. The January–March 1996 issue of the *World Bank Policy and Research Bulletin* described "World Bank Research in the Marketplace of Ideas." *That publication is distributed free to 18,000 "policymakers in developing countries, researchers and analysts interested in economic development, students . . . and members of the development community, including journalists and non-governmental organizations."* It also noted that the two journals *World Bank Economic Review* and *World Bank Research Observer* are the most cited development journals, and that citations of bank-authored articles are 10 percent-50 percent greater than the average for economics articles. Well-financed incest is effective (emphasis added).

19. See also the special issue of *Issue: A Journal of Opinion* 23 (1); Hawk (1992); and Crawford (1996). I want to thank Andia Chavaka for this reference.

20. Neta Crawford's (1996) piece on media and marginalization in Africa should be widely read as an imaginative reconstruction of America's (and perhaps even, despite its policy of "Official Multiculturalism," Canada's) fears, less about Africa than about its crisis and fears over race and of American identity itself.

21. Which is what Emmanuel U. Onyedike (1996) suggests through a kind of racialized public policy interest group approach in Re-positioning Africa: The role of African-American leaders in changing media treatment of Africa. *Journal of Third World Studies* 13 (2) (Fall 1996): 51–61. Cf. Lardner (1993), who sees the shift from emphasizing Cold War fears of the potential of the continent being awash with despotic communism to the emphasis more toward democratization and human rights issues.

22. The exception to this is Crawford (1996). See Coleman (1997); Wolpe (1966); Jones (1998); Lardner (1993). Thanks go to Andia Chavaka for these references.

23. Soyinka's (1996a) concerns, like those of other texts and articles here, look at the worst-case scenarios to argue for an amended form of sovereignty. Since the publication of this piece, Soyinka has further elaborated on this theme in numerous writings. See, especially, Soyinka, W. 1996b. *The open sore of a continent: A personal narrative of the Nigerian crisis.* New York: Oxford University Press.

24. It should be obvious that conditions 1 through 3 can be given greater content and are more likely to be accepted than the content of condition 4. In a global world dominated by market ideology, considerations of welfare are residual or are outcomes of market allocations.

25. This is one of the themes of William I. Robinson's (1996) book, where he develops the notion of "low intensity democracy" in the Third World, drawing primarily upon his work in Latin America. Whereas the colonial system depended primarily on coercive domination, the current hegemony is primarily polyarchic, which, notwithstanding the turn toward civil society, restricts democracy to the election of competing elites, and where democracy itself is given a confined institutional meaning, which focuses on the procedures and formulas for choosing leaders.

26. The "undisputed right to determine the framework of rules, regulations and policies within a given territory and to govern accordingly." See Held and McGrew (1993).

27. Despite their limitations, the late Claude Ake's (1993, 1996) last writings are a good case in point of this reassertion of a language of citizenship as sovereignty in the face of globalizing institutions. In official discourse it has been purged, of course, but perhaps not in popular discourse.

28. Contestable, because the alternative view is likely to be about the failure to deliver, and/or the impossibility of doing so with the model adopted in postindependence politics and development: the development state, with it's corrupt, inefficient, patrimonial, rent-seeking leaders.

29. As if this were possible. For a recent and less sanguine assessment of this version of such would-be liberal triumphalism, see Connell and Smyth (1998).

30. The term itself goes back to when, during the advent of nineteenth-century colonial expansion, some Southeast Asian states adopted certain values of Western civiliza-

tion in order not to be deemed barbarous, and therefore open to foreign intervention. For a discussion see Strang (1996).

31. Lest anyone feel that this is merely a conceit, these were precisely the sentiments expressed by President Museveni to a private audience of Canadian Africanists three years ago on a World Bank sponsored conference on communications. Jerry Rawlings also said as much in a number of statements, and Olusegun Obasanjo appears as the latest incarnation of this disposition (see *Africa Recovery*, Vol. 13, No. 1, 1999, 8).

32. "While the need for curbing authoritarian states is understandable, the incapacitation of the state has been extended to democratically elected ones [as] largely the anti-state ideology rarely distinguishes between democratic and authoritarian ones. Indeed, in some of the literature it is suggested that neo-patrimonialism and rent seeking will be accentuated by democracy. Consequently, the designs are to impose restrictions on the new democracies by multiplying the number of 'authoritarian enclaves' (e.g., independent central banks) that lie outside the purview of democratic politics and to limit the choices of elected bodies" (Mkandawire 1998, 27).

33. Emory Roe's (1995) notion for the basket-case diagnosis—everything works, except in Africa—is found in the popular media and also in development narratives, which simplify complex realities to legitimize intervention in and justify the management of Africa.

34. The expression is that of Ricupero, cited in Raghavan, C. 1999. From Washington consensus to Bangkok convergence. *African Agenda* 1 (2): 20.

35. Indeed, this is the fundamental position of David Held's (1995) book, where space is given for variability in the world of global institutions and what he calls "cosmopolitan" democracy.

36. Although I cannot elaborate upon this here, the other prevailing image, of empowerment through various localisms, whether communities or NGOs, and further disaggregated along ethnic and gender lines, makes no difference to this broader, globalizing framework.

37. "The conjuncture of largely non-accountable power and influence exerted by multinational corporations, transnational banks and financial arenas, and their collaborators with the ideology of consumerism and a development ethos weighted almost entirely toward return on capital, achieved mainly by maximizing growth" (Herbst (1996/1997): 69.

38. See summary by Muchie (2000, 142–143). "(1) Making the well-being of people as the centerpiece of policy, (2) eradication of poverty, (3) structural industrial transformation and diversified production, (4) self-reliance by building strong national economies, dynamic regional and continental cooperation and integration, and (5) integration into the world economy on the basis of antecedent national, regional, and even continental integrations."

39. An obvious illustration of this is Mkandawire and Soludo (1999), especially the concluding chapter.

REFERENCES

ADB. 1997. *African development report, 1997*. New York: Oxford University Press.

Ake, C. 1993. The unique case of African democracy. *International Affairs* 69 (2): 239–240.

Ake, C. 1996. *Democracy and development*. Washington, DC: The Brookings Institution.

Amin, S. 1994. The nation: An enlightened or fog-shrouded concept? *Research in African Literatures* 28 (4): 8–18.

Amin, S. 1998. *Capitalism in the age of globalization: The management of contemporary society*. Delhi: Madyham.

Appandurai, A. 1996. *Modernity at large: Cultural dimensions of globalization*. Minneapolis: University of Minnesota Press.

Aryeetey, E., J. Court, M. Nissanke, and B. Wedern. 1998. *Strengthening Africa's participation in the global economy: What lessons can sub-Saharan Africa learn from the experience of Southeast Asia?* Tokyo: World University Press.

Bhattacharya, A., P. J. Montiel, and S. Sharma. 1997. How can sub-Saharan Africa attract more private capital inflows? *Finance and Development* 34 (2): 3–7.

Bush, R., and M. Szeftel. 1998. Commentary: "Globalization" and the regulation of Africa. *Review of African Political Economy* 25 (June): 1–8.

Calamitsis, E. A. 1999. Adjustment and growth in sub-Saharan Africa: The unfinished agenda. *Finance and Development* 36 (1): 6–9.

Castles, S. 1998. Globalization and migration: Some pressing contradictions. *International Social Science Journal* 50 (2): 179–207.

Chossudvosky, M. 1997. *Globalization and poverty*. London: Zed Books.

Clapham, C. 1996. *African in the international system: The politics of state survival*. Cambridge: Cambridge University Press.

Coleman, T. W. 1997. Africa: Beyond war, tragedy, misrule. *The Masthead* 49 (1): 25–26.

Collier, P. 1995. The marginalization of Africa. *International Labor Review* 134 (4/5): 541–558.

Connell, D., and F. Smyth. 1998. Africa's new bloc. *Foreign Affairs* 77 (2): 80–95.

Crane, G. T. 1997. Economic nationalism: Bringing the nation back in. *Journal of International Studies* 27 (1): 75–97.

Crawford, N. Imag(in)ing Africa. *Harvard International Journal of Press and Politics* 1 (2): 30–34.

Davis, R. H. Jr. 1997. A comment on Ron Kassimir's article "The internationalization of African studies: A view from the SSRC." *Africa Today* 44 (2): 71–75.

Deng, F. M., S. Kimaro, T. Lyons, D. Rothchild, and I. Zartman, eds. 1996. *Sovereignty as responsibility: Conflict management in Africa*. Washington, DC: The Brookings Institution.

Du Boff, R. B., and E. S. Herman. 1997. A critique of Tabb on globalization. *Monthly Review* 49 (6): 27–36.

Edoho, F. M. 1997a. Globalization and marginalization: Toward an understanding of the African political economy. In *Globalization and the New World Order: Promises, problems, and prospects for Africa in the twenty-first century*, edited by F. M. Edoho. Westport, CT: Praeger.

Edoho, F. M. 1997b. Overview: Africa in the age of globalization and the New World Order. In *Globalization and the New World Order: Promises, problems, and prospects for Africa in the twenty-first century*, edited by F. M. Edoho. Westport, CT: Praeger.

Ekanem, N. F. 1997. An analysis of economic instability and Africa's marginal role in the New World Order. In *Globalization and the New World Order: Promises, problems, and prospects for Africa in the twenty-first century*, edited by F. M. Edoho. Westport, CT: Praeger.

Africa at the Crossroads

Fair, R. 1993. War, famine, and poverty: Race in the construction of Africa's media image. *Journal of Communication Inquiry* 17 (2): 5–22.

Falk, R. 1999. *Predatory globalism: A critique.* Cambridge: Polity.

Foroutan, F. 1993. Regional integration in sub-Saharan Africa: Past experience and future prospects. In *New dimensions in regional integration,* edited by J. de Melo and A. Panagariya. Cambridge: Cambridge University Press.

Founou-Tchuigoua, B. 1996. The state sub-region in the future of Africa. *Social Justice* 23 (1/2): 151–170.

Gibbon, P. 1996. Structural adjustment and structural change in sub-Saharan Africa: Some provisional conclusions. *Development and Change* 27 (4): 751–784.

Gill, S. 1995. Theorizing the interregnum: The double movement and global politics in the 1990s. In *International political order,* edited by B. Hettne. London: Zed Books.

Green, R. H. 1998. A cloth untrue: The evolution of structural adjustment in sub-Saharan Africa. *Journal of International Affairs* 52 (1): 207–232.

Greene, J. 1989. The debt problem of sub-Saharan Africa. *Finance and Development* 26 (2): 9–13.

Harbeson, J. W., and D. Rothchild, eds. 1999. *Africa in world politics.* Boulder, CO: Westview.

Harris, E. 1999. Impact of Asian crisis on sub-Saharan Africa. *Finance and Development* 36 (1): 14–17.

Hawk, B., ed. 1992. *Africa's media image.* Westport, CT: Greenwood.

Held, D. 1995. *Democracy and global order: From modern state to cosmopolitan governance.* Stanford: Stanford University Press.

Held, D., and A. McGrew. 1993. Globalization and the liberal democratic state. *Government and Opposition* 28 (2): 261–289.

Herbst, J. 1997. Responding to state failure in Africa: A reply to Richard Joseph. *International Security* 22 (1): 182–185.

Hernandez-Cata, E. 1999. Sub-Saharan Africa: Economic policy and outlook for growth. *Finance and Development* 36 (1): 10–12.

Hountonji, P. 1995. Producing knowledge in Africa today. *African Studies Review* 38: 1–10.

Jameson, K. 1998. Development ethics: A guide to theory and practice. *Economic Development and Cultural Change* 46 (3): 644–645.

Jewsiewicki, B., and V. Y. Mudimbe. 1995. Meeting the challenge of legitimacy: Postindependence black Africa and post-Soviet European states. *Daedalus* 124 (3): 191–208.

Jones, D. W. 1998. Aversion to Africa. *World and I* 13 (7): 80–86.

Joseph, R. A. 1997. Responding to state failure in Africa: Response to Jeffrey Herbst. *International Security* 21: 175–181.

Kaplan, R. *The ends of the earth: A journey at the end of the 21st century.* New York: Random House.

Kassimir, R. 1997. The internationalization of African studies: A view from the SSRC. *Africa Today* 44 (2): 155–162.

Keller, E. E., and D. Rothchild, eds. 1996. *Africa in the new international order.* Boulder, CO: Lynne Rienner.

Lardner, T. 1993. Rewriting the tale of the "Dark Continent." *Media Studies Journal* 7 (4): 94–103.

MacEwan, A. 1999. *Neoliberalism or democracy: Economic strategies, markets, and alternatives in the 21st century*. Halifax, NS: Zed/Fernwood.

Martin, W. G., and M. O. West, eds. 1999. *Out of one, many Africas: Reconstructing the study and meaning of Africa*. Urban-Champaign: University of Illinois.

Mkandawire, T. 1998. *Thinking about developmental states in Africa*. Geneva: U.N. Conference on Trade and Development.

Mkandawire, T. 1999. Crisis management and the making of choiceless democracies. In *State, conflict, and democracy in Africa*, edited by Richard A. Joseph. Boulder, CO: Lynne Rienner.

Mkandawire, T., and C. C. Saludo. 1999. *Our continent, our future: African perspectives on structural adjustment*. Dakar: CODESRIA.

Munchie, M. 2000. Searching for opportunities for sub-Saharan Africa's renewal in the era of globalization. *Futures* 32 (2): 1–16.

Ng, F., and A. Yates. 1997. Open economies work better! Did Africa's protectionist policies cause its marginalization in world trade? *World Development* 25 (6): 889–905.

Nnadozie, E. U. 1997. Trade and regional cooperation strategy for African economic development in the twenty-first century. In *Globalization and the New World Order: Promises, problems, and prospects for Africa in the twenty-first century*, edited by F. M. Edoho. Westport, CT: Praeger.

OAU. 1981. *The Lagos Plan of Action for the economic development of Africa 1980–2000*. Geneva: International Institute for Labor Studies.

O'Brien, S. 2000. Africa in the global economy: Issues of trade and development for Africa. Paper presented at the Africa Knowledge Networks Forum Preparatory Workshop, Addis Ababa, August 17–18.

Ochwada, H. 1996. African studies: A reassessment of academic tourism since 1960. *Africa Development* 21 (4): 123–140.

Onyedike, E. U. 1996. Repositioning Africa: The role of African-American leaders in changing media treatment of Africa. *Journal of Third World Studies* 13 (2): 51–61.

Ouattara, A. D. 1999. Africa: An agenda for the 21st century. *Finance and Development* 36 (1): 2–7.

Oxfam. 2000. Oxfam international briefing report: HIPC leaves poor countries heavily in debt—New analysis. Retrieved from http://caa.org.au/oxfam/advocacy/debt/enhanced_hipc/, September 2000.

Raghavan, C. 1999. From Washington consensus to Bangkok convergence. *African Agenda* 1 (2): 20.

Ricupero, R. 1997. Growth and globalization. *U.N. Chronicle* 34 (4): 42–46.

Rieger, E., and S. Leibfried. 1998. Welfare state limits to globalization. *Politics and Society* 26 (3): 363–391.

Robinson, W. I. 1996. *Promoting polyarchy: Globalization, U.S. intervention and hegemony*. New York: Cambridge University Press.

Roe, E. 1995. Postcript: Except Africa. *World Development* 26 (6): 1065–1070.

Roe, E., and S. Leibfried. 1998. Welfare state limits to globalization. *Politics and Society* 26 (3): 363–391.

Rothkopf, D. 1997. In praise of cultural imperialism. *Foreign Policy* 107 (Summer): 38–53.

Sahn, D. E., ed. 1996. *Economic reform and the poor in Africa*. New York: Oxford University Press.

Sahn, D. E., P. A. Dorosh, and S. D. Younger, eds. 1997. *Structural adjustment reconsidered: Economic policy and poverty in Africa.* Cambridge: Cambridge University Press.

Sassen, S. 1996. *Losing control? Sovereignty in an age of globalization.* New York: Columbia University Press.

Schatz, S. 1994. Structural adjustment: A failing grade so far. *Journal of Modern African Studies* 32 (4): 679–692.

Schatz, S. 1996. A continuing failing grade. *Journal of Modern African Studies* 33 (2): 239–247.

Scholte, J. A. 1997. Global capitalism and the state. *International Affairs* 73 (3): 427–452.

Sharer, R. 1999. Trade: An engine of growth for Africa. *Finance and Development* 36 (4): 26–30.

Soyinka, W. 1996a. The National Question in Africa: Internal imperatives. *Development and Change* 27: 279–300.

Soyinka, W. 1996b. *The open sore of a continent: A personal narrative of the Nigerian crisis.* New York: Oxford University Press.

Strang, D. 1996. Contested sovereignty. In *Sovereignty*, edited by T. J. Biersteker and C. Weber. Cambridge: Cambridge University Press.

Tabb, W. 1997. Globalization is an issue, the power of capital is the issue. *Monthly Review* 49 (2): 20–31.

Thompson, G. 1999. Introduction: Situating globalization. *International Social Science Journal* 160 (June): 139–152.

UNECA. 1998. *African economic report, 1998.* Addis Ababa: U.N. Economic Commission for Africa. Retrieved from
http://www.afbis.com/analysis/eca%20report.htm

UNECA. 2000. Economic report on Africa 1999: The challenges of poverty reduction and sustainability. Addis Ababa: UNECA. Retrieved from
http://www.uneca.org/eca_resources/Publications/ESPD
/economic_report_1999.htm, November 2000.

UNICEF. 1999. *The state of the world's children, 1998: Focus on nutrition.* New York: UNICEF.

Van de Wall, N. 1994. Review essay: Adjustment alternatives and alternatives to adjustment. *African Studies Review* 37 (3): 103–117.

Weiss, L. 1997. Globalization and the myth of the powerless state. *New Left Review* 225 (September-October): 3–27.

Wolpe, H. 1996. The media and South Africa. *Brookings Review* 14 (2): 47–48.

World Bank. 1997. *World development report, 1997.* New York: Oxford University Press.

World Bank. 1998. *World development report, 1998.* New York: Oxford University Press.

World Bank. 1999a. *African development indicators, 1998–99.* Washington, DC: World Bank.

World Bank. 1999b. *World development report, 1999.* New York: Oxford University Press.

World Bank. 2000. *World development report, 2000.* New York: Oxford University Press.

Yeats, A. J., A. Amjadi, U. Reincke, and F. Ng. 1996. What caused sub-Saharan Africa's marginalization in world trade? *Finance and Development* 33 (4): 38–42.

5

Regionalism and Regional Cooperation in Africa: New Century Challenges and Prospects

Faced by the advance of world market forces crowding out nationally inspired development, Africa's own international and transnational relations reflect the growing challenges faced by relatively vulnerable states. The continent, the most fragmented in the world (Ramutsindela 2000, 5), has, since the early 1990s, witnessed the collapse of several states (e.g., Sierra Leone, Liberia, and Somalia), the advent of regional war (in the Great Lakes region), and jerky pulls toward integration across its five loosely defined regions: the Horn, West, North, East, and Southern Africa. These regions have been recognized by the Abuja Treaty and the African Economic Commission (AEC) as "definitive" regions on the continent.[1] Many students of the continent's political economy, as well as several of its policy makers, believe that regional integration, in one form or the other, can provide the continent with the wherewithal to effectively confront its multifarious problems and finally engage in sustainable development.

What exactly is regional integration? It has been defined as a "process by which a group of states voluntarily and in various degrees" accesses "each other's markets and establish[es] mechanisms and techniques that minimize conflicts and maximize internal and external economic, political, social, and cultural benefits of their interactions" (Harlow 1997, 15). It is thought that the product of regional integration, regionalism, is the best possible response to the demands of transnationalism, fission, and fragmentation (Hurrell 1995, 346).

The desire and enthusiasm for regional integration as a way to deal with Africa's many development problems is tempered by the fear national leaders have about the possible loss of sovereignty by their respective states. Sovereignty, of course, is the one precious strategic and political asset political elites have to hold on to. As such, the various responses by African states to security and regionalism vary considerably. In other words, there has always been a high degree of ambiguity in the regional processes found on the continent (Mazzeo 1984, 3). Thus, while consensus on the desirability for unified African development is long standing, there has been serious disagreement on the scope, level, and strategy for attaining it. This has had its effect on the level of implementation. The commentary on the first phase of regional integration started after independence (when about 200 sets of institutions were created in support of regional cooperation) and has been anything but damning. All major projects, except the Southern African Development Coordination Conference (SADCC), were found to have been "disappointing" (Seidmann and Anang 1992, 8).

Nevertheless, the end of the Cold War and the subsequent cessation of superpower rivalry has significantly reduced the continent's strategic importance to the Cold War protagonists and offered Africans an opportunity to engage in a more serious and meaningful way in integration efforts. However, in this new post–Cold War effort the African state has found it politically and economically useful to opt for *subregionalism* as opposed to an all-encompassing continental regionalism. After all, subregional integration remains one way of promoting unity and "relaunching development" in what is a different world economic and political context (Asante 1997, 1) without having to enter into the vexed debate of whether or not to redraw boundaries (Ramutsindela 2000, 12). As such, subregionalism has been a convenient way of deferring the question of continental political unity, an issue permanently posed by Pan-Africanism since at least the late 1950s. But then, Pan-Africanism has lacked any meaningful structure, with the feebleness of the Organization of African Unity (OAU) serving as testimony to the largely symbolic character of political unity at the continental level in the 1990s. Aside from the Economic Commission for Africa (ECA), a U.N. body, subregional economic entities, encouraged by the ECA, have stood more chance of attracting outside donor support than continentally based development schemes.[2]

However, while at the level of rhetoric most states identify with regional cooperation projects, at the level of implementation this support tends to be fed by the immediate or purely national benefits regional membership can bestow, principally that of obtaining extra sources of official development aid (ODA) from the developed industrial economies. A real commitment at the implementation stage to forms of regional cooperation based on a closely shared vision and commonly felt values that translate into concrete and progressive attempts at long-term region building cannot happen often enough in a situation where the state is concerned about the politics of its own rather more immediate stability and year-on-year survival. In the context of a reliance on foreign sponsors who influence policy direction, regional organizations remain distant to the people on the ground. Region building is seen as the business of states where civil society plays no direct part: for states, the practical commitment to regional integration can, at will, be either turned up or down.

Even at the best of times, state-driven integration is strong on rhetoric and weak on implementation. Apart from the issue of scarce resources and limited capacity to devote to foreign policy matters in a difficult economic climate, there are other hangovers: Given the rather ephemeral nature of much inter Afri-can relations in the past, there is a long history of the politicization of inter-state relations (Calvert 1986, 95). Attempts at economic integration between 1965 and 1995 failed largely for reasons that, set against the background of ubiquitous foreign donor influence, have included the failure to translate regional agree-ments into substantive changes in national policy, the unwillingness to subordi-nate immediate political interest to long-term economic goals, an absence of developed regimes to enforce treaties, endemic political instability and uncer-tainty for policy makers, the noncommercial objectives pursued by parastatals, little consideration paid to the potential benefits consumers could derive from regional cooperation, antipathy toward markets and free enterprise, World Bank and International Monetary Fund (IMF) structural adjustment policies that dis-counted regional scenarios, and the absence of popular identification with re-gional schemes (Mistry 2000, 558–559). But amidst the growth in transregional relations on the ground, especially in the wake of structural adjustment programs (SAPs) imposed by the World Bank and the IMF, which have encouraged eco-nomic openness and the growth of market forces, both formal and informal, re-gionalization increasingly happens despite the singular preoccupations of states (Sorensen 1995, 253).

Thus, in West Africa, state-driven ventures aimed at achieving integration do not necessarily overlap with transnational economic relations on the ground. In the Horn of Africa, fratricidal conflict between Ethiopia and Eritrea mitigates against continuing regional cooperation amongst states and nongovernmental organizations on the pressing issues of drought, desertification, and the preven-tion of conflict. As such, the state can be considered an obstacle towards pro-ductive socioeconomic interaction around common regional issues. The propo-sition that regionalism probably flourishes best where the state is, economically speaking, on the retreat and less prone to preoccupy itself with matters of bor-ders and territory and, at the same time, of a more open, possibly liberal-democratic disposition toward regional neighbors and regional issues, needs further investigation. But, if we wish to accommodate the notion of "new" or "second-wave" regionalism, which distinguishes itself by its wide range of pur-pose (not purely economic but encompassing broad security considerations), it is certainly important to consider the inclusion of nonstate actors in cooperation projects and region building and the creation of regional structures more adap-tive or responsive to change (Sorensen 1995, 251). In Southern Africa, with its investment in democracy, direct state involvement in the economy and regional economic projects would seem to be on the wane. This has given scope to pri-vate actors who wish to get involved in sectors previously driven by state-sponsored activity, such as transport, communications, energy, water, and the like (Soederbaum, Schulz, and Oejendal 1998, 11–13).

As such, there are forces that encourage regionalism and there are trajectories that stand in the way of regionalism and regional cooperation. In order to look at the challenges faced by Africa in the new millennium and the practical implications for policy makers who deal with regional cooperation, this chapter wishes to look at the sources that propel Africa toward and away from regionalism and regional cooperation. With reference to the new regionalist approach, the chapter gauges the social and economic manifestations of regionalism. Then it seeks to identify the forces promoting and opposing regionalism and regional cooperation. Finally, an attempt will be made to describe the current visions on African integration and to offer a conclusion on the practical course of action that may be taken to promote sustainable forms of regional cooperation in the continent.

REGIONALISM

Regionalism is the study of issues in a particular geographic setting that add up to a set of distinct though interrelated activities of visible benefit to either individuals or governments (Taylor 1993, 7). In an African context, given the Eurocentric tenor of the neofunctionalist studies of the past, as well as the continued predominance of external influences, the study of regionalism would seem to amount to the study of issues lacking in any one predominant theoretical framework (Smith 1997, 73). Regionalism on the continent is characterized by two features: It amounts to both state-sponsored activities and those driven by economic, commercial, military, political, and societal interactions, where governments, if at all, play only an indirect part.

Globalization, peripheralization, and conflict, as well as Africa's integration into an emergent world political structure explain this seeming growth in transnational activity. On the economic front, nonstate interactions are driven by the need for economies of scale; on the social front, the search for physical and economic security is a source of transnational activity;[3] while on the welfare front, the discovery of advocacy work and the development of civil society structures make use of coalitions across borders and, as such, broader constituencies in order to obtain resources and achieve a greater political profile on a variety of issues, including constitutional rights, democratic participation, freedom from discrimination and action on HIV/AIDS.[4]

Following global trends, therefore, African states are ever more made aware of and called on to respond to nonstate sponsored regionalist phenomena, be it in the form of migratory flows (in response to humanitarian, political, or economic crises), warlordism or insurgency (obtaining sustenance from communities across borders as well as governments), regional crime syndicates (engaged in narcotics, arms trafficking, contraband, or vehicle theft), multinational investment (with its effect on the domestic business sector or trade policy for instance), health pandemics (such as HIV/AIDS), or international economic regulatory regimes (such as the World Trade Organization) bearing in on any region.

At a regional level, all this encourages greater cooperation in areas of humanitarian relief, security and policing, consultation on social, health, and welfare policy, as well as regional economic matters to do with a common approach to foreign investment, the promotion of regional business ventures, and the provision of a regionally regulated and standardized infrastructural environment.

At stake here is nothing more than the nature and effectiveness of Africa's integration into an emergent world political economy. When there is a world debate about whether or not Africa can be made part of global economic development (couched largely in a debate for and against Afro-pessimism), there are questions regarding the effectiveness of the regions promoted by African governments. The issues raised relate to whether (1) nonstate regionalist activity corresponds with regions legally defined by governments (Hurrell 1995, 334); (2) states that remain central to promoting the regionalist project (Gamble and Payne 1996, 250) and all positive forms of regionalism (set to increase the welfare and happiness of those living in it) remain fully fledged and committed participants over time; and (3) the regional responses of governments effectively contribute to the greater security and welfare not just of themselves as states, but also to that of communities and individuals living in particular regions.

State-promoted regional economic cooperation, according to Peter Smith (Hurrell 1995, 337), is measured by the scope or the range of issues covered by cooperation (from security to welfare issues), depth (the degree of policy harmonization or integration which takes place), institutionalization (formal institutions that emerge), and centralization (the degree to which formal institutions wield any authority).

A combination of these processes will produce a cohesive regional unit. Cohesion can be said to happen when at least two features occur: First, the regional institution plays a defining role in organizing the international relations of the region, and second, the formal interstate region corresponds with growing regional and transnational nonstate activity.

In Africa, donor dependency, the lack of own resources, the absence of any "tight fit" between interstate regions, and transnational regionalism (which in a military form are forces of destabilization) contribute to the ambiguity of African regionalism.

FORCES FAVORING REGIONALISM

Factors favoring regionalization and regionalism revolve around those promoting and responding to globalization as well as its attendant—though not "necessary"—phenomenon of democratization.

The withdrawal of the superpowers, the demise of apartheid in South Africa, changes at the United Nations, the promise of aid and trade concessions, conditionalities laid down by the structural adjustment programs of the World Bank and the IMF and a new uniformity in polities away from one-party states to multiparty democracy and a similar, "liberal" outlook toward cooperation have all been factors in the reconstitution of regional organizations. Much of this has its origins in the period after 1990 and revolves around issues of how to positively change the terms and conditions by which Africa relates to the rest of the world. On Africa's political interactions and presence in world politics, a number of issues can be raised to contextualize the growth in the continent's regional organizations.

After 1990, North–South relations were no longer obscured by the superimposition of the East–West struggle. Africa now had to relate to one institutional force in world politics, that of a globalizing North. With regionalism becoming a force to contend with and the division of the world economy into three trading blocs based on North America, Europe, and East Asia, a real possibility at the beginning of the 1990s, Africa's response was to readopt regionalism as a means to arrest its decline in the world economy and achieve, irrespective of the immediate economic situation, longer-term sustainable development (Laporte 1993, 3). It was against this background that the Abuja Treaty flowed out of the *Lagos Plan of Action* (OAU 1981) in 1991 and established a legal framework to realize economic integration, with the latter being considered as "a major historic undertaking . . . vital for Africa's economic survival." But, while regional economic organizations are made the cornerstone of the treaty, the eventual economic unification of the continent is kept in mind. For this, the regional organizations (regional economic communities, or RECs in AEC parlance) are an important link. They are meant to be the vital levers to assist the African Economic Community, which was established in 1994 in realizing its goal of bringing about an African economic union within not more than forty years.

In the 1990s, ideological disagreements that may have stood in the way of relations in the past no longer mattered as much. The disappearance of superpower rivalry and the related readiness to politically and militarily intervene directly in African affairs, removed some of the political and ideological aspects of Africa's relations with the industrial North. Of issue were now the larger economic terms under which Africa related to Western Europe and North America. African political elites had largely accepted that the (free) market was central to economic activity and in deciding questions of welfare. Regional organizations, it was understood, were a bridging stone toward one's reintegration into the world market on the one hand, but also provided an opportunity to retain or enlarge on one's ability to control change emanating from the global level downward. Further, policy elites view regionalism as one instrument among others to assist them in negotiating the terms and impact of globalization (Lambrechts 1997, 2). In a sense, the new regionalism is an important political construct in influencing the project of globalism. As such, there is no longer a clear dividing line between economic and political regionalism (Hurrell 1995, 333). Regional organizations, which were traditionally seen as rather narrowly defined vehicles for economic integration, are now tasked to contribute to the maintenance of economic, military, political, and social security.

This thinking was encouraged by other events at both a global and continental level. The United Nations, unable to finance, train, activate, and maintain extensive peacekeeping forces at short notice to deal with African crises, has increasingly looked to regional organizations to contribute toward peacekeeping and peace-enforcement operations. It is an approach that seeks to Africanize conflict resolution and crisis management in the continent. While some foreign support has been given to the OAU in setting up and maintaining the Conflict Resolution Mechanism (established in 1995), support has principally gone to regional bodies such as ECOWAS's ECOMOG that has been engaged with the civil wars in Liberia and Sierra Leone. The prevalence of everwidening circles of conflict across regions, the Great Lakes region at the end of the 1990s being a classic example, also brought home the urgent need for effective African diplomacy at a formal regional as well as an interregional level.

But wider conflicts and the Africanization of conflict management implies obtaining greater support from the rest of the world: here regional organizations serve to test Africa's collective ability to extract such support on issues of conflict from a global political community. Comparable to a successful regional organization in the South—the Association of Southeast Asian States (ASEAN)—is one which finds such Northern recognition and support.

THE INSUFFICIENCIES OF CONTINENTWIDE INTEGRATION

Africa's outlook on integration is a divided one. For one thing, there is the issue of differentiating between Africa as a region in world terms and Africa as an entity made up of various subregions and the way these relate to the world. One needs to ask to what extent a continental body such as the OAU (or its designated successor, the African Union) as opposed to the various regional organizations on the ground, is likely to give direction to Africa's future development and participation in global affairs.

The OAU has represented Africa as a region in regard to matters of self-determination, peace, and security, while the Economic Commission for Africa, a body of the United Nations up to 1994 when it was joined by the African Economic Community, has represented the continent at an economic level in matters regarding development. In addition (and not unlike the United Nations at a universal level), the OAU makes allowance for subregionalism.

For the first thirty years of its existence, the OAU strove to achieve unity on the question of decolonization, self-determination, and national liberation, while the ECA, the body ostensibly meant to deal with African development, came about in part as a response to the early advocacy for a continental approach to African development. Even though the global and regional balance with regard to peace and security very much favored the OAU, its inability as an institution in matters of security and peacemaking was self-inflicted: Its charter and the consensus to uphold the principle of noninterference, buttressed by the need to achieve unity on how best to support the anticolonial and anti-apartheid struggles, allowed for lack of development in these areas. Apart from the formal institution of the African Commission on Human and People's Rights in 1986, serious institutional and policy changes in regard to conflict prevention, resolution, and mediation, the imposition of sanctions on military dictatorships, and the setting up of human rights commissions were only considered after the full liberation of the continent in 1994.

On the economic side, calls for a common African market and economic community were goals set by the All African Peoples Conferences held in 1958, 1960, 1961, and that of the Second Conference of Independent States in Addis Ababa in 1960, the charter of the OAU, and summits of the OAU in 1968, 1970, 1973, 1976, 1977, and 1979. Yet the OAU only added integration to its institutional brief in the wake of the all-important Abuja Treaty of 1991, which made the OAU coordinate and administer the activities of the newly formed African Economic Community (Asante 2000, 5). By the early 1990s, the subregions had become the cornerstone of the plan to build an African economic community. But while the process toward an AEC already shows signs of inertia (the Abuja Treaty took three years to be ratified and it took three years more thereafter to convene the first summit of the AEC, while the OAU in terms of its ability to oversee the process has found itself overstretched) (Asante 2000, 9), the regional economic communities (RECs) themselves were already developing at different speeds and with different priorities as regions in their own right. This raises the issue of whether the OAU and the African Union, as well as the AEC, will, in practice, be able to either coordinate or effectively control the potential independence of these regions in serving the goal of eventual economic unification.[5]

The divided nature of African regionalism—the division between the political and the developmental on the one hand and the adherence to both continental and subregional regionalism on the other—has to do with the historical compromise reached between the "softer" and "harder" versions of Pan-Africanism in the wake of independence so evident in the founding role and structure of the Organization of African Unity in 1963. Exploiting this gap in the past have been extracontinental or neocolonial forces, as well as the former apartheid regime in South Africa.

The gap between the political and economic structures meant to work toward African unity and African development is evident in a number of contradictions. These have challenged the OAU's own role as laid down in its charter of promoting the unity and solidarity of African states, to coordinate and intensify their cooperation to achieve a better life for all the peoples of Africa, and promote international cooperation.

The OAU strictly defended the borders of small and economically very vulnerable, if not, nonviable states. At the same time, the AEC was committed to projects that transcended the individual state and aimed at trans-African integration. These were "two conflicting predispositions" whose product has been "confusion about means and ends" and a level of political and economic performance that compares "very unfavorably" with the rest of the developing world (Mistry 2000, 553–554).

Not surprising, therefore, African integration efforts have generally not been driven by the evolution of common value systems leading to common rules, regional regimes, and institutionalized behavior. The need to satisfy national pretensions while nonetheless subscribing to African development has meant that integration has often been driven by non-African sources or pursued in parochial contexts. The SAPs promoted by the World Bank/IMF concentrated on the individual state rather than on the needs of regions (Mistry 2000, 566), while, in Francophone Africa, cooperation-cum-integration efforts have been overshadowed by the preponderance of France as an outside power intent on preserving its influence among its former colonies (Martin 1992, 92). This has obstructed any opening to the wider West African region on the key issue of monetary integration, for instance. In Southern Africa before 1994, the Southern African Customs Union (SACU) and the Rand Monetary Arrangement (RMA) between apartheid South Africa on the one hand and states who opposed apartheid only worked because they were seen to be to the national advantage of both sides (Zacarias 1999, 163–164); the makeup of their states and long-term dispositions, however, remained totally different. The Southern African Development Coordination Conference and its successor body, the Southern African Development Community (SADC) are run on the basis of foreign donor project aid, which is often country specific rather than regionwide. This means that the approach to integration in the region as a whole is deflected by bilateral relations with a donor state or national considerations that underwrite the sovereignty and foreign policies of individual states. This does not necessarily promote regional integration or interdependence. Overlapping functions and multiple membership in regional organizations (one thinks of those between the SADC and the Common Market for Eastern and Southern Africa [COMESA] as well as the *Union économique et monetaire ouest-africaine* [UEMOA] and the Economic Community of West African States [ECOWAS]) are also most often driven by political rather than socioeconomic or developmental considerations.[6]

As evident from the area of development, in security matters the continental approach equally left much to be desired. By the time the post–Cold War era ended, the continent had begun to witness the proliferation of conflict. This was in part due to the fact that with the withdrawal of the superpowers from the continent, domestic and external sovereignty could more easily be challenged. At the same time, the OAU Charter did not provide for any collective security arrangement. The OAU could only address the evident crisis of the legitimacy of the African state (Jackson and Rosenberg 1986, 259–282) if a good number of its members themselves first democratized and in so doing relegitimized themselves. In the context of a shift toward multiparty democracy and in the wake of the genocide in Rwanda, the OAU did establish a formal structure—the Mechanism for Conflict Prevention Management and Resolution—to monitor, preempt, and manage conflict. In addition, in 1999 the OAU took steps to modify its defense of the notion of sovereignty when it no longer permitted military regimes to be part of its deliberations. Despite this tinkering, both the OAU and, running parallel to it, its economic counterpart, the AEC, have remained subordinate if not peripheral to the developments that balkanize the continent. As such, they have not been able, as yet, to serve as a catalyst to any continentwide process of integration.

Accompanying this has been the disintegration of an all-African consensus as it once existed. In 2000–2001 the planned demise of the Organization of African Unity, the product of an All-African consensus at a particular point in time, is indicative of this change. The political theme to politically charge, reunify, and inform foreign policy has to be refound. If the African Union, unlike its predecessor, the OAU, is to be given the means to intervene pro-actively in cases where human rights are under threat, the new continental entity will provide a new focus for African politics and diplomacy in a way that was not the case with the OAU. But given the genesis of the new body—with Libya as progenitor whose concern would seem to be the development of African foreign policy toward the outside rather than major inward reform—the organization is unlikely to spearhead change on its own. In this context, subregionalism rather than continentalism would still seem to stand the best chance of becoming the driver of regionalism on the continent.

It is these subregions that have obtained prominence, not least by the prescriptions of the Abuja Treaty, but also by the centrifugal forces unleashed by globalization, which encourage the activities and movements of nonstate actors at both global and subregional levels. These are, in the words of Fidel Castro, "not an invention (but) . . . a consequence of the development of the productive forces" (Lipalile 2000, 2). Among these nonstate forces are not only economic but also social, political and military actors who compete with, and at times challenge, the African state.

Thus, in the 1990s, as the realities of the post-Cold War period set in, African countries came to realize that the loss of the continent's strategic importance to the Cold War protagonists meant that national governments were no longer able to attract as much government-to-government aid as they had done during the Cold War. In fact, the West no longer considered it strategic to support African statehood by supplying the continent's governments with budget subventions. Northern states were now preoccupied with geoeconomic considerations, the state's withdrawal from the economy, and making global arrangements for the management of world economic issues. Their preoccupation was with financial support intended to prop up capitalism and the crumbling government structures in the area covered by the former Soviet Union and her allies. For Africa, this meant a drop in Northern interest and Northern aid. As international support declined and sources of revenue dried up—not least due to the ongoing implementation of the structural adjustment programs decreed by global financial institutions—the African state itself found that the cost of maintaining government had increased. The state continued to struggle for survival and against decay from within as well as from without (Clapham 1996, 17, 246). Faced by an all-encompassing security dilemma within and beyond the state (the most dramatic evidence for which were the political use of ethnicity to serve a campaign of genocide in Rwanda and the collapsed state scenarios of Somalia, Liberia, and Sierra Leone), African diplomacy responded by taking recourse to regional security responses.

CHALLENGES TO REGIONALISM AND REGIONAL COOPERATION: AFRICAN POLICY AND A SHARED VISION OF REGIONALISM

The peripheralization of continental bodies is accompanied by the weakness of regional bodies at the subregional level. In order to explain this, factors such as the waning of an all-African consensus and the absence of a shared value system centered around autocentric development, the political costs of making a choice between policies of nation building as opposed to those of region building, asymmetries within regions, weak infrastructural links, and the failure to set aside resources for foreign policy can be seen to serve as contributing factors.

The Disintegration of an All-African Consensus

A number of factors, including the end of the rivalries between East and West, the ideological disintegration of the Non-Aligned Movement (NAM), the fading of colonial memories among the younger generation, the demise of apartheid, all amidst a decline in living conditions, particularly for the urban classes from the late 1980s onward, has brought about a decline in an all-African consensus on a continent where already "division and lack of unity is the *sine qua non* for African marginalization, discrimination and exploitation" (Nabudere 2000, 11). The political theme that can politically charge, reunify, and inform foreign policy needs to be rediscovered. This is best found in the response Africa can muster to the challenge of globalization, a central feature in the transformation of today's international relations.

The Peripheralization from World Economic Development

The continuation of the debt crisis despite attempts to address the issue, the promotion of structural adjustment programs tailored for national not regional needs (Mistry 2000, 566), the absence of any substantial growth in multinational investment, and the export of savings abroad, as well as the slow development of information technology and the infrastructure needed to sustain it, are only a few of the problems that have pushed Africa to the periphery of the global economy. In fact, the failure of the continent to develop capabilities in information technology has prevented most of the countries in the continent from participating in an electronically managed world service economy involved in strategically important sectors such as commerce, tourism, and finance. Presently, only a handful of countries are being integrated into a virtual but real-value economy. Since only a few African countries are in step with worldwide developments in information technology, this uneven integration into the global economy continues to hamper regionalization.

The Absence of a Consensus on Common Values to Inform Regional Security

Similarly, the maintenance of regional security would seem to be a precondition for any efforts made at regional cooperation and development. Regional security can best be maintained where there is a basic understanding of democracy; a confluence of values on what constitute forms of governance that best encourage political participation and have the capacity to peacefully handle political dissent.

The Persistence of Nationalism and Nation Building

Adherence to nationalist positions and the continued attempts at nation building detract from region building. For instance, South Africa has sought to balance a policy of reconciliation and the promotion of national feeling for a "rainbow nation" at home with one of openness toward its neighbors and the revival of Africa abroad: This has its own political and economic costs in regard to immigration, the treatment of Africans who are not South African citizens, levels of emigration, and the capacity of policy makers to adequately address both domestic and external issues. Zimbabwe in the period after 2000—despite domestic and outside pressures—instituted a very restrictive policy of nation building centered around the rapid and unplanned dislodging of white commercial farmers. This put her out of step with liberal-cum-regionalist concerns for the general upholding of constitutionality, property rights, the institution of orderly and planned processes, the deemphasis of nationalism and ethnicity, as well as human rights. Generally, states are reluctant to open their polities toward a region, since "economic integration has uneven consequences for groups within particular societies, groups that may exert political influence to arrest or offset the process of integration" (Kahler 1995, xxv).

Asymmetry in Size and the Distribution of Resources

Among the large regional powers and their neighbors (Nigeria, South Africa, and Egypt), there is an asymmetry in size and the distribution of resources and this is a perennial source of anxiety and fear, making it difficult for one country (e.g., South Africa) to take leadership and push for regional integration.[7]

Border Disputes and Contests over Resources

The Ethiopian–Eritrean border conflict in 1999–2001 and territorial conflicts between Botswana and Namibia, Eritrea, and Yemen in the late 1990s negatively affected regional cooperation and integration.

Fragmenting Political Cultures

Collapsing or collapsed states or so-called warlord states (e.g., Democratic Republic of Congo [DRC], Somalia, Liberia, and Sierra Leone in the 1990s) are in part the result of the failure of nation-building programs that have not delivered a better way of life for the people. Ethnicity or religion are used as instruments by deprived groups (i.e., groups excluded from participation in political and economic processes) to mobilize for increased participation or simply for the resources they need to survive. Of course, renewed interest in ethnicity is also a way for many communities to seek either new identities or reenforce old ones in an effort to survive in a globalizing environment. There is the real possibility that these developments can cause an implosion in the postcolonial nation-state and result in the breakup of big states such as Nigeria. This complicates the construction of regions and "further complicates the search for African unity" (Nabudere 2000, 12, 15).

Weak Infrastructural Links

Communication links between many regions in Africa are nonexistent. For example, in the Horn of Africa, the Great Lakes region, and across the vast area covered by COMESA, for instance, building integrative regimes is very difficult because of the lack of effective infrastructural links that allow for cost-effective communications.

Assignment of Foreign Policy Resources to Regional Cooperation

Within many African countries, foreign policy is poorly developed and many of these countries lack the appropriate resources to engage effectively in international relations. The lack of "foreign policy resources" implies that effective cooperation at the regional level is most likely to be made quite difficult (Mazzeo 1984, 231).

AFRICAN REGIONAL COOPERATION AND INTEGRATION

By the 1980s, many regional organizations, mostly intergovernmental, created in the 1960s, the heyday of regional integration experiments, had become moribund. Successful economic development and integration efforts have been few and far between. Those cited as relatively successful include the *Com-*

munauté Financière Africaine (CFA) Franc Zone, the *Union économique et monetaire ouest-africaine*, the SACU and Common Monetary Agreement, the Gambia River Development Organization, the Organization for the Development of the Senegal River, the Liptako–Gourma Integrated Development Authority, and the Niger Basin Authority (NBA), as well as the Organization for Coordination and Cooperation in the Control of Major Endemic Diseases, the Joint Organization for Control of Desert Locust and Bird Pests, and the West African Rice Development Association (WARDA) (Soederbaum, Schulz, and Oejendal 1998, 16–17).

What follows is a selection of the larger regional organizations, some of which were restructured in the 1990s to enhance their ability to contribute to regional as well as continental integration:

The Union of Arab Maghreb

The Union of Arab Maghreb (UAM) encompasses five North African states situated on the Mediterranean with strong historical, cultural and linguistic ties. In existence since 1964, when Algeria, Libya, Morocco, and Tunisia set up a Permanent Maghreb Consultative Council, the UAM has sought to coordinate negotiations with Europe on trade and coordinate as well as harmonize the development plans of the region. By the late 1980s, the Union, however, was no longer active. It was only then that the organization experienced a revival when, in 1988, the Maghreb High Commission with a number of specialized commissions attached to it was set up, a decision ratified with the Treaty of Marrakesh in 1989. The new UAM was armed with a secretariat based in Rabat, a consultative assembly to advise the annual summit of heads of state (preceded by a council of foreign affairs ministers), and a Court of Justice. By early 1997, the work of a reestablished UAM had resulted in thirty-seven regional conventions and thirty multilateral agreements. Several of the multilateral agreements were ratified by all five members of the Union and these included those on tariffs and trade in relation to industrial products and trade in agricultural products, investment guarantees, double taxation, and sanitary standards. The main objectives of the UAM are to promote regional stability and policy coordination, especially in such areas as agriculture, industry, commerce, food security, and the setting up of joint projects. On the security side, the body has committed itself to the development of a common defense policy but has not assumed any powers in respect to intervention in the internal affairs of member states. Failures of the Union include not having met the targets of a free trade zone in 1992, a customs union by 1995, or a common market by 2000; the inability to successfully implement cooperation agreements; the Union's failure to resolve Algeria's extremely bloody internal conflict; the persistence of nontariff barriers, dependence on trade with the EU, and the absence of links with the rest of the continent; and the weaknesses of intra-UAM links (Mistry 2000, 562).

Union économique et monetaire ouest Africaine

The Francophone West African countries formed the *Communauté économique de l'Afrique de l'ouest* (CEAO) in 1971 in order to help member countries achieve economic integration. The community reestablished itself in 1994 with a membership that includes Benin, Burkina Faso, Côte d'Ivoire, Mali, Niger, Senegal and Togo. On the security side, the organization possessed the *Accord de non-aggression et d'assistance en matière de défense* (ANAD), which followed the border dispute between Mali and Burkina Faso. Its brief was enlarged during the course of the 1980s with the addition of a number of protocols. In 1994 the CEAO constituted itself as the *Union économique et monetaire ouest Africaine* while ANAD, whose primary function was to offer assistance in the defense of member states, became a separate organization with its own institutions (Yoroms 2000, 2). Major issues confronting the UEMOA today include defining the organization's relationship with the AEC, the role of donor states such as France, and the wish to establish a customs zone while its members retain their membership in ECOWAS (Asante 2000, 11).

Communauté économique des états de l'Afrique centrale

The leaders of the *Union douanière et économique de l'Afrique centrale* (UDEAC) agreed in 1981 to set up a wider economic community of Central African states called the *Communauté économique des états d'Afrique centrale* (CEEAC). Created in 1983, the CEEAC includes Burundi, Cameroon, Central African Republic, Chad, Republic of Congo (Congo-Brazzaville), Democratic Republic of Congo (Congo-Kinshasa), Equatorial Guinea, Gabon, Rwanda, and São Tomé and Principe. Functioning since 1985, its primary objectives are, to achieve economic development, promote regional economic cooperation, and establish a Central African Common Market. A Standing Committee was created to oversee the implementation of associated resolutions. It was largely inactive between 1992 and 1998 for lack of funds. Relaunched at a summit in February 1998, Angola, hitherto an observer, made known its intention to join the organization. As part of its revival, a twofold summit, including the EEC and the Economic Community of Central African States was held in 1999.

Issues confronting the CEEAC include the nonpayment of membership dues, conflict between Rwanda, Burundi and the DRC, the disruptions caused by civil war (as in Angola, the DRC, and the Republic of Congo), the spillover effects of refugees from the Great Lakes conflict, the inability of these countries to participate effectively and gainfully in trade with their neighbors as well as with the rest of the world, and the issue of membership by each country in several regional organizations (i.e., the multiple membership issue). Despite current difficulties, there is, great potential for future comprehensive cooperation in defense and security matters in this region of the continent.

The Economic Community of West African States

The Treaty of Lagos established the Economic Community of West African States in May 1975. Signed by fifteen states with a population of 120 million at the time and from a plurality of backgrounds, ECOWAS straddles the all-important Anglophone–Francophone–Lusophone divides. ECOWAS's aim is to promote trade, cooperation, and self-reliance in West Africa. In 1993 ECOWAS was revised with the objective of bringing about a common market and a monetary union. Politically, it strives to establish a West African parliament, an economic and social council, and a regional court to replace the existing tribunal. On the security side, ECOWAS has built on various security instruments. These include, the Protocol relating to Non-Aggression signed in 1978, as well as the Protocol on Mutual Assistance of 1981 (which took effect in 1986). The former puts structures in place that control international subversion and transnational insurgency, while the latter declares that "any armed threat or aggression directed against any member state shall constitute a threat or aggression against the community" and thus makes allowance for the constitution of an intervention force. Yet ECOWAS's decision to establish the Economic Community of West African States Monitoring Group (ECOMOG) and intervene in Liberia in 1990 and later in Sierra Leone was taken outside this elaborate security framework (Yoroms 2000, 1–3) and that of the OAU/U.N. Chapter VIII framework for regional peacekeeping forces. The shortcomings associated with ECOMOG (revolving around the legitimacy of its security operations, the controversial use of force, and the predominance of Nigeria in it) led to the establishment of a Mechanism for Conflict Prevention, Management, Resolution and Security (MCPMRS) in 1998. Issues confronting ECOWAS include the low level of formal intraregional member trade (it is important to note that "informal" regionalism is alive and well, with significant annual increases in informal trade); the failure to fully integrate markets in capital, goods, and labor; uncertainty and violent conflict in Liberia and Sierra Leone; worsening sectarian conflict and other domestic tensions in a democratic Nigeria; the cumbersome security architecture in the region; the inability to integrate the Protocol on Mutual Assistance and ANAD with the new MCPMRS and a lack of funds and logistics to make it work (Yoroms 2000, 1,6).

The Southern African Development Community

The Southern African Development Community was founded in 1992 when it replaced the Southern African Development Coordination Conference. The latter was originally formed in 1980, ostensibly to counter apartheid South Africa's attempt to use regional cooperation as a means of overcoming its isolation in the region. Protocols signed so far by members of the SADC include those on trade, shared water resources, transport, mining, a SADC Tribunal, communication, education, and training (Bischoff 2001). In 1997 SADC set up a parliamentary forum and a consultative body with the intention of setting up a regional parliament in the longer term (Seymour 1997, 11). The SADC hopes to establish a free trade area by 2004. In 1996, the SADC set up the Organ for Defense and Politics (OPDS); unfortunately, it has largely been inoperable. However, the region is in the process of giving itself a regional peacekeeping capacity and, through the Inter-State Defense and Security Council (ISDSC) (to be made a constituent part of the OPDS), hopes to be able to engage in greater regional police cooperation.

Considered to be one of the most promising regional institutions in Africa, SADC faces a number of challenges that, inter alia, include a strategy on how to involve the people of the region in the integration process and overcome the differences in the common political will and national capacity to promote integration. There is the need to strengthen the secretariat so that it can more effectively identify and manage wide-ranging integration projects, instead of relying, as is currently the case, on small and ill-defined donor projects, most of which are not structured to produce significant benefits for the region. Another major issue that SADC members are wrestling with is how to offset the effects of South Africa's economic predominance in the region and best manage polarized and asymmetrical development in the wake of implementing an ambitious trade protocol agreed to in September 2000, as well as overcome regional dependence on foreign donors. There is also the desire to make all members—including those with overlapping membership in other organizations such as COMESA or CEEAC—full participants in regional cooperation and negotiations with the EU over Economic Partnership Agreements between the ACP and the EU (*South Scan*, Vol. 15, No. 25 [2000], 199). Other worries include South Africa's capacity to divert resources away from reducing its fiscal deficit, as well as boosting local employment and manufacture toward long-term regional goals aimed at lifting the productive capacity of neighboring states; excessive fears among smaller states about the political, military, and economic might of South Africa (Mistry 2000, 563–564); and the need to define the terms under which SADC intervention in the affairs of a member state can take place, while at the same time building a peacekeeping capacity informed by a confluence of opinion on democratic values and those relating to gender sensitivity at a regional level.[8]

The Common Market for Eastern and Southern Africa

COMESA was established in 1994 to replace the former Preferential Trade Area (PTA) for Eastern and Southern Africa, which had been in existence since 1981. With twenty member states inhabited by 380 million people, the body has a wide-ranging series of objectives aimed at achieving economic integration and the promotion of peace and security in the region. COMESA hopes to have successfully established a common tariffs zone by 2004, and a single central bank and monetary union by 2025. Several institutions have been created, including a trade court with the power to overturn national laws, a court of justice, a trade and development bank, a clearinghouse, and an association of commercial banks. On the security side, a security policy has been drafted for the organization.

Challenges include the organization's large and divergent membership, with some members currently engaged in open conflict with each other (for instance, Ethiopia and Eritrea); the collapse of several economies (e.g., Somalia, Rwanda, Burundi, Sudan, and Zaire/DRC) (Mistry 2000, 562); and duplication of effort as a result of the existence of other integration schemes in the region (Khalil and Ezzat 2000, 1).

The East African Community

The demise of the East African Community in 1978 was largely due to the differing national dispositions of its member states—Kenya, Uganda, and Tanzania—which had become unmanageable under the Amin regime in Uganda during the 1970s; accusations by the weaker members (Tanzania and Uganda) that the benefits of the scheme accrued primarily to the stronger member (Kenya) of the union; and the lack of political will by national leaders. In tune with its commitment to national liberation in Southern Africa, Tanzania joined the Southern African Coordination Conference in 1980 and is now a member of its successor body, the SADC. However, the demise of nationalist positions and the realization of the need to jointly tackle the problem of economic survival in a competitive international climate led to the revival of the idea of an East African Community. On November 22, 1991, therefore, a presidential summit of all three heads of state helped to revive regional cooperation. This led to the establishment of a permanent body, the Tripartite Commission, consisting of the finance ministers and a secretariat in 1993, a precursor to the eventual EAC with a population of 82 million relaunched in Arusha at the end of 1999 to promote a common market via a free trade area, a customs union, and the facilitation of the free movement of capital and labor. So far the EAC has achieved a number of objectives, including the issuing of a common East African passport, allowing for the free convertibility of currencies, and the simultaneous presentation of annual budgets to the Community's respective parliaments (a first step in harmonizing fiscal and monetary policies and having a common budget with the aim of establishing common institutions such as a common parliament, court, and trade council). On the security front, the emphasis has been placed on joint military exercises, meetings of the police, and a commitment to resolve conflicts by peaceful means (Nyakwaka 2000, 7, 8, 10). As such, the EAC hopes to overcome the problems identified in the demise of its predecessor, the most important of which were the uneven distribution of benefits of integration; institutional difficulties, which are expected to be overcome by putting in place conflict-resolution mechanisms (which the original EAC did not have); political and ideological differences (which are of lesser issue in countries that, in terms of their own development perspectives, are now outward rather than inward looking); and continued dependence of member countries on the economies of the developed countries. The latter issue is expected to be resolved as the community becomes economically more mature and provides members with more benefits (Martin 1992, 83; Nyakwaka 2000, 10). In addition, there are problems of the EAC treaty's compatibility with the WTO and the negotiations between Europe and the ACP states on a successor treaty to that of the several Lomé agreements (i.e., Lomé I, II, III, IV, V), as well as the extent to which Tanzania is committed to the community, considering the fact that the country is also a member of the bigger and economically more viable SADC. Recently, Uganda has indicated its intention to seek membership in the SADC—this could become another problem for the EAC (Achieng 1999, 1–2).

The Intergovernmental Authority on Development

The Intergovernmental Authority on Development (IGAD)[9] was created in 1986 in response to the humanitarian-cum-ecological challenges faced by the Horn of Africa as it experienced desertification, periodic drought, and conflict. Djibouti, Kenya, Ethiopia, Somalia, Sudan, Uganda and Eritrea are members. The organization currently has a population of about 117 million people. When relaunching the institution in 1996, the IGAD Council of Ministers identified three priority areas of cooperation, including conflict prevention, and management and resolution and humanitarian affairs, infrastructure development and food security, and the protection of the environment. In trying to foster regional security and development, the organization, whose secretariat serves as a regional contact point or forum for discussing issues such as food security, environmental protection, natural resource management, economic cooperation and conflict management, is empowered to implement decisions taken during such discussions (USGS 1999, 1). Its role in confidence-building measures has been effective in managing and resolving conflict, especially within Sudan, but also with respect to Somalia. Issues in the past have included a hierarchical, top-down administrative structure, a lack of political space for civil society and donor communities to participate in the design and implementation of policy (Sorensen 1995, 257), the progressive erosion of "positive sovereignty" in the region, the conflict between Ethiopia and Eritrea (whose tensions have affected the functioning of the organization), the collapsed state in Somalia, and the prevalence of nonstate actors with national, regional, continental, and global interests. These issues add to the complexity of the organization's attempts at conflict resolution (Adar 2000, 42).

CHALLENGES FOR REGIONALISM

The dream of a continent without poverty, disease, and ignorance remains just that—a dream. Such a dream still needs to be concretized and made a reality. Regional cooperation remains one viable way through which Africans can improve economic conditions on the continent and generate the resources needed to deal effectively with poverty, disease, and ignorance. Unfortunately, even as the coutinent begins life in the 21st century, competing views remain on regional integration and there does not seem to be agreement on how best to tackle the continent's enormous development problems or what to do right away in the area of regional integration. Mu'ammar al-Qadhafi of Libya argues for immediate political unity, which he believes would create the appropriate environment for economic development. The Abuja Treaty, on the other hand, aims at promoting processes of economic cooperation that advance regional development before there can be any consideration of political unity. On the issue of development itself, while there is broad agreement on what needs to be addressed, it is not clear what emphasis should be placed on the one as opposed to the other. Related to the issues of debt forgiveness, compensation for colonialism, the nature and volume of aid, trade concessions, and the planning of the proper interface between a globalizing world economy and Africa is the issue of how the continent ought to relate to the industrial world. There are questions regarding to what extent Africa should engage in alliances with the developed North and with whom any cooperation agreements should be entered into. For example, what state and nonstate actors should Africa be involved with as it seeks to improve its participation in both global affairs and the global economy, especially in this new era of rapid globalization? As stated by South African president Thabo Mbeki (1999, 7; 1998, 1), "[t]he challenge we have to meet is to develop our own sovereign continental capacity to participate in the global processes . . . to promote our own interests," which include supporting a strong rules-based international system that can protect Africa against the market, which is a cannibal that feeds on "its most robust children." Presidents Mbeki, Obasanjo, and Bouteflika's Millennium Plan, adopted as the New African Initiative (NAI) by the OAU in 2001, is meant to put forth the strategies for a new, more substantive phase of African engagement and development and further the development of an African Economic Community. However, difficulties in meeting Western conditionalities with respect to "good governance" so that additional resources could be secured to finance critical development projects may lead to a postponement of the NAI. While such uncertainty amongst states and donors is likely to frustrate African development efforts, it may also encourage regionalist endeavors and the need for African countries to seek greater levels of cooperation with each other on poverty alleviation in particular and development in general.

Regionalism should help to stabilize Africa to the point where further spontaneous transregional development is able to take place. Some regional organizations hold out the promise of this while others exist for other reasons: to project power, prestige, and support for vested interests, something that is particularly true for the Anglophone–Francophone divide (Soederbaum, Schulz, and Oejendal 1998, 16), which sustains somewhat anomalous divisions (say, in the context of monetary integration in West Africa). After all, true regionalism should be able to hold out the scope for collective Southern action, reduce one's vulnerability to linkages with the North, and offer protection against dominant regional as well as global players (Ravenhill 1985, 206).

What the continent needs is a common language to push all regional efforts in a direction that is of benefit to the continent as a whole and serves the long-term goal of continental unity. South Africa's proposal for an African Renaissance is an attempt to find a common language or vision by which to identify development priorities at this historical juncture (Vale and Maseko 1998). What encourages this are the opportunities presented by the technological developments in the service sector—notably in the areas of health, education, commerce, and tourism—which can generate postindustrial growth without the need for industrialization. To make use of these opportunities there is a need for an appropriate institutional framework in areas such as the creation of common currencies, a reduction in the number of regional integration arrangements, the toleration of free markets, and donor recognition of regions rather than countries (Mistry 2000, 567). Regional organizations remain building blocks in all of this, but in order to work they do need to be able to count on stable states pursuing constant policies and forego short-term for longer-term goals. Strategic engagement with global role players (as seen in and around the African Millennium Plan proposed by the troika of Mbeki, Obasanjo and Bouteflika in 2000) as sources of know-how, investment, and political support is another building block. An All African Forum with the ability to enforce peace, support democracy, and promote an environment conducive to regional growth is a third platform.

In the meantime, probably because of the continued persistence of a vulnerable state at a subregional level, the political and economic fruits of integration remain all too modest. Integration remains extensive rather than intensive, and national concerns remain more important than regional ones. Yet "regional cooperation as being advocated in the 21st century (for) Africa . . . is that which goes beyond the narrow confines of trade integration to include regional infrastructural development, liberalization of labor and capital flows and [the] harmonization of politics" (Nwonwu 2000, 25).

The study of regionalism (see, e.g., Hettne and Soederbaum 1998) suggests that if states can only half-heartedly promote regional togetherness, nonstate actors working from below should be given the scope to integrate across a region. As argued by Notshulwana (2000, 171), "[p]ressure for institutional change should also come from the proliferating array of new regional and global actors and increasingly vociferous non-establishment domestic elites who are elbowing their way into the national and regional integration debate." The social constructivists say that reality is the product of individuals and their imaginations. The more people interact with each other in a regional context, the more they will be able to change the perceptions of each other and through enquiry and debate make friends out of former enemies. Karl Deutsch's transactionalism (Taylor 1993) implies that greater levels of interaction generate reciprocity, new forms of trust, and collective identities. As such, with such interaction and greater regional understanding and consciousness about each other, regional integration stands the best chance of becoming a lived reality, institutionalized and permanent. Regional integration ought to flow from the bottom upward.

What evidence is there for bottom-up regionalism in Africa? Is it in any way able to create greater cooperation between and among states? This would seem to depend on the degree of regionalization and also, to some extent, that of democratization. If one looks at West Africa and Southern Africa, the degree of regionalization depends largely on the rise of market forces (Soederbaum, Schulz, and Oejendal 1998, 8–9). This would of itself leave little room for civil society actors. Accommodation to market forces on a regional scale ideally ought, however, to be accompanied by degrees of greater political openness toward a common regional center, which allows for the activities of inter- and transregional society actors. The growth in the institution of election monitoring is a case in point, as are regional parliamentary bodies, trade union gatherings, issue groups, and those of academics and specialists. But, as stated in reference to the regional conferences on national human rights institutions, "while regional interactions serve as a useful opportunity to exchange ideas, it is important that these meetings do not become pro forma gatherings where weak human rights institutions can gain legitimacy through their attendance without being pushed to account for their activities" (Human Rights Watch 2001, 2).

Creating an enabling environment for civic society may need much more and encompass the reconstitution of democratic states on the basis of the recognition of equality, where "the economic, social and cultural rights of all communities are recognized on the principle of autonomy for all groups that desire it" (Nabudere 2000, 20). Regionalism, the effort undertaken by both state and nonstate actors to establish relationships across a particular geographic expanse, combined with federal and confederal solutions, may well awaken a new sense of developmental coherence. It constitutes one possible emerging source of order in Africa (Blaauw and Bischoff 2001, 53).

The conditions of integration revolve around politically relevant elites identifying and agreeing on what constitute common values to allow mutual forms of responsiveness to happen on an ongoing basis in a way that institutionalizes interaction and cooperative behavior across a region over time. Identifying these values without prompting from donors, conditionalities attached to aid and trade is a challenge. As such, the aim must be some form of "autocentric regionalism" as opposed to "dependent regionalism" (Onwuka 1991, 41). The best route would seem to be for states and their elites to allow themselves to be pushed from below by articulate, voluntary groups that have congruent or complementary interests across a region and engage in regional solidarity (Plano and Riggs 1967, 518). For instance, the rebirth of associations in sub-Saharan Africa is resulting in new forms of cooperative development: grassroots practices that challenge Western systems of development, especially those that include the "logic of violence and exclusion in the ethos that the West is seeking to impose on the whole of the planet" (Ela 1998, 4). However, such groups also need conditions of security and peace as well as democratic freedom: As Asante (1997, 173) has stated, "African countries must open up to ensure the full participation of all sections of their societies in a process of developmental regionalism." Regions that uphold and, if need be, enforce broad democratic principles and rights of self-determination fulfil the first essential step toward building sustainable regions with recognizable ideas and interactions that are understood and supported by all layers of any emergent regional society. Successful regional organizations are those that encourage and respond to regionalism or rapid economic change, domestic political demands, and changing paradigms of knowledge (Kahler 1995, viii). All people, in full recognition of their human worth and dignity, ought, after all, to be central to regional cooperation and region building.

NOTES

1. The subregions formally recognized by the AEC as regional economic communities include ECOWAS, ECCAS, COMESA, and the SADC, with IGAD and the AMU developing links. The Abuja Treaty, in Article 28, encourages the establishment of economic communities where these do not as yet exist.

2. The ECA, through its five subregional development centers, works closely with Regional Economic Communities in fostering cooperation and integration.

3. For example, in the first eight months of 2000 at least 1.5 million people in Africa fled their homes because of war, violence, and repression.

4. In Southern Africa the Swazi trade union movement and party political opposition to the absolutist monarchy in Swaziland has on occasion in the 1990s relied on solidarity action from the SA trade union movement under the Congress of South African Trade Unions and the South African Communist Party to embargo traffic to and from the kingdom. This is in order to pressure Swaziland into constitutional reform that would allow for a parliamentary democracy based on a multiparty system. Similarly, organized gay groups in Zimbabwe have drawn support from similarly aligned forces in South Africa in order to highlight socially discriminatory legislation on homosexuality in Zimbabwe.

5. Asante (2000, 9, 11) finds that "officials of the RECs have not been as cooperative with the OAU/AEC secretariat as could be expected. . . . There are lingering doubts about the positive benefits RECs can expect from the AEC in the implementation of its mandate to 'strengthen regional economic communities.' . . . It is not clear that the RECs have the long-term continental Sintegration in view. . . . There is, as yet, no firm indication of the political will within some of the REC's party to the Protocol to submit regional concerns to the overriding concerns of the AEC."

6. In the case of multiple membership in COMESA and the SADC, for instance, this is used as a possible counterfoil to the economic predominance of the South African giant and has little to do with purely developmental considerations. Accession to membership in the SADC by the DRC was equally driven by political rather than developmental considerations.

7. This was clearly demonstrated at the Windhoek summit of the SADC in March 2001, when South Africa's efforts at rationalizing and strengthening the organization were opposed by SADC smaller members.

8. Thus, the DRC's choice to negotiate with the EU not through the SADC but through ECCA, for instance, seems to have been guided by political considerations rather than trade issues. One of the aims seems to have been to show South Africa and Botswana that their refusal to come out more openly against Rwanda's and Uganda's military interventions in the DRC from 1998 had, in this way, to be "punished" (*Business Day*, March 7, 2001).

9. Initially it was the Intergovernmental Authority on Drought and Desertification.

REFERENCES

Achieng, J. 1999. Regional integration under fire. World News (Inter-Press Service), February 11. Retrieved from www.oneworld.org/ips2/feb99/16_41_58.html.

Adar, K. G. 2000. Conflict resolution in a turbulent region: The case of IGAD in Sudan. *African Journal on Conflict Resolution* 1/2: 39–66.

Asante, S.K.B. 1997. *Regionalism and Africa's development*. London: Macmillan.

Asante, S.K.B. 2000. Towards an African economic community. Paper presented at the fortieth anniversary conference of the Africa Institute, Pretoria.

Bischoff, P.-H. 2001. How far, where to? Regionalism, Southern African Development Community and decision-making into the millennium. In *African foreign policy-making*, edited by K. Adar and R. Ajulu. Aldershot, UK: Ashgate.

Blaauw, L., and P.-H. Bischoff. 2001. Directing our future? Regionalism and SADC in Southern Africa. *Africa Insight* 30 (3): 51–57.

Calvert, P. 1986. *The foreign policy of new states*. Brighton, UK: Wheatsheaf.

Clapham, C. 1996. *Africa and the international system: The politics of state survival*. Cambridge: Cambridge University Press.

Ela, J. M. 1998. Looking to a new Africa. *Le Monde Diplomatique* (English Online Edition), October: http://MondeDiplo.com/.

Gamble, A., and A. Payne, eds. 1996. *Regionalism and world order*. New York: St. Martin's Press.

Harlow, J. 1997. *Regional cooperation and integration with industry and trade in Southern Africa*. Aldershot, UK: Avebury.

Hettne, B., and F. Soederbaum. 1998. The new regionalism approach. *Politeia* 17 (3): 6–21.

Human Rights Watch. 2001. Protectors or pretenders? Government human rights commissions in Africa. Retrieved from www.hrw.org/hrw/reports/2001.

Hurrell, A. 1995. Explaining the resurgence of regionalism in world politics. *Review of International Studies* 21 (3): 331–358.

Jackson, R. H., and C. G. Rosenberg. 1986. Why Africa's weak states persist. In *The state and development in the Third World*, edited by A. Kohli. Princeton, NJ: Princeton University Press.

Kahler, M. 1995. *International institutions and the political economy of integration*. Washington, DC: Brookings Institution.

Khalil, N., and D. Ezzat. 2000. The quest for integration. *Al Ahram Weekly* (Online) 471 (March 2–8). Retrieved from http://weekly.ahram.org.eg/.

Lambrechts, K. 1997. The regional and the global in an emerging order. *Global Dialogue* 2 (3): 2.

Laporte, L. 1993. Regional cooperation and integration in Africa. Paper presented at the First Open Forum, Maastricht, April 20.

Lipalile, M. 2000. Globalization, regional integration and development in Southern Africa. Paper presented at the fortieth anniversary conference of the Africa Institute, Pretoria.

Martin, G. 1992. Africa regional cooperation and integration. In *21st century Africa*, edited by A. Seidman and F. Anang. Trenton, NJ: Africa World Press.

Mazzeo, D., ed. 1984. *Africa regional organizations*. Cambridge: Cambridge University Press.

Mbeki, T. 1998. Statement of the deputy president of the Republic of South Africa at the XII Summit of the Heads of State and Government of the countries of the Non-Aligned Movement, Durban, South Africa.

Mbeki, T. 1999. Statement of the president of South Africa, Thabo Mbeki, at the thirty-fifth Ordinary Session of the OAU Assembly of Heads of State and Government, Algiers, Algeria, July.

Mistry, P. S. 2000. Africa's record of regional cooperation and integration. *African Affairs* 99: 553–573.

Nabudere, D. W. 2000. African unity in historical perspective. Keynote address delivered at the fortieth anniversary conference of the Africa Institute, Pretoria, South Africa.

Notshulwana, M. 2000. The political economy of regional integration in Southern Africa. In *The political economy of peace and security in Africa*, edited by L. A. Jinadu. Harare, Zimbabwe: AAPS Books.

Nwonwu, F.O.C. 2000. The formation of an African economic community: Problems and prospects. Paper presented at the fortieth anniversary conference of the Africa Institute, Pretoria, South Africa.

Nyakwaka, D. 2000. Globalization and regional integration: The case of the East African Community. Paper presented at the fortieth anniversary conference of the Africa Institute, Pretoria, South Africa.

OAU. 1981. *The Lagos plan of action for the economic development of Africa 1980–2000*. Geneva: International Institute for Labor Studies.

Onwuka, R. I. 1991. *The anguish of dependent regionalism*. Ile-Ife, Nigeria: Obafemi Awolowo University Press.

Plano, J., and R. Riggs. 1997. *Forging world order*. New York: Macmillan.

Ramutsindela, M. 2000. De-territorialization and the African super-state. Paper presented at the fortieth anniversary conference of the Africa Institute, Pretoria, South Africa.

Ravenhill, J. 1985. *The future of regionalism in Africa*. London: Macmillan.

Seidman, A., and F. Anang. 1992. *21st century Africa*. Trenton, NJ: Africa World Press.

Seymour, V. 1997. Regional integration: Can SADC deliver? *The Reporter*, September 5–11.

Sorensen, J. 1995. *Disaster and development in the Horn of Africa*. Basingstoke, UK: Macmillan.

Smith, M. 1997. Regions and regionalism. In *Issues in world politics*, edited by B. White, R. Little, and M. Smith. Basingstoke, UK: Macmillan.

Soederbaum, F., M. Schulz, and J. Oejendal. 1998. Comparative regionalism: The case of Africa and Asia. Paper presented at the Third Pan-European International Relations Conference, Vienna, September 16–19.

Taylor, T. 1993. *International organization in the modern world: The regional and global process*. London: Pinter.

USGS. 1999. *IGAD and the IGAD Secretariat.* Washington, DC: U.S. Department of the Interior.

Vale, P., and S. Maseko. 1998. South Africa and the African renaissance. *International Affairs* 74 (2): 9–22.

Zacarias, A. 1999. *Security and the state in Southern Africa.* London: Tauris Academic Studies.

Yoroms, J. G. 2000. Mechanisms for conflict management in ECOWAS. Occasional Paper No. 8/99, ACCORD, Durban, South Africa.

6

The New East African Community: A Defense and Security Organ as the Missing Link

P. GODFREY OKOTH

In 1991 the Soviet Union disintegrated, signaling the end of the Cold War and the subsequent cessation of superpower rivalry (see, e.g., Hyland 1990; Garthoff 1994). In place of the bipolar superpower rivalry that dominated global affairs from 1945 to 1991, emerged several regionally based arrangements designed to ensure the peaceful coexistence of groups and nationalities and enhance sustainable development. Unfortunately, these new post–Cold War regional security and development schemes lack a worldview and do not have the proper structures to enhance their ability to cooperate for the mutual benefit of their constituents. As a consequence, unhealthy competition and confrontation seem to be on the rise, resulting in significant levels of insecurity among many nations and regions around the world. The security of human collectivities is affected by military, economic, political, societal, and environmental factors. Military security concerns the two-level interplay of the armed offensive and defensive capabilities of states and their perceptions of each others' intentions. Political security deals with the organizational ability of states, as well as systems of government and ideologies that give them legitimacy. Economic security encompasses such things as adequate access to resources, finance, and markets necessary to sustain acceptable levels of welfare and state power. Societal security concerns the sustainability within acceptable conditions for the evolution of traditional patterns of language, culture, religion, national identity, and customs. Environmental security deals with the maintenance of the local regional and planetary biosphere as the essential support system on which all the other human enterprises depend (see, e.g., Buzan 1991, 19–20).

These five security sectors do not operate in isolation. Instead, within a given polity there is usually cooperation between these sectors to provide the people with a safe environment to maximize individual as well as societal interests and objectives. The better integrated these systems are, the more effective they are in delivering benefits to the people. To create an environment conducive to development, a framework must be instituted to ensure that those whose job it is to provide society with security do not abuse their positions and engage in opportunistic behaviors (e.g., coups d'état by military officers) for their own benefit. For example, armed forces that are subordinate to civilian and constitutional control are more likely to serve the interests of the nation than those of their leaders. As a consequence, it is necessary that all security agencies within a nation be adequately constrained by the law so as to minimize opportunism by their leaders and ensure that they serve national objectives and not those of some interest groups within or without the polity.

Presently, African countries are engaged in institutional reforms to provide themselves with democratic governance structures, those that enhance popular participation in both governance and the economy. It is critical that each nation also provides itself with professional and constitutionally well-constrained security systems so as to create an environment that enhances peaceful coexistence and productive use of scarce resources and improves the country's ability to participate gainfully in global affairs. Unfortunately, many African countries may not be able to provide themselves with the security systems that they need as a result of resource constraints. As a consequence, it may be necessary for them to form regional security agencies that allow them to more efficiently and effectively exploit economies of scale in the provision of these services. This chapter examines the new East African Community and attempts to provide a justification for the establishment of a new defense and security organ for the subregion.

During the Cold War, Western interest in Africa was determined by geopolitical considerations. The latter centered primarily around what role Africa could play in the struggle between the United States and its Western allies, on the one hand, and the Soviet Union and its satellite states, on the other, for control of global affairs. Thus, as Soviet interest in Africa increased, so did that of the United States and its allies (see, e.g., Clough 1992; Schraeder 1996). When the Soviet Union disintegrated in 1991, bringing the Cold War to an end, superpower rivalry ceased and Africa became virtually irrelevant to the geopolitical interests of the Western countries. As a result of the significantly altered international environment, Western strategic interest in Africa has fallen significantly, and today the West views the continent simply as a region littered with (1) poorly governed countries with ill-managed economies and (2) societies consumed by severe ethnic, racial, religious, and class conflicts (Baker 1991–1993, 139–152).

Many African countries have reacted to the end of the Cold War by abandoning the old tactics of playing each superpower against the other in an effort to maximize foreign development and military aid. In some parts of the continent there has been an increased and renewed interest in the formation of regional intergovernmental organizations to promote economic development and political solidarity. The emergence, among many countries in the continent, of a strong desire to promote regional cooperation is a clear reaction to the realities of the end of the Cold War and the subsequent demise of superpower rivalry.

Since the end of the Cold War, many countries around the world have rediscovered the importance of regionalism, especially to small and often nonviable domestic economies. Many of these countries hope that regional integration would expand the size of domestic markets and enhance their ability to more effectively exploit technological economies of scale and in the process allow them to participate more effectively in the new global economy. In recent years, many countries in Africa have joined the economic integration bandwagon and are now actively seeking ways to form regional and subregional integration schemes. Today, many African countries realize that the exploitation of regional as well as subregional interdependencies can provide them with significant economic, social, and political benefits. It has become clear that collective regional activities can give individual states a greater competitive edge and higher bargaining power in international negotiations than would otherwise be the case. At international forums such as the World Trade Organization, African countries are likely to secure greater individual benefits if they negotiate from a regional, as opposed to a national, perspective. One must note, however, that regional and subregional integration is only part of the overall effort to transform African economies and make them more efficient and relevant to the lives of the people. For many countries in the region, the most important priorities are (1) poverty elimination, (2) food security, (3) equitable allocation of resources, (4) sustainability of the ecosystem, (5) HIV/AIDS prevention, and (6) peaceful coexistence. Thus, regional integration is only part of the overall process to transform economic structures and enhance the ability of each country to improve the welfare of the people.

Subregional integration provides the foundation for greater levels of integration in an effort for countries, especially those located in the same geographic area, to pursue common economic, social, and political goals. The desire to have a subregional body has been fostered in East Africa by Tanzania, Kenya, and Uganda, three countries that are located in the same geographic area. On November 30, 1999, these three countries signed the treaty reestablishing the East African Community. Ratification of the treaty establishing the new EAC required that member states put into effect all the parts of the treaty that they are party to (see, e.g., *The Treaty for the Establishment of the East African Community*, Arusha, Tanzania, November 30, 1999). The old EAC disintegrated in 1977 as a result of, among other things, disagreements between the leaders of Tanzania (Julius Nyerere) and Uganda (Idi Amin) and the claim by both Tanzania and Uganda that most of the benefits of the scheme had accrued primarily to Kenya, which had the strongest economy in the union (see, e.g., Mbaku 1997, 33–60).

However, as the new EAC becomes operational there seems to be several problems that must be dealt with by member states. The most important of them is the absence of a fully functioning policing and security apparatus, one that can adequately and effectively police the treaty and make sure that its provisions are being carried out as intended. Whenever a group of individuals sign an agreement to cooperate for their mutual benefit, there is always the possibility that some of the members would attempt to cheat in an effort to secure, for themselves, benefits above and beyond what they would have received had they cooperated. Thus, postcontractual compliance is an important issue that all participants in any contractual scheme must be worried about. In addition to providing the integration scheme with an appropriate and fully functioning policing organ, it is also necessary that a defense structure be provided that can effectively protect members from external aggression as well as deal with internal conflicts that threaten the security of the Community. In the following sections we will attempt to critically assess the failure by the EAC Treaty to give consideration for a defense and security organ. In addition, we also examine other subregional integration schemes that were originally designed to foster economic cooperation but have since included security issues in their agendas. These include the Economic Community of West African States and the Southern African Development Community.

THE EAST AFRICAN COMMUNITY

The desire to cooperate in matters of trade and industry in East Africa dates back to 1900, when Uganda entered into a trade agreement with the port city of Mombasa (in Kenya). The latter was to serve as a center for the collection of customs duties on goods imported into Uganda. Increased economic cooperation between Uganda and Kenya came in 1905 with the formation of the East African Currency Board and a postal union for the two colonies (Delupis 1970, 21; Adar and Ngunyi 1994, 395–425). The former German colony of Tanganyika joined the postal union in 1923 after it became a League of Nations mandate under British administration. Mutually beneficial arrangements continued to develop among these three colonies, and in 1948 the East African High Commission (EAHC) was formed and consisted of the governors of Kenya, Tanzania, and Uganda. The EAHC had two main organs, the High Commission and the Legislative Assembly. The High Commission was given the power to make laws based on advice provided by the legislatures of each territory (Delupis 1970, 21).

Today's East African Community closely reflects the Nairobi Declaration of 1963, which was supposed to provide the three British colonies a framework for political and economic integration. The idea of a political federation for the three territories was rejected. However, in 1967 the three countries signed a treaty dealing primarily with economic cooperation. That treaty established the East African Community between Tanzania, Uganda, and Kenya. Like the present EAC, the one established in 1967 pursued primarily economic issues (see *The Treaty for East African Cooperation*, Nairobi, Kenya, 1967). It provided the formation of a common market that would strengthen and regulate the industrial, commercial, and other relations of partner states. The treaty also provided for the eventual integration of the economies of the three countries to form a single market with no barriers to the movement of goods and services. Unfortunately, as already mentioned, the cooperation arrangement between the three countries collapsed in 1977. To reiterate, the collapse was blamed on (1) disagreements between the political leaders of the countries involved, especially between Nyerere of Tanzania and Amin of Uganda; (2) differences in the levels of development of member states—Kenya, with the most developed and industrialized economy, was accused by the other members of extracting the most benefits from the arrangement; (3) changes in the political economy of the region, especially the military coup that brought Idi Amin to power in Uganda and the subsequent political turmoil that eventually enveloped the country; and (4) lack of political commitment by the leaders of member states (Mbaku 1997, 33–60).

The idea for the new EAC was hatched on May 4, 1984, when officials from the three countries met to dispose of the assets of the defunct EAC. Heads of state of the three countries—Uganda, Kenya and Tanzania—were interested in developing a framework to increase and improve cooperation among their citizens. A working program was recommended on November 22, 1991. This led to the establishment of the Permanent Tripartite Commission (PTC), which was confirmed by the three states on November 30, 1993. The PTC was charged with the responsibility of identifying areas for cooperation and suggesting the modalities to implement them. The commission subsequently recommended that cooperative agreements be developed in economic, immigration, political, legal, judiciary, and security areas. Later, in November 1994, a permanent secretariat was created to begin work on developing the treaty for the establishment of the new EAC. Such a treaty was signed on November 30, 1999, establishing the new Community.

THE SUPPORTING PARADIGM OF THE EAC

In order for member states to benefit from the cooperation scheme made possible by the EAC, there must be peace in the region. As a consequence, there is a need for some form of security apparatus. Of course, one can argue that there already is enough security, considering the fact that each member country has its own army, police force, and other paramilitary units. Could not these agencies provide the security for the new union? In other words, could not these national agencies cooperate in ensuring security at the Community level? National security agencies are concerned, as they should be, primarily with issues that affect the nation. They must respond to the needs of the people in the political jurisdiction of which they are a part and hence are not equipped to or capable of dealing effectively with issues of a regional or subregional level. In other words, national security organizations are not structured to deal with security at the regional level. There is a need to redefine subregional security away from the traditional preoccupation with state security. Unlike several researchers (e.g., Carr 1939; Morgenthau 1995) who argue that nation-states are the primary actors in international politics and thus adopt a traditional security paradigm that privileges the state and its security agents, we seek a wider perspective of looking at subregional security, one that includes both military and non-military threats to the liberty of individuals within a nation or region. Thus, we include in our working definition of security threats such things as poverty, hunger, food insecurity, lack of clean water, environmental degradation, severe inequalities in the distribution of resources, inadequate access to health care, bad governance, and HIV/AIDS and other pandemics. In other words, military security is just one of several dimensions of the overall concept of security. Although these things are mentioned in the EAC treaty, it is important to emphasize them. Regarding governance, there is a need to make certain that the people are provided the facilities to participate fully and effectively in policy design and implementation: in other words, popular participation is maximized.

The EAC treaty declares that the new integration agreement will seek to promote economic, political, and social development and do so in a way that preserves the environment. In other words, development will be undertaken in such a way as to ensure sustainability of resource exploitation. In addition, the treaty encourages popular participation in the new community's decision-making structures (see *The Treaty for the Establishment of the East African Community*, Articles 6, 7). However, there is a need to have a communitywide security apparatus, one that will make certain that the Community's programs are implemented in each member state as envisaged and not hijacked by opportunistic interest groups and used for their own benefit. It is important to consider the fact that national governments may be unable to bring under their control regional movements, many of which have become quite sophisticated and are using new technologies to bypass local constraints and avoid being subjected to local laws and institutions. Thus, to make certain that EAC policies and programs are implemented in a uniform manner throughout the Community, one cannot depend on local governments alone, especially given the fact that some of them may not have the resources to perform the job effectively. It is necessary to develop transnational (i.e., regional) security agencies that can supplement the work of the local police and other security groups and thus enhance the implementation and proper functioning of the Community's development programs.

THE INSTITUTIONS AND ORGANS OF THE EAC

To help the new EAC carry out its mission, the treaty makes allowance for the creation of several agencies, as elaborated in Chapter 3, Article 9 of the treaty. Seven substantive organs are provided: (1) the Summit, (2) the Council, (3) the Coordination Committee, (4) the Sectional Committee, (5) the East African Court of Justice, (6) the East African Legislative Assembly, and (7) the Secretariat. Although the core organs for the new Community have been provided by the treaty, the authority to bring into existence other organs that the Community feels are needed to improve its ability to advance peace and development in the region does not appear to have been included in the organization's charter.

As defined by the treaty, the actual functioning of these organs may create problems for the Community. For example, Article 11 (5) authorizes the Summit to delegate the exercise of its functions, subject to any conditions that it sees fit to impose, to a member state, to the Council, or to the Secretary General. One can interpret this article of the treaty to imply that upon approval from the Summit, a member state can actually interfere in the internal affairs of another country. In fact, there is already a conflict associated with this particular article, as evidenced by Uganda's insistence that the matter of the religious cult called the Lord's Resistance Army (LRA), whose activities have resulted in the deaths of many people, is an internal affair that is not subject to intervention by member states of the union. Unfortunately, the LRA affair and many other conflicts in Northern Uganda have had a significant impact on economic, political, and social activities in the region. Thus, the inability of the EAC to intervene and resolve these issues is negatively affecting the ability of the cooperation scheme to achieve its objectives as stipulated in the treaty.

What is missing in the treaty that authorized the formation of the EAC is a mechanism to achieve some of its objectives. In Article 5 (f), the EAC states its desire to promote peace, security, and stability within and good neighborliness among the partner states. Unfortunately, there does not exist any appropriate framework to coordinate all security issues. It is necessary that an organ be established to coordinate, at the regional level, all matters pertaining to defense and security.

Matters of defense are only mentioned in passing in Article 125. Here, pursuant to Article 5, the EAC vows to cooperate to promote peace, security, and stability within and good neigborliness among partner states. It is the casual treatment of matters of defense that requires clarification. Article 24 (5) provides for cooperation between states in the handling of cross-border crime, as well as the provision of mutual assistance in criminal matters, including the arrest and repatriation of fugitive offenders and the exchange of information on national mechanisms for combating criminal activities. However, there is no information in the treaty on how other countries should respond to the overthrow, by military coup d'état, of the head of state of a member country, or how to deal with the attack of any of the member states by the army of a nonmember state.

The treaty focuses primarily on the areas of cooperation between member states. These include immigration, political cooperation, legal and judicial cooperation, and security, as well as matters concerning trade. While economic cooperation is considered the most important aspect of the EAC, and peace is a necessary condition for such cooperation to take place, no effort is made to elaborate the specific strategies through which the peace would be secured. In fact, the issue of security is only discussed when it is acknowledged that the maintenance of a peaceful and secure political and economic environment is critical for trade, investment, and other activities needed for poverty alleviation. Although it is suggested that an interstate defense and security committee be formed and charged with the job of addressing issues related to criminal activities across borders and overall safety and security in the region, the Community has not been able to provide specific directions on the implementation of such directives. For one thing, such a security agency would be considered illegal, since its formation is not provided for in the treaty.

The critical question on matters of security remains unanswered: Can the EAC carry out viable trade and economic policies without a security and defense organ? Given the many conflicts in the subregion and the fact that most of these conflicts have a direct impact on trade, it is necessary that the new Community deal more effectively with the issue of regional security if it plans to evolve into a viable framework for poverty alleviation, development, and improved governance in East Africa.

THE NEED FOR A DEFENSE AND SECURITY ORGAN IN THE EAST AFRICAN COMMUNITY

It is probably impossible to develop an appropriate security and defense organ for the EAC without taking into consideration the political economy of the Horn of Africa, especially the region's relations with other parts of the world. The three member states of the EAC are part of the Horn of Africa, a subregion that is currently characterized by unstable, undemocratic, and authoritarian regimes. In the last decade there was implosion in Somalia, Kenya's northern neighbor; the Sudan, a neighbor to both Uganda and Kenya, has fought a bitter and bloody civil war for the last several decades; Rwanda imploded in the mid-1990s; Burundi remains quite unstable as destructive mobilization by ethnic groups for resources continues; and Ethiopia was engaged in a bloody conflict that ended in the early 1990s with the secession of Eritrea. Relations between Uganda and Kenya have been strained for many years. Although the citizens of both countries stand to benefit significantly from cooperation, the latter can only occur in an environment characterized by peace. Such an environment, unfortunately, is yet to be established. In fact, cattle rustling remains an important activity on the border between Uganda and Kenya, an activity that has contributed significantly to the deterioration in relations between the two countries. Similarly, the relation between Uganda and its northern neighbor, the Sudan, remains extremely strained. In fact, diplomatic relations between the two countries have been broken for more than six years. Despite the fact that several efforts have been made to restore diplomatic contact between the two states, border skirmishes and Uganda's continued insistence that Sudan is supporting antigovernment rebels in Northern Uganda has made the restoration of diplomatic links virtually impossible. Rebels in the northern part of Uganda remain an important constraint to the activities of the EAC. Of course, it is important to note that rebel activity in northern Uganda is an unfinished part of the civil wars that have been fought in the country since Idi Amin overthrew Milton Obote in 1973. These rebel activities continue to impact negatively on EAC economic and social activities. Given the fact that the government of Uganda has not been able to deal effectively with the destabilizing effects of the rebel activities, it is possible that a regional security force might be able to provide a more effective framework for bringing this group and others like it under control and enhance economic growth and development in the region.

At present, Kenya seems to be the most peaceful of the EAC states. Of course, Kenya has its security problems; however, most of them emanate from its strained relations with its neighbors and the need to deal with hoards of refugees from Somalia and other countries in the region. For many years, Ethiopia and Kenya feuded over the issue of the Oromo Liberation Front (OLF), with Ethiopia accusing Kenya of providing facilities for the OLF to destabilize the Ethiopian regime. Regardless of who is right, during the last several years the border between Ethiopia and Kenya has remained a hotbed of political instability, making cross-border trade virtually impossible. Kenya and Somalia have had their share of problems over the years. Somalia's desire to unite all peoples of Somali origin from throughout the region to form a so-called greater Somali polity has often resulted in the country making claims on territories in Kenya and other neighboring countries inhabited by individuals of Somali ancestry. In many instances the government in Mogadishu has encouraged these so-called sons and daughters of Somalia to secede from their existing polity and join Somalia. As a consequence, Kenya has been forced to maintain a military and security force on its border with Somalia, diverting resources that could be used to increase spending on critical social services or to provide overhead capital for development. In fact, the preoccupation of Kenya and other countries in the region with border security has significantly affected government's ability to direct economic growth and poverty alleviation. It is important, of course, to mention the fact that the continued political instability in such countries as the Sudan, Somalia, and Ethiopia have imposed on Kenya significant numbers of refugees, most of whom have settled in the urban areas. The influx of refugees from Somalia into Kenya, for example, has had a significant impact on the government's ability to provide critical public goods and services, such as education, health care, and water to the urban areas. The new Community must now deal with the continued influx of refugees from such countries as Burundi, Rwanda, Democratic Republic of Congo, Somalia, and the Sudan.

Tanzania, the third member of the EAC, has had its share of problems with neighbors and as a result only reluctantly joined the union. The conflict in the Great Lakes Region has produced a lot of refugees, many of whom have ended up in Tanzania, a country with a very fragile economic base. According to the United Nations High Commissioner for Refugees (UNHCR), more than 400 people arrive at refugee camps in Tanzania every single day. The Tanzanian economy is not equipped to deal effectively with such a large influx of refugees.

In fact, refugee camps in Kigoma, Kasulu, Kibondo, and Ngara are busting at the seams with people. In addition, the town of Arusha is burdened with the job of carrying out the judiciary trials of individuals accused of masterminding the genocide that occurred in Rwanda during the mid-1990s. As if this was not enough, Tanzania faces a lot of internal political problems, including the secessionist movement in Zanzibar. The political crisis in Zanzibar and the continued influx of refugees from the Great Lakes Region are problems that have consumed Tanzanian policy makers during a significant part of the last several years and continue to do so now. It is important, then, that any attempt to form a viable integration scheme between these three countries must take into consideration the complex problems that each country faces and how they impact their relationships with their neighbors (see, e.g., Mwagiru 1996).

INTERNATIONAL SECURITY ISSUES

Apart from the clearly discernible differences in relationships between the partner states of the EAC, as well as the Community and its neighbors, there are many other factors that in part affect the way the Community should project itself in global affairs. For one thing, in its global activities the Community must seek to produce benefits for all member countries and not place any one of them at a competitive disadvantage. Thus, the foreign policy of the EAC must take into consideration such things as nationality, religious and social factors, and other issues unique to member countries. Whatever security organ the Community chooses, it must be one that is sensitive to national issues and thus performs its job in a manner that respects such sensitivities. For example, a regional armed force must respect religious sensitivities in its choice of a menu, socialization policies, and other activities that impact on the effectiveness of the unit. Basically, regional institutions must function in such a way as to maximize not only regional objectives but those of the member countries; otherwise, some countries will be forced by their citizens to withdraw from the Community.

The new post–Cold War globalization continues to have significant impact on developing countries, including the members of the EAC. Thus, it is critical that the defense and security organ for the EAC be armed with the structures to function effectively within the new global environment. Globalization has significantly reduced the ability of states to control many critical institutions, including the media and many aspects of the national economy. In fact, the Internet has made financial transactions difficult to control by national governments. As a result, borders are now relatively more porous than they were a decade or so ago (Cheru 1997). These developments present many problems for the Community and its institutions, including those devoted to security and peace. First, recent developments in the global political economy have rendered many regional and national borders virtually irrelevant. Such developments have, in turn, significantly undermined state or subregional authority and power. A framework must be put in place to make sure that globalization does not have a significantly negative impact on the Community. In other words, it is necessary that the Community find ways to enhance the ability of its member countries to participate in a more gainful way in the new globalization (Gondwe 1999).

The Community is also likely to be challenged by the rapid changes in information technology (IT). The possibility that state or Community secrets might be accessed by unauthorized personnel requires that frameworks be designed to ensure security. In fact, developments in IT, especially in such areas as the Internet, pose many problems for nations and subregional organizations. From a national perspective, for example, the ability of governments to control public discourse, especially on issues considered too sensitive for open discussion, is significantly constrained by the existence of the Internet and e-mail facilities. An opportunity now exists for individuals denied political discussions within their own societies to engage in such discourse through the Internet. Thus, individuals, groups, and organizations have the opportunity to make significant impacts on national as well as regional politics through the new information technology (Gerger 1998, 402–408).

While the new information technology may make it easier for more people to participate in governance, it may also prove to be a problem for law enforcement. For example, acts of sabotage committed on national or regional institutions through the Internet may be difficult to prosecute, especially by security forces with very limited resources. A disgruntled individual with the technical skills and access to the Internet can sabotage communication structures in the Community from any part of the world. Thus, the EAC and its many organs, including the Secretariat, Summit, and Council, remain vulnerable to such attacks and, as a result, the Community's security organ must acquire the wherewithal to deal effectively with these threats. Of course, it may become necessary for such a security organ to assist national governments in protecting vital information from any saboteurs.

OVERLAPPING SECURITY ISSUES

An important function of the new EAC is to make sure that it provides security for the subregion. Unless that is done, it is unlikely that the new economic arrangement will produce benefits for its members. In order for the Community to adequately and effectively provide the necessary security for its members, it must carefully examine the factors that inform security. Such an examination should reveal a number of overlapping security issues. First, the East African states that comprise the Community currently have their own national armies, which differ in strength, training, professionalism, and ability to respond to provocation by an external force. The present Ugandan army is considered by many as not really a national army but what had been the National Resistance Army (NRA), a guerilla movement led by the country's incumbent president. Formed as a liberation force, the unit appears to favor such struggles as evidenced by its continued involvement in the Democratic Republic of Congo. Today, the country's army continues to be seen as primarily President Y. K. Museveni's personal security outfit, despite the claim by its leaders that it is Uganda's national army.

Although the militaries of Tanzania and Kenya exhibit significant levels of professionalism, they continue to use highly outdated and obsolete technologies, and hence are not likely to perform effectively in case of a strong external threat. Second, poverty is a major security problem in the region. Given the fact that most of the economies of the member countries have, during the last several decades, been unable to achieve the kinds of economic growth that would have provided them with enough resources to deal effectively with domestic poverty, the latter remains an important problem as the quality of life for most citizens continues to deteriorate. The quality of life for citizens of the EAC remains significantly lower than that of most regions of the world (see, e.g., UNDP 2000). Third, environmental degradation is an important security problem. The Community must design and implement policy to (1) improve land use in order to ensure sustainability of this critical resource, (2) improve water collection and utilization, (3) make certain that critical natural resources such as Lake Victoria, are exploited in a sustainable manner, (4) improve the management of arid and semiarid areas, and (5) generally minimize ecosystem degradation and ensure sustainability of the subregion's natural resources.

Of course, there are security problems unique to each state that are likely to have a significant impact on the functioning of the Community. In fact, many internal security problems often cross borders and become conflicts in other countries. Cross-border cattle thefts during the last several years have caused a lot of security problems for Kenya and Uganda and the ensuing violence has had a significantly negative impact on legitimate economic activities. Thus, the internationalization of internal security problems must be addressed in an enlarged, active, and fully functioning defense and security organ.

An important function of a Community security agency is to effectively handle those security issues that overlap and thus involve more than one country. The Community, then, must put in place a security framework that can adequately guarantee security to all member states and, hence, enhance their ability to engage in trade. Unless such security is guaranteed, Community trade would be severely constrained and very few benefits would be generated for members.

REGIONAL ECONOMIC INTEGRATION

Since the colonial period, regional economic integration has been considered an important way to expand domestic economies and improve the ability of each African territory to engage in economic growth and development. Since the 1960s, Africans have made many attempts to engage in economic integration. Some of these efforts have involved customs and monetary unions, common markets, free trade zones, as well as other trading arrangements. Included among these are the Economic Community of West African States, the Inter-

Governmental Authority on Development, the Southern African Development Community, the Common Market for Eastern and Southern Africa, the *Communauté économique de l'Afrique de l'ouest*, and the *Union douanière et économique de l'Afrique centrale*. Unfortunately, many of these integration schemes have not succeeded in significantly improving trade among members or enhancing their ability to participate in global trade (see, e.g., Mbaku 1997, 33–60; Davenport 1992).

Of interest to us is the fact that many of these trade arrangements did recognize the importance of regional security to trade and subsequently provided each organization with a security apparatus. For example, members of ECOWAS took cognizance of the fact that their region was characterized by several skirmishes, border clashes, and many military coups, all of which had raised political instability in the region to significant levels. ECOWAS decided to create a security organ to deal with the political violence and general insecurity that was affecting trade and other economic activities in the subregion. The process of creating the security framework was a two-step one: First, member states signed a protocol on nonaggression that required them, in part, to refrain from encouraging, committing, or condoning acts of subversion, aggression, and other types of hostilities (Chesoni 1997). They subsequently established the Community Standing Mediation Committee, which in turn founded the ECOWAS Cease-Fire Monitoring Group. The new defense pact was geared toward mutual assistance in the event of aggression by other states within the subregion and the international community. ECOMOG has been deployed on many occasions, including service in Liberia and Sierra Leone. In both conflicts the security organ's primary responsibility was to secure a cease-fire, create a security zone within the country, facilitate the restoration of public services, and pave the way for return to civil control of the government.

Another regional integration scheme that started out as essentially an economic arrangement but later adopted a security organ is the Southern African Development Community. After its founding the SADC functioned primarily as an economic arrangement until 1996, when it became necessary to provide it with a security and defense organ. Subsequently, the Organ on Politics, Defense, and Security was formed (Tsie 1998, 8–10). The desire to provide the Community with a defense organ was motivated by several factors. The most important of them was the end of the Cold War and the subsequent cessation of superpower rivalry, which provided a window for Africans to take control of security matters in their own region. There was also a need for the relevant stakeholders (i.e., people and governments of the region) to become more involved in conflict resolution in the Southern Africa subregion.

Since its founding, the SADC security force has engaged in peace-keeping and conflict resolution in Lesotho (when troops from South Africa and Botswana, serving under the SADC flag, intervened to prevent further violence and restore the peace) and the Democratic Republic of Congo where it is currently attempting to bring peace to that troubled region. In the DRC conflict, the

SADC has been forced to deal with hostilities from nonmember countries such as Uganda and Rwanda, who nevertheless are their neighbors. This, perhaps, is one of the reasons why the problems in the Great Lakes Region seem intractable: neighbors battling each other, often without clearly defined objectives (Jalpa 1999, 35–37).

AN APPROPRIATE DEFENSE AND SECURITY ORGAN FOR THE EAC

Without peace, the EAC cannot expect to generate significant benefits for its members. Thus, it is critical that the EAC provide itself with an appropriate security and defense organ, one that would have the capacity and capability to maintain peace within the Community and effectively defend members from external aggression. It is important to note here that aggression need not come from external actors seeking to destabilize member states. Destructive conflict, which can lead to instability, can originate internally if some members of the Community, or some groups within member states, believe that they are being systematically deprived of the benefits of the new arrangement or are not being provided the wherewithal to participate and benefit from the new trade and economic opportunities made possible by integration. Considering the fact that persistent poverty and deprivation can become significant sources of instability and thus a threat to peace, it is necessary that all relevant stakeholder groups be given an opportunity to be represented on the Community board charged with overseeing the activities of the security organ. Full and effective representation of all relevant stakeholder groups in deliberations about security matters is very critical, especially since security should not be considered a job exclusively for military elites. Civil society must be allowed to participate in all aspects of policy related to the operations of the security organ. That will keep the force's activities transparent, reducing opportunities for its officers to engage in opportunistic behaviors.

For the security organ to perform its job well and meet its objectives, it should be proactive, continuously seeking ways to prevent conflicts before they arise. This can be accomplished by working closely with the people, especially at the community level, to educate them on conflict resolution processes and other ways to avoid destructive mobilization, especially by social cleavages seeking ways to improve their participation in the economy. Since more countries are likely to join the EAC, the security organ should develop modalities to deal with any conflict situations brought about by the admission of new members. For example, Burundi has made it known that it intends to apply for membership in the Community. Should Burundi be admitted, its current internal problems would become those of the EAC, requiring the Community's security to deal with them. While one may suggest that Burundi "clean up its domestic mess" before it can be accepted for membership, this might not be practical, because the country currently does not have the wherewithal to do so, especially given the role played by external actors in the country's continuing political deterioration. Perhaps joining a larger community such as the EAC might provide Burundi with the wherewithal to deal with its internal problems.

As already mentioned, poverty is a threat to peace and hence must be attacked not only by national governments, but also by the institutions of the Community. Hence, as part of its efforts to maintain security in the subregion, the EAC Secretariat should develop both short-term and long-term programs to deal with community-wide poverty. One part of such a program would involve collecting and publishing accurate data on the extent of poverty in member states in order to provide the appropriate foundation for the design of policy to intervene. Of course, member countries, eager to safeguard their sovereignty, may frustrate the operations of Community institutions. Unfortunately, each country must understand that in order for the integration arrangement to work and generate benefits for members, each country must be willing to surrender a certain level of sovereignty. This may involve, for example, the surrender of certain research functions by national universities to regional institutions with the hope that the latter's larger size and significantly bigger budgets, will allow them to more effectively exploit the technological economies of scale and produce significantly more benefits for the Community.

CONCLUSION

Regional economic cooperation is very important for African countries given the small and often nonviable size of their domestic economies. Integration schemes such as the East African Community can significantly improve the ability of member states to participate more effectively in the global economy. In addition, a regional organization can improve the ability of African countries to negotiate at such international forums as the World Trade Organization.

In order for a regional integration scheme such as the EAC to produce benefits for its members, there must be peace in the subregion. That calls for the establishment within the organization of a security organ, one that can effectively resolve conflict and minimize political violence within the Community and defend member states against external aggressors. However, it is important to note that threats to security come not only from military incursions sponsored by external actors, but also from poverty, inequality in the distribution of resources, environmental degradation, and other social and economic phenomena. Hence, it is critical for the Community to actively consult relevant stakeholder groups so that its policies reflect the needs, desires, and concerns of the latter. It is only through a participatory process that the Community can expect to fulfil its mission of improving the welfare of the citizens of member states.

REFERENCES

Adar, K. G., and M. Ngunyi. 1994. The politics of integration in East Africa since independence. In *Politics and administration in East Africa*, edited by W. O. Oyugi. Nairobi: East African Educational Publishers.

Baker, P. H. 1991–1993. Africa in the New World Order. *SAIS Review* 10 (2): 139–152.

Buzan, B. 1991. *People, states and fear: An agenda for international security studies in the post–Cold War era.* London: Harvester Wheatsheaf.

Carr, E. H. 1939. *The twenty years crisis.* London: Macmillan.

Cheru, F. 1997. *A challenge to the New World Order: Promoting transnational civil society in Africa.* Washington, DC: American University Press.

Chesoni, S. 1997. The role of peace keeping in internal conflict in Africa: A comparative analysis of the Economic Community of West African States peace-keeping operation in Liberia and the United Nations operations in Somalia. M.A. Thesis, IDIS, University of Nairobi, Nairobi, Kenya.

Clough, M. 1992. *Free at last: U.S. policy toward Africa and the end of the Cold War.* New York: Council on Foreign Relations Press.

Davenport, M. 1992. Africa and the unimportance of being preferred. *Journal of Common Market Studies* 30 (2): 233–251.

DeLupis, I. D. 1970. *East African Community and Common Market.* London: Longman.

Garthoff, R. L. 1994. *The great transition: American relations at the end of the Cold War.* Washington, DC: Brookings Institution.

Gerger, G. 1998. International security in the information age: New structures and challenges. *German Foreign Affairs Review* 48 (4): 402–408.

Gondwe, G. E. 1999. Regional integration and globalization. *African Review of Foreign Policy* 1 (2): 23.

Hyland, W. G. 1990. *The Cold War is over.* New York: Times Books.

Jalpa, T. 1999. Conflict resolution essay: African complex war, complex peace. *East African Alternatives* 3 (March/April): 35–37.

Mbaku, J. M. 1997. *Institutions and reform in Africa: The public choice perspectives.* Westport, CT: Praeger.

Morgenthau, H. 1995. *Politics among nations: The struggle for power and peace.* Delhi: Kalyani.

Mwagiru, M. 1996. Toward an architecture of peace in the Horn of Africa Conflict System. Staff Seminar No. 1, University of Nairobi, Nairobi, Kenya, May.

Schraeder, P. J. 1996. *United States foreign policy toward Africa: Incrementalism, crisis and change.* Cambridge: Cambridge University Press.

Tsie, B. 1998. Regional security in Southern Africa: Wither the SADC on politics, defense and security. *Global Dialogue* 3 (3): 8–10.

UNDP. 2000. *Human development report, 2000.* New York: Oxford University Press.

7

The African Union: Africa's Giant Step toward Continental Unity

SURESH CHANDRA SAXENA

May 26, 2001, was a very important day in the history of Africa because it was on that day that Africans formed a new integration scheme, the African Union. The latter is expected to enhance continental unity and significantly improve Africa's ability to participate in the new globalization. The AU will replace the Organization of African Unity, which existed for thirty years. Earlier, on July 11, 2000, fifty-three African heads of state and government, meeting at Lomé, Togo, had adopted a historic document called the Constitutive Act of African Union, which contained a provision to the effect that when it was ratified by two-thirds (thirty-six in all) of African governments it would mark the birth of the African Union. This legal requirement was met on April 26, 2001, when Nigeria became the thirty-sixth African state to deposit its ratification documents with the headquarters of the OAU (OAU 2001). Out of fifty-four African states, fifty-three states have signed the Constitutive Act. Only Morocco has so far not signed the treaty. It is hoped that Morocco will join the new organization when it realizes the potential benefits of membership. Morocco has a long history of hesitation in joining African integration schemes. In fact, when the OAU was founded in 1963, Morocco did not participate in the inaugural ceremonies, which took place in Addis Ababa, Ethiopia. In addition, it did not sign the Charter until later and actually withdrew its membership in 1982 when the OAU admitted the Sahawari Arab Democratic Republic (SADR) to its membership—the disputed territory generally referred to as the Western Sahara and claimed by Morocco (Saxena 1995, 25–50). It is no surprise, then, that Morocco has declined to join other African countries in signing the treaty creating the African Union.

The structures formerly occupied by the OAU in Addis Ababa will become the headquarters of the African Union. The OAU Charter will continue to be operational for a transitional period of one year in order to enable the OAU to transfer its assets and liabilities to the new organization. However, the provisions of the Constitutive Act of African Union, in terms of Article 33, shall take precedence over, and supersede, any inconsistent or contrary provisions of the Abuja Treaty establishing the African Economic Community. Pending the establishment of an administrative structure for the new organization, the OAU General Secretariat shall be the interim Secretariat of the African Union.

The process of creating a new continental organization that is better equipped than the OAU to promote African unity was formally proposed by Libyan leader Mu'ammar al-Qadhafi in July 1999 during a meeting of the OAU in Algeria. Subsequently, this question was given serious thought by African leaders when the OAU heads of state and government met at the Fourth Extraordinary Session of the OAU Assembly in Sirte, Libya, September 8–9, 1999 at the invitation of Qadhafi. After the two-day meeting, the delegates adopted the so-called Sirte Declaration (OAU 1999), which emphasized the "imperative need and a high sense of urgency to rekindle the aspirations of our peoples for stronger unity, solidarity and cohesion in a larger community of peoples transcending cultural, ideological, ethnic and national differences." The Declaration went on to say,

In order to cope with these challenges and to effectively address the new social, political, and economic realities in Africa and in the world, we are determined to fulfil our peoples' aspirations for greater unity in conformity with the objectives of the OAU Charter and the Treaty Establishing the African Economic Community (the Abuja Treaty). It is also our conviction that our continental organization needs to be revitalized in order to be able to play a more active role and continue to be relevant to the needs of our peoples and responsive to the demands of the prevailing circumstances. We are also determined to eliminate the scourge of conflicts which constitutes a major impediment to the implementation of our development and integration agenda (OAU 1999, 1).

In the deliberations at Sirte, Qadhafi played a very important and constructive role and seemed to be determined to overcome all obstacles in the way of creating a new and pragmatic continental organization that would take the place of the OAU. It appeared at the time that after decades of struggles there was an African leader who had the political commitment and will to provide the leadership for the establishment of a continental framework for unity. Like Kwame Nkrumah before him, Qadhafi hoped to persuade his fellow African leaders to work toward the establishment of a United States of Africa. Having failed to convince his colleagues, he opted for the African Union, which he believed would pave the way for total economic and political integration of the continent sometime in the future. Although the new organization falls short of the United States of Africa that Nkrumah had envisioned, Qadhafi is confident that the AU provides a sound foundation for further continental integration and unity.

Qadhafi was naturally upbeat when the Constitutive Act of African Union was adopted. He declared, "It is a victory for Africa" (Quoted in Boateng 2000,

2). His vision for a strong and united Africa, capable of meeting global challenges and shouldering its responsibility to harness the human and natural resources of the continent in order to improve the living conditions of its peoples, had inspired the delegates, and this fact is acknowledged in the Declaration itself.

Earlier at the Sirte Conference, delegates had rejected Qadhafi's call for the formation of a United States of Africa. Instead, they had agreed to a lesser form of integration, one that did not involve complete loss of sovereignty by individual countries to a larger political jurisdiction. Thus, it was at the Sirte Conference that the decision to form the African Union was made. In supporting the idea of forming a union, President Idriss Deby of Chad declared,

Qadhafi's idea is a good one and has come at the right time. But views about the ways and means of achieving this union are different. There are some who want to go faster and others who want to go slowly. But everyone is unanimous on the principle that Africa must create an organization that will enable it to have a force that can meet the challenges of globalization. . . . I have no doubt about Qadhafi's sincerity when he speaks about Africa. It comes from his heart. He speaks with an open heart (quoted in Boateng 2000, 3).

HISTORICAL CONTEXT OF AFRICAN UNITY

The idea of forging some sort of unity among African states may be traced to the early days of the growth of the movement generally referred to as Pan-Africanism. In fact, continental unity was and continues to be one of the major objectives of Pan-Africanism. During the colonial period, Africans recognized that the only way they could free themselves from further exploitation and domination was through unity and cooperation. Thus, many of the post–World War II freedom fighters (e.g., Kwame Nkrumah of Ghana, N. Azikiwe of Nigeria, Ruben Um Nyobé of Cameroon, Sékou Touré of Guinea) saw continental unity as the only way to prevent further exploitation of Africans by Europeans. Many African elites of the time believed that unity was critical in the war against colonialism. Despite their shortcomings, colonial education systems did generate among Africans a greater awareness of their dismal conditions and the need for them to unite in order to provide themselves with the wherewithal to ameliorate these conditions. Thus, part of the struggle for independence involved efforts to unite the African peoples and found political and economic arrangements that transcended the boundaries established by the Europeans, ethnicity and language, and religious and cultural preferences. The goal was to provide Africans with structures, at the continental level, that could help them negotiate more effectively with the outside world and enhance their ability to participate more fully and gainfully in the emerging postwar economy.

The idea of African unity was part of the global movement to unite all peoples of African ancestry and improve their ability to fight against European oppression (specifically in the African colonies) and the continued "enslavement" of Africans that remained a reality even in the twentieth-century United States, nearly a century after Abraham Lincoln freed the slaves. Thus, the movement for continental unity spearheaded by such luminaries as Kwame Nkrumah benefited significantly from the works of such intellectuals and freedom fighters of African ancestry as Dr. W.E.B. DuBois, Marcus Garvey, and Sylvester Williams, as well as from several European- and American-based organizations, such as the National Association for the Advancement of Colored People (NAACP), founded in New York in 1909, and the Pan-African Federation, founded in Machester in 1944. While the aim of the NAACP was to fight racism in America, that of the Manchester group was to "promote the well-being and unity of African peoples and peoples of African descent throughout the world" (cited in Saxena 1993, 182).

It is important to note that while external actors such as DuBois and Garvey contributed significantly to African unity, the idea, nevertheless, was home-grown, arising out of the frustrations of many Africans with European colonialism. As mentioned earlier, many freedom fighters realized quite early that they were not likely to succeed in their struggle against colonial rule unless they were united. It was also determined that even after independence had been granted many of the new countries would not be able to maintain viable economies, and thus integration (to form larger and more viable economies) was considered critical to survival in the postindependence period. In fact, such was the motivation behind the desire of the people of British Southern Cameroons to unite with La République du Cameroun in 1961 to form the Federal Republic of Cameroon. Specifically, the idea of African unity received further impetus through the numerous Pan-African congresses and Pan-African conventions organized by Du Bois and Garvey, respectively, in Europe.

The first formal effort to give concrete meaning to the idea of continental unity came in 1958 with the holding of the First All-African People's Conference in December in Accra, Ghana. At this critical meeting, which was attended primarily by political parties, participants indicated their interest to form a United States of Africa. In the final resolutions of the conference, attendees expressed the need to unite all Africans and provide for the formation of a Commonwealth of Free African States. They called upon the then independent African states to provide the leadership needed to lead the African peoples toward the attainment of continental unity and expressed the hope that the day would come when Africans would gladly pledge their loyalty to an African Commonwealth instead of to individual countries (Thompson 1969, 352). The Conference further declared that, as a first step toward the attainment of the broad objective of an African Commonwealth, the independent states of Africa should amalgamate themselves into groups on the basis of geographical contiguity, economic interdependence, and linguistic and cultural affinity. The Accra conference was followed by a number of similar nongovernmental conferences, all of which supported the idea of establishing an African Commonwealth.

One of the greatest champions of African unity was Ghana's charismatic independence prime minister, Dr. Kwame Nkrumah. It was he who, even before the birth of the OAU in 1963, had strongly advocated the creation of a United States of Africa because he saw no future for the continent if it remained politically divided into numerous sovereign entities, many of which were economically nonviable units. Believing strongly that in unity lay Africa's strength, Nkrumah (1963, 217) declared,

We are Africans first and last, and as Africans our best interests can only be served by uniting within an African Community. Neither the Commonwealth nor a Franco-African Community can be a substitute. . . . To us, Africa with its islands is just one Africa. We reject the idea of any kind of partition. From Tangier or Cairo in the North to Cape Town in the South, from Cape Guardafui in the East to Cape Verde Islands in the West, Africa is one and indivisible.

Shortly after he became leader of Ghana in 1957, Nkrumah put forth very strong arguments in support of his unshakable belief that the future of Africa lay in unity. He believed that "if we developed our potentialities in men and natural resources in separate isolated groups, our energies would soon be dissipated in the struggle to outbid one another" (Nkrumah 1963, 218). He rejected the view that the formation of the United States of Africa would result in the loss of sovereignty for the independent African states that would form such a union. In his view, the African states would continue to exercise independent authority except in the fields defined and reserved for common action in the interest of the security and orderly development of the whole continent. Nkrumah was obviously inspired by the example of the United States of America, in which the states had surrendered only a portion of their sovereignty in return for the enormous benefits that accrued to them from membership in a larger economic and political arrangement. Among some of the benefits were security and sustained and rapid economic development. The American leaders who had formed the United States of America had shown a great deal of political maturity and farsightedness, which appeared to have been lacking in many African leaders in 1963. Of course, it is important to note that the circumstances under which the African leaders found themselves and the constraints they faced were significantly different from those faced by the founding fathers of the United States in the 1770s. For one thing, the new African leaders faced significant opposition from the former colonizers who saw a united Africa as not in their best interest: A unified and stronger Africa would make it much more difficult for countries such as France and the United Kingdom to have access to the resources and markets of their former colonies. In addition, the new African leaders also faced opposition to unity from the Cold War protagonists, who believed that a divided continent would greatly enhance their ability to manipulate continental leaders and coopt them into the struggle for the domination of global affairs.

Nkrumah believed very strongly in African unity and hoped that the newly independent states would form a political and economic arrangement similar to the United States of America. He was aware of the fact that the realization of such a union would result in some form of retaliation from the Western industrialized countries, many of which had pledged to the United Nations to help the African countries by sending them development and other forms of aid. Many of these countries desperately needed resources to meet rising social obligations, many of which had been heightened by the advent of independence. There were many demands on the state for improvements in education, health care, housing, water, and other services. Unfortunately, many of these countries were unable to generate enough resources domestically to meet the needs of the people. As a consequence, many of the new leaders looked to foreign development assistance from Western Europe and the United States as the salvation to many of their development problems. Despite Nkrumah's very persuasive arguments in favor of continental unity, many of the new leaders feared that such a move could spell disaster for their economies and thus threaten their political positions. Nkrumah, unfortunately, did not have the resources to replace the enormous development aid that these countries expected from the West. Thus, it was not surprising that many of the new states were lukewarm to Nkrumah's arguments in favor of continental unity.

Of course, the failure of the African countries to form a commonwealth is complex and requires more detailed study than is presented here. However, one cannot underestimate the role played by Africa's traditional benefactors and the Cold War protagonists in such failure. One could argue that although Nkrumah had a good idea, it was being presented at the wrong time. Today, the Cold War is over and Africa has lost its strategic importance to the West. In fact, during the last ten years Western interest in Africa has fallen significantly and, as was indicated during the debates for the 2000 U.S. presidential elections, Africa is of little strategic interest to the United States and its allies. Perhaps Africa could use this apparent relegation to the periphery of global affairs to invest in itself and develop those structures and institutional arrangements that would significantly improve its ability to develop and improve its global competitiveness. Integration, including the formation of a commonwealth, is one such institutional arrangement.

Today, poverty alleviation is one of the most important goals of African governments. African countries urgently need rapid economic growth in order to generate the resources needed to deal effectively with high rates of poverty and deprivation. Unfortunately, macroeconomic performance is being negatively affected by continued political violence, including destructive ethnic conflict. Thus, unless each country can achieve lasting peace it is not likely to achieve the kind of economic growth that would generate enough resources for poverty alleviation. As Nkrumah said many years ago, there cannot be peace and security in the African countries without continental unity. While they remain divided, Africans and their resources continue to be easy prey to transnational companies and opportunists from the industrialized countries, who see instability on the continent as enhancing their ability to continue the exploitation of the region's environmental resources started during colonialism. Unity, then, must precede any efforts to achieve sustainability in the exploitation of the continent's human and natural resources (see, T. M. Shaw 1982, 132).

DIFFERENT APPROACHES TO AFRICAN UNITY

African leaders, no doubt, subscribed, at least verbally, to the idea of forging African unity, but they held divergent views regarding the form and the manner in which the much-sought-after goal of African unity could be achieved. In the main, four approaches to unity were being strongly advocated by African states prior to 1963. The first approach was proposed by a group of radical African states, which collectively became known as the Casablanca bloc. The states belonging to this bloc felt that political unity was a sine qua non for the subsequent integration of African economies (Cervenka 1977, 2–3). These states felt that the continent could successfully cope with the menace of neocolonialism and apartheid and deliver Africa from the yoke of colonialism only if there was political unity among African states.

Ghana was one of the countries that strongly subscribed to this approach to continental unity, and its leader, Dr. Kwame Nkrumah, was its greatest exponent. Nkrumah had made it abundantly clear that he was in favor of creating, without delay, a Union of African States (Legum 1962, 46; Padelford 1964, 522). In other words, Nkrumah stood for unitarianism and a centralist democracy. The Ghanaian plan involved the dismantling of the existing state borders to pave the way for one sovereign Union of African States with one constitution, one flag, one anthem, and one motto (Saxena 1993, 201). Nkrumah's blueprint for continental unity called for supranational institutions such as a parliament, an African civil service, a centralized economic system (characterized by state planning), and an African military high command (Padelford 1964, 526; Charter of Casablanca, 1961, reproduced in Legum 1962, 187–192).

Nkrumah's monolithic approach, advocated by the so-called Casablanca bloc of nations, sought to promote African unity through the political fusion of all the states of Africa (Saxena 1981, xii–xiii). This naturally implied the dismantling of the existing territorial boundaries, creation of continental governmental institutions, and a union government for the entire continent with one foreign and one domestic policy.

The second approach to African unity was advocated by Libya and the Sudan. These countries regarded African unity "as necessitating no more than a single charter that would encompass the varying viewpoints—a Bandung-type of declaration" (Cervenka 1977, 2–3). Under this arrangement, supranational institutions such as a union government were not really a necessity.

The third approach to African unity was advanced by President Tubman of Liberia. It envisaged the formation of a loose association of African states within the framework of an all-African organization. Continental integration was to be patterned along the lines blazed by the Organization of American States (OAS) (T. M. Shaw 1982, 135). The charter of the OAS, also known as the Charter of Bogota, does not envisage the formation of a single continental political entity comprising all the member states. Rather, it seeks to create a sort of loose confederation, an association of independent states bound together by an international treaty into a union with organs that could be used to maximize the objectives of members and significantly improve their ability to participate in global affairs (Thomas and Thomas 1959). This approach seems to have guided the founding fathers of the OAU.

The fourth approach to African unity was advocated by what became known as the Monrovia bloc. Ethiopia and Nigeria were the leading members of this bloc. Leaders of this bloc of countries argued that if an attempt was made to forge some sort of organic unity among African states, it would result in the erosion—even total loss—of the sovereignty that African states had gained after throwing away the chains of colonialism. In many cases, sovereignty had been gained only after a hard-fought armed struggle (e.g., Algeria and Kenya), and these countries were not willing or ready to surrender it to a supracontinental political jurisdiction. Members of this bloc subscribed to a pluralist approach to African unity in contrast to the monolithic approach advocated by the radical Casablanca bloc.

The pluralists considered it premature for Africa to experiment with any ambitious approach to unity, which envisaged the dismantling of the territorial frontiers of individual states and the surrendering of their newly acquired sovereignty in favor of the larger, continentwide government. Many members of this group preferred emphasis on consultative rather than executive organs and stressed the formation of a development bank, a private investment guarantee fund, and stepped-up activities in the field of education, labor, and social welfare before political union could be achieved (*The Economist*, April 29, 1961, 455; Padelford 1964, 523). The Monrovia bloc wanted to proceed gradually, allowing each country to enjoy its hard-fought sovereignty before eventually giving it up in favor of a continental government. In practical terms, they accepted the status quo in respect to national boundaries, advocated respect for the sovereignty of each other, and pleaded for the setting up of functional institutions to promote economic, technical, and cultural cooperation among African states. This group regarded the goal of establishing a United States of Africa, as advocated by the Casablanca bloc, an unrealistic and unrealizable goal at that stage in the continent's political and economic evolution (Saxena 1981, xiii).

The issue was not whether African unity should be promoted since virtually all African leaders recognized the benefits of integration and in one way or another supported the idea. The issue, and what came to be the bone of contention, was how that unity was to be achieved and what the most practical way of achieving it was. Although four approaches to African unity were being advocated, the main tussle was between the Casablanca and Monrovia blocs. The

Casablanca bloc believed in beginning with political union, paving the way for economic and social integration. The Monrovia bloc, on the other hand, stressed that "the unity that is aimed to be achieved at the moment is not the political integration of sovereign African states, but unity of aspirations and of action considered from the point of view of African social solidarity and political identity" (Wallerstein 1967, 55). The Casablanca bloc wanted African states to cooperate in creating a political entity, whereas the Monrovia bloc strongly favored the creation of functional institutions in economic, educational, and scientific fields.

These differences among African states seemed, at one stage, to thwart the establishment of a continental organization that could promote unity among the new nations. The "radicals," represented by the Casablanca group, and the "moderates," represented by the Monrovia group, seemed not to budge an inch from their positions. In addition, there were several other practical problems that stood in the way of establishing a continental state structure. For one thing, the establishment of some form of federalism in Africa required more than just abrogated existing state boundaries. There must be a genuine desire by the people of the different countries to unite and voluntarily found a new political and economic arrangement. At the time, there did not seem to be such a desire among the people. Of course, one must caution here that most of the participation in discussions on integration was limited to national leaders and urban elites. Little effort was made to involve popular forces, so it is difficult to gauge, for example, the extent to which rural inhabitants might have supported the idea had they been provided the opportunity to join in the discourse. Thus, when we argue that the desire among many countries at the time was to preserve the status quo and to zealously guard the sovereignty and territorial integrity of each country, we are necessarily referring to the wishes of the national leaders and a few urban intellectuals. When, in 1960, Nigeria's prime minister, Sir Abubakar Tafawa Balewa, declared that "Nigeria has not the slightest intention of surrendering her sovereignty, no sooner had she gained independence, to anyone else" (*Daily Express,* January 14, 1960, 137), one wonders what the results would have been had the issue of integration been put to a national referendum.

Colonialism was based on the so-called divide-and-conquer principle. As a consequence, the colonial governments sowed the seeds of division among ethnic and other social cleavages within each colony, making postindependence efforts to unite the people, even within each new country, very difficult. In fact, throughout the continent the colonial governments used military recruits from some ethnic groups to enhance their ability to suppress and exploit other ethnic groups. The differential treatment of the several ethnic groups within each colony by the respective colonial governments meant that, at independence, some groups had more human capital than others. Those with significantly more political and educational skills were in a favored position to inherit the evacuated structures of colonial hegemony. Many such successful ethnic groups were not likely to be in favor of integration for fear of losing their lucrative political and economic positions.

Another factor working against integration was the multiplicity of languages made possible by the continent's extreme ethnic diversity. Between Cameroon and Nigeria alone, there were more than 250 ethnic groups, each with its own language. In addition, there were hardly any roads between colonies and, in many cases, even within colonies, making communication among the different groups very difficult. In fact, during the colonial period it was often easier for an African to travel to the metropole than to another colony within the continent. Thus, it was much easier for an African from the French Cameroons to travel to France than it was for him to visit the Gold Coast (which became independent as Ghana in 1957). As a matter of fact, communications between African countries remained quite difficult even after independence. The communications infrastructures of many African countries (e.g., their telephone systems) were more integrated into those of their former colonies than into those of their neighbors. Hence, during the early years of independence, Cameroonians often found it easier to fly to France than to their neighbor, Nigeria. On top of this, one can add the complicating effects of Christianity and Islam.

An important constraint, one that has been a critical factor in the failure of many integration schemes in the continent, is differential rates of economic development. In fact, one of the reasons given for the breakdown of the East African Community in 1977 was the argument that Kenya, the most developed and industrialized member of the community, was able to capture most of the benefits of integration, with the other members, Tanzania and Uganda, left to serve as dumping grounds for excess output from Kenya's factories (Mbaku 1997, 33–60). In an integration scheme, weak and less viable economies are likely to seek additional protection from the stronger and more developed ones. Unless assurances can be made that these weaker economies would be given special protection, they are less likely to agree to integration. Thus, in order for one to establish and sustain a continental federal government in Africa, these issues must be resolved. At the least, (1) a way must be found to enhance the ability of each ethnic and social cleavage to participate in the new arrangement without being pushed to the periphery, (2) structures must be put in place to make certain that the benefits of integration are distributed equitably, (3) communications systems must be improved, (4) a continental language policy and another on culture and tradition must be adopted to make sure that minority groups are not forced to give up their values in favor of those of the larger and more dominant ones, and (5) the African people, and not just urban elites, must be allowed to determine the nature of integration.

SETBACKS TO THE GOAL OF AFRICAN UNITY

The objective of establishing a continental organization and promoting African unity appeared quite unattainable in the early 1960s as a result of serious differences that had cropped up among African states on some important issues. The first such issue was that of Mauritania. Morocco claimed most of the area then under French colonialism and was opposed to the territory's independence and subsequent existence as a sovereign nation. France ignored Morocco's claims and granted independence to the territory. The new country was subsequently granted recognition by most African countries. As a consequence, Morocco boycotted the 1963 founding conference of the OAU. This was a major setback to the goal of African unity.

The second political development was in relation to the former Belgian colony of Congo (now known as the Democratic Republic of Congo), which suffered from political instability as a result of the breakdown of the central government and attempts by the Katanga province (now Shaba) to secede from the country. The situation took a turn for the worse, particularly after the assassination of the prime minister, Patrice Lumumba. Thereafter, the president of Congo, Kasavubu, whose relations with Patrice Lumumba had been extremely strained, claimed that he represented the legitimate government of the country, while Lumumba's deputy, Gizenga, who had established himself in Stanleyville, claimed his government to be the real government of the country. The pro–Western African states recognized the Kasavubu government in Leopold-ville (now Kinshasa), while the radical African states recognized the Gigenza government in Stanleyville. This division among African states was a second major setback to the cause of continental unity.

The third political development that caused a severe setback to the cause of African unity was the independence of thirteen French colonies in Africa. Because of their extremely pro-French attitude, the political leaders of these colonies did not enjoy a good reputation among other African states. The leaders of many former French colonies had failed to criticize French policy in Algeria; some of them were said to have even supplied troops to help fight the National Liberation Front, which was then waging a war to free Algeria from the stranglehold of French colonialism. In addition, many African leaders, such as Kwame Nkrumah of Ghana, were quite disappointed that leaders of the former French colonies had failed to condemn France for conducting atomic tests in the Sahara and placing the people of the region in grave danger. In fact, Togo and Cameroon had entered into defense agreements with France, allowing its troops, which had been used during the colonial period to oppress the people, to remain in the new countries and help the new governments impose authoritarian rule on the people. As a result of the pro-French attitude of the Francophone countries, Ghana, Morocco, Guinea, and Egypt provided support to the exile groups from these territories. The All-African People's Organization became a strong supporter of the opponents of some of the governments in the preindependence French territories, notably the U.N. Trust Territory of Cameroons under French administration, which gained independence in 1960 and took the name *République du Cameroun*, and Niger (LeVine 1964). These developments did not augur well for the growth and development of African unity.

The final factor that contributed to the rift among African states was the attempt to create a single All-African Trade Union Federation (AATUF). The problem was complicated by the fact that many African states had their own trade union organizations, some of which were affiliated with the Western-oriented International Confederation of Free Trade Unions (ICFTU). None of them, however, was affiliated to the communist-dominated international World Federation of Trade Unions (WFTU). The dispute among African states was not over whether the AATUF should be formed, but over the question of whether individual trade unions of African countries should be allowed to retain their affiliation with any international trade union organization. Some African countries wanted that, after the formation of the AATUF, no national trade union should be allowed to affiliate itself with any international trade union organization directly. The other group of African states, which included Kenya and Tunisia, argued that national trade unions be allowed to retain their affiliation with international trade unions.

These four reasons were responsible for creating sharp divisions among African states leading to the formation of the Brazzaville bloc, the Casablanca bloc, and then the Monrovia bloc. With such divisions existing among African states prior to 1963, Nkrumah's ideal of a United States of Africa seemed unattainable at that time. It was no doubt a noble idea presented in the best interest of Africa, but it was stillborn. Under the circumstances existing in the 1960s, the only realistic way for African countries to cooperate was to set up several organizations that could allow them to work together in various economic, social and political fields and put off continental integration until later as suggested by the Monrovia bloc.

Ultimately, the Monrovia view prevailed at the Addis Ababa Conference in 1963, since it enjoyed the support of the majority of the states in attendance. The OAU finally came into existence in 1963, largely based on the ideals of the Monrovia bloc. The African states had opted to cooperate in the context of the OAU without forming a union government. The only concession in favor of the Casablanca bloc was the provision in the OAU Charter that the organization would, besides its other functions, also promote the unity and solidarity of African states.

In the formation of the OAU in the midst of sharp disagreements among the African states about the nature of integration and how it should be carried out, Emperor Haile Selassie of Ethiopia played a historic role. He made a concerted effort to bring the leaders together and get them to reach agreement on the major issues, telling them that while they differed significantly in their methods, the goal was the same: unity of the African peoples. He encouraged them to keep their eyes and hopes on the prize and not let petty differences detract them. Thus, at the 1963 Addis Ababa Conference that established the Organization of African Unity, the Ethiopian leader declared, "Through all that has been said and written and done in these years, there runs a common theme. Unity is the accepted goal. We argue about means; we discuss tactics. But while we agree that the ultimate destiny of this continent lies in political union, we must at the same time recognize that the obstacles to be overcome in its achievement are at once numerous and formidable" (quoted in Thompson 1969, 183).

THE OAU AND THE IDEAL OF AFRICAN UNITY

One of the purposes of the OAU, as enshrined in its Charter, was to "promote the unity and solidarity of African states." Here "unity" should not be interpreted to mean territorial integration of the continent, for African leaders had not agreed in 1963 to abolish the territorial borders of their states and convert the entire continent into one state. "Unity," in the OAU context means that all ideological blocs into which African states were divided should be dissolved and that the views of African states on any issue would be expressed by the collectivity called the OAU. The OAU thus became the spokesperson of the continent. The OAU, however, was not expected to be some authoritarian outfit but an accountable, participatory, representative organization whose decisions were to be made only after proper consultation with the relevant stakeholder groups. Thus, the organization was expected to take a position on any issue, whether global or regional, only after the African people, through their representatives, had been given the opportunity to engage in frank and free discussion and had, in the process, developed a consensus on the issue. The framework for such discussions was to be provided by the OAU. Such a position, once accepted by representatives of member countries of the OAU, would become the collective position of the entire continent, and member states became, at least morally if not politically, bound by it. Thereafter, if any African state took a different stand contrary to the collective position of the OAU, it could be censured by the organization. However, no punitive action was supposed to be taken against a deviating member, since the organization was not armed with any such power. The OAU Charter does not provide for the imposition of sanctions against members who act against a position taken by the membership.

Taking advantage of this weakness (i.e., the inability of the OAU to punish recalcitrant members), many member states have openly taken positions on several issues that are in violation of the decisions and policies of the organization. For instance, several African states acted contrary to the position of the OAU on the question of apartheid. Vocally, they were all opposed to apartheid, but many of them collaborated with South Africa in violation of OAU declarations. Malawi, under Hastings K. Banda, established diplomatic relations with apartheid South Africa and engaged in both trade and other exchanges with the pariah regime. In addition, Banda and his government opposed the armed struggle against Pretoria that was led by the African National Congress. In later years, Banda's government would also oppose the armed struggle by the South West Africa People's Organization (SWAPO), against South Africa's colonization of Namibia and ignored pleas from the OAU for African countries to boycott the racist regime. During the time the French used the Sahara to test its nuclear weapons, Africa was unable to present a united resolution against such abuse. The Francophone states, which considered their continued economic and political cooperation with France more important than solidarity with their fellow Africans, refused to condemn, in the harshest manner, the morally repugnant nuclear tests that the French were conducting in the heart of the continent.

An analysis of the provisions of the OAU Charter shows that the founding fathers of the organization may have considered the transformation of Africa into a single sovereign state at that time to be quite difficult and not likely to be attained, at least not in the immediate postindependence period. They then may have settled for an arrangement that preserved the status quo as a second-best solution, hoping that the OAU would provide a forum within which independent African countries could eventually recognize the enormous benefits to be derived from complete integration and then strive for it. These leaders may also have hoped that changes in the global political economy would favor intercountry cooperation in the continent and enhance integration. In fact, Nkrumah's decision to open Ghana's universities to students from other African countries was an attempt to educate the kinds of leaders who would return to their own countries and promote the idea of an African Commonwealth.

One could argue, of course, that had the founding fathers of the OAU been interested in continental unity they would not have incorporated into the Charter of the OAU provisions that preserved the status quo. For instance, one of the principles enshrined in the Charter is that of "non-interference in the internal affairs of states." Another principle entrenched in the organization's Charter is that of "respect for the sovereignty and territorial integrity of each state and for its inalienable right to independent existence." These two provisions taken together could lead one to believe that the founders of the OAU wanted to maintain the status quo. However, as argued earlier, they may have been doing so because they faced enormous difficulties in designing and implementing a continental integration agreement and felt that, given time, the new states would be strong enough politically and economically to engage in such a monumental task. The states had to be preserved so that in the future they would lead the struggle for unity. The OAU Charter, thus, was not a blueprint for the founding of a United States of Africa (Saxena 2001, 139).

If we look at the conduct of African states during the last several years, we can see that most of them have been interested primarily in preserving their distinct identities and not in losing such identities to a continental arrangement in the form of a sovereign United States of Africa. Thus, most of them have put their sovereignty and national identities above ideological considerations of Pan-Africanism. Although many of these leaders openly criticized the artificial nature of the boundaries created by the European colonialists, these same leaders did not make any effort to adjust such boundaries after independence and make them more relevant to the socioeconomic interaction of the people. As a consequence, ethnic groups divided by colonial boundaries were unable to reunite with their kinfolk after independence. Instead, the new leaders did all they could to retain the boundaries that they had inherited from the colonialists. Engaging the African people in a process in which national boundaries are redrawn and ethnic groups given an opportunity to reunite may actually work to enhance continental unity. The process can allow the people to realize, if they have not already done so, that most boundaries are artificial constraints to socioeconomic interaction placed by individuals and groups that benefit from such restrictions.

As has been mentioned already, Western activities in Africa have contributed significantly to the inability of Africans to unite and form a single continental sovereign nation, from Western support of apartheid in South Africa and Namibia, to the present financing of the activities of the National Union for the Total Independence of Angola (UNITA), which since the 1975–1976 civil war has waged a bloody war against the government in Luanda. Through UNITA, the West, as well as the apartheid government of South Africa, contributed significantly to the destabilization of Angola. Although South Africa is no longer involved in UNITA activities, the organization continues to receive substantial aid from Western-based transnational companies that are currently exploiting the country's huge natural resources. Such destabilization, with the help of indigenous elites, has continued to make continental integration only a dream.

African leaders have also contributed significantly to the postponement of the dream of a United States of Africa. Qadhafi has accused the Sudan of giving comfort to his opponents and has in the process threatened to attack the Sudan; Gen. Jafar Numeiri, the Sudanese dictator who was considered to be pro-West, in turn accused Qadhafi of seeking to destabilize the government in Khartoum. Such interference in the internal affairs of other African countries, even if justified (as in the decision by Julius Nyerere to send an army to Uganda to oust the murderous Idi Amin), have contributed significantly to a deterioration in relations between countries, making discussions of unity difficult to undertake. In fact, attendance at the annual meetings of the OAU heads of government has often been boycotted by leaders who refused to go to the country hosting the affair, because of a standing disagreement with the leader of that country (Saxena 2001, 145).

NEED FOR A NEW ORGANIZATION

For quite some time now the most important challenge for African states has been the emergence of powerful economic blocs such as the European Union and the North American Free Trade Area. If these blocs become inward looking (i.e., protectionist), that could spell disaster for the African countries since they presently carry out a significant part of their trade with the countries of these two economic and political arrangements. Given their economic and political strengths, it is likely that the EU and NAFTA will dominate global economic and political affairs in the years to come. How well the African countries participate in and benefit from the new global economy will be determined by the extent to which they are willing to unite and form a strong and viable continental economic and political organization, one that can negotiate effectively with other existing economic unions for the benefits of global trade and enhance the ability of Africans to improve domestic macroeconomic performance. Since the end of the Cold War, African countries have come to realize that the OAU, as presently constituted, cannot perform that job. Its structures cannot meet the challenges posed by the changes taking place in the world economy.

Since the mid-1970s, African countries have attempted to engage in some form of regional integration, although without success. This is a testament to their realization that each country could not go it alone, given the fact that most of them have economies that are relatively small, are still dependent on the exportation of primary commodities, and are not able to produce goods that are globally competitive in both price and quality (Mbaku 1995). As many trading blocs emerged around the world, African countries began to realize that unless they too could successfully engage in some form of integration they were not likely to benefit from the new global economy, especially one dominated by such powerful groups as the EU and NAFTA. Therefore, the need to forge a strong and viable economic community in the continent has been recognized for quite sometime. In fact, as far back as February 1979 a symposium was held in Monrovia, Liberia, at the initiative of the secretary-general of the OAU, on the future development prospects of Africa toward the year 2000. After the symposium was over, the participants issued the following warning in their final report:

Considering the gigantic resources and achievements of such countries as the United States and the Soviet Union, considering the patiently organized labor of 900 million Chinese and considering the ever-growing economic force represented by the European Common Market, were the African countries to continue to pursue a narrow nationalistic path they would be faced with the prospect not only of an ever-widening gap between rich and poor countries but also of the progressive marginalization of the continent, condemned to accept its role as a mere branch of some former or new empire (OAU/ECA 1979).

Implied in this warning was the call for African states to begin work on establishing integration schemes that could (1) improve domestic economic performance, (2) increase the size of national markets and reduce dependence on the industrial market economies, and (3) improve the ability of Africans to participate in the global economy. The same document also stated that African unity was not "just a slogan, a pious dream or an irresponsible ambition," but an ideal worth fighting for. Participants at the forum realized that if Africa were to unite, the main aim would be to create an economically viable and strong entity that had to be reckoned with, even by the industrial giants of the West, such as the United States and what was then the European Economic Community. The symposium subsequently called for three specific measures to be taken:

- First, the creation of an African common market based on progressive coordination and integration, which would evolve in the form of concentric circles reflecting the economic areas that currently exist on the continent. The African common market could also apply to individual products: meat, cereals, textiles, etc. The Symposium called upon the OAU to make all the necessary arrangements to initiate action along those lines without delay, with the support of the United Nations Development Program and the U.N. Economic Commission for Africa.
- Second, the extension of arrangements for the free movement of persons and goods on the African continent.
- Third, the awakening of African public opinion to the idea that continental unity was no longer an ideal to be pursued only by national political elites, but one whose success required the active and full participation of all relevant stakeholder groups (OAU/ECA 1979).

By the time African leaders met in Sirte in September 1999, twenty years had passed since the aforementioned symposium was held in Monrovia. There have been many significant changes in the global economy since African leaders made those proclamations in Monrovia. While many of the world's economies have made significant progress and improved the welfare of their citizens during the last twenty years, Africa, in general, has suffered economic regression, with complete collapse occurring in Rwanda, Burundi, Democratic Republic of Congo, Liberia, Sierra Leone, and a few other countries. In fact, several African countries have been able to survive only as a result of massive flows of food aid from the United States and other Western countries. Thus, when African leaders met in Libya in 1999 many of them had concluded that it was time for them to get serious about integration. It was necessary for them to get united and collectively face the new post–Cold War global economy. In indicating their intention to move forward with their "One Africa" project, the leaders declared as follows: "As we prepare to enter the 21st century and cognizant of the challenges, we emphasize the imperative need and high sense of urgency to rekindle the aspirations of our people for stronger unity, solidarity and cohesion in a larger community of peoples transcending cultural, ideological, ethnic and national differences" (OAU 1999). They hoped to significantly transform the OAU, now considered an anachronistic organization incapable of dealing with the realities of the new globalization, and produce a more fitting arrangement for the new millennium. In their own words, "It is also our conviction that our Continental Organization needs to be revitalized in order to be able to play a more active role and continue to be relevant to the needs of our peoples and responsive to the demands of the prevailing circumstances" (OAU 1999). In addition, the participants agreed to:

- Quicken the pace of implementing the 1991 Abuja Treaty, which established an African Economic Community.

- Speed up the process of establishing all of the institutions provided in the Treaty: an African Central Bank, an African Monetary Union, an African Court of Justice, and a Pan-African Parliament.
- Strengthen and consolidate existing regional economic communities.
- Mandate the OAU's Council of Ministers to ensure implementation of those decisions, particularly to prepare the legal text necessary in light of the existing Charter and the Abuja Treaty.
- Mandate the OAU chairman and Algerian President Abdelaziz Bouteflika and South African President Thabo Mbeki to engage African creditors with the goal of securing the total cancellation of Africa's debt.

At the time of the meeting in Libya in 1999, it had become quite clear, even to a casual observer, that the OAU as currently constituted was no longer able to deal effectively with Africa's mounting political problems. The organization had outlived its usefulness and had become anachronistic, failing to deal with such complex political problems as the implosion of several states (e.g., Rwanda, Somalia, Liberia, and Sierra Leone), the economically and socially debilitating war in Angola, the issue of self-determination for the people of the Western Sahara, the North–South conflict in the Sudan, the conflict in the Great Lakes Region, the Anglophone Problem in Cameroon, and many other issues. Basically, the OAU was simply unable to deal effectively with the many inter- and intra-African conflicts that were endangering the peace and hampering the economic and social development of the continent.

It is not difficult to see why the OAU has not been able to deal with the continent's problems, especially those that deal with peacekeeping. As structured in 1963, the OAU was supposed to serve only an advisory role and was not empowered to, for example, keep the peace (C. M. Shaw 1998, 8). Hence, its Charter did not provide for the eventual establishment of a peacekeeping structure. Since 1963, then, the organization has only been able to make recommendations to member states since it has no authority to enforce its decisions. Unfortunately, many states have often found it to be in their best interest to ignore the recommendations and take a different course of action (T. M. Shaw 1982, 140). As argued by William Eteki Mbouma 1978, 21), the former OAU secretary-general, "[t]he basic problem is that the OAU, even in its Charter, is not a supra-national body. It is a sort of institution that cannot impose any solution, and consequently is sometimes unable to implement its own resolutions."

Unlike his counterparts in such regional organizations as the Arab League and the Organization of American States, the secretary-general of the OAU has virtually no power to deal with most of the problems that plague the continent, including inter- and intracountry conflict. The OAU Commission of Mediation, Conciliation, and Arbitration, which, in terms of the Charter, is required to settle all disputes in Africa by peaceful means, lacks the authority even to require that the states in conflict appear before it. It cannot even interpret the OAU Charter, unlike the International Court of Justice (ICJ). There is no provision in the Charter that enables the Commission to enforce its decisions, unlike the U.N.

Security Council, which can take enforcement measures under Chapter VII of the U.N. Charter. Thus, in structural terms the OAU is too weak an organization to resolve conflicts in Africa. There are institutional weaknesses deriving first from the discordant political voices of Africa and second from a deficiency of resources and manpower (Venter 1994, 53). According to another writer, the OAU's weaknesses include the fact that it does not enjoy a significant level of popular support, that most member states do not pay their dues on time, and that given the pervasive political instability (including violent ethnic mobilization) that has characterized most countries in the continent since the early 1960s, the governments of its member states have been pre-occupied with crisis management in their own countries and have had little time and effort to devote to the activities of the OAU (C. M. Shaw 1998, 3–12).

Added to this structural weakness is the fact that the OAU does not have sufficient financial resources to carry out its functions. A significant number of members have remained delinquent in meeting their fiscal responsibilities, and there is no provision in the Charter under which these delinquent states can be forced to pay their dues. Appeals by the administrative secretary-general and by the OAU itself, through its resolutions, have failed to improve the situation in this regard. It is true that many African countries are unable to secure enough financial resources to meet domestic obligations, let alone contribute to the OAU. As argued by Venter (1994, 58), defaulters are "very often the ones who are long on words and short on action." The OAU cannot be expected to discharge its duties without adequate financial resources (T. M. Shaw 1982, 188).

The OAU is also constrained in its ability to serve the needs of the African continent by the struggle between Pan-Arabism and Pan-Africanism. In general, many African countries that have broken diplomatic relations with the state of Israel as an expression of solidarity with the Palestinians, believe that the Arabs have not reciprocated and have failed to contribute, especially given their enormous windfalls from the sale of petroleum, to the alleviation of poverty in the continent. It is interesting to note that a significant amount of the hardship suffered by many African countries, especially those in sub-Saharan Africa, are made possible by high prices for petroleum products, a consequence of the oil-price increases imposed by members of the Organization of Petroleum Exporting Countries, a significant number of whom are Arab countries. In addition, as a result of agreements signed between France and its former colonies at independence, the economies of Francophone countries remain "integrated" into that of France. In fact, through the adoption of the franc CFA, most Francophone countries in Africa have, for more than forty years, surrendered monetary policy to the French treasury in exchange for guaranteed conversion of the CFA franc into the French franc. Despite the littering of the continent with many regional economic schemes, most of the economies of the African countries remain tied to those of Western Europe and other industrial countries. There has not been very much improvement in inter-African trade.

These are a few of the issues that were weighing on the minds of the African leaders who had assembled at the historic Fourth Extraordinary Session of the Assembly of the Heads of State and Government on September 8–9, 1999, in Sirte. At that meeting, as already mentioned, they took the decision to establish a new organization that would be able to meet the challenges posed by the post–Cold War global economy. The moribund OAU was to be replaced by an active, energetic, and powerful organization that could arrest economic deterioration in the continent and provide the wherewithal for Africans to participate in and benefit from the new globalization. The Sirte Declaration, adopted after a two-day session, emphasized the need to have a new organization that would be able to solve many problems that the continent was suffering from, and which the OAU, as it was constituted, was unable to solve. The declaration went on to say,

As we prepare to enter the twenty-first century, and cognizant of the challenges that will confront our continent and peoples, we emphasize the imperative need and a high sense of urgency to rekindle the aspirations of our peoples for stronger unity, solidarity and cohesion in a larger community of people transcending cultural, ideological, ethnic, and national differences. . . . In order to cope with these challenges and to effectively address the new social, political, and economic realities in Africa and in the world, we are determined to fulfil our peoples' aspirations for greater unity in conformity with the objectives of the OAU Charter and the Treaty Establishing the African Economic Community (the Abuja Treaty). It is also our conviction that our continental Organization needs to be revitalized in order to be able to play a more active role and continue to be relevant to the needs of our peoples and responsive to the demands of the prevailing circumstances. We are also determined to eliminate the scourge of conflicts which constitutes a major impediment to the implementation of our development and integration agenda (OAU 1999, 1).

MAIN FEATURES OF THE CONSTITUTIVE ACT OF AFRICAN UNION

The Constitutive Act of African Union, like the OAU Charter, in our view, does not contain a blueprint for the formation of a United States of Africa. Article 2 (b) of the Constitutive Act, inter alia, provides that the Union shall "defend the sovereignty, territorial integrity and independence of its member states." There is no mention of dismantling the territorial boundaries of African states as a preliminary step necessary for the formation of the United States of Africa. Not only that, Article 4 (a) and (h) also talk of "sovereign equality" of Member States, and insists on giving respect to the "borders existing on the achievement of independence," almost as the OAU Charter does in its Article III. There are other provisions in the Constitutive Act, such as "non-interference by any Member State in the internal affairs of another" (Article 4 [g]) and "co-existence of Member States" (Article 4 [i]), all of which go to prove that the new document also supports the maintenance of the status quo in Africa insofar as the question of giving institutional shape to the ideal of African unity is concerned. Of course, this does not mean that future generations cannot amend the agreement and proceed with integration when they feel that the time is right for such a move.

The Constitutive Act of the African Union, however, is a bit more elaborate than the OAU Charter. The former envisages the formation of a larger number of organs or institutions than were provided for in the OAU Charter. Whereas the OAU Charter provides for four "institutions" (Article VII), the African Union allows for the establishment of nine "organs": (1) the Assembly of the Union, (2) the Executive Council, (3) the Pan-African Parliament, (4) the Court of Justice, (5) the Commission, (6) the Permanent Representatives Committee, (7) the Special Technical Committees, (8) the Economic, Social and Cultural Council, and (9) the financial institutions (see Article 5 of the Constitutive Act).

In the African Union, the OAU Assembly of Heads of State and Government has been replaced by an "Assembly of the Union" and vested with some enlarged functions. The Council of Ministers of the OAU has been replaced by an "Executive Council" in the African Union with significant additions to its functions. The Executive Council, under the African Union, shall coordinate and take decisions on policies in areas of common interest to member states, such as (1) foreign trade; (2) energy, industry, and mineral resources; (3) food, agricultural, and animal resources, livestock production, and forestry; (4) water resources and irrigation; (5) environmental protection, humanitarian action, and disaster response and relief; (6) transport and communications; and (7) insurance (see Article 13 of the Constitutive Act). The OAU Council of Ministers was not vested with these functions; its only job was to implement the decisions of the Assembly and coordinate inter-African cooperation in accordance with the instructions of the Assembly of Heads of State and Government. Therefore, from the nature of its vast array of functions it appears that the Executive Council, under the Constitutive Act, may turn out in the end as the forerunner of the cabinet of the United States of Africa if and when it is established in the future.

The Constitutive Act envisages seven technical committees, each in charge of a special technical function. They take the place of five Special Commissions in the outgoing OAU.

The major innovation that the Constitutive Act of African Union can be credited with is the creation of a Pan-African Parliament. No similar organization or institution was provided for under the OAU Charter. The composition, powers, functions, and organization of this parliament shall be defined in a separate protocol. Whether it will be a unicameral or bicameral legislature, how many members there will be, and how they will be elected will also perhaps be provided for in the Protocol. All that the Constitutive Act provides for is that such a parliament would ensure full participation of African peoples in the development and economic integration of the continent (see Article 17 of the Constitutive Act). Since the details about the composition and powers of the Pan-African Parliament have not yet been worked out, we are unable to make further comments on the subject. However, it is believed that the Parliament would have purely consultative powers (Boateng 2000, 1).

The Constitutive Act also provides for the establishment of a Court of Justice, which, when constituted, will take the place of the Commission of Mediation, Conciliation, and Arbitration provided for under the OAU Charter. This Commission, as we know, has remained a nonstarter to this day; it is still to hold its first meeting. Comments on this feature of the Constitutive Act also will have to be deferred until its details are worked out and incorporated in a Protocol.

Another innovation in the Constitutive Act is the creation of a Permanent Representatives Committee, whose task will be to help the Executive Council in the discharge of its functions. Such a Committee did not exist under the OAU. An Economic, Social, and Cultural Council has also been created, but its composition, powers, and functions have not been defined in the Constitutive Act.

The African Union shall have three financial institutions; namely, the African Central Bank, the African Monetary Fund, and the African Investment Bank (see Article 19 of the Constitutive Act). There was no such provision in the OAU Charter, although the Abuja Treaty did envisage the creation of such institutions.

It is hoped that the Pan-African Parliament, the Court of Justice, the African Central Bank, the African Monetary Fund, and the African Investment Bank will help to achieve greater unity between African countries. As the African Union makes progress, a common currency will be introduced for the continent and a common defense force will also be eventually established.

The important thing is that the regional and subregional economic organizations that are functioning at present in the continent will not be dissolved when the African Union comes into existence, which would be one month after two-thirds of the member states have ratified the Constitutive Act. They will continue to function in their respective spheres, but the duty of the African Union will be to coordinate and harmonize their policies for the gradual attainment of continental unity.

An important feature of the Constitutive Act of African Union is that it vests the Assembly with power to impose sanctions on any member state that defaults in the payment of its contribution to the budget of the African Union. The sanctions can be in the form of denial of the right to speak at meetings, to vote, to present candidates for any position or post within the Union, or to benefit from any activity or commitments therefrom (see Article 23 of the Constitutive Act). It is also provided (in Article 23) that "any Member State that fails to comply with the decisions and policies of the Union may be subjected to other sanctions, such as the denial of transport and communications links with other Member States, and other measures of a political and economic nature to be determined by the Assembly." These provisions are expected to deter the member states from refusing to honor their financial obligations to the African Union, as well as make certain that they refrain from acting contrary to the policies and decisions of the African Union. This may be regarded as a major improvement over the provisions of the now defunct OAU, which was unable to punish recalcitrant members.

On the whole, the establishment of the African Union is a "giant" step that may lead to greater unity among African states. It is certainly a bold initiative, full of promise, taken by African governments, and has come at the right time. It is a good sign that African leaders have begun to realize that the survival of their continent lies in increased levels of political and economic integration. It will be easier for them to meet these challenges if they act collectively rather than individually. Today, a growing number of Africans is realizing that individual African countries cannot stand alone against the power of the transnational corporations that have exploited them and their resources since the colonial period for the benefit of the metropolitan economies. They need to come together in order to successfully defend their interests. An African trading bloc should significantly improve the ability of Africans to benefit from the new globalization. Politically, integration should enhance Africa's ability to participate in global affairs.

BUILDING ON THE FOUNDATION PROVIDED BY THE OAU

It would be wrong to write off the OAU as an organization that achieved nothing praiseworthy during its thirty-eight years of existence. The African Union has to build on the manifold achievements of the OAU. Despite its failures, the OAU, since its founding in 1963, has kept the spirit of unity alive among Africans. It has helped to develop "Africanness" among Africans of diverse ethnic backgrounds. The OAU has been able to project an African identity, and to solidify and enhance the Africanness of the African people. Although this unity is sometimes artificial, it nevertheless does exist and continues to remind the world of the existence of something called "Africa" (Venter 1994, 49). The OAU has also succeeded in generating a psychological need for togetherness among its member states. Unless there is this "togetherness" of African countries, individual African states would not have the wherewithal to significantly affect global affairs (Novicki 1992, 39).

One cannot deny the fact that the OAU has succeeded in providing some level of unity to Africans during the last several decades. It was because of the OAU that the Casablanca and Monrovia blocs became redundant. Despite its many problems, the OAU has enjoyed a significant level of international prestige, serving as the recognized voice of Africa. During the Cold War the OAU was regularly called upon to speak for Africa and provide solutions to the continent's problems. As Timothy Shaw (1982, 139) has stated, "the OAU has acted as an effective spokesman for the entire continent in its relation with extracontinental powers."

The OAU has, no doubt, been unable to solve many African problems, but nobody can deny the fact that it has provided a forum for promoting reconciliation between African leaders who were not otherwise prepared to share the negotiating table with their opponents as, for example, Julius Nyerere of Tanzania and Idi Amin of Uganda, Emperor Haile Selassie of Ethiopia and Said Barre of Somalia, and King Hassan of Morocco and Moukhtar Ouldh Daddah of Mauritania.

The OAU has also succeeded in mediating disputes among member states and resolving conflicts that could have required some sort of extracontinental intervention, as, for example, in the Morocco–Algerian conflict in 1963, the Chad–Sudan conflict in 1966, the on and off conflict between Rwanda and Burundi, and the Ghana–Guinea dispute in 1966. Although the OAU was unable to effectively resolve these conflicts, it did in each case, succeed in diffusing what were potentially explosive situations. The organization has made a concerted effort to create an atmosphere conducive to the resolution of seemingly intractable problems (Jonah 1974, 146).

Standing on the foundation provided by the OAU, the African bloc at the United Nations has been able to sponsor or cosponsor a large number of resolutions that were subsequently adopted by the world body. The bloc has also been able to bring about some important amendments to the U.N. Charter, particularly to Articles 23, 27, and 61, with the result that the membership of the Security Council was increased from eleven to fifteen and that of the Economic and Social Council of the United Nations from eighteen to twenty-seven. The OAU has been used by African states as an instrument for the conduct of collective diplomacy in the world forum. Of late, the OAU has taken some bold initiatives in areas that were hitherto neglected by it. In June 1981 the OAU adopted the African Charter on Human and Peoples' Rights, and in 1993 it broke new ground with the establishment of a Mechanism for Conflict Prevention, Management, and Resolution. The five areas in which the OAU is most active now are economic development of Africa, human rights, refugee problems, AIDS-related problems, and conflict management. The OAU has also thrown its weight behind many of the prodemocracy movements that became operational in the continent in the late 1980s.

With the outgoing OAU having so many significant achievements to its credit, the African Union, its replacement, will not have to start from scratch. The African Union can draw upon the experience of the OAU in handling the various social, political, and economic problems that continue to plague the continent. As already stated, while the OAU did not succeed in solving many of the problems that the continent faced, it did create a forum where representatives of African states could sit across the table and try to sort out the problems that confronted them. Prior to the establishment of the OAU there was no such forum where mutual contacts at the continental level could be made among African states. The OAU, then, was the first ever forum where African leaders could meet and discuss the problems of common concern to their countries.

Of course, there have been other organizations that have provided Africans with the wherewithal to sit and discuss their problems, especially in the area of trade and economics. Several of these organizations were created through the initiative and encouragement of the U.N. Economic Commission for Africa. The most important of these groupings are the Union of Arab Maghreb, the West African Economic and Monetary Union, the Economic Community of West African States, the Customs and Economic Union of Central Africa, the Economic and Monetary Community in Central Africa, the Economic Community of Central African States, the Common Market for Eastern and Southern Africa, the Southern African Development Community, established in July 1979 as the Southern African Development Coordination Conference, the Southern African Customs Union, and the Common Monetary Area (Africa Institute of South Africa 1998, 62–70). Working under the auspices of these organizations and trying to solve common economic problems, the African states have further developed the habit of cooperation with each other.

The African Union has to pick up where the OAU left off and work to provide a more enabling environment for increased unity and cooperation in the continent. The experience gained in working together during the existence of the OAU will help African states to move forward and further cement the bonds of unity among themselves. The numerous institutions that are being created under the African Union, such as the African Parliament, the Court of Justice, the technical committees, and various financial institutions, will go a long way in strengthening the forces of unity throughout the length and breadth of the continent. It must be emphasized that it will take time for continental unity to be realized. African states will have to work patiently toward this important goal by enlarging the area of their mutual cooperation and creating more and more opportunities for working together in pursuit of common, mutually beneficial objectives.

While the objective of achieving African unity may be within reach of African states if they continue to enlarge the area of functional cooperation among themselves, the same cannot be said about the establishment of a federation in the form of a United States of Africa. As the situation currently exists, it is not likely that such a federation would be realized any time soon. Too many constraints presently exist to the establishment of a continental-level governmental structure. The most appropriate governmental structure for an African Commonwealth would have to be one that is democratic and provides the structures for all relevant stakeholder groups to maximize their values. In other words, some form of constitutional federalism must inform the establishment of such a continental government. It is not likely that such a democratic governance system can be easily structured from the various governance systems that now exist in the continent, especially when one considers the prevalence of authoritarianism in the continent.

There will be one head of state if the United States of Africa is formed. One of the existing heads of state or even an individual outside existing political cycles may become the head of state in the new United States of Africa. What will happen to other heads of state? Will they be prepared to become the governors of their existing states, which would be turned into provinces in the federal setup? Will the King of Morocco, for example, agree to surrender his kingship and accept the governorship of his kingdom-turned-province? It is difficult to see many heads of state accepting such a demotion in their political status. Even if they do, they will first have to amend their constitutions to permit such a demotion in their status. To the best of our knowledge, only the constitution of Senegal, among the existing African constitutions, permits such a demotion in the status of the head of state. The constitution of Senegal provides for the subordination of its sovereignty to an overall African political organization. The president of Senegal, Mr. Abdoulaye Wade, said that he "was prepared to propose to the Senegalese people that I am prepared to become the governor of Senegal in a politically united Africa. It would not be degrading for us to be compared to the governors of California, Massachusetts, Ohio or any other American governorship, which are much richer than Senegal" (Boateng 2000, 3).

The creation of the United States of Africa will require many sacrifices on the part of African states and their leaders, without which a common stance cannot emerge. They will have to surrender a portion of their sovereignty to the continental government. Few African states appear to be willing to take that step at the moment. It therefore seems that the United States of Africa is many decades away. For the present, African states must try to make the African Union a success.

The establishment of the African Union has naturally not been welcomed in the West. The Western countries would like to see Africa balkanized so that they can easily exploit the rich natural resources of the continent for their own benefit. In 1963 the West tried to sabotage the creation of the OAU, and although they failed, they nevertheless made it difficult for the organization to carry out its functions. Today, as Africans embark on another integration effort, they should be aware of the fact that the West is not likely to support their efforts.

CONCLUSION

African states have created a new continental organization that is vastly different from the OAU. If the African Union is able to receive full cooperation from member states, it should be able to solve many problems that have bedeviled the continent, accelerate socioeconomic development, and promote African unity. For the success of the African Union, two things are required from member states: one, they regularly pay their annual dues to the Union; and two, they comply with the policies and decisions of the Union government. Of course, the AU must function democratically, providing all relevant stakeholder groups with the facilities to participate fully in policy design so that policies adopted reflect the interests and concerns of the member states. Such an approach to policy design will encourage compliance and minimize the chance that member states will take positions contrary to that of the Union.

As we have pointed out in this chapter, one of the most important impediments to the proper functioning of the OAU was the fact that member states defaulted on the payment of their annual dues. Paucity of funds left the OAU unable to carry out its functions and hampered many of its activities, including those relating to peacekeeping. In addition, Member States often acted in open defiance of the policies and decisions of the OAU, which had no power to take any action against such erring states.

What is the guarantee that the African Union will not be as cash starved an organization as the OAU? After all, the economic condition of African states has not improved significantly over the years. In fact, it has worsened in recent years, as evidenced by deteriorating standards of living in many countries in the continent, especially those in sub-Saharan Africa (see, e.g., UNDP 2000). Unless economic conditions for the African countries change dramatically for the better, the African Union is likely to face the same financial problems that plagued the OAU. Since the African Union is a continental organization, its costs would have to be borne by the African countries. The AU is expected to help Africans and African countries assert their independence, especially from the industrial countries of the West. It would be ironic if the same West that these countries are trying to get away from is asked to assume the costs of maintaining the African Union. If African countries are serious about asserting their independence and taking their place in the global community and having other members treat them with respect, they must come up with the funds to finance this important organization. For one thing, if they rely on external actors to finance the African Union, such groups will invariably dictate policy to the Union and, as a consequence, the programs promoted by the Union would not likely be those that serve African interests.

Despite these difficulties, the outgoing OAU secretary-general, Salim Ahmed Salim, hailed the birth of the new organization as a "genuine attempt at a new beginning in the quest for greater unity and cohesion in our continent" (quoted in Ejine 2001, 1). The Pan-Africanists say that the goal of African unity may be Herculean, but is achievable. This may be true, but we have to wait and watch until the new organization becomes fully operational. After all, the proof of the pudding is in the eating.

ACKNOWLEDGMENTS

The author wishes to thank Korwa G. Adar, associate professor of international studies, Rhodes University, Grahamstown, South Africa, for critical and useful comments on an earlier draft of this chapter.

REFERENCES

Africa Institute of South Africa. 1998. *Africa A-Z: Continental and country profiles.* Pretoria: Africa Institute of South Africa.

Boateng, O. 2000. Africa: Giant step for union. *New African* 388 (September): Retrieved from http://www.africas.com/icpubs.

Cervenka, Z. 1977. *The unfinished quest for unity: Africa and the OAU*. London: Friedman.

Ejine, P. 2001. Beyond the Sirte II Declaration. Retrieved from http://www.panapress.com/english/2001/Mar/4/eng001933.htm.

Jonah, J.O.C. 1974. The OAU and its role in the maintenance of international peace and security in Africa. In *Africa and international organization*, edited by Y. Ayouty and H. C. Brooks. The Hague: Martinus Hijhoff.

Legum, C. 1962. *Pan-Africanism: A short political guide*. London: Pall Mall Press.

LeVine, V. T. 1964. *The Cameroons: From mandate to independence*. Stanford: Hoover Institution

Mbaku, J. M. 1995. Emerging global trade blocs and the future of African participation in the world economy. *Journal of Economic Integration* 10 (2): 141–177.

Mbaku, J. M. 1997. *Institutions and reform in Africa: The public choice perspective*. Westport, CT: Praeger.

Mbouma, W. Eteki. 1978. The spirit needs to change: Interview by Godwin Matatu. *Africa* 83: 20–23.

Nkrumah, K. 1963. *Africa must unite*. London: Heinemann.

Novicki, M. A. 1992. Interview: A new agenda for the OAU. *Africa Report* 37 (3): 37–39.

OAU. 1999. *The Sirte declaration* (Fourth Extraordinary Session of the Assembly of Heads of State and Government, September 8–9), Sirte, Libya.

OAU/ECA. 1979. *Africa toward the year 2000: Final report on the joint OAU/ECA symposium on the future development of Africa*. Addis Ababa, Ethiopia: OAU/ECA.

OAU. 2001. *Press Release No. 52/2001*. Addis Ababa: OAU.

Padelford, N. J. 1964. The Organization of African Unity. *International Organization* 18 (2): 521–542.

Saxena, S. C. 1981. Introduction. In *Nigeria, Africa and the world*, edited by J. O. Omolodun. Delhi: n.p. (The book was self-published by its editor, who at the time was the Nigerian High Commissioner to India).

Saxena, S. C. 1993. *Politics in Africa*. Delhi: Kalinga.

Saxena, S. C. 1995. *Western Sahara: No alternative to armed struggle*. Delhi: Kalinga.

Saxena, S. C. 2001. *Major political issues in Africa*. Delhi: Kalinga.

Shaw, C. M. 1998. Organization of African Unity and its potential for resolving African conflicts. *Africa Quarterly* (Delhi) 38 (1): 1–20.

Shaw, T. M. 1982. *Alternative futures for Africa*. Boulder, CO: Westview.

Thomas, J. T., and A. van W. Thomas. 1959. *The Organization of American States and collective security*. Dallas: Southern Methodist University School of Law and the Southwestern Legal Foundation.

Thompson, V. B. 1969. *Africa and unity: The evolution of Pan-Africanism*. London: Macmillan.

UNDP. 2000. *Human development report, 2000*. New York: Oxford University Press.

Venter, D. 1994. An evaluation of the OAU on the eve of South Africa's accession. *Africa Insight* 24 (1): 47–59.

Wallerstein, I. 1967. *Africa: The politics of unity*. New York: Vintage.

8

Fighting Poverty and Deprivation in Africa: The Continuing Struggle

JOHN MUKUM MBAKU

During the colonial period the majority of Africans believed that high levels of poverty and deprivation among the indigenous populations were due primarily to exploitation and plunder by the Europeans. Colonialism was a cruel, exploitative, and opportunistic system designed to maximize the objectives and interests of the Europeans. As a consequence, colonial state policies were designed to enhance the ability of resident European entrepreneurs to exploit the resources of the colonies for the benefit of the metropolitan economies. In fact, throughout many of the colonies, public policies favored the production of so-called export crops (e.g., cocoa, rubber, and coffee) while neglecting the production of foodstuffs, all of which had significant domestic demand. In many instances land owned communally by indigenous ethnic groups and used for the production of essential foodstuffs to meet local needs was confiscated and converted into the plantations that were devoted to the production of these cash crops (see, generally, Rudin 1938; Burns 1963; Rapley 1993). In addition, the laws and institutions imposed on the Africans by the European colonizers stunted the development of indigenous entrepreneurship and prevented the emergence of an African business class. In those colonies with significant populations of European colonists or settlers, the effort to discourage the development of indigenous capitalism was quite intense and much more focused. Although there have been claims to the contrary, the overall aim of colonialism was not to enhance the ability of Africans to govern themselves and allocate their resources more effectively (i.e., create the wealth they needed to confront massive poverty and deprivation). Colonialism, on the other hand, was an exploitative, despotic, degradative, and extremely cruel system, designed to advance European interests at the expense of African values (see, e.g., Fatton 1990, 455–473).

Africans, especially marginalized groups and communities (e.g., women, rural dwellers, and the unemployed and underemployed inhabitants of the peripheral areas of the urban sectors), perceived independence to be an opportunity to rid their societies of the most important source of their poverty: European colonialism. Independence and the subsequent capture of the apparatus of government was expected to significantly enhance development in the former colonies. It was expected that the state, captured or inherited from the Europeans, would be dismantled and "reconstructed" to provide a new dispensation that was based on African values, traditions, interests, and aspirations. The new postindependence laws and institutions, which were to be designed through a participative, inclusive, and bottom-up process (that is, with the full and effective participation of the relevant stakeholder groups), would significantly enhance the ability of Africans to (1) live together peacefully in the new nations, and (2) create the wealth that they needed to deal with endemic poverty and deprivation. A government, now controlled and dominated by indigenous elites, was expected to design and implement only policies that enhanced the national wealth and contributed to an improvement in the quality of life of the African peoples, especially the historically marginalized and deprived groups and communities. It is important to note here, however, that this view of the postindependence state may not have been shared by all Africans, as evidenced by the behavior of several of the continent's immediate independence leaders (e.g., Mobotu Sese Seko of Zaire, K. Banda of Malawi, Ahmadou Ahidjo of Cameroon, and several others). While many ordinary Africans saw independence as bringing about new governance structures that would improve popular participation, enhance entrepreneurial activities, and advance coexistence of groups, many of the opportunistic elites who captured the governments at independence hoped to use these structures to enrich themselves. As will be argued later in this chapter, many of the new African leaders made no effort to engage the people in genuine state reconstruction through democratic constitution-making to provide them with the types of institutional arrangements that would have effectively constrained the abuse of government agency and enhanced sustainable development. Instead, they undertook opportunistic institutional reforms that increased and strengthened their ability to monopolize political spaces and the allocation of resources. Thus, during the last forty years many African leaders have been able to promote perverse economic policies that have enriched them but have increased levels of poverty and material deprivation among the general population (e.g., Ahmadou Ahidjo and Paul Biya in Cameroon, Mobutu Sese Seko in Zaire, Daniel arap Moi in Kenya, Siaka Stevens in Sierra Leone, and several military elites in Nigeria, just to name a few). It is important, of course, not to forget the political, economic, and social exploits of the apartheid regime of South Africa, which was able to manipulate national laws and institutions to create and sustain privileges for the minority white population while forcing the African peoples into a life of excruciating poverty and deprivation (see, Mbaku 1997, for a review of the literature on the postindependence misadventures of African leaders, as well as on the apartheid regime in South Africa).

Since the 1960s, when most of the colonies in sub-Saharan Africa began to gain independence, a significant number of ruling elites have viewed governance and resource allocation differently from the general populace. The latter, most of whom remain extremely poor and deprived, view proper governance as enfranchising them and providing them with the facilities to participate fully and effectively in the design and implementation of policies affecting their welfare. They expect their government, at both the federal (central) and local levels to enhance their ability to provide for themselves and their families. Government and governance are expected to enhance the ability of the people to create the wealth that society needs to meet its needs. Unfortunately, as the evidence from the last several decades has shown, most of Africa's ruling classes appear to have been interested primarily in using state structures for private capital accumulation purposes. Thus, most of the public policies promulgated during the greater part of the postindependence period have been those that have enhanced the ability of these leaders to exploit their economies for their own benefit. In the process, most Africans have been impoverished.

INDEPENDENCE AND THE ABUSE OF GOVERNMENT AGENCY

Shortly after independence, many Africans felt that the new state was the one institution uniquely qualified to confront mass poverty. Thus, many citizens were willing and actually eager to grant the government significant power to intervene in economic activities. Through such intervention it was believed that the state could more effectively meet certain pressing and critical societal goals. Of course, the most serious of this was the alleviation of poverty and the subsequent improvement of the quality of life of the several groups that had been severely exploited and marginalized by many years of colonialism. Accordingly, each new state was granted significant political and economic power and allowed to intervene in private exchange as well as own and manage productive resources. Throughout the continent, the postindependence state came to be an all-encompassing institution that turned out to be, instead, a major constraint to wealth creation and sustainable development. Rather than serve as an instrument for the alleviation of poverty, as many people had expected it to be, the state, through its economic and political policies, became the major source of violence against the people and poverty among many groups.[2]

Other reasons have been advanced to support the excessive expansion of the state in postindependence Africa. First, many of the ruling elites of the time believed that the state was the only institution capable of rebuilding societies and communities that had been destroyed by many years of colonial exploitation. Second, the state, now controlled and dominated by indigenous elites, was considered the only institution strong enough, and that possessed the wherewithal to hold together competing ethnic groups and provide the enabling environment for national integration, peaceful coexistence, and sustainable development. Third, many social scientists of the time had argued that the state was the only organization able to successfully undertake the large and complicated development projects that each African country needed to generate enough resources to meet rising societal needs. Fourth, the general ethos of the time favored expansion of the welfare state and government management of the economy. Fifth, a significant number of Africa's new leaders had been educated in Europe where, as a result of an historical process of incorporating labor into the region's democracies, many of the states had become quite involved in social engineering and had eventually come to dominate economic activities (see, e.g., Webb 1897). As a consequence, many of the former colonies adopted development models that emphasized state control and regulation of economic activities, deemphasized market processes, and relied more on the government for the allocation of resources. In the so-called Afro–Marxist states the government took control of many of the activities that during the colonial period had been undertaken by the private sector (Decalo 1992). The development projects that were supposed to (1) provide employment opportunities for the people and (2) generate the wealth needed for fighting poverty were considered too risky and not particularly appropriate for the private sector to undertake. The state was either expected to undertake these projects directly or subsidize the private sector so it could organize them profitably (World Bank 1997). In many countries in the continent, governments opted to directly undertake these activities (Krueger 1992). A significant number of opinion leaders of the time argued that rapid economic growth and development required a more activist role for the new government. Under this approach to resource allocation the government was not supposed to just provide the enabling environment in which the private sector could create wealth, but was expected to become actively involved in wealth creation itself (see, e.g., Mbaku 1997). In addition, the state was expected to use its regulatory powers to redistribute the income and wealth generated by the private sector to make certain that existing inequalities and inequities in the distribution of resources were eliminated. As a consequence, many of Africa's new leaders did not consider it inappropriate to undertake production and distribution activities that during colonialism had been handled exclusively by the private sector, such as ownership and management of hotels, marketing of agricultural products, and the provision of several other goods and services. Unfortunately, the politicization of resource allocation that emerged from this approach to economic development was to have a significantly negative effect on production efficiency and the alleviation of poverty in postindependence society.

The laws and institutions that many African countries adopted at independence failed to adequately constrain the state, allowing the new leaders to abuse their public positions and engage in many forms of opportunism (e.g., rent seeking and corruption) to enrich themselves at the expense of the rest of the people. In fact, many of the large-scale enterprises that were supposed to form the foundation for rapid economic and industrial growth were easily converted into instruments for the private capital accumulation activities of the ruling elites. In addition, the regulatory system that was supposed to enhance the government's ability to promote growth with equity became a tool for the extralegal enrichment of members of the hegemonic class. Thus, corruption, rent seeking, and rent extraction came to dominate the economies of many countries in Africa, as ruling elites frequently abused the exercise of government agency to generate extralegal income for themselves. As the evidence from the last forty years has shown, the results were increased levels of poverty and deprivation, a failure to develop and sustain viable economic and political structures, and pervasive destructive ethnic conflict (Mbaku 1997).

GOVERNMENT REGULATORY ACTIVITIES AND POVERTY IN AFRICA

Regardless of its motivation, government intervention in private exchange must be considered a hidden tax on entrepreneurial effort and the creation of wealth. Government regulation of economic activity reduces competition in the marketplace and constrains the ability of entrepreneurs to engage in wealth-creating activities. Weidenbaum (1998, 360) has provided a sampling of some of the adverse economic effects of government regulation:

- the cost to taxpayers for supporting a galaxy of government regulators;
- the cost to consumers in the form of higher prices to cover the added expense of producing goods and services under government regulation;
- the cost to workers in the form of jobs eliminated by regulation;
- the cost to the economy resulting from the loss of enterprises that cannot afford to meet the onerous burdens of government regulations; and
- the cost to society, as a whole, as a result of a reduced flow of new and better products and a less rapid rise in the standard of living.

Of course, there are several beneficial effects of government intervention in the marketplace. Many of those individuals and groups that support government regulation argue that the latter can provide society with a more livable (that is, cleaner) environment, higher-quality drinking water, safer consumer products, healthier working environments, more equitable distribution of income and wealth, and so on. In addition, one can argue that since most of the economic and social problems that the African countries now suffer from were caused primarily by colonial state intervention, resolving them requires the direct intervention of the postcolonial state. Finally, market failure (that is, the inability of the market under certain circumstances to allocate resources efficiently) has been advanced as a justification for government intervention in the African economies.

In this chapter, we will not attempt to provide the reader with an exhaustive review of the impact of government intervention on the African economies. Our main objective is to show that government intervention as a way to deal with poverty and deprivation can only be undertaken effectively and efficiently if it is carried out within an environment characterized by participatory, transparent, and accountable (i.e., democratic) institutional arrangements. The latter determine the incentive structures faced by participants in both political (e.g., civil servants) and economic (e.g., entrepreneurs) markets. In the absence of appropriate incentive structures (and proper constraints on the state) the government's power to regulate economic activities will most likely be used by civil servants, politicians, and interest groups to enrich themselves at the expense of the rest of the people. To ensure that the power of the government to intervene in private exchange is used properly and only to enhance the national wealth, existing institutional arrangements must properly constrain the state and its agents.

At independence, most of the African countries adopted laws and institutions that did not properly constrain the government. As a consequence, those who captured the evacuated structures of colonial hegemony were able to manipulate government regulations to extract extralegal benefits for themselves. Instead of using state regulatory powers to enhance entrepreneurial activities and the creation of wealth (in other words, to complement the activities of the private sector), civil servants converted government structures into instruments of plunder and in the process amassed a lot of wealth for themselves while subjecting the rest of the people to excruciating levels of poverty. During the last forty years, corruption and rent seeking have become pervasive in most African economies, and today these forms of political opportunism remain important obstacles to poverty alleviation (see, e.g., Mbaku 2000).

According to recent data released by the UNDP (2000), of the thirty poorest countries in the world, twenty-seven (or 90 percent) can be found in Africa (see Table 8.1). Perhaps more important is the fact that Africa is the only region of the world in which prospects for the future remain relatively bleak. In addition to the fact that most African countries, especially those in sub-Saharan Africa, are still unable to provide themselves with effective and sustainable wealth-creating structures, the region's most productive labor resources are being decimated by AIDS.

In the last fifty years or so, economic performance in the majority of African countries has been very poor, and as a consequence the region has not done very well in the area of human development. Although a few countries (e.g., Mauritius, Botswana, and Libya) have performed relatively well in the area of human development, most of the region continues to suffer from relatively high levels of poverty and deprivation. Table 8.2 provides information on human development in several regions of the world. The data provided here confirm sub-Saharan Africa's dismal economic performance. In 1998, nearly forty years after most colonies in the region began to gain independence, the per capita GDP was only $1,607 (measured at PPP; that is, GDP converted to U.S. dollars by the purchasing power parity exchange rate), or 25 percent of that of Latin America and Caribbean and 45 percent of that of East Asia (Table 8.2).

Table 8.1
The Thirty Least Developed Countries in the World

HDI Rank	Country	Life Expectancy at Birth (years), 1998	Adult Literacy Rate (% age fifteen and above)	Per Capita GDP (PPP U.S. $), 1998	HDI Value, 1998
145	Togo	49.0	55.2	1,372	0.471
146	Bangladesh*	58.6	40.1	1,361	0.461
147	Mauritania	53.9	41.2	1,563	0.451
148	Yemen*	58.5	44.1	719	0.448
149	Djibouti	50.8	62.3	1,266	0.447
150	Haiti*	54.0	47.8	1,383	0.440
151	Nigeria	50.1	61.1	795	0.439
152	Congo, DR	51.2	58.9	822	0.430
153	Zambia	40.5	76.3	719	0.420
154	Côte d'Ivoire	46.9	44.5	1,598	0.420
155	Senegal	52.7	35.5	1,307	0.416
156	Tanzania	47.9	73.6	480	0.415
157	Benin	53.5	37.7	867	0.411
158	Uganda	40.7	65.0	1,074	0.409
159	Eritrea	51.1	51.7	833	0.408
160	Angola	47.0	42.0	1,821	0.405
161	Gambia, The	47.4	34.6	1,453	0.396
162	Guinea	46.9	36.0	1,782	0.394
163	Malawi	39.5	58.2	523	0.385
164	Rwanda	40.6	64.0	660	0.382
165	Mali	53.7	38.2	681	0.380
166	CAR	44.8	44.0	1,118	0.371
167	Chad	47.5	39.4	856	0.367
168	Mozambique	43.8	42.3	782	0.341
169	Guinea-Bissau	44.9	36.7	616	0.331
170	Burundi	42.7	45.8	570	0.321
171	Ethiopia	43.4	36.3	574	0.309
172	Burkina Faso	44.7	22.2	870	0.303
173	Niger	48.9	14.7	739	0.293
174	Sierra Leone	37.9	31.0	458	0.252

Source: UNDP. 2000. *Human development Report, 2000.* New York: Oxford University Press.
*non-African country. HDI is human development index; the HDI varies from 0 to 1, with higher value indicating higher levels of development. CAR = Central African Republic.

Table 8.2

Regional Comparisons in Human Development

Region	Life Expectancy at Birth (years), 1998	Adult Literacy Rate (% age fifteen and above)	Per Capita GDP (PPP U.S. $), 1998	HDI Value, 1998
Arab States	66.0	59.7	4,140	0.635
East Asia	70.2	83.1	3,564	0.716
East Asia (exc. China)	73.1	96.3	13,635	0.849
Latin America and Caribbean	69.7	87.7	6,510	0.758
South Asia	63.0	54.3	2,112	0.560
South Asia (exc. India)	63.4	50.5	2,207	0.550
South-East Asia and the Pacific	66.3	88.2	3,234	0.691
Sub-Saharan Africa	48.9	58.5	1,607	0.464
Eastern Europe and the CIS	68.9	98.6	6,200	0.777
OECD	76.4	97.4	20,357	0.893

Source: UNDP. 2000. *Human development report, 2000.* New York: Oxford University Press.

In terms of other measures of human development, sub-Saharan Africa lags behind most regions of the world. As indicated by the data in Table 8.2, the subregion's life expectancy at birth of 48.9 years is the lowest of all regions of the world. HIV/AIDS infections, unless checked, are expected to significantly lower the region's life expectancy. Sub-Saharan Africa's adult literacy rate of 58.5 percent, however, is higher than that of South Asia. Overall, though, as measured by the UNDP's human development index, sub-Saharan Africa remains the world's least developed region. Despite a few bright spots, Africa remains a continent in crisis, and during the last forty years most of its rulers have been engaged primarily in crisis management, devoting little or no effort to developing structures for peaceful coexistence and sustainable development. The failure of national leaders to maintain the rule of law in many countries in the region has encouraged the mass exodus of highly valued human capital and deprived these economies of critical resources for development.

Since the 1960s several types of regulatory controls have been imposed on economic activities in the African countries. One can identify controls on (1) foreign exchange and the international trade sector, (2) goods and services markets, and (3) credit and capital markets. In the last several years government intervention in the international trade sector has involved import licensing, foreign exchange rationing, and the subsidization of exports. Many governments in Africa justify their regulatory activities by arguing that they serve some important and critical social objective or meet certain societal goals. For example, in regulating international trade many governments often argue that such activities limit imports and significantly improve the ability of struggling domestic industries to grow and become more globally competitive. In addition, it is argued that such regulation prevents the expending of scarce foreign exchange on luxury imports, saving the resources for the importation of essential materials for national development.

Regulation of the International Trade Sector

At independence, many African countries adopted international trade policies that emphasized import substitution industrialization (ISI). The primary objective of such an approach to resource allocation, as explicitly stated in national development plans, was to develop and sustain local industries that could produce the goods that the country was currently purchasing from abroad. Such a process was expected to minimize the African countries' dependence on the global economy. Foreign exchange rationing and other controls imposed on the international trade sector were expected to generate the hard currency that domestic entrepreneurs needed to purchase essential raw materials from abroad for their production activities. Strict control of imports was designed to produce a less-competitive domestic economy, one in which "infant" industries could mature and become competitive enough to participate gainfully in the global economy. Thus, foreign exchange regulation, export subsidization, and import licensing were expected to form the heart of each country's ISI program.

After gaining independence from Britain in 1957, Ghana adopted an ISI program as a way to deal with poverty and improve living conditions among the people. The government of Kwame Nkrumah, the country's first head of state, believed that ISI would enhance its ability to acquire the wealth that was needed to deal with poverty and deprivation and significantly improve the welfare of all Ghanaians. Ghana's import industrialization program was anchored on comprehensive regulation of the international trade sector by the government. Several policy instruments were introduced to aid the government in its efforts to achieve the goals of the ISI. These included (1) protection of local entrepreneurs from foreign competition through tariffs, import quotas, and foreign exchange control; (2) subsidization of foreign firms that were willing to establish and maintain import substitution production units in Ghana; and (3) the creation of public financial institutions (e.g., development banks and rural credit agencies) whose job it was to improve access to credit to those interested in investing in government-designated priority-development areas. In addition, the government created many parastatals, all of which became involved in the production of a variety of goods and services.

To implement the ISI, the Nkrumah government targeted specific areas of the economy to control. Such areas included (1) public utilities, which were considered too important to national development to be left in the hands of the private sector; (2) exploitation of the country's environmental resources; (3) management of airlines, radio, and other forms of communication; (4) health care; (5) banking; and (6) higher education. Immediate postindependence nationalist fervor created an environment that enhanced the government's ability to assume control and management of the exploitation of the country's natural resources. Industries such as mining and quarrying, air and rail transportation, electricity, and telecommunications were expected to be dominated and controlled by the state. The government was also expected to take control of the financial services industry, as well as the provision of higher education. Unfortunately, two important constraints made policy failure virtually a certainty in Ghåna. First, the country's existing institutional arrangements failed to adequately constrain the state, allowing those individuals whose job it was to design and implement the ISI program to mismanage it for their own benefit. Second, the country at the time lacked civil society organizations that were strong enough to serve as a check on the ruling elites and force the latter to become more accountable to the population. The fact that an effective civil society did not exist to check the exercise of government agency and the failure of existing laws and institutions to adequately constrain the state and its agents (e.g., civil servants and politicians) resulted in widespread policy failure. A significant number of the state-owned enterprises, which had been created to help implement the ISI program, instead became instruments for the private capital accumulation activities of politically dominant individuals and groups. The Nkrumah government used these enterprises effectively as instruments of patronage and corruption, helping to enhance his ability to monopolize the Ghanaian political system. In the process, the Ghanaian people were impoverished and further marginalized. In fact, by the time the Nkrumah regime was overthrown by military coup in 1966 the country had been turned into a venal society in which access to economic markets was regularly being sold by the civil service (see, e.g., Leith 1974; Werlin 1972; LeVine 1975).

Most scholars who have examined Nkrumah's ISI (Leith 1974; LeVine 1975; Werlin 1972) report that the perverse incentive structures (made possible by the laws and institutions adopted at independence) that existed in the country at the time encouraged and enhanced corruption, destroyed the program's chances for success, and allowed ruling elites and other politically dominant individuals to use the state's regulatory powers to enrich themselves at the expense of greater Ghanaian society. While it made a few Ghanaians rich, import substitution industrialization impoverished the bulk of the people and stunted wealth creation. Leith (1974, 25) observes that the system that had been designed by the Nkrumah government to "meet the apparent national needs and to minimize capricious discrimination among importers was frequently set aside in favor of Mr. Djin [then Ghana's trade minister] and his associates." Officials at the trade ministry regularly used the foreign exchange rationing and import licensing programs, which had been designed to benefit ISI, to extort bribes from prospective importers, discriminating against entrepreneurs who were unwilling or unable to pay the bribes requested. Eventually the regulatory system set up at independence became an instrument for the private capital accumulation activities of members of the ruling class. The ease with which bureaucrats and politicians in Ghana turned the country's ISI program into a self-enrichment scheme was due primarily to the existence of institutional arrangements that failed to adequately constrain the government and consequently the behavior of its agents. Of course, the absence of a strong and viable civil society to force accountability in government also contributed to this massive policy failure (Ampofo-Tuffuor, DeLorme, and Kamerschen 1991, 537–559).

Political opportunism in the international trade sector have not, of course, been limited to Ghana. During the last forty years many other African countries have attempted to deal with poverty by implementing ISI programs similar to those adopted by the Nkrumah government. Unfortunately, poor and perverse incentive structures have produced results similar to those obtained in Ghana. Like those in Ghana, civil servants and politicians in many of these countries have turned these programs into schemes for their personal enrichment, thanks to institutional arrangements that have failed to adequately constrain the government and force state custodians (civil servants and politicians) to be accountable to the people they are supposed to serve. In the process, levels of poverty and material deprivation have increased significantly in these countries (Gould 1980; Mbaku 2000).

Goods and Services Markets

Regulatory activities in the goods and services markets involve the manipulation of the prices of agricultural output in an effort to transfer income from the rural to the urban sectors.[3] Usually, the primary reason given by the government for such intervention is protection of poorly educated and vulnerable rural farmers against exploitation by unscrupulous middlemen. The government establishes price control regimes that require farmers to sell their foodstuffs in the urban centers at below free-market prices. In addition, so-called export crops (e.g., coffee, cocoa, bananas, rubber, and palm kernels) cannot be traded directly in the global economy. Producers of these commodities must sell them to government-sanctioned agricultural marketing boards (AMBs). The AMBs purchase the commodities from the rural sector at below market prices and then sell them competitively in the global economy. According to the government, the surplus extracted through this process is supposed to be used to effect development in the relevant rural areas, including helping the latter better integrate into the modern industrial sector. During the last several years in the continent the surplus extracted from farmers has been used primarily to subsidize the urban sectors, especially through huge salaries and other benefits to groups (e.g., the military, civil servants, labor union leaders, and other politically dominant groups) that help keep incumbents in power. Also important is the fact that government price-control programs have enhanced the ability of civil servants to extort bribes from consumers seeking access to stockpiles of commodities in government storage facilities. Since the 1960s the regulation of goods and services markets, especially the agricultural sector, has failed to improve macroeconomic performance or lower levels of poverty and deprivation in the majority of African countries. Instead, such government intervention in private exchange has significantly distorted resource allocation and increased inequality in the distribution of income and wealth through the transfer of resources from the poorly organized and politically weak rural sectors to the politically powerful, well-organized, and influential urban dwellers. In the process, many individuals, groups, and communities have been impoverished. In fact, data from the UNDP (2000) show that most Africans (especially those in the rural areas) are poorer now than they were in the 1960s. Of course, there are many other contributing factors to poverty in the continent besides government intervention. However, perverse economic programs designed and implemented by opportunistic civil servants and politicians seeking ways to enrich themselves must be considered one of the most important obstacles to human development in postindependence Africa.

Credit Markets and Financial Repression

At independence the agricultural sector was regarded by many of the new African leaders as the foundation for each country's industrialization and modernization efforts. The rural sector was expected to (1) provide jobs for a significant number of restless youth, (2) produce enough food to feed an exploding population, and (3) provide the capital that could be used to industrialize the national economy and help integrate it into the postwar global economy. To enhance the ability of the rural agricultural sector to serve as the proper foundation for national development, the government passed laws that favored entrepreneurs who invested in this sector.

Access to credit was considered critical for the development of the agricultural sector. Accordingly, many African governments decided to intervene in credit markets in order to make certain that farmers and other rural entrepreneurs were provided full and effective access to the credit that they needed. Controls imposed on the loanable funds markets included (1) credit rationing, (2) interest rate ceilings, and (3) the creation of special financial institutions that were expected to provide farmers with subsidized loans. Each set of five-year development plans emphasized certain so-called government priority development areas—in the early days, most of these were in agriculture—and entrepreneurs engaged in these areas were supposed to be given preferential treatment in the lending activities of financial institutions (DeLorme, Kamerschen, and Mbaku 1986; DeLancey 1989).

Regulatory programs in the credit markets, like those in other sectors of the African economies, did not achieve their stated objectives. As a result of perverse incentive structures, the civil servants whose job it was to administer these programs easily manipulated them to extract additional income and other benefits for themselves. Thus, instead of being used to enhance efficiency in the agricultural sector, these programs were converted into instruments for the enrichment of politically dominant groups. In many of these countries interest rate ceilings, for example, created shortages of loanable funds and provided managers of financial institutions opportunities to extort bribes from individuals and enterprises seeking access to cheap or subsidized credit. Although many governments in the continent have continued to argue that regulation of credit is important for making resources available to the credit-poor farm sector and providing indigenous entrepreneurs with badly needed working capital, most of the beneficiaries of financial repression continue to be large enterprises owned by civil servants, politicians, and transnational companies that are either able to pay the necessary bribes or have significant political clout. Most poor rural farmers still do not have full and effective access to credit.[4]

During the last several decades in Africa it is only in rare cases that the regulatory powers of the government have been used to enhance the national wealth and to meet critical societal goals. Instead, regulation has been utilized primarily to (1) help incumbent politicians monopolize political power and the allocation of resources, and (2) generate extralegal income and other benefits for civil servants, politicians, and other politically dominant groups. In the process, significant social, economic, political, and human costs have been imposed on the African peoples, especially the historically marginalized (women, children, rural peasants, and the urban poor). The result has been the failure to deal adequately with mass poverty and deprivation.

GOVERNMENT REGULATION AND THE ALLEVIATION OF POVERTY: THE APPROPRIATE BALANCE

Within the appropriate institutional environment, government regulatory activities are expected to enhance the ability of the private sector to create wealth. In such an environment, government activities should improve macroeconomic performance and enhance the ability of the entrepreneurial class to undertake productive activities. In serving such a function, government activities should complement, not overcrowd or replace, those of the private sector. It is important to note that the latter should be the primary party responsible for wealth creation. Thus, state regulatory activities should complement those of entrepreneurs, enhance the functioning of markets, maximize entrepreneurial effort in the creation of wealth, and generally promote free exchange. Specifically, government regulatory activities should be designed to achieve the following (World Bank 1997):

- provide a worker-friendly environment for the nation's labor resources;
- enhance entrepreneurial activities in order to maximize the creation of wealth;
- provide entrepreneurs and investors with reliable and predictable information;
- minimize the abuse of monopoly and monopsony power; and
- generally improve economic performance.

Given the extremely poor performance of the African state during most of the postindependence period and the fact that civil servants and politicians have regularly abused government regulatory powers in an effort to enrich themselves, in each country the people should seriously debate the appropriate role for the state. The postcolonial state should be reconstructed through democratic (i.e., participatory, inclusive, bottom-up, and people-driven) constitution-making to provide the society with more effective governance and economic structures. In the process the state should be constitutionally limited to the performance of two main functions: (1) the production of those goods and services that cannot be organized efficiently by the private sector, and (2) the provision and sustaining of a legal framework within which entrepreneurs can create the wealth that society needs to confront poverty and deprivation.[5]

REVISITING THE ROLE OF THE STATE IN POVERTY ALLEVIATION IN AFRICA

Social scientists have for many years viewed governments as benevolent agents of the people. The primary objective of the government and the latter's main raison d'être was to maximize the public welfare. Proponents of this approach to governance have usually been aware of and accepted the fact that civil servants (and politicians) could occasionally be incompetent, poorly educated, ill-informed, and not capable of effectively performing their assigned duties. However, the state was portrayed in this model of government as benevolent, well-intentioned, and dedicated to maximizing the national welfare. The government was considered some organic entity that always made those choices that enhanced the national welfare, and one that was able to deal effectively with instances of market failure (Gwartney and Wagner 1988, 6). Thus, in macroeconomic performance the state was considered or seen as an exogenous factor.

In the early 1960s James M. Buchanan and Gordon Tullock introduced the public choice perspective on governance, which has come to represent a much more intellectually satisfying paradigm for studying collective choice and public policy. The argument advanced by Buchanan and Tullock is that the government is an endogenous variable, which along with several other variables (e.g., voters, interest groups, bureaucrats, and politicians) determine outcomes to public policy. Public policy outcomes, according to this perspective, are endogenously determined through the activities of well-organized interest groups, a poorly organized voting public, and legislators and civil servants. In this process, interest groups attempt to manipulate public policy to generate benefits for themselves and their members, civil servants work to maximize their bureau budgets, and legislators attempt to maximize reelection and the control of the apparatus of government. Seen from the perspective of public choice theory, then, what may first appear to be policy mistakes made by supposedly incompetent and unskilled public servants may actually be programs deliberately and purposefully advanced by opportunistic civil servants in an effort to secure benefits for themselves. In Africa there is an abundance of evidence to indicate that many postindependence ruling elites designed and implemented perverse economic programs that imposed significant social, political, and economic costs on their societies but provided enormous benefits for members of the ruling coalitions and their supporters (e.g., military elites and urban groups).[6] Although these programs failed to promote or enhance the national welfare, they were still pursued vigorously because they served as a conduit through which income and wealth were transferred to the politically dominant class (see, Mbaku 1997, for a review of the literature).

Of course, one can view regulatory failures in postindependence African countries as honest mistakes made by well-intentioned but incompetent, poorly educated, and unskilled public servants. However, if the evidence is reexamined using the tools of public choice theory, especially when one looks at who benefits and who loses (i.e., who pays the costs of these programs and to whom the benefits accrue), such perverse economic programs are seen as deliberate and purposeful attempts by civil servants and other political leaders to plunder their national economies for their own benefit and that of their supporters and benefactors. During the last forty years, as discussed earlier, many government regulatory programs in the African economies have provided civil servants with extralegal compensation (e.g., through bribery and illegal taxation of private exchange) and allowed politicians to secure the additional resources that they need to purchase regime security; but have imposed severe costs on the rest of society. According to Bates (1987, 128), "economic inefficiencies afford governments means of retaining power." Resources generated through the capricious and inefficient application of existing rules can be utilized to secure critical support for the incumbent regime and enhance its ability to monopolize political spaces. Many African dictators of the Cold War era (e.g., Ahidjo of Cameroon, Mobutu of Zaire, and Banda of Malawi, just to name a few) could not have monopolized power as long as they did without the opportunistic use of the state's regulatory powers. The big losers from this process are society at large, especially historically marginalized and deprived groups such as children, women, rural dwellers, and minority ethnic groups, as well as members of the urban periphery (Mbaku 1997).

From racially based perverse economic and social policies in apartheid South Africa to opportunism by military elites in Nigeria, Ethiopia, Somalia, Zaire (Democratic Republic of Congo), Ghana, Benin and several other countries in Africa, there is significant evidence to support the claim that many postindependence policy failures cannot be attributed entirely to civil service incompetence. A significant number of these failures were engineered by opportunistic civil servants and politicians seeking ways to plunder their economies for personal gain. In South Africa the apartheid regime established in the country in 1948 promoted programs that underdeveloped and impoverished the black majority in an effort to ensure that the latter remained permanently marginalized and dependent on the white minority (see Mbaku 1997, for a review of the literature, especially pp. 139–165). In other African countries, corrupt, bloated, and parasitic bureaucracies designed and implemented economic programs that enriched politically dominant groups but imposed severe costs on the rest of society. Existing evidence appears to support the argument that the most important determinant of public policy failure in Africa during the last forty years has not been the existence of poorly educated, incompetent, and ill-informed civil servants per se, but perverse incentive structures that have encouraged and enhanced political opportunism (e.g., corruption, rent seeking, and rent extraction).[7] Today only a small number of African countries can boast of institutional arrangements that can adequately constrain the government and prevent those who serve in it from engaging in opportunistic behaviors. In fact, few African countries have viable institutions (e.g., a professional and neutral armed forces, an independent media, a professional civil service, a police force that is adequately constrained by the law, an efficient and professional legislature, an independent judiciary) that can help maintain law and order and create the appropriate environment for entrepreneurs to generate wealth.

During the last several decades many African governments have contributed significantly to the suffocation of civil society, the stunting of indigenous entrepreneurship, and the proscription of institutions for popular participation. An important outcome of this approach to governance has been the failure of viable civil societies to develop and become important checks on the exercise of government agency. It is true that at independence in the 1960s there was a shortage of skilled, well-educated, and competent indigenous elites in the new countries. It is important to note, however, that the existence of such resources as skilled manpower is not a necessary precondition for development; these resources can be created in the process of development. Many African countries have relatively large endowments of resources. However, in order for these resources to be used productively and efficiently to generate the wealth that they need, they must provide their economies with the appropriate (or enabling) institutional environment; one that is characterized by institutional arrangements that (1) adequately constrain the state and thus, minimize the ability of civil servants and politicians to engage in opportunism, (2) promote peaceful coexistence of population groups, and (3) enhance indigenous entrepreneurship and wealth creation. In such an environment, government regulations are used to enhance the ability of the private sector to create wealth and not as an instrument of plunder for the benefit of politically dominant groups.

CONCLUSION

Since the late 1980s many countries in Africa have been engaged in a transition to more democratic governance. Part of the motivation for this effort has been the fact that the model of government that has existed in many of these countries since independence has failed to enhance the national welfare. Instead, it has served as an instrument of plunder and exploitation, used by politically dominant groups to enrich themselves at the expense of the rest of society. In the process levels of poverty and material deprivation have risen significantly. As a consequence, many Africans are today poorer than they were at independence in the 1960s.

Several studies have attempted to determine why African countries remain essentially underdeveloped even after nearly fifty years of independence. One of the most popular reasons advanced to explain continued poverty and underdevelopment in the continent is the lack of both physical and human capital. The shortage of human capital (e.g., skilled and competent bureaucrats), for example, is blamed for many of the policy failures that have resulted in a squandering of the continent's development potential. In this chapter, we argue, however, that policy failure in postindependence Africa is due primarily to opportunism on the part of politicians and civil servants. While during the last forty years many countries in the continent have suffered from a shortage of both physical and human capital, it is important to recognize that availability of these resources is not a precondition for economic development. Such resources can be created in the process of development. However, in order for each country to create the wealth that it needs to meet its needs, it must arm itself with (1) economic infrastructures that guarantee economic freedoms (i.e., the right of individuals to freely engage in exchange and contract) and thus maximize entrepreneurial effort and wealth creation, and (2) governance structures that adequately constrain civil servants and politicians and effectively minimize their ability to engage in opportunism. Unless each African country engages in state reconstruction through democratic constitution-making to provide itself with such structures, political opportunism is bound to remain pervasive and poverty and high levels of material deprivation will continue to characterize the economies of these countries.

ACKNOWLEDGMENTS

An earlier version of this chapter was published in *Global Focus*, Volume 13, Number 2 (Summer 2001): 213–226.

NOTES

1. See Bates (1981) for a review of agricultural policies that benefited primarily ruling elites and their urbanized supporters; and Mbaku (2000) for a review of the litera-

ture on corruption and other forms of opportunism that provided the ruling elites with many benefits but imposed significant costs on society in general.

2. Apartheid South Africa is a case in point. Most of the violence directed at African groups was orchestrated by the government. In other countries throughout the region (e.g., Zaire under Mobutu, Uganda under Idi Amin, Cameroon under Ahidjo and Biya, Nigeria under several military governments, etc.), government-engineered violence became a major source of the intimidation suffered by the people.

3. The seminal work on government regulation of the agricultural sector in Africa was done by Robert H. Bates. See Bates (1981, 1987).

4. See, DeLorme, Kamerschen, and Mbaku (1986), and DeLancey (1989). Note that throughout most of rural Africa informal financial institutions remain the most important source of credit for the people. Unfortunately, these institutions are not capable of functioning effectively and fully as financial intermediaries.

5. These ideas are examined more thoroughly in Mbaku (1999).

6. See, e.g., Bates (1981), on the regulation of agriculture in postindependence Africa and Mbaku (1997), for a review of the literature on postindependence opportunism on the part of African ruling elites. Note, especially, the system of apartheid in South Africa, which promoted economic and social policies that severely impoverished the majority black population but provided significant benefits to the white minority. Also see Mbaku (1998).

7. For a thorough examination of rent extraction in postindependence Africa, see Rowley (1999).

REFERENCES

Ampofo-Tuffuor, E., C. D. DeLorme Jr., and D. R. Kamerschen. 1991. The nature, significance, and cost of rent seeking in Ghana. *Kyklos* 44 (4): 537–559.

Bates, R. H. 1981. *Markets and states in tropical Africa.* Berkeley and Los Angeles: University of California Press.

Bates, R. H. 1987. *Essays on the political economy of rural Africa.* Cambridge: Cambridge University Press.

Buchanan, J. M., and Gordon Tullock. 1962. *The calculus of consent: Logical foundations of constitutional democracy.* Ann Arbor: University of Michigan Press.

Burns, Sir A. C. 1963. *History of Nigeria.* London: George Allen.

Decalo, S. 1992. The process, prospects and constraints of democratization in Africa. *African Affairs* 9 (362): 7–35.

DeLancey, M. C. 1989. *Cameroon: Dependence and independence.* Boulder, CO: Westview.

DeLorme, C. D. Jr., D. R. Kamerschen, and J. M. Mbaku. 1986. Rent seeking in the Cameroon economy. *American Journal of Economics and Sociology* 45 (4): 413–423.

Fatton, R. Jr. 1990. Liberal democracy in Africa. *Political Science Quarterly* 105 (3): 455–473.

Gould, D. J. 1980. *Bureaucratic corruption and underdevelopment in the Third World: The case of Zaire.* New York: Pergamon Press.

Gwartney, J. D., and R. E. Wagner. 1988. Public choice and the conduct of representative government. In *Public choice and constitutional economics*, edited by J. D. Gwartney and R. E. Wagner. Greenwich, CT: JAI Press.

Krueger, A. O. 1992. *Economic policy reform in developing countries: The Kuznets Memorial Lectures.* Oxford: Blackwell.

Leith, J. C. (1974), *Ghana*, National Bureau of Economic Research: New York.

LeVine, V. T. 1975. *Political corruption: The Ghanaian case.* Stanford: Hoover Institution.

Mbaku, J. M. 1997. *Institutions and reform in Africa: The public choice perspective.* Westport, CT: Praeger.

Mbaku, J. M., ed. 1998. *Corruption and the crisis of institutional reforms in Africa.* Lewiston, NY: Edwin Mellen Press.

Mbaku, J. M. 1999. Making the state relevant to African society. In *Preparing Africa for the twenty-first century: Strategies for peaceful coexistence and sustainable development*, edited by J. M. Mbaku. Aldershot, UK: Ashgate.

Mbaku, J. M. 2000. *Bureaucratic and political corruption in Africa: The public choice perspective.* Malabar, FL: Krieger.

Rapley, J. 1993. *Ivorien capitalism: African entrepreneurs in Côte d'Ivoire.* Boulder, CO: Lynne Rienner.

Rowley, C. K. 1999. Rent seeking and rent extraction from the perspective of Africa. In *Institutions and collective choice in developing countries: Applications of the theory of public choice*, edited by M. S. Kimenyi and J. M. Mbaku. Aldershot, UK: Ashgate.

Rudin, H. R. 1938. *Germans in the Cameroons, 1884–1914.* New Haven: Yale University Press.

UNDP. 2000. *Human development report, 2000.* New York: Oxford University Press.

Webb, S. 1897. *Industrial democracy*, Vol. 2. London: Longman, Green.

Weidenbaum, W. E. 1998. Recasting the role of government to promote economic prosperity. *Business & the Contemporary World* 10 (3): 355–366.

Werlin, H. H. 1972. The roots of corruption—The Ghanaian enquiry. *Journal of Modern African Studies* 10 (2): 247–266.

World Bank. 1997. *World development report, 1997.* New York: Oxford University Press.

9

Internet Connectivity and Development in Africa: Look before You "Leapfrog"

The Internet is a relatively new medium, not only in Africa but around the world. It is an unprecedented amalgamation of technological innovations that have had a profound impact on political, economic, social, and cultural systems around the world. The Internet has led to the convergence of the instrumentalities and technologies of communication; namely, telecommunications, information technology, and the traditional mass media (radio, television, film, newspapers, magazines, and music).

Information, mass communication, and telecommunications technologies, which converge on the Internet, are innovations that have "shrunk" the world, transforming it into what McLuhan (1964) called the "global village," and revolutionized human relationships. Indeed, the vast, unprecedented potential for communication created by the Internet has further changed the world from a global village to an interactive planetary "palaver tree" teeming with countless interconnected microcommunication environments. From its origin in the United States, the Internet has spread to the rest of the world. As a new medium or a collection of new media, the Internet has spurred new technologies, and laws, as well as political and economic activities in Africa and elsewhere.

The fact that the Internet has come to dominate African development communication discourse is amazing, considering its top-secret origins and aims. The secret origins of the Internet can be contrasted with its revolutionary impact on the world. In effect, the Internet was originally conceptualized, designed, and developed to serve military purposes. As early as 1969, at the height of the Cold War, the Defense Advanced Research Projects Agency (DARPA), an agency of the U.S. Department of Defense, created the precursor of the Internet, the Advanced Research and Projects Network (ARPANET) as a highly decentralized, redundant command and control communication system that could survive a nuclear first strike (Straubhaar and LaRose 2000). With the end of the Cold War, large sections of the Internet were opened up, first to universities and research centers and later to businesses and the general public.

No other assemblage of communication technologies has seen such explosive growth in such a short time. The lightning speed with which the Internet has grown and spread around the world is due in part to the invention, in 1990, of the World Wide Web (WWW), a protocol (computer rules and languages) that transfers computer files from place to place. The WWW was invented at the *Centre Européen de Recherche Nucléaire* (European Particle Physics Laboratory, CERN), in Geneva, Switzerland. It was designed to be a universal protocol that could run on almost all computers. The greatest impetus for the explosion of the Internet around the world was the decision by CERN to make the WWW technology available to all who wanted it, free of any charge. Today, true to the dream of the inventors of the WWW, the Internet works in all corners of the globe on all kinds of computers. African Internet registries are bursting at the seams as demand for services increases. However, despite the demand, the supply (diffusion) of the Internet in Africa has been problematic.

The Internet is a very new medium in Africa. Indeed, African countries took concerted action in Internet connectivity for the first time only in 1995, and the first African countries became connected to the Internet only in 1997. Though the African continent is at the "periphery" of global communication and Internet nodes, the influence of the medium is being felt in all countries, from Algeria to Zimbabwe.

From a culturist perspective, the Internet is slowly but surely taking its place in Africa's informal networks of parallel communications, which have for centuries bypassed official communication channels. The Internet is helping Africans recreate, with modern digital media, communications methods and patterns that they have used from time immemorial. Electronic mail is becoming the new talking drum, which is available to all and sundry. Messages "encoded" and sent out by e-mail are like messages "encoded" in aesoteric languages and music and sent out on the talking drum. Governmental authorities are bypassed for the most part and messages are restricted only to parties who can "decode" and understand them. Furthermore, the extreme decentralization of the Internet has effectively created disorganized and uncertain but interrelated public and private fora—village palaver trees—under which the rich and the poor, the powerful and the weak, the honest and the dishonest, the moral and the immoral from all parts of the planet meet, haggle, and seek to do business or stake cultural territorial claims.

The aim of this chapter is to survey Internet adoption and diffusion in Africa, analyze the rationale for Internet connectivity, regulations, and policies, point out their shortcomings, and advance ideas that would make the Internet culturally relevant to the African continent.

THEORETICAL FRAMEWORK OF THE STUDY

This study of the Internet in Africa was carried out within the framework of the diffusion of innovation perspective, which holds that the world is in a perpetual state of innovation and change, and this change requires the penetration of inventions. These inventions diffuse or spread through a process of imitation. As new innovations are introduced, there are certain factors that enable some of these innovations to be widely diffused and adopted while others fail and do not spread beyond the areas in which they were invented or introduced. The diffusion of innovation perspective also holds that when innovations diffuse or spread from the areas in which they were developed or introduced, certain communication processes enable them to follow certain empirically observable and measurable patterns, the so-called curves of diffusion. Curves of diffusion are S-shaped curves that represent the initial small numbers of adopters of innovations. As circumstances change, the rate of adoption accelerates, and after reaching a maximum reduces over time and becomes stabilized (Lowery and DeFleur 1995). The diffusion of innovation perspective was pioneered by a French sociologist, Tarde (1962), and tested by Pemberton (1936), Ryan and Gross (1943), and Rogers (1983), among others. According to Tarde, inventions usually diffuse from their geometrical center as waves or concentric circles created by a drop of water in a quiet pool. Thus, each innovation has a center from which it is spread to other areas. Furthermore, innovations are often modified or reinvented in the course of the diffusion process, such that they fit each existing culture or environment, which they come into contact with (Kinnunen 1996).

Diffusion of innovation studies have found that adoption of innovation tends to be a slow process (Ryan and Gross 1943). Indeed, different types of innovations diffuse at different rates (Lowery and DeFleur 1995). Thus, the process of diffusion of innovation starts with an invention, the development of a solution to a perceived problem or shortcoming (Schumpeter 1939). It can also be said to be a process through which innovation is communicated through certain channels over time among members of a social system (Rogers 1983). Once there is an invention or innovation, it moves from the invention or innovation center, spreads to subinnovation centers, and finally into the periphery.

Studies of the adoption of innovations by a number of countries or a continent are very rare. Pemberton (1936) carried out a diffusion of innovation study that included adoption of a nineteenth-century international communication innovation, postage stamps, by thirty-seven independent European and North and South American countries. He studied data from 1836, when stamps were first introduced, to 1880 when they had spread to thirty-seven postal administrations in three continents. He found that adoption of an innovation like postage stamps results from more or less chance cultural encounters and interactions. Few countries adopted the innovation (i.e., issued postage stamps) when it was first introduced in the 1830s. However, nearly ten years later, several countries adopted the innovation and issued stamps of their own. The trend tapered and

stabilized in the 1870s, when most independent countries had adopted the innovation. Pemberton showed that adoption of this communications innovation
followed the normal curve of diffusion.

In contrast to the adoption of postage stamps by countries, the spread of the
Internet around the world has not followed the normal curve of adoption. The
rapid spread of the technology compressed and abbreviated normal adoption
patterns and processes. As a result, countries on the periphery of the world
communication system have been obliged, through the forces of globalization, to
connect themselves to the Internet without the luxury of enough time to con-
ceptualize, define, adopt, and evaluate policies that spell out the role of the Internet in their political, economic, cultural, and social systems.

RESEARCH QUESTIONS

The following research questions have been addressed in this study:

- How did the greatest communication innovation of the twentieth-century, the Inter-
  net, come to the attention of Africa's political leaders?
- What were the perceived needs that could be served by the Internet?
- What was the adoption process of the Internet in Africa?
- How long did it take between awareness of the innovation and action?
- Did African countries modify or reinvent the Internet to suit their national cultural
  realities?

The Internet was introduced to Africa by the "international community"
(mostly the United Nations and international aid agencies), which saw it as a
potential tool for economic development of the continent. African governments
were initially unenthusiastic about the Internet because they could not control its
content due to its extremely decentralized nature. African countries reacted to
the promise of the Internet in two ways: (1) The countries of sub-Saharan Africa, under pressure from the international community, adopted the Internet and
facilitated its diffusion in their specific territories through legislative action; and
(2) for purposes of political and social control, North African countries implemented an adoption program that allowed the government significant control
over access to the Internet. The government, thus, became the gateway to and
from the Internet (Eko 2001).

ORIGINS OF THE POLICY OF INTERNET CONNECTIVITY IN
AFRICA

The contemporary situation of growing Internet use in Africa is very different from the reality that obtained just a few years ago. Telecommunications
were traditionally regulated as common carriers of person-to-person communication lines, while information technology and computers were hardly regulated.

The mass media were regulated as "one to many" communication channels. The "one" who controlled the mass media and did most of the communicating was the government. The "many" were the so-called masses at whom governmental mass-mediated messages were directed. The convergence of the mass media, information technology, and telecommunications changed the fundamental basis of communication and posed complex public policy problems that had profound impact on societies around the continent.

The importance of the Internet as an instrument of development was impressed upon African leaders, as a group, by international, bilateral, and multilateral aid and development agencies. In 1990 the International Telecommunications Union (ITU) convened the African Telecommunications Development Conference (AF-RTDC) in Harare, Zimbabwe. This conference set up an African Telecommunications Policy Study Group (ATPSG), which produced an "African Green Paper" that set out the orientations and policy outlines for future telecommunications development on the African continent. These included the creation of an enabling environment for telecommunications, privatization of the telecommunications sector, as well as the establishment of policies and legal and regulatory frameworks in the sector.

The kickoff to Africa's official venture into the Internet was the African Symposium on Telematics for Development (ASTD), which was held in Addis Ababa, Ethiopia, in 1995. The meeting was held under the auspices of the United Nations Economic Commission for Africa and the International Telecommunications Union (ITU). At this meeting, representatives from thirty-eight African countries, building on past telecommunications policy initiatives undertaken under the ambit of the ITU (notably, the Harare telecommunications development conference), recommended that African countries connect their telecommunications infrastructure to the Internet and include information technology in their development policies and plans. The African Green Paper, which was produced by the Policy Study Group set up by the Harare conference, was adopted in 1996 at an African Regional Telecommunications Development Conference that was held in Abidjan, Côte d'Ivoire (Info Development 1998).

Thereafter, the ECA spearheaded, with the support of the International Telecommunications Union, the World Bank, and other international aid agencies, the African Information Society Initiative (AISI). In 1997 the AISI was officially approved by African ministers responsible for economic and social development. All African countries thus agreed to accord Internet connectivity high priority in their development plans.

PERCEIVED NEED FOR INTERNET CONNECTIVITY IN AFRICA: THE DEVELOPMENTALIST APPROACH

Adoption of the Internet in Africa did not follow the traditional process of adoption of innovations advanced by Rogers (1983) and others. Indeed, the traditional, five-stage adoption process— awareness, interest, evaluation, trial, and adoption—are not applicable to Internet adoption in Africa. Under pressure from international finance institutions (namely, the World Bank and the International Monetary Fund), as well as aid agencies, African governments seem to have simply gone from awareness to adoption. International leaders called on African governments to connect their respective countries to the Internet and by so doing leapfrog or skip years ahead in the development process. By connecting to the Internet, these poor countries were told that they would be able to bypass expensive information and telecommunications technologies. According to the secretary general of the United Nations (cited in Trombly 2000), by connecting their countries to the Internet, African countries would "leapfrog" or bypass certain painful stages and processes of development and become part of the global economy, leaving behind decades of stagnation, underdevelopment, and poverty. It was envisaged that by being connected to the Internet, African countries would have increased access to information (markets, news, weather, health, and so on) and have greater access to educational materials, online journals, books, courses, and so on. The proposition that the Internet could be instrumental in the socioeconomic and political development of Africa has been wholeheartedly embraced by the international community and some African intellectuals (Ngwainmbi 2000).

Indeed, the "technological leapfrogging" metaphor used by Kofi Annan was taken out of the diffusion of innovation perspective. Diffusion of innovation theory holds that countries on the political and economic periphery of the world usually join innovations at a late stage. These countries learn from the experiences of the innovation centers and subinnovation centers and "leapfrog" decades of evaluation, experimentation, and testing of a specific innovation. These countries on the fringes of the global economy can be described as late adopters who manifest an accelerated diffusion rate over a short span of time and arrive at an approximate stage in technological innovation as the innovation center and innovation subinnovation centers (Grubler 1996). This seems to be the reasoning behind international efforts to encourage African countries to connect to the Internet and thereby leapfrog or bypass decades of expensive communication technology. Internet diffusion and connectivity in Africa thus came out of an international developmentalist agenda (Eko 2001).

The developmental model of the Internet and the regulatory regime it engenders is rooted in an understanding of the role of mass communication in social and economic development that was first applied to "Non-Self-Governing Territories" (European colonies in Africa, Asia, and Latin America) during the colonial era (U.N. General Assembly 1958b). Great Britain, France, the Netherlands, and other colonial powers stressed the importance of the mass media in stimulating economic and political development in their respective colonies and territories around the world (U.N. General Assembly 1958a). The principle of using the mass media as instruments of development in the colonial territories soon became the official policy of the United Nations and especially its specialized agency, the U.N. Educational, Scientific, and Cultural Organization. This was the origin of the concept of "development communication."

As formulated by Wilbur Schramm (1964) and other Western experts and consultants, the development communication perspective postulated that developing countries do not have the resources to indulge in the luxury of the liberal, watchdog journalistic model of the Western countries. As such, all media were to concentrate on the task of disseminating information and messages that would help improve agricultural production, health, education, national security, and other vital areas. Such "strategic use" of information would lead to nation building and provide a "climate" for national development. The development communication model became the framework of UNESCO's engagement in the developing countries of the world.

Virtually all the countries of Africa embraced this model when they became independent in the late 1950s and early 1960s. Developmental communication, as practiced in Africa, was based on the principle that African countries were fragile, fledgling societies with many internal and external problems. Achieving national unity and cohesion was considered more important than freedom of the press. Most politicians argued that in situations of extreme poverty, having mass media that concentrated on checking government action and criticizing it was a misuse of scarce resources. The result was strict government control of the mass media, censorship, and sometimes violent elimination of dissent. The developmentalist approach soon found its way into the Internet policy formulations of the international community and its African partners.

INTERNET FOR DEVELOPMENT: CASE STUDIES

With the spread of the Internet around the world in the 1990s, the development communication model was applied to this new medium by the "international community." Donor agencies in Europe and North America conceptualized the Internet as a catalyst for rapid economic and social development in the Third World. International organizations like the World Bank and the IMF, U.N. specialized agencies, bilateral aid organizations like the U.S. Agency for International Development, and diverse international nongovernmental organizations have advanced the view that the Internet offers poor countries of the Third World a golden opportunity for rapid economic development.

This perspective was spelled out in a World Bank document (Baranshamaje et al. 1995) aimed at rallying the international aid community behind the idea of helping developing countries connect to the Internet and using the latter as a tool for development. The basic premise of the document was that the information revolution offers Africa a dramatic opportunity to leapfrog into the future, breaking out of decades of stagnation or decline. To this end, it was suggested that the World Bank and the international aid community "dialogue with national governments to emphasize the importance of taking advantage of the information revolution to accelerate economic development, as well as the need

for liberalization, deregulation, privatization, and competition in the telecommunications sector." The document stated that concrete ways in which the "liberating effects" of Internet technologies could be felt in economic development
in Africa included distance education (countries were to be transformed into "e-
learning nations"), training, health, electric power, and private-sector development.

The major international proponent of this developmentalist posture, which
became the guiding principle of all communication-related aid to the developing
countries, was the U.N. Development Program. In the mid-1990s, under its
Sustainable Development Networking Program (SDNP), the UNDP promoted
the use of information technology tools in developing countries as a way to help
them "leapfrog themselves into the 21st century." Today, ninety-two "developing" countries, virtually all of which are in Africa, Asia, or Latin America, have
participated in the UNDP's SDNP. In addition, virtually all international organizations, U.N. agencies, and nongovernmental aid organizations have developed
an "Internet for development" component in their aid activities in the developing
countries.

In Africa alone there are tens of "Internet connectivity" projects sponsored
by regional, subregional and international agencies of all political and economic
persuasions. Besides the UNDP, other major Internet for development projects
include the World Bank's "Internet for Development" program, the International
Telecommunications Union's "Electronic Commerce for Developing Countries," UNESCO's "Information Society for All," the Internet development project of the French-led *Organisation Internationale de la Francophonie*, (the
French-speaking countries of the world), and USAID's "Leland Initiative."

AFRICAN RESPONSE TO INTERNET FOR DEVELOPMENT

Despite the groundwork that had been laid for Internet penetration in Africa, as late as 1998 many countries were still not ready to take the plunge. Some
African countries initially felt "lost" and overwhelmed by the Internet technology and content that flooded them from other parts of the world. In effect, African newspapers, and social, political, cultural, tribal, and even insurgent groups,
with the help of friends in Europe and North America—and free e-mail services—created hundreds of e-mail discussion and chat groups, as well as Web
pages that linked Africans with the major communication centers of the world.
Virtually all African governments were unprepared for this. During a meeting in
South Africa in 1998, African ministers of communication stated that their first
priority was to develop a "road map" for the continent's formal entry into the
information age. The ministers envisioned an African information society anchored by a broad policy and regulatory framework that would make information the engine for African development (Naidoo 1998).

At that meeting the governments of Africa's fifty-three countries officially
endorsed the international community's conceptualization of the Internet as a

tool for rapid economic and social development. In 1998, on the occasion of the 34th Assembly of African Heads of State and Government, the Organization of African Unity and the African Economic Community organized an African Exhibition on New Information Technologies, in Ouagadougou, Burkina Faso. Speaking at the opening of the exhibition, president Blaise Compaore, then acting chairman of the OAU, said that for Africa the new information and communication technologies must serve as an instrument for the development of the continent, within the context of its cultural identity.

One of the first African countries to recognize the potential of the Internet as a tool for development was Burkina Faso, a West African country that is classified as one of the least developed countries of the world. Burkina Faso incorporated the Internet in its development plan. In 1995 Burkina Faso had one of the first Internet nodes in Africa. In addition, by 1997 it had set up a regulatory and policy framework to coordinate the management of the Domain Name Server for its zone, as well as for a number of neighboring countries. It also coordinated its national Internet infrastructure with international aid projects. The country subsequently created a policy framework, which included the creation of information technology regulatory and advisory bodies, and enacted laws stipulating conditions for licensing information technology professionals. Today, Burkina Faso has one of the best Internet sectors in Africa in terms of regulation and service.

THE INTERNET IN AFRICA: CONTEMPORARY REALITIES

Today, all African countries are linked to the Internet; many have national Internet backbones, and the medium has become an important part of international and to a lesser extent, national communications, business, and commerce. All African countries have constructed their own "webs" or networks and connected them to the Internet. As a new medium, the Internet has spurred new technologies, laws, as well as political and economic activities in Africa. An Internet culture is slowly but surely developing in Africa's urban areas (Barlow 1999). More and more Africans are using the Internet for communication and commerce. From Dakar in the West, to Nairobi in the East, and from Cairo in the North to Cape Town in the South, small, private Internet cybercafés and "i-kiosks" have sprung up in virtually all African cities. These electronic palaver trees are usually very busy. Due to limited bandwidth, electronic mail is the most popular Internet function in Africa. For a modest fee, Africans can send and receive e-mail from relatives and friends around the world from one of these Internet kiosks (Bray 2001).

In addition, there are tens of African listservs, bulletin boards, and electronic discussion groups on the Internet. Africans living outside the continent generally set up these worldwide fora. Discussions on these fora take place in tens of African languages, ranging from Amharic to Zulu. Though most of these discussion groups are hosted on servers based in the United States or Europe,

Africans in the continent who have access to the Internet are joining these discussion groups. It has, therefore, become very easy for news and information about countries, regions, or ethnic groups to travel instantaneously from anywhere in the world to the village or community level.

Eritrea, Africa's newest nation, which emerged after a thirty-year civil war with Ethiopia, had one of the first online discussion groups. It was set up in 1993, the year Eritrea got its independence. Indeed, the nation of Eritrea was virtually "born" on the Internet (Rude 1996). By 1996, about 500 Eritreans from every continent belonged to this online discussion group, which dealt with issues ranging from the draft constitution of the emerging nation to women's rights. The online group has also sponsored or worked together on several projects that benefited the people of the new nation. Indeed, many of the African Internet discussion groups are used to raise funds from Africans abroad for development or cultural projects in specific African villages. Many African political and traditional rulers have used e-mail discussion groups to post messages to political, ethnic, or linguistic communities scattered in cyberspace.

In addition, the Internet is breaking down geographic and communication barriers in Africa. It has become an outlet for virtually all African newspapers, which use it as a window on the world. Sometimes these newspaper Internet sites are the only sources of news in areas of conflict.

In the early days of the Internet, some African governments showed signs of fear of the new medium, which *Jeune Afrique* (see, e.g., January 16, 1999), an African magazine based in France, describes as Africa's new freedom space. Since national telecommunications administrators were for the most part Internet service providers and domain name service administrators, they tended to provide direct access to the Internet only to embassies and nongovernmental organizations. However, after a wave of privatization of African telecommunications services urged on African governments by the IMF and the World Bank as part of structural adjustment programs, governments are no longer the sole Internet access providers. Furthermore, technology like IP multicast, which enables Web sites to provide multiple feeds to users around the world, e-mail message attachments, and re-mailing from generic servers around the world have rendered government controls ineffective.

For many African newspapers, the World Wide Web has become a showcase, an outlet where journalists, cartoonists, caricaturists, and comic strip artists who have had a brush with the law or have either been banned, censored, or seized can present their work. The Gabonese Written Press Association, which has deplored government excesses in the past, uses the Internet to tell its story to the world. Newspapers that are censored or whose reporters get arrested quickly post such information on the Internet and the international human rights community quickly condemns the government in question. This has helped to bring the plight of persecuted journalists to the attention of the world. Electronic mail has also changed the practice of journalism in Africa, since it is being used extensively for newsgathering and reporting.

Independent newspapers in Zimbabwe, Zambia, Cameroon, and other countries that trample on freedom of the press have sought refuge on the Internet whenever objectionable editions—usually those critical of the government or of political leaders—of their newspapers have been banned, seized, or censored. In many cases, newspapers that are censored appear on the Internet unhindered or their content is mirrored in Web sites hosted outside the country in which they are banned (Leone 1996).

In Nigeria, the military government of General Sani Abacha resorted to confiscation of the computers and servers of some newspapers in order to silence them. To the surprise of all, versions of the banned newspapers resurfaced on the streets after enterprising editors published them using hidden computers, e-mail, and secret printing presses. Electronic mail is a revolutionary tool that has enabled journalists and readers to receive and distribute information, thereby circumventing government censors (Olorunyomi 1996).

Today, the Internet, and specifically electronic mail, is used as a forum of free expression and promotion by all types of people and groups, ranging from the Pan-African News Agency to insurgents and rebel groups. Africa's rebel groups have become "cyber rebels" who use the Internet to tell the world their side of the story. No matter where they are physically located in the African bush, rebels maintain Web pages hosted in sympathetic African countries and use these pages to distribute information about their activities, raise funds, and recruit new members. These groups call or send e-mail massages to newsrooms around the world to give their side of the story. Rebels in Sierra Leone, Liberia, Senegal, Democratic Republic of Congo, Congo-Brazzaville, Angola, Sudan, and Ethiopia, as well as the Islamic groups in Algeria and the Moslem Brotherhood in Egypt, all make extensive use of the Internet to get their message across, raise funds and recruit members (Kpatindé 1999).

It is clear from this discussion that the Internet was officially introduced into Africa in a series of stages over a relatively short time span. In 1990 the International Telecommunications Union (ITU) sponsored the African Telecommunications Development Conference, which was held in Harare, Zimbabwe. The U.N. Economic Commission for Africa formally launched an Internet/Telematics symposium in 1995 and African ministers formally accepted ITU and ECA recommendations for Internet connectivity in 1996. Internet connectivity in Africa was driven by the need and promise of economic development. Between 1995 and 1999 virtually all African countries had nodes connected to the Internet. Thus, in terms of diffusion of innovation, the Internet was introduced and adopted in Africa in record time. As soon as they were convinced of the importance of the Internet in economic development, most countries connected their telecommunications networks to the Internet, created nodes, and their public telecommunications organizations became the domain name registries and Internet access providers for their countries. Since reinvention is part of the diffusion of innovation process, the question is whether African countries had the time to "digest" or be acculturated to the Internet enough to reinvent it to suit their political, economic, and cultural needs. The evidence suggests that the Internet is a cultural medium that has been recontextualized, for political and cultural reasons, only in North Africa. The medium has been barely reinvented in sub-Saharan Africa. The results are a serious cultural disconnect between the Internet as it operates in the United States and Western Europe and the way it operates in Africa.

CONTEXTUALIZATION OF THE INTERNET: THE AFRICAN EXPERIENCE

One of the elements of the adoption of innovation is the ability and willingness of individuals and countries to modify, reinvent, or recontextualize innovations that are adopted. Now that most African countries have adopted the Internet, few have modified it to suit their national political and cultural realities. Though post and telecommunications administrations and other government agencies still control a significant segment of the telecommunications infrastructure in the African continent, Internet activity has not been limited to the public sector. The private sector, small as it is, is leading the drive to contextualize and reinvent the Internet to suit African realities. One of the most successful African Internet ventures is Africa Online. Founded by three African young people who were students at the Massachusetts Institute of Technology, Harvard, and Princeton universities in 1989, Africa Online became a subsidiary of Prodigy in 1994. The relationship was terminated in 1998, but Africa Online has since become the foremost Internet service provider on the African continent, with branches in ten countries. Africa Online is a pioneer and leader in Internet connectivity retail, making access to the Internet available to as many people as possible for a very small fee. In order to make Internet access universal on the African continent, where the vast majority of people cannot afford computers and modems, Africa Online has pioneered the concept of "e-touch." These are small independent Internet centers that enable people to walk in and obtain free e-mail addresses. Users are charged a small fee to send and receive e-mails, type documents, use the fax, or surf the Web. E-touch centers are not cybercafés. They are just Internet access sites. Anyone with a working telephone line can start an Africa Online e-touch center. Most centers are retail stores, shops, or other small businesses to which Africa Online provides modems, bonuses, and rebates for the service. E-touch centers started in Nairobi, Kenya, in 1999. There are over 200 of them in Abidjan, Côte d'Ivoire, in West Africa (Dioh 2000). These centers, which bring the Internet down to the level of the people, are being modified to handle electronic commerce and banking (Bray 2001). Uganda has one of the most competitive and least expensive Internet markets in Africa. This is due to the fact that the government liberalized the Internet market as soon as connection was established. Today, more and more people use Internet services, particularly e-mail, to communicate with friends and relatives in Africa and around the world (Sandouly 2000).

A few countries in sub-Saharan Africa have tried, without success, to control the content of the Internet, due mostly to technological limitations. The failure of sub-Saharan African governments to control the Internet can be contrasted with the situation of North Africa, where the predominantly Arab countries have succeeded, through the use of the latest technologies, in strictly controlling and limiting the Internet content available to their citizens.

In the North African countries—Algeria, Morocco, Libya, Tunisia and Egypt—a government or government agency serves as the de facto or de jure gateway to the Internet for the whole country or specific regions. Access to the Internet, or certain sites thereof, is granted or denied in the name of national security, culture, morality, or some other government interest. This gateway model is possible because these countries have political cultures and traditions that give little or no room for freedom of speech and of the press. In addition, in these contexts authorities place severe limitations on the gathering and dissemination of news and information. In these countries there is no separation of duties between the government, Internet regulatory authorities, Internet service providers (ISPs) and Internet hosts. In most cases the government is the Internet operator, regulator, and host. Indeed, government ministries or agencies own and control telecommunications infrastructure, are the principal telecommunications operators and regulators, the domain name registries for their respective countries, the sole ISPs, the Internet Content Providers, and the Internet hosts. This type of arrangement not only stifles competition, it ensures that transmission of "undesirable" (as determined by government censors) material to and from the regulating country is prevented. Universal access to the Internet is neither desirable nor encouraged. Using electronic, legal, and other means, governments serve as electronic sluice gates that hold back the flood of undesirable Internet information that they think threatens their countries and cultures. The government selects and directs multiple inputs or sources of information from the Internet into a single, well-monitored output for consumption by the people in the country. This is done basically for purposes of control. The result is that the rate of information diffusion or propagation is slowed down considerably. In these so-called gateway countries, fast Internet access is a vice not a virtue. The thinking behind the gateway model is that the Internet is an electronic conveyor belt for Western decadence and debauchery, which, if allowed into these countries unimpeded, would infect their religious, political, and cultural systems and way of life.

CASE IN POINT: TUNISIA AS GATEWAY REGULATOR OF THE INTERNET

Tunisia is part of the predominantly Arab belt of North Africa. This region lags behind the rest of the African continent in terms of freedom of speech and of the press. According to the U.N. Commission on Human Rights, the government of Tunisia controls all Internet communications through an organization called *Agence Tunisienne d'Internet*. The government is the sole Internet service provider in Tunisia. This enables the authorities to permanently block access to a number of objectionable Internet addresses, Web sites, and portals throughout the country. These banned sites include free electronic mail services like Hotmail, as well as Web sites maintained by human rights organizations like Amnesty International, the Committee for the Protection of Journalists, the International Human Rights Federation, and Reporters without Borders. Furthermore, in order to restrict the flow of information to and from the Internet, the Web sites of French newspapers like *Le Monde*, *La Libération*, and *Le Nouvel Observateur* are systematically blocked. In addition, the two government-owned Internet service providers and content hosts are required by law to submit a list of Internet subscribers and clients, as well as their online surfing profiles, to the government every month. Tunisian police regularly pay visits to Web users in order to question them about specific objectionable Web sites they may have visited in violation of government regulations. Furthermore, the restrictive press laws regarding media content codified in the *Code de la presse* (press code) are fully applicable to the Internet (Gharbi 2000).

Reporters Sans Frontières (Reporters without Borders), a human rights organization campaigning for freedom of the press around the world, notes that forty-five countries of the world restrict access to the Internet. Of these, twenty are described as "enemies of the Internet." Tunisia is classified as one of these countries that censor, filter, or block access to objectionable Web pages and e-mail services because they are considered subversive and dangerous for national security or unity. Whether Tunisia's attempts to recontextualize the Internet will be successful in the long run will depend on technology and the response of the Tunisian people.

THE INTERNET AS CULTURAL INSTRUMENT: LOOK BEFORE YOU LEAPFROG

While the Internet has helped improve communication and information flow among a small segment of Africa's population—and this communication is mostly directed outside the continent—its very existence is unknown to the vast majority of the continent's people. Internet connectivity, therefore, raises very serious priority issues. In a continent where the vast majority of the people have no electricity, no safe drinking water, no school buildings, no books, no healthcare, and no access to telephones (to name just a few of the deprivations suffered by the African people), there are serious questions whether Internet connectivity as promoted by the international community is really the panacea for Africa's fundamental structural and institutional problems, which are the root cause of its poverty. Indeed, the collapse of the much-vaunted electronic commerce (e-commerce) in the United States and elsewhere shows that the magical powers of development and prosperity attributed to the Internet were exaggerated. The problem is that the external actors (i.e., the international business, finance, corporate, and aid industries) that are pushing for Internet connectivity in Africa have never given Africans an opportunity to determine for themselves the priority, as well as the social and cultural relevance of the Internet, or at least most of its content. Internet connectivity without the basic telecommunications and electricity infrastructure and an enabling legal and economic environment to create indigenous or local content is worse than an exercise in futility. It is no secret that Africa's decision makers and planners who endorsed the ITU and ECA Internet initiatives did so because that offered the possibility of financial assistance in the development of their tenuous or nonexistent telecommunications infrastructures

Internet connectivity for its own sake does nothing but transform African countries into consumers of Internet content produced from all parts of the world except their own. This has serious cultural implications. In effect, the Internet and its telecommunications infrastructure, as well as the information technology that drives it, have unmistakable cultural dimensions. Indeed, the Internet is an amalgamation of culture industries (radio, television, film, book publishing, music, tourism, the arts, and so on), as well as culture-bound technologies and content. The Internet, like most other technologies, can only operate within the cultural parameters imposed by its creators and software writers.

Furthermore, the Internet is based on a culturally determined technological architecture, a highly decentralized system that fits the individualistic logic of the Anglo-American culture better than most African cultures. The Internet is a network of computer networks that has no central control or choke point—at least not that we know of so far—and its technology, packet switching, makes centralized control by governments prohibitively expensive, if not virtually impossible. In addition, the extreme decentralization, electronic commerce, and free flow of information models on which the Internet functions are based on Anglo-American principles like laissez-faire economics, free trade, free flow of information, and the marketplace of ideas.

Due to their very nature, information technology and the Internet lend themselves to the development of cybercultures that are sometimes detrimental to real cultures (Star 1995; Slouka 1995; Kaye and Medoff 1999). Thus, aid projects, programs, and policies that stress Internet connectivity without addressing its detrimental cultural aspects open promoters of such projects to charges of being agents or facilitators of cultural imperialism and monoculturalism. Indeed, some European, Asian, and Middle Eastern governments have opted for a culturist posture in their regulation of the Internet. This posture is based on the assumption that culture and cultural protection should be the overriding goals of Internet regulation. As such, these countries have enacted Internet laws and adopted policies aimed at protecting the specific intellectual, aesthetic, and moral values of their national or regional civilizations or cultures (Eko 2001).

The European theoretical foundations of the culturist perspective of Internet regulation can be traced to the U.N. Educational, Scientific and Cultural Organization. As early as 1997, Philippe Quéau, a UNESCO official, succinctly articulated the culturist view of the information superhighway: "The computer and the Internet are not ordinary technologies. Beyond (the technology), they introduce a new society with its political, economic and cultural dimensions. Besides introducing a new society and culture, Internet addresses and data bases directly phagocyte or swallow existing cultures, threaten the very intimate essence of individual privacy, and lead to 'cyber brotherization', governmental and commercial intrusion on the right to privacy" (Agnus and Blanchard 1997, 48–49).

Indeed, the American-dominated governance and perceived overcommercialization of the Internet have rekindled old, international ideological debates. UNESCO (1998) has said that lack of access to the Internet by the poor countries of the world is unfair, and use of the Internet by the rich countries to transfer their values, languages, and cultural norms to these poor countries raises issues of cultural imperialism.

Koichiro Matsuura, the director general of UNESCO, spelled out the position of his organization with respect to the regulation of the Internet within the framework of the World Trade Organization. He said that cultural goods and services—audiovisual products including the Internet—because they are both electronic and cultural, cannot be treated like any other goods. Therefore, flooding the Third World with "cultural products" from the industrialized countries (through the Internet) could lead to global cultural impoverishment, homogenization, and uniformization (Caramel and Laronche 2000).

Thus, within the framework of the culturist model, communication technology, the Internet, and online content are not viewed as neutral. They are conceptualized as value-laden, social institutions or cultural instruments whose products transfer the economic and cultural values and serve the interests of the specific nations and societies from which they originate. Indeed, culturist countries like France view the Internet as an instrument for the propagation of American culture and interests. To them, inasmuch as the source code of computer hardware, software, and Internet protocols is written almost entirely in English, it follows that information technology functions within the framework of Anglo-American culture, logic, and values. As such, a computer connected to the Internet is a ramp, an entryway into the information superhighway that is a technological and social system rooted in Anglo-American Puritan cultural values and work ethic. The cur-rent Internet regulatory system is increasingly being viewed with a lot of suspicion in other countries. Even sections of the Roman Catholic Church in the United States have described the overcommercialization of the Internet as "electronic feudalism" (Allen 1998).

According to the culturist perspective, then, connectivity is not a neutral activity. The Western languages, which are the medium of Internet communication, are alien symbols that are steeped in specific and explicit philosophies (Huxley 1954). Therefore, connecting African countries to the Internet and granting Africans access to the vast treasure trove of information conveyed by the Internet would not be very beneficial to Africans as long as the content is not culturally relevant. Globalization leads to pressures to change or conform to universal norms of culture, development, aesthetics, and so on. As such, all countries and peoples are squeezed into a ready-made global cultural mold. This can be counterproductive.

Therefore, for Africans to really benefit from the Internet, they have to reinvent it and recontextualize it to fit their cultural realities. In other words, Africans have to be producers of at least some of the Internet content they are expected to consume. The key, then, is to have an African presence on the Internet. The building blocks include adopting policies and laws that spur the creation of enabling environments that facilitate home-produced content. African governments have to liberalize and encourage the development of the traditional mass media sectors that produce content—radio and television production, advertising companies, broadcasting, book publishing, music production, and so on—within African countries. Africans have always favored the consumption of local media content over imported content whenever available. The Internet should be no different.

FUTURE PROSPECTS: LOOKING BEYOND THE "LEAPFROG" METAPHOR

The short history of the Internet in Africa shows that the technology has not been the magic bullet of development that it was made out to be in the early 1990s. By all measurements the concept of developmental and technological leapfrogging that was advanced as the main benefit of the Internet has not materialized. This may be due to the fact that most diffusion of innovation studies, out of which the concept came, dealt with less complex innovations than the Internet. The model was based on diffusion of specific innovations by individual farmers or members of the community, not governments, and certainly not a complex continent like Africa, which has fifty-three independent countries and as many political and economic systems. Africa is not culturally, politically, and economically homogeneous for technological leapfrogging to be expected on a grand scale.

In addition, the Internet for development model is premised on technological determinism, the idea that "the medium is the message" (McLuhan 1964). That is to say, technologies determine culture and development and the presence of a new technology in and of itself leads to its adoption, and ultimately to change and development (Straubhaar and LaRose 2000). It is immaterial whether the technology is culturally relevant or not. The reality in Africa shows otherwise. The presence of Internet nodes in the capital cities, and even e-centers in poor urban neighborhoods, does not mean much to the vast majority of Africans who have no access to electricity or telephone connections. For the Internet to become relevant to the majority of Africans, telecommunications infrastructure has to be extended to the rural areas and the amount of relevant African Internet content increased. That is to say, Africans must first philosophize or determine for themselves the role they want the Internet to play in their societies and develop a regulatory framework to promote these roles. Thereafter, in order to reflect African cultural realities of the Internet, Africans must produce their own Internet content. The Anglo-American electronic commerce model that currently dominates the Internet and places undue emphasis on distribution and consumption of goods and services is probably not very relevant to the vast majority of Africans whose daily aspiration is survival. Furthermore, the potential of the Internet cannot be exploited in the type of highly centralized bureaucratic political environments that obtain in most African countries. Over-centralization and political control is inimical to the logic of the Inter-net. In addition, the Internet operates best in environments where the underlying mass media industries—radio, television, film, newspapers, book publishing, music production, advertising, and so on—are free and thriving. The mass media are the foundation of the Internet. In order to increase African cultural and other content on the Internet, the mass media, which converge on the Internet, must be able to produce the local content that ultimately gets streamed on the Internet. In order to prevent Africans from becoming nothing more than consumers of the homogenized, American-dominated, decadent mass culture that is the stock-in-trade of the Internet, Africans must have a cultural presence on the Internet.

CONCLUSION

Human history is one of adaptation to changing communication technologies. The history of human communication and culture is a history of our attempts to catch up with technology, which is culture-bound and comes in incremental steps. Human beings basically choose the pace at which they change in order to adapt to technological innovations, which have today virtually become a flood. If Africans choose to adapt all "the latest" technological and communications innovations at the speed with which they are developed, they will be setting themselves up for frustration, alienation, and dislocation, not to mention financial ruin. Each communication technology has a certain learning curve in every society. Technology has to be adapted to local circumstances to be relevant.

The history of the Africanization of radio and television on the continent is instructive. Radio is probably the first electronic technology of the twentieth-century to be Africanized. Africa's oral culture is tailor-made for radio, which has been around for close to forty years in most countries. The incredible range of programming content on African radio stations in hundreds of African languages is testimony to a medium that has been localized and put to the service of local cultures. Television is in the process of being Africanized and given an African hue by indigenous phenomena like the "juju video" industry in Nigeria. These are profitable private production companies that use portable video cameras and electronic and computer-generated special effects to retell African folk tales and myths (Sotinel 2001). They have become a cultural phenomenon that stretches across West Africa. Needless to say, Nigerian television producers have experimented with the medium for over forty years. Most Africans do not know what the Internet is. Africans must choose for themselves whether, in a continent where millions of people are without electricity and telephone services, they want to become part of the global culture, live in the fast lane, and thus be-come the testing and dumping ground for failed and obsolete technologies, or whether they want to go at it at their own pace.

Rather than allow the IMF, the World Bank, and the international aid industry to shove them willy-nilly into the vortex of an ever-accelerating technological whirlwind, Africans need to take a long-term view of technology and culture. Even in the midst of the technological revolution, it is important to remember that the development of communication technology has been incremental and systematic. The process of mass media development has been evolutionary rather than revolutionary. Technologies that are adopted and become widely used lay the foundation for newer technologies. The experience gained from mastering and using "old" technologies enables people to make optimum use of newer technologies. Thus, technological leapfrogging without the benefit of an enabling political, social, economic, and cultural environment is tantamount to constructing a technological society without a foundation. Indeed, technological leapfrogging in environments where the sine qua non of Internet technology—electricity and telecommunications infrastructure—are largely nonexistent ultimately becomes an exercise in creating more markets for Western electronic commerce.

REFERENCES

Agnus, C., and P. Blanchard. 1997. Internet, un objet encore mal compris, mal maitrisé, mal philosophié (The Internet, an object that is misunderstood, hardly mastered, and badly philosophized). *L'Express*, April 4: 47–48.

Allen, J. 1998. Commercial interests lust for cyberspace. *National Catholic Reporter*, May: 3.

Baranshamaje, E., et al. 1995. Increasing Internet connectivity in sub-Saharan Africa: Issues, options, and World Bank Group role. Unpublished World Bank document. Washington, DC: World Bank.

Barlow, J. 1999. Tout ce que vous savez sur l'Afrique est faux (Everything you know about Africa is wrong). *Jeune Afrique*, January 12: 30.

Bray, H. 2001. Africa goes online. *Boston Sunday Globe*, July 24: A1, A24–A25.

Caramel, L., and M. Laronche. 2000. Il faut mener un combat pour la diversité culturelle (We must fight for cultural diversity). *Le Monde* (Dossier), October 3: II.

Dioh, T. 2000. Ils font bouger l'Internert en Afrique (They make the Internet work in Africa), *Jeune Afrique/L'Intelligent*, July 11: 82–90.

Eko, L. S. 2001. Many spiders, one World Wide Web: Toward a typology of Internet regulation. *Communication Law and Policy* 6 (3): 445–484.

Gharbi, S. 2000. Tunisie libertés: Le diagnostic de l'ONU (Freedom in Tunisia: The diagnosis of the U.N.). *Jeune Afrique/L'Intelligent*, May 23: 38–45.

Grubler, A. 1996. Time for a change: On the patterns of diffusion of innovation. *Daedalus* 125 (3): 19–43.

Huxley, A. 1954. *The doors of perception*. New York: Harper and Row.

Info Development. 1998. International Telecommunications Newsletter. Retrieved from http: www.intitunenews/199606/development.htm.

Kaye, B., and N. Medoff. 1999. *The World Wide Web: A mass communication perspective*. Mountainview, CA: Mayfield.

Kinnunen, J. 1996. Gabriel Tarde as a founding father of innovation diffusion research. *Acta Sociologica* 39 (4): 430–442.

Kpatindé, F. 1999. On the tracks of the "Cyber Rebels". *Jeune Afrique*, January 1: 8–13.

Leone, M. 1996. Under the boot, out on the Net. *Columbia Journalism Review* 35 (4): 18–19.

Lowery, S., and D. DeFleur. 1995. *Milestones in mass communication research*. 3rd ed. White Plains, NY: Longman.

McLuhan, M. 1964. *Understanding media*. New York: McGraw-Hill.

Naidoo, J. 1998. *The African connection: Report of the African ministers of communication*. Pretoria: Ministry for Posts, Telecommunications and Broadcasting, Government of South Africa.

Ngwainmbi, E. 2000. Africa in the global infosupermarket: Perspectives and prospects. *Journal of Black Studies* 30 (4): 534–552.

Olorunyomi, D. 1996. Defiant publishing in Nigeria. *Media Studies Journal* 10 (4): 65–74.

Pemberton, H. 1936. The curve of cultural diffusion rate. *American Sociological Review* 1 (4): 547–556.

Rogers, E. 1983. *Diffusion innovations*. 3rd ed. New York: Free Press.

Rude, J. 1996. Birth of a nation in cyberspace. *The Humanist* 56: 17–22.

Ryan, B., and N. Gross. 1943. The diffusion of hybrid seed corn in two Iowa communities. *Rural Sociology* 8 (1): 15–24.

Sandouly, P. 2000. Ils font bouger l'Internet en Afrique (They make the Internet work in Africa). *Jeune Afrique*, July 11: 82–90.

Schumpeter, W. 1939. *Business cycles: A theoretical, historical, and statistical analysis of the capitalist process*. vol. 1. New York: MacGraw-Hill.

Schramm, W. 1964. *Mass media and national development: The role of information in the developing countries*. Stanford: Stanford University Press.

Slouka, M. 1995. *War of the worlds*. New York: Basic Books.

Sotinel, T. 2001. Le cinéma nigérien sans salle ni pellicule (Nigerian cinema has neither hall nor film). *Le Monde*, May 10: VII.

Star, S., ed. 1995. *The cultures of computing*. Oxford: Blackwell.

Straubhaar, J., and R. LaRose. 2000. *Media now: Communications media in the information age*. Belmont, CA: Wadsworth.

Tarde, G. 1962. *The laws of imitation* (first published in 1903). Clouchester, MA: Peter Smith/Holt and Company.

Trombly, M. 2000. World leaders: IT can ease globalization woes. *Computer World* 34 (37): 14.

UNESCO. 1998. Report of the 5th annual conference on adult education. Retrieved from http://www.unesco.org/opi/eng/contintea/, October 20.

U.N. General Assembly, Committee on Non-Self-Governing Territories. 1958a. *Mass communication in the non-self-governing territories, Resolution No. A/AC.35/L273.* New York: U.N.

U.N. General Assembly, Committee on Non-Self-Governing Territories. 1958b. *Social conditions in non-self-governing territories A/AC/35/SR.180.* New York: U.N.

10

Decentralization and Privatization of Infrastructure

MWANGI S. KIMENYI AND WILSON S. K. WASIKE

In developing infrastructure, Africa faces problems more severe than any other region. Vast distances and low population density make service provision costly. The division of sub-Saharan Africa into forty-eight states, many of them land-locked, makes the barriers more inhibiting in the provision of goods and services because small national markets limit economies of scale, reduce competition, and increase risk. Poor economic policies and institutions are also to blame. Weak states have played a large role in these sectors, with disappointing results. State capacity has been overstretched or even undermined to the extent that service provision has been inadequate. In its current state, the infrastructure, rather than promoting development, is a barrier to it.

Recently, efforts to strengthen decentralized government administration and finance in Africa have intensified substantially and attracted much support from the donor community. The need for decentralization may seem obvious in a continent where a highly centralized system has successfully generated significant development. Structural adjustment policies initiated during the 1980s have begun to transform some African economies, with manufacturing-led economic growth accelerating urbanization and generating a rise in real disposable incomes. These trends have led to a steep increase in demand for infrastructure and economic services in Africa's cities and towns, and also in rural areas, exacerbating already serious backlogs in public service provision. The size of the continent, the regional diversity of the population and resource base, and substantial spatial variations in development needs suggest that the magnitude of investment and service provision capacity required to meet this mushrooming demand cannot be managed effectively by relying on a highly centralized system.

Most central governments currently spend about 30 percent of their development budget on local infrastructure projects, a substantial proportion of which is planned and managed entirely by sectoral ministries. Indeed, over three-quarters of aggregate local development expenditures are often financed from the central governments' resources (Steffensen and Trollegaard 2000; World Bank 2000, 1994). Several significant problems result from this highly centralized service provision structure. First, delays in loan-financed infrastructure projects, administered by overburdened central technical departments, are widespread, leaving substantial foreign loan resources idle for long periods of time. Second, responsibility for the full range of infrastructure required to support economic development is fragmented across various central government sectoral ministries. Without an effective coordination mechanism to take adequate account of project complementarities, the public sector is unable to respond in a timely and comprehensive way to the needs of many areas. Third, excessive central control almost certainly reduces the average quality of the regional development projects undertaken because it is often exercised with little flexibility in project selection and design, such that insufficient consideration is given to unique local conditions. Fourth, the lack of fiscal accountability of local governments under the present system compromises incentives for efficient service provision and cost recovery. Since many local development projects are financed and implemented by central technical departments, there is no compelling reason for local officials to mobilize resources for constructing and operating such facilities. Fifth, the present system places an unnecessarily heavy burden on central government budgets. Most donor funds for local infrastructure are disbursed as grants, even to local governments with sufficient fiscal capacity to repay loans, and even for many projects that should be self-financing. Since debt-service obligations cannot be met from direct returns to investment projects, the central government must cover them with general revenues. Finally, redundant administrative structures that plan and implement development projects on behalf of sectoral ministries are wasteful. Many of the large deconcentrated sectoral ministry offices operating parallel to local agencies are only involved in development projects occasionally, perhaps once every few years. These conditions should be expected to collectively inhibit efficient provision of critical services on which successful private-sector investment depends, depress the financial and economic rates of return generated by the portfolio of foreign-loan-financed projects, make loan repayment more burdensome for central governments, and constrain the development of genuinely responsive local institutions.

Development of subnational fiscal systems, intergovernment financial relations, and the private sector to provide the best infrastructure and services to the citizens involves many and often conflicting economic and political challenges. It is one of the most complex reform processes in the area of public finance. This chapter examines the imperatives, extent, and impact of decentralization and privatization of infrastructure in Africa, thereby delineating the opportunities and challenges to the continent's development in the twenty-first century. In the next section we deal with fundamentals of decentralization and strategies for the participation of the private sector. Following that we explore the extent and impact of decentralization and privatization of African infrastructure on improvements in efficiency, resource availability, economic activity, equity, and participation, as well as how decentralization and privatization have proceeded in each sector of the infrastructure, highlighting distinguishing characteristics and issues. Finally, we conclude and provide a few policy recommendations.

DECENTRALIZATION AND PRIVATIZATION IMPERATIVES

Generally, decentralization can be described as the devolution of power to lower tiers of government as a means of improving urban management as well as promoting closer relationships between local administrations and citizens.[1] Decentralization is also seen in the context of the shifting of responsibility for providing direct services and infrastructure by central governments to regulate and/or facilitate their provision. Certainly, this concept and process idea represents the hope of giving greater access to the people in government and the government to people, thus stimulating national participation in development planning. However, it must be stated that the process is not boundless, rather, it should be subject to the social welfare constraint that any privatization or decentralization process satisfy the core conditions of good governance; namely, transparency in the political regime and in the process by which authority is shared and exercised in the management of a country's economic and social resources for development as well as in the capacity of local authorities to design, formulate, and implement policies and discharge their functions.

Privatization, on the other hand, can be described as the gradual process of disconnecting state-owned enterprises or state-provided services from government control and subsidies and replacing this duct with a conduit linked to market forces. However, such a definition assumes the existence of a market-centered economy with a private economic regime, which clearly is not the reality of many African countries. Taking this factor into consideration, a more relevant and, indeed, complete definition is one that goes further to characterize privatization as the entire process of expanding the sphere of the market through a host of regulations that create an enabling environment for free enterprise to operate as a strategy for sustainable economic development. Thus, the process of privatization not only includes the outright transfer of economic activities from the public sector to the private sector, but may also include contracting out, leasing, concessions, build–operate–transfer arrangements, and so on.

In the context of the broader goals of human settlements and economic development, when properly conceived and implemented, decentralization and privatization are envisaged to foster efficiency and encourage investment in infrastructure and economic services. Indeed, privatization can be viewed as a form of decentralization of management functions from government to private enterprises.

INFRASTRUCTURE DECENTRALIZATION AND SUBNATIONAL GOVERNMENT FINANCING

Africa lags behind the rest of the world on almost all dimensions of infrastructure development: quantity, quality, cost, and equality of access. Moreover, over the past fifteen years, the gap between Africa and the rest of the world in infrastructure development has widened (World Bank 1999, 2000).

The value of infrastructure for growth and development is much more important than any other type of production; it lies in its consumption, as it is an input to all other production. Consequently, Africa pays a high price for its inadequate infrastructure in lost opportunities for growth, for poverty reduction, and for access to services that could improve people's lives. Research has shown that poor infrastructure is one of the main causes of Africa's low competitiveness, weak market integration, slower growth, poverty, and inequality (ADB 1999).

The African region is experiencing an accelerated demand for infrastructure. This arises in part from the rapid growth of rural and urban populations that require basic infrastructure for well-being and productivity. Well-functioning infrastructure is a prerequisite for productive investment and economic growth. In most African countries, fiscal resources are woefully inadequate to meet these demands and/or the fiscal arrangements (e.g., composition of revenues or design of user charges) are not appropriate for this purpose. In addition, the structure of intergovernmental fiscal relations often does not provide adequate resources or incentives for improving the provision of infrastructure and services.

Decentralization efforts in the African region are shifting much of the burden of infrastructure management and finance to subnational levels. The definition of "decentralization" varies across countries and between actors within various countries. As noted, however, in the present chapter "decentralization" is defined as "devolution" of power to independent subnational governments (SNGs) which are given responsibilities for determining the level and the quality of service to be provided, the manner in which those services will be provided, and the source and types of funds to finance the delivery of those services.[2] Consequently, our emphasis is on the relationship between the central governments and the SNGs and not on a deconcentration or delegation of power within the central government system to regional or local agencies/offices. In essence, our focus is on the transfer of decision-making powers to largely autonomous local units.

Many governments are choosing to pursue decentralization/subnational strengthening programs for a variety of reasons. The transfer of responsibility for services to SNGs can help limit demands on overstretched central budgets. Decentralization can also lead to more efficient responses to the needs of rapidly growing populations dispersed across extensive hinterlands. Broader government objectives to foster local democracy and accountability may also be supported through decentralization processes (e.g., by bringing about a closer relationship between the assignment of tasks and the financing of these tasks).

Multilateral and bilateral donors have also been broadly supportive of decentralization initiatives in Africa and throughout the developing world in recent years. Many donors share the common objectives of linking efficiency gains in service and infrastructure provision with promotion of democratic processes and improved governance. Donors have naturally tended to focus their support on aspects of the decentralization process that match their institutional strengths. Among the diverse motivations and approaches of both governments and donors, the factors common to all decentralization initiatives are the need for coordinated access to finance for critical infrastructure and services in tandem with capacity building at the local level.

Analytically, indicators of decentralization relate to the following five main dimensions: (1) the government's commitment to and objectives for decentralization and the context of the SNGs; (2) subnational finance systems, including indicators on SNG revenues, expenditures, and intergovernmental fiscal relations; (3) elements of well-functioning SNG infrastructure delivery systems and infrastructure investment inventories; (4) the regulatory environment and reforms; and (5) the institutional framework and basic capacity-building requirements.

In addition, two cross-cutting indicators are often applicable (Steffensen and Trollegaard 2000): the principle of subsidiarity—operational capacity and the accountability of SNGs to their citizens.

PRIVATE-SECTOR PARTICIPATION IN INFRASTRUCTURE

As part of their decentralization efforts, many African countries have begun to address fiscal resource allocation and mobilization. This is an absolute necessity, but several studies (e.g., Steffensen and Trollegaard 2000) have shown that public resources are clearly not enough. Considerable private financing is also needed to meet the demand for infrastructure and services. In general, Africa has yet to attract significant private investment in infrastructure (especially electricity, urban water, and solid waste), although some successes are starting to be registered.

The resurgence of private infrastructure in the past decade should have large benefits for African countries (Table 10.1).[3] PPI also offers enormous scope for cutting budgetary costs and improving business services. Complete reliance on public ownership and provision of infrastructure has created inefficiencies in management and put an undue financial and managerial burden on the state. With the right incentives and regulations, the private sector and other nonstate institutions can deliver services that satisfy the socioeconomic objectives of public goods, often more efficiently than the state. For instance, introducing competition and private involvement in maritime transport in Côte d'Ivoire generated many benefits for consumers.[4] In particular, measures toward liberalization and privatization of maritime transport substantially lowered import prices for consumers and shipping costs for exporters, increasing the competitiveness of Ivorian exports.[5]

Essentially, privatizing infrastructure establishes an arm's-length relationship between the infrastructure provider and short-term political pressures. Several subsequent benefits of PPI follow from this fundamental change in the institutional framework. These include increased efficiency in investment, management, and operation, which results from the commitment to cost-covering tariffs; improved incentives for operational efficiency; opportunities to draw on competitive discipline; and access to management expertise and technology.

Table 10.1
Selected Private Participation in Infrastructure in Africa

Form	Sector	Country	Year
Management contract	Water	Gabon, Ghana, Mali	NA
	Railways	Cameroon, Togo Malawi Burkina Faso Democratic Rep. Congo	Pre-1996 1993 1997 1998
	Electricity	Gabon, The Gambia, Ghana Guinea, Guinea-Bissau Mali, Rwanda, Sierra Leone	NA
	Airports	Guinea, Madagascar, Togo	Pre-1996
	Seaports	Cameroon, Sierra Leone	Pre-1996
	Telecoms	Benin, Botswana Guinea, Madagascar	NA
Lease	Water	Central African Republic, Côte d'Ivoire, Guinea, South Africa	NA
	Railways	Côte d'Ivoire Gabon Cameroon	Pre-1996 1997 1998
	Electricity	Côte d'Ivoire, Guinea	NA
	Airports	Mauritania Côte d'Ivoire	Pre-1996 1996
	Seaports	Mozambique Zambia	Pre-1996 1998
Concession/ BOT	Railways	Malawi Mozambique	1993 1998
	Airports	Senegal	1996
	Seaports	Mali	Pre-1996
	Telecoms	Guinea-Bissau	NA

Table 10.1 (*continued*)

Form	Sector	Country	Year
Demonopol- ization/BOO	Electricity	Côte d'Ivoire, Mozambique	NA
	Seaports	South Africa	Pre-1996
	Telecoms	Burundi, Ghana, Guinea Madagascar, Mauritius Namibia, Nigeria, South Africa Tanzania, Uganda, Zaire	NA
Divestiture	Airports	South Africa	1997
	Telecoms	Sudan	NA

Sources: ADB. 1999. *African development report, 1999: Infrastructure development in Africa.* New York: Oxford University Press; Kerf, M., and W. Smith. 1996. *Privatizing Africa's infrastructure: Promise and challenge.* World Bank Technical Paper No. 337. Washington, DC: World Bank.

Second, PPI can improve access to private infrastructure finance. Last, PPI can enhance opportunities for developing local capital markets and reverse capital flight. The large-scale and predictable cash flows associated with appropriately regulated infrastructure projects allow them to issue debt and equity instruments that are often highly valued by institutional investors. In a divestiture of infrastructure enterprises, privatization may also be used to widen participation in local markets.

Compared with government enterprises, private firms typically have stronger incentives to build and run infrastructure businesses effectively and at low cost. To the extent that prices reflect costs and market conditions, private firms will tend to choose projects that are viable. Privatization also encourages and facilitates the imposition of cost-covering tariffs, thus addressing the problem of underpricing that has afflicted many publicly provided infrastructure services. Greater efficiency and cost-covering prices allow firms to make investments and provide services that might not otherwise have been possible. They simultaneously improve the government's fiscal position by making available the same quantity and quality of service with smaller budgetary subsidies.

Infrastructure development subjects private investors to major risks because the investments are often large and their costs can be recouped only over long periods of time. Two special features of infrastructure create additional risks. First, the investments are largely sunk; the assets cannot be used elsewhere except at great cost. In other words, exit is not costless. Second, infrastructure projects often provide services that are considered essential and are provided by monopolies. As a result, services are highly politicized. This combination of factors makes investors especially vulnerable to opportunistic government actions.

Before the investment is made, the government has every reason to promise to treat the investment fairly, to allow cost-covering tariffs, and to avoid changing regulations in ways that would adversely affect the investor. Once the investment is made, however, the government has an incentive to renege on its promises. The government can satisfy political demands to reduce prices or otherwise appropriate the investor's profits. Such opportunistic behavior lowers the returns to the private investor. A win–win situation for governments, private investors, and consumers can be attained through well-designed guarantees by host governments (Irwin, Klein, Perry, and Thobani 1999).[6]

The London-based Control Risk Group (CRG) identifies the four main risks for investors in Africa:[7] (1) contract frustrations and problems arising out of government corruption, (2) conflict and instability prompted by regional and ethnic tensions, (3) poorly managed economic programs, and (4) risks to assets and personnel posed by crime (Williams 2001). Despite having most of the world's "extreme-rated" areas, such as Angola, DRC, and Sierra Leone, the CRG sees the prospects of Africa as relatively promising (Table 10.2). Forecasting continuing, gradual political and economic reforms within the region, albeit accompanied by phases of political instability and renewed conflict, the CRG identifies areas of concern to be Liberia, the Central African Republic, Chad, Kenya, Zimbabwe, Guinea-Conakry, and Equatorial Guinea, while Mozambique, Tanzania, and Zambia are singled out as rising stars.

Table 10.2
Investment Risk in Africa

Risk	*Examples of Countries*
Security Risk	
Insignificant	Botswana, Burkina Faso, Ghana, São Tomé & Principe
Low	Egypt, Mali, Mauritania, Namibia, Senegal, Tanzania, Uganda, Zambia
Medium	Algeria, Côte d'Ivoire, Kenya, Nigeria, South Africa, Northern Sudan
High	Angola, Democratic Republic of Congo, Liberia
Extreme	Central African Republic, Sierra Leone, Somalia, Southern Sudan
Political Risk	
Insignificant	São Tomé & Principe
Low	Botswana, Ghana, Madagascar, Namibia, South Africa, Tanzania, Uganda
Medium	Chad, Côte d'Ivoire, Ethiopia, Kenya, Liberia, Mozambique, Nigeria, Rwanda
High	Angola, Burundi, Democratic Republic of Congo, Somalia, Zimbabwe
Extreme	Central African Republic, Sierra Leone

In order to attract private-sector participation in infrastructure, the SNGs must be well managed, creditworthy, and sufficiently autonomous to enter into and honor contracts. To achieve these goals in the region, work needs to be done on macroeconomic fundamentals, good governance, development of capital markets, regulatory and institutional capacity, strengthening of intergovernmental relationships, and creditworthiness of utilities and SNGs. In addition, the right mix of public financing, and the administrative framework for it (e.g., taxes, grants, and user charges), is crucial for an efficient public sector.

Capital markets in most African countries remain underdeveloped, and macroeconomic stability, an essential requirement, is often lacking. Banking systems are weak, with ineffective regulatory frameworks. An enabling environment does not exist in most cases for long-term investments by social security agencies, pension funds, and insurance companies. On the demand side, a viable financing system for basic infrastructure and services requires SNGs to become creditworthy and to do their part to create favorable conditions for private-sector participation. Technical assistance is necessary, but it is not effective unless the policy incentives for the SNGs are favorable.

AN ASSESSMENT OF THE EVIDENCE

How is the existing evidence on impact and extent of African infrastructure decentralization and privatization to be interpreted?[8] Although several methodological difficulties emerge in comparing decentralization studies and using them to generate reliable propositions that can guide government decision makers and aid agency professionals, it is nonetheless possible to undertake an appraisal of the effect of decentralization and privatization upon various dimensions of performance.[9]

Efficiency

As in many other aspects of decentralization, efficiency raises countervailing factors.[10] The design of public goods and services may be more in accordance with local preferences under a decentralized system (allocative efficiency), but weighing against this are central standards that can ensure a minimum degree of quality and quantity of provision. The utilization of local resources, information, and technology may lower costs (technical efficiency), but the existence of economies of scale points in favor of more centralized provision (provided that diseconomies do not thereby appear). The presence of externalities (i.e., absence of a market) also tends to justify provision and control by higher levels of government. Finally, regarding implementation and maintenance (especially in the long term), the literature and evidence favor decentralization, provided that this approach obtains a higher degree of user participation than would have been the case in a centralized system.

Inefficiencies associated with centralization include weakness in attaining and maintaining beneficiary participation, underutilization and inadequate maintenance, irrelevance to local needs and conditions, and lack of flexibility, adaptability, and speed. All these observations impact upon the relative efficiency of the decentralization/centralization alternatives, and suggest that thoroughgoing devolution of decision making and authority will aid the effective implementation of infrastructure programs and projects.

Clearly, then, simple generalizations are not likely to help us to know whether and how the structure of government affects efficiency. Nonetheless, on balance it appears that theoretical and empirical considerations tend to favor local, rather than central, responsibility. This is especially the case with public goods and services that have primarily local effects and where local adaptation is important.

Ultimately, the question of relative efficiency is largely empirical—unfortunately, little quantitative evidence exists that directly supports or refutes the various competing claims. Few sectoral studies rigorously evaluate the comparative cost of centralized versus decentralized provisions.

Decentralization, however, leads to more efficient provision of economic infrastructure in terms of both product design, unit costs, and maintenance. As to construction, the relevant possibilities lie in the use of local construction materials and labor, and the more appropriate selection of the type and location of facilities. Where infrastructure policies are applied generally across-the-board, rather than directed specifically toward particular localities, the resulting provision may be more costly and inefficient than what would have been the case where local conditions were taken directly into account. Infrastructure programs that fail to develop or apply technologies for small-scale applications typical of rural areas and instead require rural areas to use facility designs that were developed for large-scale urban operations tend to impose higher operating costs onto local residents than they can afford to pay.

Resource Availability

There are basically three interrelated themes on the link between decentralization and privatization, on the one hand, and resource availability, on the other. The first concerns the distribution of taxation and expenditure under the centralization/decentralization alternatives, or, in other words, the assignment problem of "who collects and gets what." Another relates to the degree of financial autonomy of the SNGs versus dependence on central transfers. The final theme raises an efficiency issue: whether decentralization increases the total amount of resources mobilized for public expenditures. A substantial body of literature exists that relates generally to each theme, although the empirical aspects of the third are less often addressed.

In general, the distribution of revenue sources and expenditure responsibilities between different levels of government is such that local public expenditures tend to exceed own-source revenues. The SNGs typically face practical difficulties in raising revenue, particularly because of the limitations set nationally and administrative problems. The SNGs are often actively discouraged from fully exploiting potential revenue sources by a wide variety of central checks, controls, and hindrances (Bird and Miller 1990). This may be motivated by economic considerations, as well as by popular sentiments. Generally, central governments tend to reserve for themselves the most buoyant and lucrative revenue instruments (although there may be sound efficiency reasons why this should be the case).

Moreover, there are many examples of centrally imposed legal restrictions upon local revenue raising. National governments often require explicit prior approval for local tax rates, property revaluations, and "almost everything else that affects local budgets" (Bird and Miller 1990, 284). If the power to set the rate is part of the "generally accepted definition of a local tax" (Prud'homme 1989), then many locally collected taxes would fall outside this definition. In Nigeria, for instance, central approval is required before any levy can be included in the revenue estimates of a local council (Rondinelli 1990a).

Administrative feasibility places severe limits on the revenue-raising capability of all levels of government in developing countries. The practical obstacles that inhibit efficient revenue collection and cause substantial revenue shortfalls are by no means peculiar to local government. The prerequisites of staff competence, well-defined tax legislation, and effective means of enforcement present acute problems at the national level. The tax system is typically in a state of flux, with compliance low and enforcement lax. Institutional, political, administrative, structural, and cultural constraints characterize the tax systems of developing countries at both national and local levels. The interest here, therefore, lies in assessing the relative revenue competence of local versus central government.

The heavy reliance of the SNGs upon central transfers means that their degree of financial autonomy tends to be quite limited; hence, such authorities may in reality be less independent than it first appears. However, fiscal imbalances do not necessarily indicate an inappropriate allocation of governmental responsibilities and powers. The goals of fiscal equalization, principles of "good" taxation, and administrative considerations may all point to a substantial role for central transfers. The task is to structure these transfers in such a way that any adverse incentive and efficiency implications are minimized. Finally, while the impact of decentralization on revenue raising is controversial, the most relevant evidence (e.g., Oates 1985) suggests that governmental structure and public resource mobilization have little to do with each other.

Participation

To what extent does decentralization and privatization enhance the ideal of freedom and equality through people's full participation in the formulation,

planning, and passage or implementation of infrastructure development strategies?[11] This question may be addressed by considering three issues in turn: the
mode, the intensity and quality of participation, and then the impact of decentralization and participation upon the nature of decisions made. First, as to
whether decentralization improves the modes of participation, we see that decentralization typically involves the creation of additional formal structures,
ostensibly aiming to increase local participation. An overview of country experiences suggests that decentralization is more likely to be thoroughgoing, in the
sense that there is genuine devolution of authority and efforts to promote participation under liberal democratic/pluralist national regimes.[12] Where the nation-state is authoritarian or one-party, the mode of decentralization tends to
follow deconcentration, which effectively preserves central control. This applies
equally to capitalist and socialist regimes, where small cliques have captured the
power of the state. At the same time, however, the converse does not necessarily
hold: Democracy need not lead to decentralization. The foregoing proposition is
supported by the already mentioned country cases, as well as the experience of
particular countries over time.

Second, in addressing the question as to who effectively makes decisions at
the local level, it is found that national officials and/or local elites often tend to
dominate the process (e.g., Mutizwa-Mangiza 1990; Vengroff and Johnston
1987; Samoff 1990a, 1990b). Finally, and most important from our present point
of view, the impact of local participation upon decision making and priorities is
important.[13] Even in the absence of broad based participation, the actual decision
makers may be responsive to interests other than their own, so that the quality of
decision making is enhanced.

The Impact upon Economic Activity

The impact of governmental structure upon economic activity is difficult to
pinpoint, especially given the multitude of associated variables, such as macroeconomic policy, development strategies, and ideology. Yet in principle, decentralization may promote local economic activity through several means, including an increased infusion of capital and other resources, the more extensive provision of infrastructure, and a more effective "enabling environment" than
would have been the case under a centralized system. In this light, therefore,
countries with effective SNG systems have been much more dynamic and successful economically than those under centralized control (Mutizwa-Mangiza
1990).

The potentially positive implications of decentralization for private sector
activity are various. First, where decentralization is accompanied by increased
public resource availability and capital inflows, this will have direct and secondary stimulative multiplier effects. For example, the construction and maintenance of local infrastructure such as roads, water supply, and electricity is likely
to involve local contractors and wage labor. Second, decentralization is likely to

lead to more appropriate selection of the type and location of facilities, and better long-term maintenance. Thus, decentralization can contribute to improved physical conditions (transportation, energy sources, communications, etc.), which reduce rural isolation and improve the profitability of local enterprises, and thereby stimulate local economic activity. Third, the SNGs may be more supportive of "endogenous entrepreneurial development."[14]

Finally, less immediate benefits might also be forecast, such as those flowing from a labor force whose skills better meet the needs of local employers. Devolution of decision-making power to the local level may also benefit local entrepreneurship by helping to overcome structural constraints. The rural economic environment is characterized by large distances from the urban centers where both public and private decision-making tends to be conducted and financial resources and management information concentrated. Dispersed rural enterprises have tended to be relatively isolated and have poorer knowledge of the economic activities in their immediate environment and beyond. The SNGs may be well positioned to formulate and implement policies that are supportive of local business, including such services as management assistance and market information. Physical and social distances that separate central officials from rural entrepreneurs and the indiscriminate character of regional policies may inhibit the development of fruitful policies by the national administration (OECD 1986).

Simply put, programs for supporting small businesses are best promoted at the local level. At the same time, the influence of national macroeconomic policies must be borne in mind: Where central economic managers are seeking to stabilize or contract the economy, any local stimulatory measures may well be overwhelmed in the larger context. Moreover, national development policies—industrial, agricultural, trade, and so on—will generally have a substantial impact. A national system of direct communications, highways and railways is also important, especially for local "export" industries.

In practice, there are a number of cases where decentralization has stimulated local economic activity. Sometimes this has followed the construction of economic infrastructure; in other places, it has been attributed to the capital injected through transfers to impoverished localities under a decentralized system. According to Maro (1990), for instance, the decentralization in Tanzania that sought to promote small-scale industries in a self-reliant fashion increased the use of local resources, raw materials, and skills. There was also evidence that the reformed industries produced goods and services that could otherwise only have been obtained at the expense of high foreign exchange costs.

Industrial decentralization generally refers to the relocation of industry from the metropolitan areas to the periphery therein (see, e.g., Bell 1987; Wellings 1988). The dominant opinion is that it is primarily a result of government intervention in the provision of incentives and development of infrastructure. An alternative view is that industrial decentralization is largely a spontaneous response to market forces.[15] In sum, community, local, and private-sector devel-

opment of infrastructure on a comprehensive basis is likely to positively stimulate subnational entrepreneurial activity, employment, and economic growth.
However, the effect of decentralized and privatized infrastructure on economic
activity is contemporaneously linked to national macroeconomic policies, especially fiscal and monetary management, pricing, and sectoral policies.

Equity

There are several critical factors that determine how decentralization influences equity between rural and urban areas, regions, and income groups. These
include central grants, expenditures and taxation effects. Clearly, then, no uniform generalizations can be made about the impact of decentralization on aggregate inequality, since the impact of the various factors often work in different
directions.

From a theoretical perspective, inequalities within specific localities (intradistrict) could worsen under decentralization, because the redistributive functions of the SNG are thereby limited for two related reasons (Oates 1985): (1)
On the taxation side, "sorting out along Tiebout lines" will imply relatively little
scope for redistribution from the wealthy to the poor within jurisdictions; and (2)
local redistributive expenditures will be constrained by the fear of attracting the
mobile poor with relatively generous local support programs. This suggests that
the actual scope for assistance to the poor within the locality will be more cir-
cumscribed under a relatively decentralized fiscal system.

Empirical studies support the proposition that interdistrict (spatial) disparities may be reduced through the wider provision of public goods and services.
Rondinelli, Nellis, and Cheema (1983, 50), talking about the positive results of
decentralization, say that "the access of people living in previously neglected
rural regions and local communities to central government resources and institutions has increased, if only incrementally, in most developing countries that
have decentralized." On balance, however, aggregate inequality is likely to be
predominated by worsening interregional equity, largely because of the absence
of effective central redistributive policies (also see Cheema and Rondinelli
1983).

The Extent and Impact of Central Grants

The center has a potentially powerful redistributive role in collecting revenue on the basis of ability to pay and allocating funds on the basis of need. The
latter can be done either through a bias towards poorer areas (tackling interditrict
inequality) or via specific grants that tend to benefit the less well off (e.g., for
primary education), thereby enhancing intradistrict equity. The available evidence relates mainly to the impact of grants upon interdistrict equality.

Economics of fiscal federalism asseverates that the central government has
the primary responsibility for initiating and coordinating policies so as to

achieve horizontal equity (i.e., policies for redistribution are most appropriately set and implemented centrally). This is partly because there should be a single level of government that plays a role in determining the extent of redistribution, lest different decisions made by various levels of government undo the redistributive actions of the other. Moreover, the marked spatial variations in resource availability point to the need for the center to assume the predominant role in redistribution. There is also the "Tiebout effect" of population mobility, which limits the feasible extent of variance between independent redistributive measures at the local level (Helm and Smith 1987) and suggests the need for a strong central role in promoting an equitable distribution of public resources. It is noted that the need for redistributive grants conflicts, to some extent, with the presumed need for a substantial degree of financial autonomy. The central government may undertake substantive schemes of redistribution through grants that favor the SNGs in poorer parts of the country. In practice, however, it appears that the prevailing fiscal arrangements under decentralization—by design or otherwise—generally fail to enhance interdistrict equity (Tordoff 1988; Hinchcliffe 1989).

The Expenditure Effect

Decentralization and privatization may enhance equity through increased total and subnational spending on pro-poor public infrastructure. This is possibly because SNGs' choices in terms of quality and quantity of infrastructure differ from central governments' choices. The common argument is that when the benefits of an infrastructure service are mostly local and there is little scope for economies of scale, decentralized provision is most effective.

How has increased decentralization affected spending levels on infrastructure? The outcome reflects the net outcome of opposing effects. Spending increases if the SNG makes infrastructure a higher priority than the federal government did, if they are less effective at delivering services, or if they give up the benefits of economies of scale to get more autonomy. Spending decreases if they assign infrastructure a lower priority, or if most projects are more cost-effective.[16]

The Taxation Effect

The nature of local taxes tends to suggest that the burden is not very regressive. The main progressive revenue sources available to the SNGs in developing countries are automobile use and ownership and real property. Taxes on motoring—vehicles and gasoline—may be progressive insofar as the demand tends to be highly income elastic. Of nineteen studies in thirteen developing countries reviewed by Bahl and Linn (1991), most found the property tax to be generally or very progressive. However, the actual distributive impact of such taxes obviously depends largely upon its details (Bird and Miller 1990)—for example, the treatment of rental versus owner-occupied, of land versus improvements, and so on. On the negative side, the multitude of local revenue sources, levied on entertainment, sumptuary items, small businesses and so on, may be regressive in net impact.[17]

SECTORAL-SPECIFIC CONSIDERATIONS

Energy Services

While hydroelectricity is often cited as an example of appropriate technology, many localities are unable to exploit hydropower, given seasonal stream flow fluctuations and rapidly increasing demand for electricity. The SNG authorities have, therefore, generally exploited the only remaining options through the construction of small coal-fired thermal plants and/or off-grid diesel generation. Decentralized development has been successful in providing rural areas with much-needed energy (Webb and Derbyshire 2000; Barnes, Jechoutek, and Young 1998). The incentives to expand local capacity via small plants lie in local control, the ability to set down prices (and make and keep profits), and significantly shorter lead times.[18]

Providing energy services to the poor is replete with a unique set of problems. In particular, these relate to the balance between total cost structure and poor consumers' ability and willingness to pay.[19] Traditionally, electricity has been provided by government-owned utilities through the extension of existing grid networks. In many parts of the world this model has been extremely effective in expanding access to electricity. However, sub-Saharan Africa continues to lag behind, despite policies over many years emphasizing the importance of expanding access to electricity. Since 1970, increases in the numbers served have lagged behind increases in population, and projections show biomass to comprise more than 80 percent of total energy consumption in the region well into the first decade of the twenty-first century.

There is widespread recognition of the need to adopt different approaches to the choice of institutional and market structure to deliver electricity, the choice of technology, and the nature of property rights regimes. In recent years, some countries in Africa (notably Cameroon, Kenya, Lesotho, Morocco, and Uganda) have experimented with alternative forms of service delivery (Webb and Derbyshire 2000).

Advances in technology in recent years have reduced the costs of these forms of supply to the point where in many cases they form a feasible alternative to either grid supplies or off-grid diesel generation. However, the lower cost may be associated with lower service quality. The resulting trade-off can only be effectively resolved through greater consumer involvement (e.g., allowing communities to contract directly with alternative suppliers) in the selection of technologies, reemphasizing the need for greater community involvement in the process.

There are many different means of signaling local requirements. These include allowing local communities to contract directly with providers, using pilot projects to help to bring local communities and alternative suppliers together, and setting up a central procurement process to which communities submit their demands. In some countries, such as Lesotho and Uganda, rural electrification (RE) programs are being implemented as part of major power-sector reforms. They involve the vertical separation of the national monopoly, the decentralization of rural schemes, and the introduction of new regulatory regimes. In Lesotho, the RE schemes are based on the creation of locally elected community representatives who contract directly with alternative suppliers. In Uganda, RE is carried out by an autonomous government body with responsibility for selecting projects based on a least-cost approach and the amount of money available for subsidies.

In addition to rural programs based on larger institutional reforms, other countries have begun programs to encourage increased connections in the absence of (or prior to) larger reforms. The program in Morocco is based on a large national survey that identified a least-cost expansion plan. In Cameroon the program was based on increased decentralization following the use of pilot projects to demonstrate the viability of rural electrification to potential private-sector providers. In Kenya RE has developed following local demand for an alternative to the slow expansion of the national electricity grid. Local demand resulted in the development of a strong distribution network for one particular technology, PV cells. The strong demand allowed expertise to be developed and the benefits arising from the economies of wholesale purchase to bring down costs and increase the quality of service.

Finance, policy reform, and the evolving roles of public–private partnerships are primary issues in energy infrastructure and supply (Webb and Derbyshire 2000, 22):

Financing: Sourcing finance, especially for working capital at the start of projects, is a central problem. Concerns over the ability of rural communities to pay and the lack of private-sector expertise combine to make financing of the initial capital costs difficult. In Uganda, the Rural Electrification Unit (REU), under the Ministry of Energy and Minerals Development was created to overcome this hurdle. In Cameroon, pilot projects were used to kick start the process.

Reform: Decentralization of decision making is central to allowing communities to signal their preferences (i.e., the balance between willingness to pay and required quality of service). Of the countries examined by Webb and Derbyshire (2000), only Morocco has not explicitly decentralized and the difference is evident—a much greater reliance on grid extension in Morocco compared to elsewhere. For countries with bankrupt, or near-bankrupt central utilities this is not an option.

Government: While the process of reform involves the gradual removal of government from direct participation in the process of electrification, its participation in the initial phases is crucial. In Lesotho the process of the new regulatory and institutional frame-work is critically dependent on government support. Similarly, the success of the REU in Uganda depends on government financial support and the pilot projects in Cameroon depend on government involvement.

Private Sector: All the schemes depend on the use of private-sector expertise, both technical and commercial, for their success. This, in turn, depends on the private sector having ready access to local communities and the ability of local communities to signal their requirements. In addition to such measures as minimizing taxes on necessary technologies (e.g., PV cells), this will often require central government support of local communities with little experience dealing with the private sector. For example, in Lesotho the Department of Energy is charged with supporting communities with model contracts, and in Uganda the REU conducts the competitive bidding process to find private-sector contractors.

To date, rural electrification schemes across the vast majority of sub-Saharan Africa have failed to meet the commercial energy needs of the rural poor. Future success depends on developing institutional and regulatory frameworks that devolve power to local communities while providing them with the support they require. The devolution of power allows for different responses to meet the needs of individual communities and provides both the communities and the providers with incentives to appropriately meet the demand in rural areas for commercial energy. In summary, global experience with renewable energy development offers a simple but important message: There is no magic fix for the challenge of renewable energy finance. Responding to the challenge involves patiently cultivating the right mix of supporting institutions, reforms, policies, markets, and infrastructure, based on the country and circumstances.

INFORMATION AND COMMUNICATIONS TECHNOLOGY

In the emerging knowledge-based economy of the twenty-first century, information and communications technology (ICT) will invariably be of critical importance. Generally, central governments are still responsible for many ICT infrastructure services, such as broadcasting, telecommunications, and the Internet, but this is changing as the responsibility is increasingly transferred to SNGs. Recent technological innovations reduce the need for services to be provided by monopolistic utilities. Parts of some local telephone monopolies are increasingly meeting competition from wireless telephones and rival wireline systems. In addition, there is a new global paradigm in ICT planning for optimizing regional integration and growth (Katz and Dichter 1997). This is the movement away from the current system of centralized hierarchical networks focussed on large urban centers to a decentralized system of regional networks with cross-border focus. The new paradigm presents opportunities and challenges for both service providers and policy makers in terms of their influence on the supply of services and the coordination of national ICT policies into a single regional framework.

A key step toward a single regional cooperative framework for ICT development in Africa is the Regional African Satellite Communications initiative, which plans to launch Africa-based satellite systems. In 1998, communication ministers from more than fifteen African countries agreed to support an ICT infrastructure called the African Connection, and development efforts are under way by the Southern Africa Development Community, the Common Market for Eastern and Southern Africa, the Economic Community of West African States, and the East African Community (World Bank 2000).

Recent empirical results of the telecom competition, privatization, and regulation in Africa (e.g., Wallsten 2000) are largely consistent with conventional wisdom. Competition appears to have tangible benefits across the board, on mainline penetration, pay phones, connection capacity, and prices. Privatization by itself does not appear to generate many benefits, and is negatively correlated with mainline penetration. Privatization, combined with an independent regulator, however, is correlated with increased connection capacity and pay phones per capita. Moreover, this interaction mitigates the negative effects of privatization on mainline penetration. These results suggest that reformers are correct to emphasize regulatory reforms along with privatization, since privatization without attention to regulation may be costly to consumers. Because competition appears to be the most successful agent of change, reformers should give careful thought to the notion of granting exclusivity periods to their incumbent telecom providers. While temporary monopoly rights undoubtedly raise the value of the incumbent to potential investors, it may delay the arrival of improved services to consumers.

Roads

The conceptual framework for analyzing links between decentralization and road service delivery is presented by Humplick and Moini-Araghi (1996). First, in considering the decentralization of roads it is important to distinguish between various types of decentralization. Depending on the technology and type of resources used in road works, different entities may be suited for the proper assignment of responsibilities. In this respect, three different types of decentralization may be distinguished: (1) decentralization of construction, which requires heavy equipment and machinery and lump-sum and large resource allocations; (2) decentralization of maintenance operations, which may be labor based or equipment based but require in general fewer resources periodically; and (3) administrative decentralization, which may serve as a measure of functional decentralization, as it concerns the organization and management of road activities.

The types of decentralization defined borrow from phases of road development. As a matter of fact, the impetus for the distinction between construction and maintenance activities derives from Oates's (1972) definition of determinants of centralized versus decentralized provision of a public good; mainly, the technical character of the good and the diversity in the individual preferences for the good. Arguably, construction activities are more technical in nature, requiring more coordination and complex technology compared to maintenance. Hence, in the absence of possibilities for private provision through competitive contracting out, economies of scale savings may be realized if construction activities are centrally provided through force account.[20] This may be the reason why when service provision responsibilities are decentralized, more contracting out to the private sector takes place, since these lower levels of government are no longer able to realize economies-of-scale savings.

Individual preferences for varying levels of road condition, however, would suggest potential savings in the form of lower costs to meet diversity of demands locally if SNG provision of maintenance is followed.[21] For the case of administrative activities, according to Buchanan and Tullock (1962), we expect that the resource costs involved in the SNG decision-making processes would differ from those in more centralized ones, and would be captured by the level of decentralization of administrative functions.

In the Humplick and Moini-Araghi (1996) study based on analyses of experiences with SNG road provision in eight countries, decentralization is defined in terms of how it relates to efficacy of service delivery or performance. As a measure of performance, the authors employ the extended-double-cost approach. They distinguish between two categories of costs: (1) resource costs, which are simply the costs of provision, administration, and management of roads (input costs); and (2) preference costs, which are defined as costs incurred because of insensitivity to local demand for road services. In line with economic theory, a suitable social objective is to minimize total cost, which is the sum of preference costs and resource costs. The analysis recognizes that differing levels of effort can be applied to achieve the same level of service delivery.[22] The cross-country study finds that decentralizing the responsibility for roads costs more at first, mostly through losses in economies of scale. But those losses may be outweighed by increases in efficiency when the locus of roadwork is closer to the people.

The Advantages or Limitations of Decentralization are Function-Specific

Maintenance, repair, and rehabilitation functions are best provided locally. If both resource and preference costs are considered, the SNG should have more than 40 but less than 70 percent of fiscal responsibility. If only resource cost efficiencies are considered, there should be complete decentralization. To minimize resource costs, construction should be either completely centralized or completely decentralized. The efficiency of construction is more sensitive to the degree of competition in awarded contracts than to the degree of decentralization. (3) Administrative activities are more efficiently provided by local units similar to local maintenance units. At early stages of decentralization, it is more costly to administer a growing number of road agents, making the optimal level more than 50 percent but less than 80 percent local fiscal responsibility.

The typical picture of decentralized road performance in Africa with respect to the availability of roads and the maintenance standard, including the prevalence of potholes, which increase transport time, is that half of the studied SNGs have a performance level of slightly more than 50 percent of the needs, and the rest have a performance level substantially below 50 percent coverage (Steffensen and Trollegaard 2000, 86). In Uganda, for example, the provision of feeder roads is one of the means of fighting against poverty. There, trunk, feeder, and community roads are managed, respectively, by the central government, the district, and the community. The central government has a conditional grant for maintenance of feeder roads. Under this grant the SNGs are to involve the private sector. This grant is inadequate to address the SNG maintenance needs. The government has divested itself from provision of transport services. Generally, the transport network is very poor, especially in the rural areas, where roads become impassable during the rainy season. Road maintenance performance in the sample SNGs comprises one SNG at level 3 (good) performance (Kampala), one SNG at level 1 (poor) performance (Kotido), and the remaining SNGs at level 2 (fair).

In Kenya, high levels of local participation in earlier generations of the ILO/IBRD Rural Access Roads Program contributed to savings in construction and maintenance costs, as well as higher implementation rates. Active local involvement encouraged people to donate land for project roads; the amount thereby saved was estimated to equal the cost of constructing about 150 km of additional roads (Lisk 1985; Wasike 2001).

Irrigation, Water Supply, and Sanitation

Water is increasingly being managed as an economic rather than a social good, and decentralization—in various forms—has been useful in supporting this new approach. Governments and other reformers are now trying to link service levels and costs, and provide incentives that increase the efficiency of water resource allocation, reduce costs, and increase sustainability of water service systems. Evidence from new decentralized approaches confirms that users are willing to pay for water services that are tailored to their needs. A 1993 World Bank study found this to be true across income levels (see also Litvack, Ahmad, and Bird 1998). It showed that even poor rural farmers and households are willing to pay for levels of service above the minimum usually supplied under centralized systems. However, the key is to design systems that have the capability as well as the incentive to identify and respond to consumers' demands.

Three main trends in decentralization of water services have emerged: private-sector participation (PSP), delegation, and devolution:

Private-Sector Participation: The PSP is a spectrum ranging from full privatization to contracting out for services such as irrigation, water supply, and sanitation. In the latter, the PSP is increasingly common in the urban sector and has led to better-quality services and higher operational efficiency in several African countries. The PSP does not work as well for rural water supply, however, because private, profit-seeking companies tend to neglect harder-to-reach segments of the population.

Delegation: Under the delegation model, governments transfer water management to public or semiprivate water companies. These companies are responsible for providing services within a specified region. This approach has often worked well: Provision of water in Tunisia is one example. However, as in the "pure" private sector, there are strong incentives to underserve rural areas. Delegation may not necessarily be an improvement on public provision, for public and semiprivate companies are frequently plagued by the same inefficiencies and incentive problems (such as lack of profit motive) of other government agencies.

Devolution to Subnational Governments and Users: Small-scale irrigation and rural and urban water supply/sanitation are often devolved to the SNGs. Ideally, responsibilities vary with capacity: The strongest SNGs can undertake activities ranging from interaction with communities to technical planning to supervising construction. Other SNGs might focus more on interacting with the communities, while relying on staff from central or intermediate governments for technical support. Sometimes stronger urban municipalities provide services to neighboring rural areas.

The new push toward participatory management processes has enabled decentralization to user groups. These comprise the intended beneficiaries, who weigh all technically feasible options, consider capital and recurrent cost implications, make choices, and then manage systems. The approach pays dividends for both governments and communities: Communities get what they need, and governments are relieved of the long-term operation and maintenance burden. User groups, referred to as Water Users' Associations (WUAs) or Water and Sanitation Committees (WSCs), are common to irrigation and rural water supply and sanitation.

Successes of the decentralized approach have been recorded in both water supply and sanitation and irrigation (Easter and Hearne 1994; Litvack, Ahmad, and Bird 1998). In Egypt, cropping intensity nearly doubled where farmer-managed systems were introduced, and user associations also were able to reduce some environmental impacts, such as salinity level of water applications. There have also been many successes in water supply and sanitation, particularly in extending services to relatively inaccessible rural areas. The Ghana Community Water and Sanitation Project reports that 78 percent of the target population is now benefiting from improved water sources.

A number of management options, ranging from full agency control to full WUA or WSC control, are used in water systems. Forms of joint agency–user management are the most popular.

Intermediate and Central Government Functions

In most cases, regulatory functions remain the domain of central agencies, while operating functions are more likely to be devolved in some way. Central agencies often have a primary role in establishing the legal and regulatory frameworks for water rights, pricing policies, and environment standards. These regulatory functions are the most susceptible to capture by local interest groups, and the concerns that they address—potential for environmental degradation and disputes over the distribution of water—often affect multiple subnational jurisdictions. Central governments' broader perspective gives them a comparative advantage as arbiters in disputes between communities as well as various broad user groups (such as agricultural, residential, etc.).

Central and intermediate governments also have a financial and technical comparative advantage in managing and financing capital-intensive trunk systems. End users are better able to manage feeder systems that require local knowledge and ingenuity, local resource mobilization, and enforcement of contracts among secondary and tertiary users (e.g., irrigation channels, water and sewage networks).

Role of Water User Groups

Water user groups are usually formed around a group of potential users, farmers, or rural/urban households for the purpose of accessing water resources. Two types of groups are common, Water Users Associations in irrigation and Water Supply and Sanitation Committees in rural water supply and sanitation. These groups usually have some sort of legal character (e.g., are legally registered, have elected leadership and a constitution, etc.), and are held together by common interests of members, the public good characteristics of the service, and the expected gains from collective action. User groups work well and fully internalize costs and benefits of schemes when they are certain that they will not be rescued by public agencies if they fail to mobilize the required funds for operation and maintenance.

Financing

Although high-level capital-intensive systems are usually financed by central or intermediate agencies, user charges are increasingly common for operations and maintenance of feeder systems. Experience suggests that in order for feeder systems to be sustainable, users must commit to paying the full cost of operation and maintenance, in cash in kind, or a combination. This approach links choice with costs, and given all technically feasible options, users will choose levels and types of service that they can afford to maintain and address their needs.

While O&M should be financed by users, there is considerable good experience with capital subsidies for water supply and sanitation and irrigation. Subsidies offset some of the substantial start-up costs associated with water services provision. Governments often agree to subsidize a fraction of capital costs, leaving users to then provide any additional funds required. The subsidy is borne by the level of government with functional responsibility.

The structure of tariffs used to support operations and maintenance are important for determining equity and efficiency. For example, in developing countries, an increasing block tariff is often applied to improve access and discourage wasteful water use. This is a price structure in which a commodity is priced at a low initial tariff/rate up to a specified volume of use, then at a higher rate for additional consumption. In many developing countries, however, households do not have individual water meters (i.e., several households share one meter), and thus the impact of the IBT is actually to worsen equity. Informational constraints make it advisable to leave tariff setting and collection to the municipality, as it can better monitor water use (Rondinelli 1990b).

PROBLEMS AND CHALLENGES

Development of subnational fiscal systems and intergovernment financial relations together with increased reliance on the private sector to provide infrastructure and other services to the citizens involves many and often conflicting economic and political challenges. It is one of the most complex reform processes in the area of public finance.

Political Constraints

It is predictable that change will be resisted by those who perceive their vested interests threatened by a new structure of governmental arrangements. This, coupled with bureaucratic inertia, can constitute formidable obstacles to the implementation of decentralization and privatization reforms. Political will at the highest level may not, per se, be sufficient to overcome such obstacles.

A number of authors criticize the assumption that national governments are "unitary, neutral actors." McGinn and Street (1986) argue that policy makers evaluate organizational reforms in terms of the impact upon their own power and control over the use of public resources, so that different actors react differently to the same policy. For instance, the Rawlings government in Ghana (1983–2000) pursued a decentralization proposal that transferred virtually all ministerial activities through the regions to the localities. In 1988, District Assemblies were elected that were supposed to take command of district-level administrations onto which the resources and expertise of central ministries were to be devolved. Olowu (1989) reported that progress was very slow because of powerful forces within the administration against the plan, the distrust of elected councilors by military and civil servants alike, and the widespread feeling that decentralization was a diversion from national economic policies. In the meantime, the old structures continued through selected management committees presiding over deconcentrated administration at the SNG levels (also see Wunsch 1991; Wunsch and Olowu 1990).

Bureaucratic and Coordination Obstacles

Beyond the political tensions involved in decentralization and privatization attempts, significant problems often arise related to the nature of the bureaucracy: its structure, technical competence, and resource base. The creation of new systems of the SNG especially requires considerable administrative skill and resources. There may be basic problems with respect to personnel needs, attitudes (held both locally and centrally), and training in the SNG.

Despite stated objectives and government directives from relevant ministers to strengthen regional and district offices and deconcentrate the infrastructure development process, there is often minimal local participation and capacity building as well as poor interministerial coordination of the various activities. First, many infrastructure sectors continue to operate under strong central control. Sectoral directorates in central ministries or departments that control services such as road construction and improvement, water supplies, irrigation, and sanitation often ignore proposals brought up from the SNG level through decentralized programs. They continue to exercise significant power over funds allocation and project approval, often favoring projects identified by their own offices.

As a result, regional government officials often perceive the plans and projects (prepared fully or substantially by outside consultants appointed, controlled, and paid by central government technocrats) to be essentially external, and therefore fail to identify with them and strongly support their implementation. In addition, there has been little genuine effort to build capacity at the local level.[23] Such a situation is not conducive to successful decentralized infrastructure planning.

Second, mechanisms for coordinating infrastructure, decentralization, and privatization policy development have been largely ineffective. In most cases, years after decentralization, infrastructure activities remain poorly coordinated across ministries, and they are also not harmonized with—and somewhat duplicative of—other efforts being undertaken by government. This development is inevitable wherever there is lack of a suitable forum for working out policy-making and implementation problems.

Institutional Weaknesses

Most evaluations of the institutional frameworks for decentralized infrastructure provision and PPI in the continent show that little has been accomplished in the way of reform. Repeatedly, the evaluations (e.g., Nwankwo 1984;

Wallis 1990; Nellis 1983; Rakodi 1988; Tordoff 1988) have identified the following weaknesses: (1) shortages of professional skills; (2) responsiveness of
the appointed mayor and council to their superiors, rather than local residents;
(3) inadequate revenue and weak fiscal discipline; (4) uncoordinated development programs; and (5) failure to enforce local regulations.

Staff shortages at the local level appear to be a crucial constraint in many
developing countries. An IMF survey conducted in 1982 showed that 57 percent
of all government employment in industrial countries is at the "local" (as opposed to the central) level, compared to only 15 percent for developing countries, with Africa averaging only 6 percent, Latin America 21 percent, and Asia
37 percent (World Bank 1983). This can be seen to reflect personnel shortages
as well as the fact that SNGs account for a greater share of public expenditure in
industrial, relative to developing, countries.

Regarding inappropriate institutional assumption of responsibilities, it is
notable that most major regional infrastructure projects initiated under recent
decentralization projects have been prepared and implemented largely by engineering consultants employed by central government ministries. Many of these
project proposals are overly focused on technical matters, often failing to give
adequate or competent attention to institutional, economic, and financial feasibility concerns. Financial concerns are also poorly dealt with because finance
ministries are rarely sufficiently involved in many efforts. Lack of attention to
good fiscal analysis and project evaluation can result in exaggeration of a SNG's
financial capabilities, leading to default on debt-service obligations and undermining the success of particular infrastructure projects. More important from a
national perspective, finance ministries are ultimately confronted with the
broader consequences of approving SNG development projects of doubtful financial viability, such as problems with loan repayments or the rescheduling of
loan agreements.

Fiscal Decentralization and Financing Risks

Lessons learned in many countries clearly indicate that negative outcomes
result both when capacity building takes place in the absence of access to significant finance and, conversely, when finance is provided to SNGs that lack
adequate management capacity. Lessons have also been learned from various
countries around the word; for example, some regional studies (e.g., Ehdai
1994) in Europe and Latin America show that transfer of responsibilities for
tasks to the local level without a parallel transfer of financial responsibilities (or
the opposite) may lead to inappropriate results. This has also been proved by the
results of the six African case studies summarized in Steffensen and Trollegaard
(2000).

In apparent contradiction to the principle of decentralizing regional finance,
both African local and provincial governments are still dependent for infrastructure finance on central transfers. The local dependence on central funds is

not inherently undesirable if scale economies in revenue generation are being realized and equity goals are being met; the fact that the balance is being shifted to funds over which the SNGs have little discretion seems to undermine genuine decentralization. This situation is made more serious by the slow progress in improving the productivity and buoyancy of regional own-source revenue and ensuring that potentially self-financing services more fully recover costs. The limited headway made in these areas suggests that SNGs may be unable to generate sufficient resources to operate and maintain facilities being built with rapidly growing earmarked transfers.

More generally, the most problematic issue in SNG finance has been the failure of central governments to think systematically about regional revenue generation in a broader framework of economic development and service provision needs. Little is understood about equity and efficiency consequences of using different sources of revenue (own-source, grants, loans) for regional service development, and there have been few explicit efforts to create linkages across sources (e.g., to make grants conditional on regional tax capacity and effort, to make loans only to those SNG authorities with demonstrated capacity to repay them, etc.).

CONCLUSION

The African experience, with decentralizing and privatizing infrastructure to date suggests that changes must be implemented in a rational and incremental fashion and in ways and places that maximize the probability of success. Clear achievements early on, even if quite modest, will justify taking additional steps toward decentralization/privatization and are likely to generate further support for doing so.

The broader reality is that the African governments' need to make better use of available resources will slowly propel the continent to continue to adopt—and to enforce—appropriate policies regarding institutional reform. Concurrently, technocrats and politicians at both central and the SNG levels will gradually grow accustomed to new ways of thinking about infrastructure development and the role of subnational levels of government. With careful sequencing and planning of the stages of the decentralization and privatization processes, those involved in this reform effort can steadily push the system in the right direction.

Ultimately, however, the goals of decentralization and privatization cannot be achieved without more explicitly expressed government support and better institutional coordination of the numerous agencies involved in urban and regional development. For effective private participation in African infrastructure, governments need to create favorable incentives to foreign capital by providing macroeconomic stability, competitive taxes, freedom to repatriate capital, and good governance through contract enforcement, no corruption, and adherence to transparent rules, including for privatization. Furthermore, to protect consumers against exploitation by private monopolies, governments should develop appropriate legal and regulatory frameworks that conform to international good practices for governance and pricing. Overall, decentralization and privatization appear promising institutional arrangements for the provision of infrastructure that in many ways are superior to centralized provision.

NOTES

1. It is generally agreed that there are four forms of decentralization: political, administrative, spatial, and market. Since the 1950s there have been three periods during which research output on the topic of decentralization interventions and reforms has accelerated. Each period has had a different focus. The first period occurred in the early 1960s, when the focus was primarily on decentralization as an administrative approach for local-level governance in the postcolonial era. During this period the focus was largely on administrative aspects of decentralization, with particular concern with the legal organization of center–field office relationships and the role of local authorities or municipalities within a centrally managed government. The second period took place in the early 1980s, when aid agencies were urging governments to consider decentralization strategies both to better reach the rural and urban poor and to increase their participation in the development process. A third and currently ongoing period emerged in the early 1990s. It focuses primarily on political economy aspects of decentralization, seeking to understand whether decentralization of any form or type can stimulate the emergence of good governance, constrain subnational ethnic conflict, promote democratic practices, facilitate the growth of civil societies, and increase the privatization of public sector tasks (e.g., Klugman 1994).

2. This is in line with the definition of Richard M. Bird and colleagues (Bird, Ebel, and Wallice 1995). The term "decentralization" implies the transfer of responsibility and competence to democratically independent lower levels of government. This term is to be viewed as opposed to the term "deconcentration," which implies transfer of responsibility from central ministries to field officers at the local or regional levels, thereby becoming closer to the citizens while remaining part of the central government. In this chapter, the term "subnational government" is used to describe the level of government below the central government. The type of subnational government varies from country to country, but in all cases emphasis has been placed on selecting authorities that to some extent are directly accountable to local populations through some kind of an electoral process.

3. Private participation in infrastructure ranges from management contracts and leases to concessions and build–operate–transfer (BOT), demonopolization and build–own–operate (BOO), and full divestiture (sale) of enterprises. Under a concession, the private operator manages the infrastructure facility, operates it at its own commercial risk, and accepts investment obligations (whether to build a new facility or to expand or to rehabilitate an existing facility). At the end of the concession term, the assets are returned to the state. The concession is a common model for water, ports, airports, and toll roads, where governments desire private investment but do not wish to relinquish rights to ownership of sector assets in the long term.

4. Private involvement in Cote d'Ivoire's maritime transport evolved over three steps: (1) restrictive practices favoring the state-owned shipping line, SITRAM, were first eroded in 1993, when the banana and pineapple exporters association chartered its own vessels at much lower costs, halving freight rates for banana exports to Europe and cut-

ting those for cocoa exports to the United States by one-quarter; (2) SITRAM was liquidated in 1995 to make way for COMARCO (a new carrier with majority private Ivorian ownership); consequently, COMARCO and other domestic shipping lines benefited from a reservation of 50 percent of bulk and refrigerated traffic for the three product groups that had been previously handled by SITRAM (bananas and pineapples, palm oil, wine); and (3) all nonconference shipping traffic was liberalized in December 1996.

5. Even though Côte d'Ivoire is one of Africa's leaders in attracting private investment, it lags behind many other countries. Among industrial countries the United Kingdom has fully privatized telecommunications, power, and sewerage, while France and Germany retain almost total public ownership in these sectors. In developing countries, private participation in infrastructrure could reach 40 to 50 percent (DBSA 1998).

6. Poorly designed guarantees threaten to undermine the benefits of privatization. First, they can blunt private investors' incentives to choose only good projects and to run them efficiently. Second, guarantees may impose excessive costs on the host country's taxpayers or consumers and expose them to too much risk. Guarantees also may lead to asset stripping, in which a firm's insiders extract value from the firm even as they drive into bankruptcy or excessive foreign borrowing.

7. CRG is an international business risk consultancy that provides ongoing assessments—whether by country, region or topic, of political and security risks (culminating in annual Risk Maps), as well as providing confidential investigation services, security consultancy, and crisis response. The independent private company investigates fraud, conducts detailed due-diligence studies, traces and recovers misappropriated assets, and provides litigation support.

8. The impact of decentralization upon human development will obviously depend upon the relative importance of local government. Steffensen and Trollegaard (2000), on the basis of six sub-Saharan African country studies, developed comparative indicators of decentralization and subnational government finance.

9. Difficulties include analytical problems generated by careless use of conceptual definitions and terms, misconceptions and unrealistic expectations, unsystematic presentations, an overemphasis on cases of failure, lack of comparability among diverse case studies, neglect of historical patterns that generate complexity, inappropriate linear assumptions, and naïve assertions by some that bureaucracies should be dramatically reduced and power and responsibility for public-sector tasks be transferred to local communities and private-sector organizations.

10. Efficiency is a multifaceted concept that can be used in at least three senses. Allocative efficiency involves the consideration of what is produced, preferences, and how it is allocated between agents. From a neoclassical economic point of view, the basic proposition is that local governments are better able, given differing local circumstances and preferences, to satisfy varying local demands for public goods and services. X- or technical efficiency refers to cost-minimization. In practice, attention tends to focus upon the relationships between decentralization and unit costs, the use of local resources, technical adequacy or quality, and the comparative extent of malfeasance. It is also important to view efficiency over time, or the intertemporal allocation of resources, which brings the issues of implementation and maintenance to the fore.

11. Although not always clearcut, a distinction can be drawn between participation viewed in terms of active, broad-based local participation in political decision making as an end in itself and participation as a means to affect the appropriateness of decisions and enhance the impact of public expenditures upon efficiency, equity, private initiative, and

so on. These aspects can be referred to, respectively, as the developmental and instrumental values of participation (Parry 1972).

12. For instance, Olowu (1989) and Rakodi (1988) on Zambia, Norris (1983) on the Sudan, and Wallis (1990) on Kenya.

13. Instrumental theories portray participation as a means by which individuals can ensure that their interests are defended and promoted, and as a way to facilitate better information and communication, and, therefore, more effective government (Bulpitt 1972). Participation is also expected to induce enterprise, initiative and imagination that will benefit the whole community.

14. This is defined by the OECD (1986) as development built on local assets, expanding existing enterprises and creating new ones, which is initiated and managed locally. Governments at the local level may be better able to formulate policies that are appropriate to local conditions. Entrepreneurial energies may be unleashed from the burden of central bureaucratic regulation (assuming, of course, that these are not replaced by local red tape). Thus, it has been observed that "because they need support that is individualized to local conditions, entrepreneurial initiatives appear to survive and flourish best in settings that permit flexible and localized public management" (OECD 1986, 33).

15. In the South African context, where a "vast quantity of money has been paid towards incentives and the development of infrastructure in far-flung industrial decentralization points" (Wellings 1988), the IDPs were able to offer infrastructure and services to industrialists. Surveys of local companies have shed some light on the factors bearing upon firm-location decisions, revealing that the incentives were often the major attraction of the IDPs and that many firms would relocate if the subsidies were removed. On the other hand, it has been argued that although incentives may have been decisive in some cases, the scale was substantially in excess of what was required, and that the process of relocation would have continued in any case (Bell 1987). The areas were also attractive to unskilled labor intensive industries, since labor was relatively cheap and unorganized.

16. In an international analysis, Estache and Sinha (1995) focus on spending levels and ignore the reasons these levels change, so no conclusions can be made about whether decentralization makes spending more or less efficient. Among the conclusions they offer are the following: (1) Decentralization tends to increase both total and subnational spending on infrastructure, possibly because the preferences of subnational governments, in terms of quality and quantity of infrastructure, are different from the central government's preferences; (2) the conventional wisdom is true: For decentralization, policy makers everywhere must guarantee a balance between revenue and spending assignment. A good way to offset the impact of decentralization on spending levels is to increase the imbalance between revenue and spending assignments; (3) be careful about applying lessons learned in industrial countries to decentralization in developing countries. What happens in industrial countries may help assess the decentralization's impact on total spending in developing countries, because the elasticity of per capita infrastructure spending is roughly similar in both countries (about 0.3 in developing countries and about 0.2 in industrial countries). But that is not a good indicator for subnational spending, for which the elasticity is greater than 1 in developing countries (between 1.1 and 1.3, depending on how decentralization is measured) and less than 1 in industrial countries (between 0.7 and 0.9).

17. The equity effects of local taxes can be typically seen as follows. Motor vehicle taxes are relatively equitable, since car ownership is limited to upper income groups. Taxes on entertainment are reasonably equitable, because the tariffs vary according to

type of entertainment, with traditional performances having the lowest rates. Taxes on restaurants and hotels are progressive, since the rich are likely to spend proportionately more on these items and small establishments and itinerant vendors are exempt. The effects of the registration taxes levied on businesses are uncertain, depending on who the final consumers are and what proportion of the tax is passed on. Finally, the tax on non-motorized vehicles can be regarded as regressive, since users of bicycles and mikokoteni (Swahili term for handcarts) are likely to be among the poorer members of the community.

18. At the same time, however, in terms of thermal efficiency, capital and operating costs, dispatching capacity, and environmental impact, the small plants are inferior to the large plants. There is a tendency, therefore, to reverse policy on decentralized power plants by banning their construction.

19. Supplying energy services to rural areas, where levels of poverty are usually higher, is generally at a higher cost per consumer compared to urban areas because of the large capital costs of electrification, the relatively low load density in rural areas, and the generally higher proportion of domestic to total consumption in rural areas. This aggravates the low average levels of consumption in these areas.

20. When construction activities are contracted out to the private sector, there is still the question of managing the contracts, which requires capacity and skills in procurement and supervision of civil works that may be better provided centrally in some cases.

21. Exceptions include for the case of roads, transit users and their demands, as well as externalities (air pollution, damage, etc.).

22. This term is borrowed from economics of the firm, where it is defined as the degree of attention paid by a manager to reduce costs or improve performance.

23. In Botswana, the recruitment, posting, training, promotion, and discipline of local authority staff is generally the responsibility of the centrally directed Unified Local Government Service (ULGS). The ULGS staff at headquarters has been strongly criticized by the District Councils for not being sufficiently aware of, and responsive to, local problems and needs (Tordoff 1988, 198).

REFERENCES

ADB. 1999. *African development report, 1999: Infrastructure development in Africa.* New York: Oxford University Press.

Bahl, R., and J. Linn. 1991. *Urban public finances in developing countries.* New York: Oxford University Press.

Barnes, D., K. Jechoutek, and A. Young. 1998. *Financing decentralized renewable energy: New approaches.* Washington, DC: World Bank.

Bell, T. 1987. International competition and industrial decentralization in South Africa. *World Development* 15 (10): 1291–1308.

Bird, R. M., R. D. Ebel, and C. L. Wallice, eds. 1995. *Decentralization of the social state, intergovernmental finance in transition economies.* Washington, DC: World Bank.

Bird, R. M., and B. Miller. 1990. Taxes, user charges and the urban poor. In *Taxation in developing countries*, edited by R. M. Bird and O. Oldman. Baltimore: Johns Hopkins University Press.

Buchanan, J. M., and G. Tullock. 1962. *The calculus of consent: Logical foundations of constitutional democracy.* Ann Arbor: University of Michigan Press.

Bulpitt, J. G. 1972. Participation and local government: Territorial democracy. In *Participation in politics*, edited by G. Parry. Manchester: Manchester University Press.

Cheema, G. Shabbir, and Dennis A. Rondinelli. 1983. *Decentralization and development: Policy implementation on developing countries*. New Delhi: Sage Publications.

DBSA. 1998. *Infrastructure: A foundation for development—development report 1998*. Midrand, South Africa: Development Bank of Southern Africa.

Easter, K. W., and R. Hearne. 1994. *Water markets and decentralized water resources management. Staff Paper No. P94–24*, Department of Agricultural and Applied Economics, University Minnesota, Minneapolis.

Ehdai, J. 1994. *Fiscal decentralization and the size of government*. Policy Research Working Paper No. 1387. Washington, DC: World Bank.

Estache, A., and S. Sinha. 1995. *Does decentralization increase spending on public infrastructure?* Working Paper No. 157. Washington, DC: World Bank.

Helm, D., and S. Smith. 1987. The assessment: Decentralization and the economics of local government. *Oxford Review of Economic Policy* 3 (2): i–xxi.

Hinchcliffe, K. 1989. Federal financing of education: Issues and evidence. *Comparative Education Review* 33 (4): 437–449.

Humplick, F., and Azadeh Moini-Araghi. 1996. *Decentralized structures for providing roads: A cross-country comparison*. Policy Research Working Paper No. 1658. Washington, DC: World Bank.

Irwin, T., M. Klein, G. E. Perry, and M. Thobani. 1999. Managing government exposure to private infrastructure risks. *The World Bank Research Observer* 14 (2): 229–245.

Katz, R. L., and A. Dichter. 1997. Decentralizing telecommunications in Latin America. *Journal of Strategy and Business* 9: 52–61.

Kerf, M., and W. Smith. 1996. *Privatizing Africa's infrastructure: Promise and challenge*. World Bank Technical Paper No. 337. Washington, DC: World Bank.

Klugman, J. 1994. *Decentralization: A survey of literature from a human development perspective*. Occasional Paper No. 13. New York: Human Development Office.

Litvack, J., J. Ahmad, and R. Bird. 1998. *Rethinking decentralization in developing countries*. Sector Studies Series, PREM. Washington, DC: World Bank.

Lisk, F., ed. 1985. *Popular participation in planning for basic needs*. Aldershot, UK: Gower.

Maro, P. 1990. The impact of decentralization on spatial equity and rural development in Tanzania. *World Development* 18 (5): 673–693.

McGinn, N., and S. Street. 1986. Educational decentralization: Weak state or strong state? *Comparative Education Review* 30: 471–490.

Mutizwa-Mangiza, N. 1990. Decentralization and district development planning in Zimbabwe. *Public Administration and Development* 10: 423–435.

Nellis, J. 1983. Tutorial decentralization in Morocco. *Journal of Modern African Studies* 21 (3): 483–508.

Norris, N. 1983. Local government and decentralization in the Sudan. *Public Administration and Development* 3: 209–222.

Nwankwo, G. 1984. Management problems of the proliferation of local government in Nigeria. *Public Administration and Development* 4: 63–76.

Oates, W. 1972. *Fiscal federalism*. New York: Harcourt, Brace, Jovanovich.

Oates, W. 1985. Searching for Leviathan: An empirical study. *American Economic Review* 75 (4): 748–757.

OECD. 1986. *Rural public management*. Paris: OECD.

Olowu, D. 1989. Local institutes and development. *Canadian Journal of African Studies* 23 (2): 201–231.

Parry, G., ed. 1972. *Participation in politics*. Manchester: Manchester University Press.

Prud'homme, R. 1989. Main issues in decentralization. In *Strengthening local government in sub-Saharan Africa, EDI Policy Seminar Report No. 21*. Washington, DC: World Bank.

Rakodi, C. 1988. The local state and urban local government in Zambia. *Public Administration and Development* 8: 27–46.

Rondinelli, D. 1990a. Decentralization, territorial power and the state: A critical response. *Development and Change* 21: 491–500.

Rondinelli, D. 1990b. Financing the decentralization of urban services in developing countries: Administrative requirements for fiscal improvements. *Studies in Comparative International Development* 25: 43–59.

Rondinelli, D., J. Nellis, and G. Shabbir Cheema. 1983. *Decentralization in developing countries: A review of recent experience*. World Bank Staff Working Papers No. 581. Washington, DC: World Bank.

Samoff, J. 1990a. Decentralization: The politics of interventionism. *Development and Change* 21: 513–530.

Samoff, J. 1990b. The politics of privatization in Tanzania. *International Journal of Educational Development* 10 (1): 1–15.

Steffensen, J., and S. Trollegaard. 2000. *Fiscal decentralization and subnational government finance in relation to infrastructure and service provision: Synthesis report on six sub-Saharan African country studies*. Copenhagen: The National Association of Local Authori-ties in Denmark.

Tordoff, W. 1988. Local administration in Botswana. *Public Administration and Development* 8: 183–202.

Vengroff, R., and A. Johnston. 1987. Decentralization and the implementation of rural development in Senegal: The role of rural councils. *Public Administration and Development* 7: 273–288.

Wallis, M. 1990. District planning and local government in Kenya. *Public Administration and Development* 10: 437–452.

Wallsten, S. J. 2000. *An econometric analysis of telecom competition, privatization, and regulation in Africa and Latin America*. Discussion Paper. Stanford, CA: Stanford Institute for Economic Policy Analysis.

Wasike, W.S.K. 2001. *Road infrastructure policies in Kenya: Historical trends and current challenges*. Working Paper No. 1. Nairobi: Kenya Institute for Public Policy Research and Analysis.

Webb, M., and W. Derbyshire. 2000. Delivering energy services to the poor: Case studies from Africa. Paper presented at the PPIAF Conference on Infrastructure for Development: Private Solutions and the Poor, May 31–June 2, London.

Wellings, P. 1988. International competition and industrial decentralization in South Africa: A comment. *World Development* 16 (12): 1547–1549.

Williams, S. 2001. Investment risk in Africa: Where to invest and where not to. *African Business* 262: 16–18.

World Bank. 1983. *World development report, 1983*. New York: Oxford University Press.

World Bank. 1993. *Water resources management: A World Bank policy paper*. Washington, DC: World Bank.

World Bank. 1994. *World development report, 1994: Infrastructure for development.* New York: Oxford University Press.

World Bank. 1999. *World development indicators, 1999.* Washington, DC: World Bank.

World Bank. 2000. *Can Africa claim the 21stt century?* Washington, DC: World Bank.

Wunsch, J. 1991. Sustaining Third World infrastructure investment: Decentralization and alternative strategies. *Public Administration and Development* 11: 5–23.

Wunsch, J., and D. Olowu, ed. 1990. *The failure of the centralized state.* Boulder, CO: Westview.

11

Beyond Rhetoric: Peacekeeping in Africa in the New Millennium

KORWA G. ADAR

Africa's place in the new millennium is characterized by recurring instability, inter- and intrastate wars, and economic and political problems. The intensity of these problems and conflicts has accelerated in the post–Cold War era, posing more complex challenges for the peaceful resolution of conflict in particular and the advancement of peaceful coexistence of population groups in general. Whereas most African countries made economic progress during the 1990s, with an average annual rate of growth of nearly 4 percent between 1994 and 1999, Africa as a region contributed less than 1.2 percent of the world's gross domestic product, down from 1.8 percent in the 1980s (Mills 2000, 31). Of the nearly 600 million sub-Saharan Africans, more than 45 percent of them live on less than $1 a day. Of the forty-one countries categorized in 2000 by the World Bank and the International Monetary Fund (IMF) as Heavily Indebted Poor Countries (HIPC), thirty-three can be found in sub-Saharan Africa. The total external debt of the African countries increased from $288 billion in 1990 to $324 billion in 1996 (World Bank 2000, 176).

Against this background of economic difficulties lies endemic instability and intra- and interstate conflicts. One in every five Africans lives in a country or region engulfed in conflict (Fleshman 2000, 8). These conflicts continue to serve as significant impediments to economic growth and the generation of the wealth that could be used to deal with endemic poverty. Perhaps more important is the fact that these conflicts have stalled the continent's transition to democratic governance. Thus, in countries that during the last several years have been embroiled in some form of civil strife (e.g., Somalia, Liberia, Sierra Leone, Rwanda, and the Democratic Republic of Congo), political liberalization and transition to more democratic governance structures have not been carried out as envisioned in the late 1980s, and these countries either have no legitimate central authority or remain under the control of authoritarian regimes. The results have been continued suffocation of civil society and increased poverty and material deprivation, especially among historically marginalized groups (e.g., women, rural inhabitants, children, and the unemployed and underemployed residents of the urban periphery).

In addition to the fact that Africa's domestic conflicts have continued to constrain wealth creation, they have also created a significant refugee problem. For example, in 1998 Africa accounted for 25 percent of the world's refugees (U.S. Committee for Refugees 2000). In 1992 and 1993 the total number of refugees in Africa reached 5 million and 6 million, respectively. The figure rose to 7 million in 1994, dropping to 4 million and 3 million in 1996 and 1998, respectively. Sudan and Angola, which have been embroiled in some form of domestic conflict during most of their existence as sovereign nations, have the largest number of internally displaced persons (IDPs) in the world, accounting for 4 million and 2 million, respectively. Apart from Sudan and Angola, the other countries that accounted for a high number of Africa's nearly 10 million IDPs in 1998 included, among others, the Democratic Republic of Congo (960,000), Burundi (800,000), Liberia (725,000), Sierra Leone (700,000), Uganda (622,000), Mozambique (500,000), Nigeria (470,000), Somalia (350,000), and Kenya (300,000). Indeed, these figures vary every year depending on the level of intensity of intra- and interstate conflicts (U.S. Committee for Refugees 2000).

These problems pose more complex and interlocking security crises for Africa, particularly with respect to conflict resolution, as well as poverty alleviation and peacekeeping efforts. The post–Cold War era has ushered in a new epoch amenable to tangible promotion of conflict resolution and peacekeeping in Africa. Specifically, the emerging New World Order has set in motion an environment conducive to conflict resolution and peacekeeping centered within the context of the paradigm, African solutions to African problems. The central purpose of this chapter is to examine the role of the African state and that of nonstate actors in the area of peacekeeping in the continent. Specifically, it assesses the extent to which Africans themselves have initiated and participated in peacekeeping efforts in the continent in the post–Cold War era. The central premise of the study is that whereas the African state and nonstate actors increasingly play important roles in peacekeeping in the continent, they still lack the political will to establish a standing African peacekeeping force.

Whereas "peacemaking" refers to diplomatic efforts initiated to handle conflict according to Chapter VI of the U.N. Charter, "peacekeeping," on the other hand, refers to forces positioned with the belligerent parties' consent to monitor a peace agreement not specified in the Charter. While "peace enforcement" refers to a situation where military personnel are deployed to bring belligerent parties under control as provided for under Charter VII of the U.N. Charter, "peace building" means the establishment of structures to prevent the recurrence of conflict once peace has been achieved (Boutros-Ghali 1995, 45–46). One of the main functions of peacekeeping personnel is to promote confidence between the parties involved in war by implementing the provisions of the agreement (Carey 1998, 15). Inherent in the success of peacekeeping is impartiality, a situation that in most cases is difficult to ascertain (United Nations 1990).

Peacekeeping is centered on the premise that the belligerent parties have accepted international assistance to help them reestablish stability and the status quo ante. Even though peacekeeping, at least in the U.N. context, was designed to deal with interstate conflicts, in Africa virtually all conflicts that have involved peacekeeping efforts have been intrastate conflicts (Cilliers 1999a, 20). This is not to argue, however, that intrastate conflicts in Africa have not had regional and global dimensions.

Intrastate conflicts in Africa, as in other parts of the world, have usually been internationalized (Adar 1998). What is important to emphasize is that even in situations where conflict is internal, the consent of the belligerents is a sine qua non for a peacekeeping force to be deployed. The maintenance, success, and effectiveness of peacekeeping are contingent upon the continuing cooperation of the relevant parties (James 1994, 24).

CONTEXTUALIZING AFRICAN PEACEKEEPING PERSPECTIVES: THE COLD WAR SCENARIO

Peacekeeping is not an alien concept in the context of postcolonial African international relations. The first time that the African countries were directly involved in peacekeeping and peace enforcement operations was in 1961 in Tanganyika (later Tanzania) to protect the leadership from mutinous soldiers (Vogt 1997, 65). Once again, in 1964, with the help of Britain, African countries were involved in peacekeeping operations in Kenya, Uganda, and Tanzania, necessitated by instability caused by mutinous soldiers in these East African countries (Clapham 1996, 84). However, the absence of an established institutional structure responsible for such operations undermined the legitimacy of what were ad hoc peacekeeping missions. The first time that the need for the establishment of institutional structures for peacekeeping and peace enforcement was discussed was during the formation of the Organization of African Unity. Proposed by President Kwame Nkrumah of Ghana, the concept of the African High Command was envisaged to be a viable African-centered institutional mechanism responsible for peacekeeping and peace enforcement in the continent consistent with Pan-African idealism (Amate 1986, 170–174; Schraeder 2000, 302–303). It can therefore be argued that the concept of African solutions to African problems was not far removed during the time the OAU was being conceived. However, the African High Command, together with the other Pan-African ideals, remained distant concepts following the adoption and legitimization of the *Realpolitik* Westphalian state centrism in the OAU Charter as the guiding principle for African modus operandi (Adar 1999).

The concept of state sovereignty acquired more significance in the OAU Charter, undermining the legitimacy of the Pan-African norms. Indeed, structurally, the OAU, until its replacement by the African Union in the summer of 2001, remained a weak organization without capacity to manage the responsibilities of peacekeeping (Saxena 1996, 15). The OAU founding fathers were unwilling to confer peacekeeping responsibilities on the continental body, leaving the organization without the appropriate structures to keep the peace. Articles II and III of the Charter underpin the original intentions of the founding fathers of the OAU with respect to the maintenance of *Realpolitik* state centrism as the guiding norm of African diplomacy. Peacekeeping, as a concept, therefore, was not inscribed in the OAU Charter. Instead, Article XIX provides for a Commission of Mediation, Conciliation, and Arbitration, an organ that never became operational (Patel 2000, 10). It is important to stress that Articles XIII (2), XIV, and XX of the Protocol establishing the Commission, concluded in Cairo, Egypt, in 1964, did not provide for a system of compulsory jurisdiction, but instead was based on the consent of the parties.

Without established institutional structures to deal with peacekeeping, African peacekeeping efforts during the Cold War remained ad hoc in character. The proposal by Sierra Leone for the formation of an African Political Security Council (APSC) during the seventeenth summit of the OAU in Freetown, Sierra Leone, in July 1980, never succeeded. It was the ongoing civil war in Chad that led to the proposal for the establishment of an APSC. The OAU Neutral Force in Chad (1981–1982), comprising 4,800 troops from Nigeria, Senegal, and Zaire, was the only case in which an African peacekeeping force was deployed within the continent during the Cold War era. However, the interlocking interplay of the lack of a clear mandate given to the contingent, insufficient funds, lack of adequate equipment, the involvement of regional (Libya), extracontinental (United States, France, and Britain) powers, and the unwillingness by some OAU member countries to interfere in the internal affairs of Chad led to the failure of the peacekeeping operations (Berman and Sams 2000, 51; Jonah 1994, 6–9). Apart from this major initiative in Chad, the African states have participated in peacekeeping operations within the framework of the United Nations. However, this study is not specifically concerned with the U.N. peacekeeping missions in the continent.

TOWARD A NEW PEACEKEEPING PARADIGM IN AFRICA: THE POST–COLD WAR ORDER IN PERSPECTIVE

The post–Cold War period is witnessing a shift toward isolationism within the ranks of the Western powers' foreign policy–making establishments, particularly with respect to their recommendations for direct military involvement in Africa. Instead, they are now more willing to use U.N. institutions as mechanisms for peacekeeping in Africa. For example, between 1988 and 1998, 47 percent or fourteen of the thirty U.N. peacekeeping operations largely funded by the Western powers were in Africa (Goulding 1999, 161). In 1994 alone, Africa accounted for 70 percent of all U.N. peacekeeping troop deployment. On their part, the African states, as well as regional and subregional organizations, are more willing to participate in peacekeeping operations in the continent. Specifically, a consensus is emerging in Africa in the post–Cold War period, centered on the need to establish and promote institutional mechanisms for conflict prevention, management, and resolution, as well as for states and nongovernmental organizations to be more proactive in peacekeeping in the continent consistent with the notion of African solutions to African problems. What is lacking is for the African leaders to institutionalize this emerging willingness into a clearly established peacekeeping institutional framework at the continental level. As this book goes to press, African leaders have launched the African Union, a continental organization that is supposed to replace the OAU. As discussed by S. C. Saxena in Chapter 7 of this book, the AU is expected to be provided with the appropriate framework for peacekeeping in the continent. Of course, the AU is still in the embryonic stages and it remains to be seen whether this new organization will be able to effectively carry out the function of peacekeeping. Perhaps more important is whether African countries will be willing to arm the organization with the power and facilities to perform such a function. The discussion in this chapter is limited, however, to OAU activities vis-à-vis conflict resolution and the maintenance of peace in the continent.

During their summit meeting in Dakar, Senegal, in July 1992, the OAU heads of state and government agreed in principle to establish a mechanism for conflict prevention, management and resolution (OAU 1992). It was at the 1992 Dakar summit meeting that a clear consensus on a new peacekeeping paradigm in Africa centered on the concept of African solutions to African problems emerged. The momentum was tangibly manifested at the 1993 summit in Cairo, Egypt, with the adoption of the OAU's Mechanism for Conflict Prevention, Management and Resolution (MCPMR). In their declaration at the end of the Cairo summit, the heads of state and government stated, inter alia, that "in circumstances where conflicts have occurred, it will be its responsibility to undertake peacemaking and peace building functions. . . . In this respect, civilian and military missions of observation and monitoring of limited scope and duration may be mounted and deployed" (OAU 1993, Article 15). The Cairo Declaration, as it is known, laid the foundation for a proactive African conflict resolution and peacekeeping initiative, with normative and institutional dimensions.

The MCPMR seems to have redefined the norms governing African diplomacy and African international relations in general, particularly with respect to questions pertaining to intervention in internal conflicts in the African countries. Even though it is still inchoate, the MCPMR is reincarnating the dormant concepts of preventive diplomacy, conflict resolution and management, as well as peace building, peacemaking, and peacekeeping. There are certain important institutional structures provided for in the MCPMR that require some appraisal.

The central decision-making structure of the MCPMR is the Central Organ, whose responsibilities include, among others, sanctioning the deployment of African military observers and peacekeepers (OAU 1993, Articles 18–21). The

Central Organ consists of nine OAU members who are elected yearly, with regional rotation as the guiding principle. The Organ is headed by the country chairing the OAU proceedings (Busumtwi-Sam 1999, 267). During its summit meeting in Tunis, Tunisia, in 1994, Benin, Chad, Egypt, Ethiopia, Côte d'Ivoire, Mauritius, Nigeria, South Africa, and Tunisia became the first countries to serve in the Central Organ. It needs to be noted that the chairman of the Central Organ and the OAU secretary-general have the right to convene a meeting at any time. However, whereas under normal circumstances the heads of state and government and the ministers meet once and twice a year, respectively, the ambassadors meet once a month. All the decisions of the Organ are arrived at on the basis of a consensus (OAU 1993, Article 20).

Under Article 22, the secretary-general is empowered to establish early warning systems designed to gather and analyze information on conflicts in Africa with the objective of defusing any escalation. The other important structure provided for in the MCPMR is the OAU Defense Commission charged with the responsibility of providing advice on peacekeeping in the continent (Busumtwi-Sam 1999, 267). At their first meeting in June 1996 in Addis Ababa, Ethiopia, the Chiefs of Defense Staff of the members of the Central Organ "recognized the primordial responsibility of peacekeeping and international security . . . and reaffirmed that some exceptional circumstances might emerge . . . which would lead to the deployment by the OAU of limited peacekeeping and observation missions" in Africa (OAU 1997c).

The concept of African peacekeeping operations was discussed in more detail during the second meeting of the Chiefs of Defense Staff in Harare, Zimbabwe, in October 1997, attended by twenty-four OAU members and nine members of the Central Organ (OAU 1997b, para. 32–32.9). The Chiefs of Defense Staff reiterated the importance of the recognition of certain concerns with respect to African peacekeeping operations. They recommended that in the event that the OAU deploys peacekeeping operations, this should be an all-African force. Second, in circumstances where the United Nations deploys peacekeeping operations in Africa, the Chiefs of Defense Staff recommended that the U.N. principle of universality should be recognized, with the Force Commander being an African if the majority of the forces are from the continent (OAU 1997b, para. 32.7).

The African peacekeeping or peace support operations are centered on the premise that Africa, particularly the OAU, needs to be "proactive, and not depend on others to initiate action in conflict situations in Africa" (OAU 1997a, para. 26). Specifically, the OAU Military Experts, at their October 1997 meeting in Harare, Zimbabwe, recommended the need for the promotion of African solutions to African problems in the new millennium. Indeed, African states are increasingly demonstrating their willingness to participate in peacekeeping operations in the continent (Bakwesegha 1997). Between 1993 and 1997, for example, African observers were dispatched to a number of conflict-torn countries in the continent. This is not to argue that Africa has established an operational standing army to deal with conflict situations. What is crucial to note is the emerging willingness of the African countries to involve themselves either individually or collectively in the internal affairs of other African countries. For example, between 1992 and 1997 African peacekeeping observers were dispatched to three conflict areas in the continent.

In 1992, prior to the creation of the MCPMR, an African peacekeeping observer mission, code named Neutral Military Observer Group (NMOG) (also known as *Groupe d'Observations Militaires Neutres* [GOMN]), comprised of fifty personnel from Egypt, Nigeria, Senegal, and Zimbabwe with the United States providing the funds for both its deployment and maintenance, was deployed in Rwanda to secure a cease-fire between government forces and the Rwandan Patriotic Front. The mandate of NMOG I was extended in August 1993 to NMOG II with a peacekeeping mission of 180 troops (though the target was 240) drawn from African countries (Anglin 2000, A45). NMOG II merged with troops belonging to the U.N. Mission in Rwanda (UNAMIR) in November 1993, with a broader mandate to secure peace in the country. UNAMIR, with its 2,217 troops, 331 military observers, and 60 civilian police, had more impact in the country than NMOG. However, it did little to prevent the genocide.

Following the assassination of President Melchier Ndadaye of Burundi on October 21, 1993, an African peacekeeping team known as the Military Observer Mission in Burundi (*Mission d'Observation au Burundi* [MOBU]), comprised of sixty-seven personnel from Burkina Faso, Cameroon, Mali, Niger, and Tunisia was deployed in the country. The new leadership in Burundi rejected the deployment of a U.N. peacekeeping mission in the country. Thus, under Resolution S/RES/1049 of March 5, 1996, the United Nations requested the OAU to expand its peacekeeping mission in Burundi. Even though the MOBU contributed positively to peace in Burundi, the financial limitations and size of the personnel hampered its effectiveness. Apart from the genocide, which claimed over 900,000 and 100,000 lives in Rwanda and Burundi, respectively, the United Nations only set up its Human Rights Field Operations in Rwanda (HRFOR) and Human Rights Field Operations in Burundi (HRFOB) in mid-1994.

NMOG and MOBU cannot be considered full-fledged African peacekeeping operations. They remained extremely limited in scope and capability, serving primarily an observer function. However, they are useful as confidence and peace-building measures in the evolving concept of peacekeeping in the continent. Following the Anjouan Island's (part of the Comoros) unilateral declaration of independence in August 1997, an African military contingent, the Observer Military in Comoros, comprised of twenty military observers and four civilians from Egypt, Niger, Senegal, and Tunisia, was deployed in the Comoros's capital city, Moroni, and the island of Moheli to restore confidence in the country and to establish an environment conducive for negotiations. Even though the African peacekeeping mission was eventually withdrawn in 1999 without achieving its objective, its presence, symbolic as it was, signified a new paradigm shift with respect to the increased interest in the involvement in the internal affairs of OAU members by the African states. The concept of absolute sovereignty considered sacrosanct during the Cold War is becoming increasingly undermined in the new millennium as continental leaders find ways to keep the peace and provide an environment within each country that is conducive to economic growth and development.

In order to strengthen and enhance their peace-building and peacekeeping capacities and capabilities, the African countries have adopted various strategies. They participate in regional, continental, and extracontinental peacekeeping training exercises, both at the theoretical and practical levels. Indeed, their participation in peacekeeping operations within the framework of the United Nations, the OAU, and the other African regional organizations provide useful opportunities for expanding their experience in dealing with complex conflict situations. Cognizant of the global role and responsibilities of the United Nations on issues pertaining to international peace and security, the African heads of state and government, during their summit in Addis Ababa, authorized the establishment of specially trained peacekeeping units within African militaries that can be deployed in conflict areas in the continent (Akinrinade 2000, 4). In their 1997 report, the Chiefs of Defense Staff underscored the importance of encouraging cooperation between the OAU and the United Nations and the OAU and subregional organizations in Africa in the areas of training, staff exchanges, and logistical and financial support to deal more effectively with inter- and intrastate conflict (OAU 1997b, para. 9).

STRENGTHENING AFRICAN PEACEKEEPING CAPACITY: THE EXTERNAL DIMENSION

African–United Nations Initiatives

In order to strengthen their peacekeeping capacities, the African states, as well as regional (subregional) and continental organizations, have engaged in a number of bilateral and multilateral cooperative initiatives. To this end, the U.N. Training Assistance Team (UNTAT), with the acquiescence of the African countries, has participated in training activities to strengthen African peacekeeping capacity. For example, while the U.N. training staff members were involved in large-scale multilateral exercises in Zimbabwe in April 1997, UNTAT conducted seminars in Ghana in June 1997 on African peacekeeping capacity. In 1998 UNTAT was involved in different aspects of training in Kenya, Senegal, Swaziland, and Zambia, as well as in Nigeria and Zimbabwe in 1999 (United Nations 1999, para. 30). Similarly, in 1997 and 1998 the U.N. Civilian Police (UNCIVPOL) at the invitation of Egypt, Ghana, and Senegal, conducted training for police officers in those countries. UNCIVPOL also provided training for police from the Southern African Development Community in 1998. It needs to be noted that Africa is the first continent where extensive collaborative bilateral and multilateral peacekeeping initiatives are taking root. The guiding principles behind the establishment of UNCIVPOL include, among others, protection of human rights and fundamental freedoms and the maintenance of law and order (United Nations 1995, 9–10).

Cognizant of the obligation of the United Nations to reinforce the African peacekeeping capacity, the U.N. secretary-general has also stressed the inherent responsibilities of the African countries and organizations to enhance their own capabilities. In other words, the U.N. secretary-general views the United Nations mainly as a complementary instrument for African peacekeeping operations (Annan 1998).

Table 11.1
African Peacekeeping Training Capacity: African–U.N. Initiatives, 1997–1998

Year	*Location*	*Main Activity*	*Participating African Countries*
April 1997	Zimbabwe	Training assistance to exercise "Blue Hungwe"	Multinational peacekeeping exercise (U.K.)
April 1997	Italy	U.N. Train the Trainers	Djibouti, Kenya
June 1997	Ghana	UNTAT	Burkina Faso, Chad, Côte d'Ivoire, Ethiopia, Gabon, Ghana, Kenya, Mali, Senegal, South Africa, Tanzania, Togo, Tunisia, Uganda, Zambia, Zimbabwe
October 1997	Italy	U.N. Train the Trainers	Ethiopia, Mali
December 1997	New York	Meeting on Enhancing African Peacekeeping Capacity	Algeria, Cameroon, Côte d'Ivoire, Egypt, Ethiopia, Gabon, Kenya, Nigeria, Rwanda, Senegal, Tanzania, Togo, Tunisia
January 1998	Singapore	UNTAT	Egypt
February 1998	Senegal	Training assistance to exercise "Guidimakha"	Multinational peacekeeping exercise (France)
February 1998	Zambia	Peacekeeping mission management	Botswana, Kenya, Lesotho, Madagascar, Malawi, Namibia, Tanzania, Zambia, Zimbabwe
March 1998	Swaziland	Training assistance visit	Swaziland
April 1998	Central African Rep.	Training assistance visit	U.N. mission in the Central African Republic
April 1998	Italy	U.N. train the Trainers	Namibia, Swaziland, Zimbabwe

Table 11.1 (*continued*)

Year	Location	Main Activity	Participating African Countries
May 1998	New York	African peacekeeping training strategy	Egypt, Nigeria, Zimbabwe, OAU
June 1998	Kenya	U.N. logistics training	Botswana, Chad, Ethiopia, Ghana, Côte d'Ivoire, Kenya, Malawi, Namibia, Senegal, Swaziland, Tanzania, Zambia, Zimbabwe
July 1998	Zimbabwe	Training assistance to SADC peacekeeping	SADC countries
October 1998	New York	Launch of African peacekeeping training database	All African countries
November 1998	Italy	U.N. train the Trainers	Gabon
November 1998	South Africa	Training assistance to exercise "Blue Crane"	SADC countries

Source: U.N. 2001. *UN initiatives towards enhancing African peacekeeping training capacity.* Retrieved from http://www.un.org/Depts/dpko/training/list2a2.htm, February 17, 2000.

The failures of the U.N. Operation in Somalia (UNOSOM II) in 1994 and the U.N. Mission of Observers in Angola (MONUA) in 1999 signaled the inherent limitations of U.N. peacekeeping operations in Africa. This is not to argue that the United Nations has failed to perform its responsibilities as provided for in Chapters VI and VII of its Charter. The establishment of the U.N. Department of Peacekeeping Operations (UNDPKO) in 1993 was a clear testimony of the proactive commitment on the part of the United Nations in, among other things, preventive diplomacy and peacekeeping functions. By 1996, eleven African countries—Botswana, Chad, Egypt, Ghana, Kenya, Nigeria, Senegal, Sudan, Tanzania, Zambia, and Zimbabwe—had registered their willingness to participate in peacekeeping operations within the framework of UNDPKO (Malan 1997, 23).

Both the United Nations and the OAU encourage the development and institutionalization of peacekeeping capacity based on the concepts of cooperation and partnership. The U.N. secretary-general, Kofi Annan, observed in one of his reports that the success of peacekeeping and peace-building capacity in Africa depends on the cooperation between the United Nations, the OAU, and subregional organizations (United Nations 1998, par. 20). Similar collaborative and collective roles of the United Nations, the OAU, and African subregional organizations were also inscribed in MCPMR. In the report of their second meeting in Harare, Zimbabwe, in October 1997, the Chiefs of Defense Staff recommended that, inter alia: "all peace operations in Africa should be conducted in a manner consistent with both the UN and the OAU Charters," with the OAU taking the first initiative (OAU 1997b, para. 32.1, 32.4).

As indicated in Table 11.1, there is clear evidence of growing collaboration between Africa and the United Nations and between Africa and Western countries in the area of building the necessary capacity for peacekeeping. Whereas in 1997 twenty-eight or 52 percent of the fifty OAU members participated in collaborative programs with the United Nations and Western countries to develop and sustain the continent's peacekeeping capacity, in 1998 all of the countries in Africa were involved in similar activities at least once.

The appointment of a panel of experts by U.N. secretary-general Kofi Annan, in March 2000, headed by the former Algerian foreign minister, Lakhdar Brahimi, to provide a comprehensive report on the structure and functions of the U.N. peace operations indicates a growing concern and interest of the organization of its obligations and responsibilities on global peace and security. The Brahimi Report, as it is known, submitted in August 2000, recommended the extensive restructuring of UNDPKO and the establishment of a new information and strategic analysis unit to service all U.N. departments concerned with the issues of peace and security and the formation of the Executive Committee on Peace and Security (ECPS), the Executive Committee on Information and Strategy Analysis Secretariat (ECISAS), and an integrated task force at headquarters to plan and support every peacekeeping mission from the time it is established. It also recommended the need for preventive diplomacy, peace-building strategy, the promotion of international human rights instruments, maintenance of high standards of performance with built-in accountability, rapid deployment of forces, and on-call expertise (United Nations 2000a; United Nations 2000c, para.VII; 2000a). The Brahimi recommendations dominated the September Millennium Summit at the United Nations, particularly with respect to U.N. peacekeeping missions in Africa (Fleshman 2000, 1; Chawla 2001, 10).

The reluctance on the part of the Western industrialized countries to donate troops for U.N. peacekeeping operations in Africa and the Third World in general is a worrying trend in the new millennium (Chawla 2001; Lynch 2000, A36). For example, by December 2000, of the fifteen U.N. peacekeeping missions abroad with nearly 30,000 troops, members of the Non-Aligned Movement, particularly Africa and Asia, contributed more than 75 percent of the contingent. Of the 30,000 troops, India, Nigeria, Jordan, Bangladesh, and Ghana were the largest contributors, with a total of 13,700 soldiers. Lakhdar Brahimi has echoed these concerns by stressing that "you can't have a situation where people contribute blood and some contribute money . . . that is not the UN we want" (quoted in Lynch 2000, A36). Of the twenty-one U.N. Mission in Sierra

Leone peacekeeping troops killed in early 2001, all were from Africa (Nigeria, Guinea, Kenya, and Zambia), the Middle East, and Asia (India and Jordan).

African–Industrialized Countries Peacekeeping Capacity Initiatives

The 1992–1994 U.N. Task Force/U.N. Operation in Somalia debacle in Somalia, which caused what has become known as the Somali syndrome, solidi-fied the developed countries' disillusionment with the practice of involving themselves directly in African peacekeeping operations. Instead, their foreign policy–making establishments are increasingly becoming more interested in the pursuit of policies that encourage African solutions to African problems. To this end, the industrialized countries, particularly Belgium, Canada, Denmark, France, Germany, Ireland, Italy, Norway, Sweden, the United Kingdom, and the United States, now pursue a number of complementary foreign policy options. Apart from using the United Nations to enhance their individual and collective interests, the industrialized countries have also participated in joint African peacekeeping capacity-building programs. Specifically, the Afri-can–industrialized countries' peacekeeping capacity initiatives—joint military exercises and training—are perceived to be more viable options that will prepare the African countries and organizations for future peacekeeping operations. In-deed, the industrialized countries continue to provide funds for the inter-African states' and African organizations' peacekeeping capacity building.

The concept of the African Crisis Response Initiative (ACRI), conceived during the Clinton administration in 1996 with the objective of establishing an African Crisis Response Force (ACRF), comprised of an all-African force of 10,000 troops, was designed to achieve the objective of African solutions to African problems. U.S. officials observed that ACRI is a "training program which envisions a partnership with African and other interested nations to en-hance African peacekeeping capabilities, particularly the capacity to mount an effective, collective response to humanitarian and other crises" (McCallie 1998). After consultation with African leaders and military experts, ACRI trainers de-signed training curricula useful to African units for service in Africa and the other parts of the world in conformity with Chapter VI of the U.N. Charter (Levitt 1998, 101).

In 1997, the United States, the United Kingdom, and France also agreed to coordinate their respective countries' peacekeeping capacities. Since then, the concepts of ACRI, the French *Renforcement des Capacités Africaines de Main-tien de la Paix* (RECAMP), and the U.K. African Peacekeeping Initia-tive—known within U.N. circles as P3 because of the three countries' member-ship in the U.N. Security Council—have laid the groundwork for the frequent participation by the three countries in peacekeeping capacity building in Africa (Cilliers 1999b, 135; Berman and Sams 1998).

In 1997, for example, the U.S. 3rd and 5th Special Forces Groups (Air-borne) from Fort Bragg, North Carolina, and specialists from the 18th Airborne

Corps of the U.S. Army European Command completed peacekeeping training exercises with 2,400 troops from Malawi, Senegal, and Uganda (Levitt 1998, 101). The ten-day peacekeeping military exercises, dubbed operation *Guidimakha* in Senegal, brought together 3,700 troops from Senegal, Mali, Mauritania, Cape Verde, Guinea-Bissau, Gambia, Guinea, and Ghana, with the P3 providing trainers, finance, and military equipment (Malan 1999b, 274).

Designed to operate in conjunction with the OAU and UNDPKO, ACRI's main objective is to provide peacekeeping and humanitarian-relief training and equipment to 10,000–12,000 African soldiers. Apart from providing peacekeeping capacity building to the African states, the OAU and regional organizations, nongovernmental organizations are also invited to participate in the nonmilitary-oriented training. NGOs, both local and international, provide useful humanitarian relief to victims in conflict situations. The United Kingdom, under its African Peacekeeping Initiative concept—established after consultation with many African countries, the United Nations, the OAU, and African regional organizations—has conducted peacekeeping training courses in, among others, Ghana, Kenya, Swaziland, Mozambique, Malawi, Mauritius, and Uganda. It needs to be noted that it was during the presidency of Italy in 1996 that the members of the European Union intensified their interests in peacekeeping capacity building in Africa. Since then, Italy has been involved in African peacekeeping activities, such as the establishment of an Ethiopian Brigade and also in the training of deminers for the U.N. Angola Verification Mission.

Like their United States, United Kingdom, and French counterparts, Germany, Canada, Japan, and the Nordic countries have provided financial commitments and training programs aimed at the enhancement of African peacekeeping capabilities. For example, between 1997 and 2000, ten African states—Benin, Botswana, Burkina Faso, Morocco, Namibia, Zambia, Senegal, Tanzania, Tunisia, and Guinea—benefited from support and financial assistance provided by the German government, as well as German nongovernmental organizations (United Nations 2001). Whereas Japan provided a total of $500,000 to the OAU Peace Fund, Canada has provided the MCPMR with funds totaling $2.5 million. Apart from establishing a Regional Peacekeeping Training Center in Zimbabwe, Denmark also provided $3.2 million to Southern African countries for training in peacekeeping. Belgium has not only participated in the ACRI and RECAMP peacekeeping exercises in Africa, but was also instrumental in providing military equipment for the Malawian peacekeeping contingent in UNAMIR in 1994 and the Organization of African Unity's MIOBU at a total cost of $52 million. What needs to be reiterated is that most of the members of the European Union, as well as Canada, Japan, and the United States, are involved in many peacekeeping capacity-building projects in Africa. However, as I have explained, the industrialized countries are decamping from direct involvement in peacekeeping responsibilities in conflict-engulfed theaters in Africa. This concern is clearly echoed in the Brahimi Report (United Nations 2000a, para. 105).

AFRICAN PEACEKEEPING CAPACITY-BUILDING INITIATIVES: THE CONTINENTAL DIMENSIONS

The 1993 Cairo Declaration that established the MCPMR was a clear manifestation of Africa's emerging commitment to conflict prevention, resolution, management, and peacekeeping in the continent. In his February 12, 1999 report on African peacekeeping capacity building submitted to the U.N. Security Council (United Nations 1997), secretary-general Kofi Annan acknowledged that the OAU and African subregional organizations "are playing an increasingly important role in the management of conflicts on the continent and in contributing to the maintenance of international peace and security" (para. 3). Of the top ten countries that by December 2000 had contributed the largest number of U.N. peacekeeping troops, military observers, and police, Nigeria, Ghana, and Kenya ranked second, fifth, and eighth, respectively. These commitments notwithstanding, the complexities and difficulties inherent in the issues that require the participation of African countries in peacekeeping cannot be underestimated.

Cognizant of these difficulties and complexities (with their intra- and interstate and continental dimensions), the Working Group of OAU Military Experts recommended in their October 1997 report that all the peace support operations conducted by African subregional organizations should first be endorsed by the OAU (OAU 1997a, para 28.6). Peace enforcement initiatives by Angola, Namibia, and Zimbabwe in the Democratic Republic of Congo in 1998 and by Botswana and South Africa in Lesotho in 1998, all in the name of promoting the objectives of the Southern African Development Community, would therefore be considered violations of the OAU concept of PSOs. Whereas Botswana and South Africa managed to contain instability in Lesotho, it was only after the signing of the 1999 and 2000 Lusaka Peace Accords by the belligerents that the 2001 deployment of the U.N. Organization Mission in the Democratic Republic of Congo was made possible.

The OAU–subregional organizations' cooperative model of peacekeeping, centered on African solutions to African problems, is an important concept that needs to be institutionalized. Inherent in this peacekeeping model is the right of the OAU and the subregional organizations to intervene, where necessary, in the internal affairs of states in the continent. During their 1997 summit in Harare, Zimbabwe, the OAU Heads of State and Government, in their response to the 1997 military coup d'état in Sierra Leone, stipulated the right of the organization to interfere in the internal affairs of member states "under special circumstances." These special circumstances were identified to include "serious human rights abuses, grave threat to civilian populations, and unconstitutional attempt to overthrow a democratically elected government" (International Peace Academy 1998, 7). It is imperative for the African states and organizations to move

beyond the adoption of resolutions and instead institutionalize and operational-
ize these concepts.

The peacekeeping and peace enforcement operations by the Economic
Community of West African States Cease Fire Monitoring Group (ECOMOG)
in the Liberian civil war in 1990 have been well documented (Magyar and Conteh-Morgan 1998). The complications ECOMOG encountered during its mission
in Liberia notwithstanding, the organization demonstrated that the time was ripe
for African solutions to African problems concomitant with the continent's
post–Cold War efforts to provide, within each country, a more enabling environment for rapid economic growth and development. The use of the SADC in
the DRC and Lesotho, with their politicomilitary variants, as well as ECOMOG
in Liberia, demonstrate emerging interests in African peacekeeping. These
subregional peacekeeping missions are important, not only for stability in their
own contiguous regions, but also for the continent as a whole. On the other
hand, African peacekeeping troops, military observers, and police trained for
U.N. peace operations are by extension available to the OAU and the subregional organizations (De Coning 2000, 68–69). This is not to argue that the
OAU is taking over the responsibilities of the United Nations and the subregional organizations. The United Nations is ultimately responsible for the
maintenance of international peace and security. However, the world body can
help subregional organizations in the continent in their effort to resolve conflicts
and keep the peace.

Apart from the SADC and ECOWAS, the francophone signatories to
ECOWAS (Burkina Faso, Mali, Mauritania, Niger, Senegal, Côte d'Ivoire and
Togo) signed the *Accord de non-aggression et d'assistance en matière de
défense* (ANAD) in 1977. Originally conceived as a nonaggression and mutual
defense pact, the post-1990s have witnessed the reconceptualization of its role as
a potential African subregional peacekeeping organization (Malan 1999a, 2–3).
In April 1998, ECOWAS (including its ANAD members) participated in a joint
peacekeeping capacity building, *Cohesion Kompienga*, in Burkina Faso that
included 3,000 troops from eight countries.

Whereas SADC participated in Operation Blue Hungwe (Eagle) in 1997 in
Zimbabwe and Operation Blue Crane in 1998 to enhance their peacekeeping,
similar exercises were held in Kenya involving 2,000 troops from the troika of
Kenya, Uganda, and Tanzania. The proliferation of subregional-centered organizations in the 1990s, with their peacekeeping capacity-building components,
though well intentioned, may undermine coordination efforts needed in critical
situations that may warrant the immediate deployment of peacekeeping operations. Apart from ECOWAS, the SADC, and ANAD, the other subregional organizations that have been established include the Arab Maghreb Union, which
incorporated the Council for Common Defense in the pact; the Economic Community of Central African States, with its nonaggression pact; the Intergovernmental Authority on Development, a conflict resolution–oriented organization;

and the East African Community, which provides a basis for joint military operations (Adar, 2000; Berman and Sams 1998, 5).

To help prepare their peacekeeping personnel, some African countries have also established training centers. For example, in 1998 Zambia established a peacekeeping center at the Zambia Military Academy with the help of the U.N. Training School Ireland Military College, Curragh Camp, Ireland (United Nations 2001). Zimbabwe has established its own peacekeeping center at the Zimbabwe Staff College, and at the end of the meeting of the MCPMR in Addis Ababa in 1995, Egypt established the Cairo Center for Training on Dispute Resolution and Peacekeeping in Africa (Government of Egypt 1996, 11). The central objective of the Cairo center is to prepare African cadres for peacefully resolving disputes and preserving the peace.

CONCLUSION

What I have examined in this chapter indicates clear involvement of the African states in peacekeeping operations at the subregional, continental, and global levels. Africa plays a prominent role in U.N. peacekeeping operations, particularly with respect to the contributions of troops, military observers, and police. The reconceptualization of the role of the OAU and the subregional organizations to encompass peacekeeping functions has been necessitated by a number of factors. First and foremost, Africans have accepted the emerging view that the success of the continent in the areas of economic and political development is contingent upon their acceptance and operationalization of African solutions to African problems. To this end, they continue to accommodate and participate in intra- and extracontinental peacekeeping capacity-building initiatives. Second, the post–Cold War era has paved the way for peacekeeping operations. Third, with the industrialized countries' reluctance to involve themselves in peacekeeping missions in Africa, it has become imperative for African countries and organizations to fill the vacuum.

However, there are certain problems facing African peacekeeping efforts. One of the main constraints to the development of an African peacekeeping capacity is lack of financial resources, a problem that faces the United Nations as well (Saxena 1996; United Nations 2000b). The proliferation of subregional organizations and peacekeeping centers in the continent may be a hindrance to African peacekeeping efforts if proper coordinating mechanisms are not provided. It is also imperative for the OAU to go beyond frequent conclusions of resolutions and establish a standing African Peacekeeping Force endowed with all the necessary rules of engagement. Indeed, the Chiefs of Defense Staff, in their 1997 document, recommended the adoption of the command and control functions for the Central Organ, the secretary-general, and the force commander (OAU 1997b, para. 36.2). Even though these concepts are still evolving, it is imperative for the question of African peacekeeping capacity building to be tangibly put into motion.

ACKNOWLEDGMENTS

The author is indebted to the Rhodes University Joint Research Council for financial assistance that enabled him to carry out research on the project. He is also grateful to Amanda Wortmann and Zodwa Ramafalo of the Africa Institute of South Africa, Pretoria, for assistance in gathering materials for the project.

REFERENCES

Adar, K. G. 1998. A state under siege: The internationalization of the Sudanese civil war. *African Security Review* 7 (1): 44–53.

Adar, K. G. 1999. The changing pattern of "self-determination-democracy" linkage in Africa: A conceptual re-appraisal. *Journal of Humanities and Social Sciences* 8 (2): 269–284.

Adar, K. G. 2000. Conflict resolution in a turbulent region: The case of the Intergovernmental Authority on Development (IGAD) in Sudan. *African Journal of Conflict Resolution* 1 (2): 39–66.

Akinrinade, S. 2000. Sub-regional security cooperation in Africa: Toward a model for continental security community. Paper presented at the fortieth anniversary conference of the Africa Institute of South Africa, May 29–June 2, Johannesburg.

Amate, C.O.C. 1986. *Inside the OAU: Pan-Africanism in practice.* London: Macmillan.

Anglin, D. G. 2000. Peace operations in Africa: The learning years. In *Africa Contemporary Record, 1992–1994,* edited by C. Legum. New York: Africana.

Annan, K. 1998. The causes of conflict and the promotion of durable peace and sustainable development in Africa: Report of the secretary-general. Retrieved from http://www.un.org/ecosodev/geninfo/afrec/sgreport/report.htm.

Bakwesegha, C. J. 1997. Conflict resolution in Africa: A new role for the Organization of African Unity. In *Out of conflict: From war to peace in Africa,* edited by G. M. Sorbo and P. Vale. Uppsala: Nordiska Afrikainstitutet.

Berman, E., and K. Sams. 1998. *Constructive disengagement: Western efforts to develop African peacekeeping.* ISS Monograph Series No. 33. Johannesburg: Institute for Security Studies.

Berman, E., and K. Sams. 2000. *Peacekeeping in Africa: Capabilities and culpabilities.* Geneva: U.N. Institute for Disarmament Research.

Boutros-Ghali, B. 1995. *An agenda for peace,* 2nd ed. New York: United Nations.

Busumtwi-Sam, J. 1999. Redefining "security" after the Cold War: The OAU, the U.N. and conflict management in Africa. In *Civil wars in Africa: Roots and resolution,* edited by T. M. Ali and R. O. Mathews. Montreal: McGill–Queen's University Press.

Carey, M. 1998. Peacekeeping in Africa: Recent evolution and prospects. In *Peacekeeping in Africa,* edited by O. Furley and R. May. Aldershot, U.K.: Ashgate.

Chawla, S. 2001. Trends in United Nations Peacekeeping. Retrieved from http://www.idsa-india.org/an-jan-7-01html.html.

Cilliers, J. 1999a. Regional African peacekeeping capacity: Mythical construct or essential tool? *African Security Review* 8 (4): 20–33.

Cilliers, J. 1999b. Regional African peacekeeping capacity: Mythical construct or essential tool? In *From peacekeeping to complex emergencies: Peace support missions in*

Africa, edited by J. Cilliers and G. Mills. Johannesburg: South African Institute of International Affairs and the Institute for Security Studies.

Clapham, C. 1996. *African and the international system: The politics of state survival.* Cambridge: Cambridge University Press.

De Coning, C. 2000. Lesotho intervention: Implications for SADC military interventions, peacekeeping and the African renaissance. In *Contributions toward an African renaissance*, edited by H. Solomon and M. Muller. African Dialogue Monograph Series No. 1. Durban, South Africa: African Center for the Constructive Resolution of Conflicts.

Fleshman, M. 2000. Millennium summit of the United Nations: Reform plans dominate Security Council debate on peacekeeping in Africa. *Africa Recovery* 14 (3): 1, 8–11.

Goulding, M. 1999. The United Nations and conflict in Africa since the Cold War. *African Affairs* 98 (391): 155–166.

Government of Egypt. 1996. *Egypt and the OAU mechanism for African conflict prevention, management and resolution.* Cairo: Ministry of Information.

International Peace Academy. 1998. *Seminar on peacemaking and peacekeeping, Addis Ababa, November 29–December 3.* New York: International Peace Acadmy.

James, A. 1994. Problems of internal peacekeeping. *Diplomacy and Statecraft* 5 (1): 21–46.

Jonah, J.O.C. 1994. The OAU: peacekeeping and conflict resolution. In *The Organization of African Unity after thirty years*, edited by Y. Ei-Ayouty. London: Praeger.

Levitt, J. 1998. The African crisis response-initiatives: A general survey. *Africa Insight* 28 (3/4): 100–108.

Lynch, C. 2000. Providing U.N.'s peacekeepers: Critics say U.S., Europe put unfair burden on poor countries. *Washington Post*, November 15: A36.

Magyar, K. P., and E. Conteh-Morgan, eds. 1998. *Peacekeeping in Africa: ECOMOG in Liberia.* New York: St. Martin's Press.

Malan, M. 1997. Toward sounder investments in developing African peace operations capabilities. *African Security Review* 6 (2): 17–27.

Malan, M. 1999a. The OAU and African sub-regional organizations: A closer look at the "peace pyramid." *ISS Papers* (January): 1–13.

Malan, M. 1999b. Peacekeeping in Africa. In *South African Yearbook of International Affairs 1999/2000.* Johannesburg: South African Institute of International Affairs.

McCallie, M. F. 1998. The African Crisis Response Initiative (ACRI): The America's engagement for peace in Africa. Address at Emerald Express Symposim, Camp Pendleton, CA.

Mills, G. 2000. Global realities and African priorities: A view from South Africa. In *Putting people first: African priorities for the U.N. millennium assembly*, edited by P. Mathoma, G. Mills, and J. Stremlau. Johannesburg: South African Institute of International Affairs.

OAU. 1992. *Resolving conflicts in Africa: Proposals for action.* Addis Ababa: OAU.

OAU. 1993. *Declaration of the heads of state and government on the establishment, with the OAU, of a Mechanism for Conflict Prevention, Management and Resolution.* Addis Ababa: OAU Conflict Management Division.

OAU. 1999a. *Report of the meeting of the Working Group of OAU military experts.* Addis Ababa: OAU.

OAU. 1997b. *Report of the second meeting of the Chiefs of Defense Staff of the central organ of the OAU Mechanism for Conflict Prevention, Management and Resolution.* Addis Ababa: OAU.

OAU. 1997c. *Report of the secretary-general on the second meeting of the Chiefs of Staff of the member states of the central organ.* Addis Ababa: OAU.

Patel, N. 2000. Conflict resolution through regional organizations in Africa. Paper presented at the fortieth annual conference of the Africa Institute of South Africa, Pretoria, May 30–June 2.

Saxena, S. C. 1996. Conflict resolution in Africa in the post–Cold War period. Paper presented at the International Conference on Understanding Contemporary Africa: India and the South–South Cooperation, Department of African Studies, Delhi University, and Ministry of External Affairs, Government of India, February 15–17.

Schraeder, P. J. 2000. *African politics and society: A mosaic in transformation.* New York: St. Martin's Press.

United Nations. 1990. *The blue helmets.* New York: U.N. Department of Public Information.

United Nations. 1995. *United Nations civilian police handbook.* New York: U.N. Department of Peacekeeping Operations.

United Nations. 1998. *Report of the secretary-general on the causes of conflict and the promotion of durable peace and sustainable development in Africa.* U.N. Document No. A/52/871-S/1998/318. New York: United Nations.

United Nations. 1999. *Enhancement of African peacekeeping capacity: Reports of the secretary-general.* U.N. Document No. S/1999/171, February 12. Retrieved from http://www.un.org/docs/sc/reports/1999/S1999171.htm.

United Nations. 2000a. *Report of the Panel on United Nations Peace Operations.* U.N. Document No. A/55/305-S/2000/809. Retrieved from http://www.un.org/peace/reports/peace-operations/docs/full-report.htm.

United Nations. 2000b. *Report of the secretary-general on the implementation of the report of the Panel on United Nations Peace Operations.* U.N. Document No. A/55/502, October 20. New York: U.N. General Assembly, 55th Session.

United Nations. 2000c. *Security Council, responding to Brahimi Report, adopts wide-ranging resolution on peacekeeping operation.* U.N. Document (Press Release) No. SC/6948, November 13. Retrieved from http://www.fas.org/man/dod-101/ops/war/2000/11/war-001113-unpkzur.htm.

United Nations. 2001. *Germany: Initiatives and support from Germany.* Retrieved from http://www.un.org/dpko/training/ext.10.htm.

U.S. Committee for Refugees. 2000. *Scope and scale of international displacement in Africa.* Retrieved from http://www.refugees.org/news/crisis/africa.idp.htm, April 10, 2001.

Vogt, M. A. 1997. Conflict resolution and peacekeeping: The Organization of African Unity and the United Nations. In *Out of conflict: From war to peace in Africa*, edited by G. M. Sorbo and P. Vale. Uppsala: Nordiska Afrikainstitutet.

World Bank. 2000. *African development indicators, 2000.* Washington, DC: World Bank.

12

Cultural Diversity, Societal Conflict, and Sustainable Peace in Africa: Consociational Democracy Revisited

UFO OKEKE UZODIKE

After about forty years of political independence, postcolonial African states remain deeply troubled and influenced by problems that can be traced to their colonial governors. Made up of assorted political entities with varying degrees of autonomy, late precolonial Africa, arguably, was an ambiguous and highly complex system of fluid polities and societies that were at once distinct and related. The advent of the colonial enterprise saw the establishment of rigid territorial and regional boundaries that cut across existing political, social, ethnic, and religious borders. The colonial authorities were especially insensitive to issues of ethnic, cultural, social, economic, or political propinquity as they drew the boundaries of their claimed African colonial territories. It mattered little (if at all) to the metropolitan centers that the new entities were frequently made up of societies and cultural groups that either shared few interests or harbored abiding historical rivalries or animosities toward each other. Not surprising, the postcolonial period has been marked by an undercurrent tension and pervasive conflicts within states. Although some border tensions sometimes flare up between states, they remain minimal due to the decision in 1963 by the founding members of the Organization of African Unity to accept inherited colonial boundaries.

The net effect of those societal tensions has been the collective failure of postindependence African states to create and nurture the proper contexts for sustained development. By the late 1970s, African leaders and development experts were forced by the region's persistent social, economic, and political problems to reflect critically on the nature and causes of the crises. The resulting scholarship, which was geared primarily toward capturing the dynamics of the problem of nation building, focused analytical attention on the failures of the state and issues surrounding ethnicity and class. Many of those initial analyses dealt with questions pertaining to state failures and intrastate cleavages from very narrow and deterministic perspectives, especially class or ethnicity (for instance, see Cartwright 1983; Connor 1973, 1994; Diamond 1982, 1983; Falola and Ihonvbere 1985; Graf 1985; Joseph 1983; Rothchild and Olorunsola 1983; Sklar 1979; Zolberg 1968). In doing so, other useful explanatory angles such as internal and external influences (including corruption, incompetence, poor leadership, falling cash crop prices, and negative terms of trade) were lost or ignored.

It is my intention in this chapter to make a case for a relook at consociationalism (also known as power sharing) as a potentially meaningful model for Africa's segmented societies. Given the context of African political processes and organizations as well as the severe structural segmentation of many of its countries, it seems reasonable to work toward fashioning an instrument of governance that has the right ingredients for cushioning cultural cleavages while creating an enabling environment within which political and economic development can occur. Assuming the highly contestable, albeit popular view that democracy is the most suitable form of political organization, I wish to revisit and offer the idea of consociational democracy or power sharing as potentially the most useful formula for addressing Africa's societal segmentation and the associated challenges that it poses to continental efforts at development. I take the position that the resource-starved African social and political environment provides the wrong context for majoritarian experiments at democracy. The winner-takes-all format of majoritarianism is precisely why tensions have remained rife within African states despite the introduction of political liberalization and democratic politics. In Africa (as elsewhere), national integration and development involves complex and difficult choices by leaders. Unfortunately, because of the multiplicity of subcultures and the paucity of resources, those choices are often deemed (correctly or incorrectly) to reflect serious sectional biases, especially by those on the losing side of the policy decision. Consequently, policy outcomes may lead not only to a regime's loss of legitimacy in the perceptions of disadvantaged groups, but also may serve as primary causes of instability and repression. This often manifests itself in us/them perceptions within subcultures.

The theoretical merit of consociationalism is reflected in the application of its tenets over the years in analyzing accommodation and power sharing in different countries. It has been used in the study of Austria (Powell 1970; Luther and Muller 1992), Lebanon (Dekmejian 1978), Switzerland (Steiner 1990; Lehmbruch 1993; Linder 1994), Belgium (Zolberg 1977), Malaysia (Von Vorys 1975; Zakaria 1989), Netherlands (Daalder 1989; Lijphart 1969, 1989), Colombia (Dix 1980; Hartlyn 1988), Canada (Cannon 1982), the former Yugoslavia (Goldman 1985; Vasovic 1992), and a host of other countries. Quite aside from its theoretical value, consociational arrangements, fit neatly into some traditional

African palaver political arrangements such as those found among the Tiv, Igbo, and Igala (among whom the kingship is shared rotationally between four major segments, thereby dampening both social and political competition). For African states, therefore, power-sharing modes of democratic government would mean that no cultural group would be left out of the political system. The advantages would be enormous.

An important contributing factor to domestic tensions can be traced to the production and exchange patterns that were entrenched under colonial rule. By linking economic activities, transport networks, and physical infrastructure to the social and economic needs of the metropolitan centers rather than the development imperatives of the local economies, colonialism created long-term distortions in the political economies of African states. The distortions were further exacerbated by other colonial policies, including the skewing of terms of trade in favor of the metropolitan centers, the focus on primary commodities and extractive industries, the competitive and negative positioning of subcultures under "divide and rule" tactics, and frequent and deliberate alienation of native populations from land as well as meaningful educational and skills-development projects through a policy of importing a median layer of skilled labor. Lacking financial resources, transcendent vision, and adequate managerial skills, postcolonial governments retained the inherited production and exchange patterns and some of the biases of the colonial state (Uzodike 1999, 69–74). Indeed, "as political competition was not rooted in viable national economic systems, in many instances the prevailing structure of incentives favored capturing the institutional remnants of the colonial economy for factional advantage" (Annan 1998). The net effect for the postcolonial African governments has been that the process of state building and the inculcation of the ideals of nationalism have proved difficult in the face of the cultural diversity such as the ethnic, religious, racial, and regional differences that characterizes almost all the countries of Africa.

Clearly, the objective reality of state diversity in Africa cannot be deemed to be an adequate explanatory factor for the postindependence gravitation within the region toward internecine conflicts. Nevertheless, the mix of diversity and pervasive resource scarcity and diversion as well as the attendant problems of unequal distribution of whatever is available has coalesced to create and incubate societal tensions in many African states. Where a visionary, competent, or incorruptible leadership—such as Julius Nyerere in Tanzania—manages such tensions, a working societal order can be established. However, where a parochial, incompetent, or parasitical leadership—such as Mobutu Sese-Seko of Congo-Zaire—manages such tensions the eruption of conflict may only await a trigger issue. In general, such tensions tend to erupt into open conflicts in communities and countries when political leaders either fail to manage the problems adequately and in a timely fashion, or lack the necessary resources to douse aroused sensitivities before battle lines are drawn and established.

Like politics elsewhere, African politics has been characterized by the struggle for resources. The fundamental basis of such struggles can be directly linked to the personalized and nontransparent nature of leadership, overcentralization of governance structures, systemic corruption and lack of accountability, inadequate checks and balances, failure to adhere to the rule of law, disrespect for standard human rights norms, or the affixation of leadership by circumventing democratic processes. Given the ethnic and regional base of political parties and processes and the role of nearly every African state as the major employer and source of wealth, it not only becomes clear why political control is inordinately crucial but also why the stakes can get dangerously high for all competing factions. Understandably, much of such struggles focus on the imperative of acquiring political power. This is because political control gives the possessor a decisive advantage in the struggle to secure and control economic resources and rewards. Like elsewhere around the world, individuals and groups who control political power or who have access to those in political office are better placed and able to secure and maintain economic assets and the paraphernalia of development, such as paved roads, potable water, health facilities, educational institutions, and jobs in the modern sectors. Unlike elsewhere, however, access in Africa has been crucial, and even decisive, frequently not only because of the magnitude of resource starvation but also because the monopoly of political power often led (or was perceived as leading) to nepotism, relentless corruption, and abusive use of power.

Not surprising, public participation in politics has tended to be characterized by divisive struggles among societal groups over power and resources (Sklar 1986, 115). Disadvantaged groups, fearing increased marginalization, typically rally around their shared lines of affinity in an attempt to agitate vigorously for redress. As U.N. secretary-general, Kofi Annan (1998, 4) argues, "in extreme cases, rival communities may perceive that their security, perhaps their very survival, can be ensured only through control of state power." When the tensions are managed adequately, violent conflict can be prevented. However, with poor leadership the tensions may not only grow and result in economic decline but also develop into open conflict, which can lead to state failure (such as with Liberia, Somalia, Sierra Leone, and Congo-Zaire during the 1980s and 1990s).

CULTURAL DIVERSITY: A BASIS FOR CONFLICTS IN AFRICA

So strong is . . . [the] the propensity of mankind to fall into mutual animosities, that where no substantial occasion presents itself, the most frivolous and fanciful distinctions have been sufficient to kindle their unfriendly passions and incite their most violent conflicts. But the most common and durable source of factions has been the various and unequal distribution of property (James Madison, *The Federalist*, No. 10, November 24, 1787).

Variously, Africa's cultural diversity—particularly its ethnic, racial, class, religious, and regional differences—has been the continent's most abiding source of conflict in the postcolonial period. The issue of identity, especially why people see themselves and others as belonging to particular cultural groups, is beyond the immediate scope of this chapter. Nevertheless, I would like to point to the words of James Madison as a reminder about not only the timelessness and nonspecificity of social differentiation but also its continued resilience and persistence. Contemporary analysts of group strategy echo the sense in Madison's words. They maintain that the theory of collective definition suggests that, under certain conditions, "subordinate groups will tend to insist on their own 'specialness' and thus reinforce the solidarity of their group . . . *the insistence on specialness occurs when economic mobility is unlikely and group members instead opt for an improvement in their lives through political action*" (Blumer and Dustin 1980, 211–238, emphasis added). Vincent T. Maphai (2000, 312) makes the same point when he argues that ethnic conflict is "a certainty where there is competition for scarce resources like land, funds, aid or buildings." Some theorists have tackled the link between group formation and identity and competition for resources. E. Ike Udogu (1999, 155) points out that some theorists of ethnicity maintain that ethnicity is best understood "as a system of inter-group boundaries whose allure, salience, and persistence are determined partially by the level of contact and resource competition between and among ethnic collectivities." Where competition for resources and economic rewards is organized along ethnic lines, there is an increased likelihood of the following (Nagel 1995, 442–443):

- Ethnic identification;
- Racism and prejudice (against rival competitors);
- Interethnic conflict; and
- Ethnic mobilization.

Ethnic Conflicts

Ethnicity has been a major factor in the activation and fueling of conflicts throughout Africa. Ethnicity refers not only to the domination of the state by one ethnic group to the exclusion of the other groups, but also the use of and competition between different ethnic groups for power and resources. Describing the use of ethnicity in Africa, Claude Ake (1992, 4) observes that "ethnicity is politicized, politics is ethnicized and ethnic groups tendentially become political formations whose struggles with each other and competing interests may be more conflictual for the exclusivity of ethnic group membership." Assorted political problems, such as inept leadership, nondelivery of services, lack of employment opportunities in the public sector, maldistribution of resources and economic rewards, and the abuse of power, are frequently given ethnic explanations in Africa.

Not surprising, societal groups coalesce along ethnic lines to press for their own "share" of state benefits. As such, many of Africa's most serious tensions and devastating conflicts have been (and are being) played out under ethnic banners. For instance, many serious national tensions and conflicts during the 1990s in many African countries, such as Algeria, Angola, Burundi, Cameroon, Chad, Côte d'Ivoire, Democratic Republic of Congo, Ethiopia, Kenya, Liberia, Mali, Namibia, Niger, Nigeria, Rwanda, South Africa, Sudan, Tanzania, and Uganda, have seen the lifting of ethnic banners. While some ethnically inspired insurgencies seek to remove (and replace) the perceived basis of their difficulties or torment such as the government in power, many such movements harbor aspirations of full autonomy from their present state (see, e.g., Williams 1992). Horowitz (1985, 31) describes the consequences of such conflicts: "When ethnic violence occurs, unranked groups usually aim not at social transformation, but at something approaching sovereign autonomy, the exclusion of parallel ethnic groups from a share of power, and often reversion—by expulsion or extermination—to an idealized, ethnically homogeneous status quo ante."

Ethnicity in Africa has also been manifested in the entrenchment before the 1990s of one-party rule. After independence the new African leaders embarked on "the elimination of institutional checks and balances, and the centralization and concentration of state power in presidential offices, as well as the termination of open party politics and the regulation and confinement of political participation—usually within the framework of a single ruling party" (Jackson and Rosberg 1982, 23–24). These leaders often justified single-party rule as being essential for the maintenance of national unity and peace within their countries (Mamdani 2000, 228–231; also see Mamdani 1996). The logic behind it was that the one-party system brought together groups that were otherwise separated by the centrifugal forces of ethnicity, thereby providing opportunities for their reconciliation. As Nyerere argued regarding the Tanzanian one-party state, "where there is one-party and that party is identified with the nation as a whole, the foundations of democracy are firmer than they can ever be when you have two or more parties each representing only a section of the community" (Wanyande 2000, 108). Soon after independence, majoritarian democratic political arrangements were replaced by one-party systems in several states, including Côte d'Ivoire, Guinea, Malawi, Kenya, Senegal, Tanzania, Tunisia, Zambia, and Zimbabwe. As Jackson and Rosberg (1986, 54), Lofchie (1993, 436–446), Wanyande (2000, 108–119), and many others have observed, single-party rule can be an important instrument of control and incorporation in many countries throughout the continent. For instance, President Daniel arap Moi of Kenya created an ethnic electoral base anchored on the Kalenjin—an umbrella designation that refers to a diverse grouping such as Elgweyo, Kipsigis, Nandi, and Tugen—that excludes most Kikuyu, thus intensifying the relevance of ethnicity in politics and also the level of interethnic conflict.

Some African leaders have also sought to consolidate power by using ethnic cleavages in other ways. Increasingly, the issue of citizenship has become a crucial element in the ethnicity-related conflicts in Africa. Two strands of the concept of citizenship generate conflicts among groups on the continent (de Waal 2000, 47). The first strand is the idea of an ethnically homogeneous state. In such situations, as in Rwanda and Burundi, a particular ethnic group is systematically marginalized and deprived of basic human rights. The second strand pertains to the idea that citizenship is a privilege and not a right. Thus, the state arrogates to itself, through its officials in government, the exclusive right of awarding or withdrawing citizenship within the society. In Zambia and Côte d'Ivoire, for instance, rival presidential candidates have been prohibited by the rulers from contesting elections on the ground that they are not citizens of the country.

In some instances, such as in Burundi and Rwanda and, to some extent, in Sudan, ethnically based divisions may evolve over time to other forms of cleavages. For instance, in Burundi and Rwanda, conflicts have emerged with very complex characteristics. In both Burundi and Rwanda, ethnicity appears to have overlapped with social class. Furthermore, the numerically dominant Hutu now share similar language and culture with the socially dominant Tutsi. Although the deep societal divisions and genocidal conflicts that are manifested today are not without precolonial historical context, they seem to have been exacerbated by Belgian colonial policies that further distorted and entrenched aspects of the hierarchical arrangement.

Racial Conflicts

Both South Africa and Zimbabwe serve as examples of instances where recent historical experiences have served to reconfigure the basis of societal conflicts from one driven by ethnic constellations to racialism. We will take South Africa as an example. Culturally diverse and complex, South Africa is made up of an array of ethnic and racial groups with a long history of struggle for a share of resources and political power. A country of 40.6 million people, South Africa is made up of black Africans (76.7 percent), whites (10.9 percent), coloreds (8.9 percent), Indian/Asians (2.6 percent), and unspecified/others (0.9 percent). The African population includes Ndebele, Sotho, Swazi, Tsonga, Tswana, Venda, Xhosa, and Zulu, while the white population includes the English and Afrikaner/Dutch and other migrants from France, Germany, Italy, Portugal, and many other European countries (see Maphai 2000).

Between 1948 and the early 1990s, South Africa's cultural diversity served as the official basis of state action. The apartheid system was an extreme case of legalized oppression and conflict. The white minority dominated the state. Other groups, especially the black Africans, were subjugated, dispossessed, disenfranchised, and exploited. Despite the formal end of the dreaded system since the 1994 general elections that brought the African National Congress to power, the net effect of apartheid and the preceding white/colonial domination is one of the world's widest disparities of income and the socioeconomic development of subcultural groups. The disparity remains an abiding source of alarming poverty, severe social tensions, and growing criminality. As vestiges of continued white domination, brutality, and exploitation are exposed, there is a growing evidence of retributive black response in farms and rural areas around the country. All this is despite the very progressive 1997 post-apartheid constitution, which makes provision for the accommodation of cultural diversity. The document explicitly protects the rights of citizens, individually and as members of communities, to "enjoy their culture, practice their religion and use their language," and to form "associations and other organs of civil society." The constitution also prohibits the state from discriminating against its citizens on the basis of ethnic or social origin, language, or religion. The South African constitution also made provision for the dispersal of power to provinces and local communities, giving room for multiple sites of civic engagement as a means of accommodating the country's cultural diversity. In spite of these provisions, there are indications of continuing tensions and insecurities among the disparate minority communities. Troubled by some aspects of life in the new South Africa, especially growing criminality in previously shielded areas, and agitations by some individual blacks and political parties for accelerated processes of transformation (land access and ownership, and employment opportunities in all fields), many whites are contemplating the possibility of exit from the state. Some others, reputedly Afrikaners, are demanding an autonomous state.

Regional and Communal Conflicts

Some serious tensions and conflicts within Africa occur between people who claim the same ethnic and religious constellations. Largely regional or local in nature, such conflicts can become very dangerous and obdurate. The hugely genocidal Rwandan conflict of 1994 had a strong regional dimension involving Hutu people. Similarly, serious intraethnic communal tensions and violence have cropped up in Nigeria among groups such as the Igbo and Yoruba, and in South Africa amongst the Zulu. Somalia is a good example of how regional tensions can destroy a whole nation. The Somalis, it seems, are as united by ethnicity as they are divided by clans. The one thing that is clear is that conflict broke out and destroyed the state after the fall of President Siad Barre. Beyond that, however, the issues are rather complex and go back (at least) to Italian colonial rule. As Basil Davidson (1989, 207–209) has shown, the Somalia debacle was a case of "elitism" meets "tribalism." As the Italian colonialists prepared to depart from Somalia, they fashioned a "proportional representation" parliamentary system similar to what they were operating at home. Each societal class, such as landowners, businessmen, farmers, and city workers, with a party could have seats in parliament. This might have worked in Italy, where the society was divided into classes. Somalia, however, had no classes; nearly everyone lived as a farmer or cattle herder. All Somalis were divided into clans. Colonial rulers deepened the clan divisions as a control mechanism against effective challenge to their authority. The combination of clannishness and proportional representation soon led to a mushrooming of clan-based political parties. The number of competing parties grew from five political parties at independence in 1960 to sixty-two political parties in 1969. Since very few Somalis had access to Western education (which heavily influenced access to political power), the great majority had little or no chance of sharing in the responsibility of political office and public life. The control of the sovereign government and all the trappings of power and privilege that go along with it fell into the hands of a small elite who fought personal battles for narrow selfish interests. According to Davidson (1989, 209), "Whenever elections came, they went back to their clans, whether big or small, and drummed up support against their rivals. Once back in power again, they returned to their dog fights and squabbles over sharing the spoils of office. The disunity and personal rivalry led directly to bad government and corruption."

The Somali state, "was a 'winner-takes-all' state and there were no benefits to being in opposition" (de Waal 2000, 14). The net effect of the bloody competition for clan ascendancy has been the near total destruction of the nation-state. Despite concerted international efforts and intervention, Somalia remains, even in 2002, a nation of clan-based fiefdoms under the control of warlords. Since 1991 the focus of the conflict has shifted from the struggle for state power to intersectional fighting over regional resources and subsectional fighting over local resources. With an embryonic central government, the country remains divided and controlled by rival factions. A northern section of the country has broken away and declared independence as "Somaliland." As reconciliation efforts continue to sputter, other parts of the country are beginning to contemplate the same route. But will this bring peace? How many viable separate states can emerge from this clan-based and poverty-stricken society before there is peace and stability in the area? Will rival clans without adequate resources allow endowed neighbors to secure autonomy without a fight and push for national consolidation?

Interstate Conflicts

Nearly all of the conflicts in Africa at the end of the twentieth century were of the intrastate variety, which represents our main interest in this chapter. Although numerous African states are actively engaged in conflict situations beyond their borders, very few of those (such as the Nigeria–Cameroon and Algeria–Morocco conflicts) represent the classic interstate conflict scenario. An important recent example of interstate conflict is the 1999–2000 Ethiopia-Eritrea conflict. The conflict occurred despite the strong and long-standing economic, political, and cultural ties between the two countries. Before it gained independence in 1991, Eritrea had been a part of Ethiopia for about four decades. The attempt by Eritrea to gain independence from Ethiopia resulted in over thirty years of war and conflicts. Although the mediation efforts of the OAU and its members have resulted in a measure of containment of the conflict, the issues involved are emotive and seem to transcend the putative claims of border disagreement. In the main, other examples of interstate conflicts, such as the various interventions in the DRC (by Angola, Burundi, Chad, Namibia, Rwanda, Uganda, Sudan, and Zimbabwe), Lesotho (by the SADC, especially Botswana and South Africa), and Liberia and Sierra Leone (by ECOMOG, especially Guinea, Ghana, Nigeria), have tended to derive from internal factors—typically ethnic in character—within the target country.

Religious Conflicts

As elsewhere, religion in Africa can be a powerful instrument of mobilization and destabilization. Violent religious conflicts have characterized many parts of Africa since the early stages of Christianity and Islam. In the postcolonial era, religious differences have emerged as an important source of social disequilibria. Religion's destabilizing influence has been strong in many African states, particularly in North and West Africa including Algeria, Egypt, Nigeria, Senegal, and Sudan. In Algeria, where the *Front Islamique du Salut* (FIS) was denied the opportunity by the military to assume power despite its legitimate success at the polls, the entire country has been immersed in a brutal nonconventional war of attrition. Between 1990 and 2000 the death toll reached nearly 100,000 persons, mostly civilians. The real costs in damages to property, investment, and development to one of Africa's largest and most advanced economies are incalculable.

Like Algeria, Nigeria has experienced very serious religious problems since the 1980s. Although Islam, Christianity, and African traditional religions have coexisted in the country for many generations, the degree of hostilities between Islam and Christianity took a much more hostile turn as they experienced an upsurge in fundamentalist membership. Through the activities and inflammatory comments—frequently political in nature—of fanatical and intolerant religious zealots and organizations, Nigerians and different Nigerian governments have been forced to wrestle with issues ranging from personal security to matters of survival of the nation-state itself. At the heart of these problems are the "born again" Christian elements and Islamic fundamentalist groups, such as the Maitatsine group, the Izala Movement, and the Muslim Students Society. Since the 1980s, religious riots have imposed huge costs in human lives and property. In the Maitatsine case, for instance, Muhammadu Marwa and his followers engaged first the Nigerian police and then the Nigerian army in over eleven days of pitched battles after refusing all efforts to arrive at an amicable agreement. After the dust settled, more than 5,000 people had lost their lives (Ibrahim 2000, 468–475). The period since 1986 has been characterized by increasingly violent clashes between Christian and Muslim groups (Suberu, Mala, and Aiyegboyin 1999, 42). The emergence of political Sharia as a demagogic instrument has further complicated the tense religious atmosphere in Nigeria. By July 2001, twelve of Nigeria's nineteen northern states had imposed the Sharia legal system as the supreme law within their jurisdiction. The introduction of these systems has led to episodic religious clashes. For instance, clashes broke out between Muslim and Christian groups on February 21, 2000, when Christians organized a protest of the introduction of Sharia as the criminal code in Kaduna state. Sharia-triggered conflicts have led not only to the deaths of dozens of people, but also have served to obviate an enabling unifying and harmonious environment within which progressive religious dialogue and peaceful coexistence among the adherents of all religions and the business of societal development can be undertaken.

Obviously, this list of conflicts is not exhaustive in terms of the specific typologies in terms of the scope of each of the identified types. A major reason for this stems from the fluidity of identity and conflict. Sudan is a good illustration. Ethnicity, race, class, and religion are salient features in the conflict. In some ways, even regional and communal factors appear relevant. In Sudan, where 39 percent of the citizenry regard themselves as Arab (despite the ongoing Arabization project), class, religion, and ethnicity are crucial features of tension and conflict. Arabism subsumes a qualitative claim of cultural and national superiority (Prah 2000, 394–395). Furthermore, the Arab minority controls state power, provides the majority of the political elite, dominates the armed forces, the bureaucracy, commerce, banking, trade, and the judiciary, and harnesses these instruments for the explicit purpose of Arabization of the African majority (Prah 2000, 393). Given, therefore, the importance of ethnicity and class in allowing access to a qualitative improvement in life, Arabization has been somewhat effective as a cooptation instrument for state policy makers.

EFFECTS OF POLITICAL TURBULENCE AND CONFLICT IN AFRICA

The net effect of the African political problems and tensions was that about one-half of all African countries were affected by conflict by the turn of the twenty-first century. For the period from 1960 to 2000, 8 million Africans died as a result of warfare. Of those, civilians constituted the bulk of war-related deaths in Africa, accounting for about 5.5 million (DFID 2001, 10). According to a recent study, in 1990, an African was twice more likely to die because of war than a non-African (Allen 1999). In fact, the level and scale of conflicts increased at an accelerated pace during the last two decades of the twentieth century, making Africa the world's most conflict-ridden region (DFID 2001, 10). Reflecting the increased awareness about the interconnectedness of states, internal conflicts are now attracting the active interest of neighbors. This is partially because of the growing awareness that societal disturbances have net negative effects on neighbors in terms not only of domestic markets and external investments but also the disruptive effects of refugees. At the start of the new millennium, the humanitarian crises in Africa remain the largest and most serious in the entire world, with about 17 million Africans forced out of their homes as refugees (6.25 million) or internally displaced persons (11 million).

The impact of Africa's political problems and the attendant humanitarian crises goes far beyond the immediate carnage and massive movements of persons. The effects are seen in other ways:

• In the widespread use of children in armed conflicts, not only as targets but also as instruments of war. Indoctrinated into a culture of violence, to kill or be killed, child soldiers are trained to give violent expression to the hatred of adults by various armed groups, including the Lord's Resistance Army in Uganda, the RUF in Sierra Leone, UNITA in Angola, the Interahamwe in Rwanda, and the SPLA in Sudan (United Nations 2000; DFID 2001, 11).

• Conflicts have contributed immensely in the destruction of infrastructure in Africa. Transport systems (roads, rails, ports, and airports), telecommunication networks, education and health-care facilities, electricity, sewer, and water supply systems have all been severely affected over the past three decades due to conflicts within Africa. For instance, more than 50 percent of the continent's transport infrastructure has been lost over the past twenty years due to conflicts (DFID 2001, 11). Obviously, such losses and the overall degradation of infrastructure impose huge immediate and long-term costs on the region's political economies.

One of the most important effects of conflicts is in the area of agricultural productivity, where production losses in Africa have been as high as 45 percent (DFID, 2001). Nearly all African economies and households are affected directly or indirectly by the conflict problems within the region. Productivity suffers as people lose access to their lands or crops at critical growing periods, as conflict-driven inflationary pressures place input prices beyond the reach of most farmers, and as markets are disrupted, limiting the sales of the produce. The net effect has been not only the diversion of scarce resources for the import of food products but also the creation of a dependency syndrome as some of the poorer countries have had to depend on external food aid to feed their people.

Emigration of able and skilled persons is another crucial effect of conflict in Africa. For the past two decades, African countries have endured a steady outflow of skilled manpower, ranging from teachers and nurses to medical doctors, engineers, and scientists. Also, hundreds of thousands of Africans, trained externally under state auspices, have chosen not to return to their home countries. The net effect of the emigration and self-exile of these Africans has been a severe shortage of difficult-to-replace manpower, thus further deepening the development challenges facing the continent.

The overall impact of conflict centers on how it retards or reverses development processes. For Africa, violent conflicts are a major cause of poverty within the region. The World Bank estimates that Africa suffers from an economic growth loss of about 2 percent annually due to conflicts. Throughout the region, conflicts not only displace people from their homes and lands but also destroy livelihoods of individuals, households, and whole communities. Quite aside from the physical disruption, the loss of access to land, resources, and markets, conflicts create conditions under which very little savings and investment (internal and external) can take place. Overall, this context of pervasive conflicts adds much to the present severe poverty and underdevelopment, including economic stagnation, poor and decaying infrastructure, low installed capacity and capacity utilization, low levels of technical skills, high infant mortality, low life expectancy, and the prevalence of epidemic diseases.

Given the destructive effects of conflicts on African political systems and stability as well as the associated impact on individual and communal lives throughout the region, a need exists to reflect systematically on possible modalities for mediating problem areas with an eye on identifying effective mechanisms for redressing the causal bases of conflicts. That is the objective of this chapter. We will revisit and offer suggestions about how to reconfigure African political systems to reemplace accommodative and consensual political processes. This is based on the belief that if legitimate and accountable institutions that would promote less conflictual and more active participation are put in place, Africa will be on the road to recovery from the crisis and conflict that have characterized it since independence.

IN SEARCH OF SOLUTIONS: THE CONSOCIATIONAL MODEL

Recent trends in Africa have seen the introduction and adoption of an important instrument—the New African Initiative document (drawn from the Millennium Africa Recovery Plan and the Omega plan)—by the Organization of African Unity. This document, along with the birth of the African Union (slated to succeed the OAU), the efforts of external players such as the United Nations and G8, and various governance-related (democracy-building) activities throughout the continent, are believed by many to presage not only the rebirth of the region but also the evolution of stability, harmony, and prosperity for its peoples. Given where the continent has been in the recent past, such trends and developments are positive. Nevertheless, they may fall short of what is required to achieve long-term peace, stability, and sustained economic prosperity. The reason for this is simple: Postindependence Africa now sits at a political crossroads as it struggles to establish legitimate and accommodative instruments of governance that can be adjudged by most Africans as fair and just. Basically, majoritarian liberal democracy is not enough. This is especially so if simple majoritarian systems are used without soothing mechanisms for assuring fairness and equity in the distribution of resources and economic rewards. The African reality is that most of its countries are severely segmented into subcultures that view each other with hostility or, at best, some suspicion. Subcultures, as Robert Dahl (1966, 371) has noted, "are distinctive sets of attitudes, opinions, and values that persist for relatively long periods of time in the life of a country and give individuals in a particular sub-culture a sense of identity that distinguishes them from individuals from other sub-cultures." In the African environment of relative scarcities, social differences are amplified and demonized in absolutist fashion. As Claude Ake (2000, 61) notes, "the groups struggle on grimly, brutally, with little confidence in the possibility of resolving conflicts peacefully. This in turn exacerbates the problem of political instability for which Africa is deservedly notorious."

Furthermore, a contextual difference exists between Western countries where the majoritarian democratic model, arguably, has been applied successfully and African countries where its history is riddled with failures. For one thing, the robust economies of Western countries give state officials a greater capacity to address the varied societal needs of competing interests. Consequently, the political arena is more properly seen as an opportunity, more or less, to render social service to the community. While there are opportunities for personal prestige and self-aggrandizement, these are largely taken to be the by-products of social service and responsibility. Consequently, a high premium is placed on rendering level the political arena and processes. Thus, the political system is arranged to give the impression that political candidates are formally free and equal and required to compete for office in conditions that are formally identical. Quite aside from the merits of the claims of "objectivity," the point remains that because the system is formally configured to provide an even playing field for all competitors, it leaves the impression that the emergent government is legitimate. This contrasts sharply with the African experience during the postcolonial era. As Claude Ake (2000, 61) argues:

The personalized use of coercive resources prevents the achievement of any illusion of objectivity. The limited autonomization of the state and limited commodification inhibits formal freedom and equality and competitive politics. In the absence of the institutionalization of formal freedom, equality and open competition, government lacks objectivity (even in appearance) and legitimacy. This problem of legitimacy lies behind what is often called the crisis of authority, and the crisis of nation-building in Africa. These crises are tendentially explained in terms of ethnicity and the short history of Africa's post-colonial "states." However, they have much to do with the conditions of production.

Obviously, the mere existence of cultural diversity is not a sufficient reason to assume the existence of severe segmentation. However, the existence of subcultures usually points to important divisions that can be used by demagogic politicians for narrow political objectives. Therein lies one of the more important dilemmas of democracies in all societies. The existence of severely segmented societies and subcultures in Africa gives special importance to the problem of autonomous organizations and political units. Independent organizations are not merely desirable in a democracy; indeed, they are necessary for the proper functioning of democratic processes and institutions, and as a check against the excesses of the different levels of governments. However, the fundamental problem of pluralist democracies lies in the fact that organizations—like individuals—possess the capacity to do harm if they are not controlled. In essence, as with individuals, autonomy for organizations creates an opportunity to do harm. As Dahl (1982, 1) has noted, "Organizations may use the opportunity to increase or perpetuate injustice rather than reduce it, to foster the narrow egoism of their members at the expense of the concerns for a broader public good, and even to weaken and destroy democracy itself."

Consociationalism assumes that societal unity is possible despite diversity and cultural segmentation. Anchored on the works of proponents such as Arend Lijphart, Gerhard Lehmbruch, and Jurg Steiner, the theory of consociational democracy revolves around a formula that will facilitate a solution to how people of different subcultures (whether ethnic, racial, linguistic, religious, or regional) could live harmoniously and thrive together within the boundaries of a state. In other words, the theorists maintain that it is possible for people in severely cleavaged societies to enjoy equal rights, access to resources and desirable goods, and power, without having to resort to killing themselves and pursuing other avenues of conduct that harshly limit or retard national development prospects (also see Lijphart 1977).

Put simply, consociational democracy advocates a broadly based coalition government. Deduced from empirical evidence, power sharing or consociational democracy seeks to explain how societies with varied subcultures can establish peace and democracy. Such societies, it contends, should share power among their various cultural segments. As a theoretical construct, power sharing involves four basic elements:

- Executive power sharing among the representatives of all significant groups;
- A high degree of internal autonomy for groups that wish to have it;
- Proportional representation and allocation for civil service positions and public funds; and
- A minority veto on the most vital issues.

Like any other constitutional arrangement, the consociational democracy framework will not work in an environment where critical sections of the societal subcultures are unwilling to engage in cooperative projects with rival elements. As Lijphart, its most prolific advocate, points out, the most crucial characteristic of consociational democracy rests on the "overarching cooperation at the elite level with the deliberate aim of counteracting disintegrative tendencies in the system" (quoted in Steiner 1974, 22; see also Lijphart 1969, 212). Lijphart (1969, 216) maintains that successful cooperation and peaceful intersubcultural coexistence rests on four requirements:

- Ability of elites to accommodate the divergent interests and demands of the subculture;
- Ability of elites to transcend cleavages and to join in a common effort with the elites of rival subcultures;
- Elite commitment to the maintenance of the system and to the improvement of its cohesion and stability; and

- The degree of elite understanding of the perils of political fragmentation.

Lijphart (1971, 9) maintains that intersubcultural hostility and violence may be avoided in those instances where the leaders of the subcultures engage in deliberate efforts to secure broad-based decisions on key matters: "Political stability can be maintained in culturally fragmented systems if the leaders of the subcultures engage in cooperative efforts to counteract the centrifugal tendencies of cultural fragmentation." Power-sharing advocates such as Lijphart (1968) and Steiner (1974) maintain that even in severely segmented political systems the more frequently political decisions are made by amicable agreement, the higher the probability that there will be a low level of intersubcultural hostility. Many sensible advocates of constitutionalism take it for granted that majoritarian democracy is a reasonably effective political system. Perhaps the relative success of democratic arrangements in parts of Europe and North America as well as the seeming success of several other states, such as India, Japan, Botswana, and Mexico, have helped cement this outlook. The rather recent political transformation of many of those countries, anchored by reasonably prosperous economic systems (including Botswana, France, Germany, Italy, Japan, Spain, and the United States) or an ethnic, racial, or religious majority (Botswana, India, and the United States), is ignored. Further ignored are the protracted and sputtering processes of change experienced by the more severely segmented of the present democratic successes. The United States, for instance, fought a destructive civil war and, after more than 200 years of constitutional experience, continues to deal, to this day with episodic subcultural turbulence. Beyond all that, proponents of majoritarian systems seem to ignore or dismiss the numerous empirical examples of democratic failures all over the world. Before the 1980s the global landscape was littered with assorted forms of dictatorships, most under political systems that had experiences at majoritarian democratic formats. The altered post–Cold War global political environment has seen the reintroduction of political liberalization around the world. Although the present context of change is far more propitious (externally and internally), the objective realities of democratic processes under a majoritarian winner-take-all format and societal context of resource starvation cannot be ignored or wished away. This is clearly evidenced in the African experience between 1990 and 2001. During that period, election results were contested very vigorously—even violently in several cases—in Algeria, Angola, Benin, Burundi, Cameroon, Congo, Ghana, Kenya, Niger, Nigeria, Rwanda, Senegal, South Africa, Tanzania, and Zimbabwe. As the recent experiences of the United States (2000) and United Kingdom (2001) have shown, even the established majoritarian democracies are not immune from political turmoil. How many African countries would have undergone electoral confusion similar to those recently experienced in the United States without the situation ending up in a bloodbath? The United States could get away with it, not only because of ample resources but also because of a reasonably mature political system, which does not severely penalize ballot box failures. Indeed, many Americans do not even bother to exercise their right to vote because of the belief that their lives would not be affected at all, regardless of who wins the electoral contest. By contrast, electoral outcomes are hugely important in Africa due both to the dearth of resources and the importance of political power in the distribution of economic resources and rewards. Given all that, should we not seriously explore alternative democratic models? How reasonable and realistic are expectations that majoritarian systems with their winner-takes-all characteristics will provide the proper bases for sustainable peace and stability in Africa?

POWER-SHARING FRAMEWORK

In applying a power-sharing framework, it would be crucial to contextualize the actual details. Each country has its own specific imperatives. As such, specific lines of major cleavages, such as ethnicity, race, religion, and class, would have to be adequately addressed. For instance, where religion is a major line of segmentation, the political framework would need to address the objective lines of religious differences. All major groups would have to be identified and given the opportunity of being represented within the political system. In situations where dual or multiple lines of major cleavages exist, then care must be taken to simultaneously address those lines of segmentation. Also, the four basic elements of the consociational framework should be retained substantially, with an eye on abiding objectivity, vision, and flexibility. For illustration purposes, I will attempt to show how the framework might apply to the complex Ugandan context. For our purposes here, we will assume that Uganda has a dual line of segmentation—ethnicity and religion. The ethnic makeup is as follows: Baganda, 17 percent; Karamojong (cluster), 12 percent; Basoga, 8 percent; Iteso, 8 percent; Banyankole, 8 percent; Bakiga, 7 percent; Langi, 6 percent; Banyaruanda 6 percent; Bagisu, 5 percent; Acholi, 4.5 percent; Lugbara, 4 percent; Bunyoro, 3 percent; Batoro, 3 percent; and others, 8.5 percent (Kurian 1992, 2009–2010; Ness and Ciment 1999, 876). Uganda's religious breakdown is as follows: Roman Catholic, 33 percent; Protestant, 33 percent, Muslim, 16 percent, and indigenous religious groups, 18 percent (Kurian 1992, 2009–2010; Ness and Ciment 1999, 876). Because ethnicity is the major line of segmentation in this model, it could also serve as the default basis for Uganda's proportional representation. We will take each of the four power-sharing elements separately.

EXECUTIVE POWER SHARING

Under a consociational framework, the Ugandan executive branch could be structured to reflect the demographic realities of the state. The high number of ethnic groupings would require an innovative approach in structuring the executive system of authority. Whereas a straight-out rotational presidency might be feasible in less complex situations, it would be more complicated in contexts

like Uganda. Nevertheless, a multifaceted rotational approach may be feasible in
the Ugandan case. For instance, the country's ethnic map could be reconfigured
to identify and group politically coherent clusters into functional units. The for-
mulators of the power-sharing arrangement could split the country into a number
of executive zones, let us say three or four. In a four-zone arrangement, the eth-
nic-membership map and their population percentages might look as follows
(anchored imperfectly on proximate cultural or linguistic groups):

- Group A: Eastern Lacustrine Bantu (24.5 percent)—Baganda, 17 percent; Acholi,
  4.5 percent; Batoro, 3 percent.
- Group B: Western Lacustrine Bantu (24 percent)—Banyankole, 8 percent; Basoga, 8
  percent; Bagisu, 5 percent; Bunyoro, 3 percent;
- Group C: Nilotic (26 percent)—Iteso, 8 percent; Karamojong (includes Jie, Dodoth
  and others), 12 percent; Langi, 6 percent;
- Group D: Central Sudanic and Others (25.5 percent)—Bakiga, 7 percent; Lugbara, 4
  percent; Banyaruanda 6 percent; and others, 8.5 percent

The executive system may be structured in any one of two ways: an
autonomous executive system or a joint executive system. An autonomous executive system may be configured along the lines of majoritarian systems.
Within a consociational democratic format, this is a working power-sharing arrangement. In such a case, the office of the chief executive is merely rotated
between the executive zones. For instance, if a single four-year system of
authority were adopted for the chief executive, candidates from the zone responsible for providing the chief executive would be required to identify themselves
and to contest openly for the office. All eligible voters throughout the country
would then get to take a closer look and vote for one of the candidates. The candidate with a majority or plurality (depending on the constitutional framework)
of the votes wins the contest.

The joint executive system is a more active power-sharing framework. The
system may be configured as a collegial or collective arrangement. In our Ugandan example, candidates from each of the executive zones may campaign simultaneously for office. Voters are instructed to vote for a candidate from each
executive zone. The top candidate (by plurality or majority) from each zone
wins the four-year right of membership in the presidency. To entrench a culture
of stability and continuity, it would be preferable that the tenure in the presidency be staggered so that one or two members enter every year or two. The
rules of the presidency should be structured to encourage cooperation and consensus. For instance, decisions within the body should be either by consensus or
"preponderant majority" (three-to-one). No one within the body will have veto
power. Furthermore, the chairmanship of the body should be rotated yearly so
that no one within the body is allowed two presidential terms in any given four-
year period. To depoliticize the importance of presidential power, no one is allowed more than two consecutive four-year terms in the presidency. Also, the

structure is staggered so that one member of the presidency must lose his or her eligibility every two years. These steps will not only ensure that there is stability and continuity, but also that there is a constant infusion of new blood and ideas capable of giving the presidency a strong sense of dynamism.

Internal Autonomy

In a consociational democratic arrangement, there is great need to organize nonnational political units to allow significant subcultures a measure of autonomy if they wish to have it. This not only serves to enable such groups to take direct charge of their own affairs and destiny, but also enables them to develop alongside their counterparts as equals and partners within the nation-state. In our Ugandan example, for instance, the nation-state could be a federal arrangement with a cluster of state (provincial) and local government (county) subunits with varying degrees of power. Subcultures could be given substantial autonomy on internal matters within local government structures. Where a subculture is comparatively large—for instance, the Baganda—they may be split into potentially competing autonomous local government areas. Such arrangements would serve the useful purpose of protecting other subcultures within the province or country by creating a need to cultivate a culture of bargaining, cooperation, and coalition building.

Proportional Representation and Proportional Allocation

The feeling of marginalization by some subcultures is frequently one of the most important causes of conflicts in postcolonial African states. As such, it is vital that subcultures be given a fair slice of both power and resources. Since the state is frequently the biggest employer, care should be taken to ensure adequate access and representation of all significant groups in the civil service. (Where there are structural bases of inequality, the state must undertake to redress such imbalances by taking adequate corrective measures.) In regard to political representation in government, care must be taken to ensure proportionality. For instance, in our Ugandan example the representation in a 100-member national parliament could be as follows: Baganda, 17; Karamojong, 12; Basoga, 8; Iteso, 8; Banyankole, 8; Bakiga, 7; Langi, 6; Banyaruanda, 6; Bagisu, 5; Acholi, 5; Lugbara, 4; Bunyoro, 3; Batoro, 3; and others, 8. The religious lines of segmentation could be accounted for through an internal mechanism within each group. In other words, national parliamentary representation could be configured to assure not only that each major ethnic group is represented in parliament in proportion to their overall national numeric strength, but also that each delegation reflects its own internal lines of segmentation. For instance, let us assume that the Baganda are internally divided as follows (in terms of religion): Roman Catholic, 50 percent; Protestant, 30 percent; Muslim, 10 percent; and indigenous religious groups, 10 percent. The Baganda parliamentary delegation would similarly reflect the religious lines of segmentation. Of their 17 national parliamentarians, the numbers would be as follows: Roman Catholics, 8; Protestants, 5; Muslims, 2; and Indigenous Religious groups, 2.

Minority Veto

The requirement for a minority veto power on issues of vital interest to them is anchored on the possibility that the majority might outvote them on crucial legislation. The problem here is that while this element seeks to avoid the possibility of majority tyranny, it has the potential of entrenching minority tyranny. Should a minority with a vital interest in a piece of legislation have the right to hold back a majority if the matter is also of significant interest to them? Of course, it is possible that the need to protect other vital interests through coalition building may foreclose the likelihood that minorities would exercise the veto option frequently. Nevertheless, the potential exists for the veto to serve as a sabotage factor. A truculent group may overuse the privilege by constantly holding up legislation and weakening the processes of bargaining and cooperation. Given the need for a democratic system to protect its people in entirety, the destructive potential of unencumbered vetoes may serve to render such framework untenable. A limited veto power that is constructed in such a way that it places a very high premium on preserving the privilege for the truly most vital issues may provide a more effective system of simultaneous protection for minority and majority interests. For instance, each group may be given a total of ten vetoes per legislative session. If they exhaust them in one day, they would have no veto powers for the entire legislative session. To protect less powerful groups from being overwhelmed with unacceptable legislation that they feel a need to veto, any item that receives two vetoes in any given session may not be resubmitted for additional consideration. This should have the effect of encouraging bargaining and cooperative behavior on legislative matters.

LIMITATIONS OF CONSOCIATIONAL DEMOCRACY

Obviously, no theoretical framework can claim to be flawless. Being a normative theory, power sharing has attracted many supporters and critics. A crucial and damaging criticism pertains to the claim that it is not a genuinely democratic system. Obviously, this begs the operative question: What is democracy? Writing about South Africa, Vincent Maphai (2000, 335) insists,

Consociationalists are, rightly, alarmed at the prospects and reality of ethnic wars and instability, and are prescribing means considered necessary for the achievement of peace and stability. They seem to miss that this has nothing to do with democracy or rights as such. Democracy may promote stability, but it can also exacerbate instability. What consociationalists are in effect doing, is rejecting majority rule in favor of stability. They are not promoting democracy, ordinarily understood as majority rule.

This rather parochial sense of democracy is central to the problems identified by many critics of consociationalism. They seem to ignore the inherent problems of majoritarian democracy, particularly its basic unfairness to losing parties and citizens, the internal undemocraticness of the political parties themselves, the frequent instability resulting from party-based commotions, and huge human and social costs from the violent conflicts that result when the system breaks down. Clearly, if strong opposition were seen as essential to democracy, consociational democracy—by definition—would be less democratic than the British government versus opposition pattern; a grand coalition government necessarily entails either a relatively small and weak opposition or the absence of any formal opposition in the legislature. The staunch attachment to majoritarianism today is largely (and falsely) anchored on the present workings of political parties in the more mature democracies of the United States and the United Kingdom. This confidence, however, belies the reality of doubt, confusion, and fear that earlier majoritarian democrats harbored about such organizations. For instance, Thomas Jefferson, one of America' s greatest political leaders and third president, said, "If I could not go to heaven but with a party, I would not go there at all" (Hofstadter 1969, 2, 123). George Washington (1796), first president of the United States, speaking during his farewell address, warned against the "baneful effects of the Spirit of Party," especially in popular democracies (http://gwpapers.virginia.edu/farewell/index.html; also see Starr, Curti, and Todd 1961, 103–104):

This spirit unfortunately, is inseparable from our nature, having its root in the strongest passions of the human mind. It exists under different shapes in all governments, more or less stifled, controlled, or repressed; but in those of the popular form it is seen in its greatest rankness and is truly their worst enemies. . . . It serves always to distract the public councils and enfeeble the public administration. It agitates the community with ill-founded jealousies and false alarms; kindles the animosity of one part against another and foments occasionally riot and insurrection.

As I have shown in previous sections of this chapter, these prophetic words reflect, in the main, the African experience with majoritarian systems. The costs in human lives, damaged property, and stunted development opportunities have been incalculable.

Critics also question the democratic quality of consociationalism because they believe that the framework has a tendency toward bringing about further homogenization of societal lines of segmentation. They charge that the net effect of the consociational experiment is that it preempts the development of a truly national society. They maintain that by working to ensure group equality, it serves to muffle individual freedom. Also, the democratic ideals of liberty, equality, and fraternity for all societies are lost. The claim of homogenization does appear valid. However, a similar charge can be made against ineffective majoritarian models. In many countries where the system has been in operation, there are strong indications of ethnic consolidation that belie the more fluid intermingling that preceded postcolonial state structures. Consider the experiences of Angola, Benin, Cameroon, Côte d'Ivoire, Ghana, Kenya, and Nigeria, among others. In Nigeria, for instance, the Edo, Hausa, Ibibio, Igbo, Kanuri, Nupe, Tiv, and Yoruba were never more conscious of their ethnicities than they have become as a result of Nigeria's postcolonial history. The homogenization effect that would occur under a consociational arrangement can and does occur under a majoritarian system also. The difference is that it may happen later in a majoritarian system, typically after much destruction of social cohesion, political stability, lives, and property. Rather than expending much energy hoping against the odds that people would transcend human tendencies and a long line of historical evidence, the power-sharing framework accepts the objective segmentation of society and seeks effective ways of defusing the features of human social and political interactions that would tend to cause conflict. In fact, by encouraging cooperative behavior and societal cohesion, consociational arrangements are more likely than nonworking majoritarian systems to remove the bases of societal disharmony and underdevelopment.

As one might have gleaned from the preceding sections, consociational democracy depends quite heavily on elite cooperation. That dependence forms an important objection to the democratic quality of the framework. While the elitist feature of power sharing is troubling, it does not differ markedly from the reality of other forms of government, including majoritarian democracy, where elite networks and backdoor bargaining arrangements frequently dominate political institutions and processes. Indeed, despite claims to the contrary, socialist systems also tend (in the main) to do the same.

In essence, then, consociational democracies are no less democratic than majoritarian systems. They require a greater degree of consensus than majoritarian systems. Nevertheless, its basic premise of broad agreement is frequently utilized by majoritarian systems when dealing with vital issues. As Lijphart (1969, 214) has stressed,

Consociational democracy violates the principle of majority rule, but it does not deviate very much from normative democratic rule. Most democratic constitutions prescribe majority rule for the normal transaction of business when the stakes are not high, but extraordinary majorities or several successive majorities for the most important decisions, such as changing the constitution. In fragmented systems, many other decisions in addition to constituent ones are perceived as involving high stakes, and therefore require more than simple majority rule. Similarly, majority rule does not suffice in times of grave crisis in even the most heterogeneous and consensual of democracies.

The second broad category of criticisms of consociational democracy rejects its claims of stability and effectiveness. Indeed, power-sharing efforts in Cyprus and Lebanon ended up in failures. The Cypriot experiment appears to have failed because of structural problems in the adopted framework. A crucial problem pertains to the four-to-one population imbalance in favor of the Greek population, which may have reduced the predisposition toward bargaining and cooperation. Another important factor in the failure of the experiment may have been the veto power that was wielded by the comparatively small Turkish minority. The Lebanese failure, on the other hand, was precipitated by the intrusion of outside forces such as the Palestinians, Israelis, and Syrians, as well as by the weaknesses of the internal consociational arrangement, such as the rigidity of the system's power distribution, which did not allow for shifts in demography between the competing segments.

A final category of criticisms pertains to the economic implications of consociational democracy. According to Sam Nolutshungu (1983, 30), "where different segments have markedly unequal economic and social advantages, proportional distribution alone would not meet some very widely accepted notions of justice, and might even make them more unattainable: such as the view that in these cases there ought to be 'positive discrimination' or, as it is called in the United States, 'affirmative action.'" In some ways this may be a valid criticism for societies such as Burundi, Rwanda, and South Africa, with huge objective disparities in income and opportunities between important segments. Obviously, the disadvantaged segments would prefer arrangements other than proportionality, such as "affirmative action," that have the capacity to achieve redress in the shortest possible time frame. The issue, however, is if the demand for such redress results in the refusal by the dominant segments to concede any of their powers and advantages, as has happened in Burundi, Rwanda, and Sudan. Would it be preferable for such severely segmented societies to continue their slow backward march toward poverty, genocide, and crusted underdevelopment? Maphai (2000, 339) concedes grudgingly when he argues, "consociationalists also provide compelling grounds for the conclusion that there could be circumstances in which a country has to make a trade-off between the demands of [majoritarian] democracy on the one hand, and those of stability, on the other."

CONCLUSION

Writing in the Federalist Number 10, James Madison argued that the fundamental causes of factionalism are embedded in human nature. He not only maintained that such causes are so deeply ingrained that they cannot be removed, but also that reprieve may only be sought in the means of controlling their effects. That is the challenge that faces many African states and their leaders: how to construct effective political systems that would enable them to better manage their highly segmented societies in a way that allows for peace, stability, and prosperity. Majoritarian democracy has not provided a panacea to the conflicts caused by Africa's cultural diversity. Rather, it has created and nurtured the basis of elite fragmentation and ethnic homogenization by contributing to the exacerbation of tensions and the escalation of existing conflicts between competing groups in much of the continent. The objective condition in Africa is that majoritarian democratic systems provide special problems for ethnically divided societies because of a winner-take-all format that serves to imbue political contests with life-and-death characteristics. This situation is made more urgent by the resource-starved environments of many African states. Fearing continual (or even permanent) marginalization, ethnic minorities or losing coalitions often feel forced to seek redress through autonomy or secession.

The power-sharing framework will not resolve all of Africa's political problems and conflicts. However, it does provide a credible, if not superior, alternative to majoritarian democratic systems. Power-sharing arrangements would allow African states to build the bases for durable peace and stability. These, in turn, will enable the states to nurture enabling environments for effective and sustainable economic growth and societal prosperity. Huge amounts of human and financial resources now being poured into military salaries and arms purchases for unending political tensions, conflicts, and wars, such as those taking place in Angola, Burundi, Democratic Republic of Congo, Nigeria, Rwanda, Somalia, and Sudan, can be channeled into productive activities. Roads, railways, ports, potable water and health-care systems, irrigation networks, educational institutions, respect for human rights and the rule of law, and other paraphernalia of social and economic prosperity and development can be built or rehabilitated with the savings from conflicts. Consociational democracy could enable African states to harness their cultural diversity as a source of strength rather than weakness. By deflating the consequences of electoral failure, it would also provide the basis for African people to deemphasize many of the artificial differences between people while accepting amicably the objective realities of substantive differences amongst individuals and subcultures.

ACKNOWLEDGMENTS

I wish to extend my sincere thanks to Bukky Akintola for her invaluable research assistance. The usual caveat applies.

REFERENCES

Ake, C. 1992. What is the problem of ethnicity in Africa? Keynote address presented at the Conference on Ethnicity, Society and Conflict in Natal, University of Natal, Pietermaritzburg, South Africa.

Ake, C. 2000. The state in contemporary Africa. In *Government and politics in Africa: A reader*, edited by O. Nnoli. Harare, Zimbabwe: AAPS Books.

Allen, C. 1999. Warfare, endemic violence and state collapse in Africa. *Review of African Political Economy* 26 (81): 367–384.

Annan, K. 1998. SG Report on Africa: The causes of conflict and the promotion of durable peace and sustainable development in Africa. Retrieved from http://www.un.org/ecosocdev/geninfo/afrec/sgreport/report.htm, October 26, 2003.

Blumer, H., and T. Dustin. 1980. *UNESCO: Sociological theories—Race and colonialism*. Paris: UNESCO.

Cannon, G. E. 1982. Consociationalism vs. control: Canada as a case study. *Western Political Quarterly* 35 (March): 50–64.

Cartwright, J. R. 1983. *Political leadership in Africa*. New York: St. Martin's Press.

Connor, W. 1973. The politics of ethnonationalism. *Journal of International Affairs* 27 (1): 1–21.

Connor, W. 1994. *Ethnonationalism: The quest for understanding*. Princeton, NJ: Princeton University Press.

Daalder, H. 1989. The mould of Dutch politics: Themes for comparative inquiry. *West European Politics* 12 (1): 1–20.

Dahl, R., ed. 1966. *Political opposition in Western democracies*. New Haven: Yale University Press.

Dahl, R. 1982. *Dilemmas of pluralist democracy: Autonomy vs. control*. New Haven: Yale University Press.

Davidson, B. 1989. *Modern Africa: A social and political history*. London: Longman.

Dekmejian, R. H. 1978. Consociational democracy in crisis: The case of Lebanon. *Comparative Politics* 10 (January): 251–265.

de Waal, A., ed. 2000. *Who fights? Who cares?* Trenton, NJ: Africa World Press.

DFID. 2001. The causes of conflict in Africa: Consultation document. Unpublished document. London: Ministry of Defense.

Diamond, L. 1982. Cleavage, conflict and anxiety in the Second Republic. *Journal of Modern African Studies* 20 (4): 629–668.

Diamond, L. 1983. Social change and political conflict in Nigeria's Second Republic: A SAIS study on Africa. In *The political economy of Nigeria*, edited by I. W. Zartman. New York: Praeger.

Dix, R. H. 1980. Consociational democracy: The case of Colombia. *Comparative Politics* 12 (April): 303–312.

Falola, T., and J. O. Ihonvbere. 1985. *The rise and fall of Nigeria's Second Republic, 1979–1984*. London: Zed Books.

Goldman, J. R. 1985. Consociational authoritarian politics and the 1974 Yugoslav constitution: A preliminary note. *East European Quarterly* 19 (June): 241–249.

Graf, W. 1985. The Nigerian new year coup of December 31, 1983: A class analysis. *Journal of Black Studies* 16 (1): 21–45.

Hartlyn, J. 1988. *The politics of coalition rule in Colombia*. Cambridge: Cambridge University Press.

Hofstadter, D. L. 1969. *The idea of a party system*. Berkeley and Los Angeles: University of California Press.

Horowitz, D. L. 1985. *Ethnic groups in conflict*. Berkeley and Los Angeles: University of California Press.

Ibrahim, J. 2000. The politics of religion in Nigeria: The parameters of the 1987 crisis in Kaduna. In *Government and politics in Africa: A reader*, edited by O. Nnoli. Harare, Zimbabwe: AAPS Books.

Jackson, R. H., and C. G. Rosberg. 1982. *Personal rule in black Africa: Prince, autocrat, prophet, tyrant*. Berkeley and Los Angeles: University of California Press.

Jackson, R. H., and C. G. Rosberg. 1986. The marginality of African states. In *African independence: The first twenty-five years*, edited by G. M. Carter and P. O'Meara. Bloomington: Indiana University Press.

Joseph, R. A. 1983. Class, state, and prebendal politics in Nigeria. *Journal of Commonwealth and Comparative Politics* 21 (3): 21–38.

Kurian, G. T. 1992. *Encyclopedia of the Third World*, 4th ed., vol. 3. New York: Facts on File.

Lehmbruch, G. 1993. Consociational democracy and corporatism in Switzerland. *Publius* 23 (Spring): 43–60.

Lijphart, A. 1968. *The politics of accommodation: Pluralism and democracy in the Netherlands.* Berkeley and Los Angeles: University of California Press.

Lijphart, A. 1969. Consociational democracy. *World Politics* 21 (January): 207–225.

Lijphart, A. 1971. Cultural diversity and theories of political integration. *Canadian Journal of Political Science* 4 (1): 1–19.

Lijphart, A. 1977. *Democracy in plural societies: A comprehensive exploration.* New Haven: Yale University Press.

Lijphart, A. 1989. From the politics of accommodation to adversarial politics in the Netherlands: A reassessment. *West European Politics* 12 (1): 139–153.

Linder, W. 1994. *Swiss democracy: Possible solutions to conflict in multicultural societies.* New York: St. Martin's Press.

Lofchie, M. F. 1993. Trading places: Economic policy in Kenya and Tanzania. In *Hemmed in: Responses to Africa's economic decline*, edited by T. Callaghy and J. Ravenhill. New York: Columbia University Press.

Luther, K. R., and W. Muller, eds. 1992. Special issue on "Politics in Austria: Still a case of consociationalism?" *West European Politics* 15 (January): 1–226.

Mamdani, M. 1996. *Citizen and subject: Contemporary Africa and the legacy of late colonialism.* Princeton, NJ: Princeton University Press.

Mamdani, M. 2000. Democratic theory and democratic struggles in Africa. In *Government and politics in Africa: A reader*, edited by O. Nnoli. Harare, Zimbabwe: AAPS Books.

Maphai, V. T. 2000. Liberal democracy and ethnic conflict in South Africa. In *Government and politics in Africa: A reader*, edited by O. Nnoli. Harare, Zimbabwe: AAPS Books.

Nagel, J. 1995. Resource competition theories. *American Behavioral Scientist* 38 (3): 217–237.

Ness, I., and J. Ciment, eds. 1999. *Encyclopedia of global population and demographics.* Chicago: Fitzroy Dearbon.

Nolutshungu, S. C. 1983. *Changing South Africa.* Cape Town: David Phillips.

Powell, G. B. Jr. 1970. *Social fragmentation and political hostility: An Austrian case study.* Stanford: Stanford University Press.

Prah, K. K. 2000. Constitutionalism, the National Question and the Sudanese civil war. In *Government and politics in Africa: A reader*, edited by O. Nnoli. Harare, Zimbabwe: AAPS Books.

Rothchild, D., and V. Olurunsola, eds. 1983. *State versus ethnic claims.* Boulder, CO: Westview Press.

Sklar, R. 1979. The nature of class domination in Africa. *Journal of Modern African Studies* 17 (4): 531–552.

Sklar, R. 1986. Democracy in Africa. In *Governing in black Africa*, edited by M. E. Doro and M. Stultz Newell. New York: Africana.

Starr, I., M. E. Curti, and L. P. Todd, eds. 1961. *Living American documents.* New York: Harcourt, Brace and World, Inc.

Steiner, J. 1974. *Amicable agreement versus majority rule: Conflict resolution in Switzerland.* Chapel Hill, NC: University of North Carolina Press.

Steiner, J. 1990. Power-sharing: Another Swiss "export product?" In *Conflict and peacemaking in multiethnic societies,* edited by J. V. Montville. Lexington, MA: Lexington Books.

Suberu, R. T., S. A. Mala, and D. I. Aiyegboyin. 1999. Religious organization. In *Nigeria: Politics of transition and governance, 1986–1996,* edited by O. Oyediran and A. Adigun. Dakar: CODESRIA.

Udogu, E. I. 1999. Ethnicity and democracy in sub-Saharan Africa. In *Preparing Africa for the twenty-first century: Strategies for peaceful coexistence and sustainable development,* edited by J. M. Mbaku. Aldershot, UK: Ashgate.

United Nations. 2000. Child soldiers. Retrieved from http://www.un.org/special-rep/children-armed-conflict/soldiers.htm, October 26, 2003.

Uzodike, U. O. 1999. Development in the New World Order: Repositioning Africa for the twenty-first century. In *Preparing Africa for the twenty-first century: Strategies for peaceful coexistence and sustainable development,* edited by J. M. Mbaku. Aldershot, UK: Ashgate.

Vasovic, V. 1992. A plea for consociational pluralism. In *The tragedy of Yugoslavia: The failure of democratic transformation,* edited by J. Seroka and V. Pavlovic. Armonk, NY: M. E. Sharpe.

Von Vorys, K. 1975. *Democracy without consensus: Communalism and political stability in Malaysia.* Princeton, NJ: Princeton University Press.

Wanyande, P. 2000. Democracy and one-party states: The African experience. In *Government and politics in Africa: A reader,* edited O. Nnoli. Harare, Zimbabwe: AAPS Books.

Washington, G. 1796. Farewell Address. Retrieved from http://gwpapers.virginia.edu/farewell/index.html, October 26, 2003.

Williams, D. C. 1992. Accommodation in the midst of crisis? Assessing governance in Nigeria. In *Governance and politics in Africa,* edited by G. Hyden and M. Bratton. Boulder, CO: Lynne Rienner.

Zakaria, H. A. 1989. Malaysia: Quasi democracy in a divided society. In *Democracy in developing countries: Asia,* edited by L. Diamond, J. J. Linz, and S. M. Lipset. Boulder, CO: Lynne Rienner.

Zolberg, A. 1968. The structures of political conflict in the new states of tropical Africa. *American Political Science Review* 62 (11): 70–87.

Zolberg, A. 1977. Splitting the difference: Federalization without federalism in Belgium. In *Ethnic conflict in the Western world,* edited by Milton J. Esman. Ithaca, NY: Cornell University Press.

13

State Repair and Democratic Development in Africa

'KUNLE AMUWO

The historicity of the post-colonial African state has to be the starting point of any meaningful examination and, hopefully, understanding of its many manifestations and behaviors: accumulation through the use, misuse, and abuse of the state rather than production (i.e., wealth creation); external orientation of not just the economy, but also of virtually everything else; hegemony of multinational capitalism and, ipso facto, of foreign capital; capture and monopolization of the state by a group of urban-based elites; and the unwillingness of the state to make the welfare of the people a priority in public policy. In a way, the relationship between the postcolonial state and popular forces is not that different from that between the colonial state and indigenous peoples. During colonialism, state structures were used to exploit the people for the benefit of the metropolitan economies, and today in many African countries the apparatus of state is used to plunder the economy for the benefit of the ruling class. The latter often consists of a small group of urban-based indigenous elites, many of whom obtained their positions through nondemocratic processes.

The major thesis of this chapter, both implicitly and explicitly, is that whatever else the contemporary African state is, it is nothing but a public institution whose structures have been privatized and are being used by members of the incumbent government and its supporters to enrich themselves. Entrenched interest groups, who are beneficiaries of the status quo, cannot but be unenthusiastic about, if not outrightly hostile to, drives toward popular participation; "meaningful democracy" and "people's power." By pushing for further formal privatization and deregulation of the economy as part of the so-called globalization and marketization of the international political economy, ruling elites in the continent and international financial institutions are merely reinforcing their hegemonic positions in the national economies of the various states, including those in Africa. Yet the drive since the early 1990s toward popular or substantive democracy—that is, making the state responsible, responsive and account-able to the people, particularly through the agency of civil society organizations and movements—has had its own dynamics and is, indeed, in a dialectical rela-tionship with the movement, pari pasu, toward the "deresponsibilization" of the state via the market economy.

In consequence, we are confronted with a state torn between two contra-dictory and seemingly irreconcilable pressures, politics, and "logics": one from citizens to deliver the wherewithal of living, if not also seeking quick fixes to debilitating socioeconomic conditions created over the long haul by hitherto existing authoritarian governments; the other from the international sys-tem/Western capitalist states, whose deification of the market "god" assails the state on every side, thus putting it in a "neither nor" situation. In other words, to the extent that the socioeconomic rendition and material wherewithal of democ-racy are slow in coming, political democracy, however necessary, is little more than putative. To the extent that this is so, the state has been neither "develop-mental" nor "transformative," there is more of government and less of govern-ance, and the shrinking of the formal sector and state structures is more vivid and perceptible in the realm of social and economic provisioning and less in the sphere of both putative and actual coercive apparatuses of the state. Yet Africa has to develop and time is running out. A return to the people, principally through the agency of civil society organizations, seems the only way out.

The chapter concludes by rejecting the current drive toward the privatiza-tion of African economies—as was also the case, with damaging consequences, in the 1980s and 1990s—as a possible panacea. Nor does it recommend a wholesale state or public ownership, insofar as both state control or central planning and laissez faire have demonstrated the vices of their virtues. Rather, I suggest a process of "communitization" or "municipalization" of the economy, public properties, goods, and services that necessarily have to pass through a reassertion of the people as the subject of development and, therefore, their rein-sertion into the development matrix as citizens, not as subjects. The ultimate end will be the gradual repair of the state from below, as the dialectics and dynamics of state–society relations in an emergent electoral democracy begin to transform into constitutional democracy or, simply, constitutionalism, as citizens' habitual obedience to the state turns into genuine allegiance, and as the legitimacy deficit of the state begins to wither away.

THE INHERITED NEOCOLONIAL STATE

From "too much" state through "not enough" state and "no state at all" to "bringing the state back in," the African continent and her people have, in the past four decades or so, been hapless victims of sundry conceptual and ideologi-cal experimentation with the inherited colonial state. By the same token, as sev-eral variants of that state began to manifest more dysfunctional characteristics than eufunctional ones, Africanists of all conceivable hues and traditions were agog with an outpouring of epithets and catch terms to capture the nondevelopmental state: "failed," "collapsed," "expired," "lax," "soft," "swollen," "rogue," "criminalized," "rhizome" or "invisible," or "shadow." The list is, indeed, inexhaustible. While there is little doubt that many of these descriptions summarize what has virtually become a legendary ineptitude of the African state, the point to note here is that it is not the state qua state, but a particular type of state, in this case the postcolonial or neocolonial state, that has failed Africa. Similarly, there are several variants of the postcolonial state, suggesting that different polities have varying results in their attempts to reduce the reach, depth, and intensity of underdevelopment. As a social institution weaned out of a dialectical process that was capable of both catastrophe and progress, the colonial state was janus-faced (Samatar and Samatar 1987, 674): It was both dependent and autonomous, authoritarian and transformative, strong and soft, public spirited and class oriented, alien/alienating and friendly, and so on. But on account of its genesis and assigned "historic role" in both the colonial and postcolonial "international division of labor," the inherited state has shown greater potential to be more corporatist, authoritarian, and coercive than anything else. This is because the colonial state was anything but consensual, deliberative, and democratic. By the logic of the monopoly and colonial capitalism of that period, no other trajectory of the state was feasible. The much-maligned notion of the contemporary African state as an alien, alienating, and alienated social institution dates back to its colonial historiography. Also part of the latter is the rendition of that state as dependent, lacking in legitimacy, remote, inaccesible, and brutish (Ndegwa 2001, 8). Thus, coercion and arbitrariness best describe and define the inherited state: For Forrest (1986, 4–26), that state lacks coherently organized social power and has low levels of legitimacy, unity, and authority, even if it excels in coercive skills. Bayart (2000, 58) also makes the point that "coercion is a means of regulating the imported state and of laying hold on its resources." The moral here is that constructive functions of the state were more of a shrinking public province than the state's defensive functions (Goldsmith 2000, 1–20).

In a nutshell, therefore, the neocolonial state bequeathed to Africa's elite was more of a liability than an asset as far as national political and socioeconomic development was concerned. The state was excessively bureaucratic and bureaucratized; while exceedingly beneficial to the "state class" (i.e., the indigenous elites who captured the apparatus of state at independence) that would later use political power to retrench much of the state in its hand, it was snobbish and offhandish to the people's welfare. The economy itself was highly problematic: It lacked a structural production base. This was a direct consequence of the colonial political economy, as well as the logic of imperialist domination. For Bathily (2000, 40), the predatory nature of the colonial state was far from being sui generis; on the contrary, that state merely "pursued and brought to a new level the plunder function of the preceding forms of state." Analyzing the West African state from an historical perspective, Bathily argues that, unlike the primary state that was that region's "most genuinely democratic state," the predatory state that became hegemonic during the Atlantic slave trade and the colonial conquests was most visible by virtue of a "permanent resort to brutal force." Worse, not only was violence routinely used by the state and its main institutions, such as the army and judiciary, the state also tolerated "acts of individual violence carried out by the members of the new ruling class" (Bathily 2000, 25, 34). This phenomenon would resonate in the postcolonial state; the latter became the easiest, best, and most-lucrative resource for primitive accumulation by state officials or custodians. The centrality of political power via the state can hardly be overemphasized; as Clapham (1985, 41) contends, the "control of the state is too appealing to be abandoned." The result has been a veritable war of some against many, between those who have access to and control of the state and those who do not (Ake 2000, 63–64). Moreover, carried over to the postcolonial era is the notion of politics not as a positive-sum game, where all groups and individuals can potentially gain more of some and some of more, but as a zero-sum game, a development that has tended to drive a rigid wedge between ruling parties and the political opposition in many African countries, thus often rendering democratic consolidation an extremely tasking and arduous affair. Reflecting on Ghana's 1996 elections and the possibility of democratic deepening in that country, Jeffries (1998, 208) argues that politics has become a war in which each group struggles to capture the state and use it to its advantage, and hence, there usually is no room for compromise or cooperation for the sake of, say, maximizing national objectives. Rather than agree on exact rules of the game as well as observe them, Jeffries (1998, 208) contends that beginning from decolonization in 1957,

ruling and opposition parties have entertained very little respect for each other. The language of politics has always been decidedly bellicose and the reality of politics one in which the victors have rarely been kind to the vanquished. . . . Each side tends to claim a monopoly of political virtue. Not far below the surface of constitutional argument and counter-argument lies an intensity of enmity far greater than is customary between parties in stable multiparty democratic systems.

In essence, therefore, the state class, state elites, and state citizens who benefit most from the state, by virtue of their stranglehold on the inherited state, tend to overreach themselves in resorting to Machiavellian tactics to hold on to power and its beneficence. While Diamond (1987, 570) identifies the modern African state as arguably the most significant of colonial legacies, as well as the most decisive in shaping the pattern of national development, the colonial state was anything but modern; it has largely proved to be a very poor imitation, an empty shell of the European modern state (Amuwo 1997/1998). Diamond was, however, quick to point out that, for good or for ill, African societies have been stuck with a state that has, almost in all material particulars, "dwarfed in wealth and power both existing social institutions and various new fragments of modern organization." Thus, the foundations of an "overdeveloped" and highly centralized and hardly developmental state in postcolonial Africa were conveniently laid during the colonial period. For example, the Marketing Boards—one of the early targets of the World Bank and IMF's structural adjustment programs, beginning from the mid-1980s—were established to (1) enhance the exploitation of the rural agricultural areas for the benefit of the politically influential urban centers, (2) improve the development and harvesting of the cash crops that were exported to the metropolitan economies, and (3) provide necessary revenues for the government to deal with critical social and political issues, including the control of the indigenous populations of the colonies. It is important to note here that it did not matter that the choices made by the colonial government were usually not in the best interest of each colony.

The same story could be related a propos of infrastructural and mining sectors of the colonial economy, where private sector participation was outlawed and the state took total control (Diamond 1987, 571–572). In consequence, the almost unmitigated state control of the economy commenced by colonialism would be consolidated, and the theory, practice, and demands of postcolonial national development obliged, by independence governments. In the same vein, the ideology of developmentalism gave birth to state enterprises and parastatals that, save for isolated pockets, would become hotbeds of public venality. Mistry (2000, 558) is, therefore, right to assert that the main obstacle to progress in Africa are the vested interests that have profited from development failure. Implicated here are colonialism-driven delinkage between the sociological precolonial nation and the political postcolonial state largely responsible for the negative fallouts of neopatrimonialism, Africa's state class, and, to be sure, foreign interests. Specifically on the latter, Mistry (2000, 557) contends that "aid to Africa [is] driven less by concern about development than by the geopolitical agenda and priorities of donors." What this suggests is that, unlike its colonial precursor, the postcolonial state is, mutatis mutandis, fatally incapacitated by, inter alia, its external orientation. In other words, Western capitalism essays, not without success much of the time, to vitiate domestic attempts at autonomous development. Bayart (2000, 58) evokes the dialectic of "denunciation and compromise" as two sides of the same coin: political economic realism when Western strategic interests are in place—the United States and France in Mobutu's Zaire and France in Gabon, Côte d'Ivoire, Senegal, Togo, Cameroon, and so on—and democratic conditionality, including respect for human rights, when major economic and allied interests do not loom large. The ensuing debt peonage and aid dependency would add up to postpone development to the mythical calendes grecs, echoing Claude Ake's famous statement that Africa's problem is not so much that development has failed as that development was never on the public agenda.

Transposed to the independence context, has Amilcar Cabral's (quoted in Samatar and Samatar 1987, 669) statement that "the problem of the nature of the state created after independence is perhaps the secret of the failure of African independence" become a self-fulfilling prophecy?

THE "MADE IN AFRICA" STATE: TOWARD DECOLONIZATION?

Saddled with a big state that is as extroverted as it is inefficient, juridically independent Africa reached the proverbial cul-de-sac very quickly, no thanks to the modernization and diffusionist paradigm of politicoeconomic development of the 1950s and 1960s. Proponents of this "school" were concerned to underline the value-free and globalist perspective of modernization theory in diffusing, through the use of appropriate Western artifacts and institutions, development to the emergent "new states." The message driven home to Africa in particular was that what was good for the West and foreign capital was equally good for Africa; in other words, foreign interests were coterminous and coextensive with Africa's own interests. Moreover, Africa was counseled not to reinvent the wheel. This line of least resistance appeared somewhat attractive to Africa's leaders and rulers insofar as the onerous business of development was narrowly conceived in its economic sense. Catching up with the West by using Western-inspired instrumentalities—foreign investments and aid, the civil service and technical assistance/the French "coopérants" and so on—was about the only game in town in the West, the U.N. system, and Africa in the 1960s and 1970s, before "Afro-pessimism" and aid fatigue began to set in in the 1980s. The state was to drive the development process in each country.

Within this context, Nnoli (2000, 7) has underlined several factors that, historically and empirically, have accounted for the hegemonic role of the post-colonial state. One was the role of the state as the engine or *moteur* of economic development in order to act as a counterweight to foreign capital. Two, in the war against the tripartite evil of "poverty, ignorance, and disease," the state was perceived as the central command structure. Three, according to modernization theory, the state was needed to checkmate the perceived obstructionist role of tradition to development. Four, as a junior partner of capitalism, a strong state would render invaluable service to capitalism by helping it fight communism in Africa. Five, a strong state flows from the logic of this social institution as the most effective protector and purveyor of law and order and defender of the status quo. Nnoli (2000, 8) adds that the state's hegemony was further enhanced by the socialist demand "for state ownership of productive enterprises and its active intervention in the social welfare sector." However, as several events would later show, all of this was a tall order: By virtue of an insufficient capitalization of the African economy and society at colonialism, two seemingly contradictory logics and system philosophies were in place, a capitalist logic of formal rules of the game and a pre- or anti-capitalist system of relationships obeying the impulse of informal rules and regulations.

These two systems also correspond to what Crehan (1999, 149–150) refers to as a dualistic discourse of the state: The first is based on citizenship; to wit, on the notion of equality; the second is anchored on kinship and "primitive communalism," characterized by relations among unequal partners, gender insensitivity, and women unfriendliness. The two would necessarily clash with devastating effect, particularly for the legitimacy of the "modern, neocolonial, neocapitalist" state: Its legitimacy deficit increases in direct proportion to its inability to deliver basic values, goods, and services to the majority of the population, essentials that are virtually taken for granted in several other climes and climates. As Keller (1991, 140) observes, the state "tends to lack the reservoir of resources that are essential to enable it respond effectively to uncertainties during the processes of change and modernization." The result has been a resort to a precapitalist system of socioeconomic and political relations and practices that certainly are meaningful and intelligible to participants, but are often at variance with the norms and ethos of a "migrated" neocolonial state, within which context they have acquired a somewhat odious connotation as "patron-client" relationships, "politics of the belly," and "prebendalism," and these practices, no more than what Western scholars refer to as social capital in developed economies (Olukoshi 1998), are summarized as antidevelopmental. Yet an admixture of domestic bad governments and externally driven market reforms, often indifferent to national political, social, and sociological realities, have consolidated the precapitalist "mode of production and social relations" as perhaps the dominant paradigm of "development."

On face value, the big state and bloated governments Africa inherited from colonialism have remained the same. This can be true only in appearance, however. Indeed, if scholars in the 1960s were perturbed by the "authoritarian" tendencies of African governments, scholars in the 1980s and 1990s became all too aware of the actual administrative "softness" of the postcolonial state, civil or military (Amuwo 2001a, 2000b). On this, using military juntas as an example, Decalo (1986, 21) is very clear:

Their overdeveloped civil service, notwithstanding, many African states have very low extractive, regulative and administrative capabilities. Their ability to effect change, enforce policy and interact with the domestic and external environment is both limited and intermittent. The myth of the powerful state clashes with the reality of its actual limited ability to convert policy into action, resulting in a major gap between intention and fact. And the more ambitious the commitment to fundamental change (as in the Afro-Marxist state), the sharper the likely cleavage between radical rhetoric and the reality of military rule.

Even in democracies there is the phenomenon of states exhibiting a large formalism gap between precept and praxis. Since 1995, merely a year after South Africa's multiracial, multinational, and multiparty democracy was, rather understandably, heralded with much fanfare, that country, in contrast to huge expenditure on arms imports, has not been spending all the budgeted funds in the areas of human resources and infrastructural development, even though these areas beg for decisive and urgent action. For example, between 1994 and 1995 and 1997 and 1998, the Department of Social Welfare returned some 197.7 million rands (about $40 million by the exchange rate of the time) of unspent money to the state treasury. Perhaps more significant, about 1.4 billion rands of the land-reform budget remains unspent since 1995, even though only a token 5,000 land restitution applications—out of a staggering 87,000 received—have been passed. The alibi for this lacuna is that "several departments lack the capacity and the know-how to spend what they have." It is interesting to realize that a country such as South Africa, with enormous social problems, including severe inequalities in the distribution of resources made possible by many years of apartheid polices, can unashamedly speak of budget surpluses (Soggot 2001, 2). It is little wonder that the quality of life of the country's historically marginalized groups and communities continues to tumble.

Throughout the continent, states remain unable or unwilling to promote the policies that would enhance peaceful coexistence and sustainable development. In other words, states have failed to perform their traditional functions of maintaining the rule of law and providing society with essential public goods. As a consequence, social disintegration, economic decay, and political violence, including destructive mobilization by ethnic and other social cleavages, seem to have become endemic to the region. For example, by the beginning of the new century there were as many as 18 million refugees in the continent, by far the largest concentration of displaced people in the world. This figure includes more than 15 million internally displaced people, about 3.7 million of whom are Angolans, fleeing their home countries because of conflicts and similar occurrences, but who have not yet crossed the borders. Again, in the last decade or so average economic growth has been only 2 percent, as against a 2.5-percent average increase in the population, suggesting, therefore, that many an African state are in worse shape today than they were at independence, forty or so years ago. By the same token, the continent accounts for just 1 percent of world farm trade and world tourism. In addition, most of the continent's talented athletes, especially in soccer, leave for Europe as soon as they can, instead of playing for their national teams. We are equally confronted with the notion of the bankrupt state, as brought into sharp relief in August 2001 by the decision of the eleven Francophone African countries, up till then owners of Air Afrique, to hand over the running of the admittedly beleaguered carrier to Air France. The latter would now become the major shareholder, with over 50 percent holdings, while the African states would have no more than a third of the shares. Further, no one who watched Sorious Samura's documentary *Exodus from Africa* on CNN in August 2001, detailing how young, often well-educated Africans are fleeing poverty, war, unemployment, and misery at home, exposing themselves to untold dangers, hardship, and humiliation across the Mediterranean to cross to Spain, will ever remain the same again. Even then, only a handful succeed in voting for their motherland with their feet; the North African desert and the Mediterranean have become the graveyard of Africa's young poor. This phenomenon represents the tip of the iceberg in terms of what Bayart (2000, 235) refers to as "the forces of attraction and destruction" exercised by foreign capital in Africa, from the colonial period till date. Perhaps believing that the contemporary African state has few redeeming features capable of reversing the negative trend for good, Bayart (2000, 265) adds that "there is every reason to believe that the thirst for the West remains a substantial one and that there will be no lessening of the numbers of people who set off on the path of emigration." The issue, however, is not so much an insatiable desire to live in the West—as several hundreds of Nigerians residing in the United States told President Obasanjo on his first visit to that country shortly after his inauguration in May 1999—as it is the absence of a viable alternative at home. This explains the many political struggles and battles of popular social forces and civil society organizations in the last decade or so to decolonize the inherited state with a view to rendering it developmental.

The theoretical justification for state reforms—as against a wholesale privatization of state agencies and enterprises simply because they are state owned—can hardly be faulted. Blaming the economic stagnation and political decay of independent African nations on the "inexorable expansion of a state structure that was oversized even at independence," Diamond (1987, 595) argues that "it is difficult to see how African states can become more effective unless they become leaner and more efficient." He adds that "if there is to be any basis for self-sustaining growth and peaceful democratic politics, there must be a transition in the state's role from that of resource for a parasitic few to that of nurturant for a genuinely productive bourgeoisie—both *grande* and *petite*, agricultural and industrial—that will not be dependent on the state for its survival." The problem since the mid-1980s, when the fiscal crisis of African states became almost as serious and alarming as that of their homologues in Latin America, has been the nature of the monetarist, market economy-driven blueprints scripted by the World Bank the IMF, which tended, in general, to accord scant position to the state in the running of the economy while privileging foreign investments and capital over the development of a domestic saving and investment culture. Expressed differently and provocatively, if the colonial state was authoritarian, exercising immense despotic powers and little infrastructural power, the context of the "second independence" has not, four decades after, fundamentally changed. To all appearances, therefore, orthodox market reforms can only be carried out, more or less successfully, by authoritarian governments or, for that matter, by formal democracies using despotic means. As such reforms flounder and fail, the tendency toward personalization of power and informal politics is enhanced and with it pork-barrel social relations that market reforms were, at least in theory, designed to vitiate in the first instance. The more or less effective intervening variable and institution in much of Africa remains the civil society, notwithstanding its own internal problems and other limitations. The point bears repetition that if the postcolonial state has largely failed Africa's development drive, that is not enough reason to treat the state qua state as if it were no more than a footnote in development. Our emphasis is informed by the historic role of the state in somewhat efficiently and effectively driving and developing the economy in other parts of the global hamlet. Pereira

(1993, 31) has underscored the fact that while capitalist economies are essentially market oriented, they are not, by any means, only market coordinated. For him, "by policy, by some form of planning, every capitalist economy is a result of mixed market and state intervention." He also contends that "it is not enough to fight populism and to reduce the state. While fiscal discipline is an essential goal, as is a smaller state, state intervention is not intrinsically bad" (Pereira 1993, 30). Furthermore, notwithstanding the realization of some form of market liberalization in East and Southeast Asia, Pereira (1993, 33) argues that "the role of the state continues to be fundamental," concluding that while "these economies are outward-oriented," they are far from being "market-coordinated."

In a similar vein, since orthodox market reforms depend more on foreign investments and capital than national savings and investments, there is little in the script that encourages the African state and "state class" to empower the people materially and economically, or, for that matter, nurture financial muscles for themselves for investment purposes. Yet "citizens of new democracies expect them to grant social as well as political rights." Similarly, "demands for the satisfaction of "social citizenship"—a "kind of basic human equality associated with the concept of full membership of a community"—require that security and opportunity be shared by all. Social policies respond to these demands through the provision of health and education and through income maintenance" (Pereira, Maravall, and Przeworski 1993, 7). To do this, the latter argue—contrary to the orthodox paradigm—that reforms must be explicitly oriented toward a resumption of growth, protection of the welfare of those hardest hit by reforms, as well as making full use of representative institutions. By the same token, the three authors argue that market reforms can only be meaningful in developing economies transiting to democracy if they succeed in restoring the capacity of the state to mobilize savings as well as pursue development-oriented policies. Within this ambit, "state intervention in allocating resources and activities, judicious and carefully targeted, is a condition necessary to resume growth" (Pereira, Maravall, and Przeworski 1993, 7). What the foregoing suggests is that market reforms are too important to be left solely in the hands of technocrats and economists insofar as they are, primarily, a political action. Thus is the importance of the statement in November 1990 by the then general secretary of the OECD, J. C. Paye, that the transition to a market economy is not just the business of economists; rather, it is necessary "to evaluate with caution that which is politically and socially feasible" (quoted in Przeworski 1993, 186).

So, what is it about Africa that international financial institutions and donor nations find it difficult to accept or recognize the state as a major engine of economic growth and development? Perhaps a *piste of response* can be found in the argument that Africa is the only actually existing area of the globe where crass exploitation of nations and peoples can be done with impunity. It is also the only region whose state lacks the requisite autonomy and capacity to decisively intervene, plan, and implement policy, as some of the countries in question would certainly have loved to do. Adams (1997, 178) has made the important point that "the World Bank's single most destructive accomplishment has perhaps been to free Third World governments from the need to deal with their own people, thereby undermining the growth of democratic institutions and legitimate tax regimes throughout the Third World." Some, if not many, African heads of state and government, particularly the ones already "used" by power and, to all appearances, bereft of any new, redeeming ideas about how to run a complex, modern state, are not likely to gloat over or bemoan this incapacitation. This attitude would, nonetheless, not detract anything from the sinister nature of an economic thinking that criminalizes virtually everything state driven, while eulogizing the market. Yet as Goldsmith (2000, 1–20) has shown in terms of the three conventional measures of the size of government—share of public spending in GDP, size of public employment, and proportion of government ownership of business—the African state, in relation to its counterparts in, among others, Latin America and Caribbean, the Middle East, Asia and Pacific, is not in any sense sui generis. Indeed, for him, "Public sector employment in Africa did not reach the level in other regions" (Goldsmith 2000, 6). Similarly, on other scores—such as a generally poor business environment on the continent; a diverse population as a source of conflict—Goldsmith (2000, 15–17) indicates that there is hardly anything aberrant about Africa in relation to the rest of the developing world.

However, none of the foregoing is factored in when Africa's new democracies are put under pressure to choose between the state and the market. This is a false problem, for the choice, within the neoliberal economic paradigm, is little more than the Keynesian complex compromise between a strong market and a strong state; that is, the whole notion of "embedded liberalism." The issue here is that state institutions have to engage in activities from which the larger society will derive benefits, meaning that private, group, and class interests would have to be held in abeyance, in certain fundamental respects, for social interests to prevail. Furthermore, in order for growth to resume via liberalization/stabilization, key and focused state investments must take the lead and show the way for the private sector to follow (Pereira, Maravall, and Przeworski 1993, 215). After all, the essence of democracy or, simply, good government is to "discipline how states behave towards their people" (Goldsmith 2000, 9). Within this context, new democracies are expected to take fairly autonomous decisions that are informed more by the logic of the historic role of the state to citizens than by the dictates and demands of an external environment whose rationality and finality are often suspect. Without necessarily resorting to undue economic populism, new democracies are called upon, on account of the sweeping immiseration of the people, to balance between macroeconomic reforms and social responsibility. In countries like Ghana and Nigeria, whose citizens had borne the brunt, roughly from the mid-1980s till the end of the 1990s, of a largely skewed social distribution of the costs and benefits of economic reform pains, another round of such measures would require social negotiation and consensus. No matter how onerous and time-consuming such a process often appears to be, it is to be preferred to top-down, unnegotiated reforms that had failed in the past (Pereira 1993, 62). For Africa's new democracies to be socially meaningful and relevant to individual lives, a regime of social rights has to be more visible and prominent on the ledger book than another round of market reforms that are not the result of broad-based consultations and dialogue with labor and other organized social forces. A delicate balance has to be struck between the market and the state; that is, between, on the one hand, economic efficiency and long-term growth and, on the other, citizens' immediate political and social needs, particularly education, health, housing, transport, and so on. As a pertinent analyst puts it, "once democracies are reestablished after a period of dictatorial rule, new problems emerge: the efficiency of the new political system and not just its legitimacy, becomes the main issue—that is, the capacity of the democracy to solve problems and fulfil expectations" (Maravall 1993, 78). By gradually being transparent and accountable to the people in ways that dictatorships of the past were not, elected leaders will gradually change state–society relations and, in the process, facilitate the repair of the state as well as shore up its acceptance rating among the populace. According to Maravall (1993), "new democracies usually inherit states that are too interventionist in the economy and too weak in social policies," thus necessitating that "the state . . . [be] transformed until it becomes as small as possible and as large as necessary."

To be sure, new democracies do not proffer, nor are they capable of furnishing, quick fixes to the major problematic issues of their societies; on the contrary, as comparative experiences have shown in Latin America, Southern Europe and Eastern Europe (Pereira, Maravall, and Przeworski 1993), things may have to go from bad to worse before they get better. In this respect, hedged in between the constraints and opportunities that market reforms and globalization offer, and often subject more to constraints than to autonomous choices, new democracies in Africa may yet be at their most formative stages, with all the possible consequences for a vibrant and more equal relationship between the state and the civil society. In consequence, Tripp (2000, 211–212) is right to caution Africanists that the time for the use of unflattering epithets such as "democratic reversal" has not yet come. "In much of Africa," she writes, "the main problem is not that democratic rights have deteriorated qualitatively after the holding of multiparty elections, but rather that the process has not moved beyond the holding of elections." She also bemoans the result of such a process: "The patterns of neo-patrimonial rule, personal rule and state-based clientelism remain intact and are simply manifesting themselves in a multiparty context." This view is echoed by Goldsmith (2000, 10) for whom much of political reform on the continent amounts to a facade "with little grassroots involvement," thus permitting "privileged groups [to] continue to exert undue power" while the mass of the people "remain largely disenfranchised." He was quick to add, however, that "the same can be said about Third World democracies generally." Ndegwa (2001, 8) also asserts that new institutions of democratic form in Africa, including elections and political parties, have turned into "tools of furthering patronage." Tripp (2000) believes, nonetheless, that the groundswell for change is on in Africa and is to be located in nonstate actors and agencies. For her, therefore, "what has changed is the extent to which social organizations and institutions have begun to assert their autonomy from party and state control." It is to this phenomenon that we now turn.

STATE–CIVIL SOCIETY RELATIONS IN AFRICA AND THE CHALLENGE OF STATE REPAIR AND DEMOCRATIC DEVELOPMENT

In the everrecurring optimism-pessimism continuum on African politics, the tendency in much of contemporary literature is to be excessively pessimistic about, and harsh on, the state while being extremely optimistic, if not outrightly romantic, about the possibility that civil society may well be the state's nemesis in the inexorable drive toward a democratic Africa. This dichotomy is understandable insofar as the postcolonial state has virtually exhausted its admittedly limited redemptive ability. The major problem of that state has been attributed by some scholars to a lack of a people-friendly social basis in the society it was meant to propel toward all-round development. The state is thus not only alien in the eyes of the people, it is an object of severe contestation by other societal institutions that seek, sometimes by violence and civil conflict, as many examples in contemporary Africa copiously demonstrate, to wrench from the state whatever little legitimacy it still possesses. In this respect, Olowu (1999, 21) argues that "the disconnection between the state and society is one of the fundamental causes of the crisis of the African state and its civil service systems." For Goldsmith (2000, 17), the greatest undoing of the state is that its premature birth in the 1960s has left a largely negative imprint on it; namely, its "questionable right to rule in the eyes of many of its supposed citizens." He adds that "low levels of legitimacy in turn increase the cost of governing. Any authority that is uncertain of its acceptance and support finds it especially hard to govern in a cost-effective way. Extra resources have to be expended to attain collective goals." It is also suggested that except the actually existing social basis of the state withers away through genuine democratization à la civil society activities, neither the people's redemption nor societal renovation will ensue (Bathily 2000, 51).

Africa's civil society has come a long way; not only have they often been assailed by the state and its ranks infiltrated by security operatives of various hues, they have also been victims of numerous nonclass cleavages and divisions present in the wider society (Othman and Williams 1999, 61). There are also diverse experiences in relation to how some NGOs, including women's (including "state feminism"), ethnic, and self-help organizations, undermine, rather than promote, democracy (Aubrey 2001, 104; Orvis 2001, 30–31). Whatever their structural and conjectural dilemmas, the role of the civil society in the extension of the frontiers of people's rights and socioeconomic freedom in the last fifteen years or so can hardly be overemphasized. Conceptualized in a rather general sense, following Orvis (2001, 33), Africa's civil society can be regarded as "an arena in which contending political norms develop and evolve, with crucial implications for the long-term prospects for democracy." It is as a system of ideas and philosophy that canvasses and militates for a new paradigm of governance that the civil society is extremely invaluable. It is also at this level that it serves as a counterhegemony to the state, in the sense that Foucault uses the term; namely, that wherever there is power, there is, logically, a counterpower (see Amuwo 1997). Tripp (2000, 191) has made the important point that "one of the key challenges to the status quo has come from organizations that do not have a stake in the perpetuation of politics as usual and whose very existence is contingent on more thorough-going reforms." The inference, to be sure, is that beneficiaries of the status quo, both within and outside the state, are likely to fight back. The state is likely to use the same weapon it is accustomed to; namely, depoliticization woven around an elite model of transition (Gibson 2001, 65). Bayart (2000, 244) argues that the attempt to preserve the state's hegemony vis-à-vis the civil society is done "by depoliticizing the eminently political question of social inequality and making it subject to bureaucratic procedures and by provoking the multilateralization of the passive revolution which is the true force forming the state in Africa today." Gibson (2001, 68, 70, 72) has interrogated this issue at some length, with specific reference to post-apartheid South Africa.

Gibson (2001) reasons that while the hegemonic Western state paradigm was voluntarily accepted by much of Africa during the continent's decade of independence between 1960 and 1970, the historical juncture of the 1990s was one of force and dictation, but both strategies for the same purpose of state ascendancy and societal disempowerment. Thus, for him, the post-1994 South African state is a function of an ideological battle, promotive of neoliberal globalization while stifling contending worldviews. In view of this essentially technicist approach to social issues, Gibson (2001, 68) contends that "continued optimism about the benefits of [the] state's institutional capacity building is misplaced." In contradistinction to Saul (1999, 172), who evokes the notion of "an activated civil society" consisting of a "progressive range of actors" playing "assertive politics" alongside the African National Congress, as a "mass democratic movement"—he claims the same phenomenon held in Namibia—Gibson talks about the checkmating of all forms of radicalism, with consequent little elbow room for popular social forces.

Chief among the latter was the ANC itself: Its transformation from an apparently radical opposition into a probusiness group and an advocate of fiscal conservatism and free market capitalism has presaged the future. The net effect has been that the Mbeki presidency (1999 till date) represents, for Gibson (2001, 68), "the foregrounding of business and technocratic interests in the ANC who champion technocracy as an answer to the problem of national development" as well as "the victory of technology over movement politics, that is, it represents the depoliticization of politics." This type of interrogation resonates in other parts of the continent. In the emergent democratic period since the turn of the last decade, "elite pacting" has become the name of the game. In postmilitary Nigeria since 1999, sundry politicians and political organizations that had served under and benefited from the Babangida and Abacha juntas (1985–1998) are in power at virtually all levels of government. In South Africa, the tripartite alliance—the ANC, the Confederation of South African Trade Unions and the South African Communist Party—conveniently sidelined the Mass Democratic Movement, progenitor of the United Democratic Front. In other parts of the continent where the idea of a Sovereign National Conference caught on early, why was that profound expression of democracy short-lived? Why was it that after the triumph of Benin Republic's *forces vives* in November and December 1990 there was no replication in other parts of Francophone Africa? Were France and her local surrogates at work to scuttle the diffusion of the democratic gains of that model to other parts of French-speaking Africa? Where, today, are the voices of the men and women who, early in the day, fought hard for the deconstruction of authoritarianism and the construction of democracy? From the South African democratization narrative, Gibson (2001, 72) proffers a response. While from the late 1980s to 1994 there were expressions of direct democracy in the country, however flawed and limited such expressions were, they were only celebrated, but "not translated into a radical rethinking of liberation theory that mapped out paradigms of social and ethical practices for a post-apartheid society." Subsequently, "this ideological pitfall was exploited by the ANC which was able to capture these narratives and celebrate the idea of "people's power" while remaining the self-appointed future negotiators." The aftermath is that the hegemony of the ANC/SACP has marginalized other discourses that could have snowballed into a veritable oppositional culture, with all its benefits for a viable democracy and a responsible state (Gibson 2001, 76, 78). A major problem with South Africa's nascent democracy—which countries such as Nigeria seem to have avoided—is that an otherwise powerful and politically active trade union movement is in government, and thus, at least conceptually, placing itself outside the civil society. Events in August 2001—the fairly robust, and perhaps unexpected, strike action by COSATU and its affiliates—show, however, that this does not mean a fatal or permanent incapacitation of the movement.

It is within these "coordinating complex activities," to paraphrase Gramsci (1994)—that Africa's civil society has had to wage its many struggles against existing ramparts of despotic rule. It would appear that as statism deepened its stranglehold, civil society organizations tended to make their voices heard and to pursue what were really old battles against the state's arbitrariness and excesses, but which became internationalized only because of the formal end of the Cold War. On this vexed issue, Bayart (2000, 224) is forthcoming: "Contrary to a widely held opinion, the wave of prodemocracy agitation of 1989–91 was caused less by the fall of the Berlin Wall or the speech of François Mitterand at the Franco-African Summit at La Baule in June 1990 or by pressure from aid donors, than by the resurgence of old expectations and social movements of long standing, able to assert themselves once more as soon as international organizations had moderated their support for authoritarian regimes." He would quickly add, as if to underline the context of state–society antinomy, that "this venting of popular feeling was rapidly countered by the strategies taken by incumbent power-holders intent on restoring their authoritarian regimes with an artful combination of dexterity and brutality" (Bayart 2000, 224).

The verdict on the success of the civil society in engaging the state while furnishing initial building blocks for its repair is understandably mixed. Orvis (2001, 30–31) argues, using Nigeria and Kenya as examples, that civil society organizations are torn between liberal democratic norms and the moral ethnic norms of reciprocal obligation such that, while some (for example, Nigeria's hometown associations) by "articulating legitimately the demands of many members of ethnic groups" furnish a forum for the pursuit of political accountability and participation, others (the Kenyan development project association, the harambees, is evoked here) are hardly democratic to the extent that they are sometimes led by state elites, even as they also exhibit "ambiguous autonomy as state leaders try to use them to co-opt a local group or undermine locally popular opposition." As a direct reaction to this position, Aubrey (2001, 104) contends that a renegotiated social contract between the state and society is gradually evolving from the many democratic transitions Africa is experiencing.

To be sure, the extensive damage inflicted by military and monoparty authoritarianism in the past is such as to make dividends of democracy slow in coming. The democratic (re)construction of any society is necessarily a political project of the long haul, though citizens and analysts alike are entitled to interrogate whether Africa's new democracies appear to be moving in the right direction. A simple criterion is whether a democratically elected government is using the same or similar authoritarian tactics of the past in relation to labor, the media, university teachers and students, women, professional bodies, rural or peasant farmers, and so on. After all, it is not enough to say that since democracy is a long-term project its gains will come sooner or later, without doing anything to put pressure on elected governments to govern according to the constitution. This is where, both in the past and currently in several countries in Africa, civil society organizations are doing a fairly good job. People who know it feel it: Those who were or are at the barricades for the validation of one electoral consultation or the other; those whose spouses, breadwinners, relatives and friends were released from illegal detentions on account of the agitations of human rights, prodemocracy, and libertarian groups, in short, all those who bore the brunt of oppositional politics and the beneficiaries of such activities, are well aware of the invaluable contribution of the civil society to the construction of a new citizenship and a new state on the continent.

Afolayan (1999, 76ff) has shown, on the Nigerian typology, that except for the "reawakening of the civil society," it would have been difficult, if not wholly impossible, to have witnessed the demise of formal militarism. He traced the humble beginnings of the reawakening to the formation in 1981 of the Committee of Concerned Citizens, with a self-assigned objective to "monitor and consider issues connected with the development of democratic tradition in the country." The Civil Liberties Organization (CLO), in October 1987, the Constitutional Research Project (CRP) in February 1990, and the Campaign for Democracy (CD), an umbrella organization for no fewer than forty prodemocracy groups, in May 1992, among several hundreds, would follow. What these organizations had in common under the military was to fight corruption and authoritarian rule (Afolayan 1999, 78). At a time when the traditionally radical Nigerian Labor Congress (NLC) had become little more than an appendage of the militarist state, these new organizations and their leading advocates—lawyers Fawehinmi, Falana, Agbakoba, and Nwankwo; Beko Ransome-Kuti, a medical doctor and chair of the CD; as well as a new set of antiestablishment, independent press, such as *Tell* and *The News*—were in the forefront of the people's political struggles. Their sacrifice consisted of a serial detention experience, brutalization and harassment of family members, seizure of "offensive" publications with all the financial losses involved, and vandalization of office premises, but the reward was the collapse of the military government and the opening of opportunities for electoral democracy in 1999. According to Afolayan (1999, 78), "that the campaign to remove Babangida was sustained and ultimately succeeded, even after the political class had virtually capitulated, was principally due to the resilience and courage displayed by these groups and their allies in the media."

The ensuing Abacha era (November 17, 1993 to June 8, 1998) would be worse for both democratic values and their major defenders (Amuwo 2001a, 2001b), but the significance and vitality of the civil society organizations in question were underscored by the junta's worry about how to rule the country by traditional military fiat. As David Mark, a former military governor under Babangida and one of the coup planners before he was played out testified, "The CD and CLO had gained so much popularity that it would be difficult for the military to rule without bloodshed" (Afolayan 1999, 89). The resilience of these organizations and the recrudescence of similar groups, particularly socioeconomic and environmental, in the northern and southeastern parts of the country in the last couple of years, are likely to further extend the frontiers of democracy as well as gradually render the state more accountable, responsive, and responsible to Nigerians under a democracy. The NLC has recovered its voice and combativeness—it worsted the Obasanjo government in the face-off in 2000 over a large increase in fuel prices, which the government was eventually forced to lower—and has been seen by many Nigerians as an effective moderating voice on the government's seeming inexorable drive toward unabashed market reforms. The labor movement also successfully negotiated higher wages for the country's public-sector workers in 2000, making Nigeria the country, since 2000, with the highest average income on the continent. This development may gradually lead to a savings and investment culture, a phenomenon that has been a shrinking province since the military years in power. It may also contribute to progressively vitiate the negativity of patron-client networks.

CONCLUSION

There is little doubt that since juridical independence in the 1960s and, much more so, the beginning of the second wave of independence in the 1990s, a veritable political struggle has been waged at the level of legitimacy of terms, concepts, and ideologies, principally between the state and the market. The tendency of the West and foreign capital is to formulate the difference between the two models of economic development and social democracy in an ironcast manner, as a question of "either or." It is getting increasingly difficult to understand this policy stance of the great powers and the relevant international financial institutions beyond the logic and finality of multinational capitalism; that is, globalization. This is because no matter how hard African countries try to implement orthodox economic reforms, they often flounder and fail. Those, such as Ghana and Uganda, that recorded some initial successes in reducing balance of payments deficits tend to backslide and fall, notwithstanding generous World Bank and IMF loans. For the others, failure is an ever-recurring social decimal. The point to underline here is that orthodox market reforms simply do not get along with the postcolonial state that has continually been bereft of the sovereign right to take key macroeconomic and social decisions that are in tune with the reality of their populations. A major decision that looms large on the horizon, as already remarked, is the construction of a "social citizenship." For example, Hungary refused to commence the liberalization stage of her market reforms until she was able to put market institutions and a social welfare system in place (Pereira, Maravall, and Przeworski 1993, 205). What this points to is that neither the state nor the market, working separately and at cross-purposes, will deliver political democracy and socioeconomic redemption to Africa, and neither of the two has done so for any part of the world. According to Pereira (1993, 33), "if statism is inefficient and socialism infeasible, capitalism is irrational. Markets do not function out of nothing. They are institutions that depend on other institutions, particularly on a strong state and a respected government." Pereira, Maravall, and Przeworski (1993, p. 199) conclude their comparative study of Latin America, and Southern and Eastern Europe as follows: "In recent years whenever governments have pursued expansionist economic programs, the result has been inflation, a fiscal crisis and a balance-of-payments crisis. Whenever democratic governments followed neoliberal tenets, the outcome has been stagnation, increased poverty, political discontent and the debilitation of democracy."

What then is to be done? The state has to be made responsible and accountable to the people in order to finally decolonize it and give it a socially rooted base in indigenous communities, both rural and urban. As Shaw (1993, 108) argues, "disillusionment with market forces may yet come to re-legitimize the place of the state, especially if it is simultaneously made more responsive and accountable to democratic expressions and organizations." This is, again, a long-term political enterprise that civil society organizations do not appear capable of realizing alone, however popular they are otherwise. "Mass support in the absence of a strong political organization and an appropriate political strategy" writes Nzongola-Ntalaja (1999, 313) from his study of democratic transition in Mobutu's Zaire, "is not enough for effective political change." Seeking to win political power in order to concretize its vision of state–society relations, however tempting, is not a way forward for civil society organizations. Not only would they lose their status as key nonstate actors and as a more or less effective watchdog on the state and government officials; prodemocracy and human rights groups are not likely to find the transmutation to power easy, not to talk of highly probable opposition from both domestic and international forces that are not in favor of change. A more rewarding scenario is for these groups to forge a strategic alliance with labor and other people-oriented organizations, as well as with like-minded elected representatives of the people in the National Assembly with a view to protecting and enhancing democratic gains. This broad-based alliance will have to get the state, through hard-nosed negotiation and bargaining, to shelve, as the case may be, its proposed or ongoing wholesale orthodox market reforms, in particular privatization of public enterprises—perhaps the most contentious and ill-advised policy prescription—until a fairly judicious balance has been struck between state–societal priorities and market principles. The demarche of COSATU in South Africa—as well as the NLC in Nigeria—is particularly appropriate here. The former has argued that it makes little sense to privatize those state assets that aid government to deliver social services, such as electricity, public transport, and health. In other areas, the labor federation insists that assets should not only be treated case by case, each on its merit, but also that final decisions should be negotiated by all stakeholders. In nonessential areas, COSATU not only supports privatization, but its affiliates have reportedly made bids for privatized state assets (see editorial "Don't blame Cosatu for the strike," *Sunday Times* [Johannesburg], August 2001, 26: 20).

"Communitization" or "municipalization," not privatization, of the strategic, commanding heights and human resource development sectors of the economy should be the name of the game. A likely immediate consequence will be the halting of the people's exit from the state in the multifarious ways of the past (Osaghae 1999, 83–98) and a simultaneous shoring up of the state's acceptance in the eyes of the people. As Akinola (1999 361–363) has argued, "the state has to be mended, augmented, relegitimized and renewed periodically," insofar as "institution-building is an endless process." For him, "state-mending and social-institutional change generally might be energized more by autonomous local-level action than by official prerogatives." The example of tiny Benin Republic appears instructive in this respect (Amuwo, 2003). Thereafter, it may prove easier to confront the onerous business of democratic development as well as those foreign interests that are antithetical to the continent's development.

Would state and governmental officials accept this turn of events? The logic of democracy and popular political struggle would in all probability leave them with no alternative, though not without a fight. Hopefully, enlightened self-interest would oblige them to prefer this strategy of democratization, state repair, and development to the existing modus operandi by which "African governments repeatedly point out to foreigners that they have implemented all the policies would-be investors are said to want, but still don't get the investment they need" (Friedman 2001, 18). Similarly, they—and their people—by conspiring "to defend themselves . . . on how to survive in the world" in light of the G8 regular meetings "to conspire on how to run the world," to borrow a happy phrase from President Museveni (2001) of Uganda, would begin to get some respect, not undue sympathy, from the international community. By so doing, the African state will be taken seriously by a capitalist West that, for now, "certainly gives insufficient attention to a part of the world whose difficulties concern them in the first instance" (Bayart 2000, 267).

REFERENCES

Adams, P. 1997. The World Bank's finances: An international debt crisis. In *Globalization and the South*, edited by C. Thomas and P. Wilkin. New York: St. Martin's Press.

Afolayan, F. 1999. Civil society, popular culture and the crisis of democratic transition in Nigeria. In *African democracy in the era of globalization*, edited by J. Hyslop. Johannesburg: Witwatersrand University Press.

Ake, C. 1981. *A political economy of Africa*. Lagos: Longman.

Ake, C. 2000. The state in contemporary Africa. In *Government and politics in* Africa: A reader, edited by O. Nnoli. Harare, Zimbabwe: AAPS Books.

Akinola, O. A. 1999. Review of *Nigeria: Renewal from the roots? The struggle for democratic development in Nigeria*, edited by A. Adedeji and O. Otite, *Journal of Modern African Studies* 37 (2): 361–363.

Amuwo, 'K. 1997. Prospects for sustainable democracy and accountability in Afijio, Oyo State. In *Nigeria: Renewal of roots? The struggle for democratic development in Nigeria*, edited by A. Adedeji and O. Otite. London: Zed Books.

Amuwo, 'K. 1997–1998. Critical perspectives on the structure, nature and role of the public bureaucracy in Nigeria. *Quarterly Journal of Administration* 24 (1/2): 180–190.

Amuwo, 'K. 2001a. The military factor in Nigerian politics. *Strategic Review for Southern Africa* 23 (1): 22–42.

Amuwo, 'K. 2001b. Transition to democratic regression. In *The military and the struggle for democracy in Nigeria: The Abacha years, 1992–1998*, edited by D. Bach, 'K. Amuwo, and Y. Lebeau. Ibadan: African Book Builders and IFRA.

Amuwo, 'K. 2003. The state and the politics of consolidation of democracy in Benin, 1990–1999. In *Political liberalization and democratization in Africa: Lessons from country experiences*, edited by J. O. Ihonvbere and J. M. Mbaku. Westport, CT: Praeger.

Aubrey, L. 2001. Gender, development and democratization in Africa. *Journal of Asian and African Studies* 36 (1): 87–111.

Bathily, A. 2000. The West African state in historical perspective. In *Government and politics in Africa: A reader*, edited by O. Nnoli. Harare, Zimbabwe: AAPS Books.

Bayart, J.-F. 2000. Africa in the world: A history of extraversion. *African Affairs* 99 (395): 217–267.

Clapham, C. 1985. *Third World politics: An introduction*. London: Croomhelm.

Crehan, K. 1999. The rules of the game: The political location of women in North-Western Zambia. *In African democracy in the era of globalization*, edited by J. Hyslop. Johannesburg: Witwatersrand University Press.

Decalo, S. 1986. African studies and military coups in Africa. *Journal of Contemporary African Studies* 5 (1/2): 3–25.

Diamond, L. 1987. Class formation in the swollen African state. *Journal of Modern African Studies* 25 (4): 567–596.

Forrest, T. 1986. The political economy of civil rule and the economic crisis in Nigeria, 1979–1984. *Review of African Political Economy* 36: 4–26.

Friedman, S. 2001. There is reason to be skeptical. *Mail and Guardian* (Johannesburg), August 3–9: 18.

Gibson, N. 2001. Transition from apartheid. *Journal of Asian and African Studies* 36 (1): 65–85.

Goldsmith, A. A. 2000. Sizing up the African state. *Journal of Modern African Studies* 38 (1): 1–20.

Jeffries, R. 1998. The Ghanaian elections of 1996: Toward the consolidation of democracy. *African Affairs* 97 (387): 189–208.

Gramsci, A. 1994. *Letters from prison*, vol. 2. New York: Columbia University Press.

Keller, E. J. 1991. The state in contemporary Africa: A critical assessment of theory and practice. In *Comparative political dynamics: Global research perspectives*. New York: HarperCollins.

Maravall, J. M. 1993. Politics and policy: Economic reforms in southern Europe. In *Economic reforms in new democracies: A socio-democratic approach*, edited by L.C.B. Pereira, J. M. Maravall, and A. Przeworski. Cambridge: Cambridge University Press.

Mistry, P. S. 2000. Africa's record of regional cooperation and integration. *African Affairs* 99 (397): 553–573.

Museveni, Y. 2001. Museveni calls for access to EU, Japanese markets. Retrieved from http://allafrica.com/stories/2000108210364.html, November 2001.

Ndegwa, S. N. 2001. A decade of democracy in Africa. *Journal of Asian and African Studies* 36 (1): 1–16.

Nnoli, O. 2000. Introduction. In *Government and politics in Africa: A reader*, edited by O. Nnoli. Harare, Zimbabwe: AAPS Books.

Nzongola-Ntalaja, G. 1999. The democratic movement in Congo-Kinshasha, 1956–1994. In *African democracy in the era of globalization*, edited by J. Hyslop. Johannesburg: Witwatersrand University Press.

Olowu, B. 1999. Redesigning African civil service reforms. *Journal of Modern African Studies* 38 (1): 1–23.

Olukoshi, A. O. 1998. Economic crisis, multipartyism, and opposition politics in contemporary Africa. In *The politics of opposition in contemporary Africa*, edited by A. O. Olukoshi. Uppsala: Nordiska Africaninstitutet.

Orvis, S. 2001. Civil society in Africa or African civil society? *Journal of Asian and African Studies* 36 (1): 17–38.

Osaghae, E. E. 1999. Exiting from the state in Nigeria. *African Journal of Political Science* 4 (1): 83–98.

Othman, S., and G. Williams. 1999. Politics, power and democracy in Nigeria. In *African democracy in the era of globalization*, edited J. Hyslop. Johannesburg: Witwatersrand University Press.

Pereira, L.C.B. 1993. Economic reforms and economic growth: Efficiency and politics in Latin America. In *Economic reforms in new democracies: A socio-democratic approach*, edited by L.C.B. Pereira, J. M. Maravall, and A. Przeworski. Cambridge: Cambridge University Press.

Pereira, L.C.B., J. M. Maravall, and A. Przeworski, eds. 1993. *Economic reforms in new democracies: A socio-democratic approach*. Cambridge: Cambridge University Press.

Przeworski, A. 1993. Economic reforms, public opinion, and political institutions: Poland in the Eastern European perspective. In *Economic reforms in new democracies: A socio-democratic approach*, edited by L.C.B. Pereira, J. M. Maravall, and A. Przeworski. Cambridge: Cambridge University Press.

Samatar, A., and A. I. Samatar. 1987. The material roots of the suspended African state: Arguments from Somalia. *Journal of Modern African Studies* 25 (4); 669–690.

Saul, J. 1999. Liberation without democracy? Rethinking the experiences of Southern African liberation movements. In *African democracy in the era of globalization*, edited by J. Hyslop. Johannesburg: Witwatersrand University Press.

Shaw, T. A. 1993. *Reformism and revisionism in Africa's political economy in the 1990s: The dialectics of adjustment*. New York: St. Martin's Press.

Soggot, M. 2001. Budget surplus in South Africa's reach. *Mail and Guardian* (Johannesburg), August 17–23: 2.

Tripp, A. M. 2000. Political reform in Tanzania: The struggle for association autonomy. *Comparative Politics* 32 (2): 191–224.

14

Ethnicity, Agonism of Difference, and National Imagining in Postcolonial Africa

NANTANG JUA

CONFRONTING THE CHALLENGE OF ETHNICITY

"Every state a nation, every nation a state." Though seemingly an innocent slogan, it has been the prevailing ethos for over two centuries and its power is demonstrated by the fact that it has provided a rationale for ethnofascism, genocides, and politicides. Conflicts engendered by this ethos have been more pronounced in Africa, where, it has been claimed, independence left states looking for nations (Appiah 1992, 162). Resolution to this problem has so far been elusive because of the multiethnic character of most of these states. Since one man's nation easily becomes another's prison (Appadurai 1990, 295), fostering a national imagining has been problematical and elusive. Historical evidence has, therefore, not borne out independence's normative justification as a precursor for development. Rent by, inter alia, war, the best-case scenario in Africa is to celebrate stagnation. One of its disturbing implications on state efficacy is the "maximax problematique" where the state is left only with minimum resources, construed here to include not only financial but also moral, social, and symbolic resources to satisfy maximum needs. In this context, Anthony Trollope's prophecy that "the discontinuance of a sin [of colonialism] is the commencement of a struggle" (cited in Horowitz 1985, 4) seems to take on a renewed relevance.

Solutions, some of them quick fixes, have been proffered. These have included returning to the original position; that is, the recolonization of Africa, a proposal with which listeners of the BBC's African programs, such as letters written to Focus on Africa, are familiar. Innocuous as this suggestion may seem, I doubt that metropolitan countries would want to be foisted with the "white man's burden" again. Besides, Africa's ruling class would be unreceptive to it, construing it as a metaphor for its managerial incapacity. Thus, the ruling class would cling stubbornly to the twin concepts of political sovereignty and territorial integrity, even in failed or collapsed states. Granting this, the challenge is to convert these states into vibrant ones. Attainment of this goal requires policies that would promote a successful national imagining. Only an inclusionary politics can produce the synergy needed to move them forward.[1]

Contradictory views persist on the most cost-effective method that can be used to this end. An eminent statesman such as Julius Nyerere depicted ethnic groups as mortal enemies of the postcolonial state. Shared by most other heads of state in Africa, this collective perception saw the relationship between ethnic groups and states in terms of an exclusive disjuncture. Samora Machel (in Mamdani 1996, 135) captures this aptly when he argued that for the state to live the tribe must die. Accepting the first part of the slogan that "every state a nation," African leaders were allergic to the thought of "every nation a state." Thus, not even the death of the tribe ("a socio-psychological anchor") that would have caused the African to suffer from what Balzac referred to as "moral aloneness" was seen as a prohibitive price to pay.[2] Opting for the death of the tribe through the use of force would not be an African specificity, for Ernest Renan (1990) notes that "historical enquiry brings to light deeds of violence which took place at the origins of all political formations, even those whose consequences have been altogether beneficial. Unity is always effected by means of brutality" (Bhabha 1990, 11).[3] Alternatively, displacement of ethnic groups can serve as an avoidance strategy. The many manifestations of this solution have included the transfer of urban enclaves (South Africa's Group Areas Act), programs to shift rural populations (Tigrayans in Ethiopia 1984–1985), local regrouping of ethnic peoples (colonial Algeria), assisted emigration (Falasha Jews from Ethiopia), and disguised or undisguised deportations or expulsions (Asians from Uganda; blacks from Mauritania in 1989) (Rothchild 1989, 21).

Dissenting voices arguing against the foregoing policy options could also be heard. Celebrating the tribe, Nnamdi Azikiwe, the first president of the Republic of Nigeria, noted that "it takes individuals to form a community; it takes communities to form a tribe; it takes tribes to form a nation" (cited in Tamarkin 1996, 379). This plea, supported by many other politicians, sought to promote the use of the tribe as a matrix for a politics of national imagining. Since then, the decision makers who belong to this lineage have been comforted by the normative justifications provided by renowned Africans and Africanist scholars. Though endorsing the use of local languages in literature, Ngugi wa Thiongo (1994, 14–15) observes that "culture embodies those moral, ethical and aesthetical values, the set of spiritual eyeglasses, through which [a people] come to view themselves and their place in the universe" (also see Achebe 1990, 127). These values or cultural funds are crucial in constituting a political–moral space, sustained by a political–moral community. The problem, he points out, is how to increase the spread of this space to cover the national territory (Tamarkin 1996, 366).

Ethnicity should constitute a building block of the postcolonial state. It should, therefore, be more than a collateral benefit for national imagining. Since Ranger's (1992) thesis that ethnicity was invented by colonialism is now dogma, most scholarly analysis today finds it relevant to focus on the historically determined contradictions spawned by this invention. Some have argued that the sedimentation process or imagining accounts for most of the problems confronting African postcolonial states (Chabal and Daloz 1999, 57). Proposals for their resolution have included, inter alia, the modification of custom, a prominent feature of this sociopsychological anchor (Mamdani 1996, 297). Similarly, if ethnicity is a factor in the instrumentalization of disorder, as Chabal and Daloz (1999) suggest, then advocates of rationalism may see this as a cause to factor it out. Acceptance of this position, synonymous to that of Machel, would be tantamount to throwing out the baby with the bathwater. It would be to deny the relevance of the positive dialectic theory to Africa.[4] Furthermore, the need to exorcise ethnicity overlooks the fact that "a society can begin to move forward as it is, in spite of what is and because of what it is" (Hirschmann 1963, 3). It is against this backdrop that Lonsdale (1989, 23) has called for the writing of a history of African political thought in which ethnic particularity would be transcended by universal humanity. This position has an historical lineage, for the argument against detribalization had been spurned even in the colonial period. Without making any reference to the rejection of the unilinear concept of development in which it is grounded, William Watson argued that it implied "that Africans must choose between two systems of social relations and values. . . . But a man can participate in two different spheres of social relations . . . the spheres exist conjointly" (cited in Moore 1993, 15). Because of this privilege, Africans could benefit from the synergism needed to move it forward.

Arguments about the need to get ethnicity out of the process of state construction suffer from a problem particular to multiculturalist discourse, which constructs large groupings in which people are invariably different and are often strangers to each other on the model of small-scale familial or communal groupings (Calhoun 1997, 207). Granted, this approach, which portrays people as accepting a single label over their identities and identities as relatively settled, provides scholarship with requisite stereotypes for neatness. But in real life, it has been argued, one's life is more than any official definition of identity can express. That is, though one is enabled by his identity, it neither exhausts nor completely captures him (Connolly 1991, 120). Since one's identity is always in gestation, celebrating its homecoming would be premature. Historically, social anthropology's tendency to privilege social and external knowledge over the self or internal knowledge in its analysis of individual identity has been prejudicial to this position (Cohen 1992, 222). Identities are never fixed because, being relational, they are contingent on the exterior, ipso facto making the interior appear as something always contingent (Mouffe 1997, 403).

Adoption of social anthropology's position has led to the celebration of communal self-regarding frames used to define the self. This overlooks the fact that colonialism, which brought about a rupture in space, also introduced a new consciousness in the African and by that very fact his hybridization. That is, his embedding in Western culture and value systems endowed him with two consciousness, a European one that foregrounds the individual self-regarding frame in defining self as well as the pristine position. Because of this historical placement, a situational perspective always has to be used in his definition. Admittedly, it has been argued that since the African gene, to pursue the biological analogy, is stronger than the European one, the concept of Western citizenship that implies a degree in individual differentiation has not been and cannot be reproduced in Africa (Chabal and Daloz 1999, 146, 157). Genes can therefore be seen as accounting for the discredited thesis on the African's historical incapacity to change. Morphological similarities are mistakenly seen as correlated with genetic similarities (Appiah 1992, 36).

The lack of covalence between these two similarities enables the recovering of the individual from the group, a significant development in contexts where ethnic groups are locked in conflict. Focus on intergroup conflict covers over intragroup conflict and risks reifying potentially limiting or repressive group identities. Though this provides a more critical and democratically open basis for forging and reforging collective identities (Calhoun 1997, 224), I am more interested in the possibilities to forge relational identities as a result of an ethical engagement that this noncrystallization allows individuals from different groups. Fostering this implication, as Connolly (1994, 166–167) notes, is "the stirrings of unpersuaded possibilities in oneself that exceed one's identity and an engagement with pressures to resent the obdurate features of the human condition." Because this discursive ethic is engendered by partial experiences, it tends to receive a hearing likely to have disturbing results for proponents of ethnic purity. Prominent among them is the conversion of the antagonism of identity into agonism of difference, a sine qua non for the "naturalization" of citizens. Those able to make this conversion constitute a moral community needed to build bridges across ethnic boundaries. Doubts persist whether the African can make this conversion (Chabal and Daloz 1999, 19, 52, 53). Curiosity, if any, that this line of inquiry may provoke is reinforced by the observation that because of particular social developments, individuals may sense more affinity to groups other than their ethnic groups and cannot be seen as prisoners of a group (Horowitz 1998, 346, 359).

WHAT IS WRONG WITH ETHNICITY?

The preoccupation of national constitutions with the defense of the rights of ethnic groups gives the impression that Africans are allergic to ethnicity. With a view to containing this visceral hatred and legally secure ethnicity, Article 1 of the constitution of Burkina Faso, for example, outlaws discrimination based on ethnic or regional origins. A similar prescription is found in the constitutions of Côte d'Ivoire (Article 6), Namibia (Article 10), and South Africa (Article 9).

Gabon's Law No. 3/91 of March 26, 1991, also states in its Preamble that acts of racial, ethnic, or religious discrimination are outlawed and punishable by law. The fixation on outlawing ethnic discrimination caused it to be included in the Banjul Charter on Human and People's Rights. Article 2 guarantees rights and freedoms recognized by the Charter without distinction of any kind as to race, ethnic group, and color.

A strictly legal interpretation of these instruments may give the mistaken impression that ethnicity depends on law for its cover and therefore its survival. However, this would be to deny that ethnicity is a fundamental social fact of life. Outlawing or causing its death would produce negative repercussions that would be immediately visible as the ethnic group the sole moral community in Africa (Tamarkin 1996, passim). It can also serve as a matrix for imagining "the existence of a new 'tribe' that may be the best way to look outward, to embrace social progress" (Lonsdale, cited in Chabal 1996, 49). Those who seek to expunge ethnicity also fail to acknowledge its approval in the changing social context. Notably, most of the sovereign national conferences that were held in Africa in the early 1990s did not condemn ethnicity per se, but its perverse effect on states. Against this backdrop, it becomes evident that it is political tribalism rather than moral ethnicity that is an anathema. According to John Lonsdale (1992, 466–467), political tribalism flows down from high political intrigue; it constitutes communities through external competition. Moral ethnicity creates communities from within through domestic controversy over civic culture. It is the only language of accountability that most Africans have; it is the most intimate critic of the state's ideology of order. Tribalism remains the reserve currency in our markets of power, ethnicity our most critical community of thought. Ethnic nationalism has been mobilized rather than disarmed by modern states, no matter whether liberal or authoritarian.

The effects of tribalism on the postcolonial state in Africa have been unsettling, as indicated by the ubiquity of war. Novelty stems not from this per se but from change in the nature of warfare. Commenting on this, a Nuer chief in the Sudan noted in 1998, "They used to tell us that the reason why the Nuer and Dinka fight each other was because we are ignorant. We don't know anything because we are not educated. But now look at all this killing! This war between the Nuer and Dinka is much worse than anything we experienced in the past. And it is the war of the educated (elite)—It is not our war at all" (cited in Jok and Hutchinson 1999, 131). Transformation had occurred in this war, not just because of the nature of arms used (guns instead of spears), but also in tactics, as morality in war is deemphasized. Suggestive of respect for laws similar to Western *jus in belli*, earlier Nuer cattle raids had avoided killing children, women, and the elderly and the wanton destruction of property. Morality and proportionality were emphasized even in war. Reminiscing on this, a Dinka leader observed, "On our side we would mourn over the dead, recuperate from our loss, and retaliate when the time and place were appropriate" (see Jok and Hutchinson

1999, 131). Restraint enabled the conviviality of the myth of a peaceful coexistence and the reality of war.

Also perpetrating this in precolonial Africa was the fact that wars between ethnic groups rarely lasted more than a few days. Spectacle was rare and the physical, psychological, and moral violence inflicted on its victims did not affect the community as a whole. That they affected only individuals is important, not because of Margaret Thatcher's cynical remark that "society does not exist. There are only individuals," but because it enabled the society, which was not violated, to move on. Furthermore, the wars were mostly over economic rather than political differences. Antagonism was, therefore, episodic, while dissent, the trademark of democratic politics, remained an intrinsic feature of their relations. This does not obtain in the postcolonial state and explains the moral economy of crime that is part of the present-day calculus of (political) power in contemporary Africa (Chabal and Daloz 1999, 78). More concerned with self-gratification, ethnic entrepreneurs seek to access this state, which is seen as means of production. But being adepts at the art of manipulation, they cause people to misrecognize this by giving the semblance that they are fostering "enlightened public interest." Seen through this prism, they are opportunity snatchers. A former Dinka Sudan Peoples Liberation Army (SPLA) soldier attested to this thus: "Mixing political differences with economic competition, and emphasizing to each group the danger presented by the other, is the only way Riek and Garang can get us to fight their wars for them" (cited in Jok and Hutchinson 1999, 133).[5]

That the "war of the educated" was different from the skirmishes of the past became evident when some Dinkas went to the house of Gader, a prophet and Nuer, to sacrifice an ox. Such visits in spiritual search for rain were standard practice, and therefore part of social reality even during times of hostility in the precolonial era.[6] Seen through the prism of their political heurmeutics, it symbolized that even violence did not lead to a rupture in relations between the two groups and one could not become a social suzerain of the other.[7] Though this practice had never lapsed as a result of desuetude, Gader violated it by reporting the visitors to the local SSIA authorities, who arrested and indicted them for spying on behalf of the SPLA. It was a jolting experience for the Dinkas, who saw it as a refusal of their olive branch. Blame was put not on the prophet but on the soldiers. Explaining his dilemma and the smug indifference of the soldiers to culture, a Dinka chief observed that Gader simply sought to inform the military authorities of the reenactment of this practice. "He had hoped that the authorities would understand the usual protocol regarding spiritual matters, but the behavior of the military leaders was an embarrassment to him. . . . If such spiritual matters are also ignored by these armies, we have no hope that anything else would persuade them about thinking about resuming friendly border relations. Although these soldiers were our children yesterday and should understand the primacy of spiritual life, they act as if they are from a different world. They are the same on both sides" (cited in Jok and Hutchinson 1999, 140).

Claims that this rupture in consciousness is triggered mostly by political economy of warfare considerations can easily be substantiated. In Chad, for example, transhumance had caused tension between the Negroid groups who practice farming and the Berbers who engage in cattle farming. These two communities still cohabited peacefully as cattle movement to the South also occasioned familial and cultural contact. People often evoke this era "that they glorify as the years of peace and concord in the rural areas" with a lot of nostalgic feelings (cited in Tenebaye 1999, 3). A reversal in this trend, signaled by the advent of conflict, occurred only because of the emergence of a new class of pastoral farmers, comprising mostly the petty bourgeoisie (senior functionaries, army officers, and chiefs). The circular pattern of transhumance, whereby cattle moved to the South in search of pasture in the dry season but returned to the North in the rainy season, was abandoned in 1984–1985 as a result of an intensive and extensive drought. They did not return to the Sahel (Dassering 1999, 4). This brought more pressure to bear on lands in the South, whose carrying capacity was already stretched to the breaking point. Exacerbating this, some members of this new class of pastoral farmers who are connected with those in power, in defiance of customary practice, moved their cattle into areas without the prior accord of local chiefs.

Though the local chief has the statutory competence to decide on farmer–grazier disputes, in light of the changing power relations, graziers now prefer to report to the gendarmes and the administrative officers who are frontline officials of the state. Being mostly rent seekers, these frontline officials have contributed inordinately to exacerbating the conflict. Contrary to standard practice and custom, it is commonplace for them to demand cattle from graziers as reparation requested by farmers for damages caused by cattle on their farms (Tenebaye 1999, 5). Practices such as these engender comments such as, "Saras do not love the Arabs" and "farmers make us pay even for a leaf" (Tenebaye 1999, 6). Tensions between the two communities now mostly engendering conflict, the protagonists are not interested in critical reflection that would reveal that it is the implosion of the state and the subsequent conflict in authority between the traditional and modern arms of the administration that is the genesis of the problem. As I have argued elsewhere (Jua 2000, 15), conflict has disturbing implications insofar as it thrusts to the fore of people's consciousness events that had receded into memory. Evidential of this in Chad is the nurturance of feelings of accumulated hatred as the majority Sara in the South begin to remember the violence, physical and symbolic, to which the Arabized Northern ethnic groups submitted their ancestors when they raided and sold them into slavery. Lacking any compassion toward them, the requisite conditions for establishing psychic conditions cannot be met. Neither are their fears allayed by the absence of possibility. Elites play an inordinate role in this process. And their position is important because position-taking depends for force and form on the position that each agent occupies in the power relations. This thesis suggesting that rationality has a social location causes people to consign their consciousness to this class. It can have insidious effects as happens when this class becomes corrupt. Bourdieu notes that as people fail in carrying out their projects or meet with obstacles, there is a probability that they alter, not to say deform, traditional information that they have received from various others in the course of their previous interactions with a view to bringing their projects to fruition (Lipuma and Calhoun 1993, 23, 78).

Not all members of the educated class in Africa suffer from the depletion of cultural funds that explains, even if only partially, the malignancy of the present ethnic conflicts in the continent. Only opportunity snatchers in this social class benefit from this seeming irrational breakdown of order where society is being reorganized in particular ways so that beneficiaries get real material, political and psychological gains from the conflict (Cliffe and Luckham 1999, 38). Referred to by the common man as members of the *tribu du ventre* (Bayart 1993), they have converted the state into a means of production. "Eating" became the norm among this class, giving rise to what is known in popular parlance as the "politics of the belly." Venality was uncontested because of the primordiality of violence in postcoloniality. To entrench its moral hegemony, members of the *tribu du ventre* also disciplined and normalized their "citizens." The cumulative effect was the conversion of the population to "standing reserves" that could be used as instrumental value (Heidegger 1977, 18). Facilitating this was the continuing use of the African register in defining "self." Emphasizing communal-self-regarding frames, individuals tend to defer to their leaders who contribute to their collective prominence.

Cognizance of this consciousness caused the ruling class to privilege hegemonic exchange in governance. Success in suturing the elites guaranteed the uncontested functioning of the state. This practice led to the emergence of the *état reseaux* or rhizome state in postcolonial Africa with the barons at the interface between the state and society.[8] Ethnic barons set up clientelistic networks and the dyadic relations that obtained therein guaranteed the submissiveness of (disempowered) clients to their patrons. Since this involved the use of resources largely assumed to be legitimate, even if they were illicit, corruption by members of the *tribu du ventre* was construed as patrimonially legitimate (Chabal and Daloz 1999, 79) by their clients. The tendency among Africans to celebrate the coopting of their barons into what they refer to as the *mangeoire nationale* seemingly inheres from the opportunity spaces that it offers them access to this state that puts a high premium on informal channels. This is significant because the masses mostly experience the state in the exercise of its power of violence or extraction. Acquiescence should not be mistaken with approval. Construing it as the latter would be to deny that Africans are tricksters for whom the "really real" is incessantly multifaceted and ironic. This conception of the real presents them with an infinite potentiality; that is, "the capacity for individuals to virtually transform themselves into anybody they want to be" (Hecht and Simone 1994, 12, 79). Because of this, one can begin to discern the real attitudes of the masses toward their patrons from the vigor with which they equally celebrate their dismissal from government. In Cameroon, cases abound of former patrons who have been treated as if they are social plagues.

Despite the cry of the Dinka chief noted above, the common man is not unimpeachable to the extent that he has also embraced these wars and is a *homo luden*. For them, the ethnic group is not just a social construct but a firmly bounded, durable community. The common man benefits from these wars to the extent that elites are seen as contributing to the collective prominence of a people. His attitude is however ambiguous as these wars also have disturbing implications, disrupting his everyday life. Marx noted that it is life that determines consciousness rather than the reverse. This is evident from the comment of a Mozambican peasant who had been forced to relocate three times as a result of war: "Now it is different. Yesterday, I was a person, I had my own personality; now I have nothing. All that I feel, all that I own now is my suffering" (Nordstrom 1992, 268). Insofar as this state of being is a result of evil that is caused by a human agent, it can only foster a negative remembering that is not conducive to the promotion of a national imagining

Thus, whereas the failure to suture elites is a primordial cause of wars in postcolonial Africa, their causes as noted above are much more complex (also see, Graf 1988, 17; Ntumba 1998, 10; Goodhand and Hulme 1999). Whatever their cause, it is widely acknowledged that they are simply a means to power. Since power is seen as belonging to the group, the normative expectations are that such conflicts should occasion ethnic mobilization. This is not borne out by empirical studies, which show that diverse and divergent motives push and pull people, especially children, to conscript into the army. Notable among these are the satisfaction of psychological needs such as food security and the sense of security and power that is provided by possessing a gun (Furley, cited in Honwana 1998, 12). Fear, in some cases, compels parents to allow their children to be recruited. Fear in this context is exacerbated by the persistence of a precapitalist mindset where freedom is seen as a privilege rather than a right. Evidence of this is the case of a young recruit for the National Union for the Total Independence of Angola (UNITA), who was sent home due to illness after his enlistment. Unaware of this, the troops who recruited him accused his mother of causing him to desert. This accusation and the constant harassment of her husband who "is a very religious person (a catequista)" by UNITA soldiers caused the couple to allow the soldiers to take the boy again (Honwana 1998, 13). Stories similar to this one abound, showing the reluctance of the common man to be involved in conflicts fanned even by their own ethnic barons. However, countervailing evidence also exists showing that, despite the penchant of the elite for political tribalization, the common man is more interested in moral ethnicity. The competitive edge of the former according to Lonsdale derives from the success of some elites in disempowering the common man (cited in Chabal and Daloz 1999, 60; also see Lonsdale 1994).

Because of their disempowerment, clients live in ambient fear. Relegated to this status, clients are involved in a permanent quest for rights. Conferral of rights, it has been noted in another circumstance, "is symbolic of all denied aspects of [one's] humanity: rights imply a respect that places one on the referential range of self and others, that elevates one from human body to social being" (Williams 1991, 153). Concern with recovering their rights as social beings caused Africans, who paying scant attention to their ethnic origins, to collectively support the call for sovereign national conferences in several African states. Believing that only a liberal democratic system could guarantee these rights as well as development, contra modernization, they embraced this mode of governance that promised them independence from the members of the *tribu du ventre*.

DEMOCRACY AND ITS ALL-INCLUSIVENESS PROMISE

Optimism that democracy was the panacea for all the conflicts plaguing Africa was unbounded. Historical evidence, admittedly, suggests that democracy and nationalism are Siamese twins. Little does it matter whether this is a symbiotic or parasitic relationship. The case for "democratic possibilism" in Africa was sustained by the fact that this mode of governance had flourished in other developing states. Seeing democracy as fostering contingency and relationality in identities, most scholars shared the optimism that it would lead to a modification in collective identity where all are recognized as coparticipants in the creation of a common future. Presentation of inclusion as an inevitable rather than a desirous outcome increased its purchase and caused African countries to seek to deepen and expand liberal democracy. Its modular form had been imported from Europe where the countries arguably had homogenous populations. But the peculiarity of the African state is its heterogeneity. Because of this specificity, the concept is being deconstructed with a view to deepening and expanding it. This has resulted in various modules of democracy that now inform practice in Africa. They range from Ethiopia's republic of ethnics to the South African formula where any party obtaining 20 percent of the votes cast in elections participates in the cabinet. Powers are being devolved to the local level. This, it has been postulated, should lead to a replication of the American experience, where accent is put on performance politics at the national level and identity politics at the local level (Chege 1998, 391).

To a certain extent, this prescription has been respected in Mali, where, after a series of interpellations, Alpha Oumar Konaré offered to extend more local powers to the north, which had been in rebellion against the central government. Consequently, more than 700 elected "communes" were established throughout Mali. Only after this did the rebels agree to hand in their stockpiled guns for the highly symbolic destruction in what has been dubbed as the "Flame of Peace" at Timbuktu. Accompanying this was a joint declaration issued by the rival groups in which they affirmed the indivisibility of Mali, pledged their support to its constitution, renounced the use of violence, and exhorted their fellow African fighters across the continent to "celebrate their own Flame of Peace." Konaré's approach has been presented as "ambitious" and "visionary" and a paradigm for African states. These states will flourish in the 21st century "only if they are able to reconcile the need for broader economic or monetary unions with the pressures from local groups to assume their cultural identities." For this purpose, decentralization is the new framework that will make people responsible for their own lives, for mobilizing national resources, and for using them locally for productive investments" (Poulton cited in Jua 2000, 19).

The One-Nation Consensus, an assimilisationist or Tswanalization policy of the ruling party as occurred in Botswana for a long time (Werbner 2002, 676) is not an adequate solution to the problem. Comprising more than twenty ethnic groups, with more than 30 percent of its population being neither linguistically nor ethnically Tswana, the constitution for a long time recognized only eight ethnic groups. Justification for this policy was provided by Chief Justice M. D. Mokama (*Southern Africa Political and Economic Monthly*, July 1993, 6) when he argued that with a population of only 700,000, "the best protection of any group rights is far better served by entrenched protection of individual human rights." This argument is predicated on the definition of the African from an individual self-regarding perspective to the detriment of the communal-regarding self that provides him a sociopsychological anchor, and it contradicts some of the articles of the Banjul Charter on Human and People's Rights that recognize group rights. Yet there was no consensus on reintegration, the political process that decides on how the tribe is to be placed within the state (Werbner 2002, 677) as demonstrated by the formation of the Society for the Promotion of Ikanlanga Language by university students in Botswana. Its chairman argued, "If we talk of the word 'Setswana' in terms of broadening it to include all of us so that those, who speak Ikalanga, Shona or whatever, those who were born and bred in Botswana, should be seen as speaking all dialects of Setswana." Implicitly, this was an argument for the recognition of the other ethnic groups that speak these languages and by that token a claim for tolerance as right rather than grace.[9] In the face of this impediment and others, few states have been able to emulate Mali's example successfully.

Civil society is posited as a panacea to most of these problems because it privileges dialogical reciprocity and an intersubjective consensus, which are intrinsic to the democratic culture in decision making. If we accept the argument that the African gene dominates in the African hybrid, then it is axiomatic that the individual differentiation that sustains the Western concept of citizen cannot obtain in Africa (Chabal and Daloz 1999, 157). But this position goes against the grain as the existence of civil society in Africa has been largely documented; the problem that it now faces is one of thickening (Bratton 1989; Newbury 1994; Chabal 1994; Mamdani 1996). With a view to promoting this process, Mamdani has argued for the reform of rural areas, where the stress is on the equality of people. Urban areas are not insulated from the perverse effects of this system due to the chief's tendency to appoint representatives whose role is "to look after the men in a particular area, to assert control, and to protect the particular chief's interests in the cities" (Mamdani 1996, 280, 297). This proposal, which calls for a frontal attack on custom, needs to be confronted critically. Chiefs, who are basically benevolent despots, are seen as wielding uncontested power over their societies. Freedom and equality in this context, and contrary to liberal theory, are seen as privileges rather than rights.

Custom is already under siege as can be discerned from the dynamics inherent in rural–urban relations. Despite the reciprocity in influence, rural folks tend to defer to urbanites who they see as their eyes and ears. This is a seeming endorsement of the German maxim that "city air makes one free." Deference has been more pronounced with the advent of development associations led by elites from urban areas.[10] By providing a democratic space and a conduit for a development that stresses a participatory approach, they also foster cultural pluralism in rural areas. Villagers benefit as a result of osmosis in this relationship. It results in voice or another consciousness, encouraging them to participate in critical issues that touch on everyday life. Action is no longer socially but individually controlled. Its unsettling effects are reinforced by media-refracted images from urban areas as well as the West that tend to privilege a dialogic reciprocity as a method of reaching an intersubjective consensus on critical issues.

Furthermore, any reading of African custom, which foregrounds consensus, invented in the colonial state "mainly as a means to hallow officials' history," is mistaken. It overlooks the discursive neutralization underlying the supposed unanimity in these societies, where the plurality of political ideologies was also the norm (Lonsdale 1989, 23). Inherited by the postcolonial state, it was instrumentalized by the state, which used chiefs in policing their subjects in a political environment where fear was the mode of consciousness. Admittedly, this as Renan (1990, 11) observes, was the organizing principle used in fostering national imagining in Europe. Acceptable at the dawn of the democratic revolutions, its ethical justification is doubtful in postcolonial Africa today, even if it remains a politically feasible option. The present emphasis on the democratic ethos means that the use of force would cause such a political development to be out of sync with the prevailing cultural and historical context.

Against this backdrop, governments of national unity or broad consensus have been seen as the panacea (Tamarkin 1996, 376; Horowitz 1985; Mbembe 2000, 20). Nelson Mandela provided some empirical justification for this form of governance when he coopted nonmembers of his African National Congress into his government with a view to thawing the tensions and distrust that plagued post-apartheid South Africa. In the rest of Africa, however, where politicians are seen in two registers that are not necessarily compatible (as modern leaders and as fathers), there are push and pull factors that make this an attractive option to the ruling class, even if they are members of the opposition. Prominent among them is the guarantee of access to resources needed for sustaining clientelistic networks to its members. But increasingly the common man as active agent is seeing the leader not as a father who uses state resources to cater for his needs in the patrimonial state but as a modern leader.

In the changing social context, the disengagement of the state from the economic sector, ipso facto its contraction as its role, which is now limited to providing an enabling environment for development, deprives patrons of the resources needed for greasing their networks. Either clients can no longer eat or their rations are considered derisory. And because a critical mass of people in this context do not consider corruption as patrimonially legitimate anymore, they tend to demand the introduction of new modes of political accountability. Political compromises that lead to *transformismo* (Gramsci 1978, 227) or union governments that include politicians of all shades meant primarily to smooth over moments of temporary political instability are considered as made on the backs of the masses. Leaders entering into such alliances with the incumbent are perceived as "having eaten soya" (political betrayal). A palpable example is the negative press that Ni John Fru Ndi, the leader of Cameroon's Social Democratic Front (SDF), received when he had a working breakfast with a member of the incumbent Cameroon People's Democratic Movement (CPDM) government.[11]

Creation of governments of national unity in Africa has been facilitated by the absence or paucity of parties with firm ideological convictions. Carl Schmitt argues that the political system derives its energy from several sources and emerges out of different social relations, to wit, religious, moral, economic, and ethnic (cited in Mouffe 1997, 399) and blurring these political shades on the continuum prepares the ground for diverse forms of populist politics that privilege, inter alia, religious and ethnic issues. Schmitt's predications are validated to the extent that this breeds intolerance, as confrontations over essentialist identities and nonnegotiable moral values multiply (Mouffe 1997, 402). In Côte d'Ivoire, for example, Laurent Gbagbo's *Front populaire ivoirien* (FPI) was dubbed by Felix Houphouet Boigny and Konan Bedie as the "Bete party" that was instinctively prone to violence (Coulibally 2000, 22). Use of this imagery helped to convert political protagonists into enemies rather than adversaries. Whereas an enemy is seen as the "other" to be destroyed, an adversary is one whose ideas we contest but "whose right to defend those ideas we will not put into question" (Mouffe 1997, 401). Essentialist identities can easily be transcended only in adversarial relationships.

Failures to transcend these identities have made ethnically based political parties acceptable currency in Africa and energized the *autochtone/allogène* binary. Management of political coexistence where this binary exists has been problematical. Their epicenters are metropolitan areas that should serve as spaces for the making of relational identities. In Cameroon, for instance, it has been argued that this problem is restricted to the two metropolitan centers of Douala and Yaoundé (Jua 2000, 9). Ethnically based parties with a national reach contribute to the spread of ethnic antipathies and may actually serve as a fillip for the growth of monoethnic tendencies. This relegates some groups to the bottom of society's symbolic ladder causing them to see the nation-in-gestation as their political prison. Governments confronted by such a challenge need to indulge in a labor of imagination; notably, deconstruct Western liberal democracy with a view to deepening and thickening for the purpose of accommodating their heterogeneous populations. In Kenya, for example, where cabinet members must be members of Parliament, the failure of the Kenya African National Union (KANU) to win seats among the Kikuyu and the Luos in the 1992 general elections meant that these two ethnic groups, comprising more than half of the population, would not be represented in the highest instance of decision making. Estranging them, especially the Kikuyus, who already felt victimized as a result of the replacement of their cadres with non-Kikuyus in the civil service following its reform, was considered by the incumbent Arap Moi regime as politically suicidal. Only the nomination of a Kikuyu and Luo to the National Assembly as well as their appointment to the cabinet preempted this.[12]

Formation of parties that foreground ideological rather than essential or moral differences can best promote a politics of inclusion. In Nigeria, for example, the Ibrahim Babangida junta established parties in preparation for the transition to civilian rule. Two nationwide political parties, the Social Democratic Party (SDP) and the National Republican Convention (NRC), were created and similarly given their political coloration. The former leaned a little to the left and the latter to the right. Two National Caretaker Committees were appointed to administer them until the officials could be elected at their national conventions. Regimentation was so much the norm that the programs as well as the mode of electing their officials were synchronized (Federal Ministry of Information and Culture, n.d., 45, 243). Despite the issue of provenance (Mohammed, n.d., 4–5), which admittedly is important for sustainable democracy, it would be a mistake to attribute the demise of the transition program to the visible hand of the military in the creation of the parties.

Rather, the stress on regimentation eventually marred the transition program. Without getting involved in the polemics that surrounded the June 12, 1993 election that took place despite a court injunction vacating it, there was a consensus that its success was attributable "largely to the dynamics of the two-party system, which makes it difficult for tribal and religious considerations to overwhelm the tickets presented to the electorate by the parties" (Federal Ministry of Information and Culture, n.d., 22). Essentialist and moralist factors did not mar the elections that led to the choice of Moshood Abiola, a Yoruba from the Southwest, and Bashir Tofa, a Hausa from the North, as presidential candidates for the SDP and NRC, respectively. In the June 12 election, Tofa beat Abiola in the Northern states by only a slight margin. Whereas the former had 5,402,559 votes, the latter had 5,247,318. Abiola's landslide victory was due to the fact that the Southwest voted overwhelmingly for him (3,093,991 votes), while Tofa could garner only 549,528 votes there.[13]

Admittedly, determining the intentionality (that is, causal determination), is difficult in the social sciences. Some have attributed the skewed voting pattern in the Southwest to the Yoruba factor. A plausible argument, it fails to take cognizance of the fact that the population of this area is sociologically heterogeneous and the role that ideological leanings prompted by the success of members of the "tribe of democracy" in recruiting foot soldiers may have played in crossover voting among this electorate. Thus, given its option for unicausality, it simply glosses over other variables that may have had a bearing on the outcome.

AGONISM OF DIFFERENCE IN A CHANGING SOCIAL CONTEXT

That ethnic conflict seems to be the state of normalcy in Africa is not to deny the presence of ethnic conviviality that causes people to see political differences through the prism of dissent rather than antagonism. Political civility does not necessarily have a specific location, despite normative claims that the liberal ethos is commonplace among the educated class. Evidence, however, suggests that this is not their monopoly as the democratic culture, even if work in progress, is also common among the uneducated. Cultural capital of political actors though important should not throw out of focus intentions that also determine the politics of the various actors. Accommodative politics where actors are driven by nonmaterial objectives do occur. Against the backdrop of the positive dialectic theory, this form of politics augurs well for national imagining in Africa and can contribute to transcending political tribalism (Lonsdale 1989, 137). It is becoming commonplace in Africa's changing context because of the multiplicity of actors, such as women and NGOs, that now occupy public space.

Some would argue, and correctly so, that the constituency embracing this form of politics in Africa is small. Lack of universality as a handicap is made up for by the intensity of the position taking of its advocates. Margaret Mead submits on the basis of empirical evidence that "never doubt that a small group of committed people can change the world; indeed, it is the only thing that ever does." Nigeria, during the Abacha period, is a case in point. Following the annulment of the June 12, 1993, elections, a small group of people committed to its restoration formed the National Democratic Coalition (NADECO), an umbrella organization for about eight groups. NADECO and other groups that shared its aspirations were referred to as the "tribe of pro-democracy advocates" (*The News*, October 12, 1998, 25). Its members, no matter their sociological background, shared a similar conviction that Abiola's victory in the June 12 election had crossed ethnic, religious, and regional lines. Because of this conviction, they were undeterred in their challenge to Abacha's despotic powers. In other words, their commitment to the democratic principle was so strong that they were willing to forego privileges such as an unimpeded access to the state and even to risk exile as an escape from the "Burmese treatment" (house confinement).[14] The stakes were high and real as demonstrated by the killings of Ken Saro-Wiwa and other Ogoni activists, as well as Musa Yar'Adua, a retired general and one-time candidate for the presidency. Seeing democracy as the only way of guaranteeing an autonomy of outcomes in a heterogeneous country like Nigeria, they also advocated for a sovereign national conference (SNC) where a new social compact could be forged. All 250 ethnic groups that comprise Nigeria were, therefore, to be represented at the SNC (*Tell*, July 27, 1998, 12). At the SNC, according to Nobel laureate Wole Soyinka of the United Democratic Front of Nigeria (UDFN), "all the interest groups will gather, in which we will discuss . . . the relationship of the various states to the center, the issue of minorities and boundaries" (*Tell*, July 14, 1997, 10). Throughout contemporary Africa, especially in Francophone Africa, the SNC has been used to configure a new social basis for politics that is consensually acceptable. This is a prerequisite for the introduction of a transformative recognition. In this case, to paraphrase Nancy Fraser (cited in Lee 1998, 446), "The long-term goal of a deconstructive anti-ethnicity outlook would be a culture in which hierarchically ethnic dichotomies would be replaced by networks of intersecting differences that are demassifying and shifting."

Agonism of difference, insofar as it unsettles accepted orientations to identity is contested by most members of the political class despite their commitment to national integration. To preempt the growth of this transformational consciousness, they readily resort to the use of violence or symbolic violence and employ seemingly innocent strategies such as a lexical inflation. In Cameroon, for example, people like Mongo Beti, who opted for oppositional politics, were indexed by the CPDM as *les hommes des autres*. He was also presented as a French citizen, a dubious distinction insofar as Cameroonian law does not recognize dual nationality. Though he shared this distinction with other members of the regime, it was the power to name that was important at this juncture. That is, the power and visibility of members of the regime in the society enabled them to effect a symbolic imposition that deformed this reality. Symbolic power as Bourdieu (1990, 138) notes "is a power of consecration or revelation, a power to conceal or reveal things which are already there." Generally, *les autres*, in this case, were portrayed as the *les allogènes, les envahisseurs, graffis*, or *les enemies dans la maison*, who not only sought to seize power from the Beti tribe but resented them. Invariably, such a portrayal was meant to rob Mongo Beti and others who practiced his politics of their social capital. Bereft of this capital, they could not be considered role models in their communities.

Even religious space was used to preempt the spread of accommodative politics, as demonstrated in the case of Mfou in Cameroon. Attempts to scuttle the launching of the SDF in Mvog-Amoug II were frustrated by the recalcitrance of its interim coordinator, Amougou Ali who was neither consecrated nor recognized as one of the group's leaders. That his attitude was found unbecoming is not surprising, because part of the phenomenology of power is the failure of rulers to see why the ruled should resist their power. With a view to reducing Ali, who was a victim of the unequal distribution in political capital to irrelevance, the district officer sent a letter, banning the launching ceremony to the local Catholic Church. The officiating priest interrupted mass so as to read this banning order (*The Post*, September 11, 2000, 3). This was significant, because priests in this area are seen as moral authorities. As such, their pronouncements, especially when uttered from the pulpit, are considered as dogma.[15] A subtext of this message, even if unintended, was that attendance at this rally would be tantamount to connecting or sleeping with the enemy. Fraternal relations, which constitute the bedrock of a nation, cannot be forged with the enemy. Noteworthy is the fact that advocates of this ethnic fascism or political tribalism were the "Big men" of the village.[16] The heretic, Ali, who stood as an advocate of a transcendental consciousness, predicated on the logic that moral ethnicity should not be confounded with political tribalism, was a simple villager.

Preliminary evidence indicates that despite the opposition to the introduction of another consciousness, this heretical discourse is spreading. Granted, as work in progress, it is not yet the civic religion. Recruitment of its membership, a membership reputed for its civic engagement, is carried out through direct and indirect socialization, with emphasis being placed on an unobtrusive approach.[17] So far, the most visible venture has been the creation of Children's Parliaments in most African countries with the active support of UNESCO. Despite the multiple roles accorded these parliaments, I would rather foreground their role in nurturing a democratic ethos among the youth as well as their interest in politics. Eventually, participants at these parliaments may become copycats of the Ecole Normale William Ponty graduates in Dakar in colonial Africa, albeit at a national level. These graduates became nationalist leaders while also "retaining a West African camaraderie, solidarity and intimacy lost to the succeeding generation" (Anderson 1990, 113).

Anderson's remarks are pertinent, especially as he also acknowledges overtly that this generation, oppressed by colonial officers, saw colonialism as a violating experience. This became a mobilizational resource to the extent that there is nothing more potent than an imperial people to make the oppressed aware of its collective existence (Hobsbawm 1990). Following this line of reasoning, the inability of succeeding generations at (positive) "remembering," a process by which a community reconstructs itself culturally, physically, and ontologically" (Nordstrom 1992, 267), can be attributable to the absence of colonial masters and reminds us of Anthony Trollope's prescience. This inability is a fundamental cause of war on the continent. Nordstrom notes: "if the foundations of culture are jarred in war turned dirty, ontology is thrown open to question and people's sense of reality itself is rendered tenuous." Arguably, this situation can be reversed by peace-building education. In postconflict areas, "the contents and process of education should promote peace, social justice, respect for human rights and the acceptance of responsibility. Children need to learn skills of negotiation, problem solving, critical thinking and communication that would enable them to resolve conflict without resorting to violence" (United Nations 1996, para. 255).

In the long run, this consciousness raising should have a positive effect on the peace-building capacity of the country; the nurturance of a national imagining being one of its collateral benefits. Its liberation potential inheres in its possible revelation to people that the colonizers are still there even if they have now taken on black masks, that is members of *la tribu du ventre* as well as bring to the fore of their consciousness the unpersuaded possibilities in oneself that exceed one's identity. Agonism of difference, crucial in the "naturalization" of citizens, is predicated on this realization. Consequently, as in the case of the Ecole Normale William Ponty, it may trigger a new horizontal bonding among the oppressed. Evidence of this was the difference between Xhosa migrants to East London in South Africa, where the "Reds" (those who had not been to school) privileged their primal relations and experiences in the definition of self while the "schools" (those who had been to school) were more outgoing, accepting Christianity and even using whites as a reference group (for details, see Jua 2000, 23).

Prior to the advent of structural adjustment programs, with their emphasis on good governance and disengagement of the state from the economic sector, ethnic fragmentation was catalyzed by the pervasiveness of the Big Man syndrome. It led to the creation of a patronage trough that gave privileged access to the clients of Big Men. In Ghana, for example, the skewed distribution that this engendered in the opportunity structure caused the dominant ethnic group to benefit from 25 percent of the public sector's wage premium (Collier 1998, 389). And as if to maximize the state's exposure to the group, employment in the parastatal sector also tended to favor it. Insofar as this exposure caused the privileged to improve their life chances and maximize group differential, it constituted an underlying cause of tension. This was evident in Northern Nigeria where employment trends favored Northerners to the near exclusion of Ibos (*The News*, August 10, 1998,18). This nepotism that is extractive rather than productive was bound to increase the psychic distance between the in and out groups and nurture the feelings of mutual resentment. The changed social context, introduced as a result of SAPs, with their emphasis on rationalization, should lead to a leveling of the playing field.

Against this backdrop, women who in local cognitive perceptions are seen as metonymic of society, can help to foster an accommodation politics. In recognition of this, the Organization of African Unity in 1998 created an advisory body, the African Women's Committee and Development to foster women's participation in the continent's efforts to prevent, manage, and resolve ethnic conflicts. In Somalia's largely oral culture, for example, where women can recite poems that prod men to go to war or encourage them to work for peace, gendered war fatigue has caused them to establish the Wajir Peace Group that fosters agonistic respect for differences. Reviving basic methods of conflict resolution used in the precolonial era, the group has encouraged an equitable sharing of resources, one of the underlying causes of mistrust and violence in Somalia. Though their actions may have been motivated by class interests, their occupation of public space, and that commitment to accommodative politics has invariably had a positive effect beyond class boundaries (see Jua 2000, 23–24).

It is their commitment to peace building that caused them to found radio stations like the Voice of Somali Women for Peace, Reconciliation and Political Rights, which promotes national imagining in sofar as it seeks to tackle the root causes of war and create an environment that would make war and armed conflict less likely. Predicating its actions on the belief that peace is indivisible and universal, it has harnessed the energy and expertise of the Diaspora. Enthusiasm among the latter vis-à-vis the project has been unflagging, as they are affected by the lack of peace in Somalia. Because of the project's success, it has been emulated by women in Sierra Leone, and the SEMA group in Nigeria also hopes to launch a Voice of Nigerian Women project. Local groups of Rwandan and Burundi women in Toronto have embarked on the same path.

Increasingly this space that had been occupied only by women is becoming more dense as a result of the proliferation of nongovernmental organizations. Initially involved mostly in carrying out development projects, recent trends show that the reach of NGOs has spread to include peace or consensus-building ventures.[18] Plausibly, NGO involvement in peace building is attributable to the fact that development benefits from the peace dividend. Similarly, NGOs have been implicated in building bridges across ethnic frontiers with a view to promoting the agonism of difference. Paradigmatic of this is the experience of the *Association Tchadienne pour la non-violence*, a human rights organization with sixty-one local committees and regrouping more than 5,000 members. In Tchad (Chad), where farmer–grazier problems are endemic, it has been engaged in the promotion of reconciliation and mediation. To this end, it has opened training centers for nonviolent conflict resolution throughout the country and, at a different level, the Al Mouna Center in N'Djamena organized colloquia in 1996 and 1998 on the real or perceived linguistic and religious differences between the south and the north. These efforts help to reduce the psychic distance between ethnic groups, and can therefore energize social communication.

CONFRONTING THE PAST, IMAGINING A FUTURE

Forty, it is contended, is the age of maturity. Maturity is a sign of growth and a source of self-validation and affirmation. But because of the contradictions that abound in Africa, it has the reverse effect. In everyday life the penchant of the African to marry teenagers can be construed as a sign of his preference for innocence or virginity.[19] This preference has caused some Muslim women in Morocco to visit gynecologists who perform operations in which a virgin is invented "with the hymen intact sealing a vagina which no man has touched" (Mernissi, cited in Desai 1993, 127). This invention cannot be replicated at the national level, where the innocence that accounted for the nationalistic fervor at the dawn of independence as well as the euphoria that accompanied it was short lived. As maturity proved to be challenging, this gave added poignancy to Anthony Trollope's prophecy cited above that the discontinuance of sin (colonialism) is the commencement of a struggle. Ruptures have been many; closures few. As a result, a lot of psychological wounds have failed to heal. Suffering, undergone as a result of rupture, is perceived as evil because it is attributable to an agent (Connolly 1991, 1) and occasion "chosen traumas" that engender feelings of helplessness and victimization. Drawing mental representations or emotional meanings into their very identity, victims pass on emotional and symbolic meanings of incidents, which they see as traumatic from generation to generation. Though regenerative interpretations modify each generation's reading of the incident, "what remains is its role in the psychology of group identity. . . . When a new conflict . . . develops, the current enemy's image becomes contaminated with the image of the enemy in the chosen trauma" (Valkan 1991, 13). This linkage gives rise to grand conspiracies which indicate a form of political psychopathology that causes individuals to interpret unrelated events as causally linked, revealing designs of tyranny and oppression (Hofstadter cited in Zickmund 1997, 191). Against this backdrop, I doubt that even the Africans' memory of hate can be short lived as contended by Ali Mazrui (2001). It is through this prism that the "wars of the educated" are seen and cannot be allowed to recede into memory. Rather, they are always thrust to the fore of consciousness making, healing, which should not be conflated with silencing, impossible.

Good forgetting, as posited by the German psychiatrist Hinderk Emirch (quoted in Schwan 1998, 732), depends on recognizing what was/is wrong with the past. This requires "checking off" the negative elements of the past, an act that most African governments, which have a despotic view of power wherein their citizens benefit from privileges rather than rights, are unwilling to perform. In Zimbabwe, for instance, this has taken the form of a denial to issue death certificates to the families that were victims of the raids carried out by the notorious Fifth Brigade in Matabeleland. Closure cannot be effected in this circumstance, for the victims even in death continue to have a civic existence. It also traumatizes the living, as it makes it impossible for the family to retrieve the corpse of a relative from the army for a befitting burial. As such, they fail in one of their greatest obligations, a failure that preempts good forgetting. Since the army qua state is responsible for this failure, it is thus seen as evil.

Above all, in the moral and cognitive perceptions throughout Central and Southern Africa, failure to bury the dead also preempts the "respectful and punctilious transformation into an ancestor." The dead and the living are supposed to share space. That this belief is perpetuated is not surprising, for Marx notes in the *Eighteenth Brumaire* that the tradition of the dead weighs like a nightmare on the brains of the living. Validation of this is provided by Webner's "social biography" of the Ndebele family, as recounted by Jane Guyer (1995, 4). An elder was killed along with his wife and daughter for failing to surrender his mother-in-law, who was accused of being a sorcerer. While the mother-in-law was immolated, the elder was buried. Consequently as the narrative goes, "in death Dzilo became for the family and the people immediately around his home, what is called an *ngozi*, a restless and vengeful presence, innocent yet wronged, aggrieved and dangerous to the living. All of them had failed to mourn him by shedding tears for their loss in a wake that would have freed them of his presence as a ghost and sent his soul back to rest among midzimu, the divinities of the dead." Similarly, in a quest to establish a new moral order for South Africa, the Truth and Reconciliation Committee was told the story of three boys who had been murdered by a black security policeman in Mamelodi. Following this revelation, their mothers, in a "Healing of Memories" workshop, admitted, "We know what happened, we know who did it, but we don't know where their bodies are buried. We need to know, we have unfinished business. We cannot move on in our lives" (cited in Lapsley 1998, 747). A similar fear accounts for the reluctance of relatives of people that die from ebola (2000 version), a highly contagious disease, to hand over their bodies for burial to "strangers," as happened in the recent outbreak in Uganda.

That the dead are not really dead until they have been properly buried is a "social fact" and this symbolism partly renders social life possible. Its disturbing implications in the everyday life of the living are palpable. Failing to secure a death certificate for one's deceased husband in Zimbabwe, for example, can prevent a widow from inheriting his property and savings. Furthermore, and in conformity with the law, a child's birth certificate can only be issued if the father signs it or if the death certificate of the father is presented. Without these certificates, hundreds of children born in Matabeleland are unable to attend government schools because they do not have the requisite papers. Denial of this equality of opportunity prejudices their life chances, their aspirations to full citizenship, and underlies political psychopathologies (Jua 2000, 20).

No wonder, identification with the state, seen as the cause of most "chosen traumas," becomes impossible, provoking in turn a legitimacy deficit that is the trademark of most African postcolonial states. Where an ethnic group is seen to reify this state, this preempts the building of a moral community that includes that group. Plausibly, this accounts for the failure of the Ndebeles to identify with Robert Mugabe's ZANU-PF, considered a Shona party. Granted, the conflict between these two groups predates colonialism in that the former, which has Zulu roots, came to Zimbabwe as a conquering tribe early in the nineteenth century. Because of the expansionist designs of its monarchy, the British disbanded this institution. As its political fortunes continued to sag in postcolonial Zimbabwe, the Ndebeles saw the reinstitution of the monarchy as a way of reversing this trend. To the Shonas, this was an anathema. Notably, the Ndebele position resonates with that of Chief Gatsha Buthelezi of the Inkatha Freedom Party, which for a long time advocated for the creation of an autonomous KwaZulu Natal Province in South Africa.

Elsewhere in the continent, it is the failure to enforce the principle of restitution intrinsic to justice that has helped to aggravate the state's legitimacy deficit. Whether this results from a legal oversight or in cases where private persons aggrieve the victims, the state takes the rap. Justifying this in the African context is the hegemonic nature of state, which is assigned three duties in the realm of human rights: to avoid depriving a person of some necessity, to protect them from deprivation, and to aid them when deprived (Beetham 1995, 52). It is little wonder that Hutus in Rwanda, following the advent of the Rwandan Patriotic Front to power, blamed all the injustices that they had suffered and continued to suffer at the hands of Tutsis on the government.[20] A window of opportunity for legal redress was provided by the International Tribunal set up by the United Nations in Arusha, as well as participative justice under the auspices of GACACA. The involvement of sages and popular participation in this latter mode, no doubt, suggests its cultural resonance with practices in Rwandan society (Mugemzi 1999, 41). African cultural narratives are replete with other examples of indigenous modes of conflict resolution that in local modes of cognition continue to have a high purchase value.

Overcoming political psychopathologies would be possible only if a level playing field is created. With a view to guaranteeing this in the case of Rwanda, for example, the Arusha Accords of July 1992 recognized the rights of all returning refugees to regain their property. But limitation of the prescription period to claims not older than ten years, contrary to the thirty-year period provided for in civil law regimes mitigated its efficacy. Arguably, only a longer prescription period could have guaranteed "equal concern and respect," to borrow Ronald Dworkin's terminology (cited in MacKinnon 1993, 99) in the provision of uniform rights and treatment for all. Shortening it meant that all refugees who left the country before 1982 (old refugees) could no longer claim property rights to ancestral lands or property that they had left behind. That the law did not reflect prevailing morality became immediately evident with the return of most of the old refuges to the rice paddy fields in Mugusa commune. But in accordance with the laws, they were notified that they had only temporary usufruct rights over these lands, which could be reclaimed at any moment by their owners, who were mostly new refugees or Hutus. Though the old refugees (victims) blamed the Hutus (victimizers) for their plight, the accord still privileged the latter in their rights to enter into property. This disparity in treatment could only exacerbate the accumulated resentment that existed between the two groups, rather than foster good relations.

Despite the fact that new refugees are favored under the accord, front-line officials charged with its implementation, who are mostly Tutsis, have alienated Hutus by disregarding not only its provisions but its spirit. For example, it provides, inter alia, that all unoccupied houses or farmland would revert to the commune as "state property." Burgomasters who carry out the inventory of this property become real *chef de terres*. In this position they wield excessive powers because they reallocate unoccupied houses without specific guidelines. Cases of houses that have been allocated to relatives of officials as well as army officers abound. Without proper guidelines that can be used to recover the houses, which belong mostly to Hutus, it is plausible that this de facto occupation could simply give rise to de jure ownership rights. Failure to establish individual legal responsibility in these cases would be construed as a denial of justice and constitutes another "chosen trauma" that would cause Hutus to see Rwanda as their political prison.

Invariably, for Africa to "move on," it would have to confront its past. Though innocence lost cannot be regained, the "really real" past, especially when it is used to create a national memory, cannot be covered over by the "politicization of history." Because of its tendentious particularity, this history is contestable and always contested[21] as demonstrated by Kalu Ezera's *Constitutional Development in Nigeria*. Its thesis, rehashed recently by a columnist for the *Vanguard* newspaper, claims that the Egbe Omo Oduduwa, a pan-Yoruba cultural group, just like the Jammar Mutanen Arewa, served as Trojan horses of the British in its attempt to divide the nationalist forces already built up by Azikiwe, an Igbo, and Herbert Macaulay. In response to this indictment, a Yoruba columnist noted: "only a traitor to Nigerian nationalism who would seek to promote Yoruba language, art, literature and educational growth as the Egbe Omo Oduduwa was pursuing" before positing that "this kind of self-serving fiction is deployed to make sure that the quality of the arguments between the Ibos and other Nigerians career into irrelevance to sustain old animosities" (*The News*, August 10, 1998, 24). And against the backdrop of regenerative interpretations given "chosen traumas," it would not be anomalous that Yorubas see this as explanation for the failures of Ibos, especially the Group of 34 which was led by Alex Ekwueme, a former vice president in the Second Republic, to add their voice to those calling for the restoration of the June 12 election won by Abiola, a Yoruba. And the tendency is not just to get mad but get even, a reaction that increases the level of mistrust among the two communities and fails to promote "collective amnesia" that is crucial in fostering a national imagining (Anderson 1990).

Similar debates are being reenacted on new sites such as cyberspace that recreates a common spatiality for "politicos" located in disparate geographic areas. Theirs is a "new politics" characterized by new forms of political communication and political action (Scott and Street 2001, 215). Computers initially used by states for surveillance and control purposes are now used by people to create a "creolized discourse" that mixes intense bits of intense debate about home country issues and notices of cultural events to enable an identity discursively produced (Anderson 1995). Because access to the Internet is democratic, it gives people voice, a privilege denied them by the state's monopoly control over the audiovisual media in most of these countries. Popular participation enables a popular surveillance of the state and can engender unobtrusive though effective modes of popular protest, such as e-protest. Governments, in a quest for international legitimacy, are forced to enter into debate with ordinary citizens because the debate is carried out in the gaze of the international community. Cameroon's minister of territorial administration was drawn into one of these debates recently when reacting to an interview granted by Christian Cardinal Tumi in which he denounced the institutionalization of corruption in Cameroon. The minister claimed that, "the unity, cohesion, endurance, and patriotism illus-

trated for several years by the [indomitable] Lions, appear to our Cardinal as
signs of pure and hard tribalism."

Coming in the wake of the Sydney Olympics where Cameroon won the
gold medal in football (soccer), his allusion to the Indomitable Lions (the national football team), to which the Cardinal did not refer in his interview, must
be seen as a rhetorical strategy meant to divert attention away from the thrust of
the interview. In a country where football has become political religion and reference to its national team always prompts an emotional validation of *camer-
ounité*, a consensus that helps to reconfigure political space, the government
tried to benefit from an emotional legitimacy in presenting the Cardinal as de-
riding it. Its communiqué, as narrative reality, did not however produce the desired effect because it was incorporated into creolized discourse. Its posting on
the Internet elicited a flurry of reactions on the use of lie telling as an organizing
principle of the government that forces people "to live a lie" while at the same
time denying the minister any chance of plausible deniability. And as proof of
time-space compression, a copy of this communiqué as well as reactions to it
were posted to me from the United States. On the whole, the Internet's effect on
expanding the shrinking political space as well as democratizing it has rendered
difficult the production of marginality by the center. As a "parallel discursive
arena where members of the subordinated social groups invent and articulate
counter-discourses to formulate oppositional interpretations of their identities,
interests and needs" (Fraser 1992, 123), it has unsettled the social censorship
that led to the lobotomizing of the common man. Though on the cutting edge of
technology, it can be used by the African still seemingly "locked into 'backward' social and psychological conventions" (Chabal and Daloz 1999, 145), to
begin to transcend political tribalism in the immediacy.

But for this "new politics" to have maximum effect, psychological wounds
left by past conflicts in Africa must heal. New and creative ways such as SNCs
that littered the African political scene in the 1980s are being imagined. Though
they were supposed to lead to a collective exorcism, ascertaining their impact at
this historical juncture would be difficult as shown by the mixed results in
countries that opted for this mode of transition. Other modes range from the use
international (the case of the U.N.-established Arusha Tribunal for Rwanda) to
national tribunals (as proposed by President Teejan Kabah of Sierra Leone for
the trial of Fodeh Sankoh and members of his Revolutionary United Front).
Though establishing individual legal responsibility and meting out punishment
for crimes guarantees justice, its chances of fostering reconciliation in postconflict situations are problematical in the absence of expiation.[22] Of course, they
are worse in countries where official policy requires people to forget the past, a
clear indication of the government's option for stability over justice. But increasingly, more countries are adopting the use of Truth and Reconciliation
Commissions (TRCs). Nigeria established a Human Rights Commission on October 22, 2000 with a mandate similar to that of South Africa's TRC. Empowered to examine complaints as far back as the first military coup d'état in 1966,

it received more than 10,000 applications even before the start of its work. Notable among them were complaints from the Ogoni people for the killing of Ken Saro-Wiwa and the other eight Ogoni activists, and the Igbos for the ethnic cleansing carried out against them in Northern Nigeria in 1966. Only the excavation of this forgotten past enables the incorporation of its suppressed narratives into the official history.

To jumpstart this process in South Africa, Nelson Mandela's government emphasized the need for reconciliation. Since apartheid had led to the polarization of society, the interim constitution under which he was elected placed a premium on reconciliation, noting that "the adoption of this constitution lays the secure foundation for the people of South Africa to transcend divisions and strife of the past, which generated gross violations of human rights, there is a need for understanding but not vengeance, a need for reparation but not for retaliation, a need for *ubuntu* but not for victimization."[23] This provided the statutory basis for the establishment of the TRC, which started hearings in July 1995 and was expected to present its report in October 1998. These hearings, also referred to as amnesty hearings, brought about full disclosure. Though enabling justice as acknowledgment, a condition that opens up the possibility for reconciliation (Norval 1998, 254), they also caused a rewriting of South Africa's history, a history with which victims of apartheid as well as its perpetrators could identify. Initially, however, opposition parties and the white population were skeptical about the objectivity of the TRC, which was headed by Bishop Desmond Tutu (Kotzé 2000, 86). Arguably, this approach has a competitive edge over the Zimbabwean approach that grants a blanket amnesty in its constitution. Basically, this is opting for stability. Its negative spin offs were evident when Robert Mugabe threatened to try all whites for crimes committed under apartheid Rhodesia simply for their support of the opposition, the Movement for Democratic Change.

Arguably, form becomes a moot point where amnesty or the process of granting it is guaranteed by the law. The rule of law that is intrinsic to all democracies has been deemphasized by most African regimes. Lord Atkins notes that courts are among the last, if not the last line of defense in human society and if overrun by the ever advancing avalanche of moral decay or interference or pressure, then the warning shots are being fired for the inauguration of the reign of terror or chaos. A glaring case is Mugabe's decision overlooking a Zimbabwean Supreme Court ruling stipulating that the seizure of white farms without compensation is against the law and violates a basic provision of the constitution protecting private property. Only in upholding the constitution would the "veil of ignorance" that is inherent in all constitutions be preserved. This did not obtain as Mugabe carried through his decision taken prior to the court's ruling. This is a commonplace occurrence in Africa where law is the weapon of the strong. In other words, these are autocratic states in which those who make the law are above them. Constitutions on the continent, to paraphrase de Tocqueville (1990, 181) tend to treat common people as lunatics. But unlike the French constitution that he studied, these constitutions do not fear constraining Africans to the point of choking or infuriating them.

That autocracy is seemingly implanted in Africa is not anomalous because most of these states lack(ed) icons incarnating "the way of life" (Zizek 1992, 195) in their histories. Absent, collective referents, most of the first-generation leadership were advocates of political tribalism and deeply implicated in the crime that is a pasttime of the African political class (for details, see Bayart, Ellis, and Hibou 1999). Bereft of social capital, this class could not fulfil its self-proclaimed historical mission; that is, bring nation building to fruition. Cases like that in South Africa where Nelson Mandela promoted the healing process are aberrations. In acknowledgment of his role as "father of the nation," a cliché formulation mistakenly used to describe most African leaders, Mandela has been used for midwifery in most other states. Notable is his role in brokering the Lusaka Peace Accord between the protagonists in Burundi. Peace enables people to live in the same state. And though states cannot create nations, the habit of living together engenders "patriotic constitutionalism" (Cahen, 1999,155), a condition of possibility of the nation. Also notable is the venture by Colonel Mu'ammar Qadhafi to bring about peace in the Democratic Republic of Congo (DRC). The proposal entered into in Tripoli in the presence of eight African heads of state calls for the creation of an African peacekeeping force that would be stationed in a buffer zone between the DRC and Rwanda and Uganda. As laudable initiatives, the foregoing may be evidence that warring protagonists need an external catalyst to overcome their seemingly instinctive resistance to peace building, a necessary condition for self-empowerment.[24]

CONCLUSION

Lonsdale (1989, 23) posits that only delicate statesmanship can create a new moral order required for transcending political tribalism. Africa's first-generation leadership could not meet this challenge. Even those who saw its possibility failed to see its desirability. Thus, they fanned the flames of political tribalism, making ethnic explosions as well as implosions commonplace. These fragmented and emptied identities of all collective experience, causing people to follow completely different social trajectories and enabling the identification of "chosen traumas." However, to attribute the role played by the leadership in this malfunctioning to genetics is wrong. Biology cannot be confounded with their preoccupation with material interests in the absence of appropriate modes of political accountability.[25] It is in this context that the leadership paid more attention to their strategic interest, even if this was to the detriment of "enlightened public interest." Its capacity to deform the latter, in some cases, was a primary cause of the "wars of the educated." Because of their failure to respect *jus in belli* that regulated warfare in precolonial Africa, these wars generally led to a rupture in social relations among the protagonists.

Prodemocracy activists, who seek to smuggle ethnicity out of the mainstream political culture, now contest the power of those who have promoted political tribalism and the war of the educated. For the former, tribe really is a metaphor for civic virtue. Though belonging to an ethnic group, they are neither apologetic of that fact nor its apologists. Comprising members of civil society, women who are tired of "the wars of the educated" and its consequences (namely, the complete rupture that they span in social relations), as well as NGOs, see another forward position. Proof of this is their commitment to nurturing democratic identities with a view to changing the consciousness of the common man that is the foot soldier in this project. Realizing its political possibility as well as ethical feasibility, advocates of political tribalism tried to stop this "heretical discourse" on the tracks. In some cases, this has involved appealing to culture that is the vehicle par excellence of hegemony. Its results have been mitigated as the African is continuously being embedded and inserted in other cultures as a result of globalization with its time-space compression and the creation of new democratic spaces. Celebrating "flames of peace" is evidence that Africans are beginning to "move on."

John Dewey (1983, 502) remarked that the present is a continuously moving moment stretching out a hundred years in both directions from here and now. It is, therefore, always a present of the past and the future, a future of the present. Recent African history shows that for this resignification that puts the continent on a cross roads to be consensually acceptable, it has to incorporate the really real past rather than just a politicized version that tends to promote negative remembering among some groups in a state. Synergy would be gained to the extent that this past is pluralized by changing its narratives to include suppressed histories. Consequently, this should lead to a change in the space of structured possibility, thereby enabling the sustenance of democratic values invaluable in encountering what Rainer Bauböck (2001, 320) has referred to as the "fact of cultural pluralism," namely the persistence and salience of internal cultural distinctions in contemporary societies that are marked by religion, language, ethnic origin, racial category or different ways of life. So far, African states have lacked the capacity to overcome these distinctions.

NOTES

1. Given Africa's diversity, this chapter would infer generalities from specific examples. Historians, who see every generalization as overgeneralized, would undoubtedly challenge this approach, but it is privileged in the social sciences because it enables a more sophisticated and wide-ranging description of political phenomena, as well as explanation and prediction.

2. It has been noted that man identifies with nature, clan, and religion. This "gives the individual security. He belongs to, he is rooted in, a structuralized whole in which he has an unquestionable place. He may suffer from hunger or suppression, but he does not suffer from the worst of all—complete aloneness and doubt." See Isaacs (1975, 35).

3. Bhabha (1990); Senghor (1996) buys into this logic by contending that the state precedes the nation. Displacing the debate, he is more concerned with ends than with processes.

4. Using the economic crisis that Africa wallows in as an example, Shaw and Aluko (1985, p. xv), say that "the future is not just the extension of such circumstances or cycles. Rather, crisis may produce its own dialectic, its own antithesis. Notwithstanding existential or ideological differences, optimism is not to be denied altogether."

5. Jok and Hutchison (1999). As the authors point out, the manipulation of symbols was also very important. SPLA's decision to adopt the name Titweng or "cattle guards" for its civilian-based militia was not an innocent decision. Since many Dinka herders had failed to defend their cattle from successive SSIA incursions, conscription into this force offered them an opportunity to redeem their dignity. Similarly, local SSIA officers who were pitted in battle against the SPLA formed the Dec in boor or "White army," comprising mostly loosely organized groups of armed Nuer youths who protected the local herds during the dry season. Essentially, this army was a latter-day rendition of an earlier form of Nuer youth brigade known as burnam (Jok and Hutchison 1999, 134).

6. Bloch (1953, 20, 22) makes a similar plea when he calls on historians to forgo judgments of "good or evil" for the more sober task of understanding. In a world where the foreigner is invariably considered evil, "a little more understanding of people would be necessary merely for guidance, in conflicts which are unavoidable; all the more to prevent them while there is still time."

7. Thomas Packenham (1991) not only sees the backwardness of the "dark continent" as a result of the endemic interethnic conflict but also as a justification for colonialism.

8. Both terms refer to the same form of state. Eboussi (1993) uses the former and Chabal and Daloz (1999) see this as a state where the visible institutional mechanisms are less significant than the subterranean roots issued from the complex world of factional struggles and local rivalries. .

9. For an explication of these concepts, see, Yovel (1998). Writing on this form of intolerance in heterogeneous societies, Bakhtin observes that there is a historical tendency to promote monoglossia over heteroglossia. That is, one language is elevated to the status of oracle, and under its spell dissenting gestures are marginalized and the community's discourse is purified of "alien" utterances, thereby leading to a replacement of the democratic interplay of its voices by the dominant discourse's holy war against everything that it others. For an explication see Evans (1998, esp. 414).

10. For a case study, see, Nkwi (1997, 67–86) and Jua (2002, 336–358).

11. The history of mentalities, which takes a keen interest in the masses and in the social embodiment of ideas rather than in the intellectual achievement of great thinkers, has used the press as a privileged source. See Le Goff (1974).

12. Since the president has the prerogative to nominate several members, there is no doubt that Kikuyu and Luo fears of exclusion could have been assuaged if he named more people from these groups. He did not do this, seemingly, because of opposition within KANU. Hardliners in this camp believed that the Kikuyus had "eaten" enough and that the Luo being too arrogant, had merely helped them. Now it was the time for other groups to "eat." For details see Ochieng (1997).

13. These results, I must emphasize, are unofficial since the National Electoral Commission never declared them. See The Federal Ministry of Information and Culture, (n.d.).

14. Adepts such as Colonel Abubakar Dangiwa Umar lost their positions in government and were imprisoned only because of their opposition to Abacha's decision to annul the June 12 election. Contrary to Abacha, and in the company of some prominent Northerners who comprised the Group of 18, he believed that for the greater cause of national unity power should also be wielded by Southerners. For a text of the open letter, which they sent to Abacha, thereby exposing themselves to the charge of treason see, *Tell*, No. 15, April 13, 1998, 22–23. Also notable is a recent decision by the main opposition party in Gabon to expel one of its prominent members, who was indicted for practicing political tribalism (see *Africa*, No. 1, November 19, 2000).

15. The recent trial of a Catholic bishop in Rwanda on charges of preaching ethnic hate that led to the genocide by the Arusha International Tribunal is a case in point. Whereas the case against this bishop was dismissed, several priests have been convicted for this same charge.

16. In Africa, it has been pointed out, the "Big man" is powerful and rich, a benefactor far above the people whose support he seeks (see *The Economist*, May 13, 2000, 23). In this particular instance, Naah Ondoua, the minister of environment and forests distributed material and liquid cash to the tune of about 3 million francs CFA (see *The Post*, September 11, 2000, 3.)

17. Putman (1992, 167) notes that this engagement "gives rise to social capital—'features of social organization, such as networks, norms and trust, that facilitate coordination and (spontaneous) cooperation for mutual benefit.'" I would also acknowledge the fragility of this class as well as its tenuous position. Machiavelli (1952) points out that the process introducing new institutions is fraught with difficulties. Beneficiaries of the old system are apt to resist and the commitment of the reformers is easily shaken. He argues that reformers should count not only on prayers but also on force. Inasmuch as I agree with the observation, I would question his penchant to construe force as military force. Rather, Sidney Tarrow's (1995) broad definition, construed to include power in movement, is more acceptable. Thus, the challenge facing this class consists of converting a critical mass of people to its cause.

18. Admittedly, NGOs' as well as international NGOs' involvement in peace building in Africa constitutes the subject for another study. It suffices to point out here that at a symposium organized by the U.S. Institute of Peace in October 1995, it was recognized that their efficacy in this realm would be enhanced by providing short-term employment for country experts who have the requisite ethnological and sociological expertise needed to develop appropriate population profiles before an emergency erupts (see Smock 1996).

19. This assertion is an overgeneralization, since it is not true of some societies. See the case of the Mafa in van Santen (2000, 248–265).

20. The discussion in this section of the chapter is based on a conversation with Cyprian Fisiy, January 25, 1995.

21. Parelli notes that "when the past is resignified so as to explain (and thus legitimate) the present, what is at stake is more than the here and now. To the extent that the resignification bears on the projects and possibilities of the actors in question, a dispute over the past is a struggle for control over the future" (cited in Norval 1998, 251).

22. Gesine Schwan (1998, 737), noting the tendency to confound expiation with punishment in the modern secularized world, argues that the latter in Judeo-Christian tradition "is only called for if it leads to a repentance of the perpetrator and a reconciliation and restoration of the broken relationship between the perpetrator and his victim or society as a whole."

23. Ubuntu is a Zulu word that sums up the generosity of the African spirit and has been translated by Lapsley (1998, 742) as "human beingness."

24. Paulo Friere (see Shor and Freire 1987, 109) argues that this is a social feeling that should be used to help others to be free by transforming the totality of society.

25. Hobbes (1962, 63) noted in another context that "the secret thoughts of man run all over things, holy, profane, clean, obscene, grave and light, without shame or blame."

REFERENCES

Achebe, C. 1990. *Hopes and impediments: Selected essays*. New York: Anchor Books/Doubleday.

Anderson, B. 1990. *Imagined communities*. London: Verso.

Anderson, J. 1995. Comment: 'Cyberites', knowledge workers and new creoles in the superhighway. *Anthropology Today* 11 (4): 13–15.

Appadurai, A. 1990. Disjuncture and difference in the global economy. *Theory, Culture and Society* 17: 295–310.

Appiah, K. 1992. *In my father's house*. Oxford: Oxford University Press.

Bauböck, R. 2001. Cultural citizenship, minority rights and self-government. *Citizenship today*, edited by T. A. Aleinikoff and D. Klausmeyer. Washington DC: Carnegie Endowment for International Peace.

Bayart, J.-F. 1993. *The state in Africa: The politics of the belly*. New York: Longman.

Bayart, J.-F., S. Ellis, and B. Hibou. 1999. *The criminalization of the state in Africa*. Oxford: James Currey.

Beetham, D. 1995. What future for economic and social rights. *Political Studies* 43 (4): 41–60.

Bhabha, H. K., ed. 1990. *Nation and narration*. London: Routledge.

Bloch, M. 1953. *The historian's craft*. New York: Alfred A. Knopf.

Bourdieu, P. 1990. Social space and symbolic power. In *Other words: Essays on a reflexive sociology*, edited by P. Bourdieu. Stanford: Stanford University Press.

Bratton, M. 1989. Beyond the state: Civil society and associational life in Africa. *World Politics* 41 (3): 407–430.

Cahen, M. 1999. L'état ne crée pas la nation: La nationalization du monde. *Autrepart* 10: 151–170.

Calhoun, C. 1997. Multiculturalism and nationalism, or why feeling at home is not a substitute for public space. In *Cultural pluralism, identity and globalization*, edited by L. E. Soares. Paris: UNESCO/ISSC/EDUCAM.

Chabal, P. 1994. *Power in Africa*. New York: St. Martin's Press.

Chabal, P. 1996. The African crisis: Context and interpretation. In *Postcolonial identities in Africa*, edited by R. Werbner and T. Ranger. London: Zed Books.

Chabal, P., and J. P. Daloz. 1999. *Africa works: Disorder as a political instrument*. Oxford: James Currey.

Chege, M. 1998. Comment on "Structure and strategy in ethnic conflict: A few steps toward synthesis." In *Annual World Bank conference on development economics*, edited by B. Pleskovic and J. E. Stiglitz. Washington, DC: World Bank.

Cliffe, L., and R. Luckham. 1999. Complex political emergencies and the state: Failure and the fate of the state. *Third World Quarterly* 20 (1): 27–50.

Cohen, A. P. 1992. Self-conscious anthropology. In *Identity/difference*, edited by J. Oakely, H. Callaway, and W. E. Connolly. Ithaca, NY: Cornell University Press.

Collier, P. 1998. The political economy of ethnicity. In *Annual World Bank conference on development economics*, edited by E. Plaskovic and J. E. Stiglitz. Washington, DC: World Bank.

Connolly, W. E. 1991. *Identity/difference: Democratic negotiations of political paradox.* Ithaca, NY: Cornell University Press.

Connolly, W. E. 1994. Tocqueville territory and violence. *Theory, Culture and Society* 11: 19–40.

Coulibally, T. 2000. La classe politique ivorienne se cherche. *Le Monde Diplomatique* (October): 22–23.

Dassering, O. 1999. Sacheresse et pressions anthropiques: Evolution ecologique et adaptation des eleveurs Transhumants au Tchad. Paper presented at a national seminar on farmer–grazier conflicts in Chad, Ndjamena, May 11–14.

Desai, G. 1993. The invention of invention. *Cultural Critique* (Spring): 119–142.

de Tocqueville, A. 1990. *Recollections of the French revolution.* New Brunswick, NJ: Transaction Books

Dewey, J. 1983. Some historical factors in philosophical reconstruction. In *A world of ideas*, edited by L. A. Jacobus. New York: St. Martin's Press.

Eboussi, F. 1993. *Les conférences nationales en Afrique noire.* Paris: Karthala.

Evans, F. 1998. Communication and the politics of multiculturalism. *Constellations* 5 (3):

Federal Ministry of Information and Culture (Nigeria). n.d. *June 12 and the future of Nigerian democracy.* Lagos: Federal Ministry of Information and Culture.

Fraser, N. 1992. Rethinking the public sphere: A contribution to the critique of actually existing democracy. In *Habermas and the public sphere*, edited by C. Calhoun. Cambridge: MIT Press.

Goodhand, J., and D. Hulme. 1999. From wars to complex political emergencies: Understanding conflict and peace building in the new world disorder. *Third World Quarterly* 20 (1): 13–26.

Graf, W. D. 1988. *The Nigerian state.* London: James Currey.

Gramsci, A. 1978. *Selections from prison notebooks.* New York: International.

Guyer, J. 1995. Remarks for the roundtable on "Beyond the crisis." Paper prepared for the workshop, "Prospects for Peace in Africa: The State, Civil Society and the International Community," Amherst College, Amherst, November 9–11.

Hecht, D., and M. Simone. 1994. *Invisible governance: The art of African micropolitics.* New York: Autonomedia.

Heidegger, M. 1977. The question of technology. In *The question of technology and other essays*, edited by M. Heidegger. New York: Harper.

Hirschmann, A. 1963. *Journeys toward progress.* New York: Twentieth Century Fund.

Hobbes, T. 1962. *Leviathan*, edited by M. Oakeshott. New York: Collier.

Hobsbawm, E. 1990. *Nations and nationalism since 1780: Myth and reality.* Cambridge: Cambridge University Press.

Honwana, A. 1998. Negotiating post-war identities: Child soldiers in Mozambique and Angola. Paper presented at the 9th General Assembly of CODESRIA, Dakar, Senegal.

Horowitz, D. L. 1985. *Ethnic groups in conflict.* Berkeley and Los Angeles: University of California Press.

Horowitz, D. L. 1998. Structure and strategy in ethnic conflict: A few steps toward synthesis. In *Annual World Bank conference on development economics.* Washington, DC: World Bank.

Isaacs, H. 1975. *Idols of tribe*. Cambridge: Harvard University Press.

Jok, M. J., and S. E. Hutchinson. 1999. Sudan's prolonged second civil war and the militarization of the Nuer and Dinka ethnic identities. *African Studies Review* 42 (2): 125–146.

Jua, N. 2000. Preventing ethnic conflicts and peace building in Africa: Lessons from the recent past. A position paper prepared for UNESCO, Paris.

Jua, N. 2002. Small is not always beautiful: A case study of the Njinikom Area Development Association. *Nordic Journal of African Studies* 13 (3): 336–358.

Kotzé, H. J. 2000. The state and social change in South Africa. *International Social Science Journal* 52 (163): 79–94.

Lapsley, M., SSM. 1998. Confronting the past and creating the future: The redemptive value of truth-telling. *Social Research* 65 (4): 741–758.

Lee, O. 1998. Culture and democratic theory: Toward a theory of symbolic democracy. *Constellations* 5 (4): 433–455.

Le Goff, J. 1974. Les mentalités. In *Faire l'histoire: Les nouveaux objets*, edited by J. Le Goff and P. Nora. Paris: Gallimard.

LiPuma, E., and C. Calhoun. 1993. Culture and the concept of culture in a theory of practice. In *Bourdieu: Criminal perspectives*, edited by C. Calhoun, E. LiPuma, and M. Postone. Chicago: University of Chicago Press.

Lonsdale, J. 1989. Africa's past in Africa's future. *Canadian Journal of African Studies* 23 (1): 126–146.

Lonsdale, J. 1992. The politics of conquest in Western Kenya. In *Unhappy valley: Conflict in Kenya & Africa, Book One: State and class*, edited by B. Berman and J. Lonsdale. London: James Currey.

Lonsdale, J. 1994. Moral ethnicity and political trabilism. In *Invention of boundaries: Historical and anthropological approaches to the study of ethnicity and nationalism*. Occasional Paper No. 11, International Development Studies, Roskilde University, Roskilde, Denmark.

Machiavelli, N. 1952. *Oeuvres completes*. Paris: Gallimard.

MacKinnon, C. 1993. Crimes of war, crimes of peace. In *On human rights*, edited by S. Shute and S. Hurley. London: Basic Books.

Mamdani, M. 1996. *Citizen and subject*. Princeton, NJ: Princeton University Press.

Mazrui, A. A. 2001. Roundtable: Reparations in the era of globalization. At the forty-fourth annual meeting, Special Roundtable on Africa and the African Diaspora: Past, present, future, Houston, Texas, November 15–18.

Mbembe, A. 2000. Esquisses d'une démocratie à l'africaine. *Le Monde Diplomatique* (October): 20–21.

Mohammed, A. D. n.d. *The June 12 presidential election was neither free nor fair*. Ahmadou Bello University, Zaria, Nigeria.

Moore, S. F. 1993. Changing perspectives on a changing Africa: The work of anthropology. In *Africa and the disciplines*, edited by R. H. Bates, V. Y. Mudimbe, and J. O'Barr. Chicago: University of Chicago Press.

Mouffe, C. 1997. Democratic identity and pluralist politics. In *Cultural pluralism, identity and globalization,* edited by L. E. Soares. Paris: UNESCO/ISS/EDUCAM.

Mugemzi, I. K. 1999. Le Rwanda dans le processus démocratique. In *Proceedings of a regional conference on democracy, decentralization, media and good governance*. Yaoundé, Cameroon: ICASSRT.

Newbury, C. 1994. Introduction: Paradoxes of democratization in Africa. *African Studies Review* 37 (1): 1–8.

Ngugi, W. T. 1986. *Decolonizing the mind*. London: James Currey.

Nkwi, P. N. 1997. Rethinking the role of elites in rural development: A case study from Cameroon. *Journal of Contemporary African Studies* 15 (1): 67–86.

Nordstrom, C. 1992. The backyard front. In *The paths to domination, resistance and terror*, edited by C. Nordstrom and J. Martin. Berkeley and Los Angeles: University of California Press.

Norval, A. J. 1998. Memory, identity and the (im)possibility of reconciliation: The work of the Truth and Reconciliation Committee in South Africa. *Constellations* 5 (2): 250–282.

Ntumba, L. L. 1998. Ethnicité, citoyennete et gouvernementalité dans le contexte du renouveau constitutioniste Africaine. Paper presented at the General Assembly, CODESRIA, Dakar, Senegal, December 14–18.

Ochieng, P. 1997. Folly of sidelining "opposition tribes." *Sunday Nation* (Nairobi), January 26: 8, 9.

Packenham, T. 1991. *The scramble for Africa*. New York: Random House.

Putman, R. D. 1992. *Making democracy work*. Princeton, NJ: Princeton University Press.

Ranger, T. 1992. The invention of tradition in colonial Africa. In *The invention of tradition*, edited by E. Hobsbawm and T. Ranger. Cambridge: Cambridge University Press.

Renan, E. 1990. What is a nation? (Translated by M. Thorn). In *Nation and narrative*, edited by H. K. Bhabha. London: Routledge.

Rothchild, D. 1989. Africa's interethnic conflicts: The linkages, demands, regime strategies and the management of conflict. Paper presented at the research conference, "Conflict Resolution in Africa," Brookings Institution, Washington, DC, October 15–18.

Schawn, G. 1998. The healing value of truth-telling: Chances and social conditions in a secularized world. *Social Research* 65 (4): 725–740.

Scott, A., and J. Street. 2000. From media to e-protest. *Information, Communication and Society* 13 (2): 215–240.

Senghor, L. 1996. *Senghor in dialogo*. Rio de Jeneiro: IEAA.

Shaw, T., and O. Aluko. *Africa projected: From recession to renaissance by the year 2000*. New York: St. Martin's Press.

Shor, I., and P. Freire. 1987. *A pedagogy for liberation*. New York: Begin & Garvey.

Smock, D. R. 1996. *Humanitarian assistance and conflict in Africa*. Washington, DC: U.S. Institute of Peace.

Tamarkin, M. 1996. Culture and politics in Africa: Legitimizing ethnicity, rehabilitating the postcolonial state. *Nationalism and Ethnic Politics* 2 (3): 360–380.

Tarrow, S. 1995. *Power in movement*. Cambridge: Cambridge University Press.

Tenebaye, M. 1999. La probléme des conflits agriculteurs/eleveurs au Tchad. Paper presented at the national seminar on farmer–grazier conlicts, Ndjamena, Tchad, May 11–14.

United Nations Economic and Social Council, Commission on Human Rights. 1996. *The impact of armed conflict on children: Report of the secretary-general, Ms. Graca Machel*. New York: United Nations.

Valkan, V. 1991. On chosen trauma. *Mind and Human Interaction* 3: 3.

Van Santen, J. 2000. Gender and the debates on ethnicity in Africanist anthropology: Inclusion in the third millennium. In *The anthropology of Africa: Challenges for the 21st century*, edited by P. N. Nkwi. Yaoundé: Imprimerie Saint Paul.

Werbner, R. 2002. Introduction: Challenging minorities, difference and tribal citizenship in Botswana. *Journal of Southern African Studies* 28 (4): 671–684.

Williams, P. 1991. *The alchemy of race and rights*. Cambridge: Harvard University Press.

Yovel, Y. 1998. Tolerance as grace and rightful recognition. *Social Research* 65 (4): 895–919.

Zickmund, S. 1997. Approaching the radical other: The discursive culture of cyberhate. In *Virtual culture*, edited by S. Jones. London: SAGE Publications.

Zizek, S. 1992. Eastern Europe's republics of Gilead. In *Dimensions of radical democracy*, edited by C. Mouffee.

15

The Struggle for Stability in Nigeria's Contemporary Politics (1990–1999) and the Lessons for the Fourth Republic

E. IKE UDOGU

The assumption that democratic principles will serve as a possible panacea for Nigeria's political development, peace, and stability has been promoted by Africanist scholars, foreign governments, and some international agencies. However, it has been argued elsewhere that democratic and constitutional ideals are less meaningful if the people are poor. After all, democracy and respect for the rule of law are popular in developed societies in the West because of economic prosperity and the high premium placed on these values in these systems. In politics in which survival is at the heart of daily life, political and economic "isms" matter less for the majority of the population (Udogu 1997a, 3). Moreover, as Claude Ake (1990, 2) has noted, "the problem of persistence of underdevelopment is related to lack of [stability and] democracy in Africa . . . democracy is not just a consummatory value but also an instrumentalist one [in the process of developing good governance]."

It is vexing to many Nigerianists that instability and the ruination of democratic practices and values in Nigeria by the various military regimes lasted for over a quarter of a century. Therefore, the question today is how to make a clean break from military rule and institutionalize an efficacious and lasting democracy in the country in order to further stability. Whereas some political scientists argue that stability and democratization in Nigeria are possible only after the "deconstruction" of all political, economic, and social formations and the reconstruction of the state itself, this study takes a somewhat different approach from that of these scholars. It is intended, inter alia, to suggest ways for promoting political stability within the existing state formation. Within this context, therefore, the following issues, among others, will be briefly examined: leadership, constitution, human rights, civil society, and illuminating their significance in enhancing stability and a sustainable democratic genre in the polity.

LEADERSHIP

Definitionally, Robert C. Tucker (1981, 21) defined leadership as "a process of human interaction in which some individuals exert, or attempt to exert, a determining influence upon others." James MacGregor Burns (1978, 19) defined the concept as "leaders inducing followers to act for certain goals that represent the values and the motivation—the aspirations and expectations—of both leaders and followers."

The issue of leadership or lack thereof in Nigeria has been the subject of intense intellectual discourse (Achebe 1983, 1; Odunsi 1996, 66–81; Osia 1992, 175–194; Udogu 1997c, 149–188). Even military and civilian leaders have been in agreement that the republic has failed dismally in its attempts at finding nationally acceptable leaders (Olowo 1994, 1222–1223). This problem, arguably, flows in part from the country's colonial experience. Indeed, Chinua Achebe (1983, 11) has noted, "In spite of conventional opinion Nigeria has been less than fortunate in its leadership. A basic element of this misfortune is the seminal absence of intellectual rigor in the political thought of our founding fathers—a tendency to pious materialistic woolliness and self-centered pedestrianism." Achebe suggested that attitudes such as these were likely to produce individuals who pursued wealth rather than selfless leaders of their society. In any case, this behavior pattern may have been nourished by the character of the state, which was alien to the country's indigenous leaders and population in the colonial framework that existed before 1960. Nevertheless, it was an attitude that spilled over into postindependence Nigeria.

Further, it has been contended, theoretically, that numerous reasons account for leadership problems in Nigeria: ideological incongruencies, the nature of political competition and ethnic consciousness, the structural dilemmas of the Nigerian army, corruption and mismanagement, political departicipation, intolerance and inflexibility on policy issues, and minority groups' roles in national politics (Odunsi 1996, 68). These issues, which generally mitigate the legitimacy of a state, constitute some of the bases of leadership dilemmas in Nigeria.

The central question is how to address these perceived problems in order to devise a viable democratic system to advance stability at the dawn of the twenty-first century. Ladipo Ademolekun (1988, 105) suggests "a high quality leader who combines a sound and logical understanding of the different dimensions of the nation-building task with awareness of the need to cultivate the practical skills of statecraft and efficient management." Richard Sklar (1986, 127) contends that Africa (and Nigeria in particular) needs a leader that comprehends that successful democracy equals "the existence and operation of a political mechanism which can be expected to ensure the accountability of rulers to the people." Such an ideology is likely to further stability in Nigeria.

Within this framework, too, Odunsi (1996, 78–79) addresses, in a broader context, the need to craft an adequate document to address the leadership issue in Nigerian politics. He contends that given the significance of the national constitution in the governance of the country, certain provisions are necessary to influence the governing elite in attempts to enhance stability and democratic virtues. He infers that the constitution should incorporate a number of basic democratic values significant for promoting good governance. These attributes include demands for political actors to uphold and recognize the supremacy of the constitution in their role as political leaders; imposition of proper and adequate safeguards capable of holding the political elite accountable for their actions and inactions; enunciation of the role, function, and pattern of behavior for political leadership with appropriate constraints to curb or check maladministration; and adequate steps to restructure and redefine the role of the military in a democratic polity to deter further incursions into the affairs of the state in the future.

Furthermore, if one were to accept Achebe's (1983, 1) conjecture that "the trouble with Nigeria is simply and squarely a failure of leadership . . . [and that] the Nigerian problem is the unwillingness or inability of its leaders to rise to the responsibility, to the challenge of personal example which are the hallmarks of true leadership," to be plausible, how might the country go about tackling this problem? A possible strategy could be through political socialization and the development of an appropriate political culture and urging the people's commitment to it (Ake 1967, 1). In this regard, the "paraphrased" view espoused by the revolutionary Chinese leader, Mao Zeadong, in the Chinese situation, might be instructive in the Nigerian case:

It is necessary to train a great many people as vanguard of [a democratic] revolution. People imbued with the spirit of self-sacrifice. People with largeness of mind who are loyal, active and upright. People who never pursue selfish interests. . . . People who fear no difficulties, but remain steadfast and advance courageously in the face of difficulties. People who are neither high nor seekers after the limelight, but are conscientious and full of practical sense. . . . If [only Nigeria can come up with] a host of such vanguard elements, the task of [developing good leadership in the republic might] be successfully fulfilled (cited in Bertsch 1991, 76).

The bottom line is that Nigeria needs an unselfish and patriotic leader to construct an authentic and transparent government within a constitutional framework in the search for stability. How these objectives might be attained in the republic will be addressed later on in this chapter. In the meantime, however, a concise discussion of the constitution, which represents a significant social contract between the governors and the governed, is in order.

CONSTITUTION

John Mukum Mbaku (1996, 48–49) has argued that in order to design a democratic and effective constitution for African countries in the twenty-first century the process should maximize popular participation (i.e., the relevant stakeholder groups must be enfranchised and provided the facilities to participate fully and effectively in constitution making) in order to further the system's legitimacy and stability. But what is a constitution? Jack Plano and Roy Olton (1982, 427) define a constitution as "a state's organic or fundamental law, which prescribes the basic organs of government and their operations, the distribution and use of power, and the relationship between the individual and the states. In all cases, the function of constitutions is to establish the norms by which the system operates."

Nigerians have written numerous constitutions, both in the country's pre- and postindependence eras. In fact, under the military regimes alone, Nigerians have written four constitutions (1979, 1989, 1995, and 1999). Could it be said that the frequency of these constitutional convocations implies that the problem of political governance in Nigeria is based on the country's constitutional designs? Perhaps yes, many critics of military rule in Nigeria would argue. In fact, many contend that the military's invitations to attend constitutional conferences and to write "faulty" constitutions were mainly maneuvers to mollify the political class while the military attempted to consolidate its authority over the republic (Udogu 1997b, p. 7). Witness, for example, the problematic 1994 election of members to the constitutional conference organized by the Abacha regime and the time it took to produce the defunct 1995 constitution. In reality, what was wrong with the 1979 and 1989 constitutions? Couldn't they have been amended? Is it any wonder, then, that in his criticism of the Abacha constitutional conference, Olusegun Obasanjo (1994, 252) noted:

I do not know much about the 1989 constitution [for it was never implemented], but I know more than a bit of the 1979 constitution. That constitution was designed to serve Nigeria of the 21st century. Like all human contrivances it cannot be described as perfect. . . . But it can be amended rather than jettisoned in its entirety. It was designed to give everybody hope and stake in Nigeria. If this has not been realized, it is not the fault of the constitution but the fault of the operators.

Central to this concise discussion is the extent to which the Nigerian constitution could lead to a democratic political culture and a priori political stability. It is a given that constitutional and democratic consolidations in the federation will be hollow if provisions of the constitution are consistently flouted by lawmakers (Kieh 2001, 267). What is needed in view of the country's past history is the writing of an efficacious constitution that stresses the significance of its supremacy. Put another way, what Nigeria needs is a constitution with constitutionalism (Fatton 1995, 79; Ihonvbere 2000, 45), whereby the military class and political entrepreneurs cannot use extraconstitutional means to subvert the political system. In fact, it is the unwillingness of the military-cum-political class to work within the constitution that has in part impeded the development of stability, democracy, and respect for human rights in the republic.

HUMAN RIGHTS

The discussion on the human rights question in Nigeria flows from the dismal record of the various military regimes, particularly the Abacha administration. It is a fact that if stability, democracy and peace are to be furthered in the republic, respect for human rights must be practiced (Takougang 1999, 179; Welch 1992, 58). But why is the issue of human rights particularly unique in the Nigerian situation? This might be a naïve query given the authoritarian character of military regimes. Moreover, the military regime's intolerance of political debate, governance with decrees, perception that it is above the law, unpreparedness to brook opposition, and application of brute and arrogant force to carry out its agenda are some of the examples of military practices that have exacerbated human rights problems in Nigeria. But Nigeria is at the crossroads in its quest to promote stability and a priori sustain its fledgling democracy.

There is a paradox in the nature of human rights violations in Nigeria; it is a contradiction that stems from the fact that the country was a signatory to the various human rights instruments. The important 1948 Universal Declaration of Human Rights aside, there was the famous African Charter on Human and Peoples' Rights of 1981 and 1986, to which Nigeria was a prominent participant. For example, Theodore A. Couloumbis and James H. Wolfe (1990, 291) summed up the 1948 Universal Declaration of Human Rights as follows:

The right to life, liberty, and security of person; the right to freedom of thought, speech, and communication of information and ideas; freedom of assembly and religion; the right to government through free elections; the right to free movement within the state and free exit from it . . . freedom from arbitrary arrest and interference with the privacy of home and family; . . . The right to work, to protection against unemployment, and to join trade unions; the right to a standard of living adequate for health and well-being; the right to education.

The assumption is that the African Charter on Human and Peoples' Rights subsumes these declarations. Indeed, some scholars suggest that the content of the Banjul Charter exceeds the 1948 Universal Declaration of Human Rights in that it, among other things, addresses human rights within the context of civil, political, economic, social, cultural, and peoples' rights, including women's and children's rights (Gutto 1991, 5–22; Nzongola-Ntalalaja 1994, 9; Udogu 2000a, 33–35). The fundamental rights of Nigerians are enshrined in Chapter IV of the 1979 and 1999 constitutions. These rights include right to life; right to dignity of human person; right to personal liberty; right to fair hearing; right to private and family life; right to freedom of thought, conscience, and religion; right to freedom of expression and press; right to peaceful assembly and association; right to freedom of movement; and right to freedom from discrimination. The question, however, is to what extent lawmakers have in the quest to further stability, liberalization, and democracy, performed in the republic. As noted earlier, discussion on this issue is occasioned by the belief that respect for human rights will further stability, democracy, and economic revitalization in the republic.

It was the reluctance of the Nigerian state to respect the individual and, in fact, group rights of some of its minority collectivities that, inter alia, prompted the formation of the Ethnic Minority Rights Organization of Africa to demand justice from the government in the 1990s. The concern of the group was economic marginalization, which it pursued within the framework of Part 1, Article 1 of the International Convention on Civil and Political Rights. This article states, "All peoples have the right of self-determination. By virtue of that right to freely determine the people's status and freely pursue their economic, social and cultural development" (United Nations 1976). This view is supported in the preamble of the African Charter on Human and Peoples' Rights. It states, "Convinced that it is henceforth essential to pay a particular attention to the right to development and that civil and political rights cannot be dissociated from economic, social and cultural rights in their conception as well as universality and that the satisfaction of economic, social and cultural rights is a guarantee for the enjoyment of civil and political rights" (OAU 1982, 5).

Germane to this discussion is an attempt to sensitize lawmakers on the issue of human rights, its constitutional relevance, and its place in the rebirth of the republic. The unleashing of human freedom within the context of peace, justice, and fair play can only further the process of successful nation building. This is possible if the government is stable and if civil society is strengthened.

CIVIL SOCIETY AND POLITICAL DEVELOPMENT IN NIGERIA

Conceptually, civil society represents "an arena where manifold social movements . . . and civic organizations from all classes . . . attempt to constitute themselves in an ensemble of arrangements so that they can express themselves and advance their interests" (Stepan 1988, 3–4). S. F. Starr (1990, 194) notes that within the concept of Western tradition, civil society refers to that political space that is "distinct from government and that government is but one of the several institutions coexisting in a pluralistic social fabric." For Naomi Chazan (1992, p. 281), civil society refers to that segment of society that interacts with the state, exacts pressure and power on the state, and yet is distinct from the state.

The activity of civil society in Nigeria predates its birth as a sovereign nation-state in 1960. Indeed, it was the meeting of political activists in major cities, and the later articulation of their common interests, that in part resulted in the termination of colonial rule in Nigeria (Udogu 1995, 214). Today, similar activists are agitating for the construction of an effective democratic genre in the republic in order to promote stability. The issue in Nigeria's contemporary politics has been how to attain this objective in a country beset with sociopolitical and religioeconomic imbroglios.

Although many groups in Nigeria's civil society are pressing for an efficacious democratic government in the country because it could lead to stability, they have had a tough time implementing their basic objective of good governance. This was the situation in the 1990s, when the military government was determined to inoculate groups that were purported to be "antagonistic" to the cabal by using intimidation, cooptation, and sometimes bribery to assuage the opposition in civil society. Paradoxically, in instances in which civic organizations functioned with less military interference, the internal mechanisms of some have been relatively weak. In fact, Attahiru M. Jega (1997, 38–39) noted that,

Previous efforts such as Campaign for Democracy (CD), National Democratic Coalition (NADECO) and United Democratic Front of Nigeria (UDFN) have been constrained either by stigmatization, petty squabbles at the leadership levels or by the divide and rule tactics of the state and the ruling classes. . . . A major constraint to the forging of such a broad alliance for democracy has been the increasing proliferation of Human Rights NGOs gravitating around donors, and opportunistically competing with one another for grants.

Such issues generally hamper the efficacy of some NGOs in the democratization enterprise and advancement of stability because donors and supporters are likely to lose confidence in weak organizations. Note, for example, that the success scored by the prodemocracy movements in dethroning President Babangida and the eventual suffocation and dislocation of Ernest Shonekan's Interim National Government were short-lived following General Sani Abacha's coup d'état of November 17, 1993. This was probably the case because of inadequate unity among the NGOs and mutual suspicion at this time.

That notwithstanding, why has civil society become indispensable to the process of promoting good governance in Nigeria? How has civil society articulated its endeavors in the course of attaining its objectives? What are some possible roles civil society might play in constructing a transparent government based on accountability, the rule of law, and respect for human rights in the development of stability and democracy in the country?

A series of problematic events during the Abacha regime (1993–1998) led to the intensification of the activities of numerous prodemocracy and human rights groups in Nigeria. These were the Campaign for Democracy, Democratic Alternative, Civil Liberties Organization, Constitutional Rights Projects, Committee for the Defense of Human Rights, National Democratic Coalition, United Action for Democracy, Movement for the Survival of the Ogoni People, to list a few. These NGOs, in civil society, were determined to fight for democracy and stability in the polity. Additionally, the National Democratic Coalition, the United Democratic Front, and others formed the Joint Action Committee (JA-

COM) to increase their influence and pressure on the repressive Abacha regime in March 1998. The major objectives of the prodemocracy movements, human rights groups, and JACOM itself were the restoration of stability, democracy, and the formation of a Sovereign National Conference to address and thrash out the republic's lingering socioeconomic and political problems.

However, the politicohistorical prologue to the emergence of the Abacha administration, and the buoyant activities of NGOs in civil society, has its roots in President Babangida's annulment of the June 12, 1993, presidential elections between the late Moshood Abiola, of the Social Democratic Party, and Bashir Tofa, of the National Republican Convention.

General Sani Abacha, whose coup d'état took place on November 17, 1993, in his maiden address to the nation stated that his government would immediately begin the process of setting up a constitutional conference with full constitutional powers to, among other things, tackle the political malaise in the republic. In the meantime, however, groups opposed to the abrogation of the June 12 election announced their resistance to the regime. Moreover, other minority groups with pent-up anger regarding their marginalization in the political system found an outlet to vent their alienation. So, when in January 1994 the government set up a National Constitutional Conference Commission and charged it to collect memoranda from a cross-section of the country, the content of the memoranda illustrated the concerns of the various collectivities. The bone of contention between a segment of the society and the regime itself was whether the constitutional conference was going to be sovereign; that is, if its decisions were going to be binding to the nation and not to be tampered with by the government after they had been made (Udogu 1997b, 11–14). When it became clear that the process of constitutional engineering and democratization by the administration was diversionary, the negative attitude of critics of the regime started to solidify, and so too did the apathy toward the constitutional conference itself.

While the government was moving ahead with the constitutional conference, the critics, insisting on the implementation of the June 12, 1993, electoral results, boycotted the conference and proceeded to form the powerful opposition group known as the National Democratic Coalition on June 15, 1994, in civil society. The NADECO was to serve as a major opposition to the government, emphasizing the need for a sovereign national conference to be headed by the late Moshood Abiola. Indeed, the NADECO encouraged Abiola to declare himself president of the Federal Republic of Nigeria on June 11, 1994, thus placing the NADECO and the Abacha administration on a collision course in the struggle for stability and democracy in Nigeria.

At the conclusion of the National Constitutional Conference in December 1994, a series of organs were created to work toward the objectives contained in Abacha's inauguration speech and to construct a new civilian regime that could enjoy national legitimacy and, therefore, lead to political stability. In light of this assumption, the following committees were set up: the Transition Implementation Committee (headed by Mannan Nasir), the National Reconciliation Committee (chaired by Alex Akinyele), the Committee on Power (chaired by Abdularahman Okene), the Commission on Creation of States, Local Government and Boundary Adjustment (chaired by Arthur Mbanefo), the National Electoral Commission (headed by S. Dagogo-Jack), and the Federal Character Commission (chaired by Adamu Fika). These committees were to carry out their functions with the watchful eyes of the government and decrees, since the approved 1994–1995 draft constitution was inoperative. In addition, to keep the politicians busy and distracted from the military's agenda, a zero-party local-government election was conducted in early 1996 in spite of the fact that a local election for political parties was planned for December of the same year.

Furthermore, on June 17, 1996, the National Electoral Commission announced the rules for the formation of political parties. It imposed strict regulations for the formation of what it deemed as strong and "centrist" national political parties. Each party, among other regulations, was to pay a N500,000 registration fee. Out of this political engineering emerged five approved political parties: the United Nigeria Congress Party, the Democratic Party of Nigeria, the National Center Party of Nigeria, the Committee for National Consensus and the Grassroots Democratic Movement (National Democratic Movement 1998).

Elections were conducted in March 1997 for local government legislators in the thirty-six state assemblies, and the Senate and the House of Representatives in April 1998. There were to be three senators from each of the thirty-six states and one from the Federal Capital Territory, Abuja. In the House of Representatives, elections were to be held for each of the 360 federal constituencies in the federation.

To the chagrin of critics of the military-backed transition to democracy process, the five political parties sanctioned by the government endorsed General Sani Abacha as their consensus candidate for the presidency of Nigeria. In the same month, elections marked by low voter turnout were held for the Senate and House of Representatives. These elections and the endorsement of Abacha as the sole presidential candidate drew criticisms not only from the prodemocracy movements in civil society but also from other internal political groups. This was the case with respect to the Group of 34, led by former vice president Alex Ekwueme, and a group of northern professors. Moreover, it drew criticism from the international community; in particular, the European Union was vocal in its condemnation of this political development.

The activities of the Abacha administration called into question the credibility of the entire transition to democracy scheme. Indeed, numerous NGOs and opponents of the regime in civil society had continually stressed that the electoral process was a farce. As if the selection of General Abacha as the sole candidate of the five political parties was not problematic enough, a proposal was made that the vote on Abacha's candidacy was to be based on a national referendum of yes or no vote. This perplexity in Nigerian politics, and the struggle for stability and the rebirth of democracy itself, created tremendous alienation in civil society and on the electorate, as exemplified in the low (37 percent) voter turnout in the April 1998 poll.

To be sure, the pro-Abacha forces argued that Abacha would not be the first leader in the subregion to give up his military uniform, put on an *agbada* and become a civilian president. They cited Jerry Rawlings of Ghana (who, in any case, ran against other candidates) as a good case in point. The fact, though, is that Nigeria, with a population of more than 100 million and its diverse ethnic groups, is more complex than Ghana. In any case, this political development represented one of the paradoxes in Nigeria's perennial problems with the search for stability and the struggle for democratic rule. It was during this complex debate on Nigeria's political future that Abacha died on June 8, 1998, thus plunging the country into another temporary crisis.

In the federation's political development, civil society as represented by some prodemocracy and human rights organizations (e.g., Campaign for Democracy, NADECO, etc.) were insistent that Abacha's transition program, like that of Ibrahim Babangida, was a ruse, and that Abacha's self-succession bid in whatever guise could not form the basis of a genuine democracy and durable peace and stability in Nigeria. It is imperative that if political stability and democracy are to be advanced at this significant juncture in Nigeria's new political dispensation, accountability and transparency must be put in place.

ACCOUNTABILITY

There is no doubting the fact that a regime or administration that does not provide its citizens with a transparent account of its stewardship is likely to cast suspicion on itself and could a priori create a problem of legitimacy. Further, given the genre of military governance that demurred opposition party or groups, accountability, which in the words of Harold Lasswell (Lasswell, Lerner, and Rothwell 1952, 7) is a significant dimension of democracy, has suffered in the periods of military and civilian rule in Nigeria. Indeed, speaking at a lecture held at the Arewa House Conference Hall in Kaduna, a former head of state who was in power for two years before Babangida's coup (1984–1985), General Muhammmadu Buhari, noted,

It is an understatement to say that there has been a clear lack of accountability in the conduct of public affairs in this country. The public service, as the executive agency of the government of the day at its various levels—at federal, state and local levels—wields enormous powers. . . . But the public has virtually no knowledge or control over what they do in a regime when the public has no representatives in a legislature because a legislative assembly does not exist. With such ignorance and in the absence of legislative monitoring, control of public officers and ensuring accountability become impossible tasks for the public . . . the last time the annual financial account of the Federal Government was prepared and submitted for an audit was, I understand, in 1980. And at the 1984 conference of Auditor-General of the Federation and the State Directors of Audit, it was revealed to the astonishment of no one that eleven states last submitted their annual account for audit in 1967 (Udogu 2000b, 126).

It goes without saying that such an unsavory condition in the republic led to corruption, embezzlement of public funds, pauperization of the masses in a potentially rich country, and, consequently, a lack of trust in the government. Indeed, the political and economic frustrations in the polity could be visualized against this backdrop. But it is possible for the country to exculpate itself from this instability and malaise by developing an effective democratic system that emphasizes the importance of accountability and transparency in political governance. This is so because such a system might lead to trust for the custodians of power and, consequently, encourage the citizens' support for the political system.

It is, however, difficult to govern a society for close to three decades since its independence in 1960 in an authoritarian fashion and expect the politicos to alter their political behavior patterns in one fell swoop. To this end, the following discussion will center on some possible ways for advancing stability and sustaining democracy and peace in Nigeria.

CONCLUSION: SOME POSSIBLE SOLUTIONS

The writing of a superb constitution, and the construction of adequate political institutions and structures, while extremely significant, cannot guarantee good governance. The 1979 constitution was believed by many to be relatively adequate, yet it was unable to solve the nation's problems. Therefore, for the republic and its constitution, institutions, and structures to be able to produce the desired result, the political class, civil society, and military brass must be determined to work within the framework of the legal document (Udogu 1995, 216). To accomplish this task not only requires a reorientation of the political attitudes of the custodians of power toward good governance, but also the reinvigoration of civil society to serve as a watchdog against the malfeasance of some political entrepreneurs. This view is borne out by the fact that humans are not "angels," and are, on occasion, likely to pursue selfish interests at the expense of the tier of government they are elected to serve.

The desire to establish a solid and stable democratic system to move Nigeria forward is a sine qua non in light of its history. Within this context, therefore, the following strategies might be important in sustaining stability and peace in the Fourth Republic: decentralization of power to the grassroots, pluralism and decentralization of the economy, education (as it relates to human capital formation) and political education, including the inculcation of democratic values, respect for open debate, and so on, and popular participation in all aspects of the development process (Obasanjo 1990, 762).

Briefly, some of these factors approximate a process of governance that is transparent and accountable to the people, a system that can further stability, peace, and legitimacy because the citizens are able to check on the administration of the government and demand corrective measures in cases of maladministration. These views support a federal system of government in which power is devolved to the citizens at the local tier of government. The assumption within this framework is that competition for political office at the federal level may become less intense, less attractive, and less acrimonious if some federal powers were devolved to states and local governments. In short, devolution of power to the local level may promote more rapid development at the grass roots (Abacha 1995, 1556–1557), and thus slow down the exodus of citizens to cities or urban centers for jobs.

Furthermore, the decentralization of the economy could lead to "even" development among the states. In such a system, the indigenous people of the states would be encouraged to be involved in the policymaking process because they understand the local problems. Moreover, national and local political and economic problems could best be solved if there was an open and sincere debate and dialogue with mutual respect. The presumption is that this approach might further stability, democracy, legitimacy, respect for human rights, and peace within the political framework of transparency, accountability, and the rule of law.

The efficacies of these assumptions are likely to be promoted if the polity provides opportunities and facilities for human capital formation and political education. Such an endeavor would not only empower the citizenry with the knowledge to comprehend the constitution, political issues, and so on, but also provide the populace with the ability to translate the tenets of the constitution into ways that might enhance political accountability, human rights, and freedom to participate in the political process. In this respect, the proclamations of a nongovernmental organization, the People's Right Organization, are instructive. The group once declared its objective of organizing a nationwide seminar to educate rural people on how to live in a democratic system. It affirmed that "since the military which has blocked a civil democratic existence for more than 28 years would be going back to barracks, it was imperative to reorient the masses on forgotten democratic rules and principles to enable them forge ahead, in a civil society, in the [new] millennium [emphasizing] the need for education, access to basic rights and accountability as well as enforcement of fundamental human fights" (*The News*, 1998).

Administratively, the preceding conjectures could be augmented by adopting the opinion expressed by Arend Lijphart (1995, 221–231), who advanced the idea of a consociational or power-sharing device for the governance of multiethnic societies to enhance political stability. Such a scheme was reflected in the controversial formula and endorsement in the 1995 draft constitution of a modified presidential system in which key executive and legislative offices were to be zoned and rotated between six identifiable geographical groupings; namely, Northeast, Northwest, Middle Belt, Southwest, East-Central, and Southern Minorities (Abacha 1995, 1556–1557). This modality, however, is practiced in the federal character policy, which entails the recruitment of Nigerians to government jobs on the basis of geoethnic origin in order to "ensure" equity.

Moreover, Nigeria may not have been a signatory to the U.N. Universal Declarations on Human Rights of 1948, but its participation in the United Nations and endorsement of the African Charter on Human and Peoples' Rights of 1981 and 1986 suggests her acquiescence to these charters and other related instruments. Yet Nigeria's human rights record under military rule was dismal and systemic. For example, the imprisonment of opposition members without due process of law, subversion of the legal system, death penalties on trumped-up charges, and muzzling of the press and free speech are some of the areas in which the various military regimes in Nigeria have been culpable.

It might be useful to introduce instruction of "human rights values" in the country's educational system. If properly implemented, such a process could alleviate the problems of human rights violations in the republic and help to promote stability and democracy. In the meantime, however, human rights groups, especially nongovernmental organizations within civil society, might have to bear the burden of bringing to the fore human rights violations in Nigeria, because they are not beholden to government agents.

In sum, Nigeria has traveled a difficult path in its quest for a viable stability and peace since 1960; it has made several mistakes, and hopefully learned from them. Its status as a regional power and the most populous country in Africa suggests that the country must work diligently toward establishing stability and a genre of democracy that is worthy of emulation, at least, in sub-Saharan Africa. This chapter has briefly suggested some of the major areas that might be tackled at this significant juncture in its political history to move the country forward. In the final analysis, however, theories and even solutions for constructing a stable society and democracy in Nigeria might lack legitimacy if Nigerians themselves do not participate in the process of creating the institutions and structures of governance. Thus, the sort of efficacious regime that the republic needs at this crossroads of political development to propel it deep into this millennium is one based on consultation with the people and driven by the policies of transparency, accountability, the rule of law, and respect for human rights.

REFERENCES

Abacha, S. 1995. Nigeria: Abacha anniversary broadcast. *West Africa*, October 9–15, 1556–1557.

Achebe, C. 1983. *The trouble with Nigeria*. London: Heinemman.

Ademolekun, L. 1988. Political leadership in sub-Saharan Africa: From giants to dwarfs. *International Political Science Review* 9 (2): 5–20.

Ake, C. 1967. *A theory of political integration*. Homewood, IL: Dorsey Press.

Ake, C. 1990. *The case for democracy: African governance in the 1990s*. Atlanta: Carter Presidential Center.

Bertsch, G. K. 1991. *Reform and revolution in communist systems: An introduction.* New York: Macmillan.

Burns, J. M. 1978. *Leadership.* New York: Harper and Row.

Chazan, N. 1992. Africa's democratic challenge. *World Policy Journal* 9 (2): 279–294.

Couloumbis, T. A., and J. A. Wolfe. 1990. *Introduction to international relations: Power and justice.* Englewood Cliffs, NJ: Prentice-Hall.

Fatton, R. Jr. 1995. Africa in the age of democratization: The civic limitations of civil society. *African Studies Review* 28 (2): 67–99.

Gutto, S.G.O. 1991. Human and peoples' rights in Africa: Myths, realities and prospects. *Current African Issues* 12: 5–22.

Ihonvbere, J. O. 2000. *Towards a new constitutionalism in Africa.* London: Center for Democracy and Development.

Jega, A. M. 1997. Organizing for popular democratic change in Nigeria: Options and strategies for consideration. In *Strategic planning workshop on democratic development in Nigeria: Report of proceedings.* London: Center for Democracy and Development.

Kieh, G. K. Jr. 2001. Civil wars in Africa. In *Africa beyond 2000: Essays on Africa's political and economic development in the twenty-first century,* edited by S. C. Saxena. Delhi, India: Kalinga.

Lasswell, H., D. Lerner, and C. E. Rothwell. 1952. *The comparative study of the elites.* Stanford: Stanford University Press.

Lijphart, A. 1995. Prospect for power-sharing in the new South Africa. In *Elections '94 South Africa: The campaigns, results and future prospects,* edited by A. Reynolds. New York: St. Martin's Press.

Madugba, A. 1998. Buhari regrets ousting Shagari's government. *News,* May 18.

Mbaku, J. M. 1996. Effective constitutional discourse as an important first step to democratization in Africa. *Journal of Asian and African Studies* 31 (1/2): 39–51.

National Democratic Movement. 1998. Transition Watch, May 25.

Nzongola-Ntalaja, G. 1994. Violations of democratic rights in Zaire. *ISSUE: A Journal of Opinion* 22 (2): 9–11.

Obasanjo, O. 1990. Eastern promises. *West Africa,* May 7–13, 762.

Odunsi, B. A. 1996. The impact of leadership instability on democratic process in Nigeria. *Journal of Asian and African Studies* 31 (1/2): 66–81.

Olowo, B. 1994. Power play in Abuja. *West Africa,* July 11–17, 1222–1223.

Osia, K. 1992. Leadership and followership: Nigeria's problems of governance. *Scandinavian Journal of Development Alternatives* 11 (3/4): 175–194.

OAU. 1982. *African Charter on Human and Peoples' Rights.* Addis Ababa: OAU.

Plano, J. C., and R. Olton. 1982. *The international relations dictionary.* Santa Barbara, CA: ABC.

Sklar, R. 1986. Democracy in Africa. In *Political domination in Africa: Reflections on the limit of power,* edited by P. Chabal. Cambridge: Cambridge University Press.

Starr, S. F. 1990. Soviet Union: A civil society. In *Comparative politics: Notes and reading,* edited by Roy C. Macridis and B. E. Brown. Pacific Grove, CA: Brooks.

Stepan, A. 1988. *Rethinking military politics: Brazil and the Southern Cone.* Princeton: Princeton University Press.

Takougang, J. 1999. The future of human rights in sub-Saharan Africa. In *Preparing Africa for the twenty-first century: Strategies for peaceful coexistence and sustainable development,* edited by J. M. Mbaku. Aldershot, UK: Ashgate.

Tucker, R. C. 1981. *Politics of leadership*. Columbia: University of Missouri Press.

Udogu, E. I. 1995. Military, civil society and the issue of democratic governance: Toward Nigeria's Fourth Republic. *Journal of Developing Societies* 11 (2): 206–220.

Udogu, E. I., ed. 1997a. *Democracy and democratization in Africa: Toward the 21st century*. Leiden: E. J. Brill.

Udogu, E. I. 1997b. Military politics and constitutional discourse: Toward Nigeria's Fourth Republic. *Makerere Political Science Review* 1 (1): 1–21.

Udogu, E. I. 1997c. *Nigeria and the politics of survival as a nation-state*. Lewiston, NY: Edwin Mellen Press.

Udogu, E. I. 2000a. An examination of minority groups and human rights issues in Europe and Africa. *Journal of Political Science* 28: 21–43.

Udogu, E. I. 2000b. Political leadership and governance in democratic Nigeria. *Africa Quarterly* (Delhi) 40 (3): 109–131.

United Nations. 1976. *General Assembly Resolution 2200A (XXI) 21, U.N. Doc. A/6316*. New York: United Nations.

Welch, C. E. Jr. 1992. The Africa Commission on Human and Peoples' Rights: A five-year report and assessment. *Human Rights Quarterly* 14: 43–61.

16

Imperialism and Militarism in Africa: The Political Economy of French Arms Sales and Military Interventions, 1960–1980

IMMANUEL TATAH MENTAN

France has apparently abandoned its postcolonial interventionist military policies in Africa. Now she has launched military-backed diplomacy as a sign of the revival of her diplomatic fortunes in the continent. This revival follows the 1994 Rwanda genocide, the fall of Mobutu Sese Seko in 1997, and the unexpected coup d'état in Côte d'Ivoire in 1999. To demonstrate that French diplomacy is gaining influence in its West and Central African fiefs, France has stretched its diplomatic muscle to Anglophone Africa. In fact, a recent U.N. report on the pillage of Congo-Kinshasa's minerals and loud calls for sanctions against Rwanda and Uganda (*Africa Confidential*, May 4, 2001, 3) echoed French president Jacques Chirac's views on the war and its beneficiaries. The French President is also strongly backing President Joseph Kabila's new government in Kinshasa and even winning support for the replacement of Congo mediator Sir Quett Masire of Botswana with Gabon's President Omar Bongo, a Gaullist crony.

Underpinning this revival are some new ideas on a regional "peace" strategy in Africa. This strategy posits that rich African countries can help keep the peace by providing training, transport, and equipment for troops coordinated by Africa's regional organizations under French planning and supervision. Hence, France came up with the *Renforcement des capacités Africaines de maintien de la paix* (Recamp). In May 2001, Recamp completed its first big meeting in non-French-speaking southern Africa. As many as 130 military officers and diplomats from fifteen African countries and twenty non-African partners met in Dar es Salaam to prepare Tanzanite 2000–2002. Recamp has not met with any opposition in American circles because it is not viewed as a rival to their African

Crisis Response Initiative. They seem comfortable seeing France and erstwhile colonial European countries take the lead, bringing them together in multilateral form (see Nabakwe 2002).

This French "concern" for peace in Africa demands serious examination. When the war began after the 1990 invasion, the French reorganized the Rwandan armed forces, expanding it from 5,000 to 30,000 soldiers. Falcum 50 planes and pilots, heavy guns, assault vehicles, helicopters, and Milan and Apila missiles were supplied. France's concern over losing ground to English-speaking forces in Africa led Paris to support Rwanda's former Hutu government in its fight against Tutsi rebels. Its efforts to give military support to regimes whose leaders rule using a combination of corruption, patronage, and repression, like the one committed by Mobutu, is not new (Verschave 1994, 121–139).

Explanations for such French unreliability in its African policy are not lacking. In addition to serving as a major outlet for French trade, investment, and employment, and the strategic significance of maintaining *la francophonie*, the political backing of Paris's African allies in forums such as the United Nations is very crucial to France's continuing sense of itself as a world power. While late French President François Mitterrand echoed his country's colonial policy in the 1970s that "France is nothing without Africa" (Nouvaille-Degorce 1982, 6), prime minister Edouard Balladur explained that "France sees itself as a world power. This is its ambition and its honor. [And its] main field of action is Africa," especially French-speaking Africa. However, it was not just a matter of honor. Corrupt African rulers help finance French political parties, aiding with money laundering, and providing sweetheart deals to well-connected French companies such as Elf, Bollore, and many others.

France has earned the reputation of being the "gendarme of Africa." Between 8,000 and 10,000 French military personnel are based in permanent African garrisons at any given time, ready to be reinforced rapidly by an equal number of troops on standby in France (Girardet 1964, 169–185). The presence of such forces has enabled Paris to make or break African regimes, drawing criticisms from opponents on the continent and in France itself, who say Paris must break with its colonial past. The existence of permanent French bases in or near the capitals of Djibouti, Senegal, Côte d'Ivoire, Gabon, Chad, Cameroon, and the Central African Republic are widely credited with having propped up the regimes of those countries, considered key Paris allies in the region.

Today, the world is moving toward polarization. This phenomenon is no longer based on industrialization vs. nonindustrialization, but on the fief monopolies of the center. These monopolies are the monopoly of science and technology; the monopoly of controlling financial systems at the global level; the monopoly of access to, but not control of, the resources of the globe; the monopoly of communication, and through communications interference in politics, culture, and so on; and, finally, the monopoly of armaments. Therefore, Africa can only seek its salvation through fighting back the impact of these monopolies.

This has absolutely nothing to do with French strategic military calculations in Africa. Africans may think that they have put slavery, holocausts, and apartheid behind them, that mankind would never allow dehumanizing and violent systems of imperialism to shape the rules by which they live and die. Yet, noticeably, globalization is giving rise to new slavery, new holocausts, and new apartheid. Globalization is waging a war against nature, women, children, and the poor. This war is transforming every community and home in Africa into a war zone. This war is one of monocultures against diversity, of big against small states, of wartime technologies against nature.

From the fact that globalization has put profit above life and commerce above justice (i.e., international finance capital seeks profit and puts the latter above everything else, including social justice), it is clear that technologies of war are becoming the basis of production in peacetime. Agent Orange, with which Vietnam was fed for years, is now being sprayed on farms in Africa as herbicide along with Round-Up and other poisons. Plants and animals are being genetically engineered, thereby making Africa's fields sites of biological warfare. And, of course, perverse intelligence is being applied to terminate life's cycles of renewal by engineering "Terminator" seeds to be sterile (Pesticide Action Network of North America 1990).

Across Africa, hunger and malnutrition have grown by leaps and bounds as a result of structural adjustment and trade liberalization policies. Denying food to the hungry and feeding the markets is one of the genocidal contributions of globalization. African countries cannot ensure that their hungry populations are fed because this involves laws, policies, and financial commitments that are considered by their Western benefactors "protectionist." This is the ultimate crime in the globalization regime. Thus, the important question here is that: Would "merchants of death," be they French or those of any other country, curb the violence unleashed by globalization against the African people?

This is the key question this chapter seeks to explore. The exploration will be done by the examination of constituent elements of French military operations in Africa to see the extent to which they have "saved" Africa from its woes. In a word, this analysis will be informed by historical movements from the colonial to the postcolonial periods. This historical periodization is intended to delineate the ravages of French militarism and warfarism in the continent, which have been designed to secure a comfortable place for France on the Great Power chessboard while simultaneously guaranteeing hunger, genocide, and death for the African victims of its imperialist designs.

IMPERIALISM AND MILITARISM IN AFRICA: A THEORETICAL EXCURSUS

The use of iron-hand techniques to deal with political challenges has been commonplace in Africa. Nationalist leaders are gaoled. Sympathizers simply vanish. Police watch homes, confiscating uncensored literature. Torture cells litter towns and villages. In fact, military tanks, missiles, fighter bombers, and so on have been, and still are, welcome to liberation movements and beleaguered governments, but they hardly raise living standards.

First, indeed, civil wars have been smoldering or blazing on from decade to decade. They swept from Nigeria in the west to Ethiopia in the east, from Sharpeville and Soweto in South Africa to the Mountains of the Moon in Uganda. From the Cape to Cairo, from the Atlantic to the Indian Ocean, civil and transborder strife takes a countless toll of lives. In most situations, an East–West element is discernible. But hunters search for different prey. Insurrections, wars of independence, class conflicts, coups d'état, and various acts of violence scorch the earth and threaten new dangers as former colonial powers intervene, bringing their ideologies and high-grade weaponry with them.

The consequence of this grim spectacle is that the development of democratic governance systems is stunted and constitutionalism relegated to the periphery of the political spectrum. It is apparently impractical to view contemporary African politics in a constitutional framework, since constitutionalism has ceased to be the model pattern of interaction. In reality, militarism or the extension of the influence of the military into the social, economic, and political affairs of the state, an increase in the use of violence by the state, and the increased accumulation of the means of violence to maintain the ruling class of the state have been highly institutionalized in the organization, maintenance, and changing of governments in the continent.

The African military, in some cases, has increased its influence considerably. In other cases, the ruling class in some African countries has significantly increased the size of the military, or where a military did not exist, created a new one and in the process diverted resources from national economic development to these instruments of coercion. The result has been the militarization of most African societies. This phenomenon has produced two patterns of militarization. The first distinct pattern is due to external conflicts (e.g., border skirmishes, foreign invasion, etc.) that threaten the internal security of the state. The second is due to expanding internal conflicts (e.g., violent mobilization by ethnic groups for scarce resources) that threaten domestic control and use of state power by the incumbent ruling class.

Therefore, to treat politically motivated violence and the military coup as aberrations places one in the awkward position of insisting that practically all political events of the past and present in Africa are deviations. The contrary has, historically, been true. The reason is that the propensity of most African states to manifest violent conflicts based on racial, ethnic, or communal differences, but particularly on class, is generally a function of the character of production relationships, the principles that govern the ownership of resources, and the managerial mechanisms designed to exploit these resources by means of an established labor force.

In other words, in the dominant situation of capitalist imperialism in Africa today, which is invariably characterized as one of dependency by dominated and exploited African states on the industrial market economies, violent conflicts spring from the African contradictions inherent in the economic and the political "order." That is, these conflicts are rooted in the relationships inherent in the struggle to secure and maintain looting rights. This struggle is disintegrative, since it disrupts integrative social functions.

This brief explanatory sketch compels us to raise a few exploratory questions. First, how far has capitalism been rooted in Africa? Second, what have been its implications for peace and development in the whole continent? Third, what are the feasible solutions to militarism in Africa? These are assuredly not idle questions.

CAPITALISM BEGETS IMPERIALISM

Economic relations, as mentioned, are the basis of all social life. Capitalism has been the dominant mode of production in Africa since the imposition of European colonialism. All social life in the continent has, for some centuries, been dictated by relations of capitalist production and exchange.

Capitalism itself is a mode of production determined by the way in which the means of production are owned, and by the character of the social relations between individuals and the group (especially classes) arising from the production process. This is more so from the way in which work is organized and the surplus value from production is distributed. Indeed, capitalism has been the only mode of production in human history to make labor power a marketable commodity. In other words, capitalism is characterized by three main things. First, in capitalism, the production of commodities (goods and services) is the starting point and most general feature. Second, the creation of goods and services is carried out by isolated producers each of whom specializes in the creation of one product. Third, exchange value in contrast to use value is the goal of commodity production.

From this brief characterization of capitalism, it follows that precolonial socioeconomic formations in Africa were not capitalist. For one thing, they were dominated by independent peasant producers, and craftsmen who owned their own implements of production and who undertook the sale of their own products. For another, there was no distinction between ownership and the production process. In reality, what was of primary concern was the sale and purchase of inanimate objects. The sale and purchase of human labor power was never a determining feature of any of those precapitalist formations like feudalism.

However, imperialism changed this. The colonization of Africa, which took off during the later half of the nineteenth century, was the result of changes in the nature of capitalism in the European capitalist states. These changes included the following:

• The concentration and centralization of production as well as capital to such a high extent that monopolies emerged as the decisive factors in economic life.

- The export of capital, as opposed to the export of commodities, acquired paramount importance.
- The formation of international monopoly companies that divided the world among themselves.
- The territorial division, by force, of the world among the biggest capitalist powers, which subsequently organized these territories along colonial lines, giving rise to the phenomenon of modern imperialism.

The continent of Africa fell among these unfortunate territories. Europe's imperial powers divided the continent into "spheres of influence" and subsequently created an international framework for the systematic exploitation of the continent and its people. This division set up the illogical frontiers that now demarcate the states of postcolonial Africa, opening up an era of acute instability that threatens peace and produces superpower confrontation. Hence, capitalism begot militarism in Africa. The colonial stage of imperialism begot militarism in order to impose and sustain the relations of capitalist production and exploitation of the continent (see, e.g., Ake 1981).

IMPERIALISM AND THE INEVITABILITY OF MILITARISM

Imperialism is, in effect, monopoly capitalism. The growth of large-scale industrialization in nineteenth-century Europe and of the concentration of economic power in the hands of a few monopoly companies and banks compelled a change in the pattern of relations between European powers and Africa. The reason for this change in the pattern of Euro–African relations is that expanding industries in Europe required increasing quantities of raw materials; the growth in the quantity of manufactured goods, including capital equipment, needed additional outlets to that of the domestic European markets; and the possibility of earning further profits, at still higher rates, from cheap land and labor in Africa (see, e.g., Ake 1981).

These requirements of monopoly capital pushed the ruling class of the industrialized European capitalist nations, the metropolitan monopoly bourgeoisie, into using the state power of European imperialist countries to extend their domination over Africa. Following the Treaty of Berlin in 1884–1885, Africa was carved up and forcibly colonized according to the demands of monopoly capital. Thus, wrote General H. Meynier, a Frenchman, in 1911, "From the first day of their encounter Europeans affirmed the principle of their superiority over the black race. They have forced Africans into slavery, justifying it on the basis of superior strength. To open markets for their trade in Africa, they have stamped out the last vestiges of African civilization" (*L'Afrique Noire*, 1962; also cited in Delavignette 1962).

In order to ensure the total control of African territories at minimum cost, European colonialists established full state power in each colony. Ethiopia and Liberia barely escaped being colonized. The colonial state power has its specificities distinct from that in the capitalist countries of Europe. Whereas the state in imperialist European societies was a classic domination over, and exploitation of, the other classes in the capitalist society, the colonial state in Africa was different. The colonial state was, therefore, saddled with two fundamental tasks:

- To impose the capitalist mode and relations of production in African colonies in such a way that superprofits to the ruling class of the colonizing powers were guaranteed.
- To conquer and subjugate African colonies in such a way that the cheap and undisturbed exploitation of their material and human resources was equally guaranteed. That is to say, the colonial state had to exercise total domination over all African peoples, in contrast to the metropolitan state, which maintained domination only over the noncapitalist classes of Europe. Furthermore, while the state in Europe regulated the operation of capitalism in favor of the ruling bourgeois class, the colonial state in Africa had to implant capitalism, make it the dominant mode of production as well as yield surplus value for European capitalists.

This twofold task of the colonial state defines its character even up to the neocolonial epoch. The colonial state intervened directly, more actively, and more extensively in the political, economic, social, and cultural life of the African people than was the case in Europe.

The content of this intervention of the ubiquitous colonial state was also different. The colonial state was antidemocratic. It arbitrarily restricted the formation of trade unions, curbed their right to strike, suppressed criticism of colonial exploitation and dehumanization, and drastically curtailed, fundamentally, the human rights of colonized Africans. Repressive laws were enacted to impose low minimum wages, to impose a poll tax to compel peasants to take up wage labor, to impose forced labor, and to seize land from peasants or leave them with meager plots of what was often nonarable land. These measures were aimed at keeping the colonial people in such subjugation that there was a cast-iron guarantee of maximum and heartless exploitation of their labor and other resources. State power in the colonial era was, therefore, designed to maintain this ubiquitous pattern of economic and political control. European politicians, poets, and writers were, therefore, among the supporters of, or apologists for, the colonial system. Thus, "it was in vain for moralists to point out," for instance, "that every brick of the great warehouses of Bristol and Liverpool was cemented in Negro blood" (Williams, 1964).

In other words, the military–bureaucratic and other repressive governmental institutions of the colonial era were consciously developed, even overdeveloped, to contain acts of resistance and outright rebellion by the African population against the assault of colonial capitalist imperialism. The expansion and consolidation of these institutions went pari passu with the need for increasing revenue from a reluctant African populace, for imposing a European currency, and for compelling forced labor so as to coerce Africans into colonial capitalism. All these meant that the colonial civil service, the army, the police, the prisons, and the courts had to be expanded and strengthened at the expense of those institutions that benefited the African people.

In sum, the colonial state was forcibly introduced amidst pre-capitalist socioeconomic formations. Thus, the internal base of the colonial state in Africa was not only artificial but weak. It required unfailing military support from the metropolitan state so as to maintain domination over the African people or to implement its other tasks of militarized exploitation of labor and natural resources.

NEOCOLONIALISM AND MILITARISM

The colonial situation in Africa from about 1900 on and the postcolonial situation of today bear many features in common. Imperialism established a polity dominated by the agents of the metropole; today's African country is still dominated by these metropolitan agents, with the help of indigenous neocolonial collaborators working with non-African enterprises, the so-called transnational companies headquartered in the developed industrial countries. It is, indeed, not strange to hear a spokesman for the Gabonese government argue that the country has the right to seek and secure help from its friends, be they African or not, in times of need. Other Gabonese have remarked that a few countries in Africa have sought help from the Cubans, thus they do not see why Gabon should not seek help from France (see, e.g., Cohen 2000).

Besides this pauperization of the African ruling class, neocolonialism has also sustained an economic system in which the African peasant and urban worker alike have been wholly dependent on external input for earnings and employment. In brief, capitalist imperialism of the neocolonial variety continues to create the economic infrastructure that facilitates the extraction of wealth from Africa for the benefit of groups external to the continent. That is to say, the dominant economic relations in Africa today are those of capitalist imperialism of the neocolonial variant. In essence, neocolonialism is the aggregate of the economic, political, and military methods employed by the imperialist states to maintain the economic exploitation, plunder, and dependence of the African people, despite the fact that these countries are no longer colonies.

The aim of neocolonialism, therefore, is to prevent African countries from pursuing a truly independent domestic and external policy, to prevent the new states from creating truly independent economies by not allowing them to take a noncapitalist course of development (or one that more effectively serves the needs of their people), and to do everything in its power to keep these countries and their people within the world capitalist system. Indeed, the economic foundations of neocolonialism in Africa are foreign monopoly capital and the property of the local comprador bourgeoisie. The attendant ideological foundations of neocolonialism are thus anticommunism, racism, and other reactionary theories.

Within the neocolonial context, the techniques of bringing the process of industrialization to African countries under imperialist control and using these techniques to further the interests of metropolitan capital are varied. First of all, neocolonial powers instituted "disjointed production" processes in the African countries. The initial and final stages of this type of production take place in capitalist countries and the "middle" one in African countries. The latter thus came to be technologically dependent on the international monopolies that control the whole process. As a consequence, African economies are drawn even more tightly into the capitalist system of world economy than they were during the colonial era, and once more on an unequal footing.

Second, there is a growing trend toward transferring the most labor-intensive, material-intensive, and ecologically harmful industries to African countries. The urge to use rich sources of raw materials and cheap labor power on the spot prompts international monopolies to transfer production that has become too expensive and/or archaic in the centers of world capitalism to underdeveloped African states. All this leads not so much to the development of African economies as to their transformation from agrarian and raw material appendages of advanced capitalist states into industrial and raw material ones, preserving the heartless exploitation of their peoples and their natural resources.

Third, foreign trade has gained slight significance in the present period in the plunder of Africa. Since the collapse of the colonial system, the monopolies of imperialist countries have continued to dominate the African markets, so that unequal exchange between underdeveloped African states and developed capitalist ones is on the increase rather than diminishing. The prices of raw materials exported by African countries are falling, while those of industrial goods supplied by imperialist states are on the rise. As a result of this change in the balance of export and import prices alone, African countries are losing billions of dollars yearly, which can never be upset by the "foreign aid" that they receive from the industrial market economies (see, e.g., Davenport 1992; Mbaku 1995).

Fourth, state-monopoly forms of exploiting African countries are spreading their tentacles. The more the neocolonial powers lose political influence in Africa, the greater the role they assume in the economic enslavement of the continent; that is, in fulfilling all the functions that were previously the sphere of private monopoly capital.

Fifth, collective forms of neocolonialism are being developed through the establishment of international finance and credit organizations—the International Bank for Reconstruction and Development (the World Bank), the International Monetary Fund, the General Agreement on Tariffs and Trade and its successor, the World Trade Organization, and also by drawing African countries into closed economic groupings of imperialist powers, for example, as associate members with no rights of the European Economic Community. The common feeling in the European Union is that France, for historical reasons, has accumulated a significant level of experience in Africa and the rest of the Third

World that can be used to enhance the welfare of all of Europe (see, e.g., Martin 1982).

Finally, foreign monopoly capital is merging with national capital in order to use the latter as a junior partner in intensified exploitation of the toiling people of Africa, mainly through setting up "joint companies" with a national façade, but really under the control of foreign monopoly capital.

This exploitation, plunder, and domination of African peoples by neocolonial powers breeds violent conflicts characteristic of capitalist imperialism: the conflicts arising from the continued struggle of the African people to free themselves from continued domination by the imperialist powers. This restless rivalry, insecurity, and social conflicts generated by the huge concentration of economic power in African private property economies breed the philosophy of militarism. One may ask how. Through a process of "marginalization," the colonial and neocolonial capitalist mode of production and exchange has transformed precapitalist social relations into new forms of class relations in which African society has come to be differentiated into distinct strata according to economic, social, and political criteria. The international capitalist bourgeoisie and unequal distribution of wealth and power are viewed as legitimate.

In fact, the natural endowments of Africa are being exploited to the "mutual benefit" of the local African and metropolitan bourgeoisies. This exploitation has thrived on a deliberate "marginalization" of the vast majority of Africans by totally excluding them from the political process, by denying them legal protection, by abrogating their civil and political rights, and by excluding them from economic bases of power. This exclusion tends to reproduce inequalities between neocolonialist nations and impoverished African states and inequalities within African states themselves.

The classes, foreign and domestic, that are economically privileged tend to be interested in preserving the existing social order of inequalities. Those who are disadvantaged by this social order, especially as regards its distribution of wealth, have an undying interest in changing the social order, particularly its distribution of wealth. It is, therefore, not for nothing that former U.S. president Ford assured his people that, "Africa will loom ever larger in our lives for the rest of this century. The Soviet Union is waging an undeclared war, the resources war. Africa is the battleground because from it come many of the resources and raw materials essential to western society and especially to the United States" (*Business Week*, October 9, 1978).

The economic structure, in this way, sets the general trend of political interests as well as political alignments. That is, economic conditions here not only set the tone of politics, but also define the role of coercion in Africa. For instance, by the 1980s, military expenditure by and for African states burgeoned. Since independence in the early 1960s, African countries have successfully imported billions of dollars worth of military equipment, primarily from their former colonizers, as well as from the Warsaw Pact countries (U.S. Arms Control and Disarmament Agency 1992, 131–132). Economic conditions of inequality and the attendant repression involved in the seizure, consolidation, and use of state power give rise to violence as a key power factor in African politics to change or maintain the status quo.

IMPLICATIONS OF MILITARISM FOR AFRICA

Neocolonialism nurses and sustains militarism in Africa. Within the context of neocolonial capitalism, two basic strategies are used: One of the common-place strategies is to set up repressive puppet regimes. That is, the neocolonial powers create state organs in Africa that, hiding under the national flag, serve the interests of foreign monopoly capital and those of the local comprador bour-geoisie.

For instance, the Spanish authorities dropped bloodthirsty Macias Nguema when his nephew, Obiang Nguema, led a successful coup against him. By then, conscious of their across-the-board economic involvement with their former colony, the Spanish had connived with Macias's use of torture, murder, and forced labor in the cocoa plantations. Until 1976, they had banned media cover-age of all this (Cronje 1976).

Indeed, when popular forces rise up against the puppet regimes, the imperi-alist powers intervene brutally on the pretext of defending "freedom and democ-racy" to crush the liberation movement. Examples are not hard to find. The bru-tal repression of the National Front for the Liberation of the Congo in 1977 and 1978 is a case in point. In their exterminatory struggle against African govern-ments that have taken the path of progressive independent development, the imperialists do not hesitate to use such amoral methods as air raids, economic blockades, threats and/or outright withdrawal of aid, sabotage, diversion, crimi-nal conspiracies, and murder of leading figures in the liberation movement. It is little wonder, therefore, that during the anguished Algerian war years a grand total of 300,000 French servicemen were employed to try to preserve the skele-ton of France's imperial system. Similarly, Portugal used expeditionary forces exceeded 2,000,000 at the height of its war against independence movements in Angola and Mozambique (*Le Monde*, May 21–22, 1973; Harrison 1983).

Another strategy is the extensive use of the technique of drawing African countries into aggressive military blocks, of concluding bilateral agreements with them on "mutual security," and the construction of military bases, ports, and airfields. These military bases serve as support points for imperialism against the growing national liberation movement and for political pressure on contracting African governments. That is, imperialist powers, striving to strengthen their influence in one part of the continent or another, "do not hesitate to exploit African instabilities even by military means" (*The Guardian*, June 18, 1979).

In order to fulfil the military obligations imposed by imperialist powers, the contracting African governments spend enormous resources unproductively, resources that could have been used for economic development. The militarization of Africa by the end of the 1970s threatened to increase the crushing burdens for the continent's swiftly swelling population. The social and economic costs of this militarization are enormous and include (but are not limited to) the following:

- The annual spending on soldiers and their weaponry averaged about $34 per person or more than one-tenth of the annual income of many countries in the continent. The situation became alarming in the 1980s.
- On the other hand, investment in teachers, schools, and general education has amounted to only an average of $23 per person at a time when human capital development remains one of the continent's most critical development needs.
- For every 100,000 Africans, there were 290 soldiers but only 46 physicians.
- Public debts of the countries of sub-Saharan Africa alone, according to the World Bank (1979, 1980, 1981), exceeded $17 billion in 1977. By 1979, military spending was running at an annual rate of $15 billion (also see U.S. Arms Control and Disarmament Agency 1992).
- Since 1960, richer countries have contributed each year, an average of only $5 per person to help poorer fellow inhabitants of the earth, compared with $95 per person spent on military programs.
- The annual cost to the United Nations of international peacekeeping was about $35 million, while member states were spending in total 3,000 times as much on their own armed forces.
- A woman in most parts of rural Africa has to walk several hours a day to collect safe, clean water for her family, while one of the superpowers can deliver an intercontinental ballistic missile across the globe in a matter of minutes.
- For the cost of a single one of those missiles, 50 million hungry African children can be fed adequately and 340,000 primary schools can be built (see Sivard 1978).

The fact is that as far as there is militarized economic inequality in any African country, that country cannot enjoy political democracy because political power will tend to polarize around economic power. That is to say, an African society where a high degree of economic inequality exists must, of necessity, be repressive. This repression arises from the need to curb the inevitable demand of the have-nots for redistribution.

By its very nature and history, capitalist imperialism is organically incapable of assuring any optimal, or even minimal, compatibility between the economic and social aims of development profitable to the majority of the populace. Hence, capitalism itself breeds vertical and horizontal social distance between individuals, groups, and institutions. Under conditions of socioeconomic scarcity, competition, and inequality, a distinct feature of capitalism, cultural difference tends to breed mistrust, hostility, prejudice, antagonism, and conflict among individuals, groups, and collectivities (see, e.g., Ake 1981).

In like manner, wealth differentials give rise to envy, breakdown in communication, oppression of the poor by the rich, and, in general, a breakdown in the unity of the society, which creates antagonism, hostility, conflict, and eventually a breakdown of social order. Since it is in the interests of the ruling class in any of the neocolonized African states to avoid these consequences, the use of force becomes an integral part of social engineering.

In sum, militarism has been deep, selective, and sustained in Africa from colonial times till date because of the four interlocking objectives pursued by capitalist imperialism: strategic, economic, ideological, and political. Africa possesses, in immeasurable quantities, about all of the thirteen basic industrial raw materials needed by the modern economy. No jet plane, for instance, can be built without cobalt. The United States produces no cobalt, but Zambia and Democratic Republic of Congo (formerly called Zaire) do. The Americans are 88 percent dependent on imported bauxite, 95 percent on imported manganese ore, 90 percent on nickel, 100 percent on tin, and so on. The relative figures for capitalist Europe show an even greater dependency. The reliance of the West on Africa's strategic materials extends also to aluminum, zinc, chromium, iron, lead, tungsten, oil, and uranium (Feustel 1978).

The erstwhile colonial powers have been unwilling to surrender control of their protected markets, their unimpeded access to prized raw materials, and the infrastructure of their investment in the continent. These activities directly threaten the internal security of each African state in that exploitation expands internal conflicts. These conflicts also threaten the internal control of the ruling strata. To ensure the steady flow of these resources, the financial and industrial oligarchies and governments of capitalist countries collude with African puppet regimes. That is, marauding foreign capitalists, with the help of indigenous elites in the African countries, groom African heirs to take over, heirs ready and willing to settle for the shadow rather than the substance of true independence. The succession, therefore, has generally passed to leaders more concerned with achieving authority than fundamental change, despite their occasional outburst of radical rhetoric.

Indeed, the concern of these heirs has been to protect the interests of capitalist imperialism as well as those of the ruling strata in each state. The maintenance of foreign economic dominance in the commanding heights of the economies of African states and African governments, indeed, servants to the follies of faraway imperialist powers, have attracted, with notorious regularity, the use of brute force to maintain the status quo. This phenomenon is likely to continue and, indeed, escalate as a direct complement to the politicoeconomic activities and increasing internal opposition within and among African states. The repression, torture, political murders, and militarized injustices of incumbent and ousted regimes have foreshadowed a thorough house cleaning in Africa. In other words, for decolonization to herald a brave new world of true independence, capitalist imperialism must be smashed along with its handmaiden, militarism.

THE FRANCO–AFRICAN CONNECTION

Africa is the most underdeveloped and exploited continent in the world today. In 1976, Africa had 7.5 percent of the world's population, but it accounted for only 1.2 percent of the world's GNP (McLaughlin 1979, 174). Africa also trails the other continents in literacy. In 1970, 74 percent of Africa was classified as illiterate. Africa equally trails the other continents on life expectancy, infant mortality, public health expenditure, energy consumption, and so on (McLaughlin 1979, 150–224).

In 1975, the U.N. Economic and Social Council (UN-ECOSOC 1975, 5) reported that of the thirty-two least-developed states in the world, twenty-one were in Africa That situation has not improved. In fact, it has worsened, as is evident from data provided by the U.N. Development Program (UNDP 2000), which indicate that today, Africa remains the poorest continent. For example, of the thirty poorest countries in the world today twenty-seven (or 90 percent) of them are in Africa. Most African countries depend on one or two exports as their source of foreign currency (also see World Bank 2000). As Timothy Shaw and Malcom Grieve (1977, 393) have estimated, "Africa . . . contains the most land-locked and least developed states. These also tend to be more dependent on a few exports to a few states and to be those most vulnerable to drought and the new politics of food.

These goings-on in Africa have courted much scholarly attention. Essentially, all studies on Africa's predicament tend to ask the same basic question, directly or indirectly: What are the reasons for the poverty and "underdevelopment" of the continent? Almost all analysts lay the blame for Africa's poverty and underdevelopment at the door of colonialism and the structures and processes inherited from Europe. In light of the prevalent African situation inherited from colonialism, Gutkind and Wallerstein (1976, 8) note,

Indigenous economic structures largely lost their functions and autonomy as they were incorporated into the colonial capitalist state with the primary objective of extraction of resources, both physical and human. Subsistence economies were transformed into peasant or wage-labor structures. Africa's rural economy was transformed into a vast reservoir of labor to be shunted about according to the fortunes of the capitalist economies; and, as a result, there was set in motion the process of proletarianization dependency, and internal center–periphery relations, i.e., the dominance of towns over the rural areas, one region over another, or one African country over another.

Such studies point to the fact that Africa's position in the international economic order has been a subordinate one, characterized by asymmetrical and unequal economic relationships with the industrialized Western countries. However, in spite of such glaring underdevelopment and poverty, between the hard years of 1965 and 1974, Africa spent $669 million on arms purchases from France alone (Gutkind and Wallerstein 1976, 11).

Africa's massive arms purchases from France in the face of mounting economic and social problems is the key issue in the present study. To present the problem in a more lucid way, it is essential to raise some exploratory questions. Have African states seen the buying of French arms as a schematic shortcut to the resolution of their multitudinous problems of development? Is France's policy of arms sales and militarism in Africa centered on an historical mission of spreading Francophone culture according to the Gaullist tradition of "la grandeur universelle de la France" (i.e., the universal greatness of France)? Or is it a manifestation of a policy of the rational laws of historical materialism? Are geopolitical and strategic factors more relevant in understanding the French policy of arms sales and warfarism than economic ones? Is the expanding French military presence and interventionist interest in Africa merely a paternalistic relationship in the continent? Or, is it rather France's quest for strategic raw materials necessary to maintain the ruling bourgeois class in Paris? The problem of this study is, therefore, to examine the data addressing these questions in all their military, economic, political, and social ramifications.

These ramifications make it clear that economic theory and analysis of the African drama that attempt to omit imperialism and militarism from their underlying paradigm are far removed from social reality. Such theorizing and analysis can only be bankrupt at best and obscure the truth about the problems and dangers plaguing Africa in the second half of the twentieth century at worst. Neoclassical economics is bankrupt and obscurantist in handling such a phenomenon with its characteristic ramifications.

In neoclassical economic considerations, peace reigns in absolute terms. War, militarism and the "pacification of natives" are seen as ordinary elements that tend to disrupt harmonious economic equilibrium. The models of this neoclassical harmonious economic equilibrium are intended to furnish "universal truths" about the authoritative allocation of scarce resources in the international system (see U.S. Arms Control and Disarmament Agency 1976).

Neoclassical economic thinking stands in contrast to one of the distinguishing characteristics of Marxist thought. Marxian economics is convinced that economic processes must be understood and treated as part of a social organism. In this social organism, material force plays a leading role. That is, war is at least as typical as peace. Militarism and imperialism are viewed in this context as major determinants of the form and direction of technological change and of the allocation of resources between rich and poor states. According to this Marxian conviction, price and income relations, which neoclassical economics treat as the ultimate measures of economic efficiency and social justice, are evolutionary products of capitalist institutions.

Within these capitalist institutions, political force and "pure" economics are interwoven. Rosa Luxembourg (1964, 450–453) puts the Marxist case thus: "Bourgeois liberal theory takes into account only (one aspect of economic development): the realm of 'peaceful competition,' the marvels of technology and pure commodity exchange; it separates it strictly from the other aspect: the realm of capital's blustering violence which is regarded as more or less inciden-tal to foreign policy and quite independent of the economic sphere of capital."

In reality, political power is nothing but a vehicle for the economic process. The conditions for the reproduction of capital provide the organic link between these two aspects of the accumulation of capital. The historical career of capi-talism can be appreciated only by taking them together.

The facts of French imperialism, like any other, provide eloquent testimony to the accuracy of Rosa Luxembourg's diagnosis, as this study will demonstrate. Imperialism, per se, is based on international economic expansion and exploita-tion in the interest and under the direction of the capitalist bourgeoisie and the mediating state in the imperialist nations. Historically, this imperialist expansion and exploitation has acquired many dimensions of domination and international and national oppression. These dimensions of imperialist domination, exploita-tion, and oppression may be direct or indirect. The concrete manifestations of imperialism are to be found in the interstices of relations of production within the world capitalist system. They are also found within the diverse forms of in-tercourse that they enter into as dictated by the international division of labor: production, exchange, distribution, and accumulation on a world scale.

Therefore, the conceptual point of departure is the creation and develop-ment of the world market for commodities (i.e., the internationalization of capi-talist commodity production and accumulation). As a consequence of the en-gulfing spread of world capitalism, Africa became an integral part of this proc-ess from the day Europeans became masters of the continent. Africa was sub-jected to the imposition and implantation of economic specialization inextrica-bly linked with primary production within the international capitalist division of labor.

Consequent upon integration into the world capitalist mode of production, exchange, distribution, and accumulation, Africans evolved parasitic class structures under colonial dominance. The class structures reflected this capitalist mode of economic specialization and domination. Each class structure brought with it repressive class politics that reflect historical forms of contradictions between production and consumption, the national question and the class ques-tion, populism and repression, and so on, with which Africa lives uncomfortably today, flying national flags and singing anthems.

In light of this theoretical scheme, the argument of this study is that the complexity and dynamism of the circumstances conditioning French arms sales and militarism (Luxembourg 1964, 452–453) in Africa cannot be simply under-stood in terms of commercial pragmatism and peace and stability. Rather, France's Africa policy of massive arms sales and warfarism is part of imperial-ism's global strategy of maintaining the ruling bourgeoisie in capitalist centers while developing vital client relationships in underdeveloped and overexploited African societies. In line with this argument France's policy in Africa is viewed in terms of its being a "chien de garde" (watchdog) of world capitalism in states already grafted or being regrafted onto the exporting economy.

Pursuant this argument, an analytical toolbox is necessary to enable the facts to be isolated, laid bare, and classified. The analytical toolbox includes the following factors: (1) the external environment—by this is meant the structure of regional and global security and France's adaptation of its foreign and defense policies to negotiate that environment; (2) the economic motivation—these motivations may be national and/or parochial, encouraging an open arms sales policy; (3) the process by which politically authoritative decisions are made for the production and sale of arms and other forms of military technological know-how; and (4) the quest to stabilize client regimes in order to guarantee French access to cheap raw materials and markets in Africa.

Each of these four levels of analysis is essential, but each one taken singly is insufficient to explain French governmental action in stepping up the production, sale, and use of arms to nurse militarism in Africa. For example, just after World War II the security and foreign policy preoccupations of France were with the reconstruction of its defense industries. As the security of France was less menaced by German militarism of Hitler's type, its priorities, as well as the interplay of the four levels of analysis, make the distinction between foreign and domestic policy determinants as the primary sources of French arms bazaar and warfarism irrelevant. In other words, the link is so strong that French decision makers have evolved a broad-based domestic political consensus on the security and foreign policy functions of government and its responsibility for national welfare. Any changes in leadership and in political rhetoric on the Champs Elysées amount to no substantive changes in the militarization of French economic, cultural, and political dominance in Africa. French defense policy testifies to this assertion.

FRENCH DEFENSE POLICY

France's preoccupation with its national defense is rooted in its historical antecedents. Three times within the span of seventy years (1870–1940), German troops fired *feux de joie* (victory shots) as occupants of France. In 1958, when General Charles de Gaulle returned to power following his term of office from August 1944 to January 1946, military affairs became, apart from foreign affairs, the focus of his policy. The development of France's nuclear-armed force as *force de frappe* (strike force) was decided in the Fourth French Republic under the government of the radical Socialist, Gaillard.

However, General de Gaulle sought a means of guaranteeing France's independence. This independence had to be secured foremost and above all, militarily. The maintenance of French sovereignty meant remaining outside the integrated defense concept of the North Atlantic Treaty Organization while retaining membership of the alliance.

Before de Gaulle returned to power he had a vivid understanding of France's continued role in the African periphery. This understanding was part of his proselytizing about a universalistic Greater France. In the African context, this policy meant guarding France's strategic sphere of influence so that it could be safe for French capitalist interests. General de Gaulle's immediate successor, Georges Pompidou, continued with the Gaullist defense policy.

On assuming office in the summer of 1974, president Giscard d'Estaing held extensive deliberations with his military advisers. The new president confirmed Gaullist military positions, declaring, "France must secure its defense independently. And this naturally entails control over the necessary means as well as over the decision as to the conditions and contingencies under which they are to be used" (Wauthier 1974, A67). This Gaullist military strategy holds any integrated military command, like NATO, suspect. To demonstrate the continuity of French defense policy, Defense Minister Bourges said "that one must mistrust any formal theory and that it was the gravest of all dangers to have a specific preconceived system imposed on one" (quoted in Marshall 1973, 717).

Giscard d'Estaing's innovation in French defense policy lies in the area of cooperation with allies, especially in his so-called enlarged security area (expanded base—ground, scope—for maneuver) in the military program of 1977 to 1982. This program is stamped with the increasing importance of Africa to France, not only Afro-Gaullist states but also such economically and strategically important countries traditionally outside its sphere of influence as Nigeria, Zaire, and South Africa.

Today, at least 20 percent of France's foreign trade is with African countries. Nigeria and South Africa are gradually assuming importance as France's peripheral markets in the continent. For strategic raw materials, France gets them from the following African states: oil (Gabon, Algeria, Cameroon); uranium (Niger, South Africa, Gabon); oil, manganese (Gabon); iron ore (Mauritania); timber, coffee, cocoa, and palm oil (Gabon, Cameroon, Côte d'Ivoire); phosphates (Senegal, Morocco); cobalt (Morocco, Zaire); coal (South Africa); and copper (Zaire). In view of France's demand for these vital raw materials and markets, Giscard d'Estaing held the notion that all of the capitalist North is likely to be affected by a radical change in Africa (*Le Monde*, April 12, 1977; IMF 2002).

Therefore, in his opinion, Western Europe and the United States ought to collaborate to ensure that any change in Africa does not benefit the communists. To coordinate French defense policy and its economic, cultural, and political interests in Africa, there is a *présence française* (French presence) in Africa, sustained partially by a high level of bilateral assistance (including significant levels of private French investment, especially in former colonies). Militarily, France maintains a strong but controversial presence of some 12,000 troops on the African continent. No other state of the capitalist North has such a bulky military presence in Africa. France has also embarked on direct arms sales to Africans as part of its national security interests (Jospin 1978).

NATIONAL SECURITY AND ARMS SALES

The type of regimes controlling the French state—royal, imperial, or republican—hardly make any historic difference when the chips are down on arms production and transfers. France ranked as the world's third major arms producer and supplier in 1977 when its arms sales yielded $3 billion (*Le Monde*, March 27, 1975). This figure is strange in the face of international cries against the arms race, but France has a long history as a major arms producer and supplier in the world. It was France that supplied arms to the American colonies in revolt against the British in the eighteenth century. It was also France that furnished East European states in the early twentieth century the arms they needed to check German and Russian militarism.

The sale of French arms and military technology should thus be seen as a process linked to French national interests and their promotion abroad. The sales should not be seen as isolated and discrete acts. French regimes are generally singular in their pursuit of an independent weapons capability. Their bickerings are usually on who should receive French arms and who should direct their production, the state or private arms producers. The core of the debate is never on whether France should produce and/or sell arms.

World War II dislocated the traditional role of France as an arms producer and supplier. As a power initially occupied by Germany, France became dependent on Allied powers, particularly the United States, for arms with which to defeat Germany and to retain its tottering colonial empire. France received American arms through several intermediaries, as well as help in expanding and modernizing its military–industrial complex. France's dependence on arms saw in American military aid a temporary expedient for the preservation of her colonial empire. The prerequisite for preserving French independence and power was therefore the development of an independent security and foreign policy.

When World War II ended, French military engineers became jobless. There was rife disenchantment within the French security community about the nation's dependence on American arms. This dependence was heavy. For instance, between 1950 and 1968 the United States gave over $4 billion worth of military assistance to France (*Le Monde*, June 10, 1976, 1). As a military handout to bail France out of its crippling Indochina war expenses, the Truman administration subsidized the French defense budget by nearly one-quarter and half of France's rearmament. American military aid therefore fueled the French rearmament program (U.S. Department of Defense 1971–1972).

By the mid-1950s, France had reemerged as a fairly autonomous arms producer and supplier, though still propped up by America. However, arms production and sales were not the cardinal preoccupation of the French military establishment in 1950. As many as twenty-seven key tasks of the military were those of fighting colonial wars in Asia and Algeria and fulfilling French responsibility within NATO. Both the "Dassault" and state-run arms producers centered their efforts apparently on meeting the requirements of the French armed forces.

The Fourth French Republic raised the nation back to the status of a major arms producer and supplier. The Fifth Republic gave the broad policy options for French arms production and transfers of military technology. From a national security and foreign policy viewpoint, French arms sales became a device for thinning down unit costs of defense material. The Champs Elysées saw arms sales as a way of "helping" other states to develop their own defense systems.

General Charles de Gaulle rejected the philosophy of a regional or global security system based on either superpower hegemony or superpower conflict. On the one hand, France attacked the concept of regionalizing security systems as illegitimate, since only the nation-state was seen as the final repository of political authority in world politics. In this view, an independent national defense capability was the best assurance for the validity of this principle. On the other hand, the superpower struggle threatened an eruption into a global conflagration with all the attendant dangers of sucking states into wars that were neither of their own choice nor in their own interests.

France, therefore, saw the building of a *force de frappe* as both an insulation from superpower illegitimacy or instability and an independent French national security policy. French national security policy was then projected internationally as a model for other states to follow. The national policy envisaged a multipolar system comprising states possessing sufficient military capabilities to resist superpower threats and to tone down, if not eliminate, their subjection to one superpower or the other for their security or foreign policy goals. Thus, France resumed its arms production and sales as a way of promoting this conceptually fluid and decentralized world security system.

In this Gaullist concept of a multipolar world security system, the policy of French arms sales would enable Third World states to have an alternative or supplementary arms supplier to the Cold War superpower contenders and suppliers, breaking the hold on Third World states by any superpower. Paris, in such a world security system, would then stand out as the unique guardian of the weak nation-states against the hegemonic drives of emergent states. The French foreign minister between 1969 and 1973 and de Gaulle's close collaborator for over a score of years, Michel Debre (1972, 54), stated the broad security and political considerations that rationalize French arms sales as follows: "It is difficult for us to shirk the duty to respond to the requests of certain countries, solicitous of their defense and desiring to assure it freely without having recourse to the dominant powers of each of the two blocs. Not to respond to these requests would accentuate the hegemony of the two great power" (U.S. Arms Control and Disarmament Agency 1979, 11).

Debre's statement demonstrates that French arms policy was a defense and economic mechanism against superpower hegemony. The raison d'être for this French defense and security thinking was three-fold. First, an arms-sales policy would enable France to sustain its own defense efforts through increased production. Second, such a policy could help France to purchase superior weapons and back up its extensive arms-research development program to keep pace with

American and Soviet arms programs. Finally, the sale of conventional weapons could compensate for the French nuclear defense budget. In effect, a policy of increased arms sales was supporting a larger military–industrial complex than would otherwise have been possible (see, e.g., U.S. Department of Defense 1978, 17).

The French policy of massive arms production and sales fired the enthusiasm of its arms industries. The most successful was Dassault's Mirage III and VI. Twenty air forces of the world, including the French air force, bought 350 copies of the fighter airplanes. Other Dassault successes included the F-1 fighter, the Jaguar, which was developed with the cooperation of the British aircraft industry and with the German firm Dornier. Exceptional successes were scored in tactical missiles and helicopter production and sales. Prominent among the hundreds of thousands of French missiles sold abroad are the R- and super-350 and Magic air-to-air missiles, the Roland and Crotale air-to-ground missiles, the sea-to-sea Excocet and Otomat, and the ss-11, ss-12, Milan, and antitank missiles (Kolodziej 1974, 555–598). With this large-scale production, France is next only to the United States in world helicopter sales. Of 4,600 helicopters produced by Aerospatiale since 1956, approximately 3,350 have been sold abroad. The geographical sale of the helicopters is as follows: Europe (2,600 sold to eighteen countries, including France), North and South America (750 sold to twenty-seven countries), Africa (480 sold to twenty-four countries), and Asia and Oceania (600 sold to twenty countries). All 4,600 helicopters were produced in collaboration with British Westland.

In the mid-1970s, Saudi Arabia chose France as the major supplier for its ground forces. Four hundred and fifty AMX-series tanks and vehicles, as well as a specially designed ground-to-air missile, the Chabinn, for desert conditions, were bought. Sales of naval craft have been concentrated in fast patrol boats and small submarines, such as those of the Daphne class.

France gained serious arms contracts for 1978 from the following African states: Egypt obtained 20 SA-342L Gazelle helicopters; Libya also obtained an unstated number of the same helicopters, which are coproduced with Britain; Morocco obtained 400 VAB armored cars; and Nigeria bought twelve Alpha-Jet trg planes costing $80 million. These Alpha-Jet trg planes are coproduced with Germany. The four African countries named are only those whose purchases were very remarkable (see, e.g., Assemblée nationale 1981–1982).

The security and foreign policy rationale of French arms sales simply requires a bona fide state that is capable of paying its arms bills. In Michel Debre's (1972, 54) words, "If France is often solicited, it is because she does not set any political conditions, as certain powers do, in selling its arms." France's only known "restraint" in arms sales is a prohibition against a retransfer of arms bought from her. However, France is not inflexible in the enforcement of this condition. France has failed to enforce its arms embargoes. It has also failed to apply its edicts vigorously. For example, Libya violated the prohibition on retransfer with impunity by transferring some of its 110 Mirage aircraft fighters to the Egyptian air force during the Yom Kippur War in 1973. In addition, the French arms embargo against Israel, invoked partially after the Six Day War and totally after Israel's attack on the Beirut airport in December 1968 using French super-Frelon helicopters, was insufficient to stop spare parts from reaching Israel for servicing its French-made aircrafts.

Even in the "vedette affair" of December 1969, embargoed patrol boats were still spirited out of Cherbourg past French harbor security to Tel Aviv. Thereafter, France's embargo against arms sales to the Middle East was lifted as a result of France's inability or unwillingness to enforce it in view of the financial temptations from rising Arab purchases of French arms. For instance, France refused to sacrifice its lucrative $1 billion arms deal with Saudi Arabia in 1974.

France's arms bonanza with South Africa suggests few, if any, domestic checks on security and foreign policy considerations. France was the last Western arms merchant to "give up" its lucrative arms trade with the apartheid regime. It required not only sustained pressures from some black African states, but also U.N. insistence on precipitating the "abandonment." For many years France paid no attention to the fact that its military aircraft, missiles, armored ground vehicles, and naval craft were not only contributions to South Africa's external security but also equipment most likely to be used by the apartheid regime for internal repression .

The grey line distinguishing arming South Africa for its "national security" and the denouncing of any intention to support apartheid pushed president Giscard d'Estaing to declare during his tour of Zaire in August 1975 that only naval armaments would henceforward be sold to South Africa. In 1977 this exemption was dropped. In any case, the so-called French adherence to U.N. proscriptions on arms sales to Pretoria is irrelevant to South Africa's access to French arms. Pretoria enjoys licensing rights, including the authorization to produce F-1 fighters, the most sophisticated fighter in the French arsenal. France wants to gain a competitive advantage over others by selling sophisticated weapons. The introduction of military jet aircraft in its sale of fourteen Mirage Vs to Peru between 1966 and 1970 is a case in point. The ideological defense of military expenditures and arms sales through appeals to "national security" tends to obscure concrete and immediate economic and political interests.

ECONOMIC CONSIDERATIONS

Economic considerations, more than any other pressures, have motivated French arms production and sales. Strategic and foreign policy and security considerations in the French arms bazaar are peripheral issues. Even the loose political reasons attached to arms sales abroad lend weight to the thesis that bread-and-butter motivations are foremost in French arms sales. When running for office in 1974, Giscard d'Estaing announced that selling arms would be a lesser priority: "I do not think it is a sector in which we ought to accent out effort" (*Le*

Monde, August 9, 1974). This pledge, however, crumbled shortly after he had won the Champs Elysées palace.

French financial returns from arms sales rose from $1.4 billion to $3 billion between 1974 and 1977. Within the same period, orders for new military equipment rose from $3.8 billion to $5.05 billion, a 45-percent increase. With new orders being fed continuously into the French-arms delivery pipelines, there is no hope of any downslide. Table 16.1 shows the trends in French arms transfers from 1972 to 1977 (see, e.g., Assemblée nationale 1981–1982).

The growing dependence of France on arms sales is measurable in several ways. Arms sales make up the bulk of French external trade, particularly in capital goods, where military equipment may be categorized (see, e.g., Klein 1976, 578). Between 1972 and 1977, exports of military equipment rose from 3 percent of all French trade to 4.6 percent.

Between 1972 and 1977 the proportion of arms sales to other capital goods exports rose from 12.5 percent to 15.3 percent (Klein 1976, 578–579). In the 1974 to 1976 period, French capital goods exports rose by 48 percent. Arms sales swelled by 75 percent during that period. France's ability to increase its exports of capital goods and high-level technology is closely linked with the growth of its arms deliveries, which serve as a pace setter. Since the value added from French national sources improves the country's balance of payments position, the expansion of arms transfers abroad is critical in that the enterprise is a labor-intensive one.

Without arms sales, France will suffer serious economic problems, and, as a result, the strength of the French franc will be highly jeopardized. For example, between 1974 and 1977 France registered a commercial deficit of $5.1 billion in nonarms trade. In 1976, France recorded a $7.3-billion deficit. This trade deficit was the largest in the nation's postwar history. Within the 1974 and 1977 period, French arms sales averaged $1.4 billion. Without massive arms sales, France would have registered an annual external trade deficit of $6 billion.

Table 16.1
French Arms Deliveries, 1972–1977
(Hundreds of millions of dollars)

	1972	*1973*	*1974*	*1975*	*1976*	*1977*
	800	1,175	1,386	1,944	2,435	2,992
Air	607	867	871	1,166	1,695	1,830
Ground	103	104	269	316	514	688
Naval	23	64	117	196	37	174
Electronics	28	70	130	266	190	299

Source: Extracted from *French Parliamentary Reports, 1973–1978.* Paris: Assemblée nationale.

Of course, France's concentration on arms production and sales had a significantly negative impact on other investment outlets and export opportunities, which could not easily be converted to nonmilitary production in either the short or medium term. This explains the hesitancy of President d'Estaing to cut back on arms sales despite his public rhetoric. Besides, boosting French arms sales abroad negotiated the deflationary politics of Raymond Barre, the former French prime minister. While still finance minister, Raymond Barre's policies sought to increase exports while deemphasizing domestic demand. Arms sales had been identified as the most lucrative area of the French economy.

French arms sales and its oil imports are interrelated strands in all economic calculations. Two-thirds of France's energy requirements are supplied by 98 percent of its imports (Klein 1976, 578–579). About 83 percent of French imports came from the Middle Eastern Arab states and Iran in 1977. Saudi Arabia and Iran supplied 36.4 percent and 15.3 percent of French oil imports, respectively. Since 1974, France has thus signed the largest arms contracts, especially with the oil-rich Arab states. Iran alone had an arms contract of more than $2 billion with France (*Le Monde*, November 10, 1977). When France was still heavily dependent on Libyan oil (17.4 percent in 1970, as contrasted with 2 percent in 1977), its Mirage fighters to Libya covered nearly $400 million of its oil imports from Libya. Like other developed industrial countries, France sees oil as critical to its economic survival, as well as to the maintenance of its place as an important military power in post–Cold War Europe.

France's ability to have access to foreign oil supplies is tied to its role as an arms merchant. Since oil is an important factor in French economic growth and prosperity, it seems illusory to hope that France will forgo arms sales simply not to destabilize military balance in the Middle East and in Africa.

The inability of the French defense budget to support its arms industry fully demonstrates France's dependence on foreign arms sales. Defense spending has fallen from 4.3 percent to around 3 percent of French GNP. Improvements in the pay, living conditions, and social status of military personnel have caused a deterioration in the proportion of funds spent on military equipment. In 1977, only 41 percent of the budget went for military capital goods. A decade earlier, spending was fairly even between heavy equipment and operational (personnel) activities. This inability to support defense budgets has led France into some actions amounting to full endorsement of the ideology of Africa's then bete-noir, apartheid South Africa. France is the chief contributor to South Africa's own nuclear industry. France's contribution has been made in spite of opposition from other Western powers. A French consortium headed by Framatome signed an agreement to provide South Africa with two nuclear reactors. The South African nuclear industry has been enhanced by Israeli and French technology and Iranian oil. South Africa, in turn, furnishes its partners uranium for their own nuclear needs. France, in particular, is now a big importer of energy-producing minerals (coal and uranium, in which it is particularly vulnerable) from South Africa (Klein 1976).

The implications of curbing arms sales seem unbearable to France. The economic benefits are numerous. Since the 1973–1974 oil crisis and the 1974–1975 recession, France has faced chronic stagflation. Arms industries represent one of the most advanced sectors that can be used to combat high unemployment, especially among highly skilled technicians. Unemployment figures rose above 1 million by the end of 1977—the highest figure under the Fifth Republic—and consumer prices rose by more than 30 percent between 1975 and 1978. Official figures hold that of 280,000 employees in French arms industries, 90,000 work for the export sectors. Of this figure, 75,000 work for the General Delegation for Armament located in the Defense Ministry and account for the nerve center of the French military–industrial complex. An additional 25,000 employees work on atomic energy development; the remaining key sectors include the aeronautics industry (105,000 employees), electronics (40,000 employees), and other fields (3,500 employees). Any reduction in arms sales for the external market without a corresponding increase in national defense spending and unemployment benefits would therefore be a serious blow to the French economy (Assemblée Nationale 1981–1982).

It is a truism that economics and politics are interwoven strands in the fabric of the international system. Economic relations within the international system, in and of themselves, are political relations. Although security and foreign policy and domestic economic forces are complementary rather than competing in their impact on the French arms bazaar, it appears that the arms gamble cannot be adequately analyzed from the lofty heights of security and economics alone. The causes and consequences of French domestic politics on arms production and sales cannot be ignored.

DOMESTIC POLITICAL CONSIDERATIONS

The domestic explanation postulates a functional logic inherent in the structural constraints of internal political networks that shape policy responses on French arms production and sales abroad. The similarity in the domestic policy networks linking the French state and society determines the degree of similarity in government responses to problems of indiscriminate arms sales in the international system. The joint impact of international effects of arms sales and domestic political structures condition government policy on arms transfers. In the case of France, the international effects of arms sales—the rat race for arms purchases, wars, and repression—are not a conditioning factor in stunting French arms transfers. This is because the arms race, as well as wars and repression in client states, assist the growth of French arms industries and markets. Hence, domestic political considerations are more crucial to the arms enterprise than the effects of arms transfers on the international system.

Much of the domestic political maneuverings over French arms sales happen behind the scenes. Within the bureaucratic struggle over arms transfers, all the principal actors share a common interest in selling arms abroad. Different and divergent reasons for French arms trade significantly influence the outcomes of the decision-making process.

There is a noteworthy absence of broad public or interparty bickerings or even any fundamental disagreement between the major political groupings over French arms transfers. The heated debate over France's violation of the arms embargo against Israel and over the sale of Mirage fighters to Libya were exceptions rather than the rule, but the furor was related more to the ambiguity of French policy in the Middle East than to French arms sales per se.

The attempts made by the Champs Elysées to control arms sales are propaganda instruments for external consumption. The only major review commissioned by the French government on the arms industry was not even released. The review was said to have raised serious questions about internal arms operations. As a rule of thumb, public criticism of French arms sales is confined to politically inconsequential confessional groups and to peace organizations. One myth-breaking, though mild, exception was the criticism tabled by the pacifist wing of the French Socialist Party (Masquet 1982, 16).

The socialist- and communist-dominated trade unions are responsible for the organization of parts of the French military–industrial complex. The desire of the unions is to control or to influence the French military–industrial complex. They neither want to diminish its size nor the nation's dependence on remunerative foreign sales.

From this analysis of the determinants of French arms production and sales abroad, there appear to be no strong international and domestic forces opposed to the proliferation of arms transfers. The explanation is that arms sales abroad inevitably harness the French military–industrial complex to national security and foreign policy interests and point up the contradictions of the national independence philosophy energetically preached by France. This phenomenon arises because, consequent upon being an arms supplier, France becomes automatically ensnared in the security and foreign policy interests of client states, which in itself is a "back-end" problem of arms sales abroad.

Arms production and purchases are determined by the vested economic and political interests of capital accumulation. The process of accumulation is secured through capital goods and the export sector when domestic demand in the importing states is both an instrument and a consequence of this accumulation process. This arms importation spree is always in the name of "national security" to offer support to fragile regimes that help maximize French neocolonial economic interests.

The miniaturization of French economic relations with "independent" African states raises some pertinent questions; Is France's active promotion of the commercialization of its armaments in Africa in compliance with its globe-straddling posture as guarantor of political stability and national security in emergent states? Is France's extensive training of African military personnel and local "gendarmerie" and policy forces not a technique of curtaining off its economic imperialism of trade and investment in the absence of formal colonialism? Could France, which sermonizes elaborately on a policy of Afrique aux Africains, be seen to be meddling in African politics? If France is actually meddling in African politics, who are the agents and is this meddling legitimate or illegitimate? Relevant answers to these and other questions may best be obtained from an historical analysis of the interactions between the imperialist quest for a stable world market and sources of raw materials and French tank-corps imperialism in the appendages of its economy in Africa. But is there any evidence of French militarism and warfarism in Africa?

FRENCH MILITARISM IN AFRICA

The rise of French militarism and warfarism in Africa consequent upon its arms transfers with potentially disastrous opportunities for mischief on a grand scale is not a new phenomenon. It dates back to the time when France became one of the European conquering masters in Africa. However, the withdrawal of rude French colonialism left the continuity and growth of its militarism and warfarism unscathed in Africa.

General Charles de Gaulle was the chief architect of the process. In his frantic move to circumvent the independence trend in Francophone Africa, de Gaulle ensured that Franco–African military–economic unification went pari pasu with political deconcentration (*Défense: depenses en capital*, October 11, 1977, 15). That is, Francophone states being jolted into flag-and-anthem independence signed cooperation agreements with France that went "hand in hand with a certain harmonization of diplomatic and, in some cases, the existence of common political institutions" (see Tunteng 1974, 2–6).

Franco–African cooperation and defense agreements assured that French troops could handle the internal and external defense of the newcomers to the world of nations. French troops could be called to action through the resident French ambassadors in each of the new African states. French military bases were, therefore, established and reinforced in Djibouti, Dakar, Diego Suarez, and Fort Lamy (Ndjamena), with subsidiary bases in Bou-Sfer, Port Bouet, Douala, Bangui, Niamey, and Libreville (Débazies 1980; Guillemin 1981; Luckham 1982).

The host nation-states had to guarantee local public utilities, revictualling facilities, and freedom of movement for the troops. France was also given legal access to and exploitation of, raw materials and strategic products such as uranium, hydrocarbons, thorium, beryllium, minerals, and so on, by the terms of the agreements. Host states were forbidden from either limiting or deflecting the sale of raw materials and any other strategic products. In terms of trade, the agreements, which were a quid pro quo for independence, proscribed the diversification of trade relations of African states except with Europe.

The watchdog over Franco–African cooperation was the notorious graduate from the French secret services school, Jacques Foccart. With his role as Secretaire-Général à la Présidence de la République pour la Communauté et les Affaires Africaines et Malgaches, Foccart was an embodiment of all the Franco–African relations until his dismissal in 1974. Foccart's dismissal, however, did not alter the policy of French militarism and warfarism in Africa (see Ligot 1963, 517–532).

France terminated 150 years of its colonial hegemony in Africa in June 1977 with Djibouti's independence, but less than twelve months later there were more French troops in Africa than at any time since 1960. As of 1971, France had over 12,000 men of its armed forces in sub-Saharan Africa. These French troops were distributed roughly as follows: Djibouti (4,500), Senegal (1,500), Côte d'Ivoire (500), Gabon (500), Mayotte (1,000), Réunion (2,000), and Central African Republic (3,000). There are over 2,000 French military instructors in Africa. There is also an equal number in the Force d'Intervention (intervention force) in southwest France, ready to intervene at a month's notice in the African peripheries. This is in addition to its fleet in the Indian Ocean, which can be deployed very rapidly in case of any eventualities. It is difficult to establish the true figures because of the unstated number of French military personnel serving as technical assistants in African armies. As late as 1971, for instance, a majority of senior army officers in Cameroon were still French nationals. The situation could only be worse in other Afro-Gaullist states (see Joseph 1978, 160; Hollick 1979).

France has gone beyond the stationing of troops. The training of Francophone armies has been upgraded. More than 2,200 African army officers and non-commissioned officers received advanced training in France during 1978.This figure rose to some 2,500 in 1979. The French government spent 80 million French francs for this training activity. The number of French officers dispatched to African armed forces is being augmented considerably (Mertillo 1988).

French militarism in Africa is guaranteed further by exclusive Parisian control over secret services operations in Zaire (Democratic Republic of Congo), Gabon, Senegal, Cameroon, Côte d'Ivoire, and the Central African Republic in particular. These Franco–African military links are so tight that, when Paris changed its ambassador in Libreville in 1978, Gabon's President Bongo requested that Maurice Robert, an old hand of the French secret service abroad or the Deuxieme Bureau, be appointed as the new diplomatic envoy. Libreville is the nerve center of French covert operations in central and southern Africa. But why had France to stage such a military presence? Is French militarism in Africa a phenomenon? (Débazies 1980; Luckham 1982; Guillemin 1981).

The raison d'être of the proliferation of French troops in Africa was raised by Niger. When the new military regime in Niger seized power in 1974, it immediately doubted if the country had any external enemies. The new military leaders expelled the local French commander, who had had close ties with deposed president Hamani Diori. What had the French troupes coloniales (colonial troops) been protecting in Niger, like elsewhere in Gaullist Africa, for fourteen years? First, this system of French strategic bases and military detachments was part of General de Gaulle's global defense network. It was not for individual African states. Furthermore, the French troops were stationed to protect de Gaulle's replicas in Africa from Africans over whom they had been delegated to govern.

The French miniaturization of African states is aimed at infusing negative enemy images of communism, neutralism, leftist revolution, forces of subversion, revolutionary ideas, political dissidence, insurgency, extremism, ultranationalism, radicalism, and political instability. In all, the essence of militarizing Africa by advanced industrialized states like France is to establish an armed fifth column to defend "Western values" within African states. These Western values are none other than capitalist exploitation, domination, and control. Capitalism as an economic regime was historically never confined to one country. Capitalism was born, developed, and allowed to flourish as part of a world system.

It is worth adding that the specific task of capitalist imperialism has been to fill this outline and establish a complex international network of trade, finance, and investment. Given this complex international capitalist network, it follows that restrictions on trade and investment in any part of the world would equally affect free enterprise adversely in other parts of the world. The dimensions of the defense of capitalism either militarily, diplomatically, ideologically, or culturally, therefore, become universal. That is, free enterprise is like a living human being. When the leg is wounded in Africa, the head suffers in capitalist Europe or North America. To guarantee the freedom of capitalism in any part of the world, domestic and foreign threats to the system must be combated globally. So, to guarantee the health and growth of free enterprise in Africa, France has earned for itself the "credit" of being the "gendarme of Africa" (see *Le Monde*, June 1, 1974).

A curious case clearly demonstrating the shamelessness of French insatiable capitalist taste for wealth is evidenced in Franco–Nigerian relations. When the Nigeria–Biafra war broke out, France saw it as a happy accident in history. That is, the war was an opportunity to break up the African country threatening French influence in West Africa and therefore to puncture Anglo-Saxon pride and to obtain oil from Biafra. Hence, Biafra became part of the Gaullist testament in Africa. To have changed the policy would have injured Gaullist susceptibilities.

However, immediately after the war, France changed her policy toward a reunited Nigeria. She saw Nigeria as a market that could not be ignored. Since January 1970, France has lobbied Nigerian comprador bourgeoisies with a 110-million French franc loan on very favorable terms. In October 1971, Nigerian elites accepted the loan for the country's oil refinery. France embarked fully on a gradual economic annexation of Africa's most populous and powerful country.

Thus, Vladimir Lenin did not throw an empty phrase when he said, "whoever controls Africa controls Europe" (Foltz 1965, 180–184). The experiences of the two world wars and the growing undifferentiated interest of the superpowers in emergent states led France into a militant defense of its strategic interests in

Africa. France also sought to assure itself of a reservoir of men and resources for any foreseeable military confrontations in Europe or elsewhere. For instance, during the interwar years, France raised forty African battalions of some 105,000 black Africans for external service. Thus, France finds the maintenance of its strategic interests and military fifth columns in Africa a dire necessity in securing "its share" of Africa's reserves of world resources (see Adamolekun 1978, 36).

Wherever France senses a threat—real or imagined—to the continuity of its control of raw materials and markets and nostalgia for colonial status in Africa, she has never hesitated to subscribe to warfarism as a law-and-order instrument. The multitude of examples are not far to seek. The strafing, burning, and indiscriminate bombing by the French *armée de pacification* (pacification army) against the outlawed Union des Populations du Cameroun opposition party in the "maquis" at the preindependence and early independence years is but one tiny example of French imperialism in Africa (Whiteman 1970).

In February 1964, Gabon's late President Léon Mba was arrested by mutinous soldiers. He was forced to resign by a "revolutionary committee." The latter, led by four junior army and gendarmerie officers, announced the creation of a "provisional government" on February 18, 1964, under Mr. Mba's chief political rival, Mr. Jean Hilaire Aubame. On the same day, French troop reinforcements began arriving in Libreville by air from their bases at Dakar and Brazzaville. On February 19, the French troops, acting as "community forces" under the Franco–Gabonese defense agreements signed in August 1960 and supplemented in 1961, took up strategic positions in the country and quelled the rebellion. A similar military uprising came up in Congo (Brazzaville). Following a broadcast by President Youlou (August 13) asserting that the disorders in Congo Brazzaville arose from "a plot against State security fomented by discontented and jealous men," 3,000 French troops appeared in the capital on August 14. They took up guard duties outside the presidential palace and other buildings under the terms of a 1961 defense pact providing for the use of French troops to maintain internal security. But by August 16 the strength of the demonstrations was so intense that a new provisional government, backed by army and trade union leaders, was formed by a former minister, Alphonse Massemba-Debat, when French troops failed to control the demonstrations. By using such brutal military means elsewhere in Africa, France makes it clear that the neocolonial status quo had to be maintained (Lacroix 1965; Whiteman 1970).

By September 1969, French intervention forces were in active service in war-torn Chad. The 3,000-man Chadian army was assisted by 1,600 officers and men and 300 advisers and technicians, supported by four skyraiders, six transport aircrafts of the Noratlas type, and twelve H34 helicopters and reconnaissance planes—all from the French army—to fight against the northern rebels. By July 14, 1970, France had 3,600 troops in Chad: 1,400 marine infantry, 1,000 airmen, 600 Foreign Legionnaires, and 600 advisers with the Chadian forces.

French troops fought in Chad until they were forced to pull out in 1980, but were soon back again in 1983.

French secret services have always collaborated with their local counterparts to neutralize potential challenges to Gaullist replicas. In Paris, Foccart and Journiac successively ensured the red hand's liquidation or driving into distant exile of African dissidents (i.e., nationalists).

Overlapping Franco–African structures and personnel have enabled the use of French troops to maintain law and order in critical centers (army camps) of potential antiregime action in Gaullist Africa. This appears somehow contradictory with the rise of the military to power in "French Africa" since 1960. This phenomenon might be best explained by the fact that minor African replicas of de Gaulle are expendable. For instance, the case of the overthrow of Hamani Diori in Niger is understandable. The erupting public pressures against his misrule, corruption, and persistent challenging of France's unilateral pricing of Niger's uranium production were deemed to be more intolerable than initial difficulties to be faced with a successor military regime. Troop movements and plotting within the Niger army did not stampede the Elysées to forgo some rigors of the ongoing French presidential election in 1974 to short-circuit the coup d'état (*The Economist*, April 29, 1978, 20).

It must be remarked, however, that in the case of the four crucial regimes in the French enclave (which have been kept under "civilian" rule)—Senegal, Côte d'Ivoire, Gabon and Cameroon, similar developments would surely have invited different responses from Paris. The French military presence and timely interventions have bolstered the captive Gaullist regimes at decisive stages of their history: Cameroon from 1959 to 1974, Senegal from 1959 to 1960, Côte d'Ivoire in 1963, Gabon from 1964 to 1966, and Chad from 1969 to 1980 and 1983 into the present.

In the 1970s, French warfarism in Africa was intensified to make Africa safe for capitalist exploitation of raw materials and markets. Despite French courtship of Arab states in the Middle East as well as Algeria and Libya, it was not shielded from the disastrous effects of the oil crisis. France became convinced that the future of capitalist countries in the sphere of energy requirements depended on Africa, at least, in the long run. The outcome of the Angolan civil war—the Soviet–Cuban victory—further convinced France that it was the capitalist stalwart to "roll back communism" in Africa. France then signed twenty-two military pacts with African states. These pacts were ratified by the French National Assembly on November 22, 1978. In the case of Côte d'Ivoire, Djibouti, Gabon, Central African Republic, Senegal, and Togo, the military pacts included a clause on external defense, permitting the signatories to call on French troops in the event of external aggression. Togo used French paratroops to crush a domestic uprising.

France did not stop at the level of defense pacts. By 1978, French troops were actively engaged in fighting in Chad, Zaire, and Mauritania. Besides assisting the United States to ferry 1,500 Moroccan troops to the copper-rich Zairian Shaba province to push back invading ex-Katangese gendarmes, French paratroopers were dropped in the province itself for action. France claimed that its warfarism in Chad, the Western Sahara, and especially Zaire was on behalf of Common Market Europe against what President Giscard d'Estaing called "destabilizing external forces" (*The Economist*, April 29, 1978, 20). However, Denmark, the acting president of the European Council, publicly criticized French warfarism in Africa and called for its withdrawal (*International Herald Tribune*, June 7, 1978).

Belgium clashed with France over the second Shaba crisis in May 1978. France was accused of making a brazen attempt to "grab" Belgian assets in Zaire. Accusing France of being particularly interested in the wealth of Zaire, Belgium viewed it as "an international rivalry" (Bobb 1979, 16–20; Rondos 1979, 4–8; also see *Fraternité Martin* (Dakar), September 21, 1979). Belgium's accusations are linked to its ownership of 80 percent of foreign investments in Zaire. It is not unconnected with the fear that France would gain access to Katanga, which Belgium failed to dismember from the rest of Zaire to form a client state under pauperized Moïse Tshombe.

In the face of these accusations, France attempted to spread the "burden" of warfarism among client African states. Its attempt at erecting a pan-African security force (*Keesing's Contemporary Archives*, April 18–25, 1964, 20024A) to intervene around the continent faltered. Though the idea was bought by Gabon, Senegal, Côte d'Ivoire, Zaire, and Idi Amin's Uganda, the plan failed to stand the pounding opposition of Libya, Tanzania, Liberia, Angola, Mozambique, and some Francophone states. Tanzania's President Julius Nyerere (1978, 10–13) observed that the French-led arrangements in Paris and Brussels about Shaba, Zaire, and the rest of Africa,

are by no means about the liberty of Africa. They are discussing continued domination, continued use of Africa by the Western powers. These meetings, if taken together, are put on to become a second conference of Berlin [at which the colonial powers carved Africa up among themselves in 1884]. . . . The question is one of neo-colonialism in Africa, and that for economic interests . . . this [neocolonial attempt] is being led by France. The second point on the agenda is about the use of Africa in the East–West conflict. Here the US is the leader. These two intentions are being coordinated so that they will complement each other; and the distribution of the expected profits as well as the related costs are being arranged at these meetings (see also also *Keesing's Contemporary Archives*, September 28–October 5, 1963, 19659A).

French progressive militarization of and warfarism in African politics, economics, and social life is a derivative and an instrument of the exigencies of its capital accumulation activities in the continent, a process that is determined, to a great extent, by global capitalism. Without doubt, this process of militarization and warfarism in Africa is political and military. It has consequences in policy and action (domestic and foreign). The consequent implications for policy and action derive from and relate to international political, strategic and military concerns in the international system of alliances and shifts.

Superpowers and great powers seek military and ideological alliances with African states and ideological alliances in politically sensitive and strategically crucial areas. Sadat's dramatic shift from the USSR orbit in 1978 to that of the United States shows the fragility of such alliances. Ethiopia and Somalia swapped sides in the superpower military ball game in 1974, and French warfarism has domestic political, economic, and social consequences for African states (Jospin 1978).

IMPACT ON AFRICAN STATES

Originally, "grandeur" was given a topmost position by General de Gaulle to the France–African system of cooperation within his policy strategy. Hence, there is the readiness of local African heads of state to echo and reverberate Gaullism's antagonism to the OAU, or support for the dismemberment of either Zaire or Nigeria, or coziness with apartheid South Africa. Another factor is the secrecy about this Gaullist trans-Atlantic empire. The full original Cooperation Agreements, including the "revised" 1973–1974 versions, have been "top secrets." Their implementation has registered glowing consequences on African political life. It is important to make clear that France's Africa policy is color-blind and not constrained by some concept of political, moral, or legal order, nor by some form of social justice. In fact, French firms were present in and prominent among sanction busters in Rhodesia (now Zimbabwe) and apartheid South Africa. Its geoeconomic interests have usually determined and informed France's support for military actions in Africa, including support for Rwandan "genocidaires," as well as Biafra and Cabinda secessionists. The driving force of the history of French Africa policy has therefore been anchored on violence, pillage, war, murder, and thievery (see *Le Monde*, January 29, 1981; *Keesing's Contemporary Archives*, June 13–20, 1964, 20024–24035A; *Afrique Contemporaine*, January 1982, 16).

French militarism and warfarism have drastically altered the essence of political developments in terms of democratic development, national integration, and political stability in many Francophone African states (*Africa Confidential*, July 24, 1970). The freedom of political opposition and press has been ambushed and smashed. Centralization of political power and the growth of the political strength of the military as the repository of power have become shameless rules rather than shameful exceptions. These developments are inextricably linked with French economic interests (see Kazadi 1978, 11–16).

Economic crisis is accelerating the modification of the international division of labor and the mechanisms of exploitation of the African masses, and thereby generating new and more repressive puppet regimes with French backing. These transformations are not automatically tension-free, but they are imposed by coercion. This imposition is secured through the intensification of the class struggle between not only capital and labor but also among different sectors of capital, the bureaucracy, and the armed forces within each of these African states.

As the economic and political crisis aggravates, there is a penchant to eliminate or at least neutralize internal political opponents and allies by the creation of single and authoritarian party states and the rise of military or paramilitary regimes. Appeals to "national unity, peace, and stability" in the face of real, perceived, or conjured external threats, attacks, or adventures are the regular neutralizers. Wherever such techniques of internal tension management prove to be nonstarters in the face of a rat race for capital accumulation, decentralized domestic military conflicts compounded with the economic rivalry for raw materials and African armed markets supplement, reinforce, and mutually generate war or domestic political terrorism by the armed client regime. Bokassa's two consecutive expeditions into Bangui jails to club thieves and children to death in the 1970s is but one unavoidably publicized example of domestic regime terrorism (see *The Guardian* [Manchester], September 22, 1979; *Jeune Afrique* [Dakar], October 3, 1979).

The economic impact of French militarism and warfarism in Africa is no new story of wanton murder and robbery. Of all known world reserves of highly needed mineral resources, Africa possesses 13 percent of copper, 5 percent of gold, 71 percent of platinum, 14 percent of uranium, 89 percent of industrial diamonds, 61 percent of asbestos, and 17 percent of fluorite (Owen 1984, 144–146; also see *Marchés Tropicaux et Méditerranéens*, December 21, 1984, 3169). As a result of the agreements signed between France and former colonies before independence, it is able to have relatively free access to all these enormous resources. In fact, France obtains 60 percent of its minerals from Francophone Africa alone, with Niger, Gabon, and the Central African Republic providing it with most of the uranium for its nuclear technology development (see *The World Today* [London], February 1979, 72).

France's trade empire in Africa is so lucrative that no country operating an imperialist policy can afford to give it up (*Le Monde*, May 21, 1978; *Financial Times*, May 12, 1978). France imports more from than it exports to all continents except Africa. Crude oil, natural gas, and coal are the most important raw materials that France purchases from Africa for its industries. These commodities make up about 37.2 percent of France's African imports. As a novel trade phenomenon, Paris now runs a trade surplus both with Francophone African states and the other countries in the continent. Nonetheless, Franco–African trade is intensely exploitative and concentrated where the French tricolor once fluttered. Still in 1978, Francophone African states accounted for 67.9 percent of French imports from Africa and 69 percent of its Africa-bound exports. France thus dominates trade with its African client states through a system of unequal exchange in which "the spin off and spill-over effects result in a differential allocation or unequal distribution of power resources among actors or subsystems involved in the exchange" (Feig and Holm 1978, 338–389; *International Herald Tribune*, June 9, 1978; also see Médard 1995).

France, therefore, has a captive market in Africa perpetuated by a variety of imperialist structures. There are sentimentalized ties of the Franco–African commonwealth with movements like La Francophonie Universelle, as the key cohesive force. There is also the closed franc zone, which sentences African states to export at fifty times their own local currency. Such arrangements amount to no less than what Professor Tchoundjang (1980) refers to as a "form of monetary repression." Finally, there is the trap of French bilateral "aid" to African ruling classes as bribes and regime stabilizers.

CONCLUSION

By way of a theoretical reprise, this chapter has attempted a factual analysis that has by no means totally exhausted the growth of French-sponsored militarism and warfarism in Africa. French elites of all ideological persuasions are united on the policy of arms production and transfers. First, French armaments sales constitute a significant portion of French merchandise exports to the African countries. Payment for these military equipment, however, drains the foreign exchange earnings of underdeveloped African states. At the domestic level, the proliferation of arms industries creates jobs for French citizens. Within the external environment, French military bases and accords guarantee sources of raw materials for French industries and captive markets for the country's excess production. Second, the extensive training of African military personnel sharpens African military establishments, which are strong power contenders, to some form of sentimentalized ties with French national interests. Finally, the use of French economic "aid" to train African police and gendarmerie forces for domestic law and order purposes is an assurance of the loyalty of African satellite political and economic elites to French capitalist interests.

The reasons for the increase in French military outlays in Africa (military training and advisory services, the rife military assistance programs, and the stimulus given to commercial sales of French armaments) are many. One of them is certainly the sophistication of weaponry. Another is the military strength and consequent threat of Socialist bastions. Third, the substantial portion of the huge French military machine is the price being paid to maintain the French imperialist network of trade and investment in the absence of formal colonialism. Finally, the desire of captive regimes in Africa is to satisfy their personal drives for wealth, which can be obtained through the undisturbed implantation of French private capitalist enterprise with attendant "kickbacks" to the respective chiefs of state in league with French imperialism.

But politics, culture, economics, and warfarism are interwoven threads in the fabric of the international system. Capitalism emerged from a medieval European society ruled by rope, battle axe, and torture chamber. Capitalism, therefore, required little or no change in standards to rely on brute force in building and defending its economic empire. In Africa, the French capitalist ideal has been a continent of captive nation-states in which French capital can operate uninhibited by local obstacles to the making and freely disposing of maximum attainable profits and the carting away of vital raw materials at paltry prices. This means that the French are opposed to all forms of state capitalism that might tend to water down their operations or reserve potentially profitable areas of economic activity for African nationals.

As I have tried to show in the discussion in this chapter, the race for French armaments in Africa and the consequent lavish spending is rooted in the logic of capitalism. That is, violence consequent upon the militarization of economic rapports (economic relationships involving political, cultural matters) is an indispensable ingredient of capitalism. In fact, violence (domestic and/or external) is essential to the capitalist system, wherein ownership of capital is used to acquire wealth. Irrespective of how the capitalist process of perpetrating abundance for a few and poverty for the teeming masses is camouflaged, the system is one of robbery and cannot survive without the use of violent coercion or warfarism. The ease with which French military orders and brutal interventions are fed into its economic relations with Africa is living testimony. These orders and interventions act as adrenaline injections to the private sector in client states. This phenomenon of a Franco–African elite league for oppressive and exploitative purposes better explains the magnitude and structure of the postindependence militarization of French neocolonialism in Africa.

In effect, the military and paramilitary instruments of formal or informal modes of French control of African client states in the backwash of world capitalism are aimed at securing an investment and trade climate essential to an effective imperialist foreign policy. In other words, private capital responds to the incentives held out by national governments and international agencies because of both politicomilitary policies and investment conditions in satellite economies. When substitute instruments of direct colonial rule fail in terms of close currency zones, preferential trading systems, politicomilitary pacts, cultural missions, bribes to local ruling groups in the form of "aid," and so on, the other instruments of warfarist coercion and forces are brought into play, and the principle of continuity in change wins the day.

The present organization, equipment, doctrine, and self-image of African national armed forces emphasizes classical conventional military preparedness. This military preparedness and the intense competition for French arms and military assistance dramatically reduce the chances for the future health of the body politic in Africa. For one thing, secondary military disputes in the continent tend toward erupting into great-power war. For another, the rise of military preparedness and warfarism in African states is not against Africa's external enemies. Therefore, in the face of this decentralized domestic brutality and French warfarist intervention in African conflicts, what is to be done? As it now appears to have a threatening arms race under control at one site in Africa by no means guarantees preventing its outbreak at a variety of other sites. In short, the further spread of French armaments and interventions cannot be regarded as anything but a profound complication at best and a lethal menace at worst (witness Libya's military adventures in Africa). Total disarmament remains an utopian objective in Africa, although building armaments constitutes a severe and unnecessary economic drain. For instance, Libya, armed with French Mirage fighters and an ideological Islamic crusade, attempted to annex its battle-scarred neighbor, Chad. Libyan intervention brought to the fore enemy-thy-neighbor fears. It also initiated a rethinking about the nation-state system, disarmament and arms control, and "real-politic." Hence, French arms are causing as much insecurity as European firearms did during the slave trade (*The Economist*, December 20, 1980; *Daily Sketch* [London], December 23, 1980).

African dependence thus has a decisive military dimension. The evolution of African armed forces and strategic, economic, and political interests are now becoming central to contemporary international relations in postindependence Africa. The question raised by the continuity of military dependence are many. How will the vicious circle of Franco–African military relations of dominance and dependence be broken? What role will revolutionary violence play in breaking up the relations? What are the implications of growing imbalances in the forces and equipment available to different African states? Which elements of military strength are most critical for Africa to project its power to its borders and beyond? What level of African military independence is possible and essential in a world system of dominance and dependence?

Prescriptive answers to these questions may seem to be pie in the sky. For one thing, African leaders need to rid themselves of the negative images of the "enemy-thy-neighbor" mentality. For another, they have to become more committed to the "African cause" rather than continue to nurse defeatist sentiments of Africa's lack of technical know-how, finances, and cultural and military diversity. This move will set the stage for a continental agreement, formal or tacit, against arms in excess of internal security needs. Any bridge of the arms-control measure could be countered by a revival of the League of Nation's practice of giving wide publicity to such statistics. An African High Command can be formed to police arms supplies and also assume the responsibility to defend the territorial integrity of Africa and maintain continental law and order against interstate militarism.

In sum, French military intervention in Africa has been motivated and facilitated by its policy of

- promoting "la grandeur de la France eternelle" (eternal French Greatness), which depends on continued domination, exploitation, and pillaging of its former colonies;
- depending on the twin pillars of intervention and questionable arms sales to shore up fragile African regimes that enjoy a "special relationship" with French finance capital;
- preserving the persistent myth of "black Frenchmen" among African leaders;
- cementing widespread military, financial, economic, technical, and cultural cooperation agreements to protect the mutual interests of France and her EEC partners;

- securing the quiescence of the French public and international community on the legitimacy of intervention in the internal affairs of independent states; and, most importantly,
- nursing and protecting its "looting rights" in the continent (Whiteman 1969, 30).

French arms sales and military intervention, therefore, occurred in African countries that were torn by ethnic and civil turmoil, allowing unscrupulous French mining companies to take advantage of the unstable domestic environment to loot the local resources. These companies were able to fill their coffers with what has come to be called "conflict" diamonds, gold, copper, platinum, and other precious minerals, including columbite-tantalite or coltan, which is a primary component of computer microchips and printed circuit boards. French companies exploiting and pillaging Africa's most valuable mineral and natural resources are directly linked to the French political leadership, military–industrial complex, and pro-French African leaders. Thus, political, strategic, and economic considerations compelled French–Africa policy to be mercantilist and interventionist (Chaigneau 1984; Dungia 1993).

However, the upsurge of globalization with its emphasis on accountability and transparency discourages such brutal military intervention. In other words, neoliberalism demands (1) popular participation in governance, (2) accountability in the management of public resources, (3) institutionalization of the rule of law, and (4) democratic constitutionalism or rule making. These post–Cold War developments are expected to constrain French attempts to use organized and systematic military activities to affect the political authority structures of target African states.

REFERENCES

Adamolekun, 'L. 1978. The political and social ideas of Sékou Touré. In *Themes in African social and political thought*. Enugu, Nigeria: Fourth Dimension.

Ake, C. 1981. *A political economy of Africa*. London: Longman.

Assemblée Nationale. 1981–1982. *Rapport fait au nom de la commission des finances, de l'économie générale et du plan sure le projet de lois des finances pour 1982, Annexe no. 44, defense nationale*. Paris: Assemblée Nationale Document No. 470, Primière Session Ordinaire.

Bobb, F. S. 1979. Zaire: Another rescue operation. *Africa Report* 24 (2): 16–20.

Chaigneau, P. 1984. *La politique militaire de la France en Afrique*. Paris: La Documentation Française.

Cohen, W. 2000. *African Conflict Resolution Act: Interagency progress report for fiscal 1999/2000*. Washington, DC: U.S. Department of State.

Cronje, S. 1976. *Equatorial Guinea: The forgotten dictatorship*, Research Report 2 of the Anti-Slavery Society. London: London University Press.

Davenport, M. 1992. Africa and the unimportance of being preferred. *Journal of Common Market Studies* 30 (2): 233–251.

Débazies, P. 1980. *La politique militaire de la France en Afrique noire sous le Générale de Gaulle, 1958–1969, Actes du Colloque de Bordeaux, 19–20 Octobre.* Paris: Pedone.

Debre, M. 1972. *Livre blanc.* Paris: Edition Seuil.

Delavignette, R. 1962. *L'Afrique noire française et son destin.* Paris: Gallimard.

Dungia, E. 1993. *Mobutu et l'argent du Zaire.* Paris: L'Hartmattan.

Feig, D. G., and J. D. Holm. 1978. Political development theory in Africa: A reanalysis. *Journal of Developing Politics* 12 (3): 338–389.

Feustel, S. 1978. African minerals and American foreign policy. *Africa Report* 23 (5): 12–17.

Foltz, W. J. 1965. *From French West Africa to Mali Federation.* New Haven: Yale University Press.

Girardet, R. 1964. *La crise militaire française, 1945–1969: Aspects sociologiques et idéologiques: Cahiers de la fondation française des sciences politiques.* Paris: Armand Colin.

Guillemin, J. 1981. Importance des bases dans la politique militaire française en Afrique. *Le Mois en Afrique* June/July and August/September.

Gutkind, P.C.W., and I. Wallerstein, eds. 1976. *The political economy of contemporary Africa.* Beverly Hills, CA: Sage.

Harrison, C. 1983. French attitude to empire and the Algerian war. *African Affairs* 82 (326): 75–95.

Hollick, J. C. 1979. French intervention in Africa in 1978. *The World Today* 35 (2): 71.

IMF. 2002. *Direction of trade statistics yearbook, 2002.* Washington, DC: International Monetary Fund.

Joseph, R. A., ed. 1978. *Gaullist Africa: Cameroun under Ahmadu Ahidjo.* Enugu: Fourth Dimension.

Jospin, L. 1978. Plein feux sur l'Afrique. *Le Monde*, May 21–22.

Kazadi, F.S.B. 1978. Mobutu, MPR, and the politics of survival. *Africa Report* 23 (1): 11–16.

Klein, J. 1976. Commerce des armes et politique: Les cas français. *Politique Etrangère* 41 (5): 563–586.

Kolodziej, E. A. 1974. *French international policy under de Gaulle and Pompidou: the politics of grandeur.* Ithaca, NY: Cornell University Press.

Lacroix, A. 1965. Problémes de défense en Afrique noire Francophone et coopération militaire française. In *Mémoire du centre de hautes études sur l'Afrique et l'Asie modernes (CHEAM) 3995 (Mars).* Paris: CHEAM.

Ligot, M. 1963. La coopération militaire dans les accords passés entre la France et les africains et malgaches d'expression française. *Revue Politique et Jurisdique d'Outre Mer* (October–December): 517–532.

Luckham, R. 1982. French militarism in Africa. *Review of African Political Economy* (May/August): 55–84.

Luxembourg, R. 1964. *The accumulation of capital.* New York: Oxford University Press.

Masquet, B. 1982. France–Afrique: Dépasser les contradictions. *Afrique Contemporaine* 119 (January): 16.

Marshall, D. B. 1973. Free France in Africa: Gaullism and colonialism. In *The French colonial myth and constitution-making in the Fourth Republic*, edited by D. B. Marshall. New Haven: Yale University Press.

Martin, G. 1982. Africa and the ideology of Eurafrica: Neocolonialism or Pan-Africanism? *Journal of Modern African Studies* 20 (2): 221–238.

Mbaku, J. M. 1995. Emerging trade blocs and the future of African participation in the world economy. *Journal of Economic Integration* 10 (2): 141–177.

McLaughin, M. 1979. *The United States and world development: Agenda 1979.* New York: Praeger.

Médard, J.-F. 1995. La patrimonialisation des rélations franco-africaines: Échanges politiques, économiques et sociaux. In *La corruption dans les régimes pluralistes*, edited by Yves Mery and Donatella Dellaporta. Paris: Karthala.

Mertillo, M. 1988. Les armées françaises à l'étranger: Coopération militaire en Afrique. *Revue Française d'Administration Publique* (June).

Nabakew, R. 2002. France continues peacekeeping initiative for Africa. *Panafrican News Agency*, January 23, 2002. Retrieved from http://www.globalpolicy.org/security/peacekpg/region/france.htm, November 25, 2003.

Nouvaille-Degorce, B. 1982. *La politique française de coopération avec les états Africains et Malgache au süd du Sahara.* Bordeaux, France: Centre d'Etudes d'Afrique Noire, Univérsité de Bordeaux.

Nyerere, J. 1978. Foreign troops in Africa. *Africa Report* 23 (4): 10–13.

Owen, A. D. 1984. The world uranium industry. In *Raw materials report* (Stockholm) 2(4): 144–146.

Pesticide Action Network of North America. 1990. A conspiracy of silence: Herbicide battles in South Africa Chemical Workers' Industrial Union. *Global Pesticide Campaigner*, October. Retrieved from http://www.pana.org/resources/PESTIS.burst.108.html.

Rondos, A. G. 1979. Ivory Coast: The price of development. *Africa Report* 24 (2): 4–9.

Shaw, T. M., and M. J. Grieve. 1977. Dependence or development: International and internal inequalities in Africa. *Development and Change* 8 (3): 4–9.

Sivard, R. L., ed. 1978. *World military and social expenditures, 1978*, 13th ed. Leesburg, VA: ICPSR.

Tchoundjang, J. P. 1980. *Monnaie, servitude et liberté.* Paris: Edition Jeune Afrique.

Tunteng, P.-K. 1974. France-Africa: Plus ça change . . . *Africa Report* 20 (4): 2–6.

UNDP. 2000. *Human development report, 2000.* New York: Oxford University Press.

UN-ECOSOC. 1975. *Survey of economic conditions in Africa, 1974.* New York: U.N. Economic and Social Council.

U.S. Arms Control and Disarmament Agency. 1976. *World military expenditures and the arms trade, 1964–74.* Washington, DC: U.S. Government Printing Office.

U.S. Arms Control and Disarmament Agency. 1979. *World military expenditures and arms transfers, 1968–1977.* Washington, DC: U.S. Government Printing Office.

U.S. Arms Control and Disarmament Agency. 1992. *World military expenditures and arms transfers, 1990.* Washington, DC: U.S. Government Printing Office.

U.S. Department of Defense. 1971–1972. *The Pentagon Papers: The Defense Department history of United States decisionmaking on Vietnam.* Boston: Beacon Press.

U.S. Department of Defense. 1978. *Foreign military sales and military assistance facts.* Washington, DC: U.S. Government Printing Office.

Verschave, F. X. 1994. Complicité de génocide. *La Découverte*: 121–139.

Wauthier, C. 1974. *Quatre président et l'Afrique.* Paris: Seuil.

Whiteman, K. 1969. France's year in Africa. *Africa Contemporary Record* 1: 30: 241–249.

Whiteman, K. 1970. Pompidou and Africa: Gaullism after de Gaulle. *The World Today* (June): 241–249.

Williams, E. 1964. *Capitalism and slavery*. London: Andre Deutsch.

World Bank. 1979. *World development report, 1979*. New York: Oxford University Press.

World Bank. 1980. *World development report, 1980*. New York: Oxford University Press.

World Bank. 1981. *World development report, 1981*. New York: Oxford University Press.

World Bank. 2000. *World development report, 2000/2001: Attacking poverty*. New York: Oxford University Press.

Selected Bibliography

Abdi, A. A. 2002. *Culture, education, and development in South Africa: Historical and contemporary perspectives*. Westport, CT: Bergin and Garvey.

Abrahamsen, R. 2000. *Disciplining democracy: Development discourse and good governance in Africa*. London: Zed Books.

Adamolekun, L., and C. Bryant. 1994. *Governance progress report: The African region experience*. Washington, DC: World Bank.

Adams, F., S. D. Gupta, and K. Mengisteab, eds. 1999. *Globalization and the dilemmas of the state in the south*. New York: St. Martin's Press.

Adar, K. G., and R. Ajulu, eds. 2001. *African foreign policy making*. Aldershot, UK: Ashgate.

Adedeji, A., ed. 1993. *Africa within the world: Beyond dispossession and dependence*. London: Zed Books.

Adler, G., and E. Webster. 1995. The labor movement, radical reform, and transition to democracy in South Africa. *Politics and Society* 23 (1): 75–106.

Adler, G., and E. Webster. 1999. Toward a class compromise in South Africa's double transition: Bargained liberalization and the consolidation of democracy. *Politics and Society* 27 (3): 347–385.

Agbango, G. A., ed. 1997. *Issues and trends in contemporary African politics: Stability, development and democratization*. New York: Peter Lang.

Agonafer, M., ed. 1996. *Africa in the contemporary international disorder: Crisis and possibilities*. Lanham, MD: University Press of America.

Ake, C. 1990. *The case for democracy: African governance in the 1990s*. Atlanta, GA: Carter Presidential Center.

Ake, C. 1994. *Democratization of disempowerment in Africa*. Lagos: Malthouse Press.

Ake, C. 1995. *Democracy and development in Africa*. Washington, DC: Brookings Institution.

Alexander, N. 1993. *Some are more equal than others: Essays on the transition in South Africa*. Cape Town: Buchu Books.

Ali, T. M., and R. O. Mathews, eds. 1999. *Civil wars in Africa: Roots and resolution*. Montreal: McGill-Queen's University Press.

Amadiume, I. 1997. *Reinventing Africa: Matriarchy, religion and culture*. London: Zed Books.

Amate, C.O.C. 1986. *Inside the OAU: Pan-Africanism in practice*. London: Macmillan.

Ambrose, B. P. 1995. *Democratization and the protection of human rights in Africa: Problems and prospects*. Westport, CT: Praeger.

Amin, S. 1980. *Class and nation: Historically and in the current crisis*. London: Heinemann.

Amin, S. 1992. *The empire of chaos*. New York: Monthly Press.

Amin, S. 1998. *Capitalism and the age of globalization: The management of contemporary society*. Delhi: Madyham.

Amuwo, 'K., A.A.B. Agbaje, R. Suberu, and G. Herault, eds. 1998. *Federalism and political restructuring in Nigeria*. Ibadan: Spectrum Books.

Appadurai, A. 1996. *Modernity at large: Cultural dimensions of globalization*. Minneapolis: University of Minnesota Press.

Apter, D. E., and C. G. Rosberg. 1994. *Political development and the new reality in sub-Saharan Africa*. Charlottesville: University Press of Virginia.

Asante, S.K.B. 1997. *Regionalism and Africa's development*. London: Macmillan.

Ash, R. 1999. *The Third World in the age of globalization: Requiem or new agenda*. Delhi: Madhyam.

Assensoh, A. B. 1998. *African political leadership: Jomo Kenyatta, Kwame Nkrumah and Julius K. Nyerere*. Malabar, FL: Krieger.

Aubrey, L. 2000. Gender, development, and democratization in Africa. *Journal of Asian and African Studies* 36 (1): 87–111.

Ayee, J.R.A. 1997. *The 1996 general election and democratic consolidation in Ghana*. Legon, Ghana: Department of Political Science.

Baker, D., G. Epstein, and R. Polin. 1998. *The effects of globalization on policy formulation in South Africa*. New York: Cambridge University Press.

Baker, D., G. Epstein, and R. Polin. 1998. *Globalization and progressive economic policy*. New York: Cambridge University Press.

Barkan, J. D., ed. 1984. *Politics and public policy in Kenya and Tanzania*. New York: Praeger.

Barkan, J. D., G. Bauer, and C. L. Martin. 1994. *The consolidation of democracy in Namibia: Assessment and recommendations*. Burlington, VT: USAID.

Barnett, T., and P. Blaikie. 1992. *AIDS in Africa: Its present and future impact*. London: Belhaven Press.

Baskin, J. 1991. *Striking back: A history of COSATU*. New York: Verso.

Bates, R. H. 1981. *Markets and states in tropical Africa*. Berkeley and Los Angeles: University of California Press.

Bates, R. H. 1987. *Essays on the political economy of rural Africa*. Cambridge: Cambridge University Press.

Bayart, J.-F. 1993. *The state in Africa: The politics of the belly*. London: Longman.

Bayart, J-F., S. Ellis, and B. Hibou. 1999. *The criminalization of the state in Africa*. London: James Currey.

'Bayo Adekanye, J. 1999. *The retired military as emergent power factor in Nigeria*. Ibadan: Heinemann Educational Books.

Becker, D. G., and R. L. Sklar, eds. 1999. *Post-imperialism and world politics*. Westport, CT: Praeger.

Berger, G. 1998. Media and democracy in Southern Africa. *Review of African Political Economy* 78: 599–610.

Berman, E., and K. Sams. 1998. *Constructive disengagement: Western efforts to develop African peacekeeping*. Johannesburg: ISS Monograph Series 33, Institute for Security Studies.

Berman, E., and K. Sams. 2000. *Peacekeeping in Africa: Capabilities and culpabilities*. Geneva: U.N. Institute for Disarmament Research.

Berry, S. 1993. *No condition is permanent*. Madison: University of Wisconsin.

Biko, S. 1978. *I write what I like*. London: Heinemann.

Bollinger, L., and J. Stover. 1999. *The economic impact of AIDS in Botswana*. Glastonbury: Futures Group International.

Borner, S., and M. Paldam. 1998. *The political dimension of economic growth*. Basingstoke, UK: Macmillan.

Bowman, L. W. 1992. *Mauritius: Democracy and development in the Indian ocean*. Boulder, CO: Westview Press.

Bratton, M., and N. van de Walle. 1998. *Democratic experiments in Africa: Regime transitions in comparative perspective*. New York: Cambridge University Press.

Brenes, A., ed. 1999. *The leadership challenges of demilitarization in Africa, July 22–24, 1998: Conference report*. San José, Costa Rica: Arias Foundation for Peace and Human Progress.

Buijtenhuijs, R., and E. Rijnierse. 1993. *Democratization in sub-Saharan Africa (1989–1992): An overview of literature*. Leiden: African Studies Center.

Buijtenhuijs, R., and C. Thiriot. 1995. *Democratization in sub-Saharan Africa (1992–1995): An overview of literature*. Leiden: African Studies Center.

Buzan, B. 1991. *Peoples, states and fear: An agenda for international security studies in post–Cold War era*. London: Harvester Wheatshealf.

Carmody, P. 2001. *Tearing the social fabric: Neoliberalism, deindustrialization, and the crisis of governance in Zimbabwe*. Portsmouth, NH: Heinemann.

Carver, R. 1990. *Where silence rules: The suppression of dissent in Malawi*. New York: Africa Watch.

Casper, G., and M. M. Taylor. 1996. *Negotiating democracy: Transitions from authoritarian rule*. Pittsburgh: University of Pittsburgh.

Chabal, P. 1994. *Power in Africa*. New York: St. Martin's Press.

Chabal, P., and J.-P. Daloz. *Africa works: Disorder as political instrument*. Oxford: James Currey.

Charlton, S.E.M. 1984. *Women in Third World development*. Boulder, CO: Westview Press.

Chazan, N. 1992. Africa's democratic challenge. *World Policy Journal* 9 (2): 279–294.

Cheru, F. 1997. *A challenge to the New World Order: Promoting transnational civil society in Africa*. Washington, DC: American University Press.

Chrétien, J.-P. 1995. *Rwanda: Les medias du genocide*. Paris: Karthala.

Cilliers, J., and G. Mills, eds. 1999. *From peacekeeping to complex emergencies: Peace support missions in Africa*. Johannesburg: South African Institute of International Affairs and the Institute for Security Studies.

Clark, J. F., D. E. Gardinier, eds. 1997. *Political reform in Francophone Africa*. Boulder, CO: Westview Press.

Cliffe, L. 1994. *The transition to independence in Namibia*. Boulder, CO: Lynne Rienner.

Clough, M. 1992. *Free at last: U.S. policy towards Africa at the end of the Cold War*. New York: Council on Foreign Relations Press.

Cohen, J., and A. Arato. 1992. *Civil society and political theory*. Cambridge: MIT Press.

Coleman, J. S., and R. L. Sklar. 1994. *Nationalism and development in Africa: Selected essays*. Berkeley and Los Angeles: University of California Press.

Collier, P., J. W. Gunning. 1999. Explaining African economic performance. *Journal of Economic Literature* 37: 64–111.

Coolidge, J., and S. Rose-Ackerman. 1997. *High-level rent seeking and corruption in African regimes: Theory and cases*. Washington, DC: World Bank.

Copson, R. W. 1994. *Africa's wars and prospects for peace.* Armonk, NY: M. E. Sharpe.

Cross, S., and A. Whiteside, eds. 1993. *Facing up to AIDS: The socioeconomic impact in Southern Africa.* New York: St. Martin's Press.

Davenport, M. 1992. Africa and the unimportance of being preferred. *Journal of Common Market Studies* 30 (2): 233–251.

Davidson, B. 1992. *The black man's burden: The curse of nation-state in Africa.* Oxford: James Currey.

Decalo, S. 1992. The process, prospects and constraints of democratization in Africa. *African Affairs* 9 (362): 7–35.

Des Forges, A. 1999. *Leave none to tell the story: Genocide in Rwanda.* London: Human Rights Watch.

Dia, M. 1993. *A governance approach to civil service reform in sub-Saharan Africa.* Washington, DC: World Bank.

Dia, M. 1996. *Africa's management in the 1990s and beyond: Reconciling indigenous and transplanted institutions.* Washington, DC: World Bank.

Diamond, L. 1997. *Prospects for democratic developments in Africa: Essays in public policy.* Stanford: Hoover Institution.

Diamond, L. 1999. *Developing democracy: Toward consolidation.* Baltimore: Johns Hopkins University Press.

Diamond, L., and M. F. Plattner, eds. 1999. *Democratization in Africa.* Baltimore: Johns Hopkins University Press.

Dolphyne, F. A. 1991. *The emancipation of women: An African perspective.* Accra: Ghana Universities Press.

Drah, F. K., and M. Oquaye. 1996. *Civil society in Ghana.* Accra: Friedrich Ebert Stiftung.

Dunkley, G. 2000. *The free trade adventure: The WTO, the Uruguay Round and globalism: A critique.* London: Zed Books.

Du Toit, P. 1995. *State building and democracy in Southern Africa.* Washington, DC: U.S. Institute of Peace Press.

Eboussi, F. 1993. *Les conférences nationales en Afrique noire.* Paris: Karthala.

Eboussi, F. 1997. *La démocratie de transit au Cameroun.* Paris: L'Harmattan.

Ebrahim, H. 1998. *The soul of a nation: Constitution-making in South Africa.* New York: Oxford University Press.

Edoho, F. M., ed. 1997. *Globalization and the New World Order: Promises, problems and prospects for Africa in the twenty-first century.* Westport, CT: Praeger.

Ekeh, P. 1992. The constitution of civil society in African history and politics. In *Proceedings of the symposium on democratic transition in Africa.* Ibadan: CREDU.

Ekeh, P., ed. 1992. *Wilberforce conference on Nigerian federalism.* Buffalo: State University of New York Press.

Elliot, K. A., ed. 1997. *Corruption and the global economy.* Washington, DC: Institute for International Economics.

Ellis, S. 1996. Africa and international corruption: The strange case of South Africa and Seychelles. *African Affairs* 95: 165–196.

Evans, G. 1997. *Responding to crisis in the African Great Lakes.* New York: Oxford University Press.

Eyoh, D. 1995. From the belly to the ballot: Ethnicity and politics in Africa. *Queen's Quarterly* 102 (1): 39–51.

Eyoh, D. 1998. Through the prism of a local tragedy: Political liberalization, regionalism and elite struggles for power in Cameroon. *Africa* 68 (3): 338–359.

Falk, R. 1999. *Predatory globalism: A critique.* Cambridge: Polity.

Falola, T., and P. Williams, eds. 1995. *Religious impact on the nation-state: The Nigerian predicament.* Aldershot, UK: Ashgate.

Fanon, F. 1967. *Black skin, white masks.* New York: Grove Press.

Fanon, F. 1967. *The wretched of the earth.* Harmondsworth: Penguin Books.

Fatton, R. Jr. 1990. Liberal democracy in Africa. *Political Science Quarterly* 105 (3): 455–473.

Fatton, R. Jr. 1992. *Predatory rule: State and civil society in Africa.* Boulder, CO: Lynne Rienner.

Fatton, R. Jr. 1995. Africa in the age of democratization: The civic limitations of civil society. *African Studies Review* 38 (2): 67–100.

Fine, B., and D. Davis. 1990. *Beyond apartheid: Labor and liberation in South Africa.* London: Pluto Press.

Furley, O., ed. 1995. *Conflict in Africa.* New York: St. Martin's Press.

Furley, O., and R. May, eds. 1998. *Peacekeeping in Africa.* Aldershot, UK: Ashgate.

Gamble, A., and A. Payne, eds. 1996. *Regionalism and world order.* New York: St. Martin's Press.

Geisler, G. 1995. Troubled sisterhood: Women and politics in Southern Africa. *African Affairs* 94: 545–578.

Geschiere, P. 1997. *The modernity of witchcraft: Politics and the occult in postcolonial Africa.* Charlottesville: University of Virginia Press.

Gibson, N. 2000. Transition from apartheid. *Journal of Asian and African Studies* 36 (1): 65–85.

Giddens, A. 1990. *The consequences of modernity.* Cambridge: Polity Press.

Giliomee, H., and L. Schlemmer. 1994. *The bold experiment: South Africa's new democracy.* Johannesburg: Southern.

Gilpin, R. 2001. *Global political economy: Understanding the international economic order.* Princeton: Princeton University Press.

Golding, P., and P. Harris, eds. 1997. *Beyond cultural imperialism: Globalization, communication & the new international order.* London: Sage.

Good, K. 1994. Corruption and mismanagement in Botswana: A best-case example? *Journal of Modern African Studies* 32 (3): 499–521.

Goppen, S. 1997. *South Africa: The battle over the constitution.* Aldershot, UK: Ashgate.

Gordon, A. 1996. *Transforming capitalism and patriarchy: Women and development in Africa.* Boulder, CO: Lynne Rienner.

Gould, D. J. 1980. *Bureaucratic corruption and underdevelopment in the Third World: The case of Zaire.* New York: Pergamon Press.

Goulding, M. 1999. The United Nations and conflict in Africa since the Cold War. *African Affairs* 98 (391): 155–166.

Graf, W. D. 1988. *The Nigerian state.* London: James Currey.

Gray, J. 1998. *False dawn: The delusions of global capitalism.* London: Granta Books.

Gros, J.-G., ed. 1998. *Democratization in late twentieth-century Africa: Coping with uncertainty.* Westport, CT: Greenwood Press.

Hadjor, K. B. 1987. *On transforming Africa: Discourse with Africa's leaders.* Trenton and London: Africa World Press.

Hansen, E., and K. Ninsin. 1989. *The state, development and politics in Ghana.* Dakar: CODESRIA.

Harbeson, J. W., D. Rothchild, and N. Chazan, eds. 1994. *Civil society and the state in Africa.* Boulder, CO: Lynne Rienner.

Harlow, J. 1997. *Regional cooperation and integration with industry and trade in Southern Africa.* Aldershot, UK: Ashgate.

Harsch, E. 1998. Burkina Faso in the winds of liberalization. *Review of African Political Economy* 25 (78): 625–641.

Healey, J. and M. Robinson. 1992. *Democracy, governance and economic policy: Sub-Saharan Africa in comparative perspective.* London: Overseas Development Institute.

Hecht, D., and M. Simone. 1994. *Invisible governance: The art of Africa micropolitics.* New York: Autonomedia.

Herbst, J. 1990. *State politics in Zimbabwe.* Berkeley and Los Angeles: University of California Press.

Himmelstrand, U., K. Kinyanjui, and E. Mburugu, eds. 1994. *African perspectives on development: Controversies, dilemmas & openings.* Oxford: James Currey.

Hodgson, D. L., and S. A. McCurdy, eds. 2001. *"Wicked" women and the reconfiguration of gender in Africa.* Oxford: James Currey.

Hope, K. R. Sr., ed. 1997. *Structural adjustment, reconstruction and development in Africa.* Aldershot, UK: Ashgate.

Hope, K. R. Sr. 1997. *African political economy: Contemporary issues in development.* Armonk, NY: M. E. Sharpe.

Hope, K. R. Sr., ed. 1999. *AIDS and development in Africa: A social science perspective.* Binghamton, NY: Haworth Press.

Hope, K. R. Sr., and B. C. Chikulo, eds. 2000. *Corruption and development in Africa: Lessons from country case-studies.* London: Macmillan.

Horowitz, D. 1991. *A democratic South Africa: Constitutional engineering in a divided society.* Berkeley and Los Angeles: University of California.

House-Midamba, B., and F. E. Ekechi, eds. 1995. *African women and economic power: The role of women in African economic development.* Westport, CT: Greenwood Press.

Hutchful, E. 1996. The civil society debate in Africa. *International Journal* 51 (1): 54–77.

Hutchful, E., and A. Bathily, eds. 1998. *The military and militarism in Africa.* Dakar: CODESRIA.

Hyden, G. 1983. *No shortcuts to progress.* London: Heinemann.

Hyden, G., and M. Bratton, eds. 1992. *Governance and politics in Africa.* Boulder, CO: Lynne Rienner.

Iheduru, O. M., ed. 2001. *Contending issues in African development: Advances, challenges, and the future.* Westport, CT: Greenwood Press.

Ihonvbere, J. O. 1989. *The political economy of crisis and underdevelopment in Africa: Selected works of Claude Ake.* Lagos: JAD.

Ihonvbere, J. O. 1994. *Nigeria: The politics of adjustment & democracy.* New Brunswick, NJ: Transaction.

Ihonvbere, J. O. 1996. *Economic crisis, civil society, and democratization in Africa: The case of Zambia.* Trenton, NJ: Africa World Press.

Ihonvbere, J. O. 1996. Where is the third wave? A critique of Africa's non-transition to democracy. *Africa Today* 43 (4): 343–368.

Ihonvbere, J. O. 1998. *Labor, state and capital in Nigeria's oil industry*. Lewiston, NY: Edward Mellen Press.

Ihonvbere, J. O. 2000. *Towards a new constitutionalism in Africa*. London: Center for Democracy and Development.

Ihonvbere, J. O., and T. Falola. 1985. *The rise & fall of Nigeria's Second Republic, 1979–84*. Totowa, NJ: Zed Books.

Ihonvbere, J. O., and T. Falola. 1988. *Nigeria and the international capitalist system*. Boulder, CO: Lynne Rienner.

Ihonvbere, J. O., and T. M. Shaw. 1988. *Toward a political economy of Nigeria: Petroleum and politics at the (semi)-periphery*. Aldershot, UK: Avebury.

Ihonvbere, J. O., and T. M. Shaw. 1998. *Illusions of power: Nigeria in Transition*. Trenton, NJ: Africa World Press.

Ingham, K. 1990. *Politics in modern Africa: The uneven tribal dimension*. London: Routledge.

International Peace Academy. 1998. *Seminar on peacemaking and peacekeeping, Addis Ababa, November 29–December 3*. New York: IPA.

Jackson, R. H., and C. G. Rosberg. 1982. *Personal rule in black Africa: Prince, autocrat, prophet, tyrant*. Berkeley and Los Angeles: University of California Press.

Jackson, R. H., and C. G. Rosberg. 1982. Why Africa's weak states persist: The empirical and the juridical in statehood. *World Politics* 35: 1–24.

James, V. U., ed. 1995. *Women and sustainable development in Africa*. Westport, CT: Praeger.

Jega, A., ed. 2000. *Identity transformation and identity politics under structural adjustment in Nigeria*. Uppsala: Nordiska Afrikanistitutet.

Jegede, S., A. Ale, and E. Akinsola, eds. 2000. *Path to the people's constitution: A CDHR publication on constitutionalism, democracy & the rule of law*. London: Committee for Defense of Human Rights.

Jinadu, L. A., ed. 2000. *The political economy of peace and security in Africa*. Harare: AAPS Books.

Johnson, W. R., and L. Schlemmer, eds. 1996. *Launching democracy in South Africa: The first open election, April 1994*. New Haven, CT: Yale University Press.

Johnston, A., S. Stezi, and G. Bradshaw, eds. 1993. *Constitution making in the new South Africa*. New York: St. Martin's Press.

Joseph, R. A., ed. 1999. *State, conflict, and democracy in Africa*. Boulder, CO: Lynne Rienner.

Kahler, M. 1995. *International institutions and the political economy of integration*. Washington, DC: The Brookings Institution.

Kamukama, D. 1997. *Rwanda conflict: Its roots and regional implications*. Kampala, Uganda: Fountain Press.

Kerf, M., and W. Smith. 1996. *Privatizing Africa's infrastructure: Promise and challenge*. World Bank Technical Paper no. 337. Washington, DC: World Bank.

Kibwana, K. 1996. *Sowing the constitutional seed in Kenya*. Nairobi: English Press.

Kieh, G. K., Jr. 1992. *Dependency and the foreign policy of a small power: The Liberian case*. Lewiston, NY: Edwin Mellen Press.

Kimenyi, M. S. 1997. *Ethnic diversity, liberty and the state: The African dilemma*. Aldershot, UK: Edward Elgar.

Kimenyi, M. S., and J. M. Mbaku, eds. 1999. *Institutions and collective choice in developing countries: Applications of the theory of public choice.* Aldershot, UK: Ashgate.

Kohli, A., ed. 1986. *The state and development in the Third World.* Princeton: Princeton University Press.

Korten, D. C. 1995. *When corporations rule the world.* West Hartford, CT: Kumarian Press.

Kpundeh, S. J. 1995. *Politics and corruption in Africa: A case study of Sierra Leone.* Lanham, MD: University Press of America.

LeVine, V. T. 1997. The fall and rise of constitutionalism in West Africa. *Journal of Modern African Studies* 35 (2): 181–206.

Lewis, P. 1998. *Africa: Dilemmas of development and change.* Boulder, CO: Westview Press.

Leys, C. 1996. *The rise and fall of development theory.* Oxford: James Currey.

Lindauer, D. L., and B. Nunberg, eds. 1994. *Rehabilitating government: Pay and employment reform in Africa.* Washington, DC: World Bank.

Lipumba, N. H. 1994. *Africa beyond adjustment.* Washington, DC: World Bank.

Lowenberg, A. D. 1992. A post-apartheid constitution for South Africa: Lessons from public choice. *Cato Journal* 12 (2): 297–319.

MacEwan, A. 1999. *Neoliberalism or democracy? Economic strategy, markets, and alternatives for the 21st century.* London: Zed Books.

Macharia, K. 1997. *Social and political dynamics of the informal economy in African cities: Nairobi and Harare.* New York: University Press of America.

Magnarella, P. J. 1999. *Middle East and North Africa: Governance, democratization, human rights.* Aldershot, UK: Ashgate.

Magnarella, P. J. 2000. *Justice in Africa: Rwanda's genocide, its courts, and the U.N. Tribunal.* Aldershot, UK: Ashgate.

Magyar, K. P., and E. Conteh-Morgan, eds. 1998. *Peacekeeping in Africa: ECOMOG in Liberia.* New York: St. Martin's Press.

Mama, A. 1996. *Women's studies and studies of women in Africa during the 1990s.* Dakar: CODESRIA.

Mamdani, M. 1996. *Citizen and subject: Contemporary Africa and the legacy of late colonialism.* Cape Town: David Phililp.

Mandela, N. 1990. *Nelson Mandela's speeches, 1990: Intensify the struggle to abolish apartheid.* New York: Pathfinder.

Marais, H. 1998. *South Africa: Limits to change, the political economy of transition.* London: Zed Books.

Maro, P. 1990. The impact of industrialization on spatial equity and rural development in Tanzania. *World Development* 18 (5): 673–693.

Martin, W. G., and M. O. West, eds. 1999. *Out of one, many Africas: Reconstructing the study and meaning of Africa.* Urbana-Champaign: University of Illinois.

Marx, A. W. 1992. *Lessons of the struggle.* New York: Oxford University Press.

Mbaku, J. M. 1995. Military intervention in African politics: Lessons from public choice. *Konjunkturpolitik* (Berlin) 41 (3): 268–291.

Mbaku, J. M. 1996. Bureaucratic corruption and the crisis of institutional reforms in Africa. *Business & the Contemporary World* 8 (3/4): 145–170.

Mbaku, J. M. 1996. Bureaucratic corruption in Africa: The futility of cleanups. *Cato Journal* 16 (1): 99–118.

Mbaku, J. M. 1996. Effective constitutional discourse as a first step to democratization in Africa. *Journal of Asian and African Studies* 31 (1/2): 39–51.

Mbaku, J. M. 1997. *Institutions and reform in Africa: The public choice perspective.* Westport, CT: Praeger.

Mbaku, J. M. 1998. Constitutional discourse and the development of structures for sustainable development in Africa. *Journal for Studies in Economics and Econometrics* 22 (1): 1–36.

Mbaku, J. M. 1998. Constitutional engineering and the transition to democracy in post–Cold War Africa. *The Independent Review* 2 (4): 501–517.

Mbaku, J. M., ed. 1998. *Corruption and the crisis of institutional reforms in Africa.* Lewiston, NY: Edwin Mellen Press.

Mbaku, J. M. 1998. Improving African participation in the global economy: The role of economic freedom. *Business & the Contemporary World* 10 (2): 297–338.

Mbaku, J. M. 1998. Political opportunism and policy reform in Africa: The case of Cameroon. *Politics Administration and Change* 30: 1–29.

Mbaku, J. M., ed. 1999. *Preparing Africa for the twenty-first century: Strategies for peaceful coexistence and sustainable development.* Aldershot, UK: Ashgate.

Mbaku, J. M. 2000. Appropriate institutional environment for development in twenty-first century Africa. *Africa Quarterly* (New Delhi) 40 (3): 7–44.

Mbaku, J. M. 2000. *Bureaucratic and political corruption in Africa: The public choice perspective.* Malabar, FL: Krieger.

Mbaku, J. M., P. O. Agbese, and M. S. Kimenyi, eds. 2001. *Ethnicity and governance in the Third World.* Aldershot, UK: Ashgate.

Mbaku, J. M., J. O. Ihonvbere, eds. 1998. *Multiparty democracy and political change: Constraints to democratization in Africa.* Aldershot, UK: Ashgate.

Mbaku, J. M., M. S. Kimenyi. 1995. Democratization in Africa: The continuing struggle. *Coexistence* 32: 119–136.

Mbaku, J. M., and M. S. Kimenyi. 1997. Macroeconomic determinants of growth: Further evidence on the role of political freedom. *Journal of Economic Development* 22 (1): 119–132.

McKinley, D. T. 1997. *The ANC and the liberation struggle: A critical bibliography.* London: Pluto Press.

Mengisteab, K. 1996. *Globalization and autocentricity in Africa's development in the 21st century.* Trenton, NJ: Africa World Press.

Mikell, G., ed. 1997. *African feminism: The politics of survival in sub-Saharan Africa.* Philadelphia: University of Pennsylvania Press.

Mimiko, N. O., ed. 1995. *Crises and contradictions in Nigeria's democratization program, 1986–1993.* Akure, Nigeria: Stebak.

Mkandawire, T., and A. Olukoshi, eds. 1995. *Between liberalization and repression: The politics of structural adjustment in Africa.* Dakar: CODESRIA.

Monga, C. 1995. Civil society and democratization in francophone Africa. *Journal of Modern African Studies* 33 (3): 359–379.

Morris, V. A., and M. P. Scharf. 1998. *The international criminal tribunal for Rwanda,* vol. 1–2. New York: Transnational.

Mukholi, D., ed. 1995. *A complete guide to Uganda's fourth constitution: History, politics and the law.* Kampala: Fountain.

Mutunga, W. 1999. *Constitution making from the middle: Civil society and transition politics in Kenya, 1992–1997.* Nairobi: SAREAT/MWENGO.

Nahum, F. 1997. *Constitution of a nation for nations: The Ethiopian prospect.* Lawrenceville, NJ: Red Sea Press.

Ndegwa, S. N. 1996. *The two faces of civil society.* West Hartford, CT: Kumarian Press.

Ndegwa, S. N. 1997. Citizenship and ethnicity: An examination of two transition moments in Kenyan politics. *American Political Science Review* 91 (3): 599–616.

Ndegwa, S. N. 1998. Citizenship amid economic and political change in Kenya today. *Africa Today* 45 (3/4): 351–367.

Ndegwa, S. N. 2000. A decade of democracy in Africa. *Journal of Asian and African Studies* 36 (1): 1–16.

Neocosmos, M. 1998. From people's politics to state politics: Aspects of national liberation in South Africa. In *The politics of opposition in contemporary Africa,* edited by A. Olukoshi. Uppsala: Nordiska Afrikaninstitutet.

Newitt, M. D., and M. Bennum. 1995. *Negotiating justice: A new constitution for South Africa.* Evanston, IL: Northwestern University Press.

Ngoh, V. J. 2000. *Southern Cameroons, 1922–1961: A constitutional history.* Aldershot, UK: Ashgate.

Ngwainmbi, E. 2000. Africa in the global infosupermarket: Perspectives and prospects. *Journal of Black Studies* 30 (4): 534–552.

Njoh, A. J. 1999. *Urban planning, housing and spatial structures in sub-Saharan Africa: Nature, impact and development implications of exogenous forces.* Aldershot, UK: Ashgate.

Njoh, A. J. 2003. *Planning in contemporary Africa: The state, town planning and society in Cameroon.* Aldershot, UK: Ashgate.

Nnoli, O. 1980. *Ethnic policies in Nigeria.* Enugu: Fourth Dimension.

Nnoli, O. 1995. *Ethnicity and development in Nigeria.* Aldershot, UK: Ashgate.

Nnoli, O., ed. 1999. *Ethnic politics in Africa.* Dakar: CODESRIA.

Nnoli, O., ed. 2000. *Government and politics in Africa: A reader.* Harare: AAPS Books.

Nwokedi, E. 1995. *Politics of democratization: Changing authoritarian regimes in sub-Saharan Africa.* Munster, Germany: LIT Verlag.

Nyamnjoh, F. B. 1999. Cameroon: A country united by ethnic ambition and difference. *African Affairs* 98 (39): 101–118.

Nyamnjoh, F. B., and M. Rowlands. 1998. Elite associations and the politics of belonging in Cameroon. *Africa* 68 (3): 320–337.

Nyerere, J. 1966. *Freedom and unity.* Dar-es-Salaam: Oxford University Press.

Nyong'o P. A., ed. 1987. *Popular struggles for democracy in Africa.* London: Zed Books.

Nzomo, M. 1997. *The gender dimension of electoral politics in Kenya: Capacity building of women candidates for 1997 and beyond.* Nairobi: Friedrich Ebert Stiftung.

O'Brien, J. 1993. Ethnicity, national identity and social conflict. *Nordic Journal of African Studies* 2 (2): 60–82.

Ochwada, H. 1996. African studies: A reassessment of academic tourism since 1960. *African Development* 21 (4): 123–140.

O'Donnell, G., P. S. Schmitter, and L. Whitehead, eds. 1986. *Transitions from authoritarian rule: Comparative perspectives.* Baltimore: Johns Hopkins University Press.

Okome, M. O. 1997. *Sapped democracy: The political economy of the structural adjustment program and the political transition in Nigeria, 1983–1993.* Lanham, MD: University Press of America.

Olukoshi, A., and L. Laasko, eds. 1995. *Challenges to the nation-state in Africa.* Uppsala: Nordiska Afrikaninstitutet.

Onimode, B. 1992. *A future for Africa: Beyond the politics of adjustment.* London: Earthscan.

Onwuka, R. I. 1991. *The anguish of dependent regionalism.* Ile-Ife: Obafemi Awolowo University Press.

Orvis, S. 1997. *The agrarian question in Kenya.* Gainesville: University Press of Florida.

Osaghae, E. E. 1994. *Between state and civil society in Africa.* Dakar: CODESRIA.

Osaghae, E. E. 1994. *Ethnicity and its management in Africa: The democratization link.* Lagos: Malthouse Press.

Osaghae, E. E. 1995. *Structural adjustment and ethnicity in Africa.* Uppsala: Nordiska Afrikaninstitutet.

Ostrom, E., L. Schroeder, and S. Wynne. 1993. *Institutional incentives and sustainable development: Infrastructure policies in perspective.* Boulder, CO: Westview Press.

Ottaway, M., ed. 1997. *Democracy in Africa: The hard road ahead.* Boulder, CO: Lynne Rienner.

Ottaway, M. 1999. *Africa's new leaders: Democracy or state reconstruction?* Washington, DC: Carnegie Endowment for International Peace.

Oyugi, W. O., ed. 1994. *Politics and public administration in East Africa.* Nairobi: East African Educational.

Parpart, J., and M. Bastian, eds. 1998. *Teaching Africa: African studies in the new millennium.* Boulder, CO: Lynne Rienner.

Parpart, J., and K. Staudt, eds. 1989. *Women and the state in Africa.* Boulder, CO: Lynne Rienner.

Phiri, I. 2001. *Proclaiming political pluralism: Churches and political transitions in Africa.* Westport, CT: Praeger.

Poku, N., ed. 2001. *Security and development in Southern Africa.* Westport, CT: Praeger.

Prunier, G. 1997. *The Rwanda crisis.* New York: Hurst and Company.

Rapley, J. 1993. *Ivorien capitalism: African entrepreneurs in Côte d'Ivoire.* Boulder, CO: Lynne Rienner.

Ravenhill, J. 1985. *The future of regionalism in Africa.* London: Macmillan.

Reno, W. 1995. *Corruption and state politics in Sierra Leone.* Cambridge: Cambridge University Press.

Reynolds, A., ed. 1994. *Election '94 South Africa: An analysis of the campaigns, results and future prospects.* New York: St. Martin's Press.

Rothchild, D. 1997. *Managing ethnic conflict in Africa: Pressures and incentives for cooperation.* Washington, DC: Brookings Institution Press.

Rothchild, D., and N. Chazan, eds. 1988. *The precarious balance: State and society in Africa.* Boulder, CO: Westview Press.

Rowley, C. K. 1999. Rent seeking and rent extraction from the perspective of Africa. In *Institutions and collective choice in developing countries: Applications of the theory of public choice,* edited by M. S. Kimenyi and J. M. Mbaku. Aldershot, UK: Ashgate.

Ruay, D.D.A. 1994. *The politics of the two Sudans: The north and south, 1821–1969.* Uppsala: Nordiska Afrikaninstitutet.

Russell, A. 1999. *Big men, little people: Encounters in Africa.* Basingstoke: Macmillan.

Rwomire, A., ed. 2000. *Social problems in Africa: New visions.* Westport, CT: Praeger.

Sah, R., and J. E. Stigliz. 1992. *Peasants versus city-dwellers: Taxation and the burden of economic development.* Oxford: Clarendon Press.

Sahn, D. E., ed. 1996. *Economic reform and the poor in Africa.* New York: Oxford University Press.

Sahn, D. E., P. Dorosh, and S. D. Younger. 1997. *Structural adjustment reconsidered: Economic policy and poverty in Africa.* Cambridge: Cambridge University Press.

Samoff, J. 1990. The politics of privatization in Tanzania. *International Journal of Educational Development* 10 (1): 1–15.

Sandbrook, R. 1993. *The politics of Africa's economic recovery.* Cambridge: Cambridge University Press.

Saro-Wiwa, K. 1989. *On a darkling plain: An account of the Nigerian civil war.* London: Saros International.

Sassen, S. 1996. *Losing control? Sovereignty in an age of globalization.* New York: Columbia University Press.

Saxena, S. C., ed. 2001. *Africa beyond 2000: Essays on Africa's political and economic development in the twenty-first century.* Delhi: Kalinga.

Schatz, S. 1994. Structural adjustment: A failing grade so far. *Journal of Modern African Studies* 32 (4): 679–692.

Schaffer, F. 1998. *Democracy in translation: Understanding politics and unfamiliar culture.* Ithaca: Cornell University Press.

Schraeder, P. J. 1996. *United States foreign policy toward Africa: Incrementalism, crisis and change.* Cambridge: Cambridge University Press.

Siedman, A., and F. Anang. 1992. *21st century Africa.* Trenton, NJ: Africa World Press.

Selassie, B. H. 1995. *The Constitutional Commission of Eritrea: Information strategy, plans and activities.* Asmara, Eritrea: CCE Headquarters.

Serageldin, I., and J. Taboroff, eds. 1994. *Culture and development in Africa.* Washington, DC: World Bank.

Shaw, T. 1993. *Reformism and revisionism in Africa's political economy in the 1990s: Beyond structural adjustment.* London: Macmillan.

Shivji, I. G. 1989. *The concept of human rights in Africa.* Dakar: CODESRIA.

Shivji, I. G., ed. 1991. *State and constitutionalism: An African debate on democracy.* Harare: SAPES Books.

Sichone, O. 1998. *The state and constitutionalism in Southern Africa.* Harare: SAPES Books.

Sichone, O., and B. C. Chikulo, eds. 1996. *Democracy in Zambia: Challenges for the Third Republic.* Harare: SAPES Books.

Siddiqui, R., ed. 1997. *Challenges to democracy and development: Sub-Saharan Africa in the 1990s.* Westport, CT: Praeger.

Simons, A. 1995. *Networks of dissolution: Somalia undone.* Boulder, CO: Westview Press.

Sorbo, G. M., and P. Vale, eds. 1997. *Out of conflict: From war to peace in Africa.* Uppsala: Nordiska Afrikainstitutet.

Sorenson, J. 1995. *Disaster and development in the Horn of Africa.* Basingstoke: Macmillan.

Soyinka, W. 1994. Democracy and cultural apologia. *Afrika Spectrum* 29 (1): 5–13.

Soyinka, W. 1996. *The open sore of a continent: A personal narrative of the Nigerian crisis.* New York: Oxford University Press.

Stewart, F., S. Lall, and S. Wangwe, eds. 1992. *Alternative development strategies in sub-Saharan Africa*. London: Macmillan.

Suberu, R. T. 1996. *Ethnic minority conflicts and governance in Nigeria*. Ibadan: Spectrum Books.

Takougang, J., and M. Krieger, eds. 1998. *African state and society in the 1990s: Cameroon's political crossroads*. Boulder, CO: Westview Press.

Taylor, I. 2001. *Stuck in the middle gear: South Africa's post-apartheid foreign relations*. Westport, CT: Praeger.

Thomas, C., and P. Wilkins, eds. 1999. *Globalization, human security, and the African experience*. Boulder, CO: Lynne Rienner.

Throup, D., and C. Hornsby. 1998. *Multiparty politics in Kenya: The Kenyatta and Moi states and the triumph of the system in the 1992 election*. Oxford: James Currey.

Tripp, R. 2001. *Seed provision & agricultural development: The institutions for rural change*. London: Overseas Development Institute in association with James Currey.

Udogu, E. I., ed. 1997. *Democracy and democratization in Africa: Toward the 21st century*. Leiden: E. J. Brill.

Udogu, E. I. 1997. *Nigeria and the politics of survival as a nation-state*. Lewiston, NY: Edwin Mellen Press.

Udogu, E. I., ed. 2001. *The issue of political ethnicity in Africa*. Aldershot, UK: Ashgate.

UNDP. 2000. *Human development report, 2000*. New York: Oxford University Press.

Unvin, P. 1998. *Aiding violence: the development of enterprise in Rwanda*. West Hartford, CT: Kumarian Press.

Uwadibie, N. O. 2000. *Decentralization and economic development in Nigeria: Agricultural policies and implementation*. New York: University Press of America.

Van Allen, J. 2000. Women's rights movements as a measure of African democracy. *Journal of Asian and African Studies* 36 (1): 39–63.

Van de Walle, N. 1994. The politics of public enterprise reform in Cameroon. In *State-owned enterprises in Africa*, edited by B. Grosh and R. S. Mukandala. Boulder, CO: Lynne Rienner.

Van de Walle, N., and T. Johnston. 1996. *Improving aid to Africa*. Washington, DC: Overseas Development Council.

Van Zyle Slabbert, F. 1992. *Quest for democracy: South Africa in transition*. Johannesburg: Penguin.

Vasquez, I., ed. 2000. *Global fortune: The stumble and rise of world capitalism*. Washington, DC: Cato Institute.

Vaughan, O. 2000. *Nigerian chiefs: Traditional power in modern politics, 1890s–1990s*. Rochester: University of Rochester Press.

Villalon, L. 1995. *Islamic society and state power in Senegal*. Cambridge: Cambridge University Press.

Villalon, L., and P. A. Huxtable, eds. 1998. *The African state at a critical juncture: Between disintegration and reconfiguration*. Boulder, CO: Lynne Rienner.

Wasike, W.S.K. 2000. Roads and road transport policies in Kenya: Review and synthesis. Working paper, Kenya Institute for Public Policy Research and Analysis, Nairobi.

Werbner, R., and T. Ranger, eds. 1996. *Postcolonial identities in Africa*. London: Zed Books.

Widener, J., ed. 1994. *Economic change and political liberalization in sub-Saharan Africa*. Baltimore: Johns Hopkins University Press.

Wiseman, J. A. 1990. *The new struggle for democracy in Africa.* Aldershot, UK: Ashgate.

Wiseman, J. A., ed. 1995. *Democracy and political change in sub-Saharan Africa.* London: Routledge.

Woods, N., ed. 2000. *The political economy of globalization.* New York: St. Martin's Press.

World Bank. 1996. *African development report, 1996.* Washington, DC: World Bank.

World Bank. 1997. *Confronting AIDS: Public priorities in a global epidemic.* New York: Oxford University Press.

World Bank. 2000. *Can Africa claim the 21st century?* Washington, DC: World Bank.

World Bank. 2002. *World development report, 2002: Building institutions for markets.* New York: Oxford University Press.

Wunsch, J., and D. Olowu, eds. 1990. *The failure of the centralized state: Institutions and self-governance in Africa.* Boulder, CO: Westview Press.

Yeebo, Z. 1991. *Ghana: The struggle for popular power.* London: New Beacon.

Yeros, P., ed. 1999. *Ethnicity and nationalism in Africa: Constructivist reflections and contemporary politics.* London: Macmillan.

Young, C. 1997. *The African colonial state in comparative perspective.* New Haven: Yale University Press.

Young, C. 1999. *The accommodation of cultural diversity: Case studies.* New York: St. Martin's Press.

Zartman, I. W. 1995. *Collapsed states: The disintegration and restoration of legitimate authority.* Boulder, CO: Lynne Rienner.

Zacarias, A. 1999. *Security and the state in Southern Africa.* London: Tauris Academic Studies.

Index

Abacha, Sani: coup d'état, 377, 378; death of, 380; election of, 379–380; and Internet, 221

Abiola, Moshood, Nigeria, 350, 378

Abuja Treaty: Africa regions, 121, 126, 128; regional development, 140; Sitre conference, 179, 180; subregions, 130

Accord de non-aggression et d'assistance en matière de défense: CEAO, 135, 136; ECOWAS, 281

Accountability, 380

Achebe, Chinua, 70, 372, 373

Adar, Korwa G.: on ethnic violence, 14–15; on peacekeeping, 15

Ademolekun, Ladipo, 372

Advanced Research and Projects Network (ARPANET), 211–212

"Affirmative action," 309

Africa: alternatives to French influence, 19–20; ancient globalization, 28; characteristics of globalism, 95, 98–103; comparative standing, 38, 39; cultural diversity, 15–16; current choices, 4; economic development, 193–204; French impact on, 419–421; and global economic blocs, 11, 177–178; Internet connectivity, 211–229; interstate conflict, 295–296; investor risk, 240; literacy rate, 400; main concerns, 38; military expenditures of, 396–398, 400; and neoliberal theories, 26; new goals, 4–5; political failures, 8; poverty of, 4, 196, 197, 400; priorities of, 149;
regional alignment, 121–143; technological underdevelopment, 50; Western strategic view of, 148

Africa Online, 222

African, Caribbean, and the Pacific (ACP) countries, 29

African Central Bank: Abuja Treaty, 180; AU, 184

African Charter on Human and People's Rights: Nigerian signatory, 375, 376, 383; OAU, 186

African Commission on Human and People's Rights, 128

African Commonwealth, 166

African Connection, 251

African Court of Justice: and Abuja Treaty, 180; and AU, 184

African Crisis Response Force (ACRF), 278

African Crisis Response Initiative (ACRI), 278, 279, 387–388

African Economic Commission (AEC): Africa regions, 121, 127; economic integration, 128; Internet adoption, 219

African Exhibition on New Information Technologies, 219

"African Green Paper," 215

African Growth and Opportunities Act (AGOA), 29, 102–103

African High Command (AFC), 269

African Information Society Initiative (AISI), 215

African Monetary Union, 180

African National Congress (ANC): Banda opposition to, 11, 175; and Mandela government, 348; trans-

formation of, 328–329
African Peacekeeping Initiative (P3), 278, 279
African Political Security Council (APSC), 270
African Regional Telecommunications Development Conference, 215
African Renaissance, 141
African Symposium on Telematics for Development (ASTD), 215, 221
African Telecommunications Development Conference (AF-RTDC), 215, 221
African Telecommunications Policy Study Group (ATPSG), 215
African traditional religion, religious conflict, 296
African Union (AU): African unity, 11–12; Constitutive Act, 164, 182–185; economic integration, 128; foundation of, 11, 163–164, 271, 299; funding of, 189; organs of, 183, 187; peacekeeping activities, 15
African unity: approaches to, 169–172, 174; constraints/requirements, 172; future problems, 187–188, 189; historical context, 165–169; international influence, 10; limited success of, 122; OAU accomplishments, 185–186; OAU's failure, 127–128; organizations promoting, 187; revitalized efforts, 163–164; setbacks to, 172–175; value of, 178
African Women's Committee and Development, 354
Agence Tunisienne d'Internet, 223–224
Agricultural marketing boards (AMBs), market regulations, 201
Agricultural price liberalization, African exports, 99
Agriculture: colonial impact, 191; continental conflict, 298
AIDS, comparative standing, 38, 39
Airports, PPI, 238, 239
Ake, Claude: on African ethnicity, 291–292; on crisis of authority,

300; on economic development, 319; on group struggles, 300; on instability, 371
Algeria: and African unity, 173; FDI, 31; French military policy, 397; Internet regulation, 223; Internet usage, 221; religious conflict, 296; UAM, 134
Ali, Amougou, 352–353
All African People's Conference: African unity, 166, 173; economic integration, 128
All-African Trade Union Federation (AATUF), 174
Amin, Idi: and EAC collapse, 151; and OAU, 185–186; seizure of power, 155
Amin, Samir, 76
Amuwo, 'Kunle, 17
Anglophone-Francophone divide, and regionalism, 140
Angola: civil conflict, 268; Internet usage, 221; investor risk, 240; MONU, 276; Portuguese military policy, 397
Annan, Kofi: on African peacekeeping capacity, 276; peacekeeping report, 277, 280; on state power, 290; on "technological leapfrogging," 216;
Antiglobalization forces, manifestations of, 22, 97–98
Apartheid, 206
Arabism, 297
Arewa, Jammar Mutanen, 359
Aristotle, 66
Armah, Ayi Kwei, 79
Arms sales: French, 19, 400–402, 404, 406–411, 409t, 421; French domestic consideration, 411–413
Arusha Accords, Rwanda, 358–359
Ashanti system, 81
Assisted migration, 338
Association of Southeast Asian States (ASEAN), 127
Association Tchadienne pour la non-violence, 355
Aubame, Jean Hilaire, 416

"Autocentric regionalism," 142
Autocentricity, 40
Azikiwe, Nnamdi, tribal role, 17, 338

Babangida, Ibrahim, 350, 377, 378, 380
Balewa, Sir Abubakar Tafawa, 171
Balladur, Edouard, 388
Banda, Hastings K., and South Africa, 11, 175
Banjul Charter on Human and People's Rights, 341, 347, 375
Barre, Raymond, 410
Barre, Siad: fall of, 294; and OAU, 185–186
Bauböck, Rainer, 363
Bedie, Konan, 349
Belgian Congo, and African unity, 173
   See also Democratic Republic of Congo
Benin: CEAO, 135; state repair, 333
Berlin, Treaty of, 392
Beti, Mongo, 352
Big Man syndrome, 354
Birth certificates, 357
Bischoff, Paul-Henry, 8–9
Bongo, Omar, 387, 414
Botswana: ethnic politics, 347; global trade, 31
Brahimi, Lakhdar, 277, 280
Brazzaville bloc, African unity, 174
Bricolage (patchwork), 54
Buchanan, James M., 204
Buhari, General Muhammadu, 380–381
Burkina Faso: CEAO, 135; ethnic discrimination ban, 340–341; Internet connectivity, 219
"Burmese treatment," 351
Burns, James MacGregor, 372
Burundi: CEEAC, 135; and EAC membership, 160–161; ethnic conflict, 293; IDPs, 268; MOBU, 273, 279; refugees, 155
Business sector, and state patronage, 72
Buthelezi, Chief Gatsha, 357

Cabral, Amilcar, 319
Cairo Center for Training on Dispute Resolution and Peacekeeping, 282

Cairo Declaration, 15, 280
Cameroon: and African unity, 166, 173; CEEAC, 135; democracy movement, 352; ethnic political parties, 349–350; "feymen," 62, 63; French military activity, 416, 417; Internet usage, 221; patrons, 344; political compromise, 349; RE, 249
Cameroon with Egbert, 58–59
Campaign for Democracy (CD), 331, 377
Capital: and brute force, 421; description of, 391–392; globalization of, 22, 23, 35, 51, 52, 53, 71; imposition of, 391–392, 402; infrastructure development, 241; and the neocolonial state, 396; regulatory control, 198
Capitalist imperialism: and militarism, 396; and neocolonial state, 394–396; objectives of, 399; and social inequality, 398–399; specific task of, 415
Casablanca bloc, African unity, 169, 170–171, 174, 185
Central Africa, regional organizations, 135
Central African Republic, and CEEAC, 135
Central government: infrastructure grants, 246–247, 258–259; infrastructure problems, 234; regulatory functions, 255
Centre Européen de Recherche Nucléaire, and WWW, 212
Chad: accommodation politics, 355; and CEEAC, 135; French military activity, 416–417, 418; OAU peacekeeping operations, 270; warfare transformation, 343
Chazan, Naomi, 376
"Chien de garde," 402
Children, armed conflict, 298, 345
Children's Parliaments, 353
Chirac, Jacques, African policy, 387
"Chosen traumas," 356, 357, 359, 362
Chossudvosky, Michel, 101–102

Christianity, religious conflict, 296–297

Citizenship: and ethnicity, 292–293; language of, 106; postcolonial state, 320

Civil Liberties Organization (CLO), Nigeria, 331, 377

Civil servants, social classes, 74–75

Civil service, economic development, 205–206

Civil society: description of, 376; and ethnic politics, 347–348, 363; in Nigeria, 376–380; and postcolonial state, 316, 327–332

Civil war, prevalence of, 390

Clapham, Christopher, 106

The clash of color: A study in the problem of race, 70

Class, continental conflict, 291

Clinton, Bill: ACRI/ACRF, 278; African trip, 102–103; China policy, 32

Cohesion Kompienga, 281

Cold War, peacekeeping activity, 15

Colonialism: and African capitalism, 391–392; and African poverty, 400; and African unity, 171–172; and collective existence, 353; cultural tensions, 289, 294–295; economic impact of, 191; and ethnic conflict, 337; and globalization, 33; media regulation, 216–217; state structures, 315, 316–317, 319; territorial boundaries, 287

Commission of Mediation Conciliation, and Arbitration, OAU, 180, 184, 268

Committee of Concerned Citizens, Nigeria, 330–331

Common Market for Eastern and Southern Africa (COMESA), African unity, 187; and ICT; and regionalism, 8–9, 137–138, 159

Common Monetary Area, African unity, 187

Communauté économique de l'Afrique de l'ouest (CEAO): regionalism,

135; security issues, 159

Communauté économique des états de l'Afrique central (CEEAC), regionalism, 8–9, 135

Communication, and regionalism, 133

Communication technology: African self-determination, 82–83; and globalization, 49–50, 96; and infrastructure development, 172, 250–251

"Communitization," 333

Community Standing Mediation Committee, ECOWAS, 159

Comoros, military observers, 271

Compaore, Blaise, 219

Conflict: comparative standing, 38, 39; and cultural diversity, 291–297; scope of, 267–268, 297

Congress of South African Trade Unions (COSATU), 329, 333

"Consensual democracy," 81

Consociational democracy: examples of, 288; limitations of, 306–309; model description, 301–302; for Nigeria, 382–383; value of, 16, 288, 310

Constitution: definition of, 374; of Nigeria, 374–376, 378–379, 381

Constitutional Development in Nigeria, 359

Constitutional Research Project (CRP), Nigeria, 331

Constitutive Act of African Union: adoption of, 163, 164–165; and OAU, 164, 182; main features of, 182

Consumerism, 60, 61, 63, 64

Control Risk Group (CRG), investment risks, 240, 261n.7

Corruption: African leadership, 65–66, 68, 69, 79; comparative standing, 38, 39; and economic development, 195, 196, 205, 206; in Ghana, 200–201

Costa Rica, trade exports, 37

Côte d'Ivorie: and CEAO, 135; coup d'état, 387; ethnic discrimination ban, 340–341; French military activity, 417; Internet usage, 222; and PPI, 237, 260–261 n.4

Council of Common Defense, UAM, 281

Credit: neocolonial state, 395–396; regulatory control, 198, 202–203

Crisis narratives, 108–109

Cultural industry, globalization, 6

Customs and Economic Union of Central Africa, 187

Cyprus, consociational democracy, 308–309

Dahl, Robert: on organizational harm, 301; on subcultures, 299

"Les danses folkloriques," 74

Davidson, Basil, 294–295

Davis, Elizabeth, 56

Death, burial requirement, 356–357

Death certificates, 356, 357

Debre, Michel, 406–407

Debt, and African peripheralization, 131–132; and globalization, 33, 100; and SSA, 38, 267; total African, 267

Debt service, in Africa, 101, 111 nn.8, 10, 11

Deby, Idriss, on African unity, 165

Decentralization: description of, 235, 236, 260 n.2; evaluation of, 242, 243–246, 252–253; five dimensions of, 237; four forms of, 260n.1; infrastructure development, 233, 234, 256–257; institutional weakness, 257–258; in Nigeria, 381–382; road construction, 251, 252–253; water service, 253–254

Defense Advanced Research Projects Agency (DARPA), and Internet, 211

de Gaulle, Charles; defense policy, 403–405, 406, 414–415, 419; military activities in Africa, 413

Democracy: African goals, 4; consociational, 16, 288, 301–309; and economic development, 40; essence of, 325; and ethnic groups,

346–347; future development of, 55, 76–83; majoritarian, 307–308, 309; in Nigeria, 351–352, 377–378; and political instability, 371; postcolonial state, 315–316, 330–331; and regionalism, 125; and state legitimacy, 104–105; and "state repair," 17

Democratic Republic of Congo: and CEEAC, 135; diamond industry, 61–62; French influence, 18 and IDPs, 268; Internet usage, 221; investor risk, 240; NRA activity, 157; and Qadhafi, Mu'ammar al, 362; refugees, 155

"Dependent regionalism," 142

d'Estaing, Giscard, defense policy, 404, 408–409, 410

"Deresponsibilization," 316

Deutsch, Karl, 141–141

Developmental communications model, mass media, 217

Devisch, René, 72

Dewey, John, 363

Diamonds, *bana Lunda* workers, 62, 75

Dictatorships, African, 76

Diffusion of innovation theory. *See* Innovation diffusion perspective

Dinka people, warfare, 341–342

Direct foreign investment (DFI). *See* Foreign direct investment (FDI)

"Disembodied economic relationships," 97

"The Disillusioned African," 54

Djibouti, IGAD, 139

DuBois, W.E.B., African Unity, 10, 166

Dudddah, Mouikhtar Ouldh, and OAU, 185–186

East Africa: COMESA 137–138; as region, 121; regional organizations, 135, 138–139

East African Community (EAC): breakdown of, 172; formation of, 150–151; and ICT, 251; institutions of, 152–154, 157; international security, 156–157; joint military operations, 282; quality of life, 158; and regionalism, 8–10, 138–139; regional/subregional security, 148; 154–156, 157–158, 160–161; subregional integration, 149–150

East African Currency Board, 150

East African High Commission (EAHC), 150

Ecole Normale William Ponty, 353, 354

Economic and Monetary Community in Central Africa, African unity, 187

Economic Community of Central African States: African unity, 187; nonaggression pact, 281

Economic Community of West African States (ECOWAS): African unity, 187; *Cohesion Kompienga*, 281; Community Standing Mediation Committee, 159; and ICT, 251; non-aggression pact, 281; regionalism, 8–9, 127, 136, 159; security issues, 150, 151–152, 158–159

Economic Community of West African States Monitoring Group (ECOMOG): peace enforcement, 281; regional conflicts, 127, 136, 159

Economic development: and continental conflict, 298–299; post-independence, 193–195; regulatory controls, 195–204; state failure, 322, 323; and state legitimacy, 104–105

Economic security, description of, 147

Egypt: and African unity, 173; ancient globalization, 28; and FDI, 31; French arms sales, 407–408; and Internet, 221, 223; peacekeeping center, 282; religious conflict, 296; superpower politics, 419; water services, 254

Eighteenth Brumaire, 356

Eko, Lyombe S., 12–13

Ekwueme, Alex, Nigeria, 359, 379

Electricity, PPI, 238, 239

"Electronic feudalism," 226

Electronic mail (e-mail): introduction

of, 212; use of, 219, 221, 222

Electronic technology. *See* Information technology

"Elite pacing," 329

Elites: and African state, 323; African unity, 165; and consociationalism, 301–302; conspicuous consumption, 61, 66; and consumerism, 64; and development, 6, 53, 54; and globalization, 7, 53, 54, 70–71; private capital accumulation, 193; and privatization of, 315; and regional integration, 121, 126; and transformation of war, 341–342, 343–345; and Western culture, 67–68

"Embedded liberalism," 325

Emigration, continental conflict, 298

Emirch, Hinderk, 356

Employment, multinational corporations, 96

"Enabling environment," 244

Energy sector, infrastructure development, 238, 239, 248–250, 263 n.19

Enfranchisement, and democracy, 78

Entrepreneurship: colonial impact, 191; government regulation, 195

Environment: African goals, 4; security of, 147

Equatorial Guinea, CEEAC, 135

Eritrea: and Ethiopia, 295–296; and IGAD, 139; Internet usage, 220; security conditions, 154

Ethiopia: ethnic politics, 346; and Eritrea, 295–296; and IGAD, 139; Internet usage, 221; security conditions, 154; and superpower politics, 419

Ethnic Minority Rights Organization of Africa, Nigeria, 376

Ethnicity: and "chosen traumas," 356, 357, 359, 362; and civil society, 347–348, 363; and continental conflict, 14, 291–293; and custom, 348; and democracy, 346–347; and nation building, 17–18; in national constitutions, 340–341; and national unity governments,

348–349; in political parties, 349–351; in the postcolonial state, 338, 339, 343–344; and state development, 338; and state legitimacy, 104-105;

European Coal and Steel Community (ECSC), 28

European Economic Community (EEC), 28

European Union (EU), economic bloc, 11, 177, 178

Executive Committee on Information and Strategy Analysis Secretariat (ECISAS), peacekeeping, 277

Executive Committee on Peace and Security (ECPS), peacekeeping, 277

Exodus from Africa, 322

Expertise, overseas Africans, 41

Extraction industries, 33

Ezera, Kalu, 359

Falk, Richard, 109

Fanon, Franz, 58

"Feymen," 62, 63

Finance and Development (report, IMF), 99–100

"Flame of Peace," 346–347, 363

Foccart, Jacques, 413–414, 417

Force de frappe, France, 403, 406

Foreign direct investment (FDI): in Africa, 102; in extractive industries, 31; and globalization, 22, 31, 97

Foreign exchange, regulatory control, 198

Founou-Tchuigoua, Bernard, 98

Fourth Extraordinary Session, OAU, 164

France: African military pacts, 417, 418; arms production, 405–406, 407, 410, 421; arms sales, 19, 400–402, 404, 406–411, 409t, 421, 424; arms sales politics, 411–413; defense policy, 403–404, 407, 415–416, 419; and Francophone Africa, 173, 175–176, 413, 414, 417, 418, 419;

influence in Africa, 18, 129; and Internet, 226; military interventions, 18, 19, 414–418, 422, 424; military policy, 19, 147, 387, 413–419; military policy constraints, 424; OAU condemnation, 11; oil imports, 410; postcolonial military policy, 387, 388, 402–403, 423–424; trade with Africa, 404, 420

Francophone Africa: and African unity, 173, 181; and Anglophone Africa, 140; and French military, 173, 175-176, 413, 414, 417, 418, 419; and SNC, 352

La Francophonie Universelle, 421

Fraser, Nancy, 352

Front Islamique du Salut (FIS), Algeria, 296

Fundamentalism, and religious conflict, 296

Gabon: CEEAC, 135; ethnic discrimination ban, 340–341; French military activity, 416, 417; Internet usage, 220

Gaillard, Anne, 403

Garvey, Marcus, African Unity, 10, 166

Gbagbo, Laurent, 349

"Gendarme of Africa," 388, 415

General Agreements on Tariffs and Trade (GATT): African trade, 30–31; and globalization, 24

"Genocidaires," 419

Georgetown Agreement, 29

Germany, on "global information society," 51

Ghana: and African unity, 173; ancient globalization, 28; Big Man syndrome, 354; infrastructure development, 256–257; ISI policies, 199–201; 1996 elections, 318

Ghana Community Water and Sanitation Project, 254

Gill, Steven, 106

"Global village," 50, 211

Globalization: and African elites, 6, 53;

African experience of, 22, 26–30,
53–54, 98–103, 108; and African
goals, 5; in African history,
32–33; African participation, 5–7;
concept of, 22, 23–25, 93; constraints on, 97–98; cost/benefits
analysis, 22, 30–35; critical recommendations, 22, 41–42; definition of, 49; four periods of, 28;
and French policy, 389; lessons
learned, 22, 36–41; and mass
communication, 12; resistance to,
22, 97–98; and social equity, 52;
theory of, 22, 25–27; and the
world economy, 22
"Globalization of poverty," 101–102
Government regulation: adverse economic impact, 195–203; and poverty alleviation, 203; of telecommunications, 214–215
Great Lakes Region: refugee problems,
155, 156; security issues, 160
Grieve, Malcom, 400
Group of 34, Nigeria, 379
Growth rate, comparative standing, 38,
39
Guinea, and African unity, 173
Guyer, Jane, 356

Haile Selassie, Emperor of Ethiopia:
African Unity, 174–175; and
OAU, 185–186
Hassan, King of Morocco, and OAU,
185–186
Havel, Václav, 80
"Having eaten soya," 349
Heavily Indebted Poor Countries
(HIPC), World Bank report, 267
Herbst, Jeffrey, 104
HIV/AIDS policy, African goals, 5
"Homogenous" thinking, 94
Horn: African region, 121; region
building, 123; regional organiza-
tions, 139; security conditions,
154–155
Houphouet-Boigny, Felix, 349
Human development, UNDP study,
196, 198

Human development index (HDI),
UNDP study, 197
Human rights: African goals, 4; *Asso-
ciation Tchadienne pour la non-
violence*, 355, and information su-
perhighway, 51; in Nigeria,
360–361, 375–376, 383; and
OAU, 186; and state legitimacy,
104–105
Human Rights Field Operations in
Burundi (HRFOB), 273
Human Rights Field Operations in
Rwanda (HRFOR), 273
Human welfare, comparative standing,
38, 39
Humanitarian crises, scope of, 297–298
Hutu people, cultural conflicts, 293,
294, 358, 388
Hydroelectricity, development evalua-
tion, 248

Idahosa, Paul L.Ehioze, globalization,
7–8
Identities, postcolonial state, 339–340
Igala people, 288–289
Igbo people: intraethnic communal
tensions, 294; palaver arrange-
ments, 288–289
Immigrants, and globalization, 52, 53
Imperialism: and African capitalism,
391–392; and militarism,
392–394; postcolonial state, 394
Import substitution, economic strategy,
38, 39
Import substitution industrialization
(ISI), trade policy, 199
Income, UNDP study, 197
Indomitable Lions, Cameroon,
359–400
Industrialization, decentralization, 245;
multinational corporations, 96;
neocolonial state, 395; and strate-
gic minerals, 399, 420
Infant mortality, in Africa, 100–101
Information and communications tech-
nology (ICT), 250–251
Information superhighway, and globalization, 49, 50, 51, 226

Information technology (IT); and African self-determination, 82–83; and globalization, 6, 22, 50, 51, 52, 82–83, 96; infrastructure development, 250–251; Internet connectivity, 211–229; and security issues, 157; SNG's role, 236–237

Infrastructure: and African unity, 172; destruction of, 298; and privatization, 234–235; and regionalism, 133

Infrastructure development: during the colonial era, 319; development conditions, 233–235; economic constraints, 13–14; evaluation of, 241–248; obstacles to, 256–259

Innovation diffusion perspective: description of, 213, 216; five stages of, 215–216

Intergovernmental Authority on Development (IGAD): conflict resolution, 281; regionalism, 8–9, 139, 158–159

Internally displaced persons (IDPs), scope of, 268, 297–298

International Confederation of Free Trade Unions (ICFTU), 174

International Convention of Civil and Political Rights, 376

International Financial Corporation (IFC), FDI recipients, 31

International Monetary Fund (IMF): African economic policies, 98; *Finance and Development* (report, IMF), 99–100; and globalization, 24–25; and regional development, 123, 129

International Telecommunications Union (ITU), Internet connectivity, 215, 221

International trade, regulation of, 198–199, 199–201. *See also* Trade

Internet: business promotion of, 50; connectivity policies, 212–216; "creolized discourse," 359–360; cultural relevance, 212, 224–228; current realities, 219–222; development of, 211–212; introduction

of, 12–13, 212, 218–219, 221; regulation of, 212, 216–217, 223–224; technological determinism, 227;

Inter-State Defense and Security Council (ISDCS), 137

Intrastate conflict, scope of, 269

Investment: CRG report, 240; multinational corporations, 96; overseas Africans, 41

Iran, French arms sales, 410

Islam, religious conflict, 296–297

Jefferson, Thomas, 307

Jega, Attahiru M., 377

Jua, Nantang, 17–18

"Juju video," 228–229

Kabila, Joseph, 387

Kaplan, Robert, 103

Kasavubu, Joseph, 173

Kenya: civil society, 330; current military of, 158; and EAC, 138, 149, 150–151, 172; ethnic politics, 292, 350; global trade, 31: IDPs, 268; and IGAD, 139; Internet usage, 222; peacekeeping operations, 269; rural electrification, 249; refugee problem, 16; Rural Access Roads Program, 253; security conditions, 154, 155

Kimenyi, Mwangi S., 14

Labor: and globalization, 26, 52, 53, 109; and the neocolonial state, 395

Lagos, Treaty of, 136

The Lagos Plan of Action, 8, 110, 126

Language: and African unity, 172; developmental priorities, 141; Internet cultural influence, 226–227; and Internet usage, 219–220; local use, 338

Lasswell, Harold, on accountability, 380

Leadership: absence of socialization for, 82; and African society, 55, 64–70; corruption of, 65–66, 68, 69, 79; definitions of, 372; and

globalization, 54, 64–70; in Nigeria, 372–373
"Leapfrog," 216, 218, 227
"Leapfrogging," 13
Lebanon, consociational democracy, 308, 309
Lee, Philip, 52
Lehmbruch, Gerhard, consociationalism, 301
Lenin, Vladimir, 415
Lesotho: global trade, 31: rural electrification, 249, 250
Liberia: IDPs, 268; Internet usage, 221
Libya: and African unity, 169; French arms sales, 407–408, 410, 412, 423; Internet regulation, 223; and the UAM, 134
Life expectancies, UNDP study, 197
Lijphart, Arend, consociationalism, 301–302, 308, 382
Literacy rate, Africa, 197, 400
Lomé Conventions: African unity, 163; and globalization, 29, 139
Lonsdale, John, 341
Lord's Resistance Army (LRA), Uganda, 153
Lumumba, Patrice, death of, 173
Lusaka Peace Accords, 280, 362
Luxembourg, Rosa, 401–402

Maassemba-Debat, Alphonse, 416
Mabogunje, Akin, 82
Macaulay, Herbert, 359
Machel, Samora, 17, 338, 339
Madison, James, 290, 291, 309
"Magic multipliers," 55
Majoritarian democracy, 81, 307–308, 310
Makweerekwere, 61
Mali: CEAO, 135; ethnic politics, 346–347
Mandela, Nelson: consensus government, 348; Truth and Reconciliation Commissions (TRCs), 361, 362
Mangeoire nationale, 344
Mao Zeadong, 373
Maphai, Vincent: on democracy, 306,

309; on ethnic conflict, 291
Marginalization: and globalization, 7–8, 54, 94, 95, 98, 108; and the neocolonial state, 396
Mark, David, 331
Marketing Boards, colonial state, 319
Markets, regulatory control, 198, 201–202
Marrakesh, Treaty of, and UAM, 134
Marwa, Muhhammadu, 296
Marx, Karl, 356
Marxism, economic thought, 401
Masire, Sir Quett, 387
Mass communication, regulation of, 216–217
Mass media, government regulation, 215
Mathews, Basil, 70
Matsuura, Koichiro, 226
Mauritania, and African unity, 173
Mauritius, global trade, 31
"Maximax problematique," 337
Mazrui, Ali, 59, 356
Mba, Léon, 416
Mbaku, John Mukum; on African constitutions, 374; on African poverty, 12
Mbeki, Thabo: ANC transition, 328–329; on globalism, 140
Mbouma, William Eteki, on OAU, 180
"McDonaldized" society, 51, 55
McLuhan, Marshall, 50, 211, 227
Mead, Margaret, 351
"Meaningful democracy," 315
Mechanism for Conflict Prevention, Management and Resolution (MCPMR): in Cairo, 15, 280; establishment of, 136, 186; external support, 127; and peacekeeping, 271–272, 276–277, 279
Media: African representations, 103–104; globalization role, 52
Media Development, on migrants/refugees, 52
Mentan, Immanuel Tatah, 19
Mercantilists, 25, 106
"Merchants of death," 389
"Metamorphosis in the Culture Market

of Niger," 56
Métissage (hibridity), 54
Meynier, General H., 392
Migrants, and globalization, 52–53;
"Migrants, Refugees and the Right to
    Communicate," 52
Militarism: and imperialism, 392–394;
    and the neocolonial state,
    394–399; scope of, 389–391
Military bases: in Francophone Africa,
    413, 414–415; and imperialism,
    397
Military juntas, administrative capaci-
    ties, 321
Military Observer Mission in Burundi
    (MOBU), 273, 279
Millennium Plan, 140, 141
Millennium Summit, 277
Mining sector, colonial era, 319
Mitterrand, François, 388
Mkandawire, Thandika, 107
Mobutu Sese-Seko: fall of, 387; leader-
    ship, 289
Modernity: and African elites, 6, 53,
    54; as consumerism/dependency,
    55, 60–64; as cultural superiority,
    55–60; and globalization, 54
Moi, Daniel arap, 292
Monetary integration: CFA franc, 181;
    South African rand, 129
Monrovia bloc, African unity, 170,
    171, 174, 185
"Moral aloneness," 338
Morocco: and African unity, 173;
    French arms sales, 407; Internet
    regulation, 223; and OAU, 163;
    and UAM, 134
Mozambique: IDPs, 268; and Portugese
    military policy, 397
Mugabe, Robert, 361
Multinational corporations (MNCs),
    and globalization, 23, 28–29,
    96–97
"Municpalization," 333
Murphy, Dervla, 58–59

Nairobi Declaration, East African inte-
    gration, 150

Namibia, ethnic discrimination ban,
    340–341; Western support, 177
National Association for the Advance-
    ment of Colored People
    (NAACP), African Unity, 10, 166
National Constitutional Conference
    Commission, Nigeria, 378–379
National Democrátic Coalition
    (NADECO), Nigeria, 377, 378
National Front for the Liberation of the
    Congo, 397
National Resistance Army (NRA),
    Uganda, 157
National Union for the Total Independ-
    ence of Angola (UNITA), 177,
    345
National unity governments, and eth-
    nicity, 348–349
Nationalism, and regionalism, 132
Nation-state: African representations,
    103, 104; delegitimization of,
    104–105; limited sovereignty, 94,
    95, 96; and multinational corpora-
    tions, 96–97. *See also* State
Ndadaye, Melchier, 273
Ndebele family, "social biography,"
    356–357
Neoliberalism: failure of, 32; and glob-
    alization, 25–26, 107
Neur people, warfare, 341–342
Neutral Military Observer Group,
    Rwanda, 273
New African Initiative (NAI), Millen-
    nium Plan, 140, 299
Newspapers, Internet presence,
    220–221
Nguema, Macias, 397
Nguema, Obiang, 397
Niger: CEAO, 135; and French mili-
    tary, 414–415, 417
Nigeria: absence of accountability,
    380–381; accommodation politics,
    355; and African unity, 171; Big
    Man syndrome, 354; civil society,
    330–332, 376–380; constitution
    of, 374–376, 378–379, 381; de-
    mocracy movement, 351–352; de-
    velopment strategies, 38; FDI, 31;

and French arms sales, 407; and
French military, 415, 419; French
trade, 404; human rights,
375–376, 383; Human Rights
Commission, 360–361; IDPs, 268;
Internet usage, 221; intraethnic
communal tensions, 294, 308;
"juju video," 228–229; leadership,
372–373; letter scam, 62–63; political parties, 350; political transitions, 18; possible solutions,
381–383; religious conflict,
296–297
Nigerian Labor Congress (NLC), 331,
333
Nkrumah, Kwame: African High
Command proposal, 269; African
unity, 10, 164, 166, 167–168, 169,
174; ISI policies, 199–200; university policy, 176
Nnadozie, Emmanuel, 5, 6
"Noble savage," 74, 82
Nolutshungu, Sam, 309
Non-Aligned Movement (NAM), disintegration of, 131
Nongovernmental organizations
(NGOs): and democracy, 78, 327;
in Nigerian civil society, 377, 379;
peace/consensus building, 355,
363; privatized subcontracting,
100
North Africa, region, 121
North American Free Trade Area
(NAFTA), 11, 177, 178
Nuclear tests, French, 173, 175–176
Numeiri, Jafar, 177
Nyamnjoh, Francis B., globalization,
6–7
Nyerere, Julius: on ethnic groups, 338;
on French military interventions,
418; leadership of, 289; on nation
building, 17; and OAU, 185–186;
on one-party state, 3, 292

Obasanjo, Olusegun, 374
Obote, Milton, overthrow of, 155
Observer Military in Comoros, 273
Oduduwa, Egbe Omo, 359

Okoth, P. Godfrey, regionalism, 9
Olton, Roy, 374
One-party system, post-independence
governments, 3–4, 16, 79–80, 99
One Worlders, globalization defense,
22–23
Operation Blue Crane, SADC, 281
Operation Blue Hungwe (Eagle),
SADC, 281
Organ for Defense and Politics
(OPDS), SADC, 137, 159
Organization of African Unity (OAU):
accomplishments of, 185–186; African High Command (AFC) proposal, 269; African nationalism,
176–177; African Women's
Committee and Development,
354; and AU, 163–164; Charter,
176, 180–181, 182, 183, 269–270;
and colonial boundaries, 287;
Commission of Mediation Conciliation, and Arbitration, 180,
184, 270; demise of, 11, 130; establishment of, 174–175; feebleness of, 122, 175–176, 180–182,
189; Internet adoption, 219; *Lagos
Plan*, 8, 110, 126; and MCPMR,
15, 127, 129, 271–272, 276–277
280; Monrovia symposium,
178–179; Neutral Forces in Chad,
270; Peace Fund, 279; regional
integration, 8, 128–129; role of,
10–11, 127–128; and UN-
MOG/MOBU operations, 273;
Western influence, 177
Oromo Liberation Front (OLF), Ethiopia, 155

"Pacification of natives," 401
"Palaver tree," 211, 212, 219
Pan-African Foundation, African
Unity, 10, 166
Pan Africanism: and state sovereignty,
269; and unity, 10, 122, 128, 165
Pan-African Parliament: Abuja Treaty,
180; AU, 183–184
Pan-Arabism, and African unity, 181
Participation: development evaluation,

243–244; resources/power, 290; state security, 10; water service development, 253–254

Peace building, definition of, 268

Peace enforcement, definition of, 268

Peaceful coexistence: African goals, 5; state failure, 322

Peacekeeping: during the Cold War, 15; definition of, 268; functions of, 268–269; joint African-industrialized countries initiatives, 278–280; joint UN-African initiatives, 274–277; OAU, 180–181, 186; obstacles to, 282; post–Cold War, 15; premise of, 269; regional strategy, 387; training centers, 282; UN initiatives, 274–277

Peacekeeping operations: during Cold War, 269–270; post–Cold War, 270–274; UN operations, 70–271, 273

Peacemaking, definition of, 268

Peasantry, social class, 73–73

Pentecostalism, and global capitalism, 81–82

"People's power," 315, 329

Permanent Maghreb Consultive Council, UAM, 134

Permanent Tripartite Commission (PTC), 151

Petty bourgeoisie, social classes, 75–76

Plano, Jack, 374

Political parties: and ethnicity, 80–81, 349–350; in Nigeria, 379

Political security, description of, 147

Political tribalism, 341

"Politics of the belly," 344

Pompidou, Georges, defense policy, 404

Popular democracy, drive toward, 315–316

Portugal, African policy, 397

"Positive discrimination," 309

Postage stamps, innovation diffusion, 213–214

Poverty: African goals, 4–5; and African leadership, 192–193; and African unity, 168; comparative standing, 38, 39, 400; and ethnic conflict, 14; externally induced, 40–41, 191, 192; globalization of, 389; and government policies, 204–206; institutional environment, 12; and SAP, 100; as security threat, 161

Power, public control of, 80

Présence française, 404

Pricing, multinational corporations, 96

"Primitive communalism," postcolonial state, 320–321

Principe, CEEAC, 135

Private participation in infrastructure (PPI), scope of, 237–239

Private sector: infrastructure development, 234–235, 237–241; PPI risks, 239–240

Privatization: African economies, 316; description of, 235, 260 n.3; evaluation of, 243–244; and ICT, 251; postcolonial state, 315

Protectionism, policies of, 38–39

Protocols on Mutual Assistance, ECOWAS, 136

Public choice theory, economic activity, 204–205

Qadhafi, Mu'ammar al: African unity, 140; and AU, 164–165; and Democratic Republic of Congo, 362; and Sudan, 177

Quéau, Philippe, 226

Race, continental conflict, 291, 293–294

Radio, diffusion of, 228

Railways, PPI, 238

Rand Monetary Arrangement (RMA), monetary integration, 129

Rawlings, Jerry, 380

Refugees: and EAC, 155–156; ethnic violence, 15; and globalization, 52–53

Regional African Satellite Communications, 251

Regional integration: definition of, 121; economic expectations, 8–9

Regional Peacekeeping Training Center, 279
Regionalism: challenges for, 139–143; challenges to, 131–133; continental conflict, 291, 294–295; forces favoring, 125–127; global trends, 124–125; globalization response, 5–6; insufficiency of, 127–131; post–Cold War, 149; security issues, 9
Religion: and African unity, 172; and continental conflict, 291, 296–297
Renan, Ernest, 338
Renforcement des Capacités Africaines de Maintien de la Paix (RECAMP), 278, 387–388
Rent extraction, 195
Rent seeking, economic development, 195, 196
Reporters Sans Frontières, on Internet restrictions, 224
Republic of Congo: CEEAC, 135; French military intervention, 416; Internet usage, 221
"Republic of technology," 50–51
Resources: development evaluation, 242–243; and leadership, 290; and regionalism, 128, 129
"Responsible sovereignty," 105
Ricupero, Rubens, 99
Rizer, George, 51
Roads, infrastructure development, 251–253
Robert, Maurice, 414
Roman Catholic Church, on Internet, 226
Rome, Treaty of, 28
Rose, Emory, 108–109
Rothkopf, David, 96
Rule of law, and state legitimacy, 104–105
Rural development, SAP, 100
Rural electrification (RE), infrastructure development, 249–250
Rural poor: predicament of, 55, 70, 71, 73; "traditional Africa," 74
Rural sector, economic development, 202

Rwanda: CEEAC, 135; ethnic conflict, 293, 387; French support, 388, 419; International Tribune, 358; MCPMR, 129; NMOG, 273; refugees, 155; regional conflict, 294; security conditions, 154

Sahawari Arab Democratic Republic, and OAU, 163
Samura, Sorious, 322
Sâo Tomé, CEEAC, 135
Saro-Wiwa, Ken, 351
Saudi Arabia, French arms sales, 407, 408
Saxena, Suresh Chandra, African unity, 10, 11
Schatz, Sayre, 100
Schmitt, Carl, 347
Schramm, Wilbur, on mass media, 217
Seaports, PPI, 238, 239
Second Conference of Independent States, economic integration, 128
"Second liberation," 77
Second-wave regionalism," 123
Security: absence of consensus, 132; CEAO accord, 135; EAC, 150, 151–154; five factors of, 147; and OAU, 129–130; regional arrangements, 131; regional integration, 9; SADC organizations, 137
Self-reliance: African development, 19; policy of, 5
Senegal: CEAO, 135; French military activity, 417; Internet usage, 221; religious conflict, 296
Sharia, religious conflict, 296–297
Shaw, Timothy: on Africa development, 400; on OAU, 185
Shonekan, Ernest, 377
Sierra Leone: IDPs, 268; Internet usage, 221; investor risk, 240; military coup d'état, 280; and UN peacekeeping missions, 277–278
Sitre Conference, African unity, 165, 174, 179–180, 182
Sitre Declaration, adoption of, 164, 184
Sklar, Richard, 372–373
Slave trade, and globalization, 32–33

Smith, Adam, 25
Smith, Peter, 125
"Social citizenship," 324, 332
Social class: African, 55, 73–76; and ethnicity, 293
"Social shaping," 83–84
Somali syndrome, 278
Somalia: accommodation politics, 354; clan conflict, 294; IDPs, 268; and IGAD, 139; security conditions, 154, 155; superpower politics, 419; and UNOSOM II, 276, 278
South Africa: administrative ineffi- ciency, 321–322; ethnic discrimi- nation ban, 340–341; ethnic poli- tics, 346; and FDI, 31; French arms sales, 408; French nuclear support, 410; French trade, 404; as imperiled democracy, 78; intra- ethnic communal tensions, 294; and OAU, 11, 175; racial conflict, 293–294; Truth and Reconcilia- tion Commissions (TRCs), 361; Western support, 177
South West Africa People's Organiza- tion (SWAPO), 175
Southern Africa: COMESA, 137–138; as a region, 121; region building, 123, 142; regional organizations, 136–137
Southern African Customs Union (SACU): African unity, 187; monetary integration, 129
Southern African Development Com- munity (SADC): donor projects, 129; ICT, 251; peace enforcement, 280, 281; regional intervention, 159–160; regionalism, 8–9, 122, 136–137, 138, 158–159; security organs, 137, 159; UNCIVPOL, 274
Southern African Development Coor- dination Community, security is- sues, 150
Southern African Development Coor- dination Conference: African unity, 187; donor projects, 129; regionalism, 136, 138

Sovereign national conference (SNC), democracy movement, 351–352; Nigeria, 378
Sovereignty: as conditional state, 105; limited, 94, 95, 96, 107, 108; and OAU, 128–130, 269–270; and re- gional integration, 121–122
Soyinka, Wole: on nation-state crisis, 104, 105–106; on SNC, 352
Spain, African policy, 397
"Spheres of influence," 392
"Standard-bearers of globalization," 6
State: in Africa, 98; changed role of, 106–107; and civil society, 316, 327–332; collapse of, 121, 133; in colonial Africa, 393–394; and cultural diversity, 288, 289; eco- nomic regulation, 195–204; neo- colonial, 394; political govern- ance, 16–17; post–Cold War, 130–131; post-independence Af- rica, 1–2, 193–194, 196; postcolo- nial, 315, 317–327, 332–334; and region building, 122–123, 125; three duties of, 357–358
"State class," 317, 318, 324
"State repair," 17
Statism: African policy, 1–2; evalua- tion of, 2–3; goals of, 2
Steiner, Jurg, consociationalism, 301, 302
Structural adjustment programs (SAP): agricultural price liberalization, 99; rural development, 100
Subcultures, description of, 299
Subnational governments (SNG): ICT, 250; infrastructure administration, 257; infrastructure financing, 236, 243, 246, 247, 259; roads, 252–253; and small business, 245, water service, 253, 254
Subregionalism: description of, 122; East Africa, 149
Sub-Saharan Africa (SSA): debt bur- den, 38, 111nn. 9, 10; foreign di- rect investment, 31; human devel- opment, 198; income, 267; trade, 30, 102

Sudan: and African unity, 169; ancient
    globalization, 28; and Arabism,
    297; civil conflict, 268; ethnic
    conflict, 293; and IGAD, 139; In-
    ternet usage, 221; religious con-
    flict, 296; security conditions, 154,
    155
Sustainable Development Networking
    Program (SDNP), UNDP, 218
Suva Declaration, and globalization, 29
Swaziland, global trade, 31
Sylvester, Elliott, on letter scams, 62
Symbolic power, 352

Tanzania: current military of, 158; debt
    service, 101; and EAC, 138, 149,
    150–151, 172; peacekeeping op-
    erations, 269; refugee problem,
    16, 155–156; security conditions,
    154, 155
Taxation, infrastructure development,
    247–248
Tchop, Tchop, 78
"Technological leapfrogging," 216
Technology: African development, 13;
    and economic development, 50
Telecommunications, PPI, 238, 239
Television, diffusion of, 228
Thiongo, Ngugi wa, 338
Thomas, Pradip, 52
"Tiebout effect," 247
Tiv people, palaver arrangements,
    288–289
Tofa, Bashir, 350, 378
Togo: and CEAO, 135; and France, 173
Tourism, African folk traditions, 74
Trade: African global, 30, 102; and
    globalization, 22, 37, 97; neocolo-
    nial state, 395; neoliberal models,
    25–26; regulatory control,
    198–199, 199–201
Trade unions, and African unity, 174
"Traditional dances," 74, 82
Transformisimo, 349
Transnational corporations (TNCs), 24,
    26, 28–29
Transparency International, corruption
    report, 69

Tribalism: and colonialism, 57; and
    nation building, 17, 338; and the
    postcolonial state, 341–342, 362
Trollope, Anthony, 337, 353, 355
Truth and Reconciliation Commissions
    (TRCs), adoption of, 360; in South
    Africa, 357, 361
Tubman, William, 169–170
Tucker, Robert C., 372
Tullock, Gordon, 204
Tunisia: Internet regulation, 223–224;
    and UAM, 134
Tutsi people, cultural conflicts, 293,
    358, 388
Tutu, Bishop Desmond, 59, 361

Udogu, E. Ike:on ethnicity, 291; Nige-
    rian politics, 18
Uganda: consociation framework,
    303–306; current military of,
    157–158; and EAC, 138, 149,
    150–151, 172; IDPs, 268; and
    IGAD, 139; Internet usage, 222;
    LRA, 153; peacekeeping opera-
    tions, 269; security conditions,
    154–155
*Union douanière et économique de
    l'Afrique central* (UDEAC), re-
    gionalism, 135, 159
*Union économique et monetaire ouest
    Africaine* (UEMOA): CEAO, 135;
    regionalism, 8–9
Union of Arab Maghreb (UAM): Afri-
    can unity, 187; regionalism, 8–9,
    134, 281
United Nations Children's Fund (UNI-
    CEF), World Summit on Children,
    100–101
United Nations Civilian Police (UN-
    CIVPOL), 274–275
United Nations Conference of Trade
    and Development (UNCTAD), ag-
    ricultural income, 99
United Nations Department of
    Peacekeeping Operations (UND-
    PKO), 276, 277, 279
United Nations Development Program
    (UNDP): African poverty, 4, 196,

197, 400; and globalization, 29, 40
United Nations Economic Commission
for Africa (ECA): and globaliza-
tion, 29; and Internet connectivity,
215, 218, 221; regional economic
integration, 8, 122, 127
United Nations Educational, Scientific,
and Cultural Organization
(UNESCO): Children's Parlia-
ments, 353; "developmental com-
munication," 217; information su-
perhighway, 226
United Nations High Commission on
Refugees (UNHCR), Tanzania
refugee camps, 155–156
United Nations Mission of Observers in
Angola (MONU), 276
United Nations Operations in Somalia
(UNOSOM II), 276
United Nations Security Council, Afri-
can membership, 41
United Nations Training Assistance
Team (UNTAT), 274
United States: AGOA, 29–30; French
rearmament, 405
Universal Declaration of Human
Rights, 375, 383
Urban dwellers, social classes, 74–75
Urban poor, predicament of, 55, 70, 71,
72
"Urban villages," 75
Uruguay Round, GATT, 24, 30–31
Uzodike, Ufo Okeke, consociational
democracy, 16

"Vedette affair," 408
Voice of Nigerian Women, 355
Voice of Somali Women for Peace,
Reconciliation and Political
Rights, 355

Wade, Abdoulaye, 188
Wajir Peace Group, 354
Wanyande, Peter, 79
Warfare, transformation of, 341–344
Warlord states, collapse of, 133
"Wars of the educated," 341, 342, 356,
362, 363

Washington, George, 307
Water: infrastructure development,
253–254; PPI, 238
Water and Sanitation Committees
(WSCs), 254, 255
Water User's Association (WUAs),
254, 255
Watson, William, 339
West Africa: region, 121; region
building, 123, 142; regional orga-
nizations, 135, 136
West African Economic and Monetary
Union, African unity, 187
Westphalian model, sovereignty, 105
"White man's burden," 337
Whitening agents, use of, 58, 60
Williams, Sylvester, 10, 166
Witchcraft, and global capitalism, 61,
81–82
Women: accommodation politics,
354–355, 363; African goals, 5
World Bank: on African economic
performance, 40; African eco-
nomic policies, 98; on externally
induced poverty, 40–41; and globalization, 24–25, 29; and HIOC,
267; infant mortality, 101; Internet
connectivity, 215, 217–218; and
regional development, 123, 129;
water management, 253
World Federation of Trade Unions
(WFTU), 174
World Summit on Children, infant
mortality, 100–101
World Trade Organization (WTO):
African trade, 31; and globalization, 24; regional power, 149
World Wide Web (WWW), invention
of, 212

Yoruba, intraethnic communal tensions, 294

Zaire, French military activity, 417,
418, 419. *See also* Democratic
Republic of Congo
Zambia, Internet usage, 221;
Zambia Military Academy,

peacekeeping center, 282
Zanzibar, secessionist movement, 156
Zimbabwe: death certificates, 356, 357;
    global trade, 31; Internet usage,
    221; nation building, 132; racial
    conflict, 293

Zimbabwe Staff College, peacekeeping
    center, 282
Zombification, definition of, 83 n.7;
    and global capitalism, 61, 81–82
Zulu people, intraethnic communal
    tensions, 294

About the Editors and Contributors

KORWA G. ADAR is an associate professor of international studies and Research Director, Africa Institute of South Africa, Pretoria, South Africa. Prior to joining Africa Institute of South Africa in 2002, he taught at Rhodes University (South Africa) and the University of Nairobi (Kenya). His articles have appeared in many internationally refereed journals. He was one of the 1992 recipients of the Fulbright Research Fellowship for Senior African Scholars. He is the author of *Kenyan foreign policy behavior towards Somalia, 1963–1983* (1994) and coeditor of *The United States and Africa: From independence to the end of the Cold War* (1995) and *Globalization and emerging trends in African states' foreign policy-making process: A comparative perspective of Southern Africa* (2002).

'KUNLE AMUWO has, since April 2000, been Chair of the Department of Political Science at the University of the North, South Africa. From 1997 to 1999 he was the head of the Department of Political Science at the University of Ibadan, Nigeria's premier university. Between 1988 and 1990 he was the subdean (undergraduate affairs) of the Faculty of the Social Sciences, University of Ibadan, as well as the national secretary of the Nigerian Political Science Association. Professor Amuwo is well published in the areas of comparative politics and administration, civil–military relations, international political economy, and Francophone Africa. He is notably the senior editor of *Federalism and political restructuring in Nigeria* (1998) and coeditor of *The Nigerian military and the struggle for democracy in Nigeria: The Abacha years, 1993–1998* (2001). He has also authored *General Babangida, the military and the civil society in Nigeria: Anatomy of a personal rulership project* (1995), as well as *Confronting the crisis of the university in Africa: Nigerian academics and their many struggles* (1999). He is presently working on a manuscript-length work titled *The Nigerian military and the Nigerian democratic project.*

PAUL-HENRI BISCHOFF, a native of South Africa, held appointments at the Universities of Swaziland and Papua New Guinea before returning to South Africa, where he is currently associate professor and head of the Department of Political Studies and the International Studies Unit at Rhodes University in Grahamstown. His research interests range from foreign policy studies (with particular reference to African and South African foreign policy) to international organization. He has published a book on Swaziland's foreign policy and has contributed to books and journals both in South Africa and abroad.

LYOMBE S. EKO is a professor of journalism and mass communication at the University of Iowa at Iowa City. Professor Eko served as a journalist and producer with the Cameroon Radio and Television Corporation from 1984 to 1985. He also served as program editor/translator and subsequently head of program services at the Program Exchange Center of the Union of National Radio and Television Organizations of Africa in Nairobi, Kenya, from 1985 to 1994. While in Kenya, he also held the position of adjunct professor at Daystar University College, Nairobi. He produced several video documentaries in Kenya on African topics that are widely used today throughout the world for instruction. Three of these documentaries were honored at television festivals in Germany and Canada. They are held in several American university libraries and are currently part of the interlibrary loan system in the United States. He teaches mass media law and regulation, mass communication, and techniques of video production at the University of Iowa. His areas of research and academic specialization include comparative mass media law and policy regimes, Internet telecommunications, visual communication, and international communication. He has published several articles on comparative mass media law, social science and media law, and the mass media in Africa in refereed journals in the United States and elsewhere. He has also written book chapters on communication theory and the mass media in Africa. His article, "Many Spiders, One World Wide Web: Towards a Typology of Internet Regulation," won first place in the Broadcast Education Association 2000 International Division scholarly research paper competition. The paper has since been published in *Communication Law and Policy*, the refereed journal of the Association for Education in Journalism and Mass Communication. Professor Eko is a member of several learned and professional societies, including the Broadcast Education Association, the International Communication Association, and the Association for Education in Journalism and Mass Communication.

PAUL L. EHIOZE IDAHOSA is associate professor in the Division of Social Science at York University, Toronto, Canada, where he directs the African Studies Program and teaches courses in development studies, African politics, and African popular culture. He a faculty member in York University's Graduate Programs in social and political thought, women's studies, and political science. In addition, he is an associate at the Center for Refugee Studies. He has held teaching appointments in economic and social history at the Université d'Oran (Algeria), African politics and development studies at Trent University (Canada), Third World politics and public administration at Ryerson Polytechnic University (Canada), and African politics at the University of Toronto. He has published numerous articles on development theory, development ethics, political thought, and ethnicity. He is the author of *The populist dimension to African political thought: Essays in reconstruction and retrieval* (2003).

NANTANG JUA holds the Bachelor of Arts degree in political Science and the Master of Arts degree in diplomatic history from Southern Illinois University in Carbondale, Illinois. He also holds the Ph.D. degree in political science from the University of Buffalo. Since completing his doctoral studies, he has worked as Chargé de Recherche in the Institute of Human Sciences in Yaoundé, Cameroon and taught at the University of Buea. Presently, he is Maître de Recherce in Cameroon's Ministry of Scientific Research, as well as assistant coordinator of Ethno-Net Africa. During this period, he has been a visiting research fellow at the African Studies Center in Leiden, Netherlands; senior Fulbright Scholar at the School of Advanced International Studies, Johns Hopkins University, Washington, D.C.; a Copeland Fellow at Amherst College, Amherst, Massachusetts; and a Rockefeller Humanities Fellow at the University of Michigan, Ann Arbor. He has contributed several articles and book chapters in the areas of international political economy, social transformations, and state construction. Presently, he is working on a book on social transformation and democratization in Cameroon.

MWANGI S. KIMENYI is the executive director of the Kenya Institute for Public Policy Research and Analysis. He is also associate professor of economics at the University of Connecticut. He also served as vice president of the African Educational Foundation for Public Policy and Market Process between 1993 and 1999. Professor Kimenyi has also worked as a World Bank consultant attached to the National Institute of Statistics, Ministry of Planning, in Angola. He is the author of over sixty refereed journal articles, which have appeared in ranked journals such as the *Journal of Institutional and Theoretical Economics,* the *Yale Journal on Regulation,* the *Southern Economic Journal, Public Choice,* and the *European Journal of Political Economy.* He is also author and coauthor of five books. He is the editor of two book series, *Public Choice and Developing Countries,* and *Contemporary Perspectives on Developing Countries.* He is the recipient of several honors and awards, including the Georgescu-Roegen Prize in Economics and the 2001 Global Development Network Award for Outstanding Research. Professor Kimenyi's current research focuses on institutional and economic reforms.

JOHN MUKUM MBAKU is Willard L. Eccles Professor of Economics and John S. Hinckley Fellow at Weber State University, Ogden, Utah, and associate editor (Africa), *Journal of Third World Studies.* He is also president of the African Educational Foundation for Public Policy and Market Process. He has previously taught at the University of Georgia and Kennesaw State University. His present research interests are in public choice, constitutional political economy, trade integration, intergroup relations, and institutional reforms in Africa. During 1994–1995 he served as the president of the Association of Third World Studies. He is the author of *Institutions and reform in Africa: The public choice perspective* (1997), and *Bureaucratic and political corruption in Africa: The public choice perspective* (2000); editor of *Corruption and the crisis of institutional reforms in Africa* (1998), and *Preparing Africa for the twenty-first century: Strategies for peaceful coexistence and sustainable development* (1999); coeditor (with Julius O. Ihonvbere) of *Multiparty democracy and political change: Constraints to democratization in Africa* (1998), (with Mwangi S. Kimenyi) of *Institutions and collective choice in developing countries: Applications of the theory of public choice* (1999), and (with Pita Ogaba Agbese and Mwangi S. Kimenyi) of *Ethnicity and governance in the Third World* (2001).

IMMANUEL TATAH MENTAN is associate professor of politics and communication at the University of Yaoundé II. Tatah Mentan served as communication advisor to the Cameroon Ministry of Health on HIV/AIDS Media Campaign Strategies during 1998–1999, and as a researcher on ethnic conflicts in Cameroon for Services Humanus and the Center for Interdisciplinary Studies on Ethnic Relations. He has held faculty positions at the University of Yaoundé I and II, National University of Rwanda, and the University of Buea (Cameroon). In addition, he was a guest lecturer on African history at the University of Minnesota. He has published over thirty articles in refereed journals and contributed over eight chapters to published volumes. In addition, he has evaluated programs for UNESCO and reviewed papers for several scholarly journals. He is a member of many learned societies, including the Center for Democratic Studies, African Association of Political Science, African Association for Public Administration and Management, Professors World Peace Academy, and the Mid-America Alliance for African Studies. His research interests include North–South media relations, globalization, African political economy, ethnic conflict, political communication and governance.

EMMANUEL NNADOZIE is professor of economics at Truman State University, where he has been since 1989. He was visiting professor at the University of North Carolina at Charlotte during the 1996–1997 school year, and a research fellow at the University of Oxford Center for the Study of African Economies in 1994. Dr. Nnadozie has previously worked with a World Bank development program in Nigeria. His scholarly works have appeared in both academic and nonacademic journals all over the world. He has also written books on economic development, business, and investment in Africa. His publications include *African economic development* (2003), *Historical dictionary of Mozambique*, 2nd ed. (2000, coauthored with M. Azevedo and T. Joao), *African culture and American business in Africa: How to strategically manage cultural differences in African business* (1998), and *Chad: A nation in search of it's future* (1997, coauthored with M. Azevedo). An award-winning educator and advisor, Dr. Nnadozie is the current editor of the *Journal of African Finance and Economic Development* and an inductee of several honor societies, including Pi Delta Phi, Omicron Delta Kappa, and Phi Kappa Phi National honor society. He is currently president of the African Finance and Economic Association of North America and chair, Igbo Studies Association.

FRANCIS B. NYAMNJOH is a sociologist and specialist in mass communications studies. Until 1999, he was head of the Department of Sociology and Anthropology at the University of Buea in Cameroon. In 1999, he moved to the University of Botswana where he became a senior lecturer in the Department of Sociology. He is presently head of the Department of Publications and Communications at the Council for the Development of Social Science Research in Africa, Dakar, Senegal, and the editor of the *African Sociological Review*. He is a well-accomplished scholar who has published many articles in international journals, as well as several book chapters. In addition, he has served a post-doctoral research fellowship at the African Studies Center in Leiden, Netherlands, and given seminars at major international universities, including the University of Oxford. He has just completed a manuscript on media and democratization in Africa.

P. GODFREY OKOTH is professor of history and former director, Center for the Study of Lake Victoria and its Environments, Maseno University, Kenya. Professor Okoth has held teaching positions at Makerere University, University of Waterloo, the Islamic University in Uganda, the Institute of Teacher Education Kyambogo (Uganda), and the Institute of Public Administration, Kampala, Uganda. He has published over seventy articles in learned books and journals in Africa, the United Kingdom, the United States, South Korea, and India. In addition to authoring and editing several internationally reputed books, Professor Okoth has presented over 100 conference and seminar papers to scholarly fora in Africa, Europe, Asia, and North America. He has also been editor of several learned journals, including the internationally renowned *Ufahamu: Journal of the African Activist Association*, based at UCLA. Professor Okoth is a member of many learned societies, including the Association of Third World Studies, Kenya Historical Association, Kenya–American Studies Association (he has been its chairman since 1997), and the African Association of Political Science. Professor Okoth has also been a visiting scholar at institutions of higher learning such as Nuffield College, University of Oxford; the Brookings Institution; the American Studies Center, Hyderabad, India; and the American Studies Center, Salsburg, Austria. He has received such prestigious awards as the Fulbright Scholarship, the Indian Council for Cultural Relations Award, and the Carnegie Corporation of New York Research Award, among others. His research interests include diplomatic history, foreign policy, conflict management, the military, democracy, governance, and development.

SURESH CHANDRA SAXENA served for thirty-five years in the Department of African Studies at Jawaharlal Nehru University, New Delhi (India) and Delhi University (India). He retired from Delhi University in 1999. He has authored fourteen academic books on Africa, the most important of which are *South Africa: Walking the last mile* (1992), *Africa beyond 2000: Essays on Africa's political and economic development in the twenty-first century* (2000), and *Africa: Economic and strategic issues* (2001). Professor Saxena has served as editor of the *Indian Journal of African Studies* for four years, and as the assistant editor of *Africa Quarterly* (Indian Council of Cultural Relations). He has also been a freelance journalist, and in this capacity covered several nonaligned summits and the Iran–Iraq war. He served as a radio commentator for about fifteen years. He has been the secretary of the India–Africa Society since 1987. He is also a member of two prestigious institutions, the Indian Council of World Affairs and the Institute for Defense Studies and Analysis, New Delhi.

E. IKE UDOGU, professor of political science at Francis Marion University, Florence, South Carolina, is currently serving as a faculty fellow in the Department of Political Science and Criminal Justice at Appalachian State University, Boone, North Carolina. He is a consulting editor for Collegiate Press, San Diego, California, and also a member of its editorial advisory board. He was a National Endowment for the Humanities Fellow and serves as the director of research and publication for the African Studies and Research Forum. Professor Udogu is a member of the African Studies and Research Forum, African Studies Association, Association of Third World Studies, International Society for the Study of European Ideas and the South Carolina Political Science Association. His areas of research interest are African politics, ethnic politics, democracy and democratization, and human rights. He has published in the *Makerere Political Science Review*, *Journal of Asian and African Studies*, *Journal of Developing Societies*, *International Journal of Comparative Sociology*, *IN DEPTH: A Journal of Values and Public Policy*, *Canadian Review of Studies in Nationalism*, *Review of Black Political Economy*, *Journal of Black Studies*, *Journal of Third World Studies*, *Africa Quarterly* (Delhi), and other journals. He is the author of *Nigeria and the politics of survival as a nation-state* (1997) and editor of *Democracy and democratization in Africa: Toward the 21st century* (1997), and *The issue of political ethnicity in Africa* (2001). He is currently editing a volume, *Nigeria in the 21st century*. He has contributed numerous book chapters on African politics and is the recipient of the 2001 Africa Excellence in Scholarship Award for Outstanding Contribution to Scholarship on Ethnic Relations, Minority Rights and Peaceful Coexistence in Africa.

UFO OKEKE UZODIKE is the director of political studies at the University of Natal, Pietermaritzburg, South Africa. He teaches international relations and international political economy. His current research interests include issues of development, foreign policies of African states, and African leadership.

WILSON S. K. WASIKE is a policy analyst in the Infrastructure and Economic Services Division at the Kenya Institute for Public Policy Research and Analysis. Previously, he has been a senior lecturer and chairman of the Department of Economics at Egerton University (1997–2000), and a research and teaching associate in the Department of Economics, University of Stirling (1993–1997). He has also served, in 1997 and 1998, as a visiting lecturer in environmental economics at the Moi University School of Environmental Studies. Dr. Wasike has authored and coauthored several papers in refereed journals such as the *British Review of Economic Issues*, *International Journal of Environ-*

mental Education and Information, and *International Journal of Water Resources Development.* He is the recipient of several honors and awards, including the 2001 Global Development Network Award for Outstanding Research. Dr. Wasike's current research in infrastructure, environment, technology, and natural resources management focuses on decentralization, privatization, and regulation of public service delivery; water resource allocation policy; infrastructure investment, productivity, and competitiveness; and sustainable infrastructure and environmental development.